The Art of War

Great Commanders of the
Ancient and Medieval World
1500 BC – AD 1600

The Art of War

Great Commanders of the Ancient and Medieval World
1500 BC – AD 1600

EDITED BY

ANDREW ROBERTS

Quercus

CONTENTS

continued...

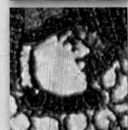

INTRODUCTION

This is the first of two volumes that seek to explore what the greatest military commanders of world history can tell us about the Art of War, from the very earliest moments of recorded history right up to the present day. By examining their genius – a word that is neither pejorative nor condoning of their very different personalities and careers – we can learn much about what it took to lead men in that harshest and most demanding aspect of the human condition: mortal conflict.

By choosing the age of gunpowder as the natural cut-off point, I hope to underline a fundamental shift that overcame the art of war in the late sixteenth and early seventeenth centuries. Before gunpowder, it took subtly different qualities to lead men into battle than those required after muskets, cannonballs and the widespread use of explosives began to dominate battlefields. Many of the phenomena of military leadership are genuinely timeless, and

include charisma, heroism, judgement, loyalty and often ruthlessness, but in the age before gunpowder – when death was dealt face-to-face and often with cold steel – such qualities were at a premium.

Some of the military leaders in this volume were born to command. Men like Alexander the Great, Julius Caesar, Henry V, the Black Prince and Akbar the Great were the heirs of kings, princes and consuls, and so were trained from birth to lead men into battle. Of course that does not guarantee genius – history is littered with the abject failures of golden-boy heirs apparent – but they had an automatic advantage over many of the others. How impressive, therefore, are those leaders who rose purely by dint of their own efforts – such as King David, Cyrus, Baibars, Genghis Khan, Joan of Arc and Cortés – who commanded the loyalty of nations in a time of deference to inherited rank. Unlike those in the second volume of *The Art of War*, most of the leaders in this volume wound up as heads of state, often as a result of their prowess on the field of battle.

As with any such collection of individuals, subjective judgement has to be exercised about who is selected. No two historians' lists will be identical. The overwhelming criterion for inclusion in this volume has not been the numbers of troops commanded, or nations subdued, or territories conquered, or even battles won, but who has shown that special spark that in music makes a Mozart, or in physics a Newton or in cosmology a Hawking. As with the elephant, it's hard to define a great military leader from first principles, but you certainly know one when you see one. Thus when Alexander Nevsky crossed the frozen waters of the lake at the Battle of Lake Chud, or Henry V chose the narrow front line for his defensive position at Agincourt, or William the Conqueror feigned retreat before the Saxons at Hastings, they each showed that exceptional gift of insight that justifies selection in a book such as this.

Military genius needs the right time and place to shine, and one common aspect of these leaders is their ability to grasp the hem of the cloak of History as it sweeps past, and to hang on tightly. Thus Alcibiades neatly swapped sides at the key turning point of the Peloponnesian War, Caesar crossed the Rubicon river when he saw, intuitively, that the use of the Triumvirate was past, and Sultan Mehmet II hauled his ships overland to enter the Golden Horn at precisely the right moment in 1453.

Whilst we can admire many of these figures, some were amongst the most vicious genocidal killers ever to stain the pages of human history. In this volume, which largely covers the period before the printing press and mass literacy, Civilization was in daily contention with Barbarism, and often on the losing side. Mass terror was frequently the easiest and most efficacious way to hold subject peoples in awe and obeisance; if leaders couldn't be loved, they reasoned, they could at least be feared. The practices of Tamerlane building pyramids of human skulls, of Genghis Khan slaughtering entire cities, then demanding the ears of the dead to prove that his orders had been effectively carried out, or of Attila treating his enemies to an agonizing death by impalement – these were all too often the natural ways of war. (Of course human nature is such that the Age of Gunpowder found equally monstrous – if less imaginative – crimes to commit.)

The ability to inspire as well as to threaten is also an integral part of leadership; what King Leonidas of the Spartans proposed at Thermopylae was nothing less than mass suicide, yet his men stood by him; Hannibal not only crossed the greatest mountain range in Europe, but did so with vast pachyderms in terrain more suited to mountain chamois; Alexander somehow marched his army across the inhospitable, pitiless terrain of the Makran desert in baking heat. Feats such as these could not have been achieved without motivational power rarely seen in ordinary life.

These leaders tended to share a keen intelligence – Themistocles, Xenophon, Caesar, Muhammad, Charlemagne, Süleyman the Magnificent and Zhuge Liang all qualify for the soubriquet 'intellectual' – but there was a calculating worldliness to almost all of them, too. The devastating combination of a commander's fast-thinking brain and his sturdy, earth-bound practicality was often enough to defeat forces many times his opponents' size, as Henry V, Cortés and Scipio Africanus were each to find. Similarly, emphasis on maintaining high morale through the exhibition of unavailing self-confidence was common to many of the greatest warriors over the three millennia covered in this volume. Victory seems to have gone to the leader who willed it the more, a phenomenon also regularly seen in the second volume, however illogical that might seem. Because warfare is so raw, so elemental and played for the highest stakes possible, outcomes can rarely be taken for granted.

The last attribute displayed by a surprisingly large number of these great commanders was resilience in defeat. However talented the general, setbacks will be experienced sometimes; virtually none of the people featured in this book or its sister volume went undefeated throughout their entire military careers. Yet they came back from adversity undaunted, having learnt the lesson of what had gone wrong and resolved not to allow it to happen again. Above all, their self-belief communicated itself to the outside world, and saw them through to ultimate victory. In that sense, this book perhaps contains lessons of value beyond the sphere of military history.

ANDREW ROBERTS
May 2008

CONTRIBUTORS

Niccolò Capponi

Born and raised in Florence in an Anglo-Italian environment, Niccolò Capponi developed a passion for history in his youth. The holder of a doctoral degree from the University of Padua, he is a former fellow of the Medici Archive Project. His well-received *Victory of the West: The Story of the Battle of Lepanto* was published by Macmillan in 2006.

Martin van Creveld

Martin van Creveld, formerly of the Hebrew University, Jerusalem, is a leading expert on military history and strategy, with a special interest in the future of war. He is the author of twenty books, including *The Culture of War* (Presidio Press, 2008); *The Changing Face of War: Lessons of Combat from the Marne to Iraq* (Presidio Press, 2007); *The Transformation of War* (The Free Press, 1991); *Command in War* (Harvard University Press, 1985) and *Supplying War* (Cambridge University Press, 1978). Between them, these books have been translated into seventeen languages.

He has acted as consultant to defence establishments in several countries, and has taught or lectured at practically every institute of strategic studies from Canada to New Zealand and from Norway to South Africa. He has also appeared on numerous television and radio programmes as well as writing for, and being interviewed by, hundreds of newspapers and magazines around the world. He is married to Dvora Lewy, a painter, and lives in Mevasseret Zion near Jerusalem.

Anne Curry

Anne Curry is a graduate of the University of Manchester and began her academic career at Teesside and Reading Universities before becoming Professor of Medieval History at the University of Southampton in 2004. She is well known for her researches on the fifteenth-century phase of the Hundred Years War and especially for her detailed work on the armies of the period, which prompted her major re-evaluation of the Battle of Agincourt and the creation of an online database, www.medievalsoldier.org, listing all known English soldiers serving between 1369 and 1453. She is now developing a new project on women and warfare. Her main publications include *Agincourt: A New History* (Tempus Publishing, 2005); *The Hundred Years War* (Macmillan Press, 1993, 2nd edn Palgrave, 2003) and *The Battle of Agincourt: Sources and Interpretations* (Boydell Press, 2000). She also edited the Rolls of the English Parliament between 1422 and 1454. She is currently President of the Historical Association and a Vice-President of the Royal Historical Society.

James Doyne Dawson

Doyne Dawson received his Ph.D. in ancient and medieval history from Princeton. He is the author of *The First Armies* (Cassell, 2001), a history of warfare to 539 BC; *Origins of Western Warfare: Militarism and Morality in the Ancient World* (Westview Press, 1996) and *Cities of the Gods: Communist Utopias in Greek Thought* (Oxford University Press, 1992). He is a visiting professor in the Asian Studies Program at Sejong University, Seoul, South Korea.

Ben Dupré

Ben Dupré read Classics at Exeter College, Oxford. He taught English in Germany before pursuing a career in reference book publishing. He was Children's Reference Publisher at Oxford University Press from 1992 until 2004 and, all told, has more than twenty years' experience of editing and writing information books for a general audience. He is the author of *Where History Was Made* (Quercus, 2008). A gifted performer on both harpsichord and viola da gamba, he lives in North Oxford with his family.

Jonathan Fenby

Jonathan Fenby has written five books on Chinese history, including *The Dragon Throne: Dynasties of Imperial China 1600 BC–AD 1912* (Quercus, 2007) and *The Penguin History of Modern China* (Allen Lane, 2008). He is also the author of *On the Brink: The Trouble with France* (Little, Brown, 1998) and *Alliance: The Inside Story of How Roosevelt, Stalin and Churchill Won One War and Began Another* (Simon & Schuster, 2007). A former editor of the *Observer* and the *South China Morning Post*, he has held senior editorial posts at the *Economist*, the *Guardian*, the *Independent* and Reuters news agency. He was made a Commander of the British Empire in 2000 for services to journalism.

Felipe Fernández-Armesto

Felipe Fernández-Armesto is Prince of Asturias Professor at Tufts University in Massachusetts and a Professorial Fellow of Queen Mary, University of London. His awards include Spain's Premio Nacional de Investigación, the John Carter Brown Medal, the Caird Medal, and the World History Association Book Prize. His journalism appears widely in Spain, Britain and the USA. Among his many broadcasting credits, he is the longest-serving presenter of *Analysis* on BBC Radio 4, and co-wrote the ten-part CNN series *Millennium*, which was based on his book *Millennium: A History of Our Last Thousand Years* (Bantam Press, 1995).

His recent books include *Amerigo: The Man Who Gave His Name to America* (Weidenfeld & Nicolson, 2006); *Pathfinders: A Global History of Exploration* (Oxford University Press, 2006); *Humankind: A Brief History* (Oxford University Press, 2004); *The Americas: A History of Two Continents* (Weidenfeld & Nicolson, 2003) and *Food: A History* (Macmillan, 2001), which won the International Association of Culinary Professionals' Prize for the best food-writing.

John Gillingham

John Gillingham studied history at Oxford and Munich Universities. He is a Fellow of the British Academy and Emeritus Professor of History at the London School of Economics and Political Science, where he taught for more than thirty years. He was awarded the Prix Guillaume le Conquérant in 1997 and for five years (2000 to 2004) was Director of the Battle Conference on Anglo-Norman Studies which meets annually on the field of the Battle of

Hastings. Three of his essays on war are reprinted in *Anglo-Norman Warfare*, edited by Matthew Strickland (Boydell Press, 1992); and he contributed to *Medieval Warfare: A History*, edited by Maurice Keen (Oxford University Press, 1999). His most recent books are *The Wars of the Roses: Peace and Conflict in Fifteenth Century England* (Phoenix Press, 2001); *The Angevin Empire* (Hodder, 2001); *The English in the Twelfth Century: Imperialism, National Identity and Political Values* (Boydell Press, 2000) and *Richard I* (Yale University Press, 1999).

Adrian Goldsworthy

Adrian Goldsworthy read Ancient and Modern History at St John's College Oxford, and remained there to complete his D.Phil. in Ancient History. His thesis was subsequently published as *The Roman Army at War, 100 BC–AD 200* (Oxford University Press, 1996). After holding a series of research and teaching posts in universities he now writes full time. His books include *Roman Warfare* (Cassell, 2000); *The Punic Wars* (Weidenfeld & Nicolson, 2000; published in paperback as *The Fall of Carthage*, 2003); *Cannae* (Cassell, 2001); *The Complete Roman Army* (Thames & Hudson, 2003); *In the Name of Rome: The Men who Won the Roman Empire* (Weidenfeld & Nicolson, 2003) and, most recently, *Caesar: The Life of a Colossus* (Weidenfeld & Nicolson and Yale University Press, 2006). He has acted as consultant on several television series and appears periodically as a talking head in documentaries on aspects of the ancient world.

Robert Hardy

Robert Hardy, CBE, is an internationally acclaimed actor with an extensive career in theatre, film and television. He is, in addition, a medieval military historian. During the Second World War he spent a year at Magdalen College, Oxford, where his tutors were C. S. Lewis and J. R. R. Tolkien, before joining up and training as a fighter pilot with the Royal Air Force, finishing his degree after demobilisation. His acting career has taken him to London, New York, California, Paris and Stratford-upon-Avon, and his many roles have included Henry V, Hamlet, Siegfried Farnon and Cornelius Fudge. He has played Winston Churchill several times on film, television and stage – including a performance in French in Robert Hossein's spectacular Paris production of *Celui qui a dit Non* (1999–2000).

An acknowledged expert on the military longbow in the late Middle Ages, his published works including *Longbow: A Social and Military History* (Patrick Stephens Ltd, 2006) and *The Great War Bow* (The History Press, 2005) with Professor Matthew Strickland, as well as various chapters in collections of medieval studies. He also lectures, speaking in Paris at the Musée de L'Armée in 2001. He is a Fellow of the Society of Antiquaries, an honorary Doctor of Literature of Reading, Durham and Portsmouth Universities, and a Consultant and Trustee of the Mary Rose Trust. He served for several years as Trustee of the Royal Armouries at Her Majesty's Tower of London.

John Haywood

John Haywood studied medieval history at the universities of Lancaster, Cambridge and Copenhagen. His doctoral research was on early medieval naval warfare. He is now a full-time historical writer with more than a dozen titles to his credit, including *The Penguin Historical Atlas of the Vikings* (1995) and *The Penguin Atlas of British and Irish History* (2001). His most recent books are *The Dark Ages: Building Europe* (Thalamus, 2008) and *The Great Migrations* (Quercus, 2008).

Tom Holland

Tom Holland is the author of *Rubicon: The Triumph and Tragedy of the Roman Republic* (Little, Brown, 2003), which won the Hessell-Tiltman Prize for History and was shortlisted for the Samuel Johnson Prize. His book on the Graeco-Persian wars, *Persian Fire: The First World Empire and the Battle for the West* (Little, Brown, 2005), won the Anglo-Hellenic League's Runciman Award in 2006. He has adapted Homer, Herodotus, Thucydides and Virgil for the BBC. He won the 2007 Classical Association prize awarded to 'the individual who has done most to promote the study of the language, literature and civilisation of Ancient Greece and Rome'.

Efraim Karsh

Professor Efraim Karsh is head of Mediterranean and Middle Eastern Studies at King's College London. He has held various academic posts – at Harvard and Columbia Universities, the Sorbonne, the London School of Economics, Helsinki University, the International Institute for Strategic Studies in London, the Kennan Institute for Advanced Russian Studies in Washington, D.C., and the Jaffee Center for Strategic Studies at Tel-Aviv University. Professor Karsh is a regular commentator for the media: he has appeared on all the main radio and television networks in Britain and the USA, and has contributed articles to leading newspapers including *The Times, The Sunday Times, The New York Times, The Wall Street Journal* and *The International Herald Tribune*.

He is the author of over a hundred academic publications, and his books include *Islamic Imperialism: A History* (Yale, 2006); *Rethinking the Middle East* (Frank Cass, 2003); *Empires of the Sand: The Struggle for Mastery in the Middle East, 1789–1922* (Harvard University Press, 1999); *Fabricating Israeli History: The 'New Historians'* (Frank Cass, 1997) and *Saddam Hussein: A Political Biography* (Free Press, 1991).

Robin Lane Fox

Robin Lane Fox has been a Fellow and Tutor in Ancient History at New College, Oxford since 1977 and the University Reader in Ancient History since 1990. His books include *Alexander the Great* (Penguin Books, 1973); *Pagans and Christians* (Penguin Books, 1986) and *The Classical World* (Penguin Books, 2006), all of which are in print in many languages. In 2003–2004 he was the historical consultant to Oliver Stone for his film *Alexander*, in which he led the Macedonian cavalry in their battle charges.

Isabel de Madariaga

Isabel de Madariaga was born in Scotland and educated in Switzerland, Spain, France and England. She studied Russian Language and Literature at the School of Slavonic and East European Studies in the University of London, where she completed her Ph.D. in History, published as *Britain, Russia, and the Armed Neutrality of 1780* (Yale University Press and Hollis and Carter, 1963). After several years as Assistant to the Editor of the *Slavonic and East European Review*, she was appointed Lecturer in History at the University of Sussex, then Senior Lecturer in History at Lancaster University in 1970 and Reader in Russian Studies in SSEES, then Professor, and now Emeritus Professor in the University of London. She is a Fellow of the British Academy, of the Royal Historical Society, and a Corresponding Member of the Royal Spanish Academy of History. She has written mainly about Catherine II and eighteenth-century Russia. Her *Ivan the Terrible* (Yale University Press) was published in 1985.

Justin Marozzi

Justin Marozzi is a travel writer, historian and a political risk and security consultant in post-conflict environments. A former *Financial Times* foreign correspondent, he is a Fellow of the Royal Geographical Society and has written widely about travel, exploration and the history of the Muslim world. His first book, *South from Barbary* (HarperCollins, 2001), told the story of a 1,200-mile expedition by camel across Libya. More recently he has written an acclaimed history of the fourteenth-century Central Asian conqueror Tamerlane. His latest book, *The Man Who Invented History: Travels with Herodotus* (John Murray, 2008), is based on expeditions in Turkey, Iraq, Egypt and Greece. He is married and lives in Norfolk and London.

Adrian Murdoch

Adrian Murdoch is a historian and journalist. Educated in Scotland and at The Queen's College Oxford, he has lived in London, Glasgow, Berlin and Singapore. He currently works for Thomson Reuters. He is the author of *Rome's Greatest Defeat: Massacre in the Teutoburg Forest* (Sutton Publishing, 2006), which was named one of the books of 2006 by the *Daily Telegraph*; *The Last Roman* (Sutton Publishing, 2006), a biography of Romulus Augustulus, the last Roman emperor in the west, and *The Last Pagan* (Inner Traditions, 2008), a biography of Julian the Apostate. He is also the co-translator of a book of Latin and Greek erotic literature, *Emperors of Debauchery: The Dedalus Book of Roman Decadence* (Dedalus, 1994). He is a Fellow of the Royal Historical Society.

John Julius Norwich

John Julius Norwich is the author of histories of Norman Sicily, Venice, Byzantium and the Mediterranean; he has also written on Mount Athos, the Sahara, English architecture, Shakespeare's histories and nineteenth-century Venice. He is at present working on a history of the Papacy and a book of memoirs. Since 1970 he has compiled an annual pamphlet anthology, *A Christmas Cracker*.

He has made some thirty historical documentaries for television, and was for four years chairman of the BBC panel game *My Word*. For three years he presented the Evening Concert, six nights a week, on Classic FM.

Formerly Chairman of Colnaghi, the oldest fine art dealers in London, he is Honorary Chairman of the Venice in Peril Fund and Chairman of the World Monuments Fund in Britain. He is a regular lecturer on art-historical, architectural and musical subjects. In 2006 and 2007 he gave one-man shows nightly for a week at two London theatres, reading from his *Christmas Crackers* and singing to the piano.

Jonathan Phillips

Jonathan Phillips is Professor of Crusading History at Royal Holloway, University of London. He is the author of *The Second Crusade: Extending the Frontiers of Christendom* (Yale, 2007); *The Fourth Crusade and the Sack of Constantinople,* (Jonathan Cape, 2004); *The Crusades, 1095–1197* (Longman, 2002) and *Defenders of the Holy Land: Relations between the Latin East and the West, 1119–1187* (Oxford University Press, 1996). He is a frequent contributor to *BBC History* and *History Today* magazines and an editor of the academic journal *Crusades*. He has acted as consultant for the television programmes *The Cross and the Crescent* (History Channel, 2005) and *Holy Warriors – Richard and Saladin* (BBC2, 2004).

Justin Pollard

Justin Pollard specialized in Anglo-Saxon archaeology at Cambridge University. A historical writer and consultant in print, film and TV, he is the author of *The Rise and Fall of Alexandria* (Viking Books, 2006); *Alfred the Great, the Man Who Made England* (John Murray, 2005) and *The Seven Ages of Britain* (Hodder & Stoughton, 2003). He was also a contributor to the *The QI Book of General Ignorance* (Faber and Faber, 2006). His film credits include *Elizabeth* and its sequel *Elizabeth – The Golden Age*, as well as *Atonement*, *The Four Feathers* and *The Boy in the Striped Pyjamas*. In television he has made over twenty-five documentary series, including *Time Team* for Channel Four, and has written for Tony Robinson, Terry Jones, Stephen Fry, Vic Reeves, Bettany Hughes and Bob Geldof. He also writes for the BBC quiz show *QI* and is the script consultant on Showtime's hit US drama *The Tudors*.

Andrew Roberts

Andrew Roberts took a first in modern history from Gonville & Caius College, Cambridge, from where he is an honorary senior scholar. His biography of Winston Churchill's foreign secretary Lord Halifax, entitled *The Holy Fox*, was published by Weidenfeld & Nicolson in 1991, followed by *Eminent Churchillians* (Weidenfeld & Nicolson, 1994); *Salisbury: Victorian Titan*, which won the Wolfson Prize and the James Stern Silver Pen Award (Weidenfeld & Nicolson, 1999); *Napoleon and Wellington* (Weidenfeld & Nicolson, 2002); *Hitler and Churchill: Secrets of Leadership* (Weidenfeld & Nicolson, 2003) and *Waterloo: Napoleon's Last Gamble* (HarperCollins, 2005).

He has also edited a collection of twelve counterfactual essays by historians entitled *What Might Have Been* (Weidenfeld & Nicolson, 2004) as well as *The Correspondence of Benjamin Disraeli and Mrs Sarah Brydges Willyams* (2006). His *A History of the English-Speaking Peoples Since 1900* (Weidenfeld & Nicolson, 2006) won the US Intercollegiate Studies Institute Book Award for 2007. Roberts is a Fellow of the Royal Society of Literature, an honorary Doctor of Humane Letters, and reviews history books for more than a dozen newspapers and periodicals. He has recently published *Masters and Commanders: How Churchill, Roosevelt, Alanbrooke and Marshall Won the War in the West, 1941–45*. His website can be found at www.andrew-roberts.net.

Francis Robinson

Francis Robinson has been Professor of the History of South Asia, Royal Holloway, University of London, since 1990, and from September 2008 will also be Visiting Professor, Faculty of History, University of Oxford. He was President of the Royal Asiatic Society, 1997–2000 and 2003–06. He was made CBE in 2006 for contributions to Higher Education and to the History of Islam. His books include: *Separatism Among Indian Muslims: The Politics of the United Provinces' Muslims 1860–1923* (1974); *Atlas of the Islamic World since 1500* (1982); *Varieties of South Asian Islam* (1988); *The Cambridge Illustrated History of the Islamic World* (1996); *Islam and Muslim History in South Asia* (2000); *The 'Ulama of Farangi Mahall and Islamic Culture in South Asia* (2001); *The Mughals and the Islamic Dynasties of India, Iran and Central Asia, 1206–1925* and *Islam, South Asia and the West* (2007). His edited volume of the *New Cambridge History of Islam, Islam in the Age of Western Domination*, is due to appear in 2009.

Jonathan Sumption

Jonathan Sumption was a History Fellow of Magdalen College, Oxford, until 1975. He is a QC practising at the commercial bar, and is the author of *The Hundred Years War*, a multi-volume history of which the first two volumes, *Trial by Battle* (Faber and Faber, 1990) and *Trial by Fire* (Faber and Faber, 1999) have appeared, and the third, *Divided Houses*, is forthcoming.

Stephen Turnbull

Stephen Turnbull took his first degree at Cambridge University, then received from Leeds University an MA and Ph.D. in Japanese Religious Studies and an MA in Military History. He is currently Lecturer in Japanese Religious and Military History at Leeds, and was until recently Visiting Professor of Japanese Religious and Military History at Akita International University in Japan. He is the author of sixty published books on religious and military topics, including *The Kakure Kirishitan of Japan* (Folkestone, 1998); *The Samurai Sourcebook* (London, 1998); *The Samurai and the Sacred* (Oxford University Press, 2006); *The Great Wall of China* (Oxford University Press, 2007) and several other illustrated monographs on the military history of Japan, China, Korea and the Mongol Empire. His other research interests include comparative military studies of Early Modern Europe and East Asia and the development of fortifications; the history of Christianity in Japan and the evolution of Shintō in the modern age.

Joyce Tyldesley

Dr Joyce Tyldesley has a degree in the archaeology of the eastern Mediterranean from Liverpool University and a doctorate from Oxford University. She is currently Lecturer in Egyptology in the KNH Centre for Biomedical Egyptology at the University of Manchester, a Fellow of the Manchester Museum, and an Honorary Research Fellow at Liverpool University. Her main area of interest is the Egyptian New Kingdom. She has worked on many excavations in Britain, Europe and Egypt.

Her many published works on Ancient Egypt include *Cleopatra: Last Queen of Egypt* (Profile Books, 2008); *Egypt: How a Lost Civilization was Rediscovered* (BBC Publications, 2005); *Ramesses: Egypt's Greatest Pharaoh* (Viking, 2005); *Egypt's Golden Empire: The Age of the New Kingdom* (Headline, 2001); *Judgement of the Pharaoh: Crime and Punishment in Ancient Egypt* (Weidenfeld & Nicholson, 2000); *Nefertiti: Egypt's Sun Queen* (Viking, 1998) and *Daughters of Isis: Women of Ancient Egypt* (Viking, 1994).

Robin Waterfield

Robin Waterfield is an internationally acclaimed scholar and author, whose publications range from abstruse academic articles to children's fiction. He has been an employed or incidental lecturer at a number of universities, mainly in Britain, but now scrapes a living as a writer and small-scale olive farmer in the far south of Greece. He has had about forty books published, most of which, these days, are scholarly works aimed at undergraduates or intelligent lay readers, rather than fellow academics. His most recent books are *Xenophon's Retreat: Greece, Persia and the End of the Golden Age* (Faber and Faber/Harvard University Press, 2006), and a translation of Plato's *Timaeus and Critias* (Oxford University Press). Forthcoming is *Why Socrates Died* (Faber and Faber/Norton/McLelland & Stewart), the definitive book on Socrates' trial and death.

'Insomuch as every prince of every northern land is enclosed within it, the capture of Megiddo is the capture of a thousand towns!' THUTMOSE SPEAKS TO HIS SOLDIERS: FROM THE ANNALS OF THUTMOSE III

THUTMOSE III

r.c. 1479–1425 BC   JOYCE TYLDESLEY

HAVING INHERITED HIS THRONE AS AN INFANT, Thutmose III ruled Egypt for fifty-three years, ten months and twenty-six days during the New Kingdom 18th Dynasty. Widely recognized as Egypt's greatest warrior king, Thutmose developed and ruled an empire that extended from Gebel Barkal, below the Third Nile Cataract in Nubia, to the banks of the River Euphrates in Syria; its sphere of influence, however, spread much further.

The great warrior pharaoh Thutmose III, wearing the *nemes* headcloth and false beard of an Egyptian king. This siltstone statue, now housed in the Luxor Museum, is considered to be one of the finest examples of ancient Egyptian royal art.

The first two decades of Thutmose's reign were spent in the shadow of his aunt, stepmother and co-regent, the formidable female pharaoh Hatshepsut. Hatshepsut's foreign policy is generally considered to have been one of peaceful trade rather than aggression, but there is evidence of at least six campaigns by her armies to quash local uprisings in both Nubia and the Levant. Towards the end of the joint reign there was a clear shift in the balance of power as the elderly Hatshepsut allowed the adult Thutmose to assume a more prominent role in matters of state. Thutmose now stood beside, rather than behind, his co-regent, and as commander-in-chief of the army he assumed responsibility for defending Egypt's borders. Egypt was already being troubled by sporadic unrest amongst its client states to the east and Thutmose was forced to commit his troops to the first of a series of military campaigns in order to reimpose firm control of the Levant.

The death of a strong king was traditionally a time of rebellion amongst Egypt's vassal states. Hatshepsut's death in *c.* 1458 BC was no different. Thutmose was compelled to act, both to protect Egypt's interests and, perhaps, to develop his own reputation as a warrior king. The long-established religious duty to defend Egypt against her traditional enemies can be traced back to the Narmer votive palette, carved over one thousand five hundred years earlier, at the dawn of the dynastic age.

The Annals

The vast majority of Thutmose's military activities were conducted to the northeast of Egypt. The minutiae of these campaigns were preserved by a band of military scribes who recorded events in an official 'day book'. Later in his reign, details of the eastern

triumphs were inscribed on the walls of two newly built halls situated behind Pylon (gateway) VI in the Karnak temple of Amen-Re at Thebes (modern Luxor): 'His majesty commanded the workmen to record the victories his father Amen had given him by an inscription in the temple which his majesty had made for [his father Amen so as to record] each campaign, together with the booty which [his majesty] had brought ...' (from the Annals of Thutmose III).

Today known as the 'Annals', this account forms Egypt's longest surviving monumental inscription. The Annals cover the events of Regnal Years 22–42, concentrating on the earliest campaign.

Two cartouches,
or oval loops, highlight the king's name 'Menkheperre Djehuty-Mes-Nefer-Kheper', in a relief from the Mortuary Temple of Hatshepsut at Deir el-Bahri. Today this king is better known as Thutmose III, fifth king of Egypt's 18th Dynasty.

They give details both of military victories and of the impressive amounts of booty, tribute and tax collected from Egypt's eastern vassals. Although they can hardly be classed as unbiased histories in the modern sense (being clearly designed to show Egypt, Egypt's king and Egypt's gods as superior to all others, and containing obvious errors, omissions and exaggerations), the Annals allow us an unprecedented insight into Thutmose's military exploits. Further details of Thutmose's campaigns can be gleaned from a series of stelae (inscribed monumental stones) erected by the king, and from a number of private inscriptions (Theban tombs, statues and stelae).

The growing threat of Mitanni

New Kingdom Egypt recognized three traditional enemies: the Libyans, the Nubians and the Asiatics or easterners. At the time of Thutmose's succession the various Libyan tribes who occupied the western desert were temporarily quiet and posed little threat to the status quo. To the south, Nubia too was relatively peaceful, a series of campaigns by the earlier 18th-Dynasty kings Ahmose, Amenhotep I and Thutmose I having ensured that it had effectively become an Egyptian province. Nubia was now governed by an Egyptian viceroy and, although there remained a chain of impressively large mud-brick forts built during the more aggressive Middle Kingdom occupation, the main instrument for Egyptian control was a series of fortified towns populated by expatriate Egyptians.

To the northeast, however, there was a growing danger. The political map was undergoing rapid change, and the city-states of Syria and Palestine were growing restive. The coastal city of Byblos retained a long-standing loyalty to the Egyptian kings. But to the north, in the lands today occupied by modern Turkey, the Indo-European Hittites had become a well-established nation whose natural expansion routes, to the southeast and southwest, would eventually bring them into conflict with Egyptian interests in north Syria. Also interested in this region were the Hurrians, an ethnic group originally from northern Zagros (modern Iran) but now based in the nation-state of Mitanni. Over thirty years earlier, Thutmose I, grandfather of Thutmose III, had raided Mitanni, and on reaching the Euphrates river had erected a boundary stela to commemorate his achievement. The elderly Thutmose had, however, died before he could complete his plans for an eastern empire. The Mitannians had rejected the Egyptians and recovered from their humiliation, spending the intervening years consolidating their hold on north Syria and Mesopotamia. Now, with the important, independent city-states of Kadesh and Tunip as friends, the Mitannian alliance posed a threat to Egypt. More specifically, the king of Kadesh, backed by the king of Mitanni, was rumoured to be preparing for war with Egypt.

Thutmose could not afford to lose his eastern territories. Control of the Levantine seaports would allow Egypt to dominate the eastern Mediterranean trade routes that underpinned the Bronze Age economy and provided Egypt with much-needed timber, while a controlling interest in Syria and the Levantine states would block the expansion of potential enemies. He therefore prepared, in his own words, to 'overthrow that vile enemy [the king of Kadesh] and to extend the boundaries of Egypt in accordance with the command of his father [the god] Amen-Re'. Thutmose was to invest seventeen years in this mission. His army – the professional and semi-professional troops of the royal household, supplemented by large numbers of non-

Thutmose III wears the red crown of Upper Egypt as he raises a mace above his head to perform the centuries-old ritual of smiting the enemies of Egypt, in a relief from the Karnak temple complex, near Luxor.

professional soldiers summoned to national service – soon developed a time-consuming yet ultimately effective technique. The soldiers fed themselves with provisions gathered as they marched; it was therefore important to march at times when food was easily available. Major, set-piece battles – two opposing armies assembled to fight – were rare. Instead, the Egyptians followed a seasonal campaign trail that led them from one fortified city-state to the next. Many city-states found it prudent to concede without fighting, effectively paying Thutmose and his army to go away and then, all too often, reverting to their previous allegiances once the Egyptians had left. Those who resisted soon found themselves under siege. Lacking any sophisticated equipment – he had no battering rams or towers – Thutmose would simply surround the city and wait for the enemy to run out of supplies. He would then sack the city and appoint a local ruler to govern on his behalf.

Thutmose soon developed the long-term policy of sending the children of the local chiefs to be educated in Egypt. Following his sixth campaign, thirty-six sons of the chiefs were sent to be taught in the palace schools alongside the sons of the Egyptian elite. After many years of indoctrination they returned home, fully Egyptianized, to govern on the pharaoh's behalf. Meanwhile the daughters of the chiefs became permanent hostages in the royal harem. The Annals tell us that Thutmose married the daughter of a chief from Retenu, who arrived in Egypt with a valuable dowry plus an assortment of attendants, while an undecorated tomb in the remote Wadi Gabbanat el-Qurud (the Valley of the Ape) on the Theban west bank has yielded the robbed burials of three foreign wives named Manuwai, Manhata and Maruta, whose names suggest that all three came from the Syrio-Palestine region.

The victorious campaigns

In his Regnal Year 22 (his first year of sole rule following the death of Hatshepsut) the Annals tell us that 'His Majesty passed the fortress of Sile on his first victorious campaign to crush the people who were assaulting Egypt's borders in valour, strength, might and right'. Thutmose crossed the north of the Sinai Peninsula using the military road known as the 'Ways of Horus', and headed for Gaza, a city loyal to Egypt since the beginning of the

New Kingdom. From there he attacked and occupied Yehem, a fortified city occupied by a consortium of enemies headed by the king of Kadesh. It was at Yehem that he planned his next move; an advance eastwards across the Carmel mountain range to the fortified city of Megiddo where he was to face a daunting coalition of enemies, again led by the king of Kadesh. Meanwhile Thutmose's general, Djehuty, was left to besiege the city of Joppa (modern Jaffa). Papyrus Harris 500, a Ramesside papyrus today housed in the British Museum, tells us that the enterprising Egyptians were smuggled into Joppa hidden inside large baskets.

Thutmose took Megiddo after a seven-month siege, instantly reaping a reward of chariots, armour and weaponry (which he used to equip his troops), gold, livestock and prisoners of war who were sent to Egypt to work. While the king of Kadesh escaped, many of his allies were captured and forced to swear an oath of loyalty to Egypt. The defeat of Megiddo was to linger in folk memory for centuries. Over a thousand years later, when the writer of the biblical Book of Revelation described the last battle of doomsday, he set it at Megiddo: 'And he gathered them together in a place called in the Hebrew tongue Armageddon.' (Revelation 16:16)

'His southern frontier is to the horns of the earth, to the southern limit of the land. His northern to the marshes of Asia, to the supporting pillars of heaven.'

GEBEL BARKAL, BOUNDARY STELA OF THUTMOSE III

Following a gap in the military records, we next see Thutmose, in his Regnal Year 29, capturing the Tunip-controlled coastal towns of Ullaza and Ardata before, in Year 30, attacking Kadesh itself. Once again the king of Kadesh experienced humiliation at Egyptian hands, but the fortified city, protected by the curve of the River Orontes, survived substantially intact.

Finally Thutmose turned his attention towards his arch-rival, Mitanni. There was to be a direct confrontation. Year 33 saw the Egyptian army sailing to the port of Byblos. Here they struck camp and waited, as the carpenters of Byblos – making good use of the plentiful Lebanese timber – built a fleet of specially designed boats. These were to be loaded in pieces on to carts, and transported with the army as the troops made their way over the mountains, along the Orontes valley and past the subdued Kadesh and Tunip. Their target was Aleppo, occupied by the king of Mitanni. Here Thutmose enjoyed three fierce, satisfactory confrontations. The enemy retreated in disarray, and Thutmose found himself standing on the west bank of the Euphrates at Carchemish, facing the Mitannian army now occupying the east bank.

The Mitannians had commandeered or scuppered all the available boats, so it should have been impossible for the Egyptians to chase them across the river. Believing themselves to be totally safe, the Mitannians relaxed. Thutmose, however, knew differently. Assembling his prefabricated boats, he crossed the Euphrates and continued his rout, advancing deep into Mitannian lands, seizing property and burning towns as he went. The Mitannian high command, fleeing before the Egyptians, was forced to hide ignominiously in caves. As had his grandfather before him, Thutmose was able to erect a celebratory boundary stela on the east bank of the Euphrates. He then paused on the long march home to enjoy a relaxing elephant hunt in Syria. He was not, however, able to retain his hold on the newly captured

Thutmose III

lands. Two years after the glorious victory the Egyptian army again faced the troops of Mitanni, and this time the enemy gained the advantage.

The final entry in the Annals shows Thutmose campaigning in the north in Year 42. Tunip was captured, and it is possible that Kadesh was also attacked. This was followed, in Year 50, by a brief and unremarkable Nubian campaign.

The Egyptian Napoleon

Although by no means vanquished, and soon to re-emerge as an important regional power, Mitanni was temporarily subdued and had learned to be wary of Egypt. With his empire secure, Thutmose found himself inundated by gifts from 'brother kings', the monarchs of Babylon, Assyria and Hatti (the Hittite kingdom) who prudently wished to become his friends. Meanwhile tribute and taxes were donated by the lesser states that wished to earn his protection. The funds now pouring into the royal coffers were used to finance an impressive temple-building programme. There was a new phase of building at the Karnak temple complex, while all the major Egyptian towns from Kom Ombo to Heliopolis benefited, as did several sites in the Nile Delta and Nubia.

Egypt's monumental inscriptions, the Annals included, were royal propaganda. They invariably depicted Egypt's kings as fit, brave and intelligent, and frequently distorted details of ancient wars to allow the Egyptians unearned victories. This makes it difficult for modern historians to develop a true assessment of a king's military prowess. Thutmose's accounts, taken from contemporaneous records and supported by archaeological evidence from Syria and Palestine, appear to be more accurate than most. They show us a man of great energy and tactical ability.

Thutmose III wears the elaborate *atef* crown on a block from a wall relief at Deir el-Bahri, now housed in the Luxor Museum.

Not only was Thutmose Egypt's greatest warrior king, he was also a skilled horseman, a superb athlete and a scholar whose interests ranged from botany to reading, history, religion and even interior design.

After fifty-four years of rule, Amenhotep II buried his father Thutmose III in a rock-cut tomb (KV 34) in the Valley of the Kings. More than three thousand years after the funeral, the mummy of Thutmose III, superficially intact and lying in its original inner coffin, was recovered as part of a cache of New Kingdom royal mummies that had been hidden in a private tomb in the Deir el-Bahri bay at Thebes. The mummy was taken to Cairo Museum and unwrapped, and it became clear that the king's body had been badly damaged in antiquity by tomb robbers. The head, feet and all four limbs had become detached and the mummy was held together by wooden paddles hidden beneath the linen bandages. His short stature (the king would have stood just over 1.5 metres or 5 feet tall, although it is not clear whether the detached feet were included in this measurement) and his unparalleled military achievements prompted historians to dub Thutmose III 'the Egyptian Napoleon'.

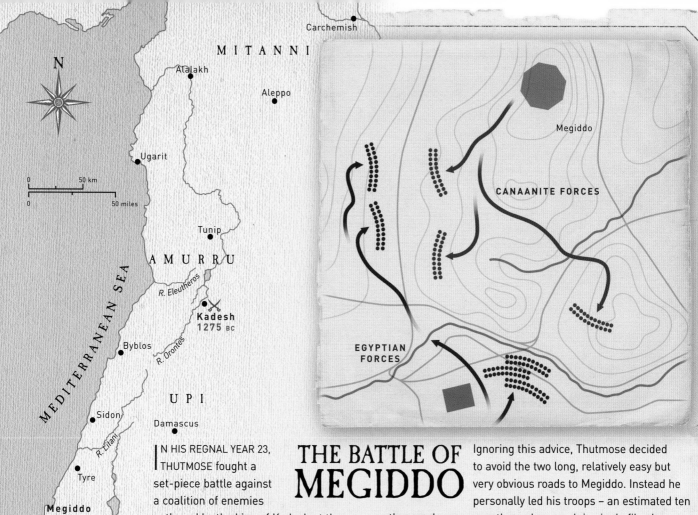

N

50 km

50 miles

MEDITERRANEAN SEA

MITANNI

Carchemish

Alalakh

Aleppo

Ugarit

Tunip

AMURRU

R. Eleutheros

Kadesh
1275 BC

Byblos

R. Orontes

UPI

Sidon

Damascus

R. Litani

Tyre

Megiddo
c.1456 BC

Beth Shean

Yehem

Taanach

R. Jordan

Shechem

CANAAN

Joppa

Ashkelon

Dead Sea

Gaza

Megiddo

CANAANITE FORCES

EGYPTIAN
FORCES

THE BATTLE OF
MEGIDDO

IN HIS REGNAL YEAR 23, THUTMOSE fought a set-piece battle against a coalition of enemies gathered by the king of Kadesh at the fortified city of Megiddo in modern northern Israel. This campaign allowed Thutmose to demonstrate his tactical ability and his personal bravery, which contrasted with the cowardice of his generals. As the king himself tells us, there were three possible ways of approaching the city. In a council of war, his generals made it clear which routes they preferred:

What will it be like to go on this path which keeps getting narrower? We have received reports that the enemy is waiting on the other side and that their numbers are constantly increasing. Will not our horses have to go in single file and our army and people likewise? Will not our vanguard have to fight while our rearguard is still standing here in Aruna unable to fight? But there are two other roads here. One of them is to our east – it comes out at Taanach. The other goes north of Djefti – and would lead us to the north of Megiddo. Our lord should go on whichever of these seems best, but do not make us march along that difficult path.

Ignoring this advice, Thutmose decided to avoid the two long, relatively easy but very obvious roads to Megiddo. Instead he personally led his troops – an estimated ten thousand men – on a three-day march in single file along a winding mountain pass, which daring move allowed him to creep up on the enemy camped outside the city walls.

As dawn broke, the rising sun illuminated the high ground which, it was plain to see, was occupied by a massive Egyptian army. At the head of his troops stood Thutmose himself: 'The southern wing of his majesty's army was at the southern hill of Kina and the northern wing was northwest of Megiddo. And his majesty was in the middle. [The god] Amen was protecting his body, the blood-lust and strength of [the god] Seth were flowing through his limbs.'

The battle was easily won when, briefly, Thutmose lost control of his men. As the defeated enemy ran back towards the city walls, the Egyptian soldiers defied orders and paused to loot the abandoned camps. The city gates were slammed shut. Enemies trapped outside the gates had to abandon their chariots and flee, and the Egyptians watched in amazement as the kings of Megiddo and Kadesh were hauled up the walls by their clothing, and 'sheets were lowered down to lift them [the enemy] into the town'. Cursing his ill-disciplined soldiers, Thutmose built a thick wall around the city and, lacking any form of siege-breaking equipment, simply waited. Seven months later, the starving citizens of Megiddo surrendered.

Thutmose III

> 'I shall go for them with the swoop of a falcon:
> killing, slaughtering and felling them to the ground.'
>
> FROM 'THE POEM', THE KADESH BATTLE INSCRIPTION OF RAMESSES II

RAMESSES II

r.c. 1290–1224 BC

JOYCE TYLDESLEY

RAMESSES II, THIRD KING of the 19th Dynasty, ruled New Kingdom Egypt for sixty-six years. The first decades of his lengthy reign were dedicated to establishing himself as a great military leader, following the glorious precedent set by Thutmose III. His proudest achievement, a tale that he told repeatedly in epic poetry, prose and a series of temple-wall illustrations, was his 'victory' against the Hittites at the Battle of Kadesh in 1275 BC. Modern historians are generally agreed, however, that Ramesses' propaganda was greater than his actual military prowess, and that his famous 'victory' may well have been nothing of the kind.

All of Egypt's kings had a religious duty to impose order (*maat*) on chaos (*isfet*). The exterior walls of Egypt's stone temples are decorated with carved images of kings fulfilling this duty by fighting – and, of course, defeating – the traditional chaotic enemies of Egypt. Some of these scenes depict purely symbolic encounters, but many, including those carved by Ramesses, are based on real battles that have been exaggerated to enhance the king's reputation. The same three enemies – Nubians from the south, Libyans from the west and Asiatics from the east – appear time and time again in these scenes. Ramesses cannot have considered the southerners to be a serious threat, as throughout his reign Nubia was effectively an Egyptian province; yet he included dark-skinned Nubians amongst his official foes. The tribes that were grouped together as 'Libyans', distinguished by their fair skins and goatee beards, were enemies of long standing who posed a constant threat to Egypt's western border. The Asiatics appear with red-brown skin and non-Egyptian profiles and beards, but although earlier periods had witnessed the occasional Syrian campaign, it was only during the New Kingdom that the Asiatics came to be seen as official enemies.

The warrior prince

Ramesses was trained in warfare by his father, Seti I, a former professional soldier, who reigned from *c.* 1306 to 1290. Seti had been determined to restore Egypt's eastern empire, created by Thutmose III and maintained by his immediate descendants, that had been lost during the atypical reign of Akhenaten, the so-called 'heretic king'.

The summer of Seti's Regnal Year 1 saw a brief campaign to reassert Egyptian control over the Sinai land bridge that connected Egypt to the province of Canaan (modern Israel). Later in the same year, Seti travelled further north to suppress disturbances in the Jordan valley. Over the next few years, he returned to Canaan and the northern province of Upi (inner southern Syria), advancing inland as far as Damascus and securing the Phoenician ports of Tyre, Sidon and Byblos. Control of the ports was important, as it allowed treeless Egypt to import much-needed timber from Lebanon.

The stabilized Egyptian empire now shared a common border with the Hittite empire. It was perhaps inevitable that the two would come to blows but, before he could commit to a full campaign, Seti's attention was diverted by trouble in the western Nile Delta. Libyan tribes were moving eastwards and attempting to settle on Egypt's fertile land. The army marched home to repel the tribes in a brief clash which allowed the 14-year-old Ramesses, 'Commander-in-Chief of the Army', to experience his first taste of battle.

Ramesses II shows his mastery over a Nubian, an Asiatic and a Libyan, representatives of the three traditional enemies of Egypt, in a painted relief now housed in the Egyptian National Museum in Cairo.

With his western border secure, Seti was free to resume his eastern mission. Ramesses accompanied his father on a campaign to subdue the province of Amurru (coastal Syria) and capture the city-state of Kadesh (modern Tell Nebi Mend) which, strategically situated at the tip of the Lebanese mountain range, was protected by the northward-flowing Orontes and an eastward-flowing tributary. A channel cut between the two rivers made the fortified city into an island. Although there was a brief moment of glory (that enabled Seti to erect a triumphal stela in Kadesh), there was no decisive confrontation with the Hittites. Instead, an agreement was reached and Kadesh and Amurru reverted to Hittite control while Egypt retained her hold on the valuable seaports.

In Year 13 a minor revolt in Lower Nubia gave Ramesses his first opportunity to take sole command of the army. This was the briefest of battles – it seems that the rebels simply lost courage and fled before the Egyptians – and there was so little danger that Ramesses even allowed his eldest sons, aged 4 and 5, to participate in the chariot charge. Nevertheless, Ramesses felt it appropriate to mark his victory by building a small rock-cut temple at Beit el-Wali. Here, alongside images of the old Syrian and Libyan campaigns, he displayed scenes of Nubians offering tribute.

Defending the Delta

The Bronze Age eastern Mediterranean swarmed with merchant boats – owned by the state, the temple and privately – sailing in an anti-clockwise trade route that linked Egypt to Cyprus, Greece, Crete and the Levantine ports. Now, at a time of general unrest and population movement in the Near East, these ships were being menaced by pirates – known as the Sherden people – who had the temerity to land and wreak havoc amongst the many towns dotted along Egypt's northern coast. Ramesses, now co-regent with his father, was entrusted with their elimination. Posting troops and ships at strategic points along the coast, he waited. When the Sherden people next appeared, they were captured and persuaded to serve as mercenaries in the Egyptian army.

The Nile Delta was still vulnerable to Libyan invasion and so, early in his solo reign, Ramesses established a defensive line of mud-brick forts along Egypt's north-western border. The ruins of three of his forts have been discovered along the coast to the west of Alexandria (at Gharbaniyat, el-Alamein and Zawiyet Umm el-Rakham) and two more are known to have been situated in the western Delta (at Tell Abqa'in and Kom el-Hisn), the remains of what was probably an impressive chain of forts stretching from Memphis to Umm el-Rakham. The forts would have dominated the coastline, offering protection and provisions for ships sailing from Crete to Egypt, although their primary purpose was almost certainly to offer a defence against overland invasion from the west.

The Battle of Kadesh

Ramesses now looked to the east. Remembering his father's earliest campaigns, he was determined to challenge the Hittites and recapture the province of Amurru and the city-state of Kadesh. The summer of his Regnal Year 4 saw the 'Campaign of Victory'. Ramesses marched along the coast to confirm his hold over Canaan and the all-important ports before turning inland. Benteshina, prince of Amurru, was easily persuaded to switch his allegiance from Hatti to Egypt (the sight of Ramesses' impressive army presumably helped to convince him), and Ramesses returned home, leaving a division of elite soldiers garrisoned in Amurru.

Unwilling to be thought a traitor, Benteshina immediately wrote to his former master explaining that his province was now, against his will, under Egyptian control. Angered by this news, the Hittite king Muwatallis swore a sacred vow to regain his lost territories. Calling on friends and allies from sixteen different provinces, he assembled a magnificent army. Egyptian records, which may be expected to contain some exaggeration, tell us that he commanded 2,500 chariots and 37,000 foot-soldiers including infantrymen, mercenaries and pirates.

In the spring of Regnal Year 5, Ramesses rode eastwards at the head of an army of 20,000 men sub-divided into four divisions of 5,000, each a mixture of infantry and chariotry and each marching under the standard of a local protective god: Amen Division (soldiers recruited from the Theban region, home of the warrior god Amen), Re Division (from the region of Heliopolis, home of the sun god Re), Ptah Division (from the region of Memphis, home of the creator god Ptah) and Seth or Sutekh Division (from the northeast Delta region, home of the mischievous god Seth). The army, and its accompanying pack animals and carts laden with provisions and equipment, took a month to pass along the coastal road through Canaan and south Syria to approach Kadesh from the south via the Bekaa valley. Meanwhile the elite force garrisoned in Amurru had also started towards Kadesh.

Four colossal seated figures of Ramesses II front the Great Temple of Abu Simbel, in southern Egypt. The figure to the left of the entrance has suffered earthquake damage. To the right and left of each figure, and between their legs, stand smaller figures representing members of the royal family.

What happened next? The official Egyptian version of the battle tells how the ignoble Hittites ambushed the brave Egyptian king; how, as disaster seemed inevitable, Ramesses prayed to the great god Amen of Thebes; how, as Amen heard his prayer, the king of Egypt was granted the power to crush the Hittites single-handedly until they pleaded for mercy. Realizing, perhaps, that this story might not be totally credible even to his uncritical Egyptian audience, Ramesses added an oath to his account: 'As I live, as Re loves me, as my father Atum favours me, everything that my majesty has told I did in truth.'

What really happened at Kadesh? The story of the ambush is almost certainly true. But Muwatallis did not commit his full infantry to the attack on Re Division. Instead, it seems that the bulk of the Hittite army waited with the over-confident Muwatallis on the east bank of the Orontes. The totally unexpected arrival of the Egyptian force from Amurru came as a demoralizing shock. Reinforced, Ramesses was able to push back the Hittite chariots whose occupants, perhaps wondering how many more troops were about to arrive, turned and fled, swimming across the Orontes. As the Hittites struggled and drowned in the water, Ptah Division arrived and the deserters of Re and Amen Divisions slowly returned to stand by their king. Seth Division arrived even later, and, with order restored, the reunited Egyptian army settled down for the night.

The following morning, Egyptian accounts tell us, there was more bloodshed. It is not, however, obvious what happened, as the texts are ambiguous. Was there a battle? Or did Ramesses, as perhaps seems more likely, punish his own troops for their

Single-handed, Ramesses II defeats the enemies of Egypt at the Battle of Kadesh in 1275 BC. The reins are tied around the king's waist so that his hands are free to draw his bow. This engraving, by the French Egyptologist Achille Prisse d'Avennes (1807–79), is based on a fresco in Ramesses' mortuary temple at Thebes.

desertion? The two greatest armies that Syria had ever seen stood on opposite banks of the Orontes, each reluctant to make a move, in what had become a stalemate. Neither side would have welcomed an open battle: the Hittites preferred to ambush their enemies; the Egyptians, accustomed to siege warfare, had never before met such a large, well-disciplined army. Eventually, or so Ramesses tells us, the Hittite king seized the initiative and sent a letter to the Egyptian camp. Negotiators were summoned and a truce was agreed, although Ramesses refused to sign a formal treaty.

So much for the Egyptian version of events. Hittite records recovered from Bogazkoy in modern Turkey (the ancient Hittite capital Hattusas), tell of a very different battle, ending with a humiliated Ramesses forced into retreat. Events after the battle do tend to support this Hittite version. Ramesses' departure without a signed treaty allowed the Hittites to reinforce their hold on Kadesh and regain control of Amurru; the unhappy Benteshina was deposed and sent to work as a servant in Hattusas. The Hittites were then able to push south through the Bekaa valley, taking Damascus and the province of Upi, which was placed under the personal control of the king's brother Hattusilis.

> 'His majesty slaughtered them all; they fell before his horse, and his majesty was alone, none with him.'
>
> FROM 'THE BULLETIN', THE KADESH BATTLE INSCRIPTION OF RAMESSES II

The Kadesh debacle and the subsequent unchallenged loss of Upi inspired several local rulers to neglect to pay their annual tribute, forcing Ramesses to reassert his authority over his vassals. With order restored, he started to think again of extending his borders. A series of Syrian campaigns are recorded on the walls of the Karnak temple, although an unfortunate lack of dates makes their precise order difficult to determine. It seems that Years 8 and 9 saw Ramesses campaigning in Galilee before marching eastwards to occupy the Hittite-held cities of Dapur and Tunip, which had been lost to Egypt for over a century. A further campaign in Phoenicia occurred in Year 10, while Syria was targeted intermittently between Years 10 and 18.

The siege of Dapur is recorded in detail both at Luxor and at Ramesses' Theban mortuary temple, the Ramesseum. Illustrations confirm that Dapur, a heavily fortified city, was situated on a hill and protected by an inner and an outer wall with towers, forcing the Egyptian soldiers to attack from below. The defenders stood on the walls and used bows and arrows to shoot down at the Egyptians who were equipped with ladders and battering rams. The Egyptians rarely lost this sort of campaign, but ultimately these sieges were an expensive and time-consuming waste of resources. A town like Dapur would submit easily to Ramesses, only to revert back to Hittite control as soon as the Egyptian army marched away.

Peace with the Hittites

The Assyrians, a new and highly aggressive enemy, were starting to threaten the Hittite territories in north Syria, and it was not long before the Hittite and Assyrian empires shared a common border. Hattusilis, who, after a brief period of misrule, had succeeded his brother Muwatallis, realized that peace with Egypt would free him to concentrate on the Assyrian danger. Having already concluded a peace treaty with the king of Babylon, he focused his considerable diplomatic skills on Ramesses. In Regnal Year 21 – sixteen years after the Battle of Kadesh – negotiations commenced and

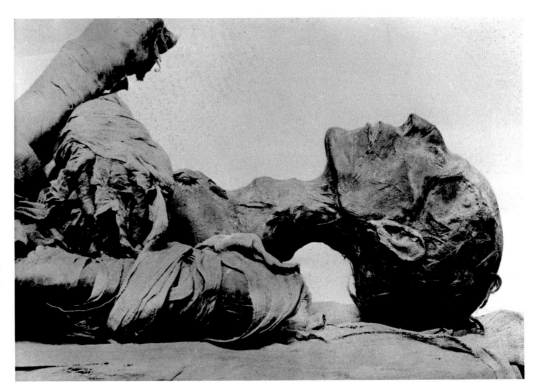

The mummified remains of Ramesses II, who ruled Egypt for more than sixty years. His mummy, today displayed in the Mummy Room of Cairo Museum, still shows traces of the pharaoh's red hair.

terms were eventually agreed. An agreement was inscribed on two matching silver tablets and witnessed, the tablet tells us, by the gods of both lands. The Egyptians and the Hittites were now pledged to respect each other's territories and to defend each other against enemy attack, an agreement intended to last beyond the death of both kings. The two courts were suddenly the best of friends. As Hattusilis started to write to Ramesses, his queen, Pudukhepa, started a correspondence with the Egyptian queen, Nefertari. Eventually Hattusilis sent Ramesses his eldest daughter as a bride.

The treaty brought to an end Ramesses' eastern campaigns. Amurru and Kadesh were now irretrievably lost, but the Syrian territories remained Egyptian and there was free access to the port of Ugarit. Ramesses never relaxed his firm control over his eastern vassals and his reign saw the start of a deliberate policy of remodelling which was to continue long after his death. Canaanite cities deemed to be of little or no commercial use were abandoned; cities considered to be of economic or strategic importance were strengthened to serve as Egyptian outposts.

Sixty-six years on the throne allowed Ramesses ample opportunity for self-promotion. By the time of his death, he was known and respected throughout the ancient world. Within Egypt he was regarded as a living legend and a great military leader; in Nubia he was already a god. Ramesses was brave, enthusiastic and ambitious, even if he was perhaps too impatient and naive. The time-honoured convention of portraying the king of Egypt as superior to all other mortals makes it difficult to understand how Ramesses himself evaluated his military career. Did he really believe his own propaganda? Or were his accounts of the Kadesh triumph merely his means of fulfilling the traditional role of the king as the vanquisher of foreigners and upholder of *maat*?

THE BATTLE OF KADESH, as told by Ramesses

RAMESSES HAD CAMPED with his army in the Wood of Labwi, some 10 miles to the south of Kadesh. Here, he had a stroke of luck. Two Shosu Bedouin joined the camp, offering the allegiance of their tribes to the Egyptians. The Bedouin were able to confirm that the Hittites were cowering near Aleppo, some 120 miles to the north of Kadesh, and that they were reluctant to fight. On the strength of this dubious information (the Bedouin were, it was later realized, Hittite spies), Ramesses decided to head straight for Kadesh, hoping to take the city before the enemy arrived. The army divided and Ramesses, riding at the head of Amen Division, forded the Orontes and marched to strike camp to the northwest of Kadesh. Re Division followed close behind, while Ptah and Seth Divisions were left on the far bank of the river.

Then two further spies – spies so obvious that even Ramesses recognized them – were captured. Their confessions, encouraged by a sound thrashing, made the true situation horribly clear. The Hittites were just 2 miles to the east of Kadesh, and were preparing an ambush. Ramesses summoned his officers to an urgent council of war. Messengers were despatched to summon the missing divisions, and the vulnerable royal family was led westwards to a position of safety.

Suddenly the Hittites launched a chariot attack on Re Division as they marched towards the Amen Division camp. The Egyptian soldiers, isolated and taken completely by surprise, scattered and fled north, running straight to Ramesses. Now it was Amen Division's turn to be taken by surprise. The Egyptians took one look at the approaching chariots, and ran. Ramesses found himself surrounded by the enemy. Only the great god Amen of Thebes – and the loyal shield-bearer Menna – could help him now. Ramesses prayed desperately to his god, and a miracle happened:

Although I prayed in a distant land my prayer was heard in Thebes. Amen came when I called to him; he gave me his hand and I rejoiced ... My heart grew stout and my breast swelled with joy ... I found the enemy chariots scattering before my horses. Not one of them could fight me. Their hearts quaked with fear when they saw me and their arms went limp so they could not shoot. They did not have the heart to hold their spears. I made them plunge into the water like crocodiles. They fell on their faces, one on top of another ...

Single-handed, Ramesses subdued the Hittites. Those who were not killed by the king turned and fled in panic; many drowned attempting to cross the Orontes. The next day Ramesses prepared to fight again, but the enemy begged for peace.

Ramesses II

> 'Fear the Lord, and serve him in sincerity and in truth.'
>
> THE BIBLE, JOSHUA 24:14

JOSHUA BIN NUN

MARTIN VAN CREVELD

1354–1244 BC

THROUGHOUT HISTORY, few commanders have received as much divine assistance as Joshua is said to have done. The little historical evidence that exists, however, suggests that he was a very effective warlord. Not only did Joshua lead his people in conquering most of the land of Israel, but he also managed to hold together their twelve quarrelsome tribes. Considering what took place under his successors, the Judges, this may have been the hardest task of all. Given the nature of the task, the fact that he also engaged in systematic acts of cruelty was perhaps inevitable.

From King David onwards, biblical heroes are frequently the subjects of books, paintings and sculptures, and have music composed in their honour. Very little of this applies to Joshua, however. Although he has an entire book in the Bible named after him, he seems rarely to have appealed to people's imaginations. His prosaic, perhaps even pedestrian, nature was reflected in the fact that, when he died, many of the Israelites he had led so successfully were too busy with their own affairs to take much notice. By the summer of 2007, he failed even to merit an entry in Wikipedia – in our digital world, surely the worst insult of all.

Taking over

Joshua ('Divine Saviour') was the son of Nun, born into the Tribe of Ephraim. If he had a private life, any secret designs, inclinations or idiosyncrasies, we know practically nothing about them. He appears for the first time in the Book of Exodus when Moses put him in command of the Israelites in their fight against their arch-enemy, the Amalekites. A little later, he was one of the two men Moses chose to accompany him to Mount Sinai and to wait while Moses, we are told, spoke to God and received the Ten Commandments.

He is mentioned again in the Book of Numbers at the time the Israelites were camping east of the River Jordan. Moses is said to have appointed Joshua as one of the twelve spies whom he sent to cross the river to explore the land of Israel. Returning after forty days, the spies reported that the country was 'flowing with milk and honey'. To verify their report, they displayed a giant bunch of grapes they had brought back with them. However, ten of the twelve also pointed out that the land of Israel was very well fortified, populated by 'giants' (they stood to ordinary people as ordinary people to grasshoppers) and that any attempt to conquer it would surely fail. Only two of them, Joshua and Caleb Ben Yepuneh, thought that such a campaign could succeed.

Judging by these brief references to Joshua, Moses clearly considered him able, God-fearing, and trustworthy. Clearly, too, he had three other qualities that every commander needs: namely, hands-on operational experience, an understanding of intelligence work, and, above all, faith in the star of his people as well as his own. When the time came for Moses to choose a successor, it was believed that the Lord told him to pick Joshua as 'a man in whom is the spirit'. A public ceremony was organized, and Joshua was duly anointed by the priest Elazar, son of the late Aron, in front of the entire people. It was shortly after this that Moses died.

One of ten gilt bronze relief panels by Lorenzo Ghiberti (1378–1455) in the Baptistery of Florence Cathedral, showing Joshua (lower right) instructing the Israelites to blow their trumpets as they circle Jericho (top) and the subsequent collapse of the city walls (lower left).

The first victory

Almost immediately after Moses' death, Joshua claimed to have had a long interview with God. 'Arise,' the Lord told him.

'Go over this Jordan, thou and all this people, unto the land which I do give to them … There shall not be a man able to stand before thee all the days of their life … [Therefore] be strong and of a good courage; be not afraid, neither be thou dismayed; for the Lord they God is with thee whithersoever thou goest.'

The Lord orders Joshua to cross the River Jordan (Joshua 1:10) in an early fourteenth-century French illumination from the *Bible historiale* of Guiard des Moulins.

Joshua's first step was to draw up a marching order and appoint sub-commanders who would oversee it. Next, he in turn sent out spies to reconnoitre the city of Jericho. Although they were almost caught, they were able to save themselves at the last minute, thanks to the efforts of Rahab, a prostitute with whom they had taken shelter. By way of gratitude, the men told Rahab to mark the window of her house with a red thread so that the invading Israelites, once they had taken the city, would know whom to spare. A much later Jewish tradition has it that Joshua ended up marrying her.

Leaving their wives, their children and their cattle behind, the men of Israel crossed the Jordan in full battle array. Their first objective was Jericho, just north of the Dead Sea. However, there was a problem. Jericho was heavily fortified with walls, the remainders of which can be seen to the present day. Though the Bible has nothing to say on the subject, it is likely that the Israelites, like all desert people throughout history, had no experience of siege warfare nor possessed the technology, such as heavy rams, to wage it. Accustomed to raiding and skirmishes, they also tended to be easily discouraged by sustained warfare.

Not for the last time, according to the Bible, God chose to help by a miraculous intervention. Appearing to Joshua, he ordered that the entire Israelite army be summoned in procession, together with all its religious paraphernalia such as the Ark of the Covenant and the trumpets made of rams' horns. His instructions were very detailed. The Israelites were to circle the city six times during six successive days. On the seventh day they were to do so not once but seven times. Next, as they blew their trumpets and raised a great shout, the walls would fall flat in front of them.

These directives were followed to the letter and events took place as promised; as the trumpets emitted their shrill sound (said, by later Jewish tradition, to be capable of piercing the heavens themselves), the walls collapsed. All that remained for the Israelites was to sack the city. This they did, 'utterly [destroying] all that was

Joshua Bin Nun

in the city, both man and woman, young and old, and ox, and sheep, and ass, with the edge of the sword'. Only vessels made out of gold, silver, brass and iron were spared, not for private use but so that they could be consecrated to the Lord.

A possible explanation for the miraculous elements in the Jericho story can be found in geological evidence. The Jordan valley lies on a major geological rift, subject to frequent earthquakes. At around the same time that the city walls fell, the Jordan supposedly parted to enable the Israelites to cross on dry land, a 'miracle' also witnessed in modern times when mudslips induced by quakes have been known to dam the river, most recently in 1927. It seems reasonable that earthquake activity dammed the Jordan and destroyed Jericho's walls (the miracle thus being one of its timing rather than the event itself).

Conquering the land of Israel

Jericho having fallen (from whatever cause), Joshua turned his efforts to a small city further up the Judean hills by the name of Ai. He succeeded in capturing it, but the extreme cruelty with which he treated its hapless inhabitants had two very different results. On the one hand, we are told, the inhabitants of at least one city, Gibeon, a few miles northwest of Jerusalem, were so terrified that they decided that they would rather make peace than war. They sent envoys, pretending to come 'from a very far country', to approach Joshua in order to draw up a treaty with them, which was duly

THE CAPTURE OF AI

THE CAPTURE OF AI was Joshua's only military failure, but one which later he succeeded in turning into his tactical masterpiece. In doing so, he displayed the qualities of a great commander, including determination, leadership (he knew how to rally his discouraged army), guile and the ability to snatch victory from the jaws of defeat. And, of course, he displayed his usual cruelty.

Unlike Jericho, Ai appears to have been a small city of no very great importance. It was, however, located east of Bethel, thus commanding one of the few routes that led west from the Jordan valley into the mountainous interior of the country.

As at Jericho, Joshua started by sending out spies. They reported that the city was weak and suggested that three thousand men should suffice to capture it. Things did not work as planned, and Joshua's men fled in front of those of Ai. They were chased downhill, and thirty-six of them were killed. 'Wherefore', the Bible tells us, 'the hearts of the people melted, and became like water.'

Clearly there was something very wrong with an army whose troops first underestimate the enemy, then run, and then lose heart because a few of them are killed. Joshua did what was necessary, given the circumstances. He started by making a big show of consulting with the Lord. He then told the people what God had allegedly told him:

namely, that the defeat was due to one of their number violating the Lord's orders and taking booty from Jericho. Lots were cast, and the name of one Achan came up. A search was made, and the stolen goods were found. Achan and his entire family were executed with great ceremony, being stoned to death and their bodies then burnt.

With the Lord thus appeased, the rest was straight-forward. 'Thirty thousand mighty men of valour' were chosen and took on concealed positions. If a true figure, this force alone outnumbered the men of Ai many times over. With Joshua himself in command, the bulk of the Israelite army attacked from another direction, pretended to be defeated and fled, drawing the enemy after them. Joshua then gave the signal for the ambush to leave its concealed positions, enter the city from the rear and set it on fire. Twelve thousand men, women and children perished, 'for Joshua drew not his hand back ... until he had utterly destroyed all the inhabitants of Ai'.

Perhaps the most interesting detail in this entire story, however, is one that reveals key information. In order to spring the trap, Joshua waved a spear. Even by men whose eyesight is keen, there are limits to the distance at which a spear can be seen, a fact which tells us how small the battlefield really was, and how few warriors it can have contained.

Joshua Bin Nun

'The face of Moses was like the sun, the face of Joshua like the moon.' THE TALMUD

signed. When he discovered the deception, Joshua, although very angry, would not go back on his word. He decided to honour the treaty, but subjugated the Gibeonites and made them into 'hewers of wood and drawers of water … even unto the present day'.

Not all of the country's inhabitants reacted in this way. 'All the kings which were on this side of the Jordan, in the hills, and in the valleys, and in all the coasts of the great sea over against Lebanon … gathered themselves together, to fight with Joshua and with Israel, with one accord.' Joshua's strategy of terror here caused growing resistance.

This resistance enabled Joshua to fight his first pitched battle. No fewer than five kings gathered 'all their hosts' near Gibeon, and it was the Gibeonites who first sounded the alarm and demanded that their newly found masters come and rescue them. At the time, Joshua and his army were based at Gilgal, further east in the Jordan valley. Having duly consulted the Lord, Joshua led his force up the mountains in what must have been an extremely strenuous night march, taking the enemy by surprise. While the Bible tells us that there was 'great slaughter', it offers no details. All we know is that the enemy ran west by way of the Valley of Beth Horon, which in turn leads down the mountain to the coastal plain below.

This was not the end of the matter. To add to the fleeing enemy's discomfiture, the biblical account has God intervening in person, raining down 'great stones from heaven' upon them. At Joshua's special request, He even stopped the sun and the moon from moving, adding some hours to the usual twenty-four so that the

A 35-feet deep cistern excavated at Gibeon (in modern Arabic, al-Jib), from the twelfth century BC. It was at Gibeon that Joshua fought his first pitched battle.

(Opposite) *Joshua's Victory over the Amorites:* a wood engraving from a drawing by Gustave Doré (1832–83), showing the Lord raining down stones on Joshua's enemies (Joshua 10:11).

Joshua Bin Nun

41

Israelites could complete the carnage. The five unfortunate kings hid in a cave, but were captured and brought in front of Joshua. First he humiliated them by forcing them to lie down while the Israelite troops put their feet upon their necks; next, he had them hanged.

Completing the conquest

Joshua's victory over the five kings meant that he was now in control of the centre of the country (although the fact that he did not conquer Jerusalem, which remained in the hands of the Jebusites until the days of King David, casts some doubt as to how firm that control really was). We do not know the location of all the remaining cities he went on to capture. Moreover, our understanding of his strategy is hampered by the fact that geography does not seem to have been the strong point of those who edited the Bible and gave it the form it has today.

All this makes his next moves, and their timing, rather difficult to follow. None the less, Joshua ended up in control of the southern Judean Hills as well as the southwestern coastal plain 'even unto Gaza' and Goshen; considering that the latter is supposed to be located in Egypt, one cannot help but raise an eyebrow. In 'all the country of the hills, and of the south, and of the vale, and of the springs, and all their kings, he left none remaining, but utterly destroyed all that breathed as the Lord God of Israel commanded'.

While Joshua was busy in the south, a second coalition, made up of a larger number of kings, was formed against him in the north, its prime mover being Yabin, king of Hazor. Some of Yabin's allies came from the hills of Samaria; others were gathered from the Plain of Esdraelon and what is today Lower Galilee, all the way to the foothills of Mount Hermon. Quantitatively and qualitatively, the forces at their disposal were far stronger than any previous enemy the Israelites had encountered. 'Even as the sand that is upon the sea shore in multitude,' the Bible says, 'with horses and chariots very many.'

Once again, Joshua turned to God, who told him that victory was guaranteed. Once again, Joshua was able to take the enemy by surprise, though

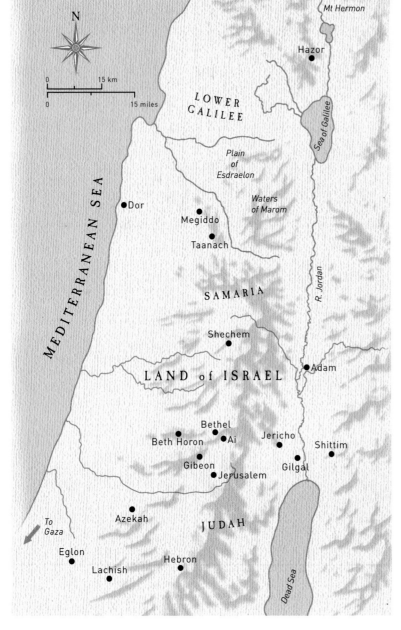

ISRAEL AND JUDAH
c. 1300 BC.

Joshua Bin Nun

42

how it was done is unknown. The battle took place at the Waters of Marom, in the Valley of Esdraelon, and was decisive. Whether this took a few months or years, we do not know.

> Joshua took all that land, the hills, and all the south country, and all the land of Goshen, and the valley, and the plain, and the mountain of Israel and the valley of the same … there was not a city that made peace with the children of Israel, save the Hivites, the inhabitants of Gibeon; all others they took in battle. For it was of the Lord to harden their hearts, that they should come against Israel in battle, that He might destroy them utterly.

The victory was not quite complete, for the Philistines, referred to as anakim (giants) were not subdued. Yet it was sufficient to enable Joshua to distribute the conquered land among the twelve tribes. In doing so, the Bible says, he followed the detailed instructions left by Moses. Feeling his death to be imminent, Joshua delivered a final speech in which he reminded the people that their triumphs had all been due to the Lord and that, should they forsake Him, they could expect Him to forsake them in return. At the age of 110 years, he died. He had ruled Israel for twenty-eight years.

The legend

Given his enormous achievement, perhaps the most surprising thing about Joshua is that there are no legends about him personally. Although he was believed to have had more than his share of divine aid, he did not have any miraculous escapes. He neither persecuted nor betrayed anybody in particular. He did not satisfy whatever lusts he may have had at the expense of others. He did not even try to argue with God, as Moses had often done. In his final message to the people, all he had to say was, 'Fear the Lord, and serve him in sincerity and in truth', advice which, however useful, must seem somewhat prosaic in comparison to the utterances of Moses, his predecessor.

Seen from a modern vantage point, he was a sort of miniature Genghis Khan, using sword and fire to invade and subdue a country whose inhabitants had done him no wrong. Wherever he went, he committed vast slaughter, only rarely sparing women and children. In his favour, all that can be said is that he was acting on the express command of God (or so he, and those whom he led, believed or affected to believe).

Subsequent generations made a few half-hearted attempts to enhance his stature. We are told that, at the time Joshua was waiting for Moses to return from his encounter with God at Mount Sinai, the Lord, showing His special consideration, made sure that he would get his portion of manna like anybody else. Another story has it that his wife Rahab – if, indeed, she did become his wife – was not a simple prostitute but 'a great soul' (whatever that may mean). A third says that his coins carried an ox on one side and a re'em (oryx), an animal with majestic horns, on the other. But that, more or less, is all.

KING DAVID
c. 1037–967 BC

MARTIN VAN CREVELD

KING DAVID OF ISRAEL is often seen as one of history's greatest commanders, known also for being an even greater poet and a talented musician who excelled at playing the harp. Above all, he was a man of God; almost everything we know about him comes from the Bible, where he is reported to have been able to talk to God face to face.

At the time that David started his ascent to power, the kingdom of Israel had just suffered its worst defeat at the hands of the Philistines, who had left their homeland in what is today southwestern Israel and the Gaza Strip. Marching north, they advanced to Mount Gilboa, not far south of the Sea of Galilee, where a battle was fought in which King Saul and his son Jonathan lost their lives, their bodies being nailed to the wall of the town of Beth Shean by the Philistines. It fell to David to restore his people's fortunes. By the time of his death, after incessant war, he had not only restored the kingdom but also expanded it, creating a mini-empire in the Middle East.

Youth and apprenticeship

David was born into the tribe of Judah in around 1030 BC. He was the youngest son of Jesse, the son of Obed, son of Boaz and Ruth the Moabite (Ruth's story is told in the Book of Ruth). He spent his youth as a shepherd near Beth Lehem. Shepherds, then as well as later, were considered to be outside civil society, always ready to fight and to engage in occasional acts of robbery and blackmail; whether David was true to type we do not know. The Bible does tell us, however, that on one occasion he killed a lion that had attacked his flock, and he himself referred to other similar events. It was at this time that the Prophet Samuel, apparently acting on God's express command, anointed David king over Israel, although the reason for his selection is unexplained.

As to what happened next, the Bible is somewhat confused. One version is that King Saul felt depressed and had the young, good-looking shepherd play the harp for him to ease his mood. According to another version, the two of them met when the Israelites were waging one of their frequent wars against the Philistines. The young

David, who had come to the Israelite camp to visit his brothers, took up the challenge issued by the Philistine giant Goliath, an encounter that ended when David slew him.

From shepherd to king

From this point, David was a national hero. He continued to play the harp for King Saul, and to form a close bond with Saul's son Jonathan, a relationship that has been the subject of speculation throughout Western culture. Saul gave him his daughter Michal to marry 'that she may be a snare to him'. By way of bride-wealth the king demanded the foreskins of a hundred dead Philistines; the number he actually received was double that. Whether because of the king's temperament or because he suspected David of plotting against him, they fell out. At first Saul himself tried to kill David by throwing a spear at him, but when that failed, he sent men to carry out his assassination. David was saved by his wife, who let him down from the window of their house by rope. In another account, Jonathan warned him of his father's plan.

The Anointing of David by Saul: a painting by Félix-Joseph Barrias (1822–1907), in the Musée du Petit Palais, Paris.

Initially David sought shelter with the Philistines, but then, fearing for his life, he left, spending most of the following years in what is today the northern part of the Negev Desert. He gathered around him some four hundred tough outlaws: 'every one that was in distress, and every one that was in debt, and every one that was discontented'. The most important of these were his three nephews, Joab, Avishai and Asael, the sons of his sister Zeruyah. With their help he skirmished against the Philistines, being careful to consult with God, who always promised him victory.

He made a living by blackmailing local landowners, killing at least one of them and marrying his widow. Twice Saul took an army and went out to hunt for him, but David proved a master of evasive tactics and an elusive commander. At one point he even caught Saul unawares and could have killed him, but he preferred reconciliation. It did not last.

At the time Saul died in battle against the Philistines, David was 23 years old. He and his men were far away, waging war against the Amalekites, traditional enemies of the Israelites. Having received news of the defeat, he went to Hebron, capital of his own Judean tribe. Saul and his heir Jonathan were dead, and his surviving sons were unfit to rule; hence they agreed to make him their king, or so the Bible says. After seven years fighting numerous small skirmishes, David finally defeated Saul's remaining supporters and became king of all the tribes of Israel.

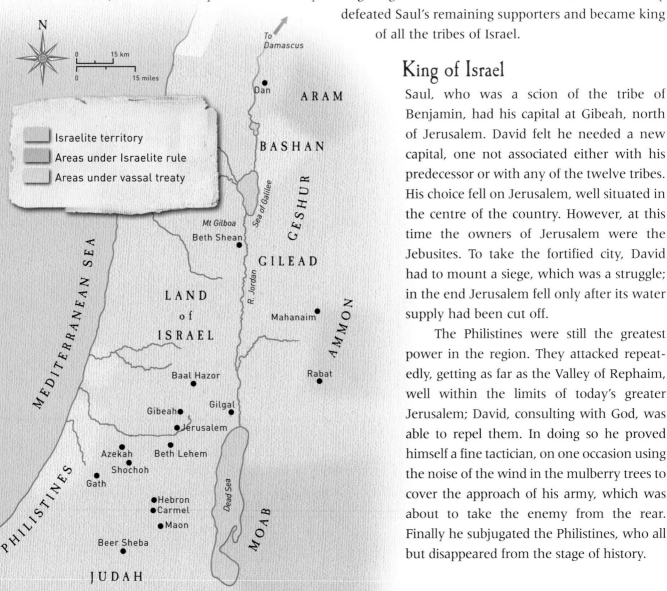

ISRAEL AND JUDAH
in the tenth century BC.

Israelite territory
Areas under Israelite rule
Areas under vassal treaty

King of Israel

Saul, who was a scion of the tribe of Benjamin, had his capital at Gibeah, north of Jerusalem. David felt he needed a new capital, one not associated either with his predecessor or with any of the twelve tribes. His choice fell on Jerusalem, well situated in the centre of the country. However, at this time the owners of Jerusalem were the Jebusites. To take the fortified city, David had to mount a siege, which was a struggle; in the end Jerusalem fell only after its water supply had been cut off.

The Philistines were still the greatest power in the region. They attacked repeatedly, getting as far as the Valley of Rephaim, well within the limits of today's greater Jerusalem; David, consulting with God, was able to repel them. In doing so he proved himself a fine tactician, on one occasion using the noise of the wind in the mulberry trees to cover the approach of his army, which was about to take the enemy from the rear. Finally he subjugated the Philistines, who all but disappeared from the stage of history.

There were, of course, other enemies: Edom to the south, Moab to the southeast, Ammon to the east and Aram to the northeast were all brought to heel. It was during the siege of the Ammonite capital, Rabat, that David saw the beautiful Bathsheba washing on the roof of her house and immediately desired her. He took her, slept with her and sent her home.

When Bathsheba informed him she was pregnant, he ordered her husband, Uriah, to be brought back to Jerusalem so he could sleep with her. Uriah, however, took life seriously: he refused to do so as long as the war was going on. Accordingly David sent him back to the front, secretly ordering Joab to expose Uriah to the enemy so he would be killed in action.

The Holy Bible is not a military handbook. It provides few details about the battles in question; the closest we come to learning about any tactical detail

David, wearing a crown and playing the harp, kneels before King Saul. This illumination, from a fifteenth-century Flemish manuscript, depicts a biblical episode described in I Samuel 18:11, in which Saul twice throws a spear at David in anger.

is when we are told that, on one occasion, two of David's nephews, Joab and Avisahi, divided their forces to confront an enemy who was advancing on them from two different directions. David was commander-in-chief, but in later days rarely commanded troops in person.

The field commander was Joab, a tough individual who had joined David early in his career. Besides being good with weapons, he quickly made himself indispensable and proved a fine strategist, able and willing to take on armies stronger than his own. Equally importantly, he could act on his own initiative and carry out necessary but unpleasant tasks of the kind that, today, would be known as targeted assassinations. (Ultimately he was killed by Salomon, David's son and heir, on the latter's express orders.)

Joab was but one of thirty-seven 'mighty men' surrounding David, though we know next to nothing about the way they and the rest of the forces were organized and commanded. The army's core consisted of three units of mercenaries, who, no doubt for reasons of security, were drawn from three different foreign peoples. The rest, probably numbering some tens of thousands, were tribal warriors who could be called upon in an emergency.

The Bible has nothing to say about the way all these forces were armed. We can only assume that, like their enemies, they consisted of both infantry – indispensable for siege warfare as well as open combat – and cavalry. Those who could afford it may have worn some elements of armour. Certainly they used the usual edged weapons, such as spears, swords and short daggers, and bows and arrows and slings. The Bible says that, at the height of David's reign, the scope of his power went as far as Damascus and he received the tribute of various client kings. Clearly his army must have been highly efficient.

DAVID AGAINST GOLIATH

THE BATTLE BETWEEN DAVID AND GOLIATH would have appeared as one in which there was simply no contest. On the one side there stood a giant – six cubits and a span tall, the Bible says – fully armed and covered by a shield so big that, until the actual moment of battle, it had to be carried for him by a special assistant; opposing him, an adolescent armed with nothing but a sling. Yet in fact it was Goliath who never stood a chance.

The Philistines were originally an Aegean people. Having left their homeland for unknown reasons, they tried to settle in Egypt but were repulsed; they ended by carving themselves a territory out of what, today, is southwestern Israel and the Gaza Strip. Joshua had fought them, but had not succeeded in subduing them. They used bronze weapons broadly similar to those described in Homer's *Iliad*. Had Goliath ridden a chariot and carried two spears instead of one, then the parallel would have been absolute. By contrast, all over the ancient Middle East the sling was considered a poor man's weapon, only fit for those who could not afford anything better.

'Saul hath slain in his thousands and David in his tens of thousands.'

HYMN SUNG IN HONOUR OF DAVID'S VICTORY OVER GOLIATH,
I SAMUEL 18:7

When David volunteered to act as Israel's champion and engage Goliath in a duel, King Saul offered him his own heavy armour and weapons to use. David tried them on but found them cumbersome; wearing them, he could barely move. To approach an opponent much stronger than himself and fight him while carrying such arms was to court certain death.

Instead he chose what, today, would be called 'asymmetrical warfare'. Having spent his youth as a shepherd, he had honed his skill with the sling during endless idle hours when he had nothing better to do. An expert with the weapon could fire one pebble every fifteen or so seconds to a distance of 100 yards, hitting his target every time. The heavily armed Goliath could not move very quickly. Hence David had plenty of time to reload his sling and hurl another pebble if, by any chance, the first one missed. If the worst came to the worst, he could always run in circles around his enemy.

Before the fight there was a slanging match that angered Goliath and distracted him. Next, breaking into a run, David approached him. While still at a safe distance, he stopped, used his sling – and missed his target. Almost certainly he was aiming at Goliath's forehead, which remained exposed under the helmet. Instead he hit him in the eye, causing a wound that, though very bad, may not have been mortal.

Thereupon Goliath crashed to the ground, his armour and weapons ringing. David went up to the fallen giant and, using the latter's own sword, cut off his head.

David with the Head of Goliath, by Michelangelo Merisi da Caravaggio (1571–1610), in the Galleria Borghese in Rome.

Quelling revolt

In some ways, the greatest military challenge David ever faced was mounted by his son Absalom (the name, paradoxically, means 'The Father of Peace'). The revolt arose out of a family quarrel after Absalom had raped his half-sister Tamar, or so she claimed. Absalom was sent into exile but was reconciled with his father by Joab who, on this occasion, proved himself a fine diplomat. The reconciliation did not last. At one point, Absalom, who is said to have been very handsome and very good at attracting popularity, rose up against David.

King David talking to God, in an illuminated letter 'O' from the Breviary of Ludovic de Teck, patriarch of Aquileia, *c.* 1350.

The revolt came like a bolt out of a blue sky. Jerusalem was threatened; of all the people David ruled, the only ones who remained loyal to him were the members of his own household, together with foreign mercenaries. With them, he fled eastward, leaving behind ten concubines to guard the palace. Allegedly, Absalom, probably in order to prove that the break with his father was final, promptly had sex with them in front of the assembled people.

Originally David seems to have hoped he could gather his forces in the wilderness west of the River Jordan and the Dead Sea. However, his spies in Jerusalem informed him that the enemy was coming for him, so he decided to cross the river. Meanwhile, inside Jerusalem, Absalom's camp was divided. One adviser in particular, Ahitophel ('Brother of Hell'), proposed that twelve thousand men be quickly called up, put under his own command, and used to hunt David down. Had this plan been carried out, it might well have succeeded.

In the end, however, the counsel of one Hushai, who was secretly loyal to David but managed to gain Absalom's favour, prevailed. Absalom was apparently no strategist. Hushai told him that 'thou knowest thy father and his men, that they be mighty men, and they be chafed in their minds, as a bear robbed of her whelps in the field; and thy father is a man of war, and will not lodge with the city'. He therefore suggested that not twelve thousand men but the entire people be mobilized and fall on David 'as the dew falleth on the ground'.

This plan was adopted. It gave David what he needed most: time. As more and more men joined him, he divided them into units and put commanders of thousands and commanders of hundreds in charge of them. The army thus hastily formed was divided into three parts, one commanded by Joab, one by Avishai, and the third by a loyal mercenary chief, Ittai the Gittite.

Apparently David wanted to command in person, but his men, claiming his life was worth that of ten thousand others, refused to allow him. Thereupon he was obliged to let them do as they wished. A battle was fought, and won, in 'the wood of Ephraim'; where that wood was located we do not know. Fleeing after his defeat, Absalom's hair, which was long and of which he had always been extraordinarily proud, was caught in the branch of a tree. His mule bolted, and he was left hanging in mid-air. When his brother Joab was told, and informed that nobody would touch the king's son, he himself went to the spot and killed him. The revolt was over.

*And the king was much moved, and went up to the chamber over the gate, and
wept: and as he went, thus he said, O my son Absalom, my son, my son Absalom!
would God I had died for thee, O Absalom, my son, my son!*
And it was told Joab, Behold, the king weepeth and mourneth for Absalom.
*And the victory that day was turned into mourning unto all the people: for the
people heard say that day how the king was grieved for his son.*
2 SAMUEL 18: 33; 19: 1–2

The aftermath

Originally David had been God's anointed; clearly he was a man who was able to
consult with God and receive answers to his questions. At one point he hoped to build
a temple to the Lord. However, God, telling him that he (David) was a warrior with
much blood on his hands, refused this offer.

Later, through committing various misdeeds, David's relationship with God began
to sour. First came the sordid affair with Bathsheba. Then there was the extermination
of some remaining sons of Saul, as well as a misguided attempt to go against the laws
of the Pentateuch and conduct a census. All this caused God to withdraw his favour.
Furthermore, if the Bible is to be believed, Absalom had been David's most dearly
beloved son, and he never came to terms with Absalom's revolt and subsequent death.

David and Bathsheba depicted in a stone pediment carving dating from the third or fourth century AD, now in the Coptic Museum, Cairo.

In old age the condition of this once
formidable warrior and lover – he had
dozens of wives and concubines – deteriorated, so much so that they brought him
a young virgin, not to sleep with, but
simply so she could provide him with
warmth. At the very end of David's life
he had to deal with another of his sons,
Adoniah who tried to usurp the throne
from the designated heir, Solomon. The
revolt was quelled, but not before Joab
had deserted David.

In all, he reigned for forty-seven
years, of which forty were in Jerusalem.
His considerable achievement lasted only
during the lifetime of his successor; after
Solomon's death, the kingdom split in
two. If Jewish tradition is to be believed,
David left behind a body of poetic work
that includes the entire book of the
Psalms as well as the lament he composed
for Saul and Jonathan. His descendants
included a long line of kings, and
ultimately Mary, the mother of Jesus.

King David

'For the first time in history the idea of centralization was introduced into politics...'

TIGLATH-PILESER III
744–727 BC

DOYNE DAWSON

TIGLATH-PILESER III is generally considered the greatest Assyrian king and one of the most successful military commanders of the ancient world. He began the process whereby the loosely organized hegemony built up by earlier Assyrian kings was replaced with history's first centralized imperial state, which became the model for all later empires. At the same time he reorganized the Assyrian army and introduced the use of combined arms, or infantry and cavalry working in cooperation.

These claims will require some historical background, for readers with any knowledge of ancient history are probably aware that very large empires had existed in the Middle East for over a thousand years before Tiglath-Pileser III. The first genuine empire based on conquest was that of Sargon of Akkad, who in the early Bronze Age (late third millennium BC) united nearly all of Mesopotamia into a state known as Sumer and Akkad. In the later Bronze Age (second millennium BC) imperial states of comparable size were assembled by the Egyptians of the New Kingdom, the Hittites of Anatolia, and the Hurrians, whose major state was the kingdom of Mitanni in north Mesopotamia and Syria. But these were not centralized empires like the later Assyrian state. They are best described as hegemonies. They were put together by successful kings who reduced their neighbours, made them pull down their walls, and exacted tribute from them; but the native dynasties of these principalities were not replaced, and as long as they paid tribute and made no attempt to rebuild their fortifications they suffered little interference from the overlord. In the Bronze Age such a state was called a 'Great Kingdom', and any king who ruled other kings could call himself a Great King. The client kings tended to be unreliable, of course, and it was frequently necessary to dispatch punitive expeditions to keep them in line.

Assyria had been a Great Kingdom in this sense for centuries before Tiglath-Pileser III, on and off. In the fourteenth century BC the Middle Assyrian kingdom succeeded in uniting all north Mesopotamia ('Middle Assyrian' is a linguistic term referring to the dialect of Akkadian spoken in Assyria in the late Bronze Age); it enjoyed a last spurt of expansion under Tiglath-Pileser I (1114–1076 BC), who sacked

Babylon and raided deep into Anatolia and Iran. After that, Assyria was devastated by the migrations of the Aramaean tribes from the Syrian Desert, who were probably the first people to make full use of the Arabian camel for transport. In the tenth century BC the Assyrian kingdom was pushed back into its original homeland, a 100-mile strip along the upper Tigris river containing the cities of Ashur (the ancient religious capital), Nimrud (the royal capital), Nineveh (the main royal capital after 700 BC), and Arbil. A second burst of expansion came between 883 and 824, when two energetic kings, Ashurnasirpal II and his son Shalmaneser III, subdued the Aramaean principalities, restored Assyrian control over north Mesopotamia, and established a block of client states stretching over northern Syria. This was a loosely organized hegemonial structure like the Middle Assyrian state and the other Great Kingdoms of the Bronze Age, and it did not last long. Between 824 and 744 there came a series of weak kings and the client kings broke away. But even during this period of weakness,

Tiglath-Pileser III established a cordon of firmly controlled client states in the Levant, finally declaring himself king of Babylon in 728 or 729 BC. He is depicted here on a stela (carved stone slab) from his palace at Nimrud.

the Assyrians kept control of north Mesopotamia, including the entire plain between the Tigris and the Euphrates as far west as the great bend of the Euphrates, with the foothills of the Zagros range to the east.

In 744 BC, the last of these weak kings was overthrown by a rebellion and the throne was seized by the governor of Nimrud, the Assyrian capital city, who claimed to be descended from an earlier king, but this is doubtful. Assyrian tradition cherished the myth that all their kings had come from the same royal family in an unbroken line since *c.* 1500 BC, and scribes tended to cover up breaks in the succession. The real name of the governor of Nimrud is unknown. Tiglath-Pileser is the biblical rendering of the Akkadian throne name, Tukulti-Apil-Esharra, meaning 'My trust is in the son of Esharra [the god Ninurta]'. The choice of this name deliberately proclaimed a programme of expansion; he called himself after the hero king Tiglath-Pileser I, who had carried the arms of Assyria further afield than any other king before him.

Campaigns of Tiglath-Pileser III

The documentation – inscriptions, chronicles, royal correspondence, treaties, parts of the Bible – is extraordinarily full for this period, compared to other earlier periods of Assyrian history, and allows a relatively full reconstruction of campaigns of conquest.

Immediately after seizing power in 744 BC, Tiglath-Pileser led an expedition into Babylonia (southern Mesopotamia) to protect his ally, the Babylonian king Nabonassar (Nabu-nasir) from the rebellious Aramaean and Chaldaean tribes who were supported by the kingdom of Elam in southwestern Iran. The Assyrians now challenged the Elamites for control of the rich and strategic territory of Babylonia. Nabonassar remained king of Babylon for the next ten years but from this time on was a vassal of Tiglath-Pileser.

However, the main threat to Assyria came from the kingdom of Urartu in the Armenian mountains directly to the north. The ethnic and linguistic affinities of the people of Urartu are uncertain; they may have been Hurrians or Armenians, or possibly an older Hurrian elite ruling an Armenian population that had moved in from western Anatolia. (The main reason for assuming an Armenian stratum in the population is that in the sixth century BC, Urartu was replaced by the kingdom of Armenia.) Early in the eighth century, Urartu became a kingdom as large as Assyria, with a block of allies stretching from northern Syria and southwest Anatolia to western Iran, forming a great crescent that hemmed in Assyria's northern frontiers and controlled the main east–west trade routes. The chronology is uncertain, but it appears that in about 743 BC, the Assyrian king attacked a league of Syrian princes, led by the city of Arpad, who were allies of Urartu. The next year, King Sarduri III of Urartu was defeated by the Assyrians at the Battle of Commagene on the upper Euphrates, and thereafter he abandoned his Levantine allies. In 740, Arpad fell after a three-year siege, following which much of northern Syria was annexed by Assyria, and the kings of Damascus and Israel offered tribute.

In 737–736 BC the Assyrian king turned eastward, occupied the central Zagros range and marched across Media, penetrating more deeply into the Iranian plateau than any Mesopotamian ruler had ever gone before. In 735 he turned north and invaded Urartu itself, crossing the formidable Armenian mountains and besieging the Urartuan capital Tushpa (modern Van) on Lake Van; the siege was unsuccessful, but the role of Urartu in Near Eastern affairs had been sharply curtailed.

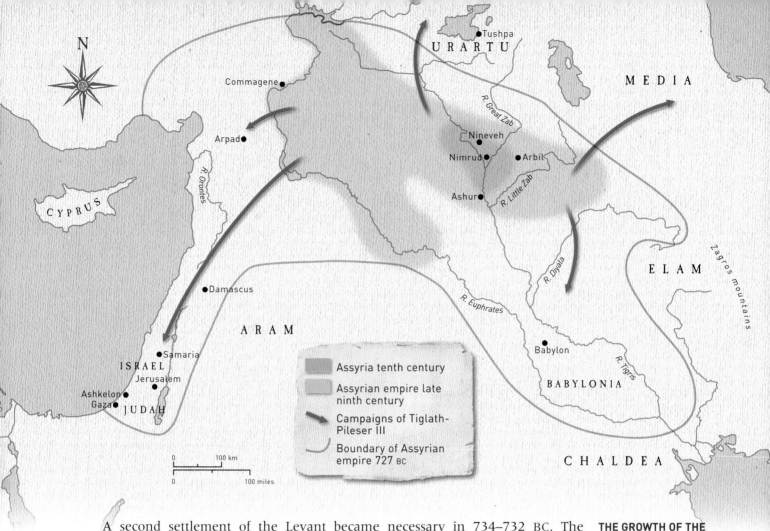

A second settlement of the Levant became necessary in 734–732 BC. The Philistine rulers of Ashkelon and Gaza organized a league of Palestinian cities against Assyria and were defeated by Tiglath-Pileser. Amon, Edom, Moab, Judah, and a queen of the Arabs paid tribute. In 732, King Ahaz of Judah was attacked by Israel and Damascus and called on Assyria for help. Tiglath-Pileser annexed Damascus and half of Israel, dividing both into provinces, but leaving Hoshea as puppet king of Israel. Judah and the Philistine cities became Assyrian clients.

Assyrian kings routinely boasted of their victories in sanguinary inscriptions. Here is an example from the palace of Tiglath-Pileser at Nimrud celebrating his triumph over King Rezin of Damascus and King Pekah of Israel:

> *Rezin the Damascene … With the blood of his warriors I dyed with a reddish hue the river … That one [Rezin] in order to save his life fled alone; and he entered the gate of his city like a mongoose. I impaled alive his chief ministers … I confined him like a bird in a cage. His gardens … orchards without number I cut down; I did not leave a single one. [Sixteen] districts of Bit-Humri [Israel] I levelled to the ground.*

The Assyrian conquests inspired the prophet Isaiah to a cosmic view of history, which was to have great influence on the Judeo-Christian tradition. All historical events were seen as part of a divine plan. The Assyrian was the scourge of God, an instrument used to punish the people of Israel for their sins:

Tiglath-Pileser III

The Assyrian! He is the rod that I [Yahweh] *wield in my anger, and the staff of my wrath is in his hand. I sent him against a godless nation* [Israel]*, I bid him march against a people who rouse my wrath, to spoil and plunder at will and trample them down like mud in the streets.*
ISAIAH 10: 5–6

Then came the final settlement of Babylonia. Nabonassar had died in 734 BC and in 731 a Chaldaean usurper seized Babylon. Tiglath-Pileser invaded the south, killed the usurper, and in 729 or 728 took the title of king of Babylonia under the throne name Pulu (by which he is sometimes called in the Bible).

By the end of the reign, all the Fertile Crescent above Egypt, with a population of several million people, had been brought within the Assyrian empire. A block of new provinces had been created extending to the Mediterranean. Beyond these provinces a series of tightly controlled client states stretched from south Anatolia to the border of Egypt. Babylonia was under direct Assyrian control. The terminal points of the major caravan routes were in Assyrian hands. It was the largest state and the most complex political structure that the human race had so far produced.

A striking feature of the new Assyrian imperialism was the massive deportation of tens of thousands of people from the conquered populations. This had been done before in the Middle East, but never on the massive scale initiated by Tiglath-Pileser. Tens of thousands were relocated by him and the policy was continued by all his successors, so that by the end of the Assyrian empire in 612 BC, if the inscriptions of the kings are to be credited, more than 4 million people had been relocated. The purpose of this policy was, of course, to punish 'rebellion' and to forestall future rebellions by breaking up disloyal populations, but also to provide agricultural labour and other manpower. After the needs of the court had been met, those deported were apportioned among temples, nobles and cities. Most were kept in family groups and settled in small communities. They were treated as Assyrians; the inscriptions often repeat the phrase: 'I carried off [deportees], I settled them, as Assyrians I counted them; the yoke of Ashur [the chief Assyrian god] my lord, like the Assyrians I laid on them; tribute and tax like the Assyrians I laid on them.' It was assumed that they would eventually become loyal subjects of the Assyrian king, and there is evidence that they often did. Most of them came from Aramaic regions, and this helped to further the Aramaicization of Mesopotamia, which was already far advanced.

Administrative reforms

As his conquests proceeded, the king began to build up a new Assyrian elite to replace the old nobility. The power of the nobles was restricted by reducing the size and multiplying the number of the provinces until there were about eighty, so that the power of any individual governor was reduced. Many eunuchs were appointed governors because they had no families and were totally dependent on the king. Each province was ruled by a governor called either a *shaknu* ('appointed one') or a *bel pihati* ('district chief'). Their duties were to keep order, to collect tribute, to supply the king and his entourage and army when they passed through, and to provide soldiers and labour gangs as needed. The system of conscription was one widely used in the ancient Middle East: individuals received land grants (*ilkum*) on the condition that they supply the king with a certain number of men for military service or labour as needed. Much of the manpower came from those deported, as described above. The empire was crisscrossed by a large road system, its use restricted to those carrying the royal seal. The court kept in contact with governors through the first efficient postal service in history, the model for the famous postal service of the Persians. The king also had at his disposal the *qurbutu*, a small staff of trusted administrators who carried out regular inspections of the provinces and made reports directly to the king. Many client states became provinces; those that remained independent were placed under the supervision of overseers (*qepu*). Failure to render tribute or other signs of disloyalty led to loss of independence and incorporation into the provincial system. The intended result of these reforms, which were continued by all Tiglath-Pileser's successors, was a tremendous strengthening of royal authority.

Military reforms

The old army, called the *sab sharri*, consisted of *ilkum* holders and peasant conscripts provided by landlords, and was distributed about the empire under the command of the provincial governors. It only campaigned in summer, between the June harvest and the October sowing. The basic unit was the *kisru*, sometimes translated as 'cohort', which was commanded by a *rab kisri*. Under the *rab kisri* were Commanders of Fifty and Commanders of Ten. The absence of any unit larger than fifty may support the assumption that the *kisru* was about the size of a Roman cohort (600 men), in which case the *rab kisri* was about the equivalent of a modern colonel. It was probably Tiglath-Pileser who added a permanent elite force under the direct

Assyrian archers marching, in a relief on a palace gate in northern Syria, dating from the time of Tiglath-Pileser III.

Tiglath-Pileser III

command of the king, a sort of Praetorian Guard, known as the Royal Cohort (*kisir sharruti*), and a smaller and still more elite force called the Royal Guard (*sha qurbuti*).

All these units held similar equipment, and all included infantry, cavalry and chariotry, recruited from native Assyrians. (It should be mentioned that these native Assyrians were actually a mix of Assyrian and Aramaean by this time. The Assyrian state had expanded in the ninth century by assimilating the Aramaean peoples of north Mesopotamia, and the widespread displacement of Aramaeans by Tiglath-Pileser continued the process of Aramaicization, so that by the end of the Assyrian empire, Aramaic had replaced Akkadian as the spoken language of Mesopotamia.) Now large numbers of non-Assyrian auxiliaries, chiefly pure tribal Aramaeans, were recruited into the light infantry, some armed as archers and some as spearmen. There were also many allied contingents contributed by the client states on the frontiers, using the equipment of their native traditions. It has been estimated that the total forces available to Tiglath-Pileser numbered half a million men.

A text from Zamua gives us a numerical breakdown of the *sab sharri* troops under the command of a provincial governor in the late eighth century BC: 10 chariots, 97 cavalrymen, 80 Assyrian heavy infantrymen, 440 auxiliary archers, and 360 auxiliary spearmen. There were also 101 Assyrian staff, and grooms and other assistants who accompanied the horse troops. It is interesting that the governor had precisely equal numbers of spearmen and archers, 440 each (counting both the heavy Assyrian and light Aramaean spearman). These were probably notional figures, but it is still significant that equal numbers of spearman and archers was the ideal.

The new model army was capable of campaigning all year round. On campaign the Royal Cohort and Royal Guard formed the core of the army, supported by *sab*

Assyrians besiege a city of the Medes using a combination of scaling and ramming tactics, in a relief from Tiglath-Pileser's palace at Nimrud, dating from *c.* 730–727 BC.

Tiglath-Pileser III

sharri troops contributed by the governors and by allied contingents as needed. Normally the king commanded in person, but there were also two field marshals (*turtanu*), the marshal of the left wing and the marshal of the right.

Cavalry were the great innovation of this army. Earlier Assyrian armies had relied on chariots, a relic of the Bronze Age. But some time in the tenth century the nomads of the Eurasian steppe had mastered the art of horseback riding. Assyrian cavalry are first mentioned in 853 BC, but for a time they worked in cooperation with chariotry; the art of managing a stirrupless horse had not been mastered, so cavalrymen rode in pairs, one holding the reins of the horses and the other shooting a bow. But by the time of Tiglath-Pileser, Assyrian cavalry consisted of single horsemen, each armed

The Assyrian defeat of the Elamites at the Ulai river in south-western Iran in 653 BC, as portrayed in a relief from Ashurbanipal's palace at Nineveh.

with bow or spear or both, and the chariot had become obsolete except as a prestige vehicle for high ranking officers.

Finally, the most dreaded service of the new army was its siege train. The Assyrians brought the art of siege warfare to a peak never surpassed until the Greeks invented catapults in the fourth century BC. The main innovation was the battering ram, invented in the ninth century, which made it possible to take cities by assault. Some cities fell to the Assyrians within a day or so, though as we have seen Arpad held out for three years.

Assyrian inscriptions do not contain realistic battle descriptions, and Assyrian art, unlike Egyptian art, never shows troops in formation. No Assyrian battle can be reconstructed in the way that we can attempt to reconstruct the Battle of Kadesh fought between Egyptians and Hittites in 1275 BC. It is clear that Assyrian armies were basically infantry armies: the ratio of foot to horse at Zamua was eight to one. The reliefs showing the battle on the Ulai river, 653 BC, from the palace of Ashurbanipal at Nineveh, the finest battle scenes in Assyrian art, appear to show spearman and archers cooperating, perhaps resembling the cooperation of pikes and muskets in early modern Europe. We may imagine the archers opening the battle under the protection of the heavy infantry, and retreating behind their shields when it came to close contact. Battles were probably won by archery. Cavalry would have operated in support of the infantry, harassing the enemy with arrows and charging in pursuit of the fleeing enemy when they broke.

Though much remains obscure about Assyrian warfare, there seems no doubt that it was the first style of war that could make use of combined arms, a variety of distinct services performing different roles in battle and supporting one another; which is to say it was the first army capable of genuine tactics such as the Greeks and Romans knew.

Tiglath-Pileser III

> 'War is a matter of vital importance to the State; the province of life or death; the road to survival or ruin. It is mandatory that it be thoroughly studied.'
>
> *ART OF WAR*

SUN TZU

JONATHAN FENBY

c. 544–496 BC

SUN WU, later accorded the honorary title of Tzu (master) in recognition of his status, has been the greatest single influence on the military strategy and tactics of the world's most heavily populated nation. The thirteen-chapter *Art of War*, which is attributed to him (though some parts may have been added later by others), has been studied by Chinese generals and strategists over the centuries. Napoleon may have read a French translation published in 1771. In the twentieth century, the eminent British military theorist, Basil Liddell Hart, placed Sun above Clausewitz for his 'concentrated essence of wisdom on the conduct of war', and judged that his treatises 'have never been surpassed in comprehensiveness and depth of understanding'.

Both sides in China's great mid nineteenth-century revolt by the Taiping rebels applied Sun's teachings. The Japanese, who inflicted a humiliating defeat on imperial China in 1894–5, had studied him. So had at least some of the warlords who ruled China in the 1920s, while the Northern Expedition of the Kuomintang Army under Chiang Kai-shek at the end of that decade put into effect Sun's advocacy of swift movement, deception, spying and political means to achieve victory.

Mao Zedong, too, was a confirmed disciple, coining aphorisms that could come straight from the *Art of War* – when the Red Army reached its haven at Yenan in Shaanxi province at the end of the Long March, Sun's work was published with a commentary for the edification of its officers. More recently, his injunctions have been presented as a guide for business, mentioned in the film *Wall Street* and hailed by an American newspaper as providing tips to rank with books of popular psychology and self-help.

For all this, little is known about the man himself. The classic Han dynasty work, the *Records of the Historian*, written soon after 100 BC and constituting the main guide to early Chinese events and dynasties, describes him as a general who worked for a king of the state of Wu in the sixth century, during an era of Chinese history known as the Spring and Autumn Period.

A bronze short sword from the state of Wu, dating from the Eastern Zhou dynasty, third century BC. A typical sword of the Warring States period, it has a bronze pommel and two ridges on the handle.

Sun Tzu, a Chinese general from the sixth century BC and author of the *Art of War*, one of the earliest known treatises on war strategy. In it he distilled his military thinking into a structured series of injunctions and aphorisms covering every aspect of warfare.

A crossbow marksman of the 'terracotta army' of Qin Shi Huangdi (221–210 BC), China's First Emperor, discovered near the city of Xian in Shaanxi province in 1974. In the wars he fought for the unification of China, Qin followed lessons learnt from Sun Tzu's *Art of War*.

The story in the *Records of the Historian* has it that the king of Wu read Sun's injunctions and asked him to conduct an exercise in troop movement using 180 beautiful women. Sun divided them into two companies headed by the king's two favourite concubines. He instructed them in handling halberds, and ordered them to perform drills. The women laughed. So Sun ordered their two commanders to be executed. The king objected to the beheading of his favourite concubines, but Sun insisted. After that, the women did as they were told. The sovereign recognized Sun's prowess as a commander, putting him in charge of a string of campaigns, which he carried out successfully.

Warring States

The timing in the *Records* given by the Han historian appears unlikely for several reasons, including the weapons and the size of the armies he mentions. As the American general and historian Samuel Griffiths has noted, the *Art of War* was written in an era when the earlier knightly code of warfare in China was breaking down. Sun appears to have lived at a time when competing regional states had emerged beneath the nominal rule of emperors who had diminishing real authority. Six major warlords ruled the nation, surrounded by smaller realms that they gradually absorbed. As the scale and intensity of warfare mounted, armies grew larger, led by professional soldiers and consisting of swordsmen, spear carriers, archers and chariots. Soldiers used iron weapons and powerful crossbows. General staffs coordinated tactics. Collective responsibility was often applied, with commanders being executed for retreating without authorization. By the time of Sun Tzu, therefore, China was well on the way to the formidable forces deployed by the kingdom of Qin, whose ruler would end the period of the Warring States in 221 BC, by claiming the Mandate of Heaven from the gods as the First Emperor, employing lessons laid out in the *Art of War*.

Sun's writings belong squarely in this new and more pragmatic age; the object is not to follow rituals or to practise courtly respect for the enemy, but, quite simply, to win at minimum cost and to maximum effect. Sun, whose teachings received glosses from subsequent military experts, was far from alone in proffering advice on how to fight wars; numerous counsellors moved between the regional courts where, in the historian C. P. Fitzgerald's words, they 'proposed and carried out schemes of the blackest treachery. Frequently they secretly served two princes at once, playing off the policy of one against the other.'

What made Sun different was the breadth of his vision, and his fundamental belief that committing an army to battle was the last resort, while 'to subdue the enemy's army without fighting is the acme of skill'. 'All warfare is based on deception,' he wrote. More than two thousand years before its modern advocates, he championed the indirect approach, avoiding the enemy's strong points and focusing on attacking weaknesses in his line. By out-thinking and outwitting the adversary, a great commander made victory inevitable before the first sword was drawn.

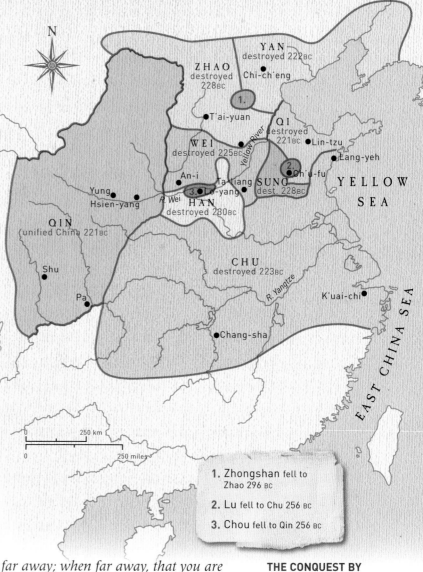

1. Zhongshan fell to Zhao 296 BC

2. Lu fell to Chu 256 BC

3. Chou fell to Qin 256 BC

The importance of the initiative

'When capable, feign incapacity; when active, inactivity,' he advised at the start of a series of short, sharp injunctions laid out in his first chapter as 'the strategist's keys to victory'.

When near, make it appear that you are far away; when far away, that you are near. Offer the enemy a bait to lure him; feign disorder and strike him. When he concentrates, prepare against him; where he is strong, avoid him. Anger his generals and confuse him. Pretend inferiority and encourage his arrogance. Keep him under a strain and wear him down. Where he is unprepared, sally out when he does not expect you.

THE CONQUEST BY THE STATE OF QIN of the main kingdoms of central, northern and eastern China in the third century BC.

Sun recognized the importance of retaining the initiative by attacking the enemy's strategy. While he laid great store by high morale, solidarity and fighting skills, bravado was not a quality he admired for itself. The lonely, outnumbered army unit fighting valiantly against the odds was not for him. Rather, numbers should be concentrated so as to produce a surrender without the need for combat. Thus, 'when ten times the enemy's one, surround him; when five times his strength, attack him; if double his strength, divide him; if equally matched, you may engage him; if weaker numerically, be capable of withdrawing; and, if in all respects unequal, be capable of eluding him, for a small force is but booty for one more powerful.'

Once war broke out, Sun thought that the aim should be to end it as soon as possible, and to capture enemy troops rather than destroying them. The first army in position was at an advantage, so a proficient general should take up his preferred place and lure the adversary on to the battlefield he had chosen. When he wished to join battle, he drew the foe from behind his fortifications by attacking a position elsewhere which the opponent had to defend; but, when he wanted to avoid fighting, he would ward off an advance by diverting the enemy from his chosen course.

Mobility, initiative and surprise were everything, to be juggled to confuse and outmanoeuvre the adversary until he grew weary and defeatist, unable to pin down the contours of the army he faced. 'The ultimate in disposing one's troops is to be without ascertainable shape,' Sun taught. Like water, war had no constant conditions, and tactics should be changed according to the nature of the battle situation.

Not knowing where he was likely to be assaulted obliged the enemy to disperse his forces to defend many positions. Attacks on cities, which were likely to be lengthy affairs that tied down troops, were to be avoided. 'No country has ever benefited from a protracted war,' Sun wrote. Defeated enemies should be treated humanely to ensure that they did not resume hostilities. Reflecting the growing professionalism of Chinese officers, he warned against interference in campaigns by rulers ignorant of military matters who would only 'hobble the army', causing confusion that would aid the enemy.

SUN TZU'S HERITAGE

Zhuge Liang

In the third century AD, Zhuge Liang (see pp. 188–95) adopted psychological warfare techniques drawn from Sun Tzu, notably in his treatment of the southern rebel leader Meng Huo, whom he released seven times in order eventually to win his loyalty. Zhuge's celebrated use of diversions and trickery was straight out of Sun's book, as was the way in which he stirred up trouble behind the lines of his stronger foe to weaken its ability to resist the offensives he launched from the kingdom of Shu. But, like Sun, he was also a highly rational commander, and ended several campaigns because of his worries about his supply chain, to avoid being caught without provisions and reinforcements on the far side of the mountains surrounding his base region of Sichuan.

The Taiping

In the mid nineteenth century, China was rocked by the huge Taiping Revolt, led by a southerner who claimed he was the son of the Christian God. Rebel armies penetrated many parts of China, establishing their capital at Nanjing and even getting within 100 miles of Beijing. Their major commanders applied Sun Tzu's strategy of avoiding imperial strong points and concentrating their attacks on weak areas, using fast marching, espionage and diversions to surprise their adversaries. After fourteen years, they were defeated by armies led by provincial gentry who had also absorbed Sun's teachings, avoiding battle until they enjoyed supremacy, under-mining the rebels by winning peasant support and establishing networks of villages protected by local militia, cutting off food and supplies and using a mixture of propaganda and threats to undermine Taiping morale.

Chiang Kai-shek and the Japanese

In the 1920s, several of Sun Tzu's tactics were employed by the Kuomintang army that marched out of Canton in the far south on its Northern Expedition to establish the Nationalist regime that ruled China until 1949. Its leader, Chiang Kai-shek, paid great attention to winning allies among the minor warlords he faced, in order to gain strength against the major militarists who had divided the country among themselves. Bribery and political persuasion were among his weapons, while his Soviet military adviser, Galen, employed flanking tactics to great effect. (Galen was the pseudonym used by Vassili Blücher, a Russian civil war hero who later headed the Red Army in the Far East before being tortured and killed in Stalin's purges.)

In the culmination of the Nationalist offensive against erstwhile allies in northern China, Chiang obtained victory by winning over the wavering Manchurian warlord, forcing his opponents to cave in without a final battle. Chiang used similar

The Confucian code

Sun's approach was deeply rooted in the behaviour code handed down from Confucius (who died in 479 BC), with its belief in reason, which was the foundation for more than two millennia of imperial rule in China – and which still has echoes in today's Communist regime. Knowing yourself and your foe was vital. 'Know the enemy and know yourself; in a hundred battles you will never be in peril,' he wrote. 'When you are ignorant of the enemy but know yourself, your chances of winning or losing are equal. If ignorant of both your enemy and yourself, you are certain to be in peril in every battle.' Invincibility, he noted elsewhere, depends on one's self, while the vulnerability of the enemy depends on him. One has, therefore, to do all one can to ensure the first by cleverness, reason, preparation and good organization.

A tale recounts a conversation between Sun and a disciple of Confucius who asked him which kind of man he should take with him if he commanded 'the Army of the Three Hosts'. 'The man who was ready to beard a tiger or rush a river without caring whether he lived or died – that sort of man I should not take,' Sun replied. 'But

The Great Wall of China, which stretches over 4,000 miles in length. At its peak during the Ming dynasty (1368–1644), the wall was guarded by more than one million men. Much further north than the current wall was that built by the First Emperor of China, Qin Shi Huangdi, between 220 and 210 BC.

tactics against a series of regional rivals, but was at a loss when faced with the full-scale offensive launched in China in 1937 by the Japanese, who had, themselves, absorbed Sun Tzu's teachings from several analyses of his work that appeared in Japan in the seventeenth and eighteenth centuries.

Mao Zedong

China's Communist leader applied Sun's teachings in the different theatres of the war he fought over two decades before the Communist victory of 1949. The evasion of frontal battle against a stronger enemy, the focus on attacking the adversary's weak points, deception, intelligence, swift movement and a readiness to run away in adverse conditions were all central to the guerrilla warfare that Mao advocated and imposed on the Chinese Communists in the 1930s.

His four slogans, coined in his first base in the mountains of Jiangxi, could have been written by Sun:

When the enemy advances, we retreat.
When the enemy halts, we harass.
When the enemy seeks to avoid battle, we attack.
When the enemy retreats, we pursue.

Or take Mao's eulogy for adaptability, which fits Sun's advocacy of tactical adaptability to perfection: 'Attack may be changed into defence, and defence into attack. Advance may be turned into retreat, and retreat into advance. Containing forces may be turned into assault forces, and assault forces into containing forces.'

In the civil war after 1945, the Communists applied elements of Sun's approach on a massive scale in the great battles with the Nationalists in Manchuria in 1947–8, and in the crucial Huai-Hai battle that won the civil war in the winter of 1948–9. Then, when it entered the Korean War, China deployed two hundred and fifty thousand men in battle positions south of the Yalu river, without the United Nations command being aware of the threat, and unleashed an attack that almost destroyed their adversary, in the tradition laid down by Sun Tzu over two thousand years earlier.

Sun Tzu

A portrait of Confucius that hangs in the Great Hall of the Confucian temple at Qufu, the legendary birthplace of the celebrated philosopher in Shandong province. Sun Tzu was a Confucian disciple, who, like the sage, venerated reason.

I should certainly take someone who approached difficulties with due caution and who preferred to succeed by strategy.'

Sun lays out practical advice, and details the tactics to adopt in different terrains and on different battlefields. He devotes twelve points in one chapter to attacks by fire. After warning of the dangers of camping in low-lying or desolate ground, he tells of the need to cross salt marshes speedily, and outlines the advantages of taking up position on the sunny side of mountains. The way birds fly can reveal an ambush, he notes. Acute observation can tell when the enemy is tired or desperate. In another practical note, he advises a commander to treat his men in a civil fashion, winning their confidence with orders that make sense and are effective. If he cares for his men as his own sons, they will march and die with a 'serene and inscrutable, impartial and self-controlled' leader.

Intelligence and spies

Sun's great achievement was in taking a broader view of war, tying together the multiple elements and insisting on the need for deep thought and planning, diplomacy, skilful manoeuvres, discipline, intelligence operations and subversion. Close attention to the terrain and the weather is important. So is the ability to avoid traps laid by the enemy – 'do not gobble up proffered baits,' Sun enjoins.

There is something quasi-mystical about the summary of military expertise which Sun lays out after detailing these multiple ways in which to get the better of an adversary. 'Subtle and insubstantial, the expert leaves no trace; divinely mysterious, he is inaudible. Thus he is the master of his enemy's fate,' Sun wrote. Later, he added that 'One able to gain the victory by modifying his tactics in accordance with the enemy situation may be said to be divine'.

Yet he is also highly realistic in noting that 'what is called "foreknowledge" cannot be elicited from spirits, or from gods, or from analogy with past events, or from calculations – it must be obtained from men who know the enemy situation.' These spies fall into five categories: natives of the enemy territory; people living there with inside knowledge; enemy spies who have been turned; agents sent in with false information who are expected to be caught and to disclose their misleading news; and, finally – the most valuable – agents who cross the lines and

Sun Tzu

> '**An army may be likened to water: water leaves dry the high places and seeks the hollows: an army turns from strength and attacks emptiness. The flow of water is regulated by the shape of the ground; victory is gained by acting in accordance with the state of the enemy.**' *ART OF WAR*

return, the best of whom are intelligent but appear stupid, and are able to 'endure hunger, cold, filth and humiliation'. When all five categories are working, they form 'the Divine Skein and the treasure of a sovereign'. Secret operations, Sun concludes in the last sentence of his work, 'are essential in war; upon them the army relies to make its every move'.

It is extraordinary that this complex but immaculately joined-up philosophy of war was evolved at a time when China was divided among warring kingdoms that lived and died by the force of arms. It seems to belong, rather, to a later, more settled period. But whatever the uncertainties about who Sun was, when exactly he lived, and whether he actually wrote the *Art of War* or whether it was a later compilation of texts, there can be no doubting its wisdom and its central role in the Chinese approach to war throughout the centuries.

Infantrymen of the period of the Western Han dynasty (206 BC–AD 9). These sculpted clay figures, found in a tomb in Shaanxi province, carry shields and are wearing red-banded caps, baggy trousers and straw sandals.

CYRUS THE GREAT

TOM HOLLAND

590 or 576–529 BC

ON A HILL-RIMMED PLAIN in southern Iran there stands a tomb of stone, looking for all the world as though a tent has been perched on a ziggurat. This striking monument was already more than a thousand years old when, in AD 640, the conquering armies of Islam first swept into Persia. Locals, keen to preserve it from the destructive zeal of the Muslims, informed their new masters that the tomb was that of Solomon's mother, and the invaders, respecting the memory of a king who had been hailed in the Koran as a prophet, devoutly preserved it. Whose tomb the monument truly was had long since been forgotten. Not even the Persians themselves had any real conception of their country's ancient past.

Only in the West, among their former enemies, was it still remembered that the Persians had once been the rulers of the most powerful empire in the world. Those who could read the histories of the Greeks knew that in distant times one of their kings had led an immense invasion force from Asia into Europe across a bridge of boats, and had almost succeeded in conquering Greece. Alexander the Great, invading Asia in turn, had claimed to be doing so in revenge. Yet even he, although he had proved himself to be the bane of the Persians' empire, had remained in awe of the achievement of its creator. Like the Muslim conquerors a millenium later, he had visited the tent-shaped tomb in southern Iran. Unlike the Arabs, he had needed no one to tell him whose it was.

'Mortal!', an inscription ran on the tomb. 'I am Cyrus, who founded the dominion of the Persians, and was King of Asia. Do not begrudge me then my monument!' Nor did Alexander begrudge it. Ordering the tomb's lavish refurbishment, he had sedulously paraded his respect for the one conqueror he was prepared to acknowledge as his peer. Indeed, the achievements of Cyrus two centuries previously had been, if anything, even more astounding than those of Alexander. The Persian, unlike the son of Philip, had seemed to emerge to his greatness from nowhere. In 559 BC, when Cyrus came to the throne, the kingdom he

Cyrus the Great

ruled was backward and inconsequential. The Persians themselves, originally nomads from the steppes of central Asia, had barely intruded upon the consciousness of the region's great powers; and yet by the time of their king's death thirty years later, they had subdued them all. From the Aegean in the west to the Hindu Kush in the east, Cyrus had made himself the master of an empire without parallel. It was the most spectacular feat of conquest that the world had ever seen.

Cyromania

The man who achieved it had been, self-evidently, a commander of exceptional prowess. Alexander was not alone among the *anairya*, as the Persians termed foreigners, in acknowledging this. Indeed, that we know as much about Cyrus as we do depends to a striking degee upon the admiring testimony of Greeks: for the Persians, with a single exception, did not write anything at all that we can identify as an account of real events. Certainly, there is no equivalent of the campaign records of the Assyrian kings, no loving descriptions of the blood spilled by Cyrus, of the cities he stormed, of the battles he won – only the odd clay tablet or cylinder, redeemed from the rubble of vanished palaces, and inscribed with details that tend to be at best

The tomb of Cyrus
the Great at Pasargadae.
'Mortal! I am Cyrus, who
founded the dominion of
the Persians and was
King of Asia ...'

Greeks from Ionia bringing the Great King tribute, as shown on a relief at Persepolis, sculpted a few decades after Cyrus' death in 529 BC.

either generalized or elliptical. Compounding the murk is the fact that even the single Persian narrative we do have, an inscription carved at Bisitun, by the side of what today serves as the main Baghdad–Tehran road, is a deliberate and skilful work of disinformation: for the king who commissioned it, Darius I, was almost certainly a usurper, who had murdered one, and conceivably two, sons of Cyrus, and wished to conceal the fact. As a result, for anything that even vaguely approaches a coherent account of Cyrus' life, we have to turn instead to the Greek historian Herodotus: an incomparable source, to be sure, and without whom our understanding of early Persian history would be truly spectral. Yet even so, ever curious and open-minded though Herodotus was, the awkward truth remains that in describing Cyrus' conquests he was often writing about remote and peculiar peoples, whose languages he did not speak, and whose lands, by and large, he had never visited. As a result, he inevitably has to be excused the occasional inaccuracy, the occasional prejudice, the occasional tendency to treat the obscurer reaches of Persian history as fantasy. That a military biography of Cyrus can be written at all owes everything to Herodotus; that it must inevitably be riddled with gaps and uncertainties owes much to him as well.

Cyrus the Great

Iron fists and velvet gloves

Nowhere is Herodotus' inimitable blend of tall stories and telling detail more flamboyantly showcased than in his account of Cyrus' youth. It is the nature of great men, of course, to attract legends, and Cyrus was no exception. Herodotus' biography of his early years frequently verges upon the fantastical: from visions of urinating princesses to grotesque tales of cannibalism, most of the events described in it bear testimony to Cyrus' posthumous status as a figure less of history than of myth. Nevertheless, a few of the details recorded by Herodotus do appear genuine. We are told, for instance, that the young King of Persia was the grandson of another and much greater king, Astyages of Media, a region occupying what is now northwestern Iran; and this may well be true. For Media, during the period of Cyrus' boyhood, was one of the great powers of the Near East; and Astyages, if a Babylonian source is to be trusted, was indeed in the habit of marrying off his daughters to neighbouring vassals. If Cyrus was truly Astyages' grandson, then it meant that he had Median as well as Persian blood in his veins; and, very probably, contacts in the Median aristocracy as well. Astyages certainly came to view him as a potential rival, for in 553 BC, six years into Cyrus' reign, he struck southwards against his vassal, resolved to topple him from his throne. The odds seemed stacked against Cyrus' survival. Not for nothing was the Median cavalry famed as the most devastating strike force in the entire Near East. Sure enough, so desperate did things appear for the Persians at one point that even their women, it is said, had to take to the battlefield. Cyrus, however, refused to submit; and for three years the war raged on. Then, abruptly, it was Astyages who was brought to defeat. So unexpected was this upset that in Babylon, it was reported, the news had been brought to the king by a god. 'The large armies of the Medes were scattered by Cyrus and his outnumbered forces,' reported the divine messenger. 'And Cyrus captured Astyages, the King of the Medes. And he took him to his country as captive.'

Brought to Persia, Astyages was not impaled or flayed or fed to animals, but set up on a country estate. Cyrus' display of mercy towards his grandfather was complemented by a no less gracious refusal to treat the conquered Medes as slaves. Prompted by a naturally magnanimous temperament this may well have been – but it was prompted, too, by a steely measure of calculation. Cyrus, having won the war, had no intention of losing the peace. The Medes were encouraged to feel, if not exactly the equals of their conquerors, then at least associates in the great adventure of their new king's reign. And this was just as well – for his campaigns, as events were to prove, were very far from over. In 547, a bare six years after Astyages had presumed to launch a pre-emptive strike against Cyrus, a second king thought to repeat the gambit. Croesus was the legendarily wealthy ruler of Lydia, a kingdom in the west of what is now Turkey; and he had long nurtured an ambition to extend his empire eastwards. Late that summer, he crossed the Halys, a river that served as the frontier between Lydia and Media – and by doing so effectively declared war on the upstart Persian king. Cyrus, even though winter was coming on, was hardly the man to duck such a challenge. That same autumn, the two kings clashed brutally but indecisively. Croesus, content to have probed Cyrus' defences, then withdraw to his capital, Sardis. Here he intended to hunker down for the winter, in a city that appeared at a perfectly safe remove from his adversary, located as it was only three days' journey from the Aegean. Certainly, it never crossed Croesus' mind that Cyrus might follow him. But follow him Cyrus did – for the Persians and the Medes, with their sheepskin coats and tough mountain horses, were ideally equipped for a winter campaign. Braving the bitter cold, they shadowed Croesus, never alerting him to their presence, allowing him time to dismiss his allies and for his conscripts to melt away. Only once Sardis was denuded did they finally strike. Frantically, Croesus cobbled together what limited forces he could. All to no avail. Riding out from Sardis to confront Cyrus, the Lydian king had made no allowance for the innnovative quality of his opponent's generalship. As his cavalry charged the Persian forces, they were startled to find themselves confronted by a line of baggage-camels. Unfamiliar with the stench, the horses duly swerved and bolted. Croesus' entire army then scattered in disarray, leaving Cyrus free to invest Sardis, storm it, and lay claim to its stupendous treasury. Lydia was duly added to the swelling dominions of the Persian king.

King of kings

Meanwhile, even as Cyrus was completing his conquest of the west, trouble had been brewing among the provinces that extended to the east of Media. Many of these, which had been tributary to Astyages, had initially proffered a shadowy submission to his conqueror; 'but then they revolted, and this defection was the cause and origin of numerous wars'. As to how and when these wars were fought, however, we are almost completely in the dark. Herodotus, whose knowledge of eastern affairs was inevitably hazy, states only that Cyrus campaigned 'across the north and the east, and ended up bringing about the subjugation of every nation, without exception'. The limit of Persian expansion appears finally to have been set at the Jaxartes, a broad, island-dotted river that flows through what is now Kazakhstan, and beyond which the steppelands extended in defiance of the ambitions of even the most prodigious conqueror the world had ever known. Intending to make good the deficiencies of the river as a natural frontier, Cyrus ordered the construction of seven frontier towns, so that the approaches to Persia from central Asia, which had always been open to predatory nomads, could be patrolled effectively. Meanwhile, behind the buffer zone, lands which had once been breeding-grounds of menace and instability – Gandhara, Bactria and Sogdiana – were transformed into bulwarks of the new superpower. Running in a great arc, they stretched from the Hindu Kush to the Aral Sea. Not only had the frontier been stabilized, but yet further reserves of manpower had been added to the armies of the Persian king.

'He is My shepherd, and shall perform all My pleasure.'
ISAIAH 44:28

This was just as well – for Cyrus was not done with his conquests yet. By 540, with both the western and eastern limits of his new empire secured, he felt ready for his ultimate test. Incomparable though the scale and range of his victories had been, yet there remained one great power with pretensions still to rival Persia as the mistress of the Near East. Babylon had long been accustomed to regard herself as the very fulcrum of world affairs. Her rulers, with a corresponding display of conceit, thought nothing of laying claim to titles such as 'King of the Four Quarters of the Earth' and 'King of the Universe'. Nor was this entirely braggadocio – for celebrated kings such as Nebuchadnezzar II had indeed cast a lengthy and fearsome shadow. 'Their quiver is like an open tomb,' the biblical prophet Jeremiah had wailed, 'they are all mighty men.' In terms of wealth, size and glamour, Babylon was certainly incomparable. No man could truly consider himself the master of the world until he had subdued her – as Cyrus well knew. Concerned to present himself as a man worthy of such a prize, and skilled as he was at overturning hostile preconceptions, he duly ensured that his assault on the city was accompanied by a masterly propaganda onslaught. Invading Babylonian territory, he claimed to be defending it; leading an army of battle-hardened veterans, he affected to be an avatar of peace. The strategy proved brilliantly successful. Even as he advanced, most enemy strongholds hurried to open their gates.

An unheroic strategy, maybe – but certainly a sensible one. Persian firepower was overwhelming, and Cyrus, who was not averse to staging the odd atrocity where necessary, made sure that the Babylonians knew it. Although his propagandists would later make much play about how Babylon fell 'without a battle', this was not the case. The initial clash, we know from a Babylonian source, took place at Opis, on the banks of the Tigris, in early October 539 BC, and was followed up by much plundering and slaughter. As Nabonidus, the king of Babylon, retreated to his capital, Cyrus pursued him. There was nothing to block his advance. Even the Tigris was easily forded: for Persian troops were practised in the crossing of rivers while clinging on to horses, camels and inflated animal-skins. One last attempt by Nabonidus to confront his nemesis outside the very walls of Babylon was disdainfully swatted aside; and by the middle of October, the great city was acknowledging its conqueror as 'King of the Universe'.

The capture of Babylon marked the climax of Cyrus' military career; but not its end. The sword of such a conqueror did not sleep easily in its scabbard. A decade after his triumphant entry into the capital of the world and Cyrus was still in his saddle, leading his horsemen ever onwards. Various stories are told of his end; but most of them are agreed that he died in central Asia, north of the Jaxartes, far beyond the limits he had once thought to set on his own ambitions. Even though it is evident that his corpse was transported back with full honours to Persia, for burial in his splendid tomb, numerous eerie stories gave a different account. According to Herodotus', for instance, the queen of the tribe which had killed him ordered his

The site of the Lydian city of Sardis, capital of King Croesus, and the scene of his defeat by Cyrus in the winter of 547/6 BC.

WHEN THE MEDE CAME: THE CONQUEST OF IONIA

EVEN MORE THAN THE TOPPLING of Astyages had done, Cyrus' victory over Croesus in 547/6 BC burst like a thunderclap across a world that seemed abruptly and spectacularly shrunken by it. On the eastern seaboard of the Aegean, the Greek cities of Ionia found themselves suddenly confronted by conquerors that they called not Persians, but Medes – a linguistic muddle that powerfully conveys just how disorienting had been Cyrus' rise. Terror filled all those who found themselves lying in the Persians' path. One Ionian city, Phocaea, went so far as to evacuate its entire population, 'women, children, moveable property, everything, in fact … leaving the Persians to take possession of nothing but an empty shell'. Those that opted for resistance were systematically broken to the yoke of the Persian king, amid 'the tearing down of walls, the tumult of cavalry charges, and the overthrow of cities'.

Not once were the Ionians able to confront the invaders successfully in open combat. Indeed, such was the shock of the Persians' coming that it would long serve to darken even the most intimate moments of joy:

> In winter, as you lie on a soft couch
> by the fire,
> Full of good food, munching on nuts
> and drinking sweet wine,
> Then you must ask questions such
> as these
> 'Where do you come from? Tell me,
> what is your age?
> How old were you when the Mede came?'

Nor was the sense of fear confined to the limits of Ionia. A dread of Persian military prowess was instilled in Greeks everywhere, an inferiority complex that would endure for decades. Not until 490 BC, and the Battle of Marathon, would it finally – and even then only to a degree – be exorcised.

THE GREEK CITIES OF IONIA
in the early sixth century BC.

corpse to be decapitated, and then dropped the severed head into a blood-filled wineskin, so that Cyrus' thirst for slaughter might be glutted at last. Such a tale powerfully suggests the terror that the great conqueror was capable of instilling in his adversaries: for vampires, demons hungry for human flesh, had long haunted the nightmares of the peoples of the Near East.

Yet a very different tradition also served to keep alive the memory of Cyrus the Great: one that bore witness less to his military prowess, perhaps, than to his aptitude for exploiting the arts of peace. Great commander though he undoubtedly was, his most distinctive achievement was to have launched a novel and far-reaching experiment in geopolitics. Cyrus had not merely conquered his enemies; he had wooed them as well. Brutal though he could certainly be in the cause of securing an enemy's speedy surrender, his preference, by and large, had been to live up to the high-flying claims of his own brilliantly crafted propaganda. Once his regime was established, over the corpses of toppled empires, further bloodshed was kept to the barest minimum. His diktats had worn a moderate and gracious tone. To kingdoms far older than his own, venerable with temples and celestial pretensions, Cyrus had presented himself as a model of righteousness, and his rule a payback from the gods. Peoples from across the vast span of his empire had duly scrabbled to hail him as their own. Astonishingly, Cyrus, the man who had, in the awed words of the prophet Isaiah, made 'the world tremble from end to end', would be remembered with an almost unqualified admiration, as the architect of a universal peace. For centuries afterwards, even among its bitterest enemies, the glow of its founder's memory would suffuse the empire of the Persians. 'He eclipsed all other monarchs, either before him, or since.' The verdict, not of a fellow countryman, but of Xenophon – an Athenian.

Persian infantrymen, from a frieze discovered at the great palace at Susa, built – like Persepolis – some years after Cyrus' death. The richness and splendour of their robes suggest that they belonged to the elite shock-force of the Persian army.

Cyrus the Great

LEONIDAS
c. 530–480 BC

BEN DUPRÉ

LEONIDAS IS A CURIOSITY in the pantheon of great commanders, for the reputation of the heroic Spartan commander who sought to stem the Persian tide at Thermopylae is built on a single battle – and on a battle, moreover, in which he was manifestly defeated.

In 480 BC, Persia's Great King Xerxes set out at the head of a colossal army, supported by a powerful fleet, to overrun Greece and make it the latest satrapy in what was already the most expansive empire the world had ever seen. The path to central Greece and the Peloponnese lay through the narrow pass at Thermopylae, and it was here that the Spartan king Leonidas and a small band of loyal Greeks attempted to block the Persian advance. Massively outnumbered, the Greeks carried their resistance into the third day. Then, betrayed by a fellow Greek, they were overwhelmed and annihilated to a man.

Though the Persian juggernaut rumbled on southwards and eventually put Athens to the torch, the almost superhuman resistance of Leonidas and his fellows was credited, from antiquity onwards, with providing the spark and inspiration for the subsequent victories at Salamis and Plataea that finally extinguished the Persian threat. As such, Leonidas has been hailed as the saviour of Greek – and by extension Western – liberty and civilization.

Greece – a festering sore

For Xerxes, Greece represented unfinished business. A decade before Thermopylae, his father Darius (the Great) had launched a punitive expedition directed principally at Athens and Eretria, which had supported the Greeks of Asia Minor in the failed Ionian Revolt. Darius' venture, however, came spectacularly unstuck at Marathon in 490, when the Greek (mainly Athenian) forces trounced a far larger Persian army. On Darius' death in 486, Xerxes inherited the crown and with it the obligation to avenge his father's humiliation at the hands of the Greeks. Making his preparations meticulously and on a quite unprecedented scale, Xerxes set about launching a second and far greater expedition, mustering tens of thousands of soldiers and hundreds of ships from every part of his

kingdom. This time the explicit aim was to subjugate those Greek states that had so far refused to bow to his authority.

The Greek response

Xerxes made no attempt to conceal his intentions, so the city-states of Greece had several years to coordinate their response. Yet their efforts, for the most part, were fragmented and inadequate. Unable to settle age-old animosities and rivalries, most remained divided and disunited. By the time the Persian threat was almost on top of them, the majority of the Greeks had either 'medized' – gone over to the Persian side – or decided to keep their heads low and stay on the sidelines. Just thirty-one of the mainland Greek states — fewer than one in twenty – agreed to set aside their differences and to resist Xerxes.

Sparta, acknowledged by all as leader of the Greek resistance, was given overall command of both the army and the fleet. As one of Sparta's two kings, Leonidas is likely to have played a leading role in devising the allies' strategy. The plan they agreed upon was to confront Xerxes in northern Greece, blocking his advance simultaneously on land and at sea. After an abortive attempt further north, the Greeks elected to take up a defensive position on the axis running from the Thermopylae pass on the Malian Gulf to Artemisium on the northern coast of the island of Euboea.

The pass at Thermopylae, seen from the foot of mountains that in 480 BC rose steeply along the coastline of the Malian Gulf. The road that today crosses the plain gives an indication of the ancient shoreline.

(Left) **The face of the defeated hero** of Thermopylae – or not. This famous marble statue of a Spartan warrior, dating from the early decades of the fifth century BC, is popularly known as the 'Leonidas bust', but there is no clear evidence for the identification, which was first made when the piece was excavated in Sparta in the 1920s.

Leonidas

The pass at Thermopylae

Whatever Leonidas' role may have been in determining the broad outlines of the Greek strategy, there can be little doubt that he would have been intimately involved in deciding the minutiae of their response, including the choice of arena and the size and disposition of the forces involved.

An ancient Greek would scarcely recognize Thermopylae today. Over the past two and a half thousand years, the Malian Gulf has silted up to such an extent that the site of the fighting is now several kilometres inland. In 480 BC the Callidromus mountains rose sharply out of the Aegean, forming a narrow pass some 3 to 4 miles (5 to 6 kilometres) long. Along the pass there were three especially narrow constrictions, or 'gates' (*pylai* in Greek; *thermo*, meaning 'hot', comes from the nearby hot sulphur springs). The gates at either end were narrower – Herodotus suggests that there was space only for a single cart to pass – but while the ground at the Middle Gate was wider, at around 65 feet, the cliffs at this point were sheer and steepled up to around 3,300 feet, making them all but impassable. It was here, at the Middle Gate, that Leonidas chose to make his stand. In addition to its natural advantages, running across the pass there was a defensive wall, largely dilapidated by this date, which had been built long before by the Phocians. The Greeks spent the interval before the arrival of the Persians rebuilding it, so gaining an excellent position from which they could make sorties against the enemy.

The opposing forces

For all these reasons, Thermopylae, and the Middle Gate in particular, was an excellent choice by Leonidas. In almost every respect this location helped to offset the Greeks' most obvious weaknesses. The Persian cavalry – which could prove devastating in open terrain – was effectively obsolete here, while Xerxes' archers – another great strength – made little impression on the serried rank of overlapping Greek shields. Most glaringly, the Greeks were massively outnumbered. It is not certain exactly by how much, but it may have been 20:1 or worse. In any case, fighting on an extremely narrow front, such numerical superiority counted for little.

By contrast, the Greek (and especially Spartan) strength lay almost exclusively in their infantry. The heavily armoured Greek infantryman, or hoplite, was virtually sheathed in metal from head to toe: crested bronze helmet covering all but the eyes, nose and mouth; cuirass or breastplate; and greaves protecting the legs. The secret of the hoplite lay in the disciplined phalanx formation. Each man carried his eponymous shield – the large, round *hoplon* – locked on his left arm, while he thrust over the shield rim with his long (around 8-feet, or 2.5-metre) spear. In the phalanx, the hoplite's vulnerable right side was covered by the shield of his right-hand neighbour. The only other essential – iron discipline in holding the line at any cost – was the Spartans' speciality.

How big were the opposing forces at Thermopylae? The Greek army is known with some degree of certainty to have numbered around seven thousand. According to the memorial at Thermopylae, which Herodotus saw, there were some four thousand Peloponnesians, including Leonidas' own hand-picked force of 300 Spartan hoplites. As they advanced north, these were joined by contingents from central Greece, whose homes were most immediately at risk: 700 Thespians, 400 Thebans (none too willing, apparently), 1,000 Phocians and the entire army of the Locrians. On the size of the Persian army we can only speculate. Herodotus himself understandably doubts his own estimate of over 5 million (including camp followers), a wildly exaggerated figure that would have been manifestly unsustainable in both food and water. No one since has attempted to defend a figure of this magnitude, and few modern estimates have gone above two hundred thousand.

Whatever the exact figures, it is clear that the Greeks were spectacularly outnumbered. Should Leonidas, as commander-in-chief, be held responsible for the grotesque mismatch? In fact it is quite explicit that the Greek army was

Hoplites, the heavy-armed infantry of the Greek city-states, depicted on a red-figure bowl (*crater*) donning their armour. The intensive training and extreme discipline required to fight effectively in the hoplite phalanx ensured that Sparta's professional soldiers remained the most feared in the Greek world.

Leonidas

intended only as an advance force, and Leonidas repeatedly (albeit vainly) requested reinforcements. Through bad luck (or good Persian planning), it happened to be the time of the Olympic festival, during which the Greeks – always scrupulously observant – were required to refrain from fighting. For the hyper-scrupulous Spartans, it was even worse, being the time of their most important annual festival, the Carneia. It is difficult at this distance to distinguish true cause from pretext, but the fact that the Greeks mustered any force at all at such a time may be an indication not of complacence but of the gravity with which they regarded the situation.

The first and second days

Over the first two days of fighting, the excellence of Leonidas' choice of position soon became apparent. On the first day, Xerxes' foot soldiers (including his 10,000 elite 'Immortals') were forced by the terrain into a head-on assault on the Greek phalanx. More accustomed to open skirmishing, with lighter armour and shorter spears, they were no match for the hoplites and rapidly incurred appalling casualties. The Greeks, on the other hand, suffered few losses. The weak point of the phalanx – the extreme right flank – was covered by the sea, while they stayed fresh by fighting in relays emerging from the protection of the Phocian Wall. To add to the discomfiture of Xerxes' soldiers, the Spartans showed off one of their parade-ground manoeuvres, by feigning a retreat and then wheeling around to inflict terrible damage on the overzealous pursuers.

Day two proceeded along similar lines, except now there was an ever-growing pile of corpses building up in front of the Greek line. Even allowing for Herodotean exaggeration (he puts the Persian casualties over three days at twenty thousand), the mountain of bodies – flesh rotting in the searing late-summer heat, the sweet, sickening stench of decay, clouds of flies amid the

The Immortals of the imperial guard, shown in relief in the Throne Hall at Persepolis, the ceremonial capital of Persian empire. According to Herodotus, the elite Immortals were so called because their number was never allowed to fall below 10,000 – any vacancy caused by death or illness was filled at once.

dust and blood – must have not only presented a major physical barrier but also shattered the morale of the frustrated attackers.

The position turned

By the end of the second day, the extreme impenetrability of the Greek line appears to have driven Xerxes to the point of distraction, but then his luck changed. A local man named Ephialtes – a name for ever after held in infamy – agreed, at a price, to guide the Persians along the Anopaea path – a track that snaked through the mountains and led to a point close to the East Gate. The Immortals were promptly dispatched to follow the path overnight with orders to attack Leonidas' position from the rear on the third morning.

We might expect local knowledge to have been a big advantage for the Greeks, so should their intelligence have been better, and should blame attach to Leonidas for

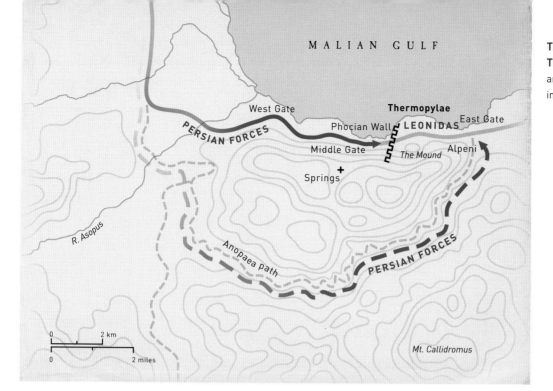

allowing his position to be encircled? In fact, the Greek states were, for the most part, fiercely independent, politically divided and often ignorant of what lay beyond their own borders. Herodotus says that the Greek force only found out about the Anopaea path when they arrived at Thermopylae, and that when he learnt of it, Leonidas did what any competent commander would have done – he posted a body of soldiers to guard it.

Was the force, then, inadequate to watch the path – a criticism also levelled at Leonidas? It is true that, in the event, the body of 1,000 Phocians did not cover themselves with glory. They apparently failed to post sentries, were taken completely by surprise, and beat a very hasty retreat beneath a hail of Persian arrows. Yet it is hard to see what better course was open to Leonidas. The size of the guard seems proportionate to his available means, while the reasons for choosing the Phocians appear sound: first, they were familiar with the terrain; and second, they were in effect guarding their own homes and could thus be expected to sell their lives dearly.

The Greeks split

In the event, the Phocians were simply bypassed by the Immortals, leaving Leonidas' position exposed on two flanks. In the hours after the news of the outflanking reached Leonidas and before the Immortals arrived, the Greek forces split: the bulk of the army moved southwards to safety, while Leonidas and his Spartans, the Thespians and the Thebans remained, facing almost certain death, to make their famous last stand.

At this point, another major question over Leonidas' leadership arises. Herodotus favours the view that the departure of the main contingent took place in an orderly manner, on the instruction of their commander. On this reading the last stand can be seen as a deliberate attempt to cover the retreat, buying time for the withdrawing soldiers as they moved through the open ground south of the pass, where they would be vulnerable to pursuit by Xerxes' cavalry. But Herodotus also gives an alternative account in which the retreat was basically haphazard – rather a case of the various contingents melting away when it became clear that the game was up. Such a reading does nothing to diminish the merit of those that remained – quite the reverse – but it does cast doubt over Leonidas' own authority and the degree of loyalty that he inspired in those under his command.

The last stand

What is not remotely in doubt is the extraordinary bravery of those who remained behind. For Leonidas himself and his fellow Spartans, there clearly can never have been any question of leaving their posts: 'for Sparta, it is not dying but fleeing that is death', as an epigram (inspired by an earlier encounter) put it. Changing their tactics, the Greeks moved forward of the Phocian Wall on to more open ground, determined to inflict the greatest possible damage before the Immortals arrived to complete the encirclement.

It is difficult to assess Leonidas' personal bravery in this context. The essence of Spartan soldiery was collective and disciplined action within the phalanx, based on intensive training since boyhood. 'Fighting singly, Spartans are as good as any,' Herodotus notes, 'but fighting together they are the best soldiers in the world.' Herodotus' account of Leonidas' death is heroic, indeed Homeric – the repeated attempts by his comrades to rescue his body from the enemy and the subsequent desecration of his body by Xerxes are reminiscent of (for instance) Hector's treatment at the hands of Achilles. But this is likely to be conventional and formulaic. There is no reason to doubt that Leonidas fought and died like a model Spartan; but that is precisely what a Spartan was supposed to do.

> 'A little of Leonidas lies in the fact that I can go where I like and write what I like. He contributed to set us free.'
>
> WILLIAM GOLDING, *THE HOT GATES* (LONDON, 1965)

'Fighting tooth and nail', according to Herodotus, is literally true of the Greeks' final act of defiance. When the Immortals finally appeared, the surviving Greeks closed their ranks and retreated to a small hill, where they fought till their spears were broken, then with their swords, and finally with their hands and teeth. They succumbed at last beneath a torrent of missiles. A Spartan named Dienekes had earlier responded to the news that the arrows of the enemy would be so dense as to blot out the sky with a typically laconic reply: 'All the better: we shall fight in the shade.' In the end, it was in that shade from Persian arrows that Dienekes, Leonidas and all their comrades fought and died.

The legacy of Thermopylae

If those Greek states set upon resistance had quickly crumbled under the wheels of Xerxes' juggernaut, it is undeniable that the course of history would have been very different. In particular, the magnificent flowering of Athenian democracy and culture in the latter half of the fifth century would not have taken place, and the significance of that for the development of Western civilization is beyond question.

There is an irony in Leonidas – a Spartan – being honoured as the saviour of Western values, for Sparta itself was the oddest and most illiberal of all the Greek states: a culture based on extreme militarism and underpinned by enslavement of fellow Greeks. But the essence of the Greco-Persian War – at least as it was presented by

A SUICIDE MISSION?

DID LEONIDAS SET OFF to Thermopylae with the express intention of dying? Various bits of evidence can be pieced together to suggest that he did.

First there is the remark, left unexplained by Herodotus, that Leonidas chose his 300 only from those Spartans who had living sons. A natural interpretation of this is that he knew that none of them were coming back and did not wish to extinguish any Spartan family line. Second, according to Plutarch, there is Leonidas' reply to his wife Gorgo, when she asked before his departure what she could do to help: 'Marry a man that will treat you well and bear him good children.' Then, just before the battle itself, Xerxes is bemused by a spy's report that the Spartans outside the Phocian Wall are combing their long tresses; the explanation given by the exile Demaratus is that such behaviour is customary when Spartans are expecting to die in battle. And on the final morning, Leonidas' gallows humour – 'Eat a good breakfast, for this evening we shall dine together in Hades' – clearly suggests that he did not expect to survive the day.

But none of this need indicate more than that Leonidas and his men were fully aware, before and during the battle, of the grave danger that they faced.

A bronze statue of Leonidas erected at Thermopylae in the 1950s. According to Plutarch, Xerxes demanded at the outset of the battle that Leonidas lay down his weapons and surrender, to which the Spartan gave the laconic reply inscribed below the modern statue:

ΜΟΛΩΝ ΛΑΒΕ
– 'Come and get them!'

This is a far cry from saying that they set out with the *deliberate* intention of dying. One piece of evidence, however, strongly supports the suicide theory. At the very outset of the war, Herodotus tells us, the Spartans received an oracle from Delphi:

Either your famed, great town must
*   be sacked by Perseus' sons,*
Or, if that be not, the whole land of Lacedaemon
Shall mourn the death of a king of
*   the house of Heracles ...*

While such utterances have always been open to retrospective manipulation, we should not underestimate their reality and significance to ancient Greeks. The Spartans, in particular, were notoriously superstitious and almost obsessively diligent in their observance of religious rituals. Religious scruple was the reason (ostensive, at least) for the small size of the Spartan contingent at Thermopylae, and it is not far-fetched to suppose that Leonidas would have taken a Delphic utterance (perhaps rather more ambiguously stated than in Herodotus' version) very seriously.

Nevertheless, even if we accept that Leonidas was set on sacrificing himself in order to save his city, it is still a big leap to supposing that he would have determined that his 300 fellow Spartans should suffer the same fate. The oracle in no way required it. And while the Spartans were notably scrupulous about making necessary sacrifices, they were just as well known for their unwillingness to make unnecessary ones.

Herodotus and others – is that it was a confrontation between freedom and slavery. As the exiled Spartan king Demaratus (as Herodotus' mouthpiece) explains to Xerxes, the Spartans' only master is the law – an insight that also underlies Simonides' famous epitaph. In effect, the Spartans act freely under their own laws – albeit a very unusual and restrictive set of laws. The fruit of Sparta's self-sacrifice at Thermopylae was a political and cultural efflorescence in other Greek states that was denied – indeed, in many respects was anathema – to Sparta itself. Leonidas' formal defeat was a moral victory. It was also a victory for morale, because it demonstrated to all, not least to the Persians, that when bent on resistance, the Greeks had the determination to defy the odds and struggle through to ultimate victory.

THEMISTOCLES

c. 525–459 BC

ROBIN WATERFIELD

THEMISTOCLES OF ATHENS was the ideal commander, equally at home and effective on the battlefield and in assembly. He was widely recognized as the saviour of Greece in the hour of its darkest peril, during the second Persian invasion of 480–479 BC. Several years before the invasion, he had equipped Athens with a sizeable fleet, the crews of which had sufficient time to master their skills. The victory single-handedly and somewhat deviously engineered by him at the Battle of Salamis in 480 made the final defeat of the Persians in 479 considerably easier, because they no longer dared to face the Greeks at sea.

At the beginning of the fifth century, Athens was a fledgling democracy, where invariably the most important military and political positions still went to members of a tight-knit, intermarrying aristocracy. Themistocles, however, was a 'new man', from a previously unremarkable family, who gained power entirely by his own merits. He was both a clear-sighted democrat and a gifted military tactician. Born around 525 BC, he was therefore old enough to greet the constitutional changes of 508 that laid the foundations for Athenian democracy.

His first major coup, in 493 BC, was to move the centre of Athens' seafaring activities a few miles north, from the old harbour of Phalerum to the Piraeus peninsula, which, with three natural harbours, was better suited to future requirements and easier to fortify. Though briefly eclipsed by rivals, especially Miltiades, Themistocles grew in power and stature during the 480s. Through the process of ostracism, he exiled powerful rivals, particularly those who were pro-Persian or anti-democratic.

In 487 BC Themistocles was instrumental in a far-reaching constitutional reform, whereby the nine most senior political officers of Athens were to be chosen by lot, rather than elected. These offices were therefore sidelined as routes to power, and ambitious Athenians instead sought one of the ten generalships, instituted in around 500, since these were now the only important posts still open to voluntary election, and to which one could be repeatedly re-elected, year after year.

The development of the fleet

By 483 BC, Themistocles was the most prominent public figure in Athens, and he used his position to push through a proposal that must have required all his rhetorical powers. A rich new vein of silver had been opened up in the Athenian mines at Laurium, and Themistocles persuaded the Athenians not to share out the surplus among themselves, but instead use it to develop a war fleet, initially of 100 triremes over and above those they had already. The immediate excuse was an ongoing war with the city's trade rival, the island of Aegina, but also the Persians were known to be planning a second invasion following their defeat by Miltiades at Marathon in 490. By the time of the pivotal Battle of Salamis, Athens was able to launch over two hundred ships with experienced crews.

As a democratic politician, Themistocles was undoubtedly also aware of the political repercussions of the development of a fleet. Every single Athenian trireme required a crew of 200, of whom 170 were oarsmen. Even though some of the oarsmen were resident foreigners and hired mercenaries, even slaves, the majority of them were poor Athenian citizens, who until that point had been denied much political power. But the more important they became, first to the defence of Athens, and then to the maintenance of its empire, the

A bust of Themistocles dating from the second century AD. Despite having been produced more than five hundred years after Themistocles' death, the bust manages to convey something of the stocky determination he needed to push through his controversial naval and political reforms.

The trireme *Olympias* during her maiden voyage in 1986. The exact design of a trireme, the standard warship of the classical period, is a matter of some controversy, but this reconstruction is widely accepted. It is rowed by 170 oarsmen (85 to each side), arranged in three tiers (hence the name).

more they were able to make their voices heard. Themistocles' development of the navy thus helped to make Athens a true democracy.

A trireme was hugely expensive to maintain; it cost about a talent a year (say, £350,000 in today's terms). Multiplied by two hundred or so, this was not a burden the state could, or chose to endure, and wealthy Athenians were themselves required to pay for the upkeep of one trireme each for a year, the development of the navy again having levelling political repercussions.

A wall of wood

Themistocles attracted many apocryphal stories in later antiquity, and even a collection of pseudonymous letters. One such story has a better claim than most to be grounded in truth.

It is certain that, in the face of the imminent Persian invasion, the Delphic oracle consistently counselled despair and surrender. So when the Athenians consulted Delphi about what they should do, they received an unequivocal reply that started: 'Fools, why sit you here? Fly to the ends of the earth …' But on consulting the oracle a second time, they received a more ambiguous reply which said, among other things, that only a 'wall of wood' would stand intact against the enemy. This provoked considerable debate, with opinions more or less evenly divided between seeing the

'wall of wood' as a reference to a palisade around the Acropolis, so that the god was advising the Athenians to stay in Athens and defend the city, and seeing the 'wall of wood' as a reference to their new navy.

The oracle ended with an equally ambiguous reference to Salamis: 'Blessed Salamis, you will be the death of mothers' sons ...' This was regarded as a hint that they should avoid Salamis at all costs, or die there. But Themistocles argued not only that the 'wall of wood' referred to the navy, but that it would be Persians who would die at Salamis, rather than Athenians – otherwise, why call it 'blessed'? Such was his influence in Athens at the time that his view prevailed even over that of the official oracular experts.

The second Persian invasion

Still smarting from their defeat by puny Athens at the Battle of Marathon in 490 BC, the Persians had long been planning a second invasion of Greece, a task that Xerxes inherited when he ascended to the Persian throne in 486. When it came, the invasion was massive: modern estimates talk of two hundred thousand land troops and a fleet of over one thousand three hundred warships. The invasion was supported by two extraordinary engineering feats: a double pontoon bridge all the way across the Hellespont from Abydos to near Sestos (a distance of some 3 miles), and a canal through the neck of the Athos peninsula in northern Greece, to avoid the tricky currents and frequent high winds there. Huge magazines of grain were established on the invasion route in what is now northern Greece, to supply the army as it passed and as it progressed further into the Greek mainland.

An ancient Greek seal, with a stylized representation of a warship, clearly showing that Greek warships had hoplite marines on board, as well as the oarsmen. The marines' job was to board enemy ships after ramming, and to be available for any fighting that took place on land.

Faced with imminent invasion, in 481 BC the Greeks convened a conference in Corinth. It was poorly attended because many Greek states, not unnaturally, preferred to capitulate or to side with the Persians, or to maintain an uneasy neutrality. At the conference, the delegates of thirty-one states – fewer than 5 per cent of those of mainland Greece – agreed to set aside their often long-standing differences, and chose the Spartans, with their military expertise and leadership of a powerful coalition of Peloponnesian states, as the overall commanders of the Greek forces. The following year, they formed two lines of defence: one in the north, directly in the line of the Persian approach, at Thermopylae and Artemisium, and one to fall back on in the south, around the Isthmus to the Peloponnese.

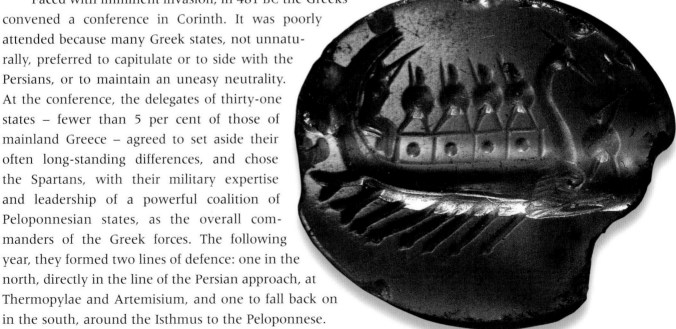

Themistocles

After – or perhaps more or less simultaneously with – the betrayal and glorious defeat of the Spartan king Leonidas and his vastly outnumbered troops at the narrow pass of Thermopylae, it was the turn of the largely Athenian navy at Artemisium, under the command of Themistocles. Perhaps they could check the inexorable advance south of the Persian forces through Greece. Even though quite a few crack Persian ships were destroyed in a storm, the Greeks were still hugely outnumbered. However, they held their own in an indecisive battle, before falling back south to the island of Salamis, in the Saronic Gulf near Athens.

> 'There was no one better than Themistocles at doing what had to be done on the spur of the moment.'
>
> THUCYDIDES, *THE PELOPONNESIAN WAR*, 1.138

The Greek army, meanwhile, withdrew to the Isthmus – the neck of land joining mainland Greece and the Peloponnese. There was nothing in the way of the Persian advance, and the Athenian fleet was used, on Themistocles' orders, to evacuate Athens and ferry its inhabitants to safety on Salamis and elsewhere. And the city was indeed soon sacked. The few defenders, those who were too stubborn or too poor to have evacuated, were massacred, and the temples were plundered and burnt to the ground. For many years after the war, the Athenians left the temples as they were, as a reminder of the atrocity – until they replaced them with the magnificent buildings the remains of which can still be seen on the Acropolis and elsewhere.

Many of the Greeks saw their position at Salamis as a dead end, a trap, and regarded the capture of Athens as the end of the war on the mainland. They were now concerned only to retreat to the Peloponnese and make a last stand there. In fact, the Peloponnesians were already in the process of building a defensive wall across the Isthmus near Corinth (close to the site of the modern canal), but this was a futile strategy: even if the wall succeeded in holding up some of the Persian troops, others could be landed beyond it. The Greek fleet could not patrol the whole coastline of the Peloponnese against the seven hundred or so enemy ships that remained after storm and battle losses – and Persia could soon bring up more ships as well.

Themistocles understood that the Greeks had to risk all on a single battle and, with his local knowledge of the waters and the weather, he saw that their position at Salamis could work in their favour, however hopeless it seemed – and maybe he bore the Salamis oracle in mind too. The victory at Salamis was decisive. Xerxes had set up his throne on a high point on the mainland in order to watch the expected victory. In the wake of the defeat, however, he returned with the bulk of his fleet to Asia Minor, to forestall opportunistic rebellions in other parts of the empire, to secure his line of retreat, and to guarantee provisions for the bulk of the land army, which wintered in northern Greece in order to continue the campaign the following year. Coincidentally, on the same day in 479, Greek forces annihilated the Persians on the mainland at Plataea and on the coast of Asia Minor at Mycale. Many of the Asiatic Greek cities rose up in revolt against their Persian rulers. The Persians withdrew, to recuperate and prepare for the future.

Themistocles after the war

Athens' prominent role in the two Persian invasions made it the equal of Sparta in authority, and it was not slow to grasp the opportunity afforded it by Themistocles. Sparta and Athens promised jointly to continue to keep the Persians at bay, but since this was largely a naval enterprise, the defence of Greece soon devolved on to Athens alone. A league was formed, the members of which contributed ships or, far more usually, money, which was used to help develop and maintain the Athenian fleet.

Themistocles had always seen that Athens would increase in power as a result of its naval expertise, and that this would eventually lead to tension and warfare with Sparta. He therefore pushed for a new defensive wall to be built around the city, and for Piraeus to be fortified. The new wall determined the size of the city of Athens for centuries to come, at about 1½ square miles, but its erection met with strong disapproval from the Spartans, who had become used to regarding themselves as the main power in Greece and wanted to curb upstart Athens. Themistocles arranged that he himself would be sent as ambassador to Sparta to discuss the matter, but delayed his departure for Sparta for a long time, and once there, delayed matters still further, until Athens' new wall was a *fait accompli*.

Themistocles' anti-Spartan stance brought him into conflict with Cimon, the son of Miltiades, who saw the future of Athens lying in cooperation with Sparta. Cimon used his enormous wealth and prestige to gain massive support, and when it came to an ostracism vote between the two men, probably in 470 BC, it was Themistocles who was banished for ten years. It is also likely that Themistocles, newly enriched by the war, was displaying rather too much arrogance: he was, for instance, playing the old aristocratic game of embellishing the city with temples and other buildings designed to aggrandize himself and his achievements.

Ostracism involved exile, but no loss of rights back in Athens, so that an ostracized man could, for instance, still hold property and do business through proxies in the city. However, while Themistocles was in exile in the Peloponnesian town of

Potsherds bearing the name of Themistocles, who was ostracized from Athens in 470 BC. Every year in democratic Athens, the people had the right to vote to send a prominent individual into exile, in order to preserve the stability of the state. Votes were cast by means of potsherds (*ostraka* in Greek, hence 'ostracism'), inscribed with the individual's name.

Themistocles

Argos, he was accused by the Spartans of collaborating with the Persians. We do not know what episode or episodes the Spartans were alluding to, unless they were referring to Themistocles' somewhat underhand dealings with Xerxes at Salamis (see below). At any rate, this charge of treachery made him a criminal exile, not a political one, and he was hounded from place to place until he fetched up – no doubt to his enemies' delight – at the court of the Persian king in Susa.

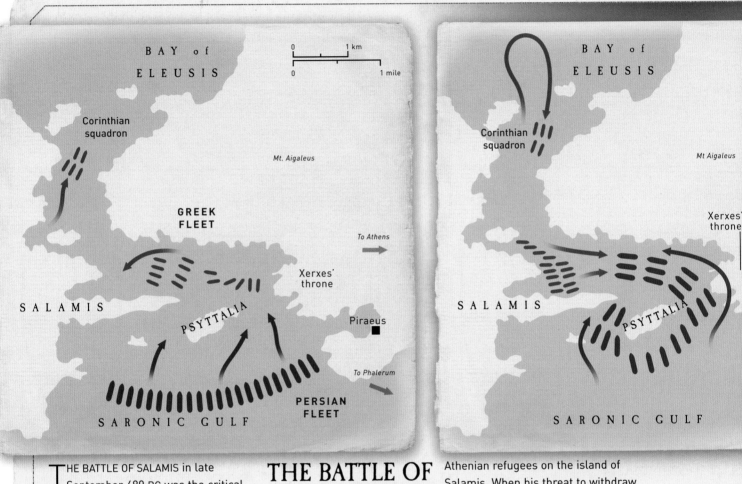

THE BATTLE OF SALAMIS

THE BATTLE OF SALAMIS in late September 480 BC was the critical battle of the second Persian invasion, involving over two hundred thousand men. After the three-day battles of Thermopylae and Artemisium (where the Greek navy worked together for the first time), the Greek army retreated south to the Isthmus, while a revived fleet of 366 ships was beached on the island of Salamis, just west of Athens and about 22 miles from the Isthmus.

The Greek senior command was undecided: the Peloponnesians wanted the fleet to link up with the army for a last-ditch attempt to defend the Peloponnese. Themistocles, however, refused to abandon Athens, or the

Athenian refugees on the island of Salamis. When his threat to withdraw the 200-strong Athenian fleet failed to tip the balance, he took matters into his own hands. He sent a secret message to Xerxes, claiming to be pro-Persian (as many Greeks were), and telling him that the Greeks planned to sneak away from the island under cover of darkness.

The Persian king therefore ordered his fleet of some seven hundred warships, recently arrived at Phalerum, to close in on the island by night, and when this was reported to the Greeks, they realized they were trapped. A squadron of two hundred Egyptian ships was detached from the Persian fleet to close off the western

The new king, Artaxerxes I, received him kindly, and gave him the income from three towns of Asia Minor as a stipend. In return, in due course of time, he demanded Themistocles' help in the ongoing war against Cimon, who was proving himself a very competent general and was laying the foundations of the Athenian empire. In 459 BC, finding himself unable to betray his native city, Themistocles, surely the most brilliant and original leader ever known to Athens, committed suicide.

(Below) **A view across** the Straits of Salamis.

To Athens

Piraeus

To Phalerum

exit and four hundred crack infantry troops were quietly landed on Psyttalia (where the next day they were cut off and massacred). The Greeks now listened to Themistocles.

It was critical to Themistocles' plan that the Persians should sail further into the narrows, where their enormous numbers would be a disadvantage, and where the Greeks' heavier ships could not be outmanoeuvred by the enemy vessels. The following morning, then, he arranged for the Greek fleet to launch in seeming disarray, with some ships even breaking off north, as if to make for the Isthmus, satisfying Persian expectations of finding disunity among the Greeks.

The Persians took the bait and sailed into the narrows, with the Greeks backing water with their oars to draw them further in and to keep a tight formation. The tired oarsmen of the Persian ships, which had been maintaining battle stations all night, began to break formation, and the swell that Themistocles had been expecting caused some of the Persian ships to heave and expose their sides. The Greek ships rowed hard into the attack, ramming the Persian triremes or breaking their oars. Many Persian ships chose flight immediately, while the Greeks succeeded in more or less surrounding the remainder. The battle was one-sided: over the course of a long day, the Persians lost over two hundred of their best ships, while the Greeks lost about forty.

Themistocles

THUCYDIDES

c. 455 – c. 398 BC

ANDREW ROBERTS

THE INCLUSION OF THUCYDIDES IN A BOOK subtitled *Great Commanders* might seem somewhat quixotic, for Thucydides was a general who failed so comprehensively in battle that he was sent into permanent exile as a punishment. Yet his right to be included stems from his philosophy of warfare, for no thinker before or since has so perceptively enunciated the great truths about what happens to human beings when they come into military conflict. Although those truths are timeless, if we are to understand how Thucydides arrived at them we need to know something of the man himself.

Because Thucydides spent nearly half his life in exile, and his sole literary work was unfinished at the time of his death, his contemporaries did not write about him, and it was not until the early years of the Roman Empire, half a millennium after his death, that his fame was really established.

From occasional references in his own writing we can surmise that he was probably over 30 years of age when he was elected a *strategos*, one of Athens' ten generals, for the year 424. That locates his birth somewhere in the mid 450s, and makes him a contemporary of some of the greatest Greeks of the ancient world, including Socrates, Phidias, Sophocles, Euripides and Aristophanes. He admired Pericles and knew Alcibiades. The Parthenon was built during his lifetime.

We know that Thucydides' father was called Oloros and that he was distantly descended from the ancient kings of Thrace, where his family still owned gold mines and had some political influence. He himself was an Athenian citizen, however, hailing from one of the 139 *medes* (constituent villages) called Halimous, which was to be found 4 miles from the city on the coast (near to today's Athens airport). From his background and the occasional political references in his work, we can assume that Thucydides was an aristocrat with marked oligarchical tendencies.

Apart from being of a sufficient age to attend the Athenian assembly at the outbreak of the Peloponnesian War in 431 BC, and possibly catching the plague of the late 420s – his description of the symptoms are thought too detailed to be anything other than first-hand – little can be even guessed about Thucydides until his election by the *demos* (the enfranchised) as a *strategos*. Sent to relieve the city of Amphipolis in the northern Aegean, he was outmanoeuvred by the great Spartan commander Brasidas, and subsequently condemned to exile by the Athenians, a sentence that he most probably served in Thrace until his death some time in the early 390s. We can picture him living in comfortable exile among the olive groves there, a disappointed ex-general thinking himself ill-used by the *demos*, and writing what is today the greatest historical work ever penned, *The History of the Peloponnesian War*.

The History of the Peloponnesian War

Thucydides' own definition of his history as an everlasting possession (quoted above) might sound extraordinarily arrogant had it not proved to be true. Thucydides tells us he began it as soon as the Peloponnesian War broke out in 431 BC, rightly 'expecting that it would be a great war'. He went about it in a thoroughly professional manner, interviewing survivors, collecting the texts of important documents, noting down speeches and adopting an accurate chronology of campaigning season by season. The historian Dr G. B. Grundy was convinced that Thucydides also visited Syracuse and walked the battlefields of the Sicilian campaign very shortly after the Athenian defeat there in 413. As Thucydides himself put it, he trusted in 'laborious investigation' rather than mere memory.

Where Herodotus would use absurd exaggeration to make his points – such as claiming that 5,283,320 Persians invaded Greece – Thucydides generally produced believable figures for amounts of tribute and numbers of ships and men. Herodotus' history of the Ionian Revolt, rather like Homer's history of the Trojan War, was more about literature and morality than objective history, while Thucydides' (by him untitled) history of the Peloponnesian War tried hard to relate, in Ranke's phrase, *'wie es eigentlich gewesen ist'* ('how it actually was'). Of the verbatim speeches that pepper his work, Thucydides wrote that he attempted to get 'as close as possible to the general gist of what was actually said'.

What also sets Thucydides apart from other ancient Greek writers – especially Homer and Herodotus – is his very modern attitude to human motivation. He excised the traditional supernatural explanations entirely; gone are the stories of gods, dreams, omens and curses. Instead the actions of the Athenians, Spartans and their respective

**A carved relief from
c. 420 BC** depicting
Chairedemos and
Lykeas, two hoplites
(heavy-armed
infantrymen) who were
killed during the
Peloponnesian War
(431–404 BC).

allies are presented as having been actuated by fear, greed, ignorance, opportunism, stupidity, the desire for honour, the lust for glory, the defence of markets, occasionally by idealism, and all the real motives for which men have gone to war throughout the centuries.

This is one of the only accounts of warfare in the ancient world – Xenophon and Julius Caesar being the other two – written by a professional soldier, and although he rarely comments on the pity of war (beyond writing in Book III of the 120 youths lost in a disastrous Aetolian mission as 'the finest men whom Athens lost in the whole war'), the work can and should be read as a tragedy.

What is certainly tragic is that the great work breaks off suddenly in Book VIII while covering the events of 411 BC, despite the fact that in earlier parts of the same volume there are mentions of Athens' final catastrophic defeat in 404. He could not possibly have wanted to finish his great work with the phrase: 'As soon as Tissaphernes arrived at Ephesus he sacrificed to Artemis', but if there were further books after the eighth, they have not survived.

The Melian Dialogue

Thucydides invented the concept of Realpolitik, which came to its apogee in his notorious Melian Dialogue of 416 BC, in which his theme was the essential amorality of relations between states. It is, of course, impossible at this distance of time to gauge the exact extent to which the speeches quoted as verbatim by Thucydides actually represent his own views or those of the speakers, despite his protestation of objective accuracy, but the speeches of the Athenians and Melians have a tautness, eloquence and literary quality that are remarkable even for that period of fine rhetoric.

Athens' great maritime power meant that in the summer of 416 BC, the weaker Aegean island of Melos lay at her mercy. Before she attacked, however, her generals sent envoys to state the case for the island to become a tributary vassal state of the Athenian empire. Refused permission to address the popular assembly, the Athenians presented their case to the magistrates and oligarchs, expressed in uncompromising form in Book V of Thucydides' work:

> *The strong do what they can and the weak follow. We will show you that we are here for the benefit of our empire and what we are going to say now will be aimed at preserving your city. We wish to rule over you without trouble and we want you to be spared to our joint advantage.*

In answer, the Melians offered benign neutrality, to which the Athenians replied with contempt: 'Your hostility does not harm us. Your friendship would be a sign to our subjects of weakness; your hatred is a sign of our strength.' When the Melians answered that their destruction would send a dangerous message to Athens' other subject peoples, their interlocutors argued that in fact the opposite was the case, because Athenian imperialism rested on the terror of the subject peoples rather than their love. Melian protestations that the gods would not allow the destruction of the righteous brought forth this cynical rejoinder: 'We think that the gods apparently and men demonstrably carry their rule as far as their power extends by a necessary law of nature. We did not make this law, nor are we the first to use it.'

After the Melians rejected Athens' demands, and decided to fight for their independence, Thucydides baldly recorded how 'The Athenians killed all the adult Melian men that they captured; the women and children they enslaved. Then they occupied the island themselves, subsequently sending five hundred settlers.' Such was the tyrannical reality of Athenian imperialism; nor was Melos the only place where the entire male population of a city was put to the sword.

The Sicilian expedition

Retribution for Athens' cruelty on Melos, Scione and elsewhere, came in the shape of the Sicilian expedition, the story of which is told in Books VI and VII. It forms by far the longest campaign sequence in Thucydides' work and there is some internal evidence to suggest it was originally written as an entirely separate book. Earlier in the work, Thucydides had described an unsuccessful Athenian expedition against Sicily in 427 BC under Laches, but eleven years later:

> *the Athenians resolved to sail against Sicily with larger forces than those which Laches and Eurymedon had commanded and, if possible, to conquer it. They were for the most part ignorant of the size of the island and of the numbers of its inhabitants, both Hellenic and native, and they did not realize they were taking on a war of almost the same magnitude as their war against the Peloponnesians.*

These failures of intelligence Thucydides put down to 'the people' of Athens, rather than to Nicias, the rich commander of the expedition, who had originally argued against it in the assembly. Was this, as some historians have assumed, a case of class comradeship between fellow millionaires, or might the expedition really have been undertaken by an over-excited *demos* in a spirit of wild overconfidence? Certainly its main advocate was one of the most mercurial, vain, charismatic, reckless but undeniably brilliant men in classical Greek history, Alcibiades the Younger, whom

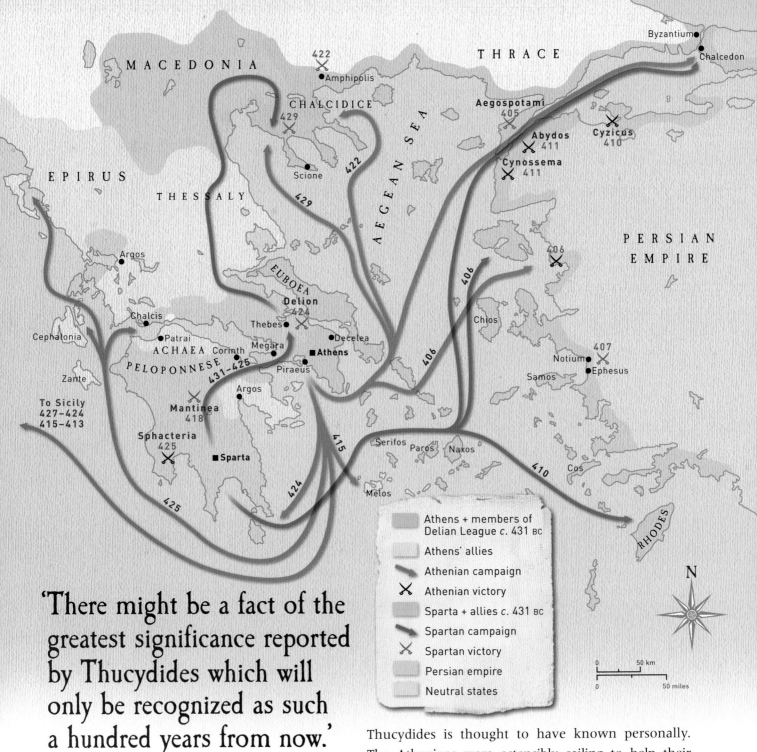

MACEDONIA

THRACE

Byzantium

Chalcedon

422 Amphipolis

CHALCIDICE

EPIRUS

THESSALY

429

Scione

422

429

Aegospotami
405

Abydos
411

Cyzicus
410

Cynossema
411

AEGEAN SEA

PERSIAN
EMPIRE

Argos

EUBOEA

406

Delion
424

Chios

Chalcis

Cephalonia

Patrai

Thebes

Megara

Decelea

Athens

406

Notium
407

Ephesus

ACHAEA   Corinth

PELOPONNESE

431–425

Piraeus

Samos

Zante

Argos

To Sicily
427–424
415–413

Mantinea
418

415

Sphacteria
425

Serifos Paros Naxos

Sparta

424

410

Cos

RHODES

Melos

425

N

'There might be a fact of the greatest significance reported by Thucydides which will only be recognized as such a hundred years from now.'

JACOB BURCKHARDT

Athens + members of
Delian League c. 431 BC

Athens' allies

Athenian campaign

✗ Athenian victory

Sparta + allies c. 431 BC

Spartan campaign

✗ Spartan victory

Persian empire

Neutral states

0   50 km
0   50 miles

Thucydides is thought to have known personally. The Athenians were ostensibly sailing to help their Sicilian allies, the Egestians, stay free of the hegemonizing influence of the town of Syracuse. But as Thucydides clearly alleges, what they really wanted was to bring the whole island under their imperium. They appointed Nicias, Alcibiades and the elderly but adventurous Lamachus as the three commanders of the expedition, notwithstanding Nicias' avowed opposition to the scheme.

Once appointed against his will, Nicias then argued that the whole expedition ought to be a massive effort of 100 triremes and 5,000 hoplites (infantrymen). He hoped to dull its appeal to the assembly, but his proposal met with general acclaim and thus had exactly the opposite result. As Thucydides recorded, 'whoever was

**CAMPAIGNS AND
BATTLES OF THE
PELOPONNESIAN WAR**
(431–404 BC).

opposed kept quiet, lest by voting in the negative he appear unpatriotic'. As a result, the largest fleet and army ever raised by Athens – eventually comprising 134 triremes and 5,100 hoplites, including contingents of allies and mercenaries – set sail in the summer of 415 BC in three squadrons, each under a *strategos*.

On arriving in Sicily, the Athenians discovered that they had been tricked by the Egestians, who were not in fact able to pay for the expedition as they had promised. The three generals then disagreed amongst themselves over the next course of action: Nicias wanted to attack the Egestians' enemy in the city of Silenus and then return to Athens; Alcibiades wanted to raise a Sicilian army against Syracuse; while Lamachus wanted an immediate attack on Syracuse.

After initially following Alcibiades' plan, which largely failed, the Athenians set up camp at Catana, midway between Naxos and Syracuse. Desultory skirmishing ashore resulted in the Syracusan cavalry drawing first blood when they attacked some Athenian light infantry. In the winter of 415 BC, the Athenians made a bold attack on Syracuse. Having lured the Syracusan army away to attack Catana, the Athenians entered the Grand Harbour of Syracuse in a dawn assault, and occupied a strongpoint opposite the temple of Olympian Zeus. When the Syracusans returned, a set-piece battle ensued, in which the Athenians lost fifty men to the enemy's two hundred. The victory could not be pressed home because for some unaccountable reason the Athenians had brought no cavalry to Sicily, whereas the Syracusans had plenty. The next day, Nicias returned to Catana to sit out the winter, requesting that cavalry be urgently sent from Athens. The Syracusans meanwhile built an extra wall around their city and protected the entrance to the Grand Harbour with sharpened stakes under the water.

Greek warriors fighting, wounded and dying, in a vase painting dating from *c.* 560–550 BC.

Thucydides

97

The following spring (414 BC) saw the Athenians unsuccessfully attacking the Syracusan fort of Megara, capturing and burning Centoripa in central Sicily, and receiving 250 cavalrymen from Athens, who absurdly enough arrived without their horses. Nicias' surprise attack on Syracuse the next morning resulted in the Athenians once more taking an advantageous strategic position, albeit at the cost of Lamachus, who was killed in battle. Nicias then settled down to besiege a seemingly doomed city.

In exile in Sparta, Alcibiades unveiled to his hosts the Athenian plans to conquer Sicily, Carthage and Italy, before they returned in force to lay waste to the Peloponnese. To forestall such a disaster, Sparta despatched her talented admiral Gylippus with a small force to try to relieve Syracuse.

Once Gylippus landed at Himera on the north coast of Sicily, he was joined by the forces of various anti-Athenian cities, in total over one thousand seven hundred men. In a lightning attack, he arrived at Syracuse just as the inhabitants were considering suing for peace, and caught the Athenians so much by surprise that he was able to enter the city unscathed. Under the cover of skirmishing over the next few weeks, Gylippus was able to build enfilading walls that prevented the Athenians from investing the city, thereby effectively raising the siege. Cut off from a regular water supply on the headlands outside the city, the situation for Nicias started to look bleak, as he explained to the Athenian assembly in a despatch in the winter of 414 BC, pointing out that he was no longer the besieger but the besieged, and begging for reinforcements.

Whereas Gylippus was an enterprising and resourceful commander, Nicias was a cautious and nerve-wracked one, whose heart had never been in the campaign from the start. As the Spartans seemed to win the upper hand, neutrals started to support them rather than the Athenians. Even when the Athenians voted to send out another large expeditionary force under the daring general Demosthenes, they could not turn

THE MORAL OF THE WORK

THUCYDIDES HAS MUCH OF VALUE to say about politics, especially the limits of democracy; about the horrors of *stasis* (civil war), especially in Corcyra in Book III; and about the morally corrosive effect of war, which diverts human progress down vicious channels towards a kind of utter hellishness where new methods of exacting retribution are constantly discovered. Although Might and Right occasionally overlap, he teaches, they are entirely separate from one another.

In Book III, Thucydides makes plain the moral of his great work, which is that:

> In peace and prosperity states and individuals have better sentiments, because they do not find themselves confronted suddenly with imperious necessities; but war takes away the easy supply of daily wants, and so proves a violent teacher, that brings most men's characters down to a level with their fortunes.

Such a phenomenon has been found again and again throughout history. War has stripped away the humanity from humans, reducing mankind to what King Lear calls 'unaccommodated man ... no more but such a poor, bare, fork'd animal'. The scenes of brutality witnessed during such struggles as the Thirty Years War, the Retreat from Moscow and Operation Barbarossa bear testament to Thucydides' iron law of war, which he believed would remain true 'as long as human nature stays the same'.

Lord Macaulay believed that the seventh book of Thucydides' history, covering the hubris and nemesis of the Sicilian expedition, represented the highest achievement of human art. Thomas Hobbes wrote that the whole work provided 'profitable instructions for Noble men and such as may come to have the managings of great and weighty actions'. Writing in the darkest days of the Second World War, in 1942, the great Harvard classicist John H. Finley equated the Athens–Sparta struggle with that of the Allies versus the Axis. In the context of 'a world in which armed nationalism is at its height', he wrote that each generation must study afresh the great authors of the past, 'because each will find in them certain qualities that its predecessors overlooked or failed to emphasize, and the statement has a special force in regard to Thucydides'.

the tide. Attacks by siege engines on the enfilading wall outside Syracuse were forced back, with the engines being set on fire by the Spartan and Syracusan-allied Sicilian defenders. Even when Demosthenes managed to start pulling the wall down after a flanking movement during a daring night attack, the Athenians were finally dispersed with heavy losses.

Sickness in the low-level marshy Athenian camp outside the city walls led to demoralization, even though in sheer numbers of ships they still had clear superiority. In defiance of Demosthenes' advice to withdraw to Catana or Thapsus, Nicias resolved to continue the half-siege of Syracuse. When finally he changed his mind and ordered an embarkation, there was an eclipse of the moon, which convinced the troops that it was ill-omened. The humanist Thucydides despised such superstition, but accurately recorded its dire result for the Athenian expeditionary force.

After a disastrous naval defeat, the Athenians attempted to escape to Catana, harried by their enemies on both flanks and the rear. Demosthenes' force was cut off, nearly destroyed and then forced to surrender. Nicias surrendered to Gylippus the next day as his troops, maddened by thirst, drank from the River Assinarus even though it was flowing thick with the blood of their comrades killed upstream.

A very few Athenians managed to escape to Catana and safety, but Thucydides' gripping account shows how the vast majority of both expeditionary forces were killed in action, executed (including Nicias and Demosthenes), enslaved or died of exposure in prison-caves. The power of Athens was broken for ever, and with it the power of Greece.

Thucydides

ALCIBIADES

c. 452–404 BC

ROBIN WATERFIELD

ALTHOUGH ALCIBIADES OF ATHENS was a skilled battlefield commander, who lost very few of the many engagements in which he was involved, he shone especially before and after battles – at diplomacy, negotiation and fund-raising for his troops. These aspects of warfare, often overlooked by historians, enabled him to keep Athens' hopes alive for a number of years in the Peloponnesian War, even when the situation seemed altogether hopeless.

Too much is made of Alcibiades' alleged treachery; it is more plausible to see him as more or less loyal to his native city – or at any rate to a version of it in which he himself could hold power. With or without him, Athens was destined to lose the Peloponnesian War (431–404 BC), but without him Athenian history in the last quarter of the fifth century BC would have been considerably less colourful.

Alcibiades was always destined for greatness. He was born no later than 452 BC into one of the wealthiest and most powerful families of classical Athens, and after his father's early death was adopted by no less a person than Pericles, who for over twenty years was the leading politician of the city. With this background, Alcibiades could well have stepped into his guardian's shoes, but his scandalous playboy lifestyle – involving heavy drinking, multiple affairs with members of either sex, and near sacrilege – was a constant hindrance to his evident ambition.

Entry into public life

Alcibiades came of age in the early years of the Peloponnesian War between Athens and Sparta. Even as a child he had shown his ambition and arrogance, and since warfare was all he knew, it was warfare that he chose to be the field in which he would rise to greatness. He served in a couple of battles in the early years of the war, but his first major coup was to stir up conflict at a time of temporary peace. In 421 BC, Athens and Sparta negotiated a truce after ten years of open warfare and half a century of cold war. This irritated Alcibiades and the other Athenian hawks. For fifty years Athens had held a maritime empire, which had enriched the city hugely and had made it the most powerful state in Greece, at least the equal of Sparta with its network of alliances and supremacy at land battle. Alcibiades wanted to see the empire not just maintained, but expanded, both for the continued enrichment of his native city and to give himself a greater field of endeavour.

The peace between Sparta and Athens was fragile, since neither side was in a position to fulfil its promises. Alcibiades' opportunity came in 420 BC, at a summit meeting in Athens, consisting of the Athenian authorities, and delegates from both Sparta and a few of its Peloponnesian neighbours, who were undecided whether to enter into an alliance with Sparta or with Athens. Alcibiades put his rhetorical skills to work and so thoroughly discredited the Spartan representatives that Athens immediately entered into an alliance with Argos and the other Peloponnesian states.

With such a threat on its doorstep, Sparta was bound to try by military means to recover Argos and the other dissident Peloponnesian states. While Sparta hastened to reassure and retain its existing friends, Alcibiades, who had been chosen as one of Athens' ten generals (a post subject to annual re-election in democratic Athens), spent much of 419 BC touring the Peloponnese, strengthening the Athenian–Argive alliance and persuading others to join it. His immediate goal was to try to force Corinth, Sparta's most powerful ally, to withdraw from the Peloponnesian alliance. He strengthened the Athenians' position at the western mouth of the Gulf of Corinth, and tried to persuade Argos to threaten the city by land also, although sabre-rattling by Sparta on Argos' borders dissuaded that venture.

Having achieved relatively little, Alcibiades was not re-elected as a general for 418 BC and when it came to a battle between the two sides, he was present only in an ambassadorial role, to strengthen the allies' resolve. At the Battle of Mantinea, Sparta crushed a combined force of Athenians, Argives and others; the Athenian alliance collapsed and all the dissident Peloponnesian states promptly went over to Sparta. Although Alcibiades' Peloponnesian policy had failed, he was able to boast that he had brought the Spartans to the brink of defeat, and had forced them to risk all on a single battle; and that he had done this without seriously endangering Athens, since the battle had taken place far from the city.

The Sicilian expedition

Even though Athenian and Spartan forces had clashed at Mantinea, both sides tacitly agreed to overlook this and to try to preserve the tattered peace treaty. Alcibiades had other plans. Having fought off his political enemies, and not least because of his actions in the Peloponnese, by 416 BC he had emerged as leader of the Athenian hawks. He also excelled gloriously at the Olympic Games of 416, when he achieved the unparalleled feat of entering seven teams for the prestigious four-horse chariot event and coming first, second and fourth. He was at the height of his influence in Athens.

The Athenian empire consisted largely of Aegean states, but many Athenians had long entertained hopes of expanding westward, into the Greek cities of Sicily and southern Italy. Apart from anything else, grain was plentiful there and Athens constantly suffered from a shortage. The pretext came in the winter of 416–415 BC, when a number of small Sicilian cities appealed for Athenian help against Syracuse, which wanted to establish hegemony over the entire island.

The debate in the Assembly was personal and furious, but in the end Alcibiades prevailed, and was chosen, along with two of his fellow generals, Nicias and Lamachus, to command the expedition. The size of the armada showed that Athens wanted not just to curb Syracuse, but to establish a powerful presence on the island. Though Syracuse was a Spartan ally, the Athenians were well aware of Spartan reluctance to campaign abroad, and they had no reason to doubt that they would be successful.

However, just a few weeks before the expedition sailed, a terrible omen rocked the city. On a single night, a great many of the herms of the city – squared blocks of stone personalized only by a bearded head of Hermes and an erect phallus – were defaced. This was sacrilege of the highest order, and smacked of a conspiracy of some

A hoplite driving a chariot, in a late fourth-century BC marble relief. Our familiarity with chariots obscures the fact that they were rare items in the ancient world. Only the very wealthy could afford to breed and rear horses; this was one of the ways in which Alcibiades flaunted his flamboyant lifestyle.

kind, even if its purpose was a complete mystery. Was it a drunken prank or politically motivated? The subsequent inquiry rapidly became a witch-hunt as fears spiralled out of control. In the course of the investigation it was revealed that this was not the only sacrilege that had taken place in the city: on a number of occasions, aristocratic men had mocked the Eleusinian Mysteries, one of the most sacred and secret rites, by performing some of the rituals out of context and before an uninitiated audience.

Alcibiades was certainly implicated in the latter sacrilege, but the terrified Athenians so compounded the two scandals that it was commonly supposed that he and his circle had also been involved in the mutilation of the herms; Alcibiades' ambition was well known, and it was assumed that he was intending to replace democracy with a narrow oligarchy or even with tyranny. The armada therefore set off with this dark cloud hanging over it.

> # 'Alcibiades had no equal: he was better than the best and worse than the worst.'
>
> CORNELIUS NEPOS, *LIFE OF ALCIBIADES* 1

The expedition's first purpose was to win over as many of the southern Italian and Sicilian states as possible, and with the help of Alcibiades' negotiating skills the Athenians began to achieve moderate success. But then an official ship arrived from Athens with orders to relieve Alcibiades of his command and to bring him home to stand trial. Alcibiades jumped ship, however, and made his way to Sparta, where he took up residence in the enemy heartland. Meanwhile, back in his native city, the Athenians cursed him, condemned him to death in absentia, and confiscated all his property.

In Sparta and Sardis

To his credit, Alcibiades did little to harm his native city during his stay in Sparta. He advised the Spartans to help the Syracusans, but in the event they sent only a small force. The Athenian defeat there was due to Athenian incompetence, not to Alcibiades' advice. He also recommended that the Spartans establish a permanent fortification close to Athens, rather than employing their old tactic of invading once a year for a few weeks, so as to threaten agriculture and generally make life difficult for the Athenians, who were no match for the Spartans on land. The Spartans duly fortified Decelea, but this was a tactic they had been contemplating for a while, so again Alcibiades' contribution as a traitor was slight.

Alcibiades spent two years in Sparta. This was a quiet period for him, but he then fell out with one of the two Spartan kings (whose wife he was rumoured to have seduced) and found it prudent to move on. He chose to go to the court of Tissaphernes, the Persian king's satrap in central Asia Minor. Persia had long been hovering on the margins of the war. The Persians claimed the Greek cities of Asia Minor as their vassal states, and had lobbied for their return ever since losing them sixty-five years earlier. They were poised to enter the war, and were prepared to finance whichever side took their fancy. Sparta desperately needed their help, because without them they could not afford to build and maintain the navy they needed to combat the Athenians at sea. The Athenians needed them because by 413 BC they had lost an entire fleet and thousands of men in Sicily. Moreover, in the wake of this disaster, some of their most important subject states seceded from the empire and deprived them of income.

Alcibiades

An image by the Swiss photographer Fred Boissonas. Dating from the early twentieth century, it shows the riverbed of the Eurotas, the river of ancient Sparta. The valley extends to the sea, but otherwise Sparta was protected by high mountains; the Taygetos mountains, usually snowcapped from November to May, are visible here.

In the early part of his sojourn in Asia Minor, Alcibiades helped Tissaphernes and his more northerly colleague Pharnabazus in their efforts to spread the coastal Greek cities' rebellion against Athenian domination. This enabled him to ingratiate himself with the Persian satraps at the same time as blunting the Spartan king's hostility towards him. But the Athenians were surprisingly quick at rebuilding a fleet, and once they had made the island of Samos their base of operations in the Aegean, they managed to staunch the potentially lethal haemorrhage of rebel states.

At this point, once again, Alcibiades helped his native city. The Persians had to decide which side to support, and Sparta was the natural choice, not just because Athens had been crippled by the Sicilian disaster, but also because Athens had been at the forefront of resistance to Persia since the start of the fifth century. Alcibiades, however, persuaded Tissaphernes to offer tepid support to both sides, arguing that he should play them off against each other and come down firmly on one side or the other only when it was clear where the advantage lay.

Tissaphernes followed Alcibiades' advice, and Athenian hopes began to rise a little. Alcibiades took advantage of this to enter into secret negotiations with the Athenian commanders on Samos. He convinced them that he could bring the Persians into the war on the Athenian side, but only if he was restored to power in Athens. Since this was impossible under the current regime, which had cursed him and condemned him to death, a regime change was the first prerequisite.

Alcibiades

There was plenty of disaffection amongst the aristocrats of Athens against the democracy, but it was far from universal, whether on Samos or in Athens itself. Nevertheless, the oligarchs on Samos stirred up matters in Athens until there was a coup, and in 411 BC the democracy was replaced by an oligarchy known as the Four Hundred. The single most important reason for the success of this coup was the prospect of the war's ending as quickly as possible with the Persian help that Alcibiades had promised. What most people did not know, however, was that Alcibiades was unable to do this: he had promised the Persians not only that they would regain their long-lost coastal territories but also that they would have the right to patrol the Asia Minor coast with their Phoenician fleet. While the Athenian oligarchs were prepared to go along with the first provision, they flatly refused to countenance the second.

Restoration, second fall, and death

A desire to end the war quickly was not, however, the Athenian oligarchs' main reason for establishing an oligarchy; they were simply committed oligarchs. But the troops on Samos remained democratic, and their leaders were also committed to ending the war as quickly as possible. Ironically, it was they who recalled Alcibiades from exile, since they too were convinced by his promise of Persian aid. The Athenian fleet wanted to sail to Athens and restore the democracy, but Alcibiades persuaded them not to: he knew that would leave the eastern Aegean undefended against the Spartans, and he also dreaded civil war.

Alcibiades abandoned the oligarchs, however, and said that he would negotiate only with a more moderate regime in Athens. Such was Athenian faith in Alcibiades' powers as a war-leader that this was one of the main levers that caused the downfall of the Four Hundred in Athens. Alcibiades was again Athens' darling, but he chose not to return home immediately. Although he held no official position, he was the effective leader of some of the Athenian forces in the Aegean, and he used them to good advantage.

By the end of 411 BC, the Spartans were dominant in the Aegean and, even more importantly, in the Hellespont. They had proved capable of absorbing any minor defeats the Athenians could inflict on them, and their control of the Hellespont meant near-starvation for the Athenians at home: in the classical period, Athens was never self-sufficient in grain and other produce that was imported from the fertile Black Sea region. Spartan dominance also encouraged discontented members of the Athenian empire to secede, and every such secession was a further blow to the Athenian war effort, since they were losing much-needed revenue.

But in 410 BC, Alcibiades was instrumental in destroying the Spartan fleet at the Battle of Cyzicus, and over the next three years he led or took part in a number of engagements that enabled the Athenians to regain control of the Hellespont. This was a complete turnaround: even after the Sicilian catastrophe, and despite political opposition at home, Alcibiades enabled Athens to recover for three whole years, and even to hope once more for ultimate victory – so much so that they rejected a Spartan offer of peace after Cyzicus.

Buoyed by his successes, in 407 BC Alcibiades returned in splendid style to Athens, where he was welcomed with adoration as the saviour of the city. All the charges against him were dropped, the curses were revoked, and his property was restored to him. Naturally, he was elected general and he soon returned to Samos to prosecute the war against the Spartans and to bring rebel states back into the Athenian fold. But by now Alcibiades had met his match in the new Spartan commander Lysander, who was not only a brilliant strategist and tactician, but had also endeared himself to Cyrus, the Persian king's son, who had been sent west from Persia to see to Athens' downfall. Lysander took advantage of Alcibiades' absence on a fund-raising campaign to defeat his lieutenant at the Battle of Notium, and Alcibiades was powerless to retaliate. His ineffectiveness made it possible for his

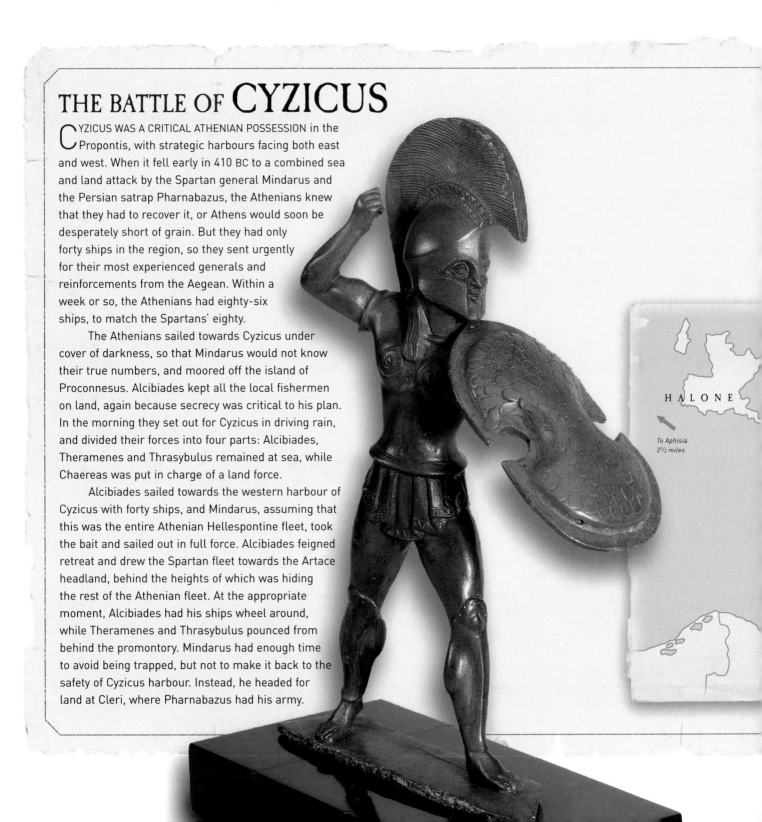

THE BATTLE OF CYZICUS

Cyzicus was a critical athenian possession in the Propontis, with strategic harbours facing both east and west. When it fell early in 410 BC to a combined sea and land attack by the Spartan general Mindarus and the Persian satrap Pharnabazus, the Athenians knew that they had to recover it, or Athens would soon be desperately short of grain. But they had only forty ships in the region, so they sent urgently for their most experienced generals and reinforcements from the Aegean. Within a week or so, the Athenians had eighty-six ships, to match the Spartans' eighty.

The Athenians sailed towards Cyzicus under cover of darkness, so that Mindarus would not know their true numbers, and moored off the island of Proconnesus. Alcibiades kept all the local fishermen on land, again because secrecy was critical to his plan. In the morning they set out for Cyzicus in driving rain, and divided their forces into four parts: Alcibiades, Theramenes and Thrasybulus remained at sea, while Chaereas was put in charge of a land force.

Alcibiades sailed towards the western harbour of Cyzicus with forty ships, and Mindarus, assuming that this was the entire Athenian Hellespontine fleet, took the bait and sailed out in full force. Alcibiades feigned retreat and drew the Spartan fleet towards the Artace headland, behind the heights of which was hiding the rest of the Athenian fleet. At the appropriate moment, Alcibiades had his ships wheel around, while Theramenes and Thrasybulus pounced from behind the promontory. Mindarus had enough time to avoid being trapped, but not to make it back to the safety of Cyzicus harbour. Instead, he headed for land at Cleri, where Pharnabazus had his army.

HALONE

To Aphisia
2½ miles

enemies in Athens to arouse hostility against him, and in 406, only a few months after his restoration, he was once again banished.

This time he retired to private estates in the Thracian Chersonese. He played no further part in the war except, in a probably apocryphal story, to offer advice to the Athenian generals before the final battle of the war at Aegospotami, not far from his estates. The advice was ignored, the battle was lost, the empire crumbled, and in 404 Athens was rapidly starved into submission. Only a few weeks later, under circumstances that must remain for ever obscure, Alcibiades was murdered in Phrygia.

Alcibiades pursued Mindarus and destroyed some of his ships. Hand-to-hand fighting began on the shore, with the Athenians hampered by fighting in the water against men on dry land. Thrasybulus therefore came up to support Alcibiades, while Theramenes landed further west and joined forces with Chaereas. This land army arrived just in time to save Alcibiades' and Thrasybulus' troops from defeat, and after a hard battle Pharnabazus ordered his men to retreat. Not long afterwards, Mindarus himself was killed, and the dispirited Spartans abandoned

their ships and fled. The remaining Spartans just had time to send a typically laconic message back home before abandoning Cyzicus: 'Ships lost. Mindarus dead. Men starving. No idea what to do.'

(Opposite) **A hoplite,** or heavy-armed spearman. Greek shields of the period were, more typically, round, but otherwise this late sixth-century statuette, found in the sanctuary of Zeus at Dodona, gives an excellent impression of a hoplite's fighting stance and fearsome appearance.

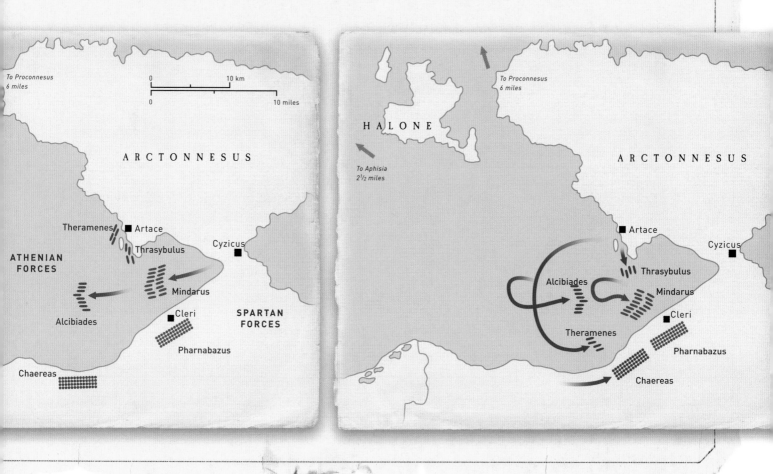

'Friendly and harsh, straightforward and subtle, a good protector and a good thief, generous and grasping, steady and aggressive.' (XENOPHON ON THE QUALITIES OF A GOOD GENERAL), *MEMOIRS OF SOCRATES* 3.1.6

XENOPHON
c. 430 – c. 354 BC

ROBIN WATERFIELD

XENOPHON OF ATHENS was a prolific writer who is best known, in military terms, as one of the leaders of the so-called 'Ten Thousand' Greek mercenaries who journeyed east on an ill-fated expedition to topple the Persian king and replace him with his brother. He himself wrote the only surviving account of the expedition, which is the world's first eyewitness campaign narrative. Although his military career was short, after retiring he continued to reflect upon his experiences as a commander and this led him to develop a theory of leadership, which features in his account of the expedition, with portraits of himself and other generals at work. These ideas also crop up in other works. His importance, then, is not just as a practitioner, but also as a theorist.

The famous expedition lasted two years (401–399 BC), and then Xenophon chose to stay on for a few years as a mercenary commander, with the remnants of the Ten Thousand, fighting for the Spartans first against the Persians in Asia Minor, and subsequently, more briefly, on mainland Greece fighting for the Spartans against other Greek states, including his native Athens. But by then he had been formally exiled from Athens, for his anti-democratic and pro-Spartan tendencies.

Xenophon was born into a well-to-do Athenian family, and was rich enough to serve in the Athenian cavalry. He probably helped the Thirty Tyrants police Athens during their brutal but shortlived regime (404–403 BC), and it was during this time that he got to know the philosopher Socrates. The restoration of the democracy in 403 BC, with which he was not in sympathy, helped to trigger his decision to travel east with Cyrus, the younger brother of the Persian king Artaxerxes II. His time as a mercenary ended in 394 or 393 BC, and after that he lived as a gentleman farmer on an estate in Scillus, in the western Peloponnese, under Spartan protection. Most of his books, which range from history to technical treatises on matters such as hunting, estate-management and cavalry command, were written during his twenty or so years at Scillus. At some point the Athenians repealed his banishment, but he chose not to return to Athens and ended his days in Corinth.

The *Anabasis*

Intermittently, Cyrus had held a command in the Persian territories of Asia Minor, but he wanted more. When he decided to try to take the Persian throne from his brother, he began to recruit Greek soldiers, because they were the best in the known world – the best-equipped and, thanks to the Peloponnesian War (431–404), the most experienced. By the time his plans came to fruition in 401, he had about ten thousand six hundred Greek hoplites (heavily armed infantry), and about two thousand three hundred peltasts (mobile infantry) from the margins of the Greek world. He also had at least the same number again of native troops, under the joint command of himself and his uncle Ariaeus.

The journey east (the *anabasis*, 'the march up country') was not too arduous, but it was the longest such march undertaken before Alexander the Great. They marched some 1,700 miles, at a fairly leisurely pace, and met Artaxerxes in battle near a village called Cunaxa, somewhere in the desert west of modern Baghdad. The battle was lost (see below), which left the Greeks in a desperate situation. They had no paymaster and were deep in hostile territory. They offered themselves for employment by Artaxerxes, but were rejected. Having decided not to surrender, they had no choice but to try to get back home, but they could not return by the route they had taken, since they had exhausted the supplies there. They had to head more or less directly north, aiming to strike the south coast of the Black Sea, then head west for familiar Greek territory around Byzantium.

Up to the mountains of northern Iraq and southeastern Turkey they were shadowed by Tissaphernes, who was on his way to take up Cyrus' former post in Asia Minor. There were occasional skirmishes, but no pitched battles, because Tissaphernes had other plans. First he suborned Ariaeus, and so deprived the Greeks of their allies; then he convinced Clearchus, the Spartan general who had the most authority among the Greek commanders, of his good intentions, and tricked most of the senior officers into a conference with him, at which they were arrested; they were taken to Babylon and killed.

If Tissaphernes had hoped that this alone would be sufficient to make the army vulnerable, he had reckoned without Xenophon, who persuaded the Greeks to choose new generals, including himself, and continue north. Tissaphernes was now content to let the winter climate and the hostile tribes of the mountains finish the Greeks off, and he turned west for Asia Minor.

The Greeks had to make their way through some of the most rugged, mountainous terrain in the world, in winter. Xenophon instigated some tough but necessary decisions, such as shedding all non-essential baggage and the cumbersome carts on which much of the baggage had been transported by lumbering oxen. At a later stage, he even insisted that the men abandon their prisoners, who when sold into slavery were one of the main sources of income for mercenaries. These decisions were essential to conserve supplies and fodder, which were hard to come by in the winter mountains.

The Ten Thousand had to fight not just the appalling weather, but running battles and skirmishes with almost every tribe they came across. The terrain was never suitable for traditional Greek hoplite tactics, and Xenophon and his fellow commanders quickly had to learn to be flexible, in order to endure the constant harrying from Persian troops and mountain guerrilla fighters; in order to take a fortress built into a cliff and a hilltop stronghold; and in order to cross rivers against strong opposition and fight with their backs against ravines.

Matters did not improve much once they reached the Black Sea – their first sight of which, and their cry 'The sea! The sea!', was so memorably recorded by Xenophon. They encountered Greek settlements there, but there were still long stretches of non-Greek coastline, and in fact their worst losses were sustained in Bithynia, when about one thousand men died in battle in one week. By the time they reached Byzantium, several thousand Greek mercenaries had been lost since Cunaxa, and countless camp followers had died too.

Moreover, on the Black Sea, the motivation of the army changed from mere survival to profit. Under the influence of greed, the army began to fall apart again into its various contingents, and they alienated every single Greek town they came to, culminating in their storming and temporarily occupying Byzantium, until Xenophon made them come to their senses. The Spartans, who were at that time the masters of the Greek world, naturally wanted them out of the way – either back in their various homelands, or employed by them for their own purposes, with a distinct preference for the former option.

A detail from a panel of the Chigi Vase (actually a jug), a striking piece of proto-Corinthian ware from around 640 BC, showing in stylized form two Greek hoplite phalanxes about to clash. It was the pipe-player's job to try to regulate the speed of advance.

Serving under the Spartans

By the end of the journey, Xenophon had emerged as the general most trusted and respected by many of the mercenaries. In fact, when they reached Sinope, and the mercenaries decided that things would go better with a single leader, it was Xenophon they nominated. But by then they were back in the Greek world, so Xenophon diplomatically made way for the senior Spartan officer among them. This episode sums up his main contribution to the campaign as a whole: in the face of potential rifts caused by divergent goals, by differences in nationality, by lack of discipline, greed and disillusionment, he bolstered morale and kept things from falling apart.

Some of the men trickled home from Byzantium, but Xenophon took several thousands of them to serve for the winter of 400–399 BC, under the Odrysian Thracian warlord Seuthes. Seuthes was in the process of expanding his personal holdings in what is now northern Greece and Bulgaria, with a view to making himself the most powerful ruler in the region. By the time this campaign had come to an end, the fragile peace between Sparta and Persia had broken down, and they were at war. The Spartans therefore changed their minds about the

Xenophon

undesirability of Xenophon's men, and offered them employment as they set about trying to drive Tissaphernes out of Asia Minor. They intended to replace the former Athenian empire with an even more extensive one of their own.

Xenophon and the remnants of the Ten Thousand fought over the next three years under Thibron and then Dercyllidas. Their *esprit de corps* and experience made them one of the Spartans' most valuable units, though their loyalty was to Xenophon and to themselves, rather than to the Spartans as such. But the war did not go well until one of the Spartan kings, Agesilaus II, was sent out in 396. He was a brilliant tactician and strategist, especially in his use of large-scale ruses, and he waged a remarkable campaign against both Pharnabazus in the north and Tissaphernes in central Asia Minor. His successes included victory in a major battle against Tissaphernes outside Sardis. Xenophon was later to write a eulogistic biography of Agesilaus.

Tissaphernes fell from grace and was assassinated on the orders of Artaxerxes, but any hopes Agesilaus had of conquering Asia Minor were dashed by the Persians' judicious distribution of cash on the Greek mainland, where resentment of Sparta was running high. Politicians were bribed, recruitment financed, and a coalition of Greek states went to war against Sparta. In 394 Agesilaus and his men, including Xenophon, were recalled from Asia Minor to meet the more immediate threat at home. It is not known whether Xenophon actually took part in any of the battles that the Spartans fought against the Greek coalition, which prominently included his fellow Athenians, though he was certainly present at the ghastly Battle of Coronea in 394. But soon after that, Xenophon's brief military career came to an end.

Theory of command

Leadership is a recurrent topic in Xenophon's works and was a live issue for debate among fourth-century intellectuals. The theory of leadership that Xenophon developed, initially as a result of his experiences and observations while campaigning in the east, goes somewhat as follows.

The first principles of any organization consisting of leaders and subordinates are that subordinates should be obedient and should meet with good leadership. These are in fact two sides of the same coin, because the only true obedience is willing obedience, and obedience is given willingly to a good leader. The essential ingredient of good leadership is knowledge, specifically knowledge of how to recognize and work for the good of the subordinates. A true leader, then, is analogous to a shepherd, who takes care of his flock, rather than being a dictator, concerned only to enhance his own wealth and position, or a demagogue, who is pulled this way and that by the whims of his community. A true leader finds the balance between leading and being led.

Successful rulers, in Xenophon's opinion, know how to care for the interests of their subjects better than the subjects themselves do. Aristocratic self-confidence is a huge advantage here, and Xenophon seems to have believed that true leaders result from a combination of nature and nurture. Certainly not everyone can do it. Good leaders lead by example and show that they are flexible and imaginative in devising the means of attaining the common good and the safety of their subjects, and strong enough to stand up to aggression and wrongdoing. 'The

'Alexander the Great would never have become "Great" without Xenophon.'

EUNAPIUS, *LIVES OF THE PHILOSOPHERS AND SOPHISTS*, INTRODUCTION

A relief from Athens, dating from the fourth century BC, showing a horseman attacking a fallen hoplite. The horseman is wearing a broad-brimmed hat known as a *petasos*. Note the lack of stirrups and saddle, which were yet to be invented.

good' may of course vary between different forms of organization: what is good for a household may not be what is good for an army. But, generally speaking, a leader works to increase and improve his community.

In a military context, this means that the leader has to not only ensure the safety of his troops and guarantee them pay and provisions, but also enhance their military capacity and do his best to ensure success on the battlefield. In most ancient military contexts, it also meant making sure that they returned home richer than they left, so the leader had to provide them with opportunities for plunder. But the improvement of subordinates also has a moral dimension: all Greek political theorists believed that moral improvement was possible for human beings chiefly in a communal setting, interacting with others. And so, in a military setting, a good general sets an example to his men by his own self-discipline and even self-denial, until, hopefully, they too learn discipline and are not motivated by greed, and refrain from plundering too much or inappropriately.

Xenophon

THE BATTLE OF CUNAXA

LATE IN SEPTEMBER 401 BC, two huge armies faced each other on a dusty plain, on the eastern bank of the River Euphrates, in what is now Iraq. The pretender, Cyrus, had marched east to wrest the throne of the Persian empire from his brother, Artaxerxes II. The exact location of the encounter is unknown: the battle came to be named after a nearby village called Cunaxa.

Artaxerxes commanded an army of forty-five thousand. Most of the king's men were foot soldiers, from all over the empire, and the dreaded Persian archers, but there were also hundreds of cavalrymen and dozens of scythed war chariots. Cyrus' men, perhaps thirty thousand in all, largely recruited from Asia Minor, were outnumbered. But Cyrus was not unduly worried about this, because he had Greeks on his side, and the Greeks were the supreme warriors of the time. Cyrus' battle formation disposed the Greeks on the right wing, himself in command of the centre, and his trusted Persian second in command Ariaeus on the left.

When the enemy were about half a mile away, the Greeks advanced. They started at a walk, but the phalanx began to bulge, and those who were being left behind picked up speed to catch up with the others. Soon they were all running forward. But before they reached the Persian lines, the Persian left wing, under the command of Tissaphernes, turned and fled. It was a feint! Tissaphernes had his men draw the Greeks further from the battlefield than they should have gone. They were supposed to circle back and outflank Artaxerxes' centre.

With the Greeks off the immediate battlefield, Artaxerxes' cavalry galloped forward, followed by the infantry, in an attempt to encircle Cyrus' right flank, now exposed by the forward movement of the Greeks. Cyrus had to act quickly to come up with a significant counter-threat. He spotted the Persian royal standard with its spread eagle, and led his elite horsemen in a reckless, headlong gallop straight for his brother. They broke through Artaxerxes' cavalry, but at the cost of Cyrus' death, which meant that the battle was lost, whatever else happened.

Meanwhile Cyrus' left wing, commanded by Ariaeus, also fared badly. Their attention was divided, since they were constantly in danger of being outflanked by the longer Persian line. At first they resisted as best they could, but the news of Cyrus' death broke their spirits

A seal showing a Persian horseman, identifiable by his exotic clothing, fighting a Greek hoplite, who is wearing the soft felt cap that often replaced the rather ineffective and cumbersome metal helmets.

Such a leader is immediately attractive to his subjects, who, as a result, respect and honour him, and obey him. Willing obedience is best, but in emergencies it may also be generated by compulsion or emulation or a sense of shame or of duty. Ideally, the leader uses praise and rewards to teach his subordinates, but at times punishment is required. However it comes about, the vertical virtue of obedience to a superior is chiefly a means of instilling discipline in his subordinates, the horizontal virtue of being able to work with others. This in turn raises morale, the value of which, especially in military success, Xenophon recognized with exceptional clarity.

A good leader needs more specific characteristics, though: courage (Greek generals were not just tacticians, but fought in the front rank), intelligence, tactical and strategic skill, self-discipline and piety; the ability to act slyly; accessibility to his men, and knowledge of their strengths and weaknesses; the ability to negotiate with foreigners and in general to communicate well. Of these qualities, self-discipline is the most critical, because, as a good Socratic, Xenophon saw self-discipline as the foundation of

Xenophon

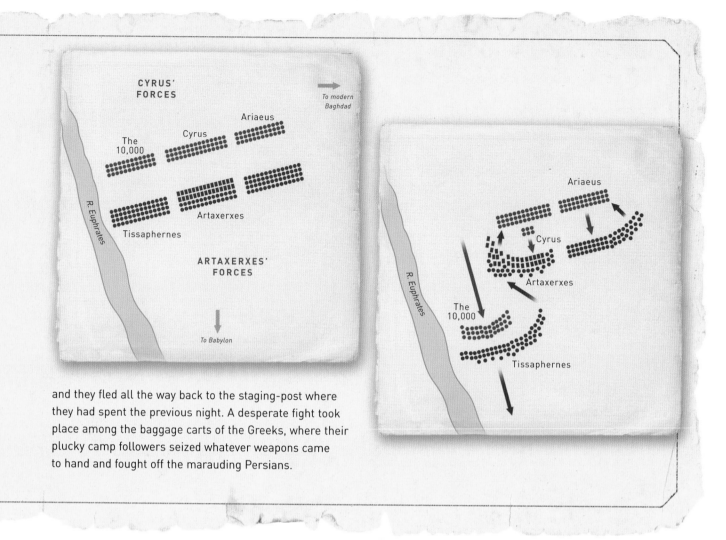

and they fled all the way back to the staging-post where they had spent the previous night. A desperate fight took place among the baggage carts of the Greeks, where their plucky camp followers seized whatever weapons came to hand and fought off the marauding Persians.

all moral virtue, including the ability to do good to others, or to inculcate self-discipline in them. Deficient leaders, on the other hand, lack the determination and strength of moral certainty. They fail to find the correct balance between coercion and the instilling of willing loyalty; they are too swayed by personal motivations; they do not tell men off when they are making mistakes, but buy them off instead with rash promises; they cause divisions in the army; and they ignore the omens sent by the gods.

Xenophon was not so naive as to think that even a perfect leader would always arouse willing obedience from all his subordinates. But a good leader is prepared to take the time to inculcate discipline in his men, to channel their competitiveness, and to develop their virtues. In the meantime, a certain degree of negative reaction from soldiers is just something a leader has to expect and use his skills to overcome, just like any other hazard of leadership.

'He makes no distinction between summer and winter and there is no chosen season which he leaves alone ...'

DEMOSTHENES THE ATHENIAN ON KING PHILIP'S STYLE OF WAR

PHILIP OF MACEDON

ROBIN LANE FOX

382–336 BC

KING PHILIP OF MACEDON was the greatest military inventor and army-trainer in the ancient Greek world. His new model army conquered from the Danube to Sparta in southern Greece, from the area around modern Dubrovnik to the west coast of the Black Sea. Philip was a master tactician and a courageous leader in battle. His new type of army was retained by his son and was a main reason for Alexander's great victories in Asia. Philip's army units remained dominant in the Greek army for the next 150 years; he is the founder of Hellenistic warfare.

Philip's genius is still overshadowed by that of Alexander, his glorious son. Philip was also unlucky in his contemporary historians. The most productive, Theopompus of Chios (*c.* 387–320 BC), lived for a while at Philip's court in Macedon, but wrote maliciously about Philip's extravagance, vice, and the supposed sexual profligacy of his courtiers. He recognized Philip as a 'man such as Europe has never borne', but even this comment may have been hostile. We know this work only in a few later quotations, but it underlies the Latin historical epitome by Justin (perhaps *c.* AD 350) which is our best brief source on Philip's campaigns. Although Theopompus called his long history work the *Philippica*, in recognition of Philip's importance, he was not a military historian. For accounts of Philip's battles we have to look to much later Greek collections of military stratagems and anecdotes (especially Polyaenus', *c.* AD 162) and the brief secondary narrative of Diodorus of Sicily (*c.* 20 BC) whose sources are uncertain and were not eyewitnesses. The discovery in 1977 of the great royal tomb, surely Philip's own, at Vergina in Macedon revealed contemporary weapons and a great painting of the king and his young royal pages armed and out hunting. Other archaeological finds have helped our understanding of Philip's military reforms and preferred weaponry.

King Philip's early military career

Philip took command of the Macedonian kingdom in northern Greece at a time of extreme crisis (359 BC). The previous king had been killed in battle and much of the kingdom's western sector had been overrun by victorious Illyrians. Philip was aged 23 and at first was only the regent for an even younger nephew. He probably did not become king until 356 BC.

The young Philip had already gone as a hostage to the Illyrians and then to the Greek city-state of Thebes in the 360s BC. There he had observed the greatest Greek generals of the age, especially Epaminondas, and the training of the Thebans' citizen army, famous for its cavalry and infantry formations, up to forty-eight ranks in depth. He was well educated, and as ruler of Macedon deployed the basic units of cavalry and infantry in a new way. His cavalry were to charge, armed with specially long spears, and his unusually equipped infantry were to advance against enemies who were broken by the 'shock and awe' of galloping horsemen.

After victories over the neighbouring barbarians in the northwest and north (359–358 BC), Philip attacked walled Greek cities which were settled on or just beyond the eastern borders of his kingdom. He had inherited siege machinery from previous kings, but his engineers improved it and Philip applied it to no less than thirty-two Greek towns in the north, including, between 357 and 354 BC, four of particular importance: Amphipolis, 357 BC; Potidaea and Pydna, 356 BC; Methone, 354 BC (during the siege of which he lost his eye to an arrow from a catapult). These conquests gave him well-watered farmland which he gave to Macedonian settlers, many of whom became new recruits for his cavalry on receipt of this good horse pasturage.

From 354/3 BC until July 348 BC, Philip, responding to an initial invitation by Thebans and Thessalians, fought a 'sacred war' which they had initiated against the lesser power of Phocis in central Greece. After a major victory at the Crocus Field in Thessaly in 352 BC, Philip settled the war by artful diplomatic skill, avoiding a major battle. Meanwhile he had captured and flattened the big Greek city of Olynthus on his eastern borders. Its walls had defied his siege engines for a year until the city was betrayed from within. The ruins are our best-preserved town plan of a fourth-century BC Greek city. They contain missiles inscribed with offensive words that were thrown by Philip's troops.

An iron breastplate with gold ornamentation that was found in the tomb of Philip II of Macedon, in Vergina, northern Greece: fourth century BC.

From peace to war

In the summer of 346 BC, Philip, ever the diplomat, made
peace with many of the Greek states, including the Athenians who
had been antagonized by his various sieges in the north. It was, as he knew,
only a temporary measure while he secured Macedon's borders with the barbarian
north and east. His greatest conquests lay here, beyond Greece. We follow Philip
nowadays in the hostile speeches of the democratic Athenian orator Demosthenes,
but thirteen of Philip's twenty-three years of campaigning were spent in the barbarian
plains and mountains where we know him only through anecdotes.

His increasingly centralized standing army allowed him to campaign abroad even
in winter. The open plains of Thrace (approximately modern Bulgaria) were well
suited to the massed ranks of his infantry, armed with long pikes, and the galloping
tactics of his cavalry. Perhaps Philip had devised them with the open terrain of Thrace
and western Asia in mind.

Philip of Macedon

At least since the late 350s his ultimate aim had been the invasion of the old Persian Empire in Asia. An invasion would require control of the Hellespont between Europe and Asia which the Athenians kept open as the vital route for their city-state's grain ships. Philip knew, as they did, that they would fight to keep control of it. Their city had formidable long walls and a potentially big navy. Philip's fleet was still very small and the Athenian walls would be impregnable, even to his improved artillery, siege towers and arrow-shooting machinery.

In 345 BC he marched northwest into Illyria and from 341 to 339 BC he campaigned against the cavalry and lightly armed infantry of the Thracian tribes. He even reached the eastern end of the River Danube. In July and September 340 BC he besieged the two important Greek cities of Perinthus and Byzantium on the nearby Sea of Marmara but failed, significantly, to take either. The attack on Byzantium damaged his deteriorating alliance with Thebes, Byzantium's old ally, in central Greece.

Late in 339 BC, Philip returned to central Greece for what he had always known would be his ultimate test there, a war with the Thebans and Athenians, who had finally combined against him. After entering central Greece in early winter by an unexpected route, Philip's army encamped near the small Boeotian town of Chaeronea. After an inconclusive winter of diplomacy Philip finally engaged battle on the plain. On 22 August 338 BC he won a hard-earned victory, reputedly by a deceptive infantry manoeuvre and a decisive charge by one wing of his cavalry led by his son Alexander. The Battle of Chaeronea was indeed fatal to liberty, as poets later said. It ushered in the Macedonian kings' domination of the Greek city-states for more than one hundred and fifty years.

Philip followed up his victory by campaigning against the still hostile Sparta, by another campaign into Illyria (probably in 337 BC) and by launching an advance invasion into Persian-ruled Asia under his senior generals in summer 336 BC. He was murdered, however, during wedding celebrations at the ancient Macedonian capital of Aigai (Vergina) in autumn 336 BC. The murder was almost certainly related to discontent in his family over the most recent of his polygamous marriages and the birth of another son. It was left to Alexander, nearly two years later, to follow up Philip's first moves in Asia and to carry them as far as India, probably much further than Philip had ever thought possible.

Philip's new model infantry

In 359 BC Philip had inherited a small kingdom with a long tradition of good cavalry but no trained or centralized infantry, no supporting units of lightly armed troops and only a simple style of siege train. His military reforms relied on changes in the Macedonians' social order and he gave new titles to the military units he created. Names like 'Royal Foot Companions' and 'Royal Shield Bearers' bound them closely to the king, not to the local nobles they had served as personal retainers. He also gave many of them new lands from his ever-increasing conquests and thus won them away from their local loyalties. Captives taken in war became slaves who would work the land and mines in his expanding Macedon. The royal infantry was then trained intensively for campaigning throughout the year (including winter). Traditionally the summer month of harvesting had been inauspicious for campaigning because

Macedonians needed to gather in their crops. Philip's new army was freed from work on the land and could fight in any month.

The reforms were complex and needed years to perfect. He planned a battle line whose central block was to be his famous phalanx of infantrymen armed with very long spears, the *sarissai*. A *sarissa* was at least 16 feet long and was made of two lengths of tough wood, preferably from the Cornelian cherry tree (*Cornus mas*) which was already used for cavalry spears by Persians in western Asia. The two pieces were held together by a central metal tube. One end carried a balancing butt-spike that could be rammed into the ground when making a stand. The *sarissa* had to be held with both hands, and when nearly horizontal the first five ranks' metal points would project beyond the front line. The central ranks could hold their *sarissas* upright so as to intercept arrows and missiles. By trained manoeuvres, the phalanx would present *sarissas* vertically, face about, then lower them in the rear ranks and march in retreat. Sideways manoeuvres were also possible, directed by trumpeters. Alternatively a *sarissa*-armed phalanx could halt and present a wall of protruding spear-points on all four sides of the rectangle. The soldiers in the front and back ranks were the finest and were paid more highly.

Sarissa-armed infantry wore leg armour, at least in the front and back ranks, metal helmets (the 'Phrygian' type, with a forward-curving crest, was popular) but no metal breastplates. They had a small convex shield slung on the neck and left shoulder by a strap, as both hands were needed for manoeuvring the long spear. The basic infantry unit began as one of ten ranks, but eights and sixteens were soon developed. Later Greek tactical manuals identify basic units of 256 men (16 x 16) in a phalanx but they may only be theoretical reconstructions. The phalanx was made up of battalions (*taxeis*) which were locally recruited according to cantons in Macedon and led by a local prince or noble. Each *taxis* was probably around one thousand five hundred strong and at least seven *taxeis* made up a phalanx at battle strength.

Later authors compared this phalanx with the Greek battle lines described in Homer's *Iliad*, but Homer was not Philip's source for it. He devised it as one part of a carefully planned line. Its long wall of sharp, slim spear-points kept off attackers with its greater outreach, but it was most useful when moving on level ground. Its unprotected right flank linked with the highly trained unit of Shield Bearers who carried bigger metal shields and wore full body armour while carrying spears and swords. They numbered three thousand in Philip's battle-plan and became the supreme military unit in all ancient history during their service with Alexander. They were also used for pursuits and dangerous 'special operations' on rough and steep ground. Presumably they could take off some of their armour to increase their flexibility on these missions.

The new style of cavalry warfare

On their right and on the phalanx's left Philip stationed cavalry in pointed formations, wedge-shaped ones for his Macedonian Companion cavalry, diamond-shaped ones for his Thessalian Greek allies. These pointed formations increased the speed of turning, as horsemen focused on their immediate leader and turned as he did, like birds, watchers said, who were flying in formation. The cavalry wore no stirrups and no toe-straps. They sat on padded saddlecloths which were sometimes the skins of wild animals. Their legs are shown in art as unprotected and they carried no shields, although they wore metal breastplates and a protective leather 'skirt' from the waist to mid thigh. Their helmets were metal, fluted round the rim in the Boeotian Greek style, and they carried a sword for close combat, the feared *kopis* which was a very sharp slashing instrument. In their right hands they carried a long spear, the *xyston*, up to 9 feet long, which gave them a longer reach than their enemies. So long as an enemy had no stirrups, a frontal charge with a *xyston* was manageable, as recent reconstructions of Macedonian battles by film armies have proved. It is most effective to ram the *xyston*'s long metal point into an opponent's shoulder just by the collarbone. The spear is not easily extractable by galloping on and pulling on its shaft when past the enemy. After using it, therefore, the cavalryman resorted to the sword, or *kopis*. A wedge-shaped charge with spears at the ready would often be enough to scatter enemies in terror.

A silver tetradrachma from *c*. 354 BC, showing Philip II of Macedon on horseback and wearing the *kausia*, the flat Macedonian hat.

These cavalry charges were trained to turn at an angle and strike into the centre of a line which was already breaking when attempting to avoid being outflanked. Previous Greek armies used cavalry only to fight opposing cavalry or to pursue infantry who were already in flight.

A balanced army

Balance and variety were the principles of Philip's new battle line. It was an integrated whole, to which Thracian javelin throwers, Greek slingers and Cretan archers added the element of the long-range missile. Experts in artillery

Philip of Macedon

THE BATTLE OF CHAERONEA

PHILIP'S FINAL VICTORY over the large Greek army led by the Athenians and Thebans exemplifies the problems in reconstructing his battles. The site has been identified as the narrow plain between the River Cephissus and the acropolis of Chaeronea in Boeotia. Both sides had been waiting for several months and it was only in mid August 338 BC that the Greek army took up a battle position. They chose it so as to limit the scope for Philip's cavalry to make an outflanking manoeuvre. The river and the hills protected the Theban infantry on the right and the Athenian infantry on the left respectively. If the line broke, the Cerata pass offered the Greeks an escape route to the southeast.

Typically we have two contradictory sources for the size of Philip's army. One says he was outnumbered, the other that he had 30,000 infantry and 2,000 cavalry, outnumbering the enemy. More than 60,000 troops probably engaged, a battle far bigger than any in western Europe in the medieval period. Our only overview of the battle is the abbreviated version of Diodorus, three centuries later. He credits Alexander with leading the cavalry on Philip's left wing in a decisive charge against the Greek infantry. Anecdotes preserved by Polyaenus credit Philip's infantry phalanx with a deceptive manoeuvre. They marched back as if in retreat, heading for high ground (which is not visible on the site) and when the Athenian infantry rashly pursued them Philip is said to have exclaimed, 'The Athenians do not know how to win a victory,' and to have ordered his retreating phalanx to halt and march forwards again with their *sarissas* unbroken. This manoeuvre is hard to accept in such a controlled fashion, but it would account for the breaking of part of the Greek line and the scope for a decisive cavalry charge into it.

The combination of anecdotes and contradictory sources typifies almost all ancient battles and the problems of reconstructing them. Nobody had a total overview and promptly wrote it up; participants knew only what was happening hand-to-hand around them. The battle site of Chaeronea has archaeologically verified burial places. A mound on the Macedonian left contained cremated bodies, spear-points and coins, presumably for the Macedonian dead. A commemorative stone lion marks another mass burial place, probably containing 254 bodies of the Theban 'Sacred Band' (linked by homosexual pairing, it was said). The sight of the bodies of these brave men, who opposed Alexander on the Greek right wing, caused Philip to weep.

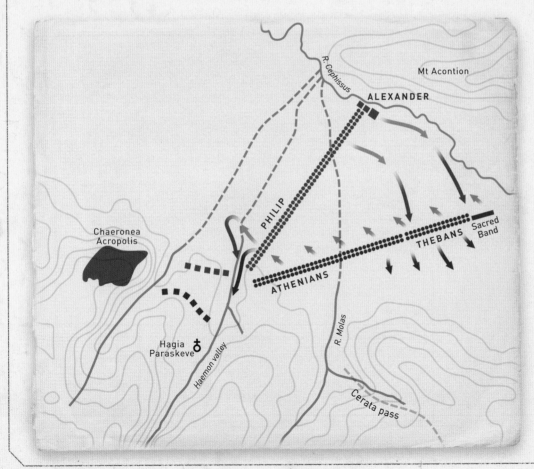

Philip of Macedon

> 'You carry on war with Philip like a barbarian who is boxing. When a barbarian is hit he always holds the place where he is hit; if you strike him on his other side, his hands go there. He neither knows nor cares how to parry or watch his opponent. So, too, you take your marching orders from Philip and try to keep up with him wherever he goes.'
>
> DEMOSTHENES ON THE ATHENIANS' WAY OF OPPOSING KING PHILIP

were brought in from Greek Thessaly in order to develop the torsion power of arrow-catapults and bigger and better siege towers. Dogs, even, were used in pursuit, while breeding mares were imported by the thousand. Stallions must have been carefully controlled in special royal studs to maintain the development of the best warhorses.

Philip led his cavalry in person, sustaining several serious wounds. Like his diplomacy, his tactics were often cunning. Twice he allowed letters announcing his troops' imminent withdrawal to be intercepted by the Athenian general Chares. On the first occasion Chares was deceived and believed him. On the second occasion he wrongly chose to believe the message again, a neat double bluff by Philip. His army's mobility depended on extreme discipline and drill. Servants were severely limited in camp, while forced marches with heavy supply packs and tents were frequent. It was said that hot baths were banned in Macedon except for women who had just given birth.

Philip seldom ended a battle on the battlefield, the usual Greek practice. In the tribal non-Greek world it was crucial to capture the king and his few courtiers by pursuit. Philip would follow up at the gallop for many miles, a practice which he passed on to Alexander. His rebalancing of cavalry and infantry, the *sarissas*, the shock charges, and the array of missiles and these long pursuits made battle with him a new and terrifying experience for conventional Greek armies.

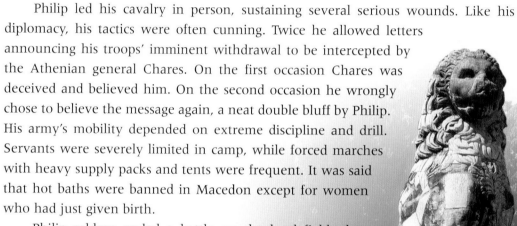

The tomb of the Sacred Band of Thebes, the elite Theban battalion that fell in the Battle of Chaeronea, 22 August 338 BC.

ALEXANDER THE GREAT

ROBIN LANE FOX

356–323 BC

ALEXANDER THE GREAT was the supreme conqueror in the ancient world. An acknowledged military genius, in three battles he defeated huge Persian armies and took the western and central parts of their empire in Asia. He then pressed on into India, aiming for the edge of the world. His personal leadership, strategic boldness and tactical ingenuity are unsurpassed, whether on the flat plains of Mesopotamia or on the peaks of the Himalayan range. He died, from uncertain causes, when he was only 32.

Even in antiquity, people argued whether his success owed more to luck than skill. The truth is that great commanders create their own luck. Alexander owed much to his father Philip's new model army and to the trained units and experienced officers Philip had prepared for him. We know far more about Alexander's campaigns than about Philip's and so we may underestimate Philip's example. An experienced army, which a much-adored king has created, is not easy for a young heir to lead. Alexander inherited a balanced army the subtle variety of which could easily have been misapplied by a lesser tactical mind. No previous Macedonian king had died peacefully from natural causes. His older officers would not have hesitated to kill him and replace him if he had failed them. Alexander was only 20 when he began leading a great army to victory. In thirteen years he was only defeated once, by the weather and dry terrain on his march home through southeastern Persia's fearsome Makran desert.

Alexander's early career

When his father Philip was murdered in the autumn of 336 BC, Alexander became king of the Macedonians and promptly asserted his role as leader of the Greek alliance that Philip had founded. His first year required campaigning to retain Thrace (approximately, modern Bulgaria) as far as the River Danube, which his troops crossed on skins of leather stuffed with hay, a time-honoured method in Asia. He deployed his father's cavalry and famous infantry phalanx with distinction against loose formations of rebellious tribes. His infantry's exceptional training showed in their advance through fields of standing corn, flattening the crops by a disciplined sideways movement of their long *sarissa* spears, which they wielded in formation with both hands. When the tribesmen released wagons at them down a steep hill, they were quick to close ranks behind a wall of shields, the bearers of which crouched to the ground and caused the wagons to fly up and over their unit's bodies. A rebellion in the Greek city of Thebes caused Alexander to march with exceptional, but characteristic speed south and issue the rebels with an ultimatum. They refused, so he besieged and took the city, levelling it to the ground and selling the thirty thousand Greek survivors into slavery. Throughout his career Alexander was utterly destructive of opponents who refused or went back on his offers in return for surrender. He was also a master-besieger, unlike his father Philip. From 332 BC onwards he was helped by siege machinery improved by his engineers, who applied torsion-power to enable catapults to throw rocks, not arrows. However, machinery alone never won him a city. His night attacks, 'special operations' and dispersed assaults on sections of wall were essential factors.

In the spring of 334 BC, Alexander invaded Asia and paid his respects at ancient Troy, where weaponry said to belong to Homer's Achilles was given to him in honour of his self-publicized rivalry with the great hero. It accompanied him into battle as far as India. The Homeric values of personal prowess in combat and individual courage were profoundly rooted in Alexander and were well adapted to the semi-Homeric Macedon in which he had grown up. He never asked of others what he would not risk himself. He even put care of their wounds before his own. He led by example in the front line, inspiring his men with a faith in his fortune and invincibility.

His invasion was matched with an effective political 'spin'. Like Philip, he claimed to be avenging the Persians' past sacrileges in Greece (back in 480–479 BC). He was liberating the Greek cities in Asia under their rule, to most of which he granted democracy, the opposite of rule by small pro-Persian cliques. In May 334 BC, he won his first victory by a bold charge across the Granicus river in modern northwest Turkey. Persian cavalry held the far bank but they were pushed back by an audacious assault by Alexander's cavalry. The infantry phalanx was less effective, being hindered by the river.

A statue representing Alexander in a war chariot in battle near Chaeronea, from the so-called Alexander Rondanini, 338–336 BC.

Alexander the Great

Alexander's genius became clear in November 333 BC at the huge Battle of Issus, near modern Iskenderun and the southeast Turkish coast towards Syria. The Persian king Darius had mustered a vastly greater army, but unintentionally passed north of Alexander's, which was hidden by the intervening Amanus mountains. Alexander then heard that his enemy was advancing down into his rear, threatening to push him out into a wide open plain where their numbers would be decisive. Brilliantly, he decided to turn his men round, march them back up the coast in a narrow formation and then line them across an enclosed plain where the sea and the hills guarded his two wings from encirclement. He regained surprise by this forced night march, countered the Persians' superior numbers and won a remarkable victory by an angled cavalry charge that drew off and weakened the Persian centre. Again, the main infantry phalanx and their long *sarissa* spears split apart on rough ground broken by a river. Again, this victory was a cavalry triumph. The deceptive shuffling of his battle line before combat began, his personally led charge on his horse Bucephalas (as at Chaeronea for his father Philip in 338 BC) and his inspiring decision to turn back and fight on narrow terrain made the Battle of Issus one of Alexander's master-pieces. As ever, he showed a brilliant grasp of space and the potential of terrain.

Other strategists might have pursued Darius directly into Asia, even though many more troops and many walled cities would have protected him there. Instead, Alexander attended deliberately to his coastline. He had disbanded his inferior fleet in the summer of 334 BC. In order to hinder the Persians' fleet, he set about capturing their main naval bases, including Tyre, which he took after a massive siege, and then Gaza after another. His machinery was now fearsome, including siege towers and collapsible bridges up to 100 feet high. Diades, his chief engineer, was remembered as the 'man who took Tyre with Alexander'. His troops included many skilled carpenters and woodworkers, trained by their years in Macedon's forests. Alexander even made them connect the island of Tyre to the mainland by an artificial causeway which is still visible, more than half a mile across the sea.

Sieges always brought out the boldest and most ingenious side of him. His overall strategy, however, was even bolder: to take Egypt, return to Tyre and then wait for most of the summer in 331 BC – while Darius gathered the biggest possible army – which Alexander wanted to knock out in one engagement. The plan was immensely daring, pitting his forty-seven thousand men against at least four times as many under Darius. These exact numbers were added as special effects to the remarkable film reconstruction of this, the Battle of Gaugamela in northern Iraq, for Oliver Stone's film *Alexander* (2004). They give us a visual sense of its scale for the first time. As at Issus or in his father Philip's battles, Alexander's winning manoeuvre

Alexander the Great, as he appears in the 'Alexander Mosaic', depicting the Battle of Issus in 333 BC. A floor mosaic removed from the Casa del Fauno at Pompeii, it is modelled on a painting by an artist contemporary with Alexander.

'When the Persian King Darius sent Alexander a letter offering him 10,000 talents, all the lands up to the River Euphrates and the hand of his daughter in marriage, his general Parmenion said, "I would accept, if I were you, Alexander." "So would I", replied Alexander, "if I were Parmenion."'

PLUTARCH, ON ALEXANDER'S REFUSAL TO ACCEPT TERMS

Alexander the Great

was again an angled cavalry charge on the right wing, led by himself, cutting back into the enemy centre which he had destabilized. The charge was supported by many minor tactical tricks, by a reserve phalanx line behind his main one, by the concealment of slingers and light troops on foot amongst units of cavalry, by the ability of one half of the phalanx to stand fixed and firm in a central rectangle although their other half had broken. Inevitable outnumbering on his left wing meant that Alexander had to abandon pursuit of Darius and return. The foul smell of the dead soon caused him to abandon the site.

He was now being called the 'King of Asia'. It remained to capture Darius and show where Asia ended.

Fighting in Asia

Alexander never had to cope with a separate political parliament: he was general and politician in one. True to his initial publicity, he took revenge and burned down the

big Persian palaces at Persepolis in early 330 BC. Like many great commanders, he often drank heavily when off duty. At Persepolis, drink helped along a riotous evening of destruction.

Before capturing Darius' dead body, Alexander changed his tone and presented himself as Darius' respectful heir, and from July 330 BC as the punisher of Darius' murderers. In reality he wanted to conquer all Asia, even beyond the Persian empire's boundaries. The aim took him through astoundingly steep and difficult landscapes, including a crossing of the snowbound Hindu Kush mountains. The next four years (330–326 BC) were typified by hardly believable mountain marches, by sieges of sheer rocks beyond the Oxus river, by a more open and fluid style of warfare and an absolutely implacable assault on all 'terrorists', or local rebels if they went back on their initial surrender. From the winter of 328 BC, Alexander's army was more often split into divisions which fought under his increasingly experienced officers. None the less, the most spectacular sieges were all led by his example, supported by the veteran Shield Bearers he had inherited from Philip and by the fearsome Agrianian–Thracian javelin men. The troops were driven by Alexander's intrepid example, the increasing promise of bonuses and the knowledge that their skills of besieging, bridging and mountaineering had already triumphed over the impossible. They even believed they were following the tracks of the ancient Greek god Dionysus and Heracles the hero.

In India the snakes and the monsoon rains dampened Alexander's misplaced aim of reaching the 'edge' of the world at the mouth of the River Ganges. His troops refused to march on, which threw Alexander into a rage; but eventually he accepted it. They had faced a few war elephants at Gaugamela but in India they had to confront so many more, a terrifying novelty. His men lost heart at the rumours of what lay beyond.

The right side of a frieze from the painted tomb façade found under the eastern part of the Agios Athanasios Tumulus, just west of Thessalonica. The men wear Macedonian outfits of leather boots, cloaks fastened on the right shoulder and the Macedonian hat, the *kausia*. Several wear helmets with high white plumes.

Their return home from the River Beas in the Indian Punjab took them in specially built ships down the River Indus. Since 330 BC, Alexander had been recruiting troops from his new subjects. His returning army was now more than one hundred thousand strong and was mostly non-Macedonian, including Indians and many Iranian cavalry, especially their fine horse archers.

During the return march home it is wrong to see him as addicted to battle and slaughter or straining to punish the men who had refused to fulfil his aims. He had to fight hard against Indian tribes, who were known to be warlike and were keen to block and defeat him. He continued to lead by example, even leaping alone off the battlements into a host of Indians inside a walled city. He was then badly wounded in the chest by an Indian long arrow. These risks were not new or desperate: they had always been part of his style.

His one major disaster followed his recovery. It was due to his miscalculation of the weather. He marched his fittest men home by the coastal route through the Makran desert, although he knew it to be a harsh landscape. Part of his plan was to dig wells for the fleet which would then follow and meet him. Arguably, the other part had been for this fleet to bring a stockpile of supplies by sea for the army. Adverse winds detained the fleet's departure, leaving Alexander already in the desert with no supply line. His losses were heavy, but they are not quantifiable. As many as half of the troops that were with him may have been lost.

He returned to Babylon, but in the spring of 323 BC was planning yet another land and sea operation, this time against the Arabian peninsula. Here too the winds at sea might have worked against him, but before setting out he died (June 323 BC) from uncertain causes. Poisoning was rumoured, but is most unlikely as he lay sick for more than a fortnight. It is possible that he had caught a malarial fever.

Alexander the Great

THE BATTLE OF HYDASPES

IN THE LATE SPRING of 326, Alexander's army reached the River Hydaspes, now the Jhelum, one of the broad Punjab rivers of northwest India. It was held on the far bank by a major army of Porus, the Indian king, complete with war chariots and many war elephants. Alexander began by waging a month-long war of nerves. He marched to and fro on his riverbank under darkness, making noises as if he was planning to cross. He wore down his opponents by deception, and only then launched one part of his army in small boats by night, leaving another part downstream to mislead Indian observers. Fearful storms broke out, but enough of his cavalry, his veteran Shield Bearers and part of his phalanx crossed to take control of the far bank. Fortunately the rains impeded the Indian advance unit of war chariots.

The Indian army was preceded by a long battle line of war elephants. Archers with longbows and cavalry were the main Indian strengths. Alexander had planned for each arm of war. He sent part of his cavalry with his general Coenus on a wide outflanking gallop to the left: the reasons for it have become clearer after Oliver Stone's recent film reconstructions of a cavalry charge against a live elephant corps. Against an elephant line, horses will pull away to the left in fright, even if they have lived for a while in the company of elephants. Alexander's plan built on this tendency and turned it to advantage as a wide outflanking movement which then cut round into the main Indian army's rear. Elephants are also prone to panic when attacked from behind.

The elephant line was then driven back by Alexander's Shield Bearers on foot, armed with special axes and cutters so as to slash the beasts' trunks and legs. They panicked and withdrew into their own lines behind them, compounding a chaos which a part (or probably, all) of the phalanx in its *sarissa*-led formation could then sweep into disarray. Alexander, as usual, led a simultaneous cavalry charge, drawing off the Indian cavalry on his right wing.

One source for the battle implies that only a few thousand of Alexander's army crossed the river and engaged in battle. The implied length of the Indians' elephant line makes such a small force most unlikely and the support of the rest of Alexander's troops has surely been omitted from this one shortened narrative. Certainly posterity remembered him as a great elephant-conqueror. After his death, the coins of his successor in Egypt, King Ptolemy, showed a portrait of Alexander wearing a symbolic headdress of an elephant's head. It had been a memorably planned victory against a river, the weather and a novel enemy. Alexander followed up by sparing King Porus because of his bravery and reappointing him as ruler, but now under his victor's command.

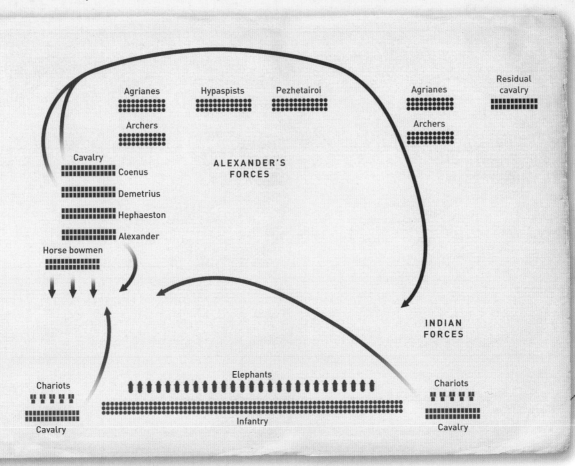

Alexander's aims and planning

The makeup of his army remained essentially Philip's, as described on pp. 116–23. In 323 BC he was experimenting with Iranian archers in the centre ranks of the phalanx, but *sarissas* were still crucial in the front and back ranks. Cavalry charges in pointed formations were his supreme shock tactic, reinforced by Persian horsemen, whom he added into his all-conquering Macedonian Companion units. His wish for an 'army of the best', whatever its origin, provoked a Macedonian mutiny, but he did not abandon it. The identity, but not the structures, of his army thus changed considerably by the end of his life. The one addition was a corps of war elephants, always ridden, however, by Indian experts.

His dash and brave example were important, but his tactical ruses, his bold 'grand strategy' and his sense of the spatial possibilities on a battlefield and the imperatives of supply were crucial. Even the Makran march had had a double supply plan, though it failed badly. Supplies were partly carried in ox-drawn wagons, partly looted from local stockpiles and livestock. Water sources were a crucial determinant of the route of his men and especially his horses. They have still not been traced systematically along his line of march. Increasingly, women accompanied the march too, at least ten thousand of them by 325 BC. Traders came as well, one reason for the high debts which the troops contracted over and above their regular pay.

Even after turning back in India, the troops revered Alexander as invincible. He himself believed he was guided by the god Zeus, to whom he had a special heroic relationship as Zeus' son. His achievements were indeed superhuman and their style was long invoked and imitated by his successor-generals. Even in his lifetime, Greek admirers and hopeful flatterers gave him honours equal to those of the gods. He had excelled even the mythical deeds of Heracles.

The Alexander Sarcophagus, from the Phoenician royal necropolis at Sidon, probably made for Abdalonymos, whom Alexander had appointed king of Sidon. The relief shows Persian and Greek soldiers in close combat at the Battle of Issus, 333 BC.

> 'Soldiers, a battle or two, and you will have Italy's
> capital, the city of Rome, in the hollow of your hands!'
>
> HANNIBAL, ON THE SUMMIT OF THE ALPS

HANNIBAL
c.247–183 BC

TOM HOLLAND

COMPILING LISTS OF GREAT GENERALS is an exercise that even great generals themselves have been known to enjoy. A celebrated example took place in 193 BC, when the two most brilliant commanders of their age met during the course of a diplomatic exchange, and one took the opportunity to ask the other who would feature on his own personal hit-parade. The man putting the question was Scipio Africanus, a Roman who only nine years previously had recorded a crushing and decisive victory over the last surviving army of his city's deadliest rival, Carthage; and the man whose opinion he was canvassing was none other than the Carthaginian whom he had defeated on that fateful day, Hannibal Barca.

Yet Scipio put his question in no mood of gloating or triumphalism. He appreciated – none better, perhaps – the full genius of his old adversary: for such was Hannibal's record of victory and devastation, achieved over sixteen years of relentless campaigning, that it had won for him, despite his final defeat, a reputation as the most dangerous enemy that Rome had ever faced. The opinion of such a man, Scipio judged, was well worth having. And so it was, in the words of Livy, 'that he asked his companion who was the greatest general of all time'.

Hannibal's choice was hardly a controversial one: Alexander the Great. At number two, with a due show of modesty, he placed King Pyrrhus of Epirus; and only at number three did he finally nominate himself. Scipio, it is said, laughed at this, and asked his companion, '"What would you be saying had you defeated me?" "In that case," replied Hannibal, "I would certainly have put myself before Alexander and before Pyrrhus – in fact, before every general who had ever lived."' The reply was, as Livy points out, a subtle one, for it succeeded in flattering both men simultaneously – and yet it also reflected, on Hannibal's own part, a haunting appreciation of the essentially tragic nature of his own genius.

He knew that he had been a failure. No matter how many and spectacular his victories had been, the fact that his career had ended in disaster ensured that all his battle honours would serve only as trophies in the triumph of his enemies. It was not Scipio alone who had brought about the ruin of his war plans. Even more fatal had been the unyielding character of the Roman republic itself, a state that had consistently refused to acknowledge any superior, or ever to sue for terms. Hannibal, by opting to declare war upon such an implacable and ruthless foe, had staked everything upon his conviction that it was possible to bring the Roman people to their knees, a miscalculation that in due course would prove as fatal to his city as to himself. Yet what set his failure as a strategist in an even bleaker light was the fact that as a tactician he had indeed shown himself incomparable – for he had inflicted upon the legions a succession of defeats so shattering that any other enemy, set to bleed as grievously as the Romans had, would surely have given up the fight. Had Hannibal combined his ability to win battles with a strategic vision capable of defeating Rome, then he surely would have deserved to outrank Alexander. As it is, even at a distance of more than two millennia, there is one victory of his in particular that has no rival as the very model of the perfectly executed battle-plan. Cannae, where some seventy thousand Romans were enveloped and wiped out by Hannibal's

Superpower death-struggle. A heated and imaginative sixteenth-century reconstruction of Rome against Carthage.

vastly outnumbered forces, remains the single engagement of the pre-modern era that is still capable of serving as an inspiration to commanders today. From August 1914 and the German attempt to execute the Schlieffen Plan, to 1991 and Norman Schwarzkopf's strategy of encirclement during the first Gulf War, Hannibal's example has loomed large in the minds of many a twentieth-century general. That is more than can be said for any other commander from the ancient world – even Alexander himself.

Like father, like son

Indeed, for all the lip-service that he paid to Pyrrhus, Hannibal has a far worthier claim to be considered Alexander's heir than any Greek. Like his great predecessor, he struck fearlessly into the very heartlands of his enemy; he combined cavalry with different classes of infantry to devastating tactical effect; and he had a god-like taste for defying the very elements. In one other obvious way as well, Hannibal's career was a striking echo of Alexander's: both were the greater sons of great commanders. Just as Philip of Macedon had done, Hannibal's father bequeathed to his heir both a formidable army and a ferocious sense of mission. Hamilcar Barca had well understood what it took to fight the Romans. War between Carthage and the upstart republic had first broken out in 264 BC, and had raged, amid escalating slaughter, for more than two decades. The principal campaigning theatre had been Sicily; and the most impressive commander operating there on either side had been Hamilcar. Although in the end it was the Carthaginians who had been brought to defeat, Hamilcar himself had remained unvanquished in open battle; and he never quite shook off a sense of resentment at being obliged to lower his arms. Resolved to see his city restored to its former pre-eminence, Hamilcar duly began to scout around for new horizons. In 237 BC, he set off for Spain.

This was a bid of some desperation, for the army available to him was limited, and Spain itself notoriously savage, swarming with barbarous tribes. Naturally, then, before leaving on such a perilous venture, Hamilcar made sure to seek the blessing of his city's gods. Hannibal, then only 9 years old, was taken by his father to watch the sacrifice. After Hamilcar had poured out a libation, he turned to his son, and asked if he too wished to embark for Spain. Hannibal, who is said to have possessed precisely 'the same vigour in his look, and the same fire in his eyes' as his father, did not

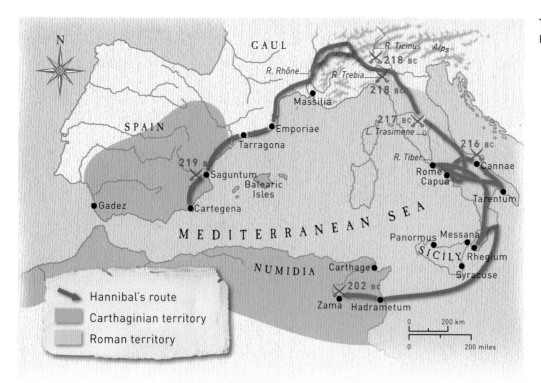

hesitate. Then came a fateful moment. Hamilcar took his son by the hand, led him up
to the altar, and commanded him to swear, upon the bloody remains of the victim,
'never to bear goodwill to the Romans'.

It was a promise that Hannibal would never forget. From that moment on, his
life, like his father's, had a single purpose. Arriving in Spain, his aptitude for warfare
was soon being forged amid the breaking of the natives to Carthaginian power.
Carving out a new empire in the west was very much a family project: after
Hamilcar's death in 228 BC, the result of a tribal ambush, his son-in-law, Hasdrubal,
took command of the imperial enterprise, successfully pushing the reach of his
dominance ever northwards, expanding the size of the army and establishing a cadre
of officers of quite exceptional experience and ability. Chief among these was
Hannibal himself, who, as commander of horse, was responsible for the training of a
cavalry arm that would prove itself more proficient than any since the time of
Alexander. By the time Hasdrubal was murdered by a disgruntled Spaniard in 221 BC,
and Hannibal stepped up to replace him, the Carthaginian empire in Spain was
possessed of a killing force that might have served to make even the Romans pause.

Elephant man

Except that it did not. In 219 BC, when Hannibal attacked Saguntum, a Spanish city
that had long been allied to Rome, a tense diplomatic stand-off culminated the
following year in the republic's decision to renew its war with Carthage. The test for
which Hannibal had been preparing all his life was now upon him – and he was
ready for it. In the previous conflict with Rome, the Carthaginians had been content
to fight defensively; this time round, however, Hannibal was resolved to take the
attack directly to the enemy. Because the Romans had command of the sea, he knew
that he would have to lead his army over the Pyrenees and through the hostile
badlands of southern Gaul if he were to reach Italy: an intimidating prospect.

Hannibal

Hannibal not only accepted the challenge, however, but positively embraced it – for it was his intention, as he marched on the Romans, to shock and awe them with the sheer Herculean scale of his boldness. This was why, along with heavy infantrymen from Libya, light horsemen from Numidia, slingers from the Balearic Islands, and sizeable contingents of both cavalry and infantry recruited from Spain, he took thirty-seven of the beasts for which his army today is chiefly remembered: elephants. Never mind that they were, as one military analyst cheerfully acknowledged, 'unsuited by their very nature to the demands of combat'; that was hardly the point. Ever since the time of Alexander, elephants had served as the ultimate in military status symbols, lumbering expressions of the taste for gigantism that had long afflicted generals raised in the military traditions of the eastern Mediterranean. None, however, had thought to do what Hannibal, as the climax of his march on Italy, intended to attempt: to lead them, and all his army, over a mountain range as towering and bleak as the Alps.

'Truly, Hannibal, you know how to win a victory – but not how to use one.'

HANNIBAL'S CAPTAIN OF HORSE, AFTER THE BATTLE OF CANNAE

What followed remains even today perhaps the most totemic exploit in all military history. To that extent, at least, Hannibal's ambitions for his Alpine crossing were more than met. That a general would lead war elephants across the roof of the world in pursuit of his burning hatred did indeed serve to astound the Romans, who were generally, as a people, unwilling to be astounded by their opponents. Yet Hannibal paid grievously for what was, essentially, a propaganda stunt. It was true that the Romans were expecting him to take the low road, and had been planning accordingly; but the advantage Hannibal accrued by outflanking them was as nothing compared to the losses that he suffered amid the snows. He had left Spain that summer of 218 BC with, at a rough estimate, some sixty thousand men; of these, by the time that he finally debouched into northern Italy, a bare twenty-five thousand were left to him. Losses on such a scale appeared devastating to all of Hannibal's hopes. It had never been any part of his plans to invade Italy with so small a force. Even though he sought, with a mounting degree of success, to recruit the local Gauls to his standard, he knew that even the hardiest of them were not the equals of the seasoned veterans he had lost on the road to Italy. There must have been many in his ranks, then, who dreaded that their great bid to overthrow Rome was doomed to failure almost before it had begun.

'Hannibal ad portas!'

But if so, their spirits were soon to be spectacularly raised. Whatever the strategic failings that had marred Hannibal's journey from Spain, his arrival on the Romans' very doorstep provided him at last with an opportunity to engage in what he did best: winning battles. His first brush with the Romans took place near the River Ticinus, by the Alpine foothills, and even though the engagement was little more than a skirmish, the Roman cavalry were routed and their commander, a consul by the name of Scipio, severely wounded. A few weeks later, amid the bitter cold of late December, Hannibal won an emphatic victory on the banks of a second river, the Trebia. Out of a Roman army of forty thousand men, some three-quarters were killed or captured: a morale-sapping demonstration to the defeated of what they were up against in Hannibal.

The concealment of troops behind the enemy's line, a brilliant exploitation of the terrain of the battlefield, and a climactic encirclement: Trebia had featured them all. So too, the following year, would an even more devastating victory. In the summer of 217 BC, as Hannibal headed south, he brilliantly outmanoeuvred a Roman army that had been stationed to block his crossing of the Apennines, and then headed on southwards, merrily burning and looting as he went. The Romans – up to thirty thousand of them in all – naturally set off in hot pursuit. In due course, on the evening of 20 June, they caught distant sight of their quarry by the banks of Lake Trasimene. The following morning, impatient to get to grips with the invaders, they advanced hurriedly through an early morning fog towards the Carthaginian rear-guard. On one side of them stretched the waters of the lake, and on the other a line of hills. It was, in other words, the perfect spot for an ambush – and Hannibal was not the man to waste such an opportunity. The fog grew thicker; the legionaries blundered along the lakeside road; and Hannibal gave the order for the jaws of his trap to close. The legions found that they were entirely surrounded. In the resulting massacre, all but the Roman vanguard, some six thousand men, were wiped out. Such was the horror of the slaughter that even an earthquake went unregarded.

From that moment on – with a single, disastrous exception – the Romans bound themselves to the grim and inglorious strategy of refusing battle to Hannibal. The general who first formulated it, Quintus Fabius Maximus, would end up being given the derisive nickname of 'the Delayer' for his pains; but, as time would show, he had correctly identified the fatal weakness in the invader's strategy. Ironically enough, the Battle of Cannae, the most extraordinary victory of Hannibal's entire extraordinary career, only served to emphasize it: for even after inflicting upon the republic the greatest calamity in its history, he could not force a final victory. Bled of manpower

Hannibal's crossing of the Alps has a good claim to be considered the most celebrated exploit in military history. Strategically, however, it was a disaster, and probably doomed the Carthaginian invasion of Italy before it had even begun.

though Rome had been, Hannibal's reserves were more anaemic still. By the spring of 217 BC, he had already lost all but one of his elephants; and over the decade and a half that followed Cannae, disease and desertion progressively accomplished what the legions no longer dared to attempt. Simultaneously, every source of reinforcements was being methodically denied him. Not only was a second Carthaginian invasion of Italy, led by Hannibal's brother, annihilated, but a Roman expeditionary force succeeded in conquering the Barcid empire in Spain. The general who pulled off this feat was none other than the son of the consul who had been wounded beside the Ticinus, Scipio; and by 204 he was ready to embark on the invasion of the Carthaginian homeland that would serve to win him his nickname of 'Africanus'. Hannibal, frantically summoned back from Italy, met with Scipio in the summer of 202, outside the town of Zama. He lost.

A PERFECT BATTLE:
CANNAE

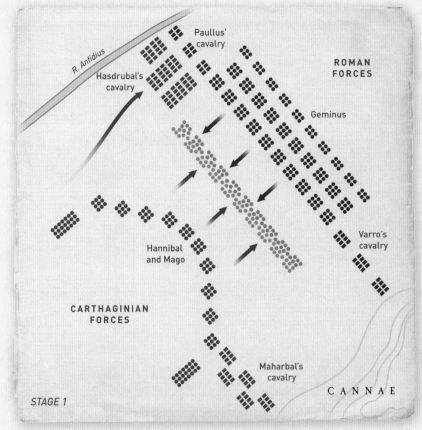

THE BATTLE OF CANNAE was Hannibal's master-piece. The Romans, having initially agreed to avoid open combat with the invader in the wake of their defeat at Lake Trasimene, had in due course wearied of such an inglorious policy. Accordingly, in the summer of 216 BC, they set about raising the largest army that the republic had ever put into the field: eight whole legions, some eighty thousand men in all. At their head rode the two heads of state, the consuls. No effort was spared in their effort to wipe out Hannibal once and for all.

Nothing daunted, Hannibal himself eagerly seized the opportunity to offer his enemies battle. As the Romans advanced southwards into Apulia, he stationed himself on an open plain near the town of Cannae, where his cavalry would be able to operate at peak effectiveness. Even though one of the two consuls refused to risk an engagement amid such terrain, the command that he held with his fellow-consul was a rotating one, and his colleague was set on battle. Accordingly, on 2 August 216 BC, the order was given, and the legions left their camp. They outnumbered their enemy two to one.

Hannibal, confronted in the centre by a massive block of infantry, but on his wings only six thousand untrained horsemen, had opted to weaken his own centre, and massively to strengthen his wings. As the legionaries advanced, they found Gauls and Spaniards arrayed against them in a curving bulge. Inevitably, the sheer weight of Roman numbers was soon serving to push the bulge flat and then back – drawing the densely ranked legionaries ever forwards. Simultaneously, however, Hannibal's wings had easily routed the Roman cavalry, and were now poised menacingly on the undefended flanks of the legions. As the Libyan heavy infantry closed in on their sides, so Spanish and Gallic horsemen fell upon their rear. The Romans, completely surrounded, were massacred. By nightfall, if the Greek historian Polybius is to be believed, the battlefield was strewn with more than seventy thousand dead.

That single defeat ended the war. Carthage no longer had the manpower to continue the struggle, and when its conqueror's terms were delivered, Hannibal advised his countrymen to accept them. What he had failed to achieve as a commander he now sought to accomplish as a statesman: to ensure the survival of his country. The Romans, however, fearful of him still, forced him in 195 BC to leave Carthage; and from that moment on he endured a wretched and spectre-like exile, 'an eagle plucked of all its feathers', forever being harried from foreign court to foreign court by Roman agents. When he eventually died in 183 BC, it was by his own hand: his enemies had cornered him at last. Their inveterate hatred of him, of course, ranked as the greatest compliment that they ever paid a foe. A failure, in the final reckoning, he may have been; but the Romans would never forget that in Hannibal, in the scale of his exertions and in the scope of his ambitions, they had met the opponent who was most like themselves.

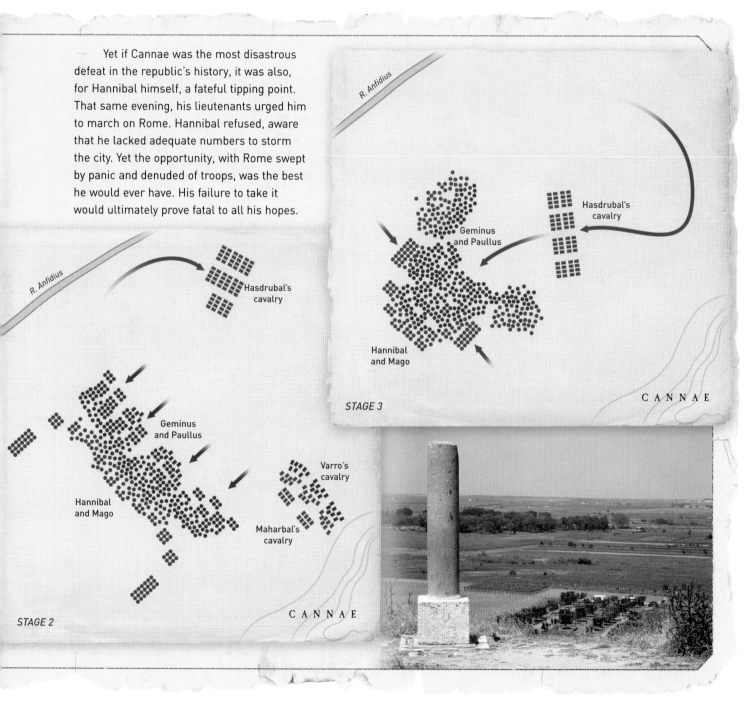

Yet if Cannae was the most disastrous defeat in the republic's history, it was also, for Hannibal himself, a fateful tipping point. That same evening, his lieutenants urged him to march on Rome. Hannibal refused, aware that he lacked adequate numbers to storm the city. Yet the opportunity, with Rome swept by panic and denuded of troops, was the best he would ever have. His failure to take it would ultimately prove fatal to all his hopes.

R. Anfidius

Hasdrubal's cavalry

Geminus and Paullus

Hannibal and Mago

STAGE 3

CANNAE

R. Anfidius

Hasdrubal's cavalry

Geminus and Paullus

Varro's cavalry

Hannibal and Mago

Maharbal's cavalry

STAGE 2

CANNAE

Hannibal

139

'Scipio ... consulted his safety as far as possible; for he had with him three men carrying large shields, who ... afforded him protection.' POLYBIUS

SCIPIO AFRICANUS
c. 236–184 BC

ADRIAN GOLDSWORTHY

PUBLIUS CORNELIUS SCIPIO WAS THE MOST GIFTED Roman general to emerge from the desperate Second Punic War fought between Rome and Carthage. After a series of Roman disasters, he was given command of Spain in 210 BC, and within five years had driven the Carthaginians from the entire Iberian peninsula. He then led the invasion of North Africa, threatening Carthage itself, ending the war with his victory at Zama in 202 BC. He was the only Roman commander to defeat Hannibal in a major land battle.

Scipio trained his men hard. Under his command the Roman legions became better drilled and more confident than ever, able to perform both complex battlefield manoeuvres and surprise night attacks. He was both methodical and meticulous in his preparations for each campaign, gathering intelligence, acquiring local allies and ensuring that adequate supplies were readily available. These were the skills that made possible his bold capture of New Carthage. In Spain he used large numbers of Spanish warriors, although never relying on them too heavily and leaving the more serious fighting to his own troops. In Africa he secured sufficient Numidian light cavalry to give him an advantage over the enemy – an essential to success that he had learned from Hannibal. He also copied the Carthaginian in ensuring that the enemy was deceived about his intentions, and that every move he made was both fast and unexpected.

Scipio's life and career were closely tied up with Hannibal's. A teenager when Hannibal invaded Italy, he served on the staff of his father, was present at the first encounter between the armies in 218 BC, and survived Rome's most serious defeat at the Battle of Cannae in 216. Scipio grew up in a time of war fought against a skilled and determined opponent. Because of this, his generation served on campaign for longer periods than was normal for Roman aristocrats and learned how to soldier in a very hard school. Such men proved to be very capable commanders, and Scipio was by far the best of them.

Yet his career, after the defeat of Hannibal, was largely one of disappointment. Although he commanded an army in one later campaign, his performance was no more than competent and his opponents merely a Gallic tribe. The long years of commanding the army in distant lands were poor preparation for political life in Rome, and he proved an indifferent politician. He eventually died in bitter and self-imposed retirement; in death as in life seemingly linked to Hannibal, who took his own life around the same time.

The hard school

Scipio was born into one of the wealthy and distinguished patrician families that held a central place in the political life of the Roman Republic. His father was elected consul for 218 BC and given the task of taking an army to Spain to confront Hannibal. En route, he realized that Hannibal had already passed him, heading for Italy, so he sent his brother with the bulk of the troops on to Spain and turned again to the east, to meet Hannibal south of the Alps. The young Scipio came with him as a member of his staff. In November 218 BC, the consul led a force of cavalry and light infantry that confronted Hannibal at the River Ticinus, where it was overwhelmed. The Roman commander was wounded and Scipio, according to family tradition, led a desperate cavalry charge that saved his life.

A detail from a relief on the sarcophagus of Domitius Ahenobarbus, c. 100 BC, which may give an idea of the appearance of Roman soldiers during the Punic Wars. Soldiers of lesser means would have substituted a simple pectoral chest plate for the expensive mail armour shown here.

Scipio was still with the army when the combined forces of the two consuls, were smashed at Trebia in December, and in 217 BC may have been present at the disaster at Lake Trasimene where a Roman army was ambushed by Hannibal and massacred. In the following year he was a military tribune with the Second Legion, part of the massive army sent to confront Hannibal. In August, despite massively outnumbering the enemy, the Romans were almost annihilated at the Battle of Cannae, but Scipio again survived. He rallied groups of other survivors, gaining fame by his dramatic response to a group of young aristocrats who were thinking of fleeing abroad; grasping his weapon, he made them all swear an oath, at sword point, never to abandon the Republic.

Scipio Africanus

The so-called 'tomb
of the Scipio' at
Tarragona in Catalonia is
one of a group of Roman
funerary monuments
dating from the imperial
period. The two carved
figures may be deities,
but have sometimes
been identified as Scipio
Africanus' father and
uncle, who fought the
Carthaginians in Spain
until their deaths in
214 BC.

In 211 BC, the Romans suffered a serious setback. On recovering from his wounds, Scipio's father had been sent to Spain to hold joint command there with his brother, but following the defection of local allies, both brothers were killed. A year later, when he was still only in his mid twenties, Scipio applied to succeed them in the Spanish command. Despite the fact that the Republic normally gave military commands only to elected magistrates in their forties, casualties among the ranks of the Senate had been exceptionally high in the previous few years. No one else appears to have been keen to serve in Spain. In addition, it was felt that the family name would command greater loyalty from the tribes in the peninsula than the distant and unknown entity of Rome. Even so, it is important to remember just how exceptional his appointment was. At a time of crisis, it demonstrated the extent to which the Romans were prepared to gamble.

The Spanish campaign

Scipio took with him reinforcements to raise the number of Roman troops in Spain to just over thirty thousand. Although massively outnumbered by the Carthaginians, the Roman army was concentrated and disciplined; the Carthaginians, on the other hand, were unable to keep their armies assembled in one place because of the difficulty of feeding them. Almost immediately Scipio decided to launch a bold stroke against the Carthaginian provincial capital at New Carthage (modern Cartagena). According to local fishermen, the lagoon protecting the western wall of the city was fordable in certain conditions. At the start of the campaigning season in 209 BC, discovering that the three Carthaginian field armies were at some distance from the city, he moved rapidly down the coast, his fleet keeping pace with the land forces. The day after arriving, he launched a full-scale assault on the wall facing the main landward approach, his forces fighting hard even to reach the wall in the face of a robust defence from the Carthaginian forces that came out to meet him.

Scipio kept the attack going for several hours. Only once the tide had fallen did he despatch a force of five hundred men to ford the lagoon. Virtually all of the defenders had been drawn away to face the 'main' Roman threat and these five hundred men were able to use ladders to climb the wall. They then followed the wall round to the main gate, while the forces outside renewed their assault. The Carthaginian defenders panicked and fled, allowing the Romans to open the main gate. Scipio then led a reserve force to seize the citadel and other key points in the town. It was a remarkable victory, showing the tribes that it was possible to beat the Carthaginians.

Scipio took possession of the enemy treasury, along with many other resources. There were also hostages in the city, from the noble families of many of the Spanish tribes, kept there as security for treaties with the Carthaginians. One of the hostages – a beautiful aristocratic woman – was brought to him by his men. In a gesture emulating Alexander the Great, Scipio refused to touch her, instead handing her over to her family with her honour intact. It was a politic as well as a noble gesture. Over the following winter Scipio was able to persuade a number of Spanish leaders to defect to his side, bringing their warriors with them.

In 208 BC, Scipio won a marginal victory over Hannibal's brother Hasdrubal Barca at Baecula, but he was unable to prevent Hasdrubal from leaving Spain to

The Greek trading colony of Emporion in Catalonia, founded in the sixth century BC, flourished during the many centuries of Roman occupation in Spain. Scipio Africanus landed here, and it was an important base in his initial campaigns.

march to Italy. In the event this did not matter, since Hasdrubal was overwhelmed by superior Roman forces soon after he arrived in Italy. The next year was spent in indecisive manoeuvring before the Carthaginians concentrated a great army under Hasdrubal Gisgo and met Scipio at Ilipa. The Romans were heavily outnumbered, and almost half of their force consisted of Spanish allies, whose loyalty was questionable and whose effectiveness was low. Yet Scipio's legions and their Latin allies were well drilled. For days the armies confronted each other, lined up with their best troops in the centre and allies on the flanks; neither side choosing to risk a battle.

Having lulled the enemy into this routine, at dawn the next day Scipio sent his cavalry and light infantry to attack the enemy outposts in front of their camp. While this attack was under way, Scipio formed up his main army, this time posting the legions on the flanks and placing his unreliable Spanish in the centre. Hasdrubal deployed in a hurry, taking up the same formation as before. He was stunned when he saw the Roman wings marching forward towards his weakest infantry on his own flanks. Scipio's Spanish allies deliberately advanced much more slowly, but still prevented Hasdrubal's centre from threatening the Roman wings. The Carthaginians watched, mesmerized, as the Roman infantry manoeuvred, quickly routing these flanks before turning against the better troops in the Carthaginian centre. Hasdrubal's army was utterly shattered. In the following months it was simply a matter of mopping up the few remaining Carthaginian strongholds.

Scipio Africanus

The invasion of North Africa

After his success in Spain, Scipio returned to Rome and was elected consul for 205 BC. Although he was still below the legal age for this office, his recent successes made the electorate and other senators willing to make an exception. Scipio then lobbied successfully to be given command of an army that would invade North Africa and threaten Carthage itself. The invasion was launched from Sicily, and at the heart of the army were two legions formed from the survivors of Cannae and other Roman defeats – now very experienced soldiers whose drill, Scipio made sure, was up to his high standard.

In 204 BC, Scipio landed and camped outside the town of Utica. He was soon afterwards joined by Masinissa, a Numidian prince, who brought with him a force of cavalry. Contingents of these superb light horsemen had been some of Hannibal's most effective troops, but after service with the Carthaginians in Spain, Masinissa had become disgruntled and was persuaded to defect. Masinissa commanded only a small force, but they soon proved their worth, luring some enemy cavalry into a carefully laid ambush. Scipio started to besiege Utica, and two large Carthaginian armies soon approached, one led by Hasdrubal Gisgo, the other by Syphax, the Numidian king, an ally of Carthage and a bitter enemy of Masinissa. Throughout the winter the two forces camped about 7½ miles apart and watched the Romans. Early in the spring of 203 BC, Scipio divided his army into two and launched carefully prepared night attacks on the separate enemy camps. The camps were burnt, and the panicking enemy soldiers were either cut down or dispersed. It was a spectacular success.

'My mother bore a general, not a warrior.'

SCIPIO (OR HIS GRANDSON PUBLIUS CORNELIUS SCIPIO AEMILIANUS AFRICANUS MINOR)

The Carthaginians took some time to regroup, allowing Scipio to strengthen the fortifications of his own camp and build substantial granaries to hold the supplies of captured enemy grain. Eventually, combining a newly arrived contingent of mercenary Celtiberian warriors from Spain with the survivors of the earlier disaster, Hasdrubal and Syphax mustered an army roughly equivalent in size to the Romans'. Scipio attacked immediately, confronting them in what became known as the Battle of the Great Plains. The Celtiberians formed the centre and put up stiff resistance. On the wings the Roman cavalry and Masinissa's men swiftly overwhelmed the enemy horsemen. The infantry on the wings – in the main survivors of the night attacks on the camps at the beginning of the year – soon joined them. Scipio's legions were up against the Celtiberians, but while the first line kept them pinned down, the second and third manoeuvred to strike at both flanks of the mercenaries. Then they too were driven off or destroyed.

This new disaster forced the Carthaginian leaders to summon Hannibal and his army back from Italy to confront the invader. In a display of confidence, Scipio ordered that some captured enemy spies should be shown around his camp and then released to make their report. After a brief attempt at negotiation, the two armies met at Zama and for the first time in his career Hannibal was utterly defeated. Aware that there was no possibility of forming another army, he returned to Carthage and told the political leaders that they had no alternative but to make peace.

Fading glory

Scipio returned to Rome and celebrated a spectacular triumph. He also took the surname Africanus as a permanent reminder to others of his great victories. Now in his late thirties, he was at the age when a senator would normally begin to seek high offices and the chance for military command. But he had already fought and won great campaigns. Elected consul for a second time for 194 BC he was given command of an army campaigning against the Gallic tribes of the Po valley. Two consuls were sent to the region and the bulk of the fighting seems to have fallen to his colleague. Scipio may have led a series of plundering expeditions, but achieved little. Furthermore, the situation had changed since the Second Punic War. There were now plenty of Romans who were eager for military commands, and he was granted only a single year in his post before being replaced.

A female war elephant with her calf, on a plate from Campania, southern Italy, dating from the early third century BC. The elephant probably represents one of the animals used by the Greek king Pyrrhus, who fought against Rome during this period. It is not clear whether or not Hannibal's elephants carried towers on their backs.

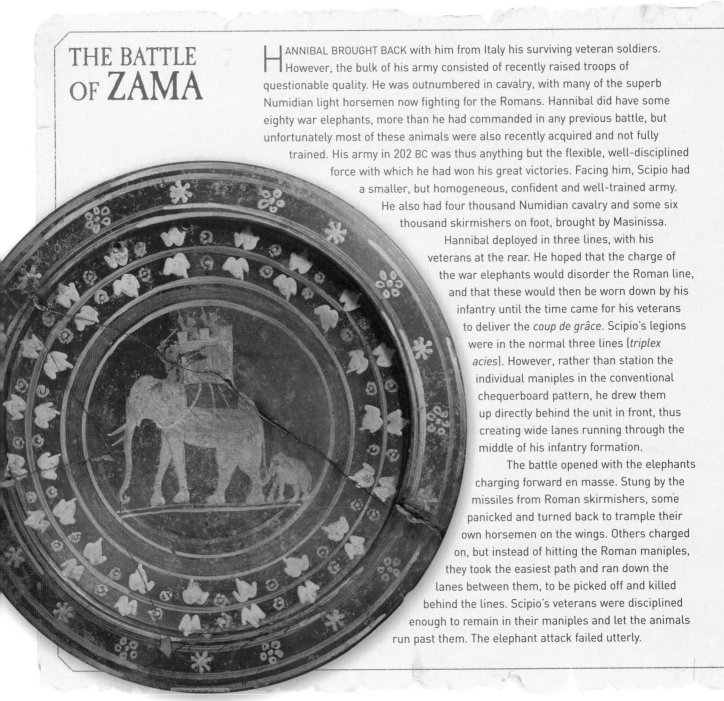

THE BATTLE OF ZAMA

HANNIBAL BROUGHT BACK with him from Italy his surviving veteran soldiers. However, the bulk of his army consisted of recently raised troops of questionable quality. He was outnumbered in cavalry, with many of the superb Numidian light horsemen now fighting for the Romans. Hannibal did have some eighty war elephants, more than he had commanded in any previous battle, but unfortunately most of these animals were also recently acquired and not fully trained. His army in 202 BC was thus anything but the flexible, well-disciplined force with which he had won his great victories. Facing him, Scipio had a smaller, but homogeneous, confident and well-trained army. He also had four thousand Numidian cavalry and some six thousand skirmishers on foot, brought by Masinissa. Hannibal deployed in three lines, with his veterans at the rear. He hoped that the charge of the war elephants would disorder the Roman line, and that these would then be worn down by his infantry until the time came for his veterans to deliver the *coup de grâce*. Scipio's legions were in the normal three lines (*triplex acies*). However, rather than station the individual maniples in the conventional chequerboard pattern, he drew them up directly behind the unit in front, thus creating wide lanes running through the middle of his infantry formation.

The battle opened with the elephants charging forward en masse. Stung by the missiles from Roman skirmishers, some panicked and turned back to trample their own horsemen on the wings. Others charged on, but instead of hitting the Roman maniples, they took the easiest path and ran down the lanes between them, to be picked off and killed behind the lines. Scipio's veterans were disciplined enough to remain in their maniples and let the animals run past them. The elephant attack failed utterly.

Scipio Africanus

Perhaps Scipio's last chance to achieve something comparable to the victories in Spain and Africa came when he accompanied his younger brother Lucius in the campaign against the Seleucid ruler Antiochus the Great, a command allocated largely because Scipio announced that he would go with him. Yet in the event Scipio played only the most minor of roles and was not present at the great Roman victory of Magnesia in 190 BC. The reason given was illness, but perhaps he chose not to be there so that his brother could win glory for himself.

Lucius celebrated a great triumph on his return to Rome, but both he and his brother were accused of misappropriating state funds during the campaign. Neither was convicted, but simply being brought to trial was a major humiliation. Soon afterwards Scipio retired to a country estate and never again took part in public life. His grandson by adoption, Scipio Aemilianus, would destroy Carthage in 146 BC.

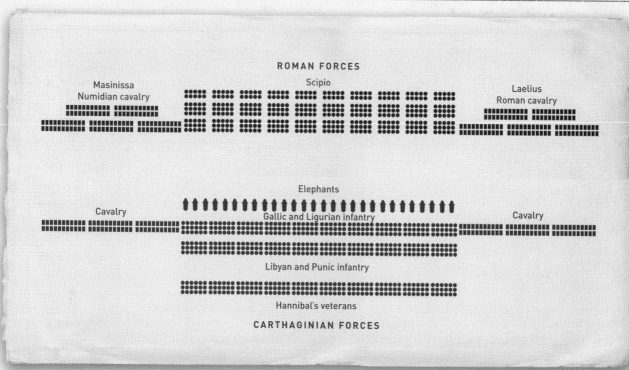

In the meantime, the Roman and Numidian cavalry charged on both wings, overwhelmed their Carthaginian counterparts and pursued them off the field. In the centre, the Roman front line struck the foremost of Hannibal's infantry lines. The Carthaginians resisted stubbornly, but after a time were driven back. There was some confusion as units from the first line withdrew and the second line was reluctant to let them pass. After a further struggle the Carthaginian second line was also routed. That these two lines failed to support each other properly showed clearly that the Carthaginian army had not had sufficient time to train together or integrate its contingents.

Hannibal's veterans had not moved from their position and closed ranks, preventing any of the fugitives from forcing their way through. The Roman first line was by now tired, and had probably already been reinforced by maniples from the second line. In another impressive display of discipline, the Romans halted and reformed. All three lines were merged to form a single block, much like the traditional phalanx formation. This then lumbered forward into contact with the veterans. A fierce combat ensued, which was only ended when the Roman cavalry returned and attacked Hannibal's veterans in the rear. Having superiority in cavalry gave Scipio a marked advantage from the start. But he also effectively countered each of Hannibal's tactics. Hannibal's army was utterly broken, having lost twenty thousand dead and almost as many taken prisoner.

'Not in a great army is victory in war, but from the Heavens comes valour.' I MACCABEES

JUDAH MACCABEUS
c.190–160 BC

MARTIN VAN CREVELD

PERHAPS the strangest thing about Judah Maccabeus is the way he is remembered: as a glance at publishers' catalogues will confirm, only a handful of books have been written about him; on the Internet, many of the hits refer not to him but to the oratorio that bears his name, *Judas Maccabaeus* – written by George Frideric Handel in 1746 to a libretto by Thomas Morell, and containing the celebrated passage:

See, the conquering hero comes!
Sound the trumpets, beat the drums.
Sports prepare, the laurel bring,
Songs of triumph to him sing.

See the godlike youth advance!
Breathe the flutes, and lead the dance;
Myrtle wreaths, and roses twine,
To deck the hero's brow divine.

See, the conquering hero comes!
Sound the trumpets, beat the drums.
Sports prepare, the laurel bring,
Songs of triumph to him sing.
See, the conquering hero comes!
Sound the trumpets, beat the drums.

Sources about Judah are relatively abundant; in addition to the two Books of Maccabees – apocryphal texts originally written in Hebrew during the second half of the second century BC but surviving only in Greek translation – we have several shorter ancient accounts of his deeds. Still we know nothing of his youth, other than that he was the third son of a priest, Matthathias the Hasmonean, and that the family lived in the village of Modiin in Judea, not far from where Tel Aviv airport now stands. His name, Judah (Judas is the Greek version), means 'Knows God'; his nickname, Maccabeus, may have derived from *makevet*, or mallet, so probably meant 'the hammerer'.

Judea was, at the time, governed from Antioch, in Syria, by the Seleucid king, Antiochus IV Epiphanes ('Surrounded by Light'). His father, Antiochus III, had been badly defeated by the Romans at the Battle of Magnesia in 190 BC, after which his kingdom began to disintegrate. In 170 BC, Epiphanes usurped the throne from his brother Seleucus, and in order to consolidate his power he then prohibited Jewish practices and demanded that religious worship focus on himself.

In 170 BC and again two years later, Antiochus IV invaded Egypt. The second campaign in particular was a great success; the king got as far as Alexandria, the capital. However, at the city's outskirts he was met by a Roman envoy who summarily ordered him to turn back, a grievous blow to his power and prestige. In 167 BC, the very next year, Matthathias raised the standard of revolt against him. When his father died in 166 BC, Matthathias designated Judah, rather than either of Judah's older brothers, to be his successor.

The Judean revolt

The first blows of revolt were directed not against the Syrian occupiers but against fellow Judeans. Apparently not everybody was delighted to join the sons of Matthathias; at one point, altars of idol worship had been destroyed and some 'Hellenizing' Jews forcibly circumcised.

The first Seleucid response was commanded by Apollonius, who was possibly the governor of Samaria. He, and what today would be called 'the forces of order', appeared at Modiin in the spring of 166 BC. Modiin being situated in a plain, the rebels were unable to resist their heavily armed enemy, and fled to the nearby hills. While details are scant, apparently Judah relied on classic guerrilla tactics, fighting at

A bronze head of Antiochus IV Ephiphanes, Seleucid king of Syria and occupier of Judea, whose policies of Hellenization triggered the Jewish revolt of 167 BC.

(Opposite) The head of a thirteenth-century statue of a king of Judah, one of twenty-eight representations of Old Testament kings that decorated the western façade of the cathedral of Notre-Dame in Paris. The head is now housed in the Musée Cluny.

Judah Maccabeus

149

night, selecting suitable places, and taking the enemy by surprise. We are told in I Maccabees that he 'made quite a number of the enemy flee ... and the fame of his courage spread everywhere'.

The victory over Apollonius was quickly followed by another skirmish. This time the Seleucid commander was one Seron, who was probably in charge of some garrisons along the coast. Seron committed the error of marching his troops into the mountains by way of Beth Horon, a route that, until a modern highway was built there a few years ago, had always been notoriously hard to travel and easy to block. The sources say Judah had about six thousand men with him – which, modern scholars believe, was considerably more than Seron had. In any case eight hundred of the royal army died, possibly including Seron himself, while the rest fled back the way they had come.

Clearly, a pattern was being established. The Seleucid army was a powerful war machine, consisting mainly of heavy infantrymen who carried long pikes and operated in a phalanx. It also included light infantry, however – the only element that was really useful outside the plain – as well as heavy and light cavalry. We have no idea what kinds of units Apollonius and Seron commanded, because the prime purpose of our main sources, I and II Maccabees (which all the rest seem to have used), was not to provide military detail but to record and praise the ways of God.

The road to Jerusalem

By this time Antiochus had realized the revolt was more than a minor affair. To deal with it, he therefore dispatched a relative, Lysias, who was governor of the western part of his kingdom. In September 165 BC this led directly to what was probably Judah's greatest triumph: the Battle of Ammaus.

By enabling Judah to switch from guerrilla to regular warfare, the victory at Ammaus changed the nature of the struggle. Lysias' army, though it had been shattered, was not annihilated. The Syrian commander succeeded in rallying his forces, and, while the sequence of events that followed is not completely clear, November–December of 165 BC found him leading another large-scale expedition against the Jews.

Wary of the mountains, this time Lysias took an altogether different route. Starting from Philistia, he marched east by way of Beer Sheba, then turned north and headed for Hebron and Beth Lehem, reaching all the way to Beth Tzur (today a Palestinian Arab village on the southernmost outskirts of Jerusalem).

Judah was waiting for him, but no major battle took place. Antiochus was, at the time, campaigning against the Parthians far away when he died of disease. The Seleucid postal services, consisting of mounted messengers working in relay, were efficient, and the news apparently reached Lysias even as he was preparing for his assault on Jerusalem. The army thereupon retreated, and its commander hastened to Antioch to look after the succession of the late king's son, Antiochus V, who was a mere child.

The citadel of Jerusalem was known as Akra or Hakra. One hundred and seventy years later, it was where Jesus was imprisoned; in 164 BC it was firmly held by a Seleucid garrison. Still Lysias' retreat enabled Judah to enter the temple – which for years had been used for idol worship – and purify it, in a ceremony which gave rise to the modern Jewish festival of Hanukkah, when candles are lit in commemoration.

In the words of the song that is sung on the occasion:

O mighty stronghold of my salvation,
to praise You is a delight.
Restore my House of Prayer and there
we will bring a thanksgiving offering.
When You will have prepared the
slaughter for the blaspheming foe,
Then I shall complete with a song of hymn
the dedication of the Altar.

Lysias, however, did not give up. The next year saw Judah and his men, who had grown from a band of guerrillas into a semi-regular army, engaged on an attempt to reduce Akra by means of siege machines. In telling us how powerful Lysias' force was, I Maccabees grows positively lyrical: 'from other kingdoms and from islands of the sea mercenary armies came to him. And the number of his armies was a hundred thousand foot and twenty thousand horsemen, and elephants thirty-two trained for war'. Considering the state of the Seleucid kingdom, the true figure was probably less than half that.

The sack of Jerusalem by the Seleucid king Antiochus IV, as depicted in an illumination from the fifteenth-century *Chronique de Jean de Coucy*. Antiochus' soldiers slaughtered many of the city's inhabitants, destroyed the temple and desecrated its sacred objects.

This time the encounter took place a little further to the south, not far from the village of Beth Zeharia, named after the biblical prophet. First came the elephants, which had been 'saturated with blood of grape and berries to rouse them for war'. Each of these moving fortresses was surrounded by a thousand heavy infantry and five hundred picked horsemen. Each elephant carried a wooden castle with four men in it, plus the mahout (elephant driver); a good example of combined arms at work. Following the normal Hellenistic pattern, the remaining cavalry was distributed on both wings to provide cover. 'And all trembled who heard the sound of their throng, and the strides of the throng and the clank of the weapons for the camp was very large and heavy.'

The ensuing battle was sharp, but short. Judah's brother Elazar sacrificed himself, diving under one of the elephants, killing it with his sword and then being crushed as it fell. This act of heroism notwithstanding, there was no resisting Lysias' superior force. Soon the Jews found themselves besieged in the Temple Mount, so recently liberated, with nothing to eat; many of Judah's men deserted. No doubt they would have succumbed, but again luck came to their aid. Back in Syria, a certain Philippus, who commanded the Seleucid army in the east, had marched on Antioch in an effort to wrest the kingdom for himself. In the end, Lysias was able to overcome him, but only at the cost of giving Judah a much-needed respite.

Judas before the army of Nicanor: a depiction by Gustave Doré (1832–83) of an episode described in II Maccabees 15:21 in which Judah Maccabeus confronted the Seleucid forces of Nicanor at Adasa in 161 BC.

Last battles

By this time the revolt had been going on for four years, the first two of which had been marked by considerable military successes. Guerrilla warfare on its own could not liberate the country, however, and once the Seleucids were able to bring even part of their mighty forces to bear – the rest were tied down in Iran – only the death of Antiochus IV and the ensuing troubles saved Judah and his men. Nor did Lysias' victory over Philippus end the kingdom's difficulties. Only in 162 BC did a new ruler, Demetrius I, succeed in consolidating his control.

A new commander, Bacchides, was sent out. Apparently Judah had learnt the lesson of Beth Zeharia in the previous campaign; his men, for all their courage, were not yet ready to face the full might of a well-organized, well-armed and well-led Seleucid army. Accordingly, when Bacchides appeared in front of Jerusalem, he gave up the city without a fight.

JUDEA in the mid second century BC.

At this stage, Bacchides appears to have considered the war as good as won; he even appointed a new high priest. Leaving a garrison at Akra, he marched from Jerusalem to the hills to the north, apparently with the intention of combing them. However, once again outside events intervened. The military situation in Babylonia was deteriorating, forcing Bacchides and some of his forces to go there. To fill his place he appointed a former subordinate, Nicanor, *strategos*.

Nicanor tried to negotiate with the insurgents, but to no avail. Next, apparently fearing that his inferior forces would be bottled up in Jerusalem, he decided to leave the city and offer battle in the mountain plateau to the north; there, some reinforcements reached him. We know nothing about their strength, or Nicanor's. However, they must have come through Samaria by way of the present road that leads from Jenin to Nablus and Ramallah.

'**How is a hero fallen, the saviour of Israel.**'

I MACCABEES

The two armies met at Adasa, the exact location of which remains unknown, in March 161 BC. Nicanor 'fell first in battle' (the thirteenth of the Jewish month Adar being thereafter called 'Nicanor Day'). His troops, dispirited by their commander's death, fled wildly to the west. Their route was the same one followed by Seron five years earlier, only in the opposite direction. As the inhabitants of the surrounding villages came out and joined in the pursuit, the survivors' plight grew worse and few of them can have survived. Nicanor's own body, or parts of it, were brought to Jerusalem in triumph and displayed on stakes.

The next year, 160 BC, brought Bacchides back to Judea. This time he chose to march by a completely different route, namely the one leading south from the Sea of

Judah Maccabeus

Galilee through the Jordan valley; next, turning west at Gilgal (where Joshua had once camped), he ascended the mountains to reach the same mountain plateau where Nicanor had been defeated.

The encounter took place at Elasa, a few miles northwest of Adasa. Attempting to explain away the defeat that was to come, I Maccabees grossly exaggerates Bacchides' strength while under-reporting that of Judah's army; still there is no doubt that the Seleucid force was much the stronger. When Judah's staff advised a retreat, however, his response was defiant: 'If our end is near, let us die bravely for our brothers!'

For the first time, we get a glimpse of Judah's tactical dispositions. Following the normal Hellenistic pattern, he deployed his light troops, armed with bows and slings, in front. The cavalry occupied the wings, while his infantry held the centre. Likewise Bacchides had his phalanx in the centre with cavalry on both wings.

Bacchides himself commanded his powerful right wing, which was standard Hellenistic practice. Apparently Judah felt he had only one chance: namely, to stake everything on a single throw by concentrating his best men against Bacchides. Coming under attack, Bacchides, resorting to a manoeuvre that had been executed many, many times before, carried out a feigned retreat, drawing the Jews after him. This enabled the phalanx to march into their rear: 'and the battle grew harder, and many fell dead of these and of these, and Judah fell, and the remaining fled.'

The aftermath

From the beginning of the revolt, Judah proved himself a tough, resourceful commander and a master of guerrilla warfare. Probably his greatest successes were the early ones. Later, as he engaged in regular warfare, things became more difficult;

Hasmonean excavations in the Old City of Jerusalem. The independent Jewish kingdom that Judah Maccabeus had fought for endured for nearly one hundred years following his death in 160 BC.

THE BATTLE OF AMMAUS

ALTHOUGH AMMAUS (165 BC) WAS NOT THE LARGEST battle Judah fought, it changed the nature of the revolt he led. Fortunately, an account of the battle was preserved in I Maccabees, containing information so detailed that modern scholars have speculated that the author may have participated in the battle.

The Seleucid king Antiochus IV was angered by the defeats of his commanders Apollonius and Seron. Having appointed Lysias as his commander, he gave him 'forty thousand men and seven thousand cavalry to go to the land of Judea and devastate it'. He also had some elephants, the tanks of the ancient world, though our sources do not say how many there were.

Along with his subordinates, Ptolemy, Nicanor and Gorgias, described as 'men of valour from among the king's friends', Lysias marched south into the land of Israel. He set up camp at Ammaus, very close to Latrun (where fierce battles were fought during Israel's 1948 War of Independence). There he was joined by auxiliary forces from Philistia and Edom. Also present was a throng of merchants with money to buy the expected Jewish prisoners and chains to put them in.

Judah's first move was to raise the morale of his troops, which had been

A terracotta figurine of a war elephant and its driver, or mahout, from Myrina, Greece, from the second or third century BC.

lowered by the mighty host being brought up against them. Jerusalem was, at the time, in the hands of a Seleucid garrison; it was 'desolate as a desert'. Accordingly, he assembled his men at Mitzpah, a hill further to the north, where there was 'a place of prayer'. They put on sackcloth, fasted and prayed. Judah then harangued them:

Gird yourselves and be valiant men, and be ready against the morning, that you may fight with these nations that are assembled against us and our sanctuary. For it is better for us to die in battle than to see the evils of our nation and of our Holy Places.

Gorgias must have heard about the ceremony, or perhaps the Jews deliberately spread the news. Taking with him five thousand infantrymen and a thousand cavalrymen, he launched a night march to take the rebels by surprise – only to find their camp empty. As he spread out to seek them in the hills, Judah and his men, probably about six thousand in number, evaded him and marched west until they took up positions south of Lysias' main base. Again Judah harangued his men, then gave the signal to attack.

The enemy fled, and the Syrian camp was soon taken and set alight. Realizing that Gorgias' force remained intact, however, Judah managed to prevent his men from dispersing and plundering it; apparently he had them well in hand. Soon after, light being reflected from shields showed that Gorgias was coming to the rescue. However, when Gorgias realized what had happened to the rest of the force he, in turn, fled.

And Judah returned to plunder the camp and they seized much gold and silver and cloth dyed blue and marine purple and great riches; and returning they sang hymns and praises to Heaven, for he is good, for his mercy endureth for ever.

in part, this was because much of the time he simply could not match the enemy in terms of numbers and armament. Twice, in 163 and 162 BC, he was saved only by his enemy's internal difficulties. In his last battle he was overwhelmed by superior forces and, fighting to the end, lost his life.

His death was a grave setback, but it did not end the revolt. His remaining brothers took over; in the end, thanks as much to the internal difficulties besetting the Seleucid kingdom as to their own abilities, they prevailed. The Hasmonean kingdom survived for just under a century, but in 64 BC was occupied by the Roman commander Pompey. With that, the curtain was drawn on Jewish independence for a period lasting more than two thousand years.

POMPEY

ADRIAN GOLDSWORTHY

106–48 BC

GNAEUS POMPEY was one of Rome's greatest generals, who won victories in Italy, Africa, Spain and Asia. Contemporaries compared him to Alexander, and he was especially delighted when the dictator Sulla gave him, too, the name Magnus or 'the Great'. His career was exceptional in every way, for unlike other Roman commanders he held no political office until he was in his late thirties, instead spending most of his early life on campaign. Pompey broke most of Rome's political rules, and spent as much time fighting other Romans as he did foreign enemies. This made it all the more ironic that he died as the defender of the Republic, fighting Julius Caesar.

A marble bust of Pompey. The Roman general is shown with his head slightly to one side, a pose associated with Alexander the Great, with whom Pompey liked to compare himself. Cicero commented that Pompey's apparently open and honest features belied his secretive nature.

Pompey's exceptional skill was in organization and planning. He had immense talent for raising and training troops, setting a personal example, even when in his late fifties, by drilling with his soldiers. Still more impressive was the scale of organization that he displayed in combating and defeating the pirates in the Mediterranean in 67 BC. Furthermore his armies rarely faced serious supply shortages; when they did, it was usually because of decisions taken by others over whom he had no control. In this he contrasted markedly with Caesar.

As a battlefield commander, however, Pompey lacked Caesar's finesse. He had immense courage, being inclined throughout his life to lead heroic cavalry charges after the manner of his hero Alexander. On one occasion, however, he had to flee, abandoning his horse, and only escaped because the pursuing enemy fell to bickering

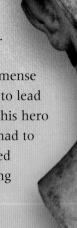

Pompey

over his mount and its rich harness. Worsted on several occasions on the battlefield, Pompey usually learned from his mistakes. Yet his aim was always to gain such a massive strategic advantage that a battle was either unnecessary or its outcome a foregone conclusion.

The private army

In his teens, Pompey served on the staff of his father, Pompeius Strabo, in the Social War fought from 91 BC to 89 BC against Rome's rebellious Italian allies. His father avoided taking sides during the civil war that followed immediately after this, but died suddenly – struck by lightning, according to one story. Pompey himself came under suspicion from one of the sides in the war, and so resolved to join the other, led by Sulla. He did not arrive empty-handed, but raised two legions from the population of his family's vast estates, paying for their wages and equipment out of his own pocket. He later added a third legion to this private army. As he marched to join Sulla, he encountered several enemy forces, all poorly trained and most abysmally led. Pompey routed them easily at every encounter. He became one of Sulla's most trusted subordinates, sent to region after region to overwhelm the enemy there. Within a few years he had fought in northern Italy, Sicily and North Africa.

Pompey's soldiers were fiercely loyal, but were not always under his full control. They mutinied when they felt that Sulla had slighted their commander, and were only restored to discipline after Pompey threatened to kill himself. Sulla – who made himself dictator in late 82 or early 81 BC – soon after dubbed him 'the Great' and allowed him to celebrate a triumph. He also arranged for him to marry his stepdaughter (although she died not long after the wedding).

Other people, however, had a lower opinion of the youthful general: older subordinates of the dictator were jealous of the favour shown him, and neutral observers felt that Pompey revelled far too much in power and took excessive pleasure in executing his defeated Roman enemies – it was at around this time that he gained the nickname of the 'young butcher'.

Sulla resigned his office in 79 BC and died a year later. As Pompey still had his army, the Senate decided to make use of it to defeat an attempted coup by the consul Lepidus in 78 BC. Pompey suppressed the rebellion with his usual speed and ruthlessness, and was then sent to

N

COLCHIS

IBERIA

ALBANIA

3

2

R. Cyrus

1

Artaxata

R. Araxes

BLACK SEA

Sinope

Trapezus
(Trebizond)

Amisus

4

ARMENIA

BITHYNIA-PONTUS

1

Nicomedia

Byzantium

Ancyra

CAPPADOCIA

2

Tigranocerta

GALATIA

Nyssa

COMMAGENE

Samosata

MESOPOTAMIA

ASIA

R. Tigris

PAMPHILIA

Aphrodisias

Cyrrhus

Zeugma

R. Euphrates

Aspendus

Side

Tarsus

CILICIA

Pompeiopolis

Antioch

5

Aleppo

Dura
Europos

Xanthus

SYRIA

Apamea

Palmyra

CYPRUS

Laodicea

MEDITERRANEAN
SEA

Paphos

Citium

Berytus

Baalbek

Curium

Damascus

Tyre

6

PHOENICIA

Bostra

Joppa

Gerasa

JUDEA

Jerusalem

Gaza

7

Masada

Pelusium

ARABIA

Alexandria

Petra

Memphis

R. Nile

EGYPT

RED SEA

0   100 km
0   100 miles

Pompey's first campaign

Pompey's later operations

3   Sequence of events

Spain to fight against Sertorius, one of Sulla's rivals who had refused to surrender. It was the first time that Pompey and his army had come up against a well-trained and competently led enemy, and in the first encounter Pompey was ambushed and completely outfought. Pompey learned from his experiences, however, realizing that it was better to attack Sertorius' inept subordinates and avoid confronting the man who had dubbed him 'Sulla's pupil'.

Although Pompey had for the first time been granted formal power as a proconsul by the Senate, there was little enthusiasm for this tough campaign from the elected magistrates, and on several occasions Pompey complained that he and his army were being inadequately supplied. Despite this, he and his fellow commander Metellus finally defeated the enemy – helped considerably by the assassination of Sertorius by jealous rivals. Pompey returned to Italy in 71 BC, where he managed to encounter and destroy a fragment of Spartacus' slave army that had survived defeat by Crassus, and began to display a petty tendency to boast about finishing wars already won by others. Finally, at the age of 36, he decided to enter the Senate, but despite being still under age, was determined to start at the most senior level by becoming consul. The Senate felt unable to resist either his popularity or the armies which he and Crassus kept camped outside Rome, and both were elected consuls for 70 BC in a landslide victory.

The people's general

Pompey revelled in his popularity, celebrating a second triumph. (Crassus, on the other hand, despite having prevailed in a gritty campaign against the slave army, was granted the lesser honour of an ovation.) Pompey had fame and massive wealth, but little experience or skill in political life. Within a few years he sought fresh military glories to reinforce his position, and in 67 BC was granted an extraordinary command by popular vote – something normally allocated only by the Senate. The exceptionally influential and popular could, however, bypass the magistrates and go straight to the People's Assembly. Pompey's challenge was to deal with the pirates infesting the Mediterranean, a task previously attempted by others but with inadequate resources and inevitable lack of success. Pompey, however, was given massive authority, along with men, ships and money on a lavish scale. The war was won in a matter of months.

'For the qualities proper to a general ... are possessed in greater measure by Pompeius alone than all other generals.'
CICERO

Publicly Pompey claimed that he wanted a chance to enjoy a peaceful life, but it was abundantly clear that he was eager for another grand command. A second bill in the People's Assembly put him in charge of the war against King Mithridates VI of Pontus. Sulla had beaten the king in an earlier war, but had negotiated a peace that allowed him to return to face his rivals in Italy. Conflict had soon restarted, and the Romans had again come very close to total victory under the leadership of Lucullus. The latter had enemies in the Senate, however, who were able systematically to starve him of resources, allowing Mithridates to recover.

Pompey was once again given all the men, supplies and money that he needed. In 66 BC, he confronted Mithridates in western Pontus, a region on the southeast coast of the Black Sea, but the latter was forced to withdraw when his food supplies

A scene from Trajan's Column in Rome, depicting Roman auxiliary cavalrymen in the uniform worn at the start of the second century AD. In Pompey's day the Romans were already reliant on foreigners as cavalrymen, but these were only slowly developing into regular units.

ran out. As usual, Pompey was far better prepared and pursued the enemy. The Pontic cavalry was lured into an ambush and badly cut up. In spite of a numerical superiority, Pompey was determined not to take risks and blockaded the enemy army, building a line of fortifications 19 miles in length. His men starving, Mithridates withdrew again, escaping under cover of darkness. In the days that followed, Pompey managed to force march his men and get ahead of the enemy column. In the ensuing ambush the king managed to escape, but his army was effectively destroyed. Soon afterwards Mithridates' ally, King Tigranes of Armenia, surrendered.

Mithridates was beaten and fled to a stronghold in the north of his kingdom. Pompey showed little interest in capturing or killing him, being eager for further military adventures before the war was formally concluded and he was forced to lay down his command and return to Rome. An attack on one of his army's winter camps by a force of Albanians prompted Pompey first to invade this Black Sea kingdom, and then extend his operations into neighbouring Iberia and Colchis. He then intervened in a civil war raging between rival members of the Hasmonean dynasty in Judea,

Pompey

backing one claimant and besieging Jerusalem, capturing the city three months later. He then moved south against the Nabatean Arab kingdom of Petra, his campaign coming to an end only when news arrived that Mithridates had committed suicide.

Pompey had added great swathes of territory to Rome's empire. These operations and those against the pirates were his only campaigns fought against unambiguously foreign enemies, and once the fighting was over he again demonstrated his genius for organization by creating a settlement to administer the new conquests. Much of the administrative structure he created would last for centuries. Not all became provinces, as some remained under the rule of local client kings. However, there was a delay before they were formally ratified in Rome. When Pompey returned in 62 BC he was granted another triumph – his third – in which he boasted that he had triumphed over Europe, Africa and now Asia, the three continents known to the Greeks and Romans. Yet again he was to display his lack of skill at political manipulation, however, and he did not seem to know how to deal with political opponents.

Civil War

A few years later, Pompey secretly allied with Crassus and Julius Caesar, forming what is known to scholars as the First Triumvirate. Caesar was elected consul for 59 BC and forced through the legislation sought by his two colleagues. Pompey secured the ratification of his eastern settlement and grants of farmland for the discharged veterans who had fought under his command. He also married Caesar's daughter Julia to cement the alliance. His new father-in-law then left for Gaul in 58 BC to begin a five-year command, later extended to ten.

The alliance was always a little uneasy. Pompey and Crassus disliked each other intensely. They came close to a split in 56 BC, but were reunited and again shared the consulship in 55 BC. Pompey was given command of all the armies in Spain, although he never went to the peninsula and instead remained just outside Rome to oversee events. Crassus went to Syria, and from there launched an invasion of Parthia, where he was killed in 53 BC. Julia died in childbirth at around the same time, weakening the bond with Caesar. As the time approached for his Gallic command to end, there was growing tension between the two former allies, Pompey being unwilling to accept Caesar as an equal. When asked what he would do if Caesar chose to fight, he disdainfully replied 'What if my son should attack me with a stick?' He also boasted that all he had to do was stamp his foot and legions would spring out of the soil of Italy. Eventually mutual suspicion, and the confident expectation that the other side would back down, led to war.

In January 49 BC, Caesar marched a legion across the border of his province – the little River Rubicon – into Italy. More troops followed. Pompey and his allies had raised many soldiers, but they were still untrained and no match for Caesar's veterans.

A coin minted by Pompey's younger son Sextus, depicting Pompey the Great on the left, and Sextus' brother Gnaeus on the right. Both of them died during the Civil War with Caesar. Sextus himself would eventually be defeated and killed by Caesar's adopted son Octavian.

THE PIRATE WAR

PIRACY HAD BEEN A SERIOUS PROBLEM throughout the Mediterranean since the start of the first century BC. Kidnappings were common – two Roman praetors with their attendants were once abducted from the Italian coast – and frequent attacks made on ships or coastal communities, including Ostia, the vital port which dealt with the huge amounts of grain needed to feed Rome. In 67 BC Pompey was voted an extraordinary command to deal with this, with power superior to that of provincial governors, to encompass the entire Mediterranean coast for a distance of 50 miles inland. His forces totalled 120,000 infantry and 5,000 cavalry, as well as a fleet of 500 warships. To assist him he had no fewer than twenty-four legates (or senior generals), many of them highly experienced.

Organization was always Pompey's great strength. He divided the Mediterranean into thirteen regions – six to the west and seven to the east of Italy. Each area was controlled by a legate, backed by strong forces, ordered to pursue only within his own zone. Pompey himself led the main strike force of sixty ships, which would attack the pirates anywhere they were found. In the spring he began in the western sectors, and within forty days had swept them free of pirates with apparently little fighting. The pirates had not been faced with serious Roman opposition for decades and appear to have been completely unprepared for this sudden concerted onslaught.

Operations took a little longer in the east, which had less land directly governed by Rome and thus more pirate strongholds. From the beginning Pompey knew that it was useless to sweep the sea of raiders if their coastal bases remained secure, and his land forces played a vital role in capturing enemy strongholds. Siege equipment had been prepared, but again there was less fighting than had been anticipated. In most cases the approach of a determined Roman force was enough to prompt a surrender. Once again Pompey confirmed his reputation for stealing other men's glory, by accepting the surrender of some pirate strongholds in Crete, placed under siege by another Roman commander.

The Romans could be utterly ruthless in punishing defeated enemies yet at other times lenient. For the pirates, Pompey had judged from the beginning that a permanent solution required conciliation. Accordingly, those who surrendered were not enslaved, but were transported and settled in new communities on better land, the aim being to enable them to feed themselves and their families without resorting to piracy. The east was settled in forty-seven days. Although Pompey claimed to have captured 846 vessels, some of these were no doubt very small. Some twenty thousand prisoners were resettled, one of the cities in Cilicia to which they were sent being renamed Pompeiopolis in his honour.

Pompey

Unlike his opponent, he was also saddled with many prominent senators who demanded important commands, but refused to obey his orders. Pompey decided that he must abandon Italy and create a massive army in the eastern Mediterranean, so that he could then return and dispose of Caesar. As Pompey himself put it, referring to Sulla's successful invasion of Italy from Greece in 83 BC – 'Sulla did it, why can't I?' Apart from some serious losses when his subordinates disobeyed his orders, his retreat was well managed, the bulk of his troops being safely evacuated from Brundisium in spite of Caesar's attempt at a blockade.

For the rest of the year Pompey concentrated on mustering a very large army in Greece, backed by strong naval forces. Although unable to catch Caesar's invasion fleet at the end of the year, they made it difficult for him to receive reinforcement and supply convoys. Caesar twice attempted to capture Pompey's main supply depot at the port of Dyrrachium. On the second attempt Pompey arrived first, and the two armies then sought to blockade each other, building long lines of fortifications on the high ground. Caesar's smaller army was on the outside, furthest from the sea, and struggled to complete their more extensive line, although they managed to repulse a series of attacks by the Pompeians. However, a major assault launched by Caesar a few days later ended in a costly failure. He commented that the enemy would have won an outright victory 'if only their leader was a winner'. Yet Pompey was content to wait. There were clear signs that his strategy of starving the enemy into submission was working; with his army desperately short of food and no prospect of beating the enemy, Caesar withdrew away from the coast.

In August, Pompey was persuaded by the many senior senators with his staff to risk battle outside Pharsalus (see also p. 171). Although a break with his strategy, it is possible that he felt the time was at last ripe. Relying on his greatly superior cavalry to outflank the enemy line, he was dismayed when these were routed, and would seem to have had no other clear idea of how to beat the enemy. Soon afterwards he fled the field. It was a lacklustre performance, perhaps explained by his age – he was now 58 – and by the fact that he had not been on campaign for over a decade before the Civil War began. Pompey escaped and took ship for Egypt, perhaps still hoping to rebuild an army there. On rowing ashore in a small boat he was greeted by officials of the boy King Ptolemy XIII, one of whom had served under him in his eastern campaigns before taking service as a mercenary in the Egyptian army. At a signal, Pompey was cut down and beheaded. Caesar arrived a few days later, but refused to look at the head when it was presented to him. Despite the nature of his death, Pompey was given a funeral that befitted his status, and his tomb was a landmark in Alexandria for many years.

(Opposite) **A relief block** from Praeneste showing a manned Roman warship, *c.* 37–32 BC. Although the Roman Republic had created a powerful navy during the struggles with Carthage (264–146 BC), by the first century BC its effectiveness had declined and it proved incapable of dealing with the problem of piracy until Pompey took charge. Most of the warships used by both the pirates and the Romans chasing them were small vessels.

Pompey

JULIUS CAESAR

ADRIAN GOLDSWORTHY

100–44 BC

CAIUS JULIUS CAESAR was Rome's most famous and successful general. In eight years of intensive campaigning from 58 to 51 BC, he conquered Gaul (roughly modern France and Belgium), crossed the Rhine into Germany, and twice landed in Britain. Backed into a corner by his political enemies at Rome, he then defeated them in the Civil War (49–45 BC) fought all around the Mediterranean. The Romans believed that he fought more battles than any other commander, won all his campaigns, and only suffered two serious setbacks, both of which proved temporary. Caesar was also a writer and consummate propagandist. His *Commentaries* on his own operations in Gaul and the Civil War were recognized from the start as one of the greatest expressions of the Latin language. Their clear, dispassionate and fast-paced narratives are models of how military history should be written. Napoleon was just one of many famous commanders who acknowledged that he had learned a good deal from them.

Like Napoleon, Caesar was a charismatic leader, able to inspire an almost fanatical loyalty in his soldiers. The stubborn determination of his legionaries carried his army through a number of desperate situations. It is also fair to say that Caesar's skills as a commander were often most spectacularly displayed when he was obliged to extricate himself from problems of his own creation. He was always bold, and at times apparently rash. Roman generals were expected to be aggressive, and Caesar's audacity is sometimes deceptive. He took risks – famously starting the Civil War with a gambler's comment 'the die is cast' (*iacta alea est*) – but only after he had done everything possible to strengthen his own position. If delaying would not improve his situation but would strengthen the enemy, then Caesar attacked even if the odds were against him. He was never wasteful with the lives of his men.

Caesar was very generous with promotions, plunder and praise. His officers, the famous and formidable centurions, he knew by name, emphasizing their heroism in his *Commentaries*. Caesar imposed a rigorous training regime on his army, but led by example. According to Suetonius, he would often order his men to keep a watchful

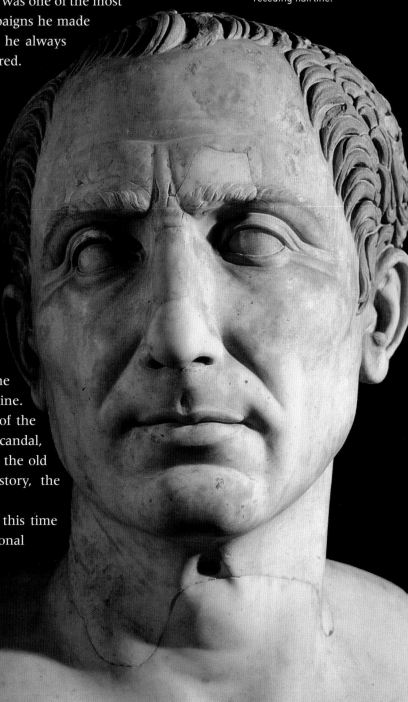

eye on him, and their ship quietly out of camp, expecting them to catch up and follow him on a tough route march. He did not worry about formal discipline in rest periods, however, and was no martinet. When he spoke to his legionaries, he always addressed them as 'comrades'. When he faced two serious mutinies during the Civil War, the second one led by his favourite Tenth Legion, Caesar broke the mutineers' spirit with just one word, calling them 'civilians' instead of 'comrades'. Soon the veteran legionaries were begging him to decimate them – executing one soldier in ten – as long as he would take them back into his service. Ultimately, however, his men always trusted him, believing that, with Caesar in charge, they would win. He boasted that he was lucky, something the Romans felt was one of the most important attributes of a general. In his campaigns he made mistakes, and took big risks, but in the end he always won. For the Romans that was all that mattered.

Early career

Caesar was born into a Republic riven by increasingly violent political rivalries. While he was in his teens, the first civil war erupted and saw Rome itself stormed three times by Roman armies. The young Caesar played no active part in this brutal conflict, but in its aftermath he angered Sulla the dictator and spent some months as a hunted fugitive. His mother and her influential relatives managed to secure him a pardon, and he was sent as a junior officer to the Roman province of Asia (80–78 BC). Here he quickly demonstrated his courage, being awarded Rome's highest decoration, the civic crown (*corona civica*) at the siege of Mytiline. However, a diplomatic mission to the court of the allied King Nicomedes of Bithynia led to scandal, when Caesar was rumoured to have become the old king's lover. Despite always denying the story, the gossip was to dog him for the rest of his life.

Caesar returned to Rome in 78 BC. By this time the Roman army was effectively a professional force, but led by aristocratic officers who interspersed periods of military service with civil and political posts. Caesar, too, embarked on this course, and for the next twenty years his career was a broadly conventional one for a young senator. He also spent some time studying rhetoric and

Julius Caesar's campaigns were predominantly fought in the last fifteen years of his life, at the start of which he was already in his forties. Up until this point his career had been flamboyant, but still essentially conventional. This bust shows his lined face and hints at his receding hairline.

This relief from the sarcophagus of Domitius Ahenobarbus, *c.* 100 BC, is one of the best depictions of the uniform worn by the Roman army in the first century BC. The legionaries wear mail armour, high bronze helmets topped with horsehair plumes, and carry oval shields.

oratory with famous lecturers in the Greek east. On one of these trips he was captured by pirates and held for ransom. Caesar charmed his captors, but promised that after his release he would return and have them all crucified. When the ransom arrived he did just that. With no authority to do so, he raised a force of ships and men from allied cities and swooped down to capture his former captors. The pirates were duly crucified, although as a gesture of mercy he had their throats cut first. In 74 BC he was on another study trip when a raiding force sent by King Mithridates of Pontus attacked the Roman province of Asia. Caesar rushed east, organized an army from the local allied cities and chased the enemy out of the province. Again he had no authority to do this, but his actions were widely praised, demonstrating both his skill and his immense self-confidence.

Caesar was building an impressive reputation which helped him climb the political ladder at Rome (at the same time gaining a less reputable name as a serial seducer of other men's wives). In either 72 or 71 BC he was elected to the post of military tribune – effectively a staff officer – and seems to have served against Spartacus and his army of rebellious slaves. It was another decade before he won a significant military post, when he was made governor of the province of Further Spain in 61 BC. He was massively in debt, having spent far beyond his means to win fame and popularity, and needed a successful and profitable campaign in Spain to restore his reputation and keep his creditors at bay. The province was garrisoned by two legions, but he quickly raised the equivalent of another and led the army on a series of aggressive operations against the border tribes.

Caesar won his victory and was awarded a triumph – a formal parade through the heart of the city of Rome – when he returned at the end of 60 BC. However, his political opponents made sure that this honour would prevent him from standing for election for the consulship, Rome's most senior magistracy. In consequence, Caesar gave up his triumph, was elected to the consulship and formed a secret alliance with Pompey and Crassus, the two most powerful men in Rome. Together the three

Julius Caesar

dominated politics for a year. Caesar's reward was a five-year command of the Gallic provinces and Illyricum. This was later extended to ten years. Still facing staggering debts, Caesar desperately needed to win victories on a vast scale.

Intervention in Gaul

Caesar may well have originally planned to fight a campaign in the Balkans, advancing from Illyricum to attack the Dacian kingdom. Instead an opportunity presented itself when the Helvetii, migrating from their homeland in what is now Switzerland, sought permission to pass through Transalpine Gaul (modern Provence). Caesar refused, fortified the line of the River Rhône, and repulsed all attempts to cross it by force. When the Helvetii turned away, Caesar answered an appeal for protection from the Aedui, a Gaulish tribe allied to Rome, and pursued them. An attempt at a night attack failed because of poor scouting, but soon afterwards Caesar managed to surprise one isolated convoy of the migrants and cut them to pieces. When his allies failed to supply him with sufficient grain, Caesar withdrew towards the Aedui's capital at Bibracte. The Helvetii took this as a sign of weakness and massed their army to attack him. But they were beaten back, suffering massive losses, the survivors being sent back to their homeland.

Later in 58 BC, Caesar turned on the Germanic war-leader Ariovistus, again claiming that he was responding to an appeal for help from Rome's allies. There was nearly a mutiny when the Roman army heard rumours of the ferocity of the German warriors. Caesar announced that he would press on, even if only the Tenth Legion accompanied him. The Tenth were flattered, and the rest shamed into following. In a brief campaign Ariovistus was brought to battle and utterly defeated. In 57 BC, Caesar answered another appeal for help and turned northeast to confront the warlike Belgian tribes. A stand-off between the two armies was broken when the tribal army ran out of food and had to disperse. Caesar began attacking the tribes individually, but they managed to re-form their army and surprised him with a large-scale ambush

Julius Caesar

beside the River Sambre. In a desperate and confused battle, Caesar rushed to his right wing and, in his own words:

> He ... took a shield from a man in the rear ranks – he had come without his own – advanced into the front line and called on the centurions by name, encouraged the soldiers, and ordered the line to advance and the units to extend, so that they could employ their swords more easily.

In the end the day was saved – but only when troops from his victorious left wing were sent back into the fray by one of his subordinate commanders.

In 56 BC, Caesar's operations were smaller scale – for much of the year he was preoccupied with political matters – although he did smash the navy of the Veneti, a tribe living on the Atlantic coast and famous for their seamanship, having constructed a fleet in order to do so. In 55 BC, an attempt by some German tribes to migrate into Gaul provoked a ferocious response, and all were massacred. Caesar followed up this success by crossing the Rhine, the legionaries building a bridge in just ten days, then led his men over the river and devastated the nearest fields before returning to the west bank. The bridge was then demolished. It was a vivid demonstration to the Germans, to show how easy it was for Caesar to reach them in their homeland.

Late in the year, Caesar took two legions across the Channel to Britain. The Romans landed and established a base, but soon afterwards most of their transport ships were wrecked in a storm, and Caesar was barely able to repair enough to get back to Gaul. In 54 BC, he returned to Britain with a much larger force, driving north and crossing the Thames. The Britons harassed him, but were persuaded to come to terms by his attacks on their main towns. However, once again the Romans lost many beached ships to a violent storm and were only just able to escape. Militarily neither expedition to Britain achieved much, while both came close to disaster. Politically, however, they were staggering successes, capturing the imagination of the Roman people.

A Gallic iron helmet – known today as the Agen type – found at Alesia. The Romans copied this pattern as well as other types of Gallic equipment, including mail armour and probably horse harness and saddle.

Rebellions

In the winter following his second British expedition, Caesar was faced with the first of a series of rebellions. One and a half legions were massacred by rebellious Belgian tribes, and another garrison besieged. Caesar led two under-strength legions and some cavalry – in total fewer than seven thousand men – to break the siege. In 53 BC, he led a series of punitive expeditions, ravaging the lands of the tribes responsible until all submitted.

In the winter of 53–52 BC, an even wider and more serious rebellion erupted throughout Gaul. The rebels were led by Vercingetorix, a talented young chieftain who was able to impose much tighter discipline on the tribes than they had displayed in the past. Caesar was initially wrong-footed, but responded with characteristic aggression by launching counter-attacks against tribes who joined the rebels. Vercingetorix planned to deprive the Romans of supplies and starve them into submission rather than risk a battle. He therefore withdrew in the face of Caesar's advance, harassed his foraging parties, and ruthlessly burnt the towns and grain stores in the Romans' path.

The townsfolk of Avaricum pleaded to be allowed to defend their strongly fortified home, yet it was stormed by Caesar after a siege lasting just four weeks. As a terrible warning to others, the town was sacked and its people massacred. Caesar then pursued Vercingetorix to the town of Gergovia. A plan to launch a limited attack on the Gauls' camp went wrong when his eager soldiers pursued too far and began to assault the town itself. They were then swept out and suffered heavy losses when the bulk of the Gaulish army came up. Caesar withdrew and the Gauls rather over-

'Caesar was known through the colour of his cloak, which he always wore in battle as a distinguishing mark ... His arrival brought hope to the soldiers and refreshed their spirits.'

CAESAR, *COMMENTARIES*

Julius Caesar

confidently chased him. An attack by the Gaulish cavalry on the Roman column was repulsed, prompting an immediate reversal as the Gauls retreated. Caesar followed.

The Gauls camped outside the hilltop town of Alesia and sent messengers to all the tribes to muster a great army to come to their rescue. Caesar surrounded the hill with 11 miles of fortifications – a line of circumvallation. He then built a second, even longer line facing outwards – a line of contravallation. A massive Gaulish army eventually arrived. As it attacked from the outside, Vercingetorix led his own men in repeated attempts to break out. Eventually there was a final day of desperate fighting around a fort sited at the weakest spot in the Roman lines. Caesar fed in reserves, and then led in his last troops to break the Gaulish attack. Vercingetorix surrendered the next day. The rebellion was not fully suppressed for another year, but the Romans systematically defeated the few recalcitrant tribes. Intensive diplomacy accompanied the military operations, for Caesar was always aware that this was the only way to create a lasting peace.

Civil War

By 49 BC, Caesar's former ally Pompey had become much closer to his opponents. Determined to prevent him from returning to public life and enjoying the fame and wealth of his Gallic victories, they backed Caesar into a corner. Rather than see the end of his public career, Caesar was willing to fight a civil war. In January 49 BC, he crossed the River Rubicon and in a matter of weeks overran Italy. He then went to Spain, forcing the Pompeian army to surrender at Ilerda. At the end of the year he crossed to Macedonia to confront Pompey himself. An attempt to capture the enemy supply base at Dyrrachium ended in failure after weeks of effort. Caesar retreated, but accepted battle at Pharsalus in 48 BC and routed the enemy army.

Pompey fled to Egypt, but was murdered by the boy king, Ptolemy XIII. Caesar arrived shortly afterwards and soon became involved in the civil war between the king and his older sister and wife Cleopatra VII. Famously smuggled into Caesar's presence – actually in a laundry bag rather than a carpet – she quickly became his lover. Unsurprisingly Ptolemy could not match her negotiating power and Caesar eventually defeated and killed him. He then spent months cruising the Nile with Cleopatra, and it was not until late in 47 BC that he again stirred himself, going to Asia to defeat King Pharnaces at Zela. It was in celebration of this rapid campaign that he coined the expression *veni, vidi, vici* – I came, I saw, I conquered.

Given time to regroup during this lull, Caesar's Roman enemies had massed a new army in Africa. He crossed there and, after an initial near reverse at Ruspina, crushed the Pompeians at Thapsus in 46 BC. The final campaign of the Civil War took place in Spain, and was concluded by the victory at Munda in 45 BC. Caesar returned to Rome and made himself dictator for life. He planned a major expedition, first to Dacia and then to Parthia (equivalent to modern Iraq and part of Iran). However, although he had won the war, he failed to make a success of the peace. On 15 March 44 BC he was assassinated by a group of senators.

A coin showing Caesar as dictator and wearing the laurel wreath of a general celebrating his triumph. Gossips said that he was delighted to be granted the honour of wearing this symbol, since it helped to conceal his growing baldness.

Julius Caesar

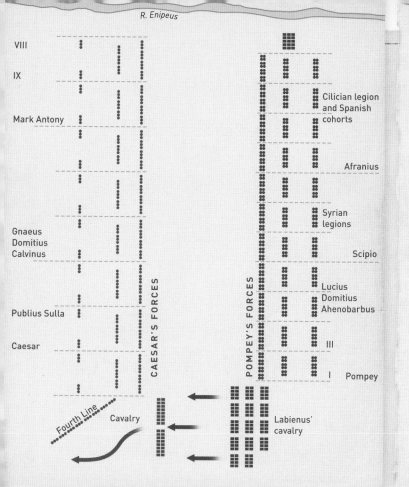

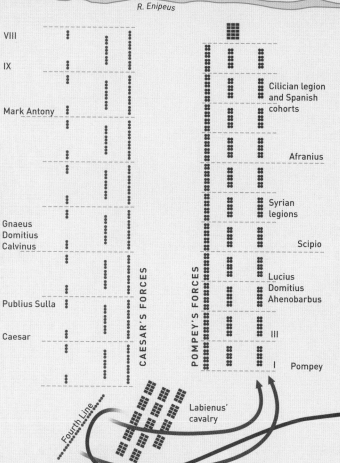

BATTLE OF
PHARSALUS

DEFEATED AT DYRRACHIUM, Caesar withdrew from the coast into Thessaly, where he was cut off from any supplies or reinforcements from Italy. Pompey pursued him and finally, on 9 August 48 BC, under strong pressure from the senior senators with his army, offered battle outside Pharsalus. Caesar's army mustered 22,000 infantry and just 1,000 cavalry. They were veterans, but were heavily outnumbered by the enemy's 45,000 infantry and 7,000 cavalry.

Pompey's cavalry was the greatest threat. The battle-field was an open plain, but Caesar was able to secure his left flank on the River Enipeus. His right flank was exposed and Pompey concentrated 6,500 horsemen on his own left: his plan was simple – overwhelm the thousand or so Caesarean cavalry, then swing round to roll up Caesar's infantry. All Pompey's less experienced infantry had to do was defend their position until this occurred.

As usual, Caesar's legions were in three lines of cohorts (the *triplex acies*). As the enemy formed up, he took one cohort from the third line of each of his legions and stationed them behind his own horsemen as an extra fourth line. These were masked by his own horsemen and so invisible to the enemy. The battle opened with Caesar's legions advancing, expecting the enemy infantry to come

forward to meet them. In a remarkable display of discipline, Caesar's veterans halted when they saw that the enemy were not moving. They re-formed, before resuming the advance and charging into contact.

Meanwhile, Pompey's cavalry had charged forward and driven back Caesar's cavalry on the right wing. In the process the massed Pompeian squadrons lost much of their order and merged into one. Although well mounted and confident, these horsemen were inexperienced and not well disciplined. When the cohorts of the fourth line came through the clouds of dust and attacked them, the Pompeian cavalry stampeded to the rear. Caesar's fourth line now swung round against the left flank of the Pompeian infantry. Under pressure from the front and the flank, these began to give ground, then collapsed into rout.

Losses were always disproportionately heavy for the side that fled in an ancient battle. Pompey's army was virtually destroyed, losing at least 6,000 dead – Caesar himself claimed that 15,000 were killed – and 24,000 taken prisoner. The Caesarean army lost just 200 men, in addition to no fewer than 30 centurions, officers who led from the front and so tended to suffer very high casualties. It was a remarkable victory.

> 'Remember only the greed, the cruelty and the arrogance of the Romans. Is anything left for us but to retain our freedom or to die before we are enslaved?' ARMINIUS, QUOTED BY TACITUS, *ANNALS*, 2.15

ARMINIUS
ADRIAN MURDOCH
c. 18 BC – AD 21

THE BATTLE OF TEUTOBURG FOREST was the greatest military setback that the Roman Empire was ever to suffer. 'The heaviest defeat the Romans had endured on foreign soil', wrote a contemporary Roman historian of the battle in September AD 9 that saw Germanic warriors wipe out three legions, three cavalry battalions and six auxiliary units under the command of Publius Quinctilius Varus. Arminius, commander of a loose coalition of Germanic tribes, achieved what no other opponent of Rome ever managed. The Carthaginian Hannibal, the Gaulish leader Vercingetorix or Boudica, queen of the Iceni, to name just three who dared challenge Rome, were all eventually punished and their territories absorbed into the Roman world. But Arminius stopped the Roman Empire in its tracks and halted any imperial pretensions east of the Rhine.

The emperor Augustus' plaintive and heartrending cry of 'Quinctilius Varus, give me back my legions!' as he paced his palace on the Palatine Hill in Rome is well known, but so serious was the loss of Legions XVII, XVIII and XIX that the few survivors of the battle were banned from ever setting foot in Italy, the legions themselves were never replaced, and the Rhine became a barrier between civilization and barbarism that was never willingly crossed even in late antiquity.

Little wonder that Arminius himself soon turned into a mythologized figure of German might. He became, in turn, the personification for German resistance to Catholic Italy, a symbol of the struggle against France in the nineteenth century, one of the voices of German nationalism and ultimately Nazism. A massive statue of Arminius, the 174-feet-tall Hermannsdenkmal near Detmold, remains one of the more popular tourist attractions in Germany. He is as popular today as he ever was, thanks to the discovery in 1987 of the battlefield itself, near the town of Kalkriese in Lower Saxony, by an amateur British archaeologist – a find justifiably trumpeted in one German newspaper as 'a second Troy'.

First contact with Rome

Arminius is a difficult man to characterize. Everything we know about him comes from inevitably hostile Roman authors, most of them writing a hundred years or more after the events took place. As a result, virtually every fact given here is open to debate.

To give just one example, it is not known for certain what Arminius was actually called, though most accept that what has come down to us is a Latinization of either a familial name or an honorific. *Erman* or *ermen* is an old Germanic word meaning roughly 'the eminent' – not implausible for a boy born into the ruling elite. Nor is it certain what he was called by the Romans. There was a convention that auxiliaries of the period took on the name Julius, so it is plausible that he was called Gaius Julius Arminius, but there is no universal agreement about the spelling of his name in the manuscripts either. Sometimes he is Arminius, sometimes Armenus.

The son of an aristocrat called Segimerus, Arminius was born in roughly 18 BC, around the time that the Romans started giving serious consideration to a conquest of Germany. His tribe, the Cherusci, dominated the area that roughly corresponds to the southern part of the modern state of Lower Saxony, between the River Elbe to the east and the River Weser to the west. Archaeological research in what was Cheruscan territory remains in its infancy. Because of the nationalist associations that tainted Arminius from the nineteenth century up to the Second World War, little work was carried out on native settlements in Lower Saxony post-war until recently. But archaeological research since the mid 1990s has painted a picture of a predominantly agrarian countryside dotted with isolated farmsteads or clusters of farms.

Apart from an occasional passing mention, the Cherusci do not enter recorded history until the turn of the millennium, when Arminius was in his late teens. For the next three years, the tribe was a participant in, though not an instigator of, a serious revolution (one Roman historian calls it 'a vast war') that gripped Germany. Following restoration of peace in AD 4, the tribe seems to have been an ally of Rome until AD 9.

In the service of Rome

From the time of Julius Caesar onwards, Celtic tribes provided the Roman army with auxiliary soldiers to serve as lightly armed infantry or cavalry. There is no doubt that the supply of troops was a condition of the peace treaty that the future emperor Tiberius signed with the Cherusci in AD 4.

It is certain that in his early twenties Arminius was an officer in the Roman army, seeing action somewhere in the northern Balkans during what are known as the Pannonian uprisings,

The Hermannsdenkmal: Ernst von Bandel's monument to Arminius on the Grotenburg near Detmold was completed in 1875 in the afterglow of Prussia's victory over France in the Franco-Prussian War. Standing 175 feet tall, it is one of Germany's most popular tourist attractions.

Arminius

M·CAELIVS
M·L·
RIVATVS

M·CAELIVS
M·L·
THIAMINVS

M·CAELIO·T·F·LEM·BON
O·LEG·XIIX·ANN·LIII
CIDIT·BELLO·VARIANO·OSSA
IFERRE·LICEBIT·P·CAELIVS·T·F

the revolts that shook the empire after AD 6. The Roman historian Tacitus writes that Arminius 'served … as commander of his fellow-countrymen', the senior officer of an auxiliary corps. He clearly distinguished himself. Arminius' service record was significant enough for him to have earned not just coveted Roman citizenship but promotion to equestrian status, the admired middle class.

No sense of his own feelings towards Rome emerge, but this period of Arminius' life certainly provided the military groundwork for what was to come. Above all, it allowed him to know his enemy. At its most basic level he became fluent in Latin. Much more importantly, Arminius learned how the Roman army worked and saw its tactical innovations in action. It is easy to forget that for the Cherusci, the majority of warfare of the period involved tribesmen fighting tribesmen – conflicts which have left no mark on history. Arminius' strength as a tactician and strategist was to find ways of using the very different Germanic mode of warfare to beat the technologically advanced Romans.

Home again

In around AD 7, Arminius left Roman service to return to his homeland. Rome may even have interfered to encourage Arminius' return to act as some kind of standard-bearer for Roman civilization. The new governor of Germany, Publius Quinctilius Varus, was attempting to speed up the Romanization of the province, and he wanted as many pro-Roman allies and senior Germanic voices around him as possible. It was one of the great failings of Roman imperialism that it never considered the possibility that someone who had once tasted the fruits of its civilization might ever reject it.

Arminius may have had some cachet because of his Roman experience but he was not universally welcomed. It took him, after all, two years to establish his position and engineer the attack on the Romans. At the time of his return there were at least three factions, or perhaps more accurately two other nobles, vying for influence in Cheruscan politics. All three had significant followers and were related to each other either by blood or by marriage.

Arminius came to represent the anti-Roman point of view. His uncle Inguiomerus was undecided. And Segestes remained consistently pro-Rome throughout. His influence and support throughout the period is a reminder that Arminius was not leading a universally popular rebellion. The relationship between Arminius and Segestes is given an additional twist after the Battle of Teutoburg Forest, when Segestes' daughter Thusnelda eloped with Arminius while betrothed to another man.

NORTHWEST GERMANY in the first century AD.

THE BATTLE OF TEUTOBURG FOREST

Arminius' skill as a commander was to make the Romans fight inefficiently. The Battle of Teutoburg Forest in September AD 9 remains a master lesson in how to neutralize the technological advantages of a superior war machine.

Arminius planned to ambush the Roman army and its retinue in what is now Lower Saxony, when it was marching west through what it believed to be friendly territory. He sprung the trap with calculated finesse. The Cheruscan leader had arranged an uprising to draw out the Roman army. News of the revolt was significant enough for Varus to lead the army in person, but not so important as to awaken suspicion.

The challenge for Arminius was how best to counteract the might of the Roman legions. Both sides were fairly evenly matched numerically. Arminius could count on approximately fifteen thousand men while the Roman commander Varus was leading a force that was around fourteen thousand strong. In a pitched battle, however, the lightly armed German forces were no match for heavily armed legionaries protected by a new, light and flexible segmented armour called *lorica segmenta*. What Arminius did was to play to the strengths of the Germanic warriors.

The first attack happened east of Kalkriese, at the end of a day when the Roman soldiers were tired. The initial targets for Arminius' men were the Roman cavalry – a strike that immobilized and demoralized the Romans, quite apart from causing them huge logistical problems.

The weather helped. Persistent storms waterlogged the Roman legionaries, while the unarmoured, spear-carrying Germanic warriors carried on their guerrilla attacks unencumbered.

The next morning, Varus led the three legions towards a narrow pass called the Kalkrieser-Niewedder Senke, where the main west–east routes from the mid Weser to the lower Rhine converged. It was the perfect spot for an ambush, a narrow corridor, some 4 miles long, but because of the high water-table at the time, only 200 yards wide. It was bounded by the Kalkriese Berg to the south and the Great Moor to the north. The analogy of a lobster pot has been used to describe the pass – the Romans could get in, but not out.

Archaeological evidence has revealed that the spot for the ambush had been well planned, with arc-shaped turf walls and sand ramparts built along the side of the hill. These preserved the element of surprise for the Germans and also narrowed the path, so that the Romans had no chance to form their impregnable legionary lines that had seen off so many enemies.

Trapped, and with no means of escape, the remainder of Varus' army was soon massacred. Varus committed what the Roman historian Cassius Dio calls the 'terrible yet unavoidable act' and killed himself. Arminius had won.

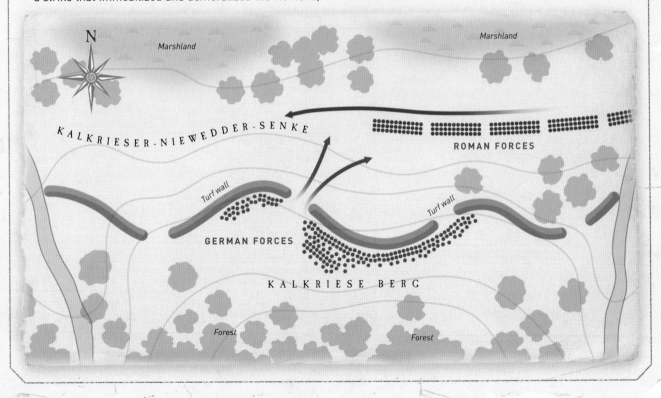

Arminius

The revolt

What tipped the young Cheruscan commander into revolution? The Greek historian Cassius Dio gives two reasons: first, the Germans were given orders 'as if they were actual slaves of the Romans'; and second, that 'Varus demanded money as he would from subject nations'.

The first was an unpalatable loss of freedom. A change from being an ally of Rome to a conquered nation meant that Cheruscan troops, for example, would now be subject to Roman discipline, pay and conditions. But the second reason was conclusive. All the costs of Romanization were borne by the province itself. The bill for roadworks, for buildings and for towns, landed on the desks of local worthies. Resentment was fuelled by the continuous presence of the Roman army in their territory. There were, of course, some economic benefits – for local businesses that supplied the camps with food, goods or amatory services – but for the most part they were loathed. It is also safe to assume that the Roman soldiers were not at their most sensitive towards natives in the young province after years of warfare.

By September AD 9, disaffection and resentment had spilled over into active revolt, and Arminius, the 27-year-old Roman officer, mutinied against his commanders, keeping his plans secret by pretending to be loyal until the trap was sprung.

After the tactically brilliant and definitive ambush at Teutoburg, virtually all the Germanic tribes joined Arminius' call. Every Roman settlement east of the Rhine was overrun. Even nascent towns such as Waldgirmes, an assimilated civilian settlement in the Lahn Valley discovered in 1993, were either abandoned or destroyed. The Germans wanted to erase any trace of the hated invaders. Only one Roman stronghold, the camp of Aliso (usually equated with the camp at Haltern) made any attempt to hold out, but that, too, was assaulted and then burned to the ground in the autumn. Little wonder that the German historian Theodor Mommsen described Arminius' campaign as the turning point in Germany's national destiny.

But for all Arminius' skill as a tactician, his great flaw as a commander was his lack of a sense of strategy. What was he trying to achieve? He cannot be spoken of as a liberator of Germany; that is too Roman a perspective. It is too much even to suggest that he was trying to unite Germany east of the Rhine. He appears to have had no imperial ambitions at this time. His aim, quite simply, was to stop the Romans from setting up a province between the Rhine and the Elbe.

After Teutoburg

Rome's reaction to this military debacle was massive mobilization. The Rhine armies were boosted from five to eight legions under the command of Tiberius throughout AD 10 and 11. A new chapter began in AD 13 with the appointment of Germanicus,

Roman weapons found at Kalkriese, in Lower Saxony, where the Battle of Teutoburg Forest was fought in AD 9. The site has yielded only one example of the head of a *pilum*, or heavy javelin (above, centre). Its 6½-inch tip was designed to bend on impact so that it could not be re-used against the Romans. The other missiles (top and bottom) are the heads of lances, the weapons of auxiliary soldiers and cavalry.

Tiberius' nephew and heir to the throne, as governor and commander-in-chief. His commission was to consolidate his uncle's work, to repair the damage caused by Varus and to pursue and punish Arminius. In all three he proved to be an abject failure.

Germanicus' lack of success, however, was not really down to Arminius so much as his own incompetence. In the years immediately after Teutoburg, the Cheruscan leader was strangely passive. He did not, for example, capitalize on the revolt among the Rhine legions, caused by news of the death of Augustus on 19 August AD 14. Instead, Arminius seems to have been preoccupied with internal politics, a power struggle that resulted in the imprisonment of Segestes.

For most of AD 15, the initiative remained with Germanicus. He embarked on a series of retaliatory campaigns against Arminius' allies, recaptured two of the three legionary standards that had been lost at Teutoburg, and buried the Roman dead on the battlefield. It took the Roman liberation of Segestes and the capture of Arminius' pregnant wife Thusnelda to shake Arminius from his torpor and to unify the Cherusci again.

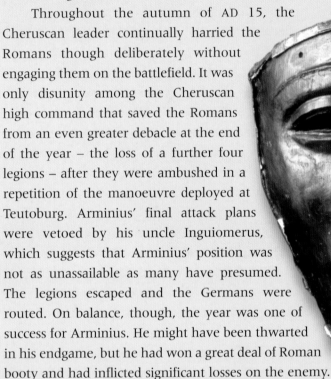

The Kalkriese mask: Found in the winter of 1989, the 6½-inch-tall iron cavalry mask of an auxiliary soldier is one of the best-known finds from Kalkriese and the oldest such mask ever found. Originally covered in silver leaf, it is the frontispiece of a face helmet that probably belonged to a senior Gallic or Thracian cavalry troop commander.

Throughout the autumn of AD 15, the Cheruscan leader continually harried the Romans though deliberately without engaging them on the battlefield. It was only disunity among the Cheruscan high command that saved the Romans from an even greater debacle at the end of the year – the loss of a further four legions – after they were ambushed in a repetition of the manoeuvre deployed at Teutoburg. Arminius' final attack plans were vetoed by his uncle Inguiomerus, which suggests that Arminius' position was not as unassailable as many have presumed. The legions escaped and the Germans were routed. On balance, though, the year was one of success for Arminius. He might have been thwarted in his endgame, but he had won a great deal of Roman booty and had inflicted significant losses on the enemy.

The Battle of Idistaviso

With Roman patience and money running out, it was clear that AD 16 would be decisive. Arminius was forced to confront for the final time what he called the 'cowardly runaways from Varus' army' at the Battle of Idistaviso, an unidentified site along the River Weser, possibly somewhere near Minden.

That it came to pitched battle is curious. Up to that point, what had made Arminius outstanding as a commander was his ability to minimize Roman military supremacy. It is tempting to suggest that Arminius found himself overruled at Idistaviso by his fellow commanders, as he had been the previous summer. Whether because of this or through overconfidence, Arminius' battle formation showed how much he had developed as a military thinker. Despite the fact that this was his first set battle, his deployment was professional and notably Roman in style. He and the Cherusci kept to the higher ground with other tribes to the fore, the River Weser to his left and forest to the right to keep the Roman attack front narrow.

None the less it was a disaster. Arminius was injured in the first moments of the battle and the Germanic tribes were routed. A subsequent engagement resulted in further German losses. Yet on that inconclusive note, Roman involvement on the eastern side of the Rhine ended. Germanicus' plea for one more campaign fell on deaf ears (Emperor Tiberius had a campaign in Armenia to fund) and he was recalled to Rome.

The final years

His defeat at the Battle of Idistaviso marked the beginning of the end of Arminius' power. Despite the recall of Germanicus, Cheruscan warriors began to move east, away from any future Roman threat. This migration brought the settlers up against the Bohemian king Maroboduus. By AD 17, war had broken out between the two commanders. Arminius was hailed as victor and an isolated Maroboduus had to appeal to Tiberius for sanctuary.

For Arminius this should have been the greatest moment of his life, the consolidation of his power. He had won. The Romans had been pushed back to the other side of the Rhine and his greatest rival was gone. But his victory and subsequent attempt to unite the tribes proved to be his undoing. He was 'aiming for royalty', writes Tacitus. As soon as Arminius began to demand authority for its own sake, he lost his power; he had become simply another oppressor.

An attempt by a disgruntled Germanic chief to get the Romans to sponsor an assassination attempt on Arminius was rejected by Emperor Tiberius. But

> 'Arminius ... defied Rome, not in her early rise, as other kings and generals, but at the height of her empire's glory.'
> TACITUS, *ANNALS*, 2.88

it was an indication of how unpopular he had become. Arminius was faced with a civil war and was soon murdered by a member of his family under somewhat murky circumstances. We do not know who killed him or how he died, though it is a tidy coincidence of history that he and Germanicus died in the same year.

His obituary at the end of the second book of Tacitus' *Annals* is one of the most extraordinary pieces of Latin prose to come down to us. In a few sentences, the historian manages to capture, with incredible pathos, both the admiration and revulsion the Romans had for their most successful opponent.

Make no mistake, Arminius was the liberator of Germany, one too who defied Rome, not in her early rise, as other kings and generals, but in the height of her empire's glory. The battles he fought were indeed indecisive, yet he remained unconquered in war. He lived for thirty-seven years, twelve of them in power, and he is still the subject of song among barbarous nations, though to Greek historians, who admire only their own achievements, he is unknown, and to Romans not as famous as he should be, while we extol the past and are indifferent to our own times.

TRAJAN

ADRIAN GOLDSWORTHY

AD 56–117

TRAJAN WAS PERHAPS THE GREATEST, and certainly the most famous, of Rome's soldier emperors. He was the last great Roman conqueror, and during his reign the empire expanded to its greatest geographical extent. After the period of expansion under Trajan, the Roman Empire switched to a more defensive posture. Trajan's successor Hadrian is famous for building Hadrian's Wall in northern Britain, as well as other frontier defence systems.

(Opposite) **A statue of Marcus Ulpius Traianus,** commonly known as Trajan. The conquest of Dacia was a high point of his reign as emperor, but his eastern campaigns – fought over a wider area and probably on an even bigger scale – were to prove much less successful.

Trajan's most important and lasting conquest was the occupation of Dacia, a powerful and wealthy kingdom in what is now Romania, which had inflicted a number of humiliating defeats on the Romans in the last decades of the first century AD. Later in his reign he embarked upon a massive offensive in the east, aimed probably at the complete conquest of Parthia. Some gains were made and a new province created in Mesopotamia, but widespread rebellions in other recently occupied territories erupted within a few years. In addition there was a major revolt by Jewish communities within the Roman Empire. Many of the new gains were abandoned before Trajan died, and Mesopotamia was later given up by Hadrian. On several occasions over the next two hundred years, the Romans managed to regain some of the lost territories, these often being a source of friction between the empire and its Parthian, later Persian, neighbours.

The Romans remembered Trajan as one of the best emperors they had ever had, setting him alongside Augustus. Although his martial achievements contributed a good deal to this, it was also due to his reputation for justice, generosity and good administration. He was one of the emperors who made the second century AD, according to Edward Gibbon, '... the period in the history of the world, during which the condition of the human race was most happy and prosperous.' We know more about his wider achievements and the broad trend of his campaigns than we do about the details of his command style. As far as we can tell, he led in the conventional way for a Roman general. Like Julius Caesar, Trajan wrote *Commentaries* describing his campaigns, but only a single sentence of these has survived. However, we do have some literary accounts, as well as evidence from archaeology and the reliefs depicting his Dacian Wars on Trajan's Column, which still stands in Rome today.

Trajan's rise to power

Trajan's family lived in Italica in Spain and boasted that they were descended from the veteran soldiers settled in the colony there by Scipio Africanus at the end of the Second Punic War. The family were part of the local aristocracy, and in time began to enter imperial service and enjoy distinguished careers. Trajan's father was a senator – we do not know if he was the first in his family – and commanded the Tenth Legion Fretensis during the suppression of the Jewish rebellion against Nero in AD 67–70. This army was led by Vespasian, who emerged as the victor from the civil war that followed Nero's suicide in AD 68. As emperor, Vespasian granted Trajan's father the post of legate (governor and army commander) in Cappadocia and later the even more prestigious province of Syria. During this time he success- fully dealt with a border dispute with the Parthians.

Trajan's own early career was typical for a man of his social class. In his late teens he became a senior tribune (*tribunus laticlavius*) in one of the legions commanded by his father. Tribunes were essentially staff officers. For some men it was merely a necessary step in a political career and they spent as little time with the army as possible, and certainly no more than a year. Others, like Trajan, were far more enthusi- astic and chose to extend their service. In his case he took a posting to a legion on the Rhine frontier. It was not uncommon for men to serve as tribunes for three years. Trajan was supposed to have held this rank for a decade, although this may well be an exaggeration. He certainly took soldiering seriously and used his time to learn as much as possible. A speech in his honour later claimed that: 'Through ten years' service you learnt the customs of peoples, the localities of countries, the

A relief from a monument at Adamklissi, a former Roman settlement in what is now Romania, commemorating the Roman defeat of the Dacians. The details on this monument, which was made by and for the Roman army on the Danube, are rougher, but more realistic than the idealized images on Trajan's Column (see opposite).

opportunities of topography, and you accustomed yourself to cross all kinds of river and endure all kinds of weather ...'

A keen horseman – like many aristocrats from Spain, he was addicted to hunting – it was said that he became an expert in all military drills and weapons handling, although again this was a fairly conventional compliment. It is unclear how much fighting was involved in his father's border dispute with the Parthians or whether the son was directly involved. Trajan certainly saw active service on the Rhine, and from the beginning displayed unusual skill.

He was an enthusiastic and serious- minded soldier, but no Roman aristocrat was ever a professional military man. Like anyone else pursuing a senatorial career, he held a series of civil posts. His next spell with the army did not come until he was 32, when he was posted as legionary legate to command the Seventh Legion Gemina at the city of Legion (modern León) in Spain. It was a peaceful province with little prospect of active

campaigning, but in AD 89 he and his legion were sent to deal with the rebellion of a governor on the Rhine against the unpopular emperor Domitian, second son of Vespasian. The revolt sputtered out before Trajan arrived, but he remained on the Rhine for some time and led a successful punitive expedition against the German tribes on its eastern bank.

In the next decade Trajan was made provincial legate, commanding first one of the German provinces, and then Pannonia on the Danubian frontier. In Pannonia he fought and defeated part of the Sueves, a large Germanic people divided into many sub-tribes and famous for wearing their hair in a topknot. When Domitian was murdered in a palace conspiracy in AD 96, the 40-year-old Trajan had a good reputation for his character and military skill. The Senate appointed one of its elderly members, the childless Nerva, to become emperor. Insecure – he faced strong pressure from the praetorian guard to execute the conspirators who had killed Domitian –

Nerva adopted Trajan as his son and heir. It was a popular choice. More importantly, Trajan was at the head of an army that could be expected to back his claim.

Wars with Dacia

Nerva died in AD 98 after a reign lasting less than two years. Trajan's succession was generally popular, but he may have realized that some great achievement would help to strengthen his position. Under Domitian the Dacian king Decebalus had raided across the Danube into the Roman provinces, on one occasion defeating and killing a provincial legate. Roman expeditions to exact punishment for these attacks had enjoyed mixed fortune. One column commanded by the praetorian prefect Cornelius Fuscus was virtually annihilated by the Dacians in AD 86. In the end, Domitian concluded a peace treaty in which he agreed to pay Decebalus an annual subsidy, as well as supplying him with military engineers to supervise the building of fortifications, and artillery. The emperor claimed victory, but this was widely seen as a major humiliation and contributed further to Domitian's unpopularity.

The heartland of Dacia lay in Transylvania, and many of Decebalus' strongholds, including his capital at Sarmizegethusa Regia, lay in the Carpathian mountains. Dacia was rich in gold and other mineral deposits, and had contact with old Greek colonies in the Black Sea. Its many fortified towns and outposts reveal an ingenious blend of indigenous, Hellenistic and Roman building techniques. Decebalus was a very strong king, and no Dacian leader had had as much power since the middle of the first century BC. His victories over Domitian strengthened his position. He not only controlled the Dacians, but also drew allies from neighbouring peoples, including the fierce Germanic Bastarnae and the Sarmatians, who were famous for their heavy cataphract cavalry. Encouragement was also given to Roman troops to desert and take service with the king.

Trajan seems to have resolved on a war with Dacia from very early on in his reign. Troops from all over the empire were massed along the Danube and in AD 101 the Romans invaded. Nine out of the thirty legions then in existence were represented, even if some were only present as detachments. There were also substantial forces of regular auxiliaries, along with irregular units of Germanic and British warriors, as well as Numidian light cavalry. Trajan supervised the operations in person. At first there seems to have been little fighting, the Dacians withdrawing in the face of this onslaught and abandoning some of their forts. The Romans pushed forward to secure the Iron Gates pass in the Carpathians.

The first major battle seems to have been fought at Tapae, where a strong Dacian force tried to block the Roman advance. There was heavy fighting – the Dacian two-handed curved sword known as a *falx* made a strong impression on Roman observers – before the Romans were victorious. Trajan's Column in Rome shows the emperor overseeing this engagement and others. It was not his job to fight hand to hand, but to supervise from close behind the fighting line, committing reserves and encouraging the troops. It was important for Roman soldiers to feel that they were closely observed, and conspicuous bravery

Trajan's Column was commissioned by Trajan and completed by his successor Hadrian to celebrate the Roman victory in the Dacian Wars. Decorated with spiral bas-reliefs telling the story of the campaigns to defeat the Dacian king Decebalus in AD 101–102 and 105–106, Trajan's Column offers the most detailed surviving images of a Roman army on campaign.

Dacian noblemen (below left), recognizable by their distinctive caps, plan the war against Rome from inside one of the many hilltop fortresses dotting their country. (Right) Roman auxiliary cavalry hasten to the scene of the action. Both of these images, and that on p. 185, are from Trajan's Column.

would be rewarded as readily as cowardice would be punished. Trajan's Column often shows the emperor rewarding or encouraging his men. Twice auxiliary soldiers present him with severed heads taken from enemies they had killed. In a later battle we hear of a wounded cavalryman who was evacuated to the field hospital, but then told that he would not survive. Inspired by the emperor, he returned to the battle and died fighting. When the aid stations ran short of bandages, Trajan ordered that his own spare clothes should be torn up and used. He always emphasized that he cared for the welfare as well as the discipline and fighting power of his soldiers.

Trajan was also directly involved in planning, reconnoitring the ground and interrogating prisoners. When the Dacians counter-attacked on the Danubian frontier and raided the Roman frontier garrisons, he went himself with his praetorians to meet the threat. They travelled by boat along the river, and then hunted down the

THE SECOND DACIAN WAR

THE SECOND DACIAN WAR began in AD 105 when Decebalus seized the commander of the small Roman garrison in the Dacian capital, hoping to use him as a hostage and renegotiate the treaty. He was thwarted when a servant smuggled poison to the officer in question and he committed suicide. It took time for a new field army to be mustered. Trajan was in Italy when the war began and had to travel to the theatre of operations. The army for this campaign may actually have been larger than the force used in the earlier conflict. Two new legions, raised by and named after Trajan himself, were sent to the area.

There were massive preparations, including construction of a road running along the Danube – and where necessary cut into the rock of the cliffs themselves – as well as a great arched stone bridge across the river. As the army mustered, great supply dumps were formed. One historian notes that 'Trajan conducted the war with safe prudence rather than with haste.'

Negotiation with individual Dacian chieftains persuaded many to submit, and also prevented many of Decebalus' old allies from joining him. The Dacians seem to have attacked Roman outposts late in 105, but were driven off.

Trajan

In 106 the Roman army crossed the Danube and advanced into Dacia. Its target was the capital at Sarmizegethusa Regia, a place of religious as well as political significance, high in the Carpathians. The city was large, situated on a mountain top and defended by a strong circuit wall. The Romans settled down to a formal siege, employing torsion catapults and other siege engines. A direct assault was mounted, which seems to have been only partially successful and may actually have been repulsed. Nevertheless it was enough to provoke the defenders to set fire to the city and escape. It is probable that the location of the site made it very difficult for the Romans to cut off all the paths leading from it. Trajan sent patrols to pursue the fugitives, with specific orders to take Decebalus. Some Roman horsemen led by a

junior officer named Tiberius Claudius Maximus caught up with the Dacian king, who cut his own throat before he could be captured. His head was taken back to Trajan and paraded before the army. There were some mopping up operations, but the war was effectively over. Sarmizegethusa Regia was slighted and abandoned, and Trajan founded a new capital for the province, naming it after himself: Colonia Sarmizegethusa Ulpia. It was situated in the valley at the foot of the Carpathians.

The Dacian king Decebalus chose to slit his own throat (above) rather than be taken prisoner. The Roman reaching out to restrain him was an officer named Tiberius Claudius Maximus. We know from an inscription on his tombstone, which survives to this day, that it was Tiberius who carried the king's head back to Trajan.

raiders and destroyed them, before rejoining the main army. Decebalus made several attempts to negotiate, but would not meet the Roman demands and so Trajan pushed on and won another battle. The approach of winter then ended the fighting for that year.

In 102 Trajan advanced again, taking stronghold after stronghold by siege. In the end Decebalus surrendered. At this stage the Romans were not bent on annexation. The king was allowed to remain in power, although a token Roman garrison was installed in his capital. He lost some territory, was made to return all Roman deserters in his service and not receive any more, and would now pay the Romans a subsidy instead of receiving one. Trajan took the title of Dacicus – victor over the Dacians. However, the peace proved to be temporary as Decebalus chafed under these new restrictions. He decided to fight again, and a second war was fought from AD 105–106. This time Trajan's victory was complete and the kingdom was turned into the province of Dacia. An extremely prosperous province, it was soon providing soldiers for the Roman army. One man named Decebalus is later attested as serving in one of the forts on Hadrian's Wall.

War with Parthia

Trajan celebrated his Dacian triumph with great splendour, using the plundered gold of Decebalus to build a massive new Forum complex in the heart of Rome. At its centre was the column 100 Roman feet high (97 feet 9 inches in modern measurements) which served as a reminder of the height of the hillside before it was excavated to form the site of the Forum. Success in Dacia confirmed the emperor's power and avenged Domitian's humiliating peace treaty. For a few years Trajan seems to have been content to remain at peace. However, in time, tension with the

(Above right) **A coin depicting Trajan in later life.** Less than a decade after his victory in Dacia, Trajan chose to mount a massive expedition against Rome's most powerful neighbour, the Parthian empire. In spite of initial successes, the war was to end in failure.

Trajan

Parthians over the border kingdom of Armenia led him to plan a massive expedition to defeat them once and for all. The desire to emulate Alexander the Great helped to fuel his ambition, but that is not to say that he did not also feel that it would be for the greater good of the empire.

In 114 Trajan led a huge army against the Parthians. Armenia and then Mesopotamia were overrun and both turned into provinces by 115. A year later the Romans marched down the Euphrates to the Parthian capital at Ctesiphon and sacked it. Trajan then pressed onwards, getting as far as the Persian Gulf. He is supposed to have looked longingly at a trading ship sailing for India, realizing that he could not follow Alexander any further. The point was rammed home when many of his recent conquests rebelled and his overstretched army struggled to cope with these new threats. When Trajan was at Babylon he heard of rebellions by the large Jewish communities in Egypt, Cyrenaica and Cyprus, although not curiously enough in Judea itself. Savage fighting involved militias from the Gentile communities as well as regular Roman troops before the revolts were finally suppressed.

As Roman columns moved to confront the various rebel groups, there were a number of reverses. Trajan was reluctantly forced to recognize the Parthian monarchy, abandoning his ambition of occupying the whole kingdom. Probably in 117, he attempted to storm the oasis city of Hatra, but was repulsed. During one reconnaissance of the fortifications, the guard cavalryman next to Trajan was killed by an arrow – the defenders' attention having been drawn by the 60-year-old emperor's grey hair. A siege was mounted, but the harsh climate and problems of supply forced them to withdraw.

> **'I should certainly have crossed over to India too, if I were young.'**
> TRAJAN

Trajan had been ill for some time and soon afterwards suffered a stroke. A few weeks later he died. He was succeeded by Hadrian, although Hadrian's 'adoption' may well have been arranged after Trajan's death in concert with the emperor's widow. Needing to establish himself more securely, Hadrian had no enthusiasm for remaining on campaign in the east. Those territories from Trajan's eastern conquests which had not already been lost were swiftly abandoned.

'Those who are skilled in combat do not become angered, those who are skilled at winning do not become afraid. Thus the wise win before they fight, while the ignorant fight to win.'

ZHUGE LIANG

ZHUGE LIANG
181–234

JONATHAN FENBY

WHAT MACHIAVELLI IS TO EUROPEAN STATECRAFT, the third-century Chinese general and strategist Zhuge Liang is to his country's military history. Known as the 'Crouching Dragon', he is more than a military commander for the Chinese. He epitomizes prized traditional virtues and skills at the start of a protracted period of national division which followed the decline and fall of the third imperial dynasty, the Eastern Han, in 220 and lasted until the Sui dynasty took the throne in 581, restoring unity and paving the way for the great era of the Tang.

Helped by a highly impressive starring appearance in the vast epic saga about the period, the *Romance of the Three Kingdoms*, where he is referred to also as 'Master Sleeping Dragon', he is seen as a byword for intelligence, a supremely skilled and loyal commander who was also a statesman, a scholar and – highly important given the status of the heavens in Chinese cosmology – an astrologer.

Much of what is attributed to Zhuge lies on the borderline between history and myth; it is virtually impossible in many cases to distinguish between the two.

Techniques and technology

If Zhuge did not actually possess the supernatural powers granted to him in the stories handed down over the centuries, he nevertheless represents a corpus of military techniques prized by the Chinese both of his time and subsequently. Furthermore, the general feeling is that such an iconic figure should have been able to summon up winds to decide naval battles, whether or not he could actually do so.

On firmer ground, he is credited with having advanced military technology through his inventions, including weaponry, mines and transport equipment. Works attributed to him outline infantry and cavalry tactics based on Taoist principles; one is said to be so finely written that it drew tears from readers – anybody who did not cry being deemed untrustworthy.

Zhuge is also credited with having been a master of trickery. In one famous example he responded to his army's inadequate supply of arrows by floating ships filled with straw close to the enemy, waiting until the enemy archers unleashed

Zhuge Liang

volleys of arrows into them, then getting his men to drag the boats back into position in order to replenish his stocks. Books and poems celebrate his achievements and character. Most recently, Zhuge has been a video-game hero, wielding his trademark – a large white feather fan.

The fall of the Han

The 'carving of the empire' to which the poem (right) refers was the division of China that followed the fall of the Han dynasty in 220. In the dynasty's last years, the country had suffered from weak rulers, factionalism and the rise of eunuch power at court, as well as natural disasters. Rebels in eastern China, known as 'the Yellow Turbans' for its members' headgear, assembled three hundred and fifty thousand followers, while other insurgents declared their independence in the west.

The death of the emperor Lingdi in 189 set off a succession struggle. A warlord took the capital of Luoyang, massacred two thousand eunuchs and put a new emperor – a boy of 8 – on the throne, but he soon fled from the competing militarists.

Zhuge was 19 at the time. He had been born in the eastern province of Shandong in 181, but his mother died when he was 9 and his father when he was 12. He and his siblings (two brothers and two sisters) were then raised by an uncle, but were forced to flee from Shandong when in 195 a northern warlord rampaged across their province. They moved to present-day Hubei in central China, and Zhuge wed the daughter of a well-known scholar – a vital conn-ection as it turned out, since the scholar's wife was the sister-in-law of a local warlord, who was giving protection to a mercenary chieftain, Liu Bei.

The Three Kingdoms

Liu Bei's career had been rackety. He had been forced to flee the court of a northern kingdom, the Wei, after being implicated in a plot to assassinate its ruler, Cao Cao, the leading general of the time. Liu's safety came under threat after the warlord who was protecting him died, and the militarist's son allied with the Wei. That led to a battle in which Liu was defeated. At some point around this time, he heard about Zhuge, and went three times to the reed hut where he was living. On the third occasion, Zhuge agreed to receive him, making such an impression that Liu said he felt like a fish being put back into water. He had found his lieutenant – his *consigliore* – who would take care of matters for him.

*Zhuge's great name
hangs over the whole world;
the revered statesman's portrait
awes with its sublimity.
The empire carved into thirds
hindered his designs,
yet he soars through the ages,
a lone feather in the sky.
…
If he had established control,
Xiao and Cao would be forgotten.
But the cycle had passed;
Han fortunes could not be restored.
His military strategy a failure,
his hopes dashed, his body perished.*

(Du Fu, 'The Temple of Zhuge Liang', eighth century, translated by David Lunde)

A seventeenth-century ink drawing of Zhuge Liang, perhaps showing him pondering a fresh strategem. The inscription reads, 'Former emperors know what a prudent person I am'.

Zhuge Liang

The times were made for ambitious soldiers. While the Wei dominated northern China, the Yangtze Valley and regions to the south were controlled by the kingdom of Wu under Sun Quant. It was there that Liu now fled, allying himself with Sun, marrying the king's sister, and – with Zhuge – joining in his confrontation with the Wei.

In 207, Zhuge presented Liu with a programme to establish himself as a major player in China and to restore the house of Han at the head of a reunited empire. Known as the Longzhong Plan, this provided for Liu to set up a strong base in wild, fertile, mountainous Sichuan as a third kingdom, under the name of Shu. Administrative, economic and legal reforms would be implemented to create a strong state. Relations would be nurtured with tribal people to the south to counter their hostility to the Han Chinese.

From Sichuan, Zhuge's plan provided for a two-pronged attack on the Wei to the north, advancing on the major cities of Chang'an (the first imperial capital outside present-day Xian) and Luoyang in the Yellow River plain. The Wu would be neutralized by an alliance, though, once the northerners had been defeated, they would also be overcome as the Shu kingdom reunited China. It was quite a programme for a wandering military adventurer and his 26-year-old adviser.

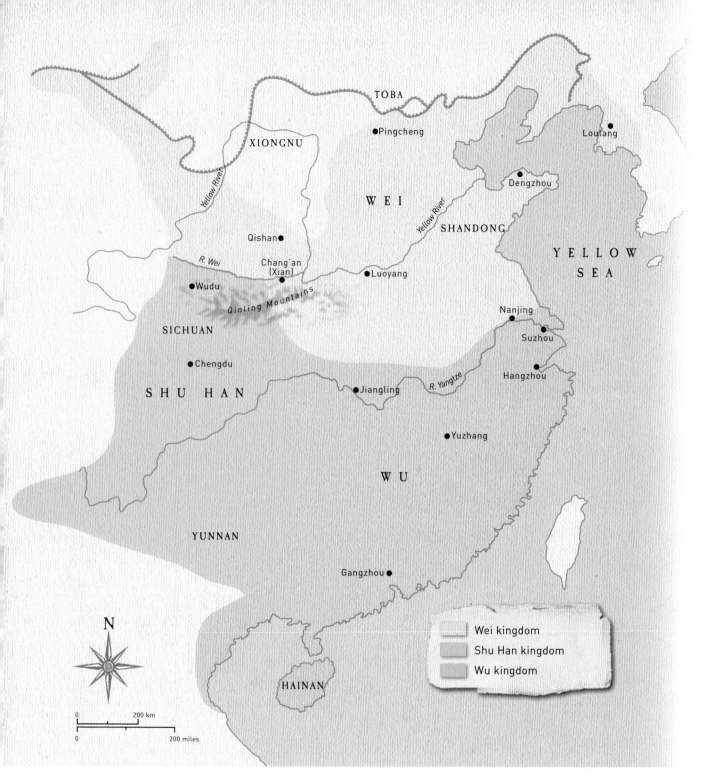

The Battle of the Red Cliffs

The vital breakthrough came a year after Zhuge unveiled his plan, when the Wei attacked the Wu kingdom along the Yangtze river being resoundingly defeated in 208, at the Battle of the Red Cliffs by a combination of trickery and the superior skills of their adversaries at naval warfare. In one celebrated episode, a Wu general offered to surrender and hand over large supplies of food. Ten ships duly appeared, but they were filled with combustible materials. Set on fire, they were blown by the wind into the numerically superior Wei armada, while the Wu fleet attacked from the other

191

side. Retreating by land, the Wei were harassed by ambushes and the king was said to have only one hundred members of his retinue left alive when he reached his northern capital.

According to the *Romance of the Three Kingdoms*, which undoubtedly exaggerates his role in the battle, Zhuge used his supernatural powers to conjure up the wind. A more prosaic version has him obtaining an accurate weather forecast and advising the Wu fleet accordingly. The grateful Wu king allowed Liu to establish himself in Sichuan to provide a base from which to seek to conquer all China.

In 220, Cao Cao died and the Han emperor abdicated. Cao's son promptly proclaimed himself emperor under the name of Wendi. In Sichuan, Liu went into mourning, but a Han ancestry was unearthed for him, and members of his entourage, including Zhuge, told him he had inherited the Mandate of Heaven, by which the gods designated emperors to govern on earth. So Liu duly declared himself the rightful ruler of China, at the head of the house of Shu Han, with its capital in the Sichuan city of Chengdu. (The Wu ruler joined the party by also declaring himself emperor.)

Liu soon ran into trouble. One of his generals alienated the Wu, who defeated him and sent his head to the Wei court. A counter-attack in 219 on the Wu from Sichuan was initially successful but then ran into difficulties as its different elements became disconnected from one another. Their supply lines were strained and, when the attackers moved out of the mountains into flat country, the Wu cavalry gained the upper hand. Zhuge did not take part in the campaign, staying in Chengdu to oversee the administration there.

Protecting the south

Having evaded direct battle with the Shu, the leading Wu general staged a night-time attack, setting fire to the adversary's positions in a dry forest, the Wu crossbow archers then cutting down the Sichuan soldiers as they ran to fetch water. After other elements in his army had been destroyed when rockslides devastated their camps, Liu took refuge in a fortified city where he was said to have died of grief at the age of 63. On his deathbed, he called for Zhuge, and named his son, Liu Shan, as his successor. If the young man proved incapable, he added, Zhuge should take the throne.

The young man did indeed fall short – Chinese historians call him 'degenerate'. But Zhuge refused to try to replace him, believing in the importance of maintaining the dynastic principle that underlay the Shu claim to the Mandate of Heaven. Still, as

Zhuge Liang

chancellor, he became the dominant figure in the kingdom, and set out to make it the dominant force in China, even though it was weaker in resources and men than the Wei or the Wu.

Zhuge saw the Wei as the prime adversary, so he formed an alliance with the Wu to protect the Shu's eastern front. To secure the rear, he launched expeditions to pacify rebel tribes in the mountains of Yunnan, to the south of Sichuan. His army defeated the much-respected main tribal leader, Meng Huo, seven times. On each occasion, Zhuge had him released as a sign of benevolence and to win his confidence. In the end, Meng submitted. 'You must be the valour of Heaven,' he told Zhuge. 'The south will not rebel again.'

Zhuge appointed Meng and other regional chiefs as administrators to win their loyalty while avoiding the expense and uncertainties of occupation. The Yunnan tribes paid the Shu tribute in gold and silver, horses and cattle, providing much-needed additional resources for the kingdom's army.

The march north

In 227, it was time to march north against the Wei in the next stage in Zhuge's Pingzhong Plan. The purpose, he told the ruler, Liu Shan, was to conquer the vast plain of northern China 'to exterminate the wicked, restore the house of Han and return to the old capital (Chang'an)'. Despite this ambition, the first northern expedition, like later Shu offensives, was marked by Zhuge's ultimate awareness of the relative weakness of the kingdom, the need to avoid putting his army at the mercy of larger

(Opposite and below) **Further scenes from the *Romance of the Three Kingdoms*** (see caption, p. 190), showing armies manoeuvring in the repeated wars as the Three Kingdoms jockeyed for power.

northern forces, and supply chain factors as the troops moved further and further from their home base.

The terrain that lay ahead was forbidding – notably the Qinling Mountains, with their deep valleys and sparse roads climbing through awesome passes. Rejecting a proposal for a frontal attack through the mountains, Zhuge opted for a typically deceptive move, sending two columns to act as diversions while his main force advanced along the upper valley of the Wei river on the way to Chang'an. The Wei ruler, Cao Rui, took personal charge of the defence. In addition to the garrisons in the area, a fifty-thousand-strong force of cavalry and infantry was sent in to oppose the attackers directly. A Shu general allowed himself to be isolated on a waterless mountain top, where he was defeated. Fearing encirclement by the Wei troops, Zhuge ordered his army to withdraw to Sichuan.

Zhuge Liang

ZHUGE'S TACTICS

Pits After capturing the rebel leader, Meng Huo, in the southern expedition, Zhuge took him on a tour of his camp before releasing him. When the rebels attacked, Zhuge ordered his men to withdraw. Meng thought he knew the camp so his army rushed in – only to fall into huge concealed pits dug to trap them.

Fire In another attack in the wars in Yunnan, the enemy used elephants and tigers to attack the Sichuan forces, but Zhuge set up fire-breathing machines which scared them away.

Mines For the final battle in the south, Meng allied with a king whose soldiers wore rattan armour that could withstand arrows and swords. Zhuge sent a force to lure then into a valley where mines were detonated beneath them, setting fire to their uniforms and burning them alive.

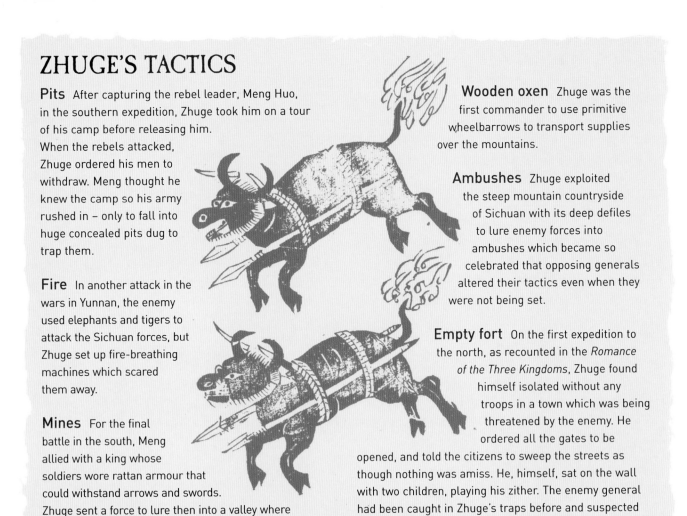

Wooden oxen Zhuge was the first commander to use primitive wheelbarrows to transport supplies over the mountains.

Ambushes Zhuge exploited the steep mountain countryside of Sichuan with its deep defiles to lure enemy forces into ambushes which became so celebrated that opposing generals altered their tactics even when they were not being set.

Empty fort On the first expedition to the north, as recounted in the *Romance of the Three Kingdoms*, Zhuge found himself isolated without any troops in a town which was being threatened by the enemy. He ordered all the gates to be opened, and told the citizens to sweep the streets as though nothing was amiss. He, himself, sat on the wall with two children, playing his zither. The enemy general had been caught in Zhuge's traps before and suspected that he was being lured into an ambush. So he marched his army away.

Fire oxen with flaming brands attached to their tails – first used as a method of siege breakout during the Warring States period – exemplified China's innovative tradition of incendiary warfare.

The following year, he was back on the offensive, seeking to take advantage of a conflict between Wu and Wei. A Shu army again marched to the Wei river basin, but, again, Zhuge ordered it to return home when grain supplies ran short. He did, however, score one signal victory when a leading Wei commander fell into an ambush set by Zhuge in the Qinling Mountains.

Back on the march again, Zhuge's troops occupied the western Qinling foothills in their third expedition in 209. They scored a significant success at the Battle of Wudu, but then ran into stiff defence from numerically superior Wei forces which led Zhuge to order the retreat, though the Shu held on to two commanderies across the mountains. By now, the Wei had had enough of the attacks from Sichuan and in the autumn of 230 invaded the Shu kingdom with an army said to total four hundred thousand men.

Zhuge sent agents to stir up anti-Wei sentiment among non-Han tribes on the route of the enemy's march, who sold weapons and horses to the Shu in return for silks. Heavy rain made the mountain tracks impassable. Shu forces operated behind the enemy lines. A Sichuan general defeated the main Wei army while Zhuge led in reinforcements on an arduous march. After a month, the Wei called off the attack and went home.

Zhuge Liang

Supply chain and rain

Building on this success, at the beginning of 231 Zhuge swiftly launched another advance into Wei territory. Having drawn the main enemy force to defend the city of Qishan, he sent troops to seize other Wei positions. When the enemy left its defensive position to try to stage a pincer attack, Zhuge put them to flight.

He then halted the advance to harvest the spring wheat before marching south to confront the main Wei army. Its general held back from battle but, eventually, let criticism of his evading tactics get the better of him and launched a frontal assault that ended in disaster – the Shu were reported to have captured 5,000 swords, 3,100 crossbows and 3,000 suits of armour.

Despite this major victory, Zhuge did not advance further, worried as he was about the supply chain. Summer rain bogged down the roads, and his king ordered a withdrawal. There was, again, a final victory typical of Zhuge's skills at laying ambushes – the leading Wei commander and his men were mown down by Shu crossbowmen as they followed the retreating army into a narrow valley.

The Shu chancellor launched his final expedition to the north in the spring of 234, with an army of one hundred thousand men. However, it faced an enemy army twice as large which blocked its initial advance into the plain of the Wei river. Disease spread through the Sichuan ranks. Zhuge became increasingly depressed, foreseeing his own death as he issued orders about how the Shu realm was to be run after him. In the autumn of 234, at the age of 54, he died. The leading Wei general thought that he was really still alive and that the pretended death was a ruse to lure the northerners into a snare – stories were told of a double impersonating Zhuge or of a wooden statue dressed in his clothes being put on display to convince the Wei that he was still alive.

Zhuge thus failed to realize his plan to dominate China, but the manner in which he took the initiative on behalf of the weakest of the three kingdoms ensured his place as a major figure among Chinese commanders. The way in which he used diversion and sudden unexpected attacks to unsettle numerically superior forces was squarely in the tradition laid down by Sun Tzu in the *Art of War*.

Zhuge's overall strategy has been criticized for not clearly defining which was the principal line of advance and which were sideshows. But his main weakness lay in the relative poverty and isolation of Sichuan and the problems of long supply lines through forbidding terrain. On top of which, the political objective – the restoration of the Han in the shape of the Shu pretenders – was deeply flawed. The Wei had developed an effective system of government in their lands, and the third kingdom, the Wu, would never have accepted the rise of the Shu to primacy.

After Zhuge's death, his protégé, Jiang Wei, led further campaigns against the Wei that ended in defeats and, in 263, the northerners conquered the southwestern kingdom. Jiang tried to continue resistance, but his troops refused to follow him, and he was killed in battle. In turn, the Wei were overcome in 264 by another dynasty, the Jin, while the Wu also went into decline. The end of the Three Kingdoms period then gave way to three centuries of disunion, before the empire was finally restored by the Sui dynasty in 581.

ALARIC I

c. 360/370–410

JOHN HAYWOOD

A HERO TO SOME, a villain to many, Alaric was the Gothic leader who exposed to the world the declining power of the Roman Empire, when he captured and sacked Rome in AD 410. Alaric's career was dominated by his quest to find a secure home for his followers. Though this did not happen in his lifetime, his achievements made possible the foundation of the Visigothic kingdom in 417, the first autonomous barbarian kingdom within the frontiers of the Western Roman Empire.

Alaric was born near the mouth of the Danube at some time between AD 360 and 370. Later writers would invent a royal genealogy to match his heroic stature, but it is likely that he was a 'new man' who rose to prominence by his leadership ability. His formative years were a time of great upheaval and insecurity for his people. The Goths were divided into two main groups: the Tervingi, to whom Alaric belonged, and the Greuthungi, who were regarded as the most powerful of the German peoples and whose defeat by the Huns in around AD 374 spread panic among the rest.

As a result, the Tervingi decided to abandon their lands and seek refuge in the Roman Empire. Some Greuthungi who had fled rather than submit to the Huns decided to do likewise. The Romans had watched the mounting chaos in the Germanic world with ill-disguised glee, but the arrival of some two hundred thousand Gothic refugees on the north bank of the Danube in the late summer of 376 was an alarming development. The emperor Valens (r. 364–378) was fully committed to a war against Persia and did not have enough troops to stop the Goths. He therefore decided to allow the Tervingi to enter and use what troops he could spare to oppose the less numerous Greuthungi.

Roman emperors were no strangers to the manipulative interpretation of facts and Valens presented the admission of the Tervingi as a great opportunity for the empire. One of the most serious problems faced by the Romans in the fourth century was that of population decline. Agriculture was suffering from labour shortages, tax yields were falling and the army was forced to recruit Germanic mercenaries to fill the ranks. The Tervingi could be settled on vacant land in the Balkans, bring abandoned fields back into production, provide recruits for the army and pay taxes. What could be better? Many thousands of Germans had been settled successfully in the empire in the past but these had always been defeated, disarmed and leaderless prisoners of war. Admitting the Tervingi was far more dangerous. They had not been defeated in war, their leadership was intact, and Valens did not have the troops to control them if his plans went wrong, which they very quickly did.

The generals whom Valens had left to manage the resettlement were corrupt: they embezzled the funds allocated to buy supplies so that the Tervingi were soon reduced to selling their children into slavery in order to survive. In 377, the Tervingi rebelled and went on a plundering spree. Bands of Greuthungi took advantage of the disorder to cross the Danube illegally and joined them. In 378, Valens made peace with Persia, finally releasing troops to deal with the Goths. On 9 August he launched a badly planned attack on the Gothic camp near Adrianople (modern Edirne, Turkey) and was defeated and killed. For four years the Balkans were ravaged by war. The

The reliefs from the base of an obelisk erected by Theodosius I in Constantinople show the emperor, his wife and sons, Arcadius and Honorius, at the hippodrome, while defeated enemies of the Roman Empire kneel to offer tribute. The triumphal imagery belies the empire's deepening problems.

Romans harassed the Goths constantly, but were unable to inflict a decisive defeat on them or expel them from the empire. In a peace treaty agreed in October 382, the emperor Theodosius (r. 379–395) allowed the Goths to settle in Thrace (roughly modern Bulgaria) as semi-autonomous *foederati* ('allies') under their own leaders. Theodosius' concession of federate status was intended to be withdrawn as soon as the opportunity arose, but because he had to spend most of the remainder of his reign suppressing two usurpers who had seized power in the west, Magnus Maximus (r. 383–388) and Eugenius (r. 392–394), it never did. Theodosius needed Gothic troops to fight these usurpers, so he could not afford to alienate them by attacking their hard-won autonomy.

The Battle of the Frigidus

Alaric first came to prominence in 391. The Balkans were in turmoil following an army mutiny and a popular uprising in Thessalonica, and the Goths had seized the opportunity to go plundering. Alaric made his name by ambushing Theodosius while he was sleeping off an alcoholic lunch during a lull in fighting, the befuddled emperor only managing to escape because some of his men still had their wits about them and fought a rearguard action. A few years later Alaric was fighting for Theodosius, as the commander of a unit of Goths in the emperor's war against Eugenius. In September 394, Theodosius led an army of regulars and Goths from the Balkan provinces across the Julian Alps into the valley of the River Frigidus (modern Vipava) on the borders of Italy. Eugenius was waiting in a well-chosen position, but two days of hard fighting saw Theodosius victorious. Eugenius was captured and executed. The Goths, whom Theodosius had deliberately placed in the first line, suffered very heavy casualties – ten thousand according to one source, around a quarter of their fighting strength. Theodosius did not enjoy his triumph for long. On 17 January 395 he died of heart disease at Milan, and the empire was divided between his two sons, the 17-year-old Arcadius becoming emperor of the east and 10-year-old Honorius becoming emperor of the west under the regency of the Vandal general Stilicho.

After Theodosius' death, Stilicho ordered most of the Gothic units to go home. Alaric, rightly suspecting that the Romans had been pleased to see the Goths weakened in the battle, was angered by this casual dismissal after the sacrifices the Goths had made at the Battle of the Frigidus. He felt that his personal contribution to the victory should have been recognized by promotion to a regular command. While travelling through the Balkans, Alaric rebelled and marched on Constantinople, the eastern capital, to demand the command he deserved. At first he was probably followed only by his own unit, but the discontented Goths rallied to him and he was accepted as king by both the Tervingi and the Greuthungi. Under Alaric's leadership

A marble bust of the eastern Roman emperor Arcadius (r. 395–408). The refusal of Arcadius' government to meet his demands forced Alaric to invade the Western Roman Empire in 401.

Seville

Alaric I

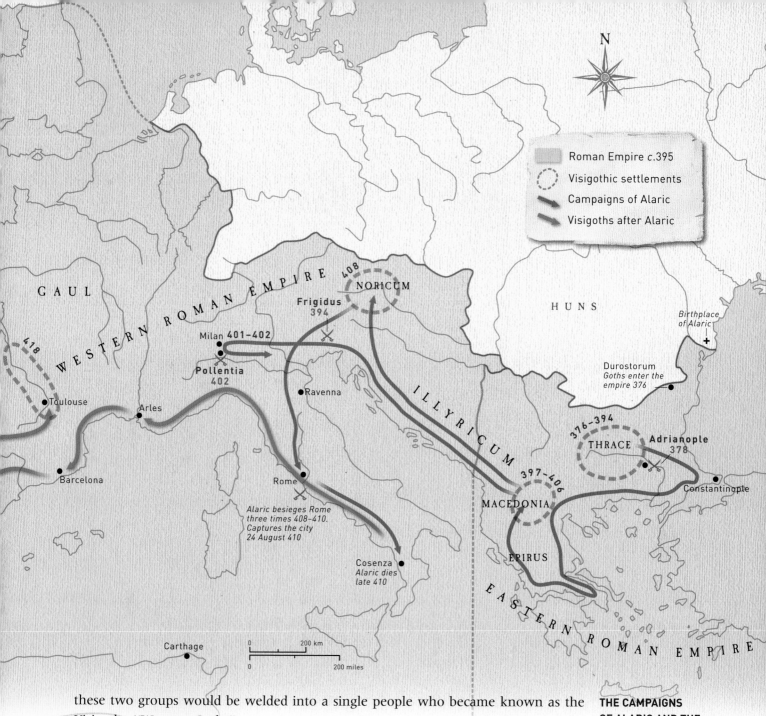

THE CAMPAIGNS
OF ALARIC AND THE
VISIGOTHS in the late
fourth and early fifth
centuries AD.

these two groups would be welded into a single people who became known as the Visigoths ('Western Goths').

Alaric found Constantinople too strongly fortified for an assault to succeed so he turned west, and spent the next two years pillaging along the Aegean coast as far south as the Peloponnese. In the spring of 395, Stilicho crossed the Alps to deal with Alaric but failed to bring him to battle. This may have been deliberate. Stilicho believed that Theodosius had intended him to be regent for Arcadius as well as Honorius, but the government of the east was dominated by the eunuch Eutropius. Stilicho may have left Alaric to pillage in the hope that it would discredit Eutropius. In 397, Stilicho intervened again, leading a naval expedition to Greece and forcing Alaric to move north into Epirus. Soon afterwards Eutropius negotiated a settlement with Alaric, more to remove Stilicho's pretext for intervention in the east than from a sincere commitment to peace with the Visigoths.

Alaric was given the generalship he craved and the Visigoths were permitted to settle on lands in the provinces of Thrace and Macedonia with tax revenues and a grain subsidy. Unfortunately, these concessions were regarded in Constantinople as appeasing the barbarians, and in 399 Eutropius was overthrown and executed by the general Gainas who, ironically, was also a Goth. The new government refused to honour Eutropius' commitments and Alaric lost his generalship and his subsidies, though the Visigoths could not be expelled from their lands. Soon after, Alaric was forcibly reminded of the precariousness of his position. Gainas was dismissed and executed and there followed in Constantinople a massacre of his Gothic followers.

Alaric's first invasion of Italy

Having failed to extract concessions from the eastern government, Alaric invaded Italy to put pressure on Stilicho and the western government. His invasion was brilliantly timed. Taking the same route he had followed with Theodosius in 394, Alaric crossed the Julian Alps in November 401, just before snow closed the Alpine passes for the winter and cut Italy off from the heavily garrisoned northern frontiers. Alaric faced little opposition as he marched west up the Po river valley and laid siege to the imperial court at Milan.

It was not until February or March 402 that Stilicho was able to bring reinforcements into Italy. Learning that the emperor Honorius had escaped, Alaric lifted the siege of Milan and went in pursuit, but was intercepted by Stilicho at Asti. After an inconclusive battle, Alaric withdrew 25 miles to Pollentia (modern Bra) where, on 6 April, Easter Sunday, Stilicho brought him to battle again. Alaric, brought up as a Christian, was apparently taken by surprise while attending a religious service. The Visigothic cavalry drove the Roman cavalry from the field but the Roman infantry captured Alaric's baggage train, along with his wife and children, and all his plunder. Alaric opened negotiations with Stilicho and agreed to leave Italy. However, he had reached only as far as Verona when he was accused of breaking the truce and was again forced into battle by Stilicho, probably in July or August. Once again Stilicho got the better of Alaric but the defeat was not serious enough to prevent him from withdrawing in good order back to the lands the Visigoths had held in 397. One of the consequences of Alaric's invasion of Italy was that Honorius moved the western capital to Ravenna, which was protected by marshlands and strong fortifications, and had good sea communications with Constantinople.

The failure of his invasion of Italy left Alaric in limbo until, late in 406, Stilicho offered him everything that Eutropius had previously offered him in 397 in return for an alliance against the eastern government. Stilicho's aim was to force the east to give him control of the Balkan province of Illyricum, which was one of the major recruiting grounds of the Roman army. The military situation in the western empire was deteriorating. In 405, Stilicho had defeated an invasion by a group of Goths under their king Radagaisus and it was clear that more trouble could be expected

> 'Alaric the Visigoth [is] equalled, as it seems to me, by only three men in succeeding times as a changer of the course of history. And these three are Muhammad, Columbus, Napoleon.'
>
> THOMAS HODGKIN, *ITALY AND HER INVADERS* (1880)

from that direction. Then in Britain, in 406, the field army mutinied and proclaimed as emperor its general, Constantine. To face these threats, Stilicho urgently needed to be able to recruit troops from the Balkans, since manpower shortages were more acute in the western than in the eastern empire. However, his plan backfired badly.

Alaric's second invasion of Italy

Alaric moved south into Epirus, where he waited to be joined by Stilicho and his regular Roman troops for a campaign against Constantinople in the summer of 407. Before that could happen, however, events began to spin out of Stilicho's control. On the last day of 406, a coalition of Vandals, Sueves and Alans crossed the frozen Rhine and invaded Gaul. Then early in 407, the usurper Constantine crossed the Channel

An ivory diptych featuring the master general Flavius Stilicho, his wife Serena and son Eucherius. Stilicho's Germanic origins made him suspect in the eyes of the Roman elite, but his execution in 408 left the Western Roman Empire without effective military leadership to face Alaric's invasion.

to save Gaul from the barbarians. Stilicho had no choice but to abandon his plans and Alaric was again left in the lurch. In 408, Alaric led the Visigoths to occupy the Alpine province of Noricum, where he was well placed to invade Italy again, and threatened war if he did not receive a subsidy of 4,000 pounds of gold to maintain his people. Stilicho, who did not wish to add a third enemy to the two he already faced in Gaul, persuaded a reluctant Senate to pay up, but his reputation was fatally damaged. Now a grown man, Honorius was desperate to be rid of his overbearing general. In August 408, Stilicho was arrested on trumped-up treason charges and executed.

An anti-barbarian reaction flashed through Italy. German soldiers in the Roman army were massacred in their thousands, together with their families. The survivors fled and joined forces with Alaric. In the autumn of 408, Alaric invaded Italy for a second time and, plundering as he went, headed for Rome, where he set up camp outside its walls in November. Visigoth numbers were swelled by thousands of runaway slaves, many of them Goths who had been captured by Stilicho in 405. With these reinforcements, Alaric had a fighting strength of perhaps forty thousand, a large force by the standards of the time. Alaric's men were also much better equipped than most barbarian armies. While in the Balkans, Alaric had taken over Roman arms factories and forced the craftsmen to make weapons and armour for his troops.

Over a year of fruitless negotiations followed. Alaric lifted his blockade when there appeared to be progress and imposed it again when talks broke down. Military confrontation was not an option for Honorius, as he needed to save his troops to combat Constantine in Gaul. Despite his strong position, Alaric was conciliatory, dropping his demands for a generalship and gold and asking only for the province of Noricum and a grain subsidy. Even many Romans thought his demands were astonishingly moderate but Honorius would not give ground. Alaric's patience ran out in August 410, and after a brief siege the Visigoths captured Rome. After having plundered the city for three days, Alaric withdrew. Though no longer the capital, Rome remained a potent symbol of Roman history and power; news of its fall to an invader, for the first time since it was sacked by the Celts eight hundred years before, sent shock waves through the empire. Alaric had done his worst but, safe in Ravenna, Honorius still refused his demands.

Frustrated, Alaric led his troops into southern Italy. Recognizing its importance as the major exporter of grain to Italy, Alaric threatened to invade North Africa, but he died before the year was out. His successor, Athaulf, turned and took the Visigoths to Gaul. After helping the Romans defeat the Vandals in Spain, only seven years later they were finally given control of fertile lands in Aquitaine.

Alaric's achievement

The surviving sources give few clues as to Alaric's true character, but it is clear that he was never bent on destruction for its own sake, nor was he a would-be empire builder. His restraint in the face of repeated Roman bad faith was outstanding but this reflects his real concern for the future of his people. Alaric was always prepared to trade a short-term military advantage for a long-term political settlement with the Romans. Though he is most famous for the sack of Rome, the significance of this act was largely symbolic. In itself it did not make the fall of the Western Roman Empire inevitable or even likely. Alaric was not the first barbarian to play an influential role

THE SACK OF
ROME

ALARIC'S ON–OFF SIEGE OF ROME, which began in November 408, moved towards its climax in the summer of 410. Hoping to increase the pressure on Honorius, Alaric had lifted the siege of Rome late in 409 and persuaded the Senate to elect its own emperor, Attalus. Attalus proved less cooperative than Alaric had hoped, and he deposed him in July 410 and reopened negotiations with Honorius. Alaric went to meet Honorius outside Ravenna, but while he waited for the emperor he was ambushed by a small Roman force. Outraged, Alaric returned to Rome and renewed the siege. On the night of 24 August the Visigoths entered Rome through the Salarian Gate on the northeast side of the city. It is not known exactly how the city fell. One story is that Alaric had earlier given Gothic slave boys to several wealthy senators and it was this unsuspected fifth column who opened the gate. Another account implies that the Visigoths had to fight their way in.

The sack that followed was remarkably restrained considering the years of hardship and uncertainty suffered by the Visigoths. Alaric gave orders that churches were not to be damaged and advised his men to concentrate on pillaging movable wealth rather than on killing and destruction. The basilicas of St Peter and St Paul were nominated as places of sanctuary, and people who took refuge there were not disturbed. There were inevitably some who were killed or beaten to make them reveal where valuables were hidden, but the Visigoths seem generally to have heeded Alaric's advice. Refugees from the city would tell how some Visigoths had even escorted nuns to safety. Movable wealth, however, did include people – one of whom was the emperor's sister, Galla Placidia – and many were taken prisoner to be ransomed or sold as slaves. The Visigoths were mindful enough of their Christianity to leave the church most of its treasures and only one important building, the Senate House, was seriously damaged. When the Visigoths withdrew after three days of plundering, Rome was a great deal poorer but still substantially intact and life quickly returned to normal.

in Roman politics. Many Germans – Stilicho, for example – had served in the Roman army, risen to high rank and played a dominating role in the empire's politics. Like them, Alaric became a Roman general but, unlike them, he never commanded a regular army unit or became absorbed into the Roman military hierarchy. Alaric was a king but he never had a kingdom or any secure territory to which he could retreat if things went wrong. Yet, despite this, he successfully resisted all military efforts to assimilate his people into the Roman system. The Visigoths lived in the empire but were not Roman subjects, and their only connection to the empire was through Alaric and his relationship with the imperial government. By proving that it was possible for a barbarian king to maintain an independent power base within the empire, Alaric pointed the way to the establishment of the barbarian kingdoms and the eventual dismemberment of the Western Roman Empire.

A heavily armed Visigothic warrior with full chain-mail coat and helmet, from a twelfth-century Spanish manuscript. By the time of the sack of Rome in 410, Visigothic warriors were equipped in a similar way to Roman regular soldiers.

'[Aetius was] the great protector of the western republic ...
and with him the Hesperian realm fell, and up to the present
day has not been able to raise its head.' MARCELLINUS COMES, *CHRONICLE*, C. 534

AETIUS
c. 400–454

JOHN HAYWOOD

FLAVIUS AETIUS WAS THE LAST GREAT GENERAL of the Western Roman
Empire. Supreme commander of the western Roman armies from 433 until his
death in 454, he skilfully maintained Roman control of Gaul by playing one
group of barbarians off against another. His death is often seen as marking the
beginning of the end for the Western Roman Empire.

Born in around 400, Aetius was the son of Gaudentius, a common soldier from the
Balkans who had joined the elite Praetorian Guard and risen to high command in the
cavalry. His mother was an Italian heiress from a senatorial family. Aetius began his
military career by following in his father's footsteps and joining the Praetorians while
still in his teens. Because of his family's importance, Aetius spent part of his childhood
as a hostage with the Visigothic king Alaric and he later spent several years also as a
hostage among the Huns. Although their lives might be forfeit if diplomatic relations
broke down, young hostages were normally treated more like foster children than
prisoners. During his time with the Huns, Aetius learned horsemanship and archery
and formed a friendship with one of their kings, Ruga (d. 434), and with his nephew
Attila. Aetius married a Visigothic princess and one of their sons, Carpilio, was sent as
a hostage to Ruga in 425. These relationships that the young Aetius forged with
Visigothic and Hun royalty served him well in his subsequent career.

Rise to power

When the western emperor Honorius died in 423 without a male heir, the eastern
emperor Theodosius II (r. 408–450) appointed Honorius' 4-year-old nephew
Valentinian III (r. 425–454) as his successor under the regency of his mother, princess
Galla Placidia (d. 450). A child emperor was the last thing the embattled Western
Empire needed. The army rebelled and raised an official called John to the throne
instead. Refusing to accept the coup, Theodosius gave Galla Placidia an army to place
Valentinian on the throne by force. To stop her, John sent Aetius to recruit troops of
mercenaries from his friends the Huns. Aetius returned at the head of sixty thousand
Huns to find that John had already been defeated and executed. Under different

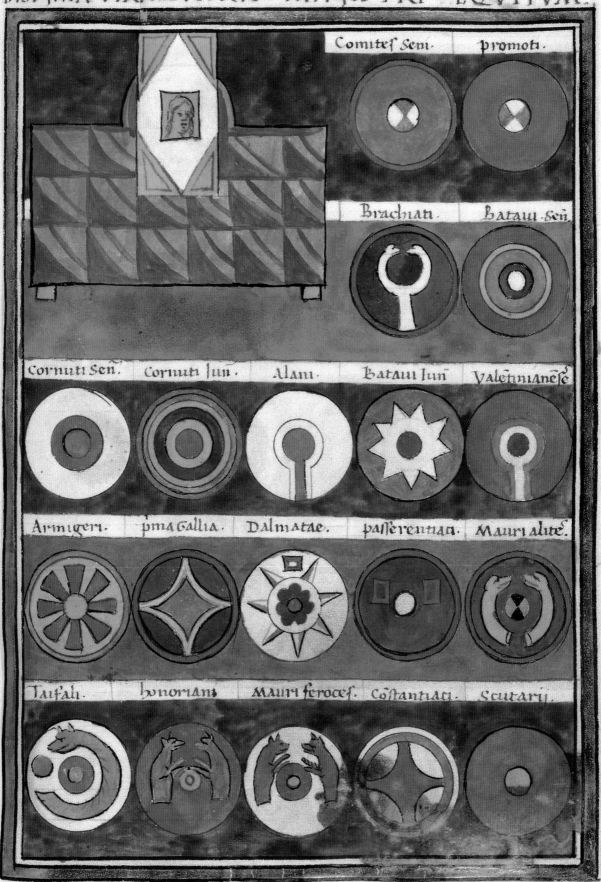

An ivory diptych
showing Aetius
presiding over circus
games held to
celebrate one of the
three occasions (432,
437 or 446) when he
was appointed consul
of Rome.

circumstances Aetius would have shared John's fate, but the Huns would have gone on the rampage in Italy if he had been killed. Expediently, Galla Placidia appointed Aetius master of horse with command of the field army in Gaul.

The situation that Aetius inherited in Gaul was a desperate one, with the Romans steadily losing ground to Germanic invaders. In 417 the Romans had been forced to allow the Visigoths to settle in Aquitaine as *foederati* ('allies'). The Visigoths, who had entered the empire as refugees from the Huns in 376 and who had sacked Rome in 410, were granted the tax revenues of the province in return for serving in the Roman

armies. Though technically still subject to Rome, they gradually exploited its weakness to increase the territory under their control. In the north, the Romans faced a similar problem with the Franks, who were extending their control over the province of Belgica. Much of eastern Gaul was occupied by the Burgundians, while even those areas still nominally controlled by the Romans were insecure because of the activities of peasant brigands called *bagaudae*.

To deal with all these problems, Aetius had only around forty-five thousand regular troops, assuming that all his units were actually up to strength. Because of this he depended heavily on Hun mercenaries to supplement his forces and, without them, he would have achieved little. Aetius' first success came in 425 or 426 when he defeated the Visigothic king Theodoric (r. 418–451) who was attempting to capture Arles. In 427 he defeated the Franks, who were trying to extend their territory to the River Somme. In 430 he defeated an invasion by the Alamanni. In the following year he suppressed a rebellion in the Alpine province of Noricum and again drove the Visigoths from Arles. In 432 Aetius inflicted another defeat on the Franks. This run of victories greatly increased his prestige and influence. In 429 Aetius was made second in command to Felix, the master general of the western armies. The following year he forced Galla Placidia to dismiss Felix and appoint him master general in his place. Felix ('Lucky') was then executed for treason and in 432, Aetius was appointed consul of Rome.

Civil war

Galla Placidia had never forgiven Aetius for supporting John and she had been merely waiting for an opportunity for revenge. In 432 she dismissed Aetius and appointed in his place Boniface, the commander of the army in Africa. Aetius refused to submit and met Boniface in battle near Rimini. Though Boniface won, he died of wounds soon after and was succeeded as master general by his son-in-law, Sebastian. Aetius fled to the Huns and with the support of Ruga was able to return to Italy and dictate terms to Galla Placidia in 433. Sebastian was exiled, Aetius was reinstated as master general and was made a patrician, the highest rank of the Roman aristocracy. Aetius' dominance of the Western Empire became complete in 437, when the regency of Galla Placidia came to an end with Valentinian's eighteenth birthday. Valentinian was a weak and ineffectual character and, with his mother politically sidelined, Aetius effectively became the ruler of the Western Empire. For all his ambition, Aetius never aspired to seize the throne for himself. To have tried would have invited the hostility of the east and Aetius had the political acumen to understand that he needed its support if the Western Empire was to survive: far better to be the power behind the throne.

The 430s saw the development of a new and serious threat to the Western Empire. In 429 the Vandal king Geiseric led his people on an invasion of North Africa from Spain, where they had been repeatedly attacked by the Visigoths. It is possible that Boniface, who was in rebellion against the western government at the time, may have encouraged Geiseric in the hopes of using the Vandals to support his ambitions in much the same way that Aetius used the Huns. If so, it was a plan that quickly went badly wrong as Geiseric swept Boniface's forces aside and began to advance on Carthage, North Africa's richest and largest city. North Africa was the only region of the Western Empire still untouched by war. It was the main source of tax revenues for the western government and of grain for Italy. Fully engaged in Gaul, Aetius had few troops to spare for Africa, so to save Carthage he recognized Vandal control of Mauretania (roughly modern Algeria) in 435.

The destruction of the Burgundians

To do anything about the Vandals, Aetius first had to stabilize the position in Gaul. In 436 he dealt a decisive blow to the Burgundians by unleashing an army of Huns against them. In a ferociously genocidal campaign it was said that twenty thousand Burgundians were slaughtered, including their king Gundahar. The cowed and demoralized survivors were settled by Aetius a few years later on lands south of Lake Geneva. The devastating defeat of the Burgundians passed into legend and forms the background to the German medieval epic, the *Niebelungenlied*. At the same time Aetius destroyed most of the bands of *bagaudae* that were plaguing the Gallic countryside, suppressed a rebellion in Armorica (Brittany) and, taking advantage of the departure of the Vandals for North Africa, restored Roman control to all of Spain other than mountainous Galicia which remained under the control of the Suevi, former allies of the Vandals. Two more years of difficult campaigning against the Visigoths culminated in a major victory at the Battle of Snake Mountain in 438.

With a lot of help from the Huns, Aetius had achieved much in a decade and more of constant campaigning. He had restored the Rhine frontier for the first time since it was overrun by the Vandals in 409. Most of the German tribes who had followed in their wake had been either expelled or thoroughly chastened and the Visigoths had been confined again to the lands granted to them by treaty back in 417. Peace and order were being restored in the countryside of Spain and Gaul, promising much-needed increases in tax revenue for the western government. Soon Aetius would have the resources he needed to deal with the Visigoths once and for all.

The treaty of 435 had left Geiseric dangerously close to Carthage, but the constant campaigning to restore order to Gaul left Aetius with little alternative other than to cut the city's garrison to the bone. By far the cleverest and most ruthless of

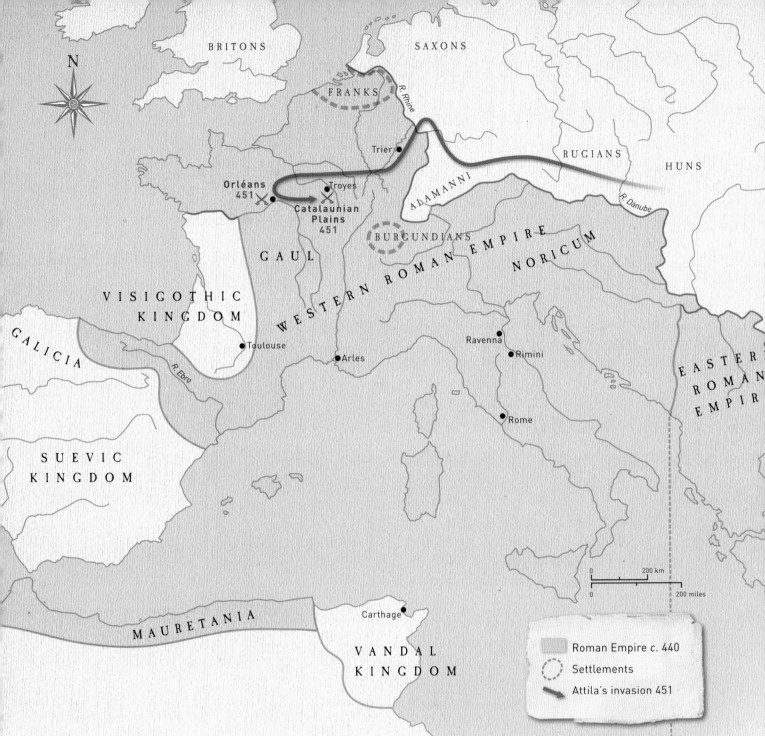

Map labels:

BRITONS

SAXONS

N

FRANKS

R. Rhine

Trier

RUGIANS

HUNS

Orléans
451

Troyes

R. Danube

Catalaunian
Plains
451

ALAMANNI

GAUL

BURGUNDIANS

WESTERN ROMAN EMPIRE

NORICUM

VISIGOTHIC
KINGDOM

GALICIA

Toulouse

R. Ebro

Arles

Ravenna

Rimini

EASTERN
ROMAN
EMPIRE

Rome

SUEVIC
KINGDOM

200 km

200 miles

MAURETANIA

Carthage

VANDAL
KINGDOM

Roman Empire c. 440

Settlements

Attila's invasion 451

THE WESTERN ROMAN EMPIRE at the time of the invasion of Attila the Hun, 451.

the barbarian kings of his day, Geiseric was not a man to resist such temptation, and in 439 he seized Carthage and with it the richest provinces of North Africa. The loss of Carthage was by far the most serious setback yet suffered by the Western Empire in its struggle for survival. Without the tax revenues of North Africa, the western government was not fiscally viable: without its grain, the population of Rome would starve. Though Ravenna had been the administrative capital of the west since 402, Rome remained the symbolic heart of the empire. Aetius' authority would not survive a famine there. To keep the grain flowing, Aetius had no choice but to recognize Geiseric's possession of Carthage, but he almost immediately began planning a counter-attack. Realizing that his resources were insufficient for the task, Aetius successfully appealed to Theodosius for eastern support. Late in 440 a fleet of eleven hundred ships and a massive army from both halves of the empire began to gather in Sicily. If it succeeded, the expedition would transform the fortunes of the Western Empire at a stroke. With North Africa returned to Roman control, the reconquest of the remaining barbarian enclaves in Gaul and Spain would surely soon follow. Flavius Aetius would be hailed as the saviour of Rome.

The great expedition never sailed. Attila's invasion of the Balkans in 441 forced Theodosius to withdraw his troops and the expedition was abandoned. From this moment on, the Western Empire was living on borrowed time. The failure did not diminish Aetius' personal prestige. Even the Britons, who had expelled the Roman administration in 410 and had been independent ever since, came to him in 446 asking for help against the barbarians who were attacking Britain. However, his hard-won successes of the 430s began slowly to unravel. Taking advantage of his preoccupation with North Africa, the Suevi emerged from Galicia and began to take over Spain. The limited forces Aetius could send to oppose the Suevi suffered a succession of defeats and by 443 almost everything south of the Ebro river was lost to them. At least Aetius' friendship with Attila protected the west from Hun raids. To keep Attila sweet, Aetius found a face-saving way to pay him a subsidy by making him an honorary master general, a post that brought with it a substantial salary.

> 'Your breastplate is not so much a defence as a garment ... not a magnificent display but a way of life.'
>
> FLAVIUS MEROBAUDES, *PANEGYRIC ON AETIUS*, c. 446

Aetius versus Attila

In 450 Aetius' friendship with Attila broke down and he was forced to prepare for a Hun invasion. Attila probably had ambitions to replace Aetius as the military strongman of the Western Empire and announced his intention to attack the Visigothic kingdom as an ally of the emperor. Attila received further encouragement from what he took to be a proposal of marriage from Valentinian's rebellious sister Honoria and the chance to intervene in a succession dispute among the Franks. Because Attila was simultaneously threatening the interests of the empire, the Visigoths and the Franks, Aetius was able to build an unlikely coalition to oppose him. At the head of an army comprising Romans, Visigoths and Franks, Aetius won his greatest victory, defeating Attila at the Battle of the Catalaunian Plains in 451. Attila was allowed to withdraw in good order; the Huns had been far too useful to Aetius for him to want to destroy them. It was at this point that Aetius made the most serious miscalculation of his career. Assuming that Attila was chastened by his defeat and would be ready to restore friendly relations, Aetius neglected to garrison the Alpine passes. In 452 Attila, who had not given up his ambition to marry Honoria, was able to invade Italy almost unopposed and subject it to ravaging before supply problems forced him to withdraw. The following spring, Attila died unexpectedly and his empire immediately began to fall apart.

A coin issued by the emperor Valentinian III to celebrate 'his' victory over Attila at the Catalaunian Plains in 451. In the Roman Empire, it was normal for the emperor to take the credit for his generals' victories.

Aetius

The fall of the Hun empire left Aetius militarily and politically bankrupt. Not only had he lost an irreplaceable source of ferociously effective troops, but also the delicate balance of power by which he maintained Roman authority in Gaul was shattered. With the Huns gone, there was no longer any good reason for the Germans to cooperate with him. Aetius' influence at the imperial court was also undermined. He alone had been able to manage the Huns: now he no longer seemed quite so indispensable.

Downfall and death

Even before the death of Attila, Valentinian was growing increasingly resentful of Aetius' power. After the death of Theodosius in 450, Valentinian had conceived a hare-brained plan to reunite the empire under his sole rule. Realizing that this would cause a civil war that the empire could ill afford, Aetius blocked the plan. Valentinian and Aetius soon disagreed again over a marriage alliance. Perhaps sensing that his position was weakening, Aetius proposed a marriage between his son Gaudentius and Valentinian's daughter Placidia. Since Valentinian had no male children, this would not only have made Aetius' position unassailable, but it would also have made Gaudentius heir to the throne. This was too much for Valentinian. At a meeting to discuss tax revenues on 21 or 22 September 454, he suddenly drew his sword and murdered Aetius. A contemporary chronicler commented that Valentinian might as well have chopped off his own right hand. Valentinian lasted barely six months: on 16 March 455 he was cut down by two of Aetius' loyal Hun officers as he practised archery in the fields outside Rome. With no general of comparable ability to replace Aetius and no obvious successor to Valentinian, the Western Roman Empire entered its final decline. By the time its last feeble emperor was deposed by a barbarian general in 476, the Western Roman Empire consisted of Italy and little else.

The fall of the Western Empire did nothing to diminish Aetius' posthumous reputation, and in the sixth century the Byzantine historian Procopius described him simply as 'the last of the Romans'. Aetius' failure to save the Western Empire was largely the result of circumstances

The sarcophagus of Valentinian III in the mausoleum of his mother, Galla Placidia, at Ravenna. Valentinian was murdered in 455 by two of Aetius' officers seeking to avenge his death at the emperor's hands.

THE BATTLE OF THE CATALAUNIAN PLAINS

ETIUS' LAST AND MOST IMPORTANT VICTORY, the Battle of the Catalaunian Plains, was as much a masterpiece of diplomacy as of generalship. Faced with an invasion of Gaul by his former ally Attila in 451, he built an unlikely coalition of his former German enemies in Gaul, including the Visigoths (under their veteran king Theodoric), Franks, Burgundians, Saxons and Alans (a former nomad people who had been driven off the steppes by the Huns). Most of Aetius' regular Roman troops were also Germans, so his army was Roman in name only. Attila's army also had a large German component drawn from his subject peoples, chief among them the Ostrogoths and the Gepids.

Attila advanced as far west as Orléans but was unable to take the city. Harassed by Aetius' forces, Attila withdrew to the more open country of the Catalaunian Plains (modern Champagne) where he could exploit his superiority in cavalry more effectively. On 20 June near the village of Châtres, between Châlons and Troyes, Attila laagered his wagons and prepared to make a stand against his pursuers. Attila formed his battle line with his Huns in the centre and his German allies on the flanks. Aetius placed the regulars on the left of his line and the Visigoths and the other Germans on the right. The Alans, whose reliability Aetius doubted, were placed in the centre, to stop them running away.

Fighting began around three o'clock in the afternoon with a struggle over possession of a low hill on the left of the battlefield. Aetius spotted the advantageous position slightly sooner than Attila, and Visigothic cavalry under Thorismund (Theodoric's son) managed to occupy the summit just ahead of the Huns. The fighting then became general. The Roman infantry formed an impenetrable formation behind interlocking shields so Attila

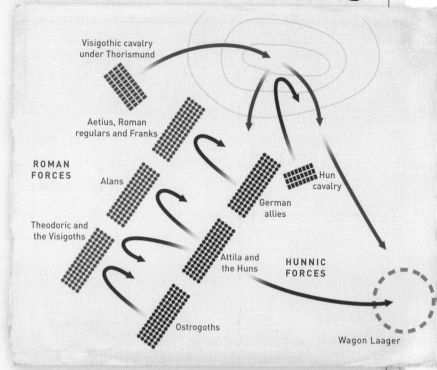

Visigothic cavalry under Thorismund

Aetius, Roman regulars and Franks

ROMAN FORCES

Alans

Theodoric and the Visigoths

German allies

Hun cavalry

Attila and the Huns

HUNNIC FORCES

Ostrogoths

Wagon Laager

concentrated his attack on the Germans, most of whom were also fighting on foot. In the mêlée, King Theodoric was thrown from his horse and trampled to death by his own men. Ferocious fighting was still continuing when darkness began to fall, some seven hours after it had begun. Attila began to withdraw into his wagon laager pursued by Thorismund. In the darkness and confusion Thorismund was wounded in the head and thrown to the ground, to be saved from his father's fate only by the quick action of one of his men. Aetius had had the better of the fighting and he called off the action rather than risk continuing in the dark. Casualties on both sides were heavy – sources speak improbably of one hundred and sixty-five thousand dead. Aetius did not order a pursuit when Attila began to withdraw the next day, probably because he wished to preserve the Huns to counterbalance Visigothic power in Gaul.

beyond his control. His military record speaks for itself – he lost only one battle in his career and was adored by his troops – and his political judgement was usually sound. His greatest weakness was his reliance on the Huns, which was forced on him by the chronic manpower shortage of the later Roman Empire. Aetius was rarely able to do more than contain one threat to the empire before he had to divert his limited resources to face a new one. What he did brilliantly was to use his military and political skills to buy time for the empire while he waited for a lucky break that never came.

ATTILA

JOHN HAYWOOD

c. 406–453

ATTILA THE HUN is quite probably the most notorious figure of what it is now unfashionable to call the 'Dark Ages'. King of the Huns from 434 to 453, Attila terrorized the declining Roman Empire and conquered an empire of his own that stretched from the Black Sea to the Rhine. Ultimately, however, he destroyed far more than he built and his achievements did not outlive him.

Of Attila's early life nothing much is known. His father was Mundzuk, brother of Ruga, who had become joint king of the Huns in the 420s. At this time, the Huns were a society in transition. A Turkic nomad people, they had migrated from central Asia to eastern Europe in the later fourth century and settled on the Hungarian plain. This was the most westerly area of steppe grassland suitable for pasturing the vast herds of horses on which the nomads depended for their military power. The area was also strategically well placed for raiding the Germanic peoples of central and northern Europe and both the western and eastern halves of the Roman Empire.

The Huns in the fifth century

At the time of their arrival in Europe, the Huns did not acknowledge a single ruler but had several power-sharing kings who operated within a ranking system, with one of their number recognized as senior king. To avoid overgrazing, the Huns needed to

Attila

be dispersed over a wide area, and this led naturally to the formation of a devolved power structure. In the fifth century, the Huns began to abandon nomadic pastoralism and settle in villages. They became wealthy from raiding, collecting tribute from subject peoples and wages for mercenary service with the Roman armies. This made possible a process of political centralization that led to Ruga becoming sole king of the Huns in 432. Kings ruled with the support of a chosen elite called the *logades*, but the Huns still lacked formal institutions of government and their unity depended solely on their leaders' success in war. Loyalty had, in effect, to be paid for by distributing the spoils of war: a king who lacked the means to reward his followers would not last long.

Ruga died in 434 and was succeeded as king jointly by Attila and his brother Bleda. Their first act was to conclude a peace treaty that their uncle had been negotiating with the Eastern Roman Empire at the time of his death. Attila and Bleda declined to dismount for the peace conference, forcing the Roman ambassadors to conduct negotiations on horseback to maintain the impression that both parties were equals. In fact the Romans were desperate for peace – they needed to free troops to fight the Vandals who had invaded North Africa – and the brothers drove a hard bargain. Escaped Roman prisoners were to be returned or ransomed for eight golden solidi apiece and the annual tribute that the Romans would pay for peace was doubled from 350 to 700 pounds of gold a year. The Romans also had to hand over to certain death members of the Hun royal family who had unsuccessfully opposed Ruga and become refugees in the empire.

Invasion of the Balkans

For several years after the peace treaty, Attila and Bleda were fully occupied conquering what Roman writers vaguely called 'Scythia', meaning barbarian Europe. The exact bounds of their conquests are not known, but they certainly extended to the Baltic Sea in the north and to within a short distance of the Rhine in the west and the Black Sea in the east. During this time the Romans failed to pay the Huns their annual subsidy. Then in 439 the Vandals captured Carthage and threatened to cut off Rome's corn supply. All of the Romans' military resources needed to be marshalled to recapture Carthage, presenting Attila and Bleda with an opportunity to exact vengeance. The Roman failure to abide by the terms of the treaty gave the Huns an unimpeachable reason for war and in 441 they crossed the Danube and invaded the Balkans. First Viminiacum (Kostolac, Serbia) fell and was razed to the ground, its population being marched off into slavery. Next to fall was Margum, then Singidunum (Belgrade), and with the fall of the great fortress city of Sirmium (Mitrovica) the defences of the Danube frontier collapsed. With a large swathe of Roman territory under his control, Attila agreed a truce with the eastern emperor Theodosius II (r. 408–450). Attila warned that any attempt at offensive action by the Romans would result in a renewal of war. Despite this, Theodosius used the respite to cancel the planned attack on the Vandals and transfer his troops to the Balkans.

As he had threatened, Attila went back to war. In 443 he captured the base of the Romans' Danube fleet at Ratiaria (Archar, Bulgaria). With his lines of communication now secured against Roman attacks, he marched south and sacked the major arms-manufacturing centre at Naissus (Nish, Bulgaria) before turning east and meting out the same treatment to Sardica (Sofia). He then moved quickly down the main road towards the eastern capital city of Constantinople. Up until then, he had met little opposition, but between Attila and Constantinople lay the main Roman field army under the master general Aspar. In a succession of battles Attila comprehensively outmanoeuvred Aspar, cut him off from the capital and scattered his remaining forces. Though Constantinople itself was so heavily fortified as to be impregnable, the Balkans were now completely defenceless and Theodosius sued for peace. Attila demanded payment of the arrears of tribute and in future an annual payment of 2,100 pounds of gold. The price of ransoming Roman prisoners was to rise from 8 to 12 solidi. The arrears were paid, peace was agreed in autumn 443 and the Huns withdrew from Roman territory.

Sole ruler of the Huns

In 444 or 445 Attila murdered his brother Bleda and became sole king of the Huns. It is not known why they fell out, but the brothers seem to have had very different characters. Bleda had a wantonly cruel and sadistic side to his character while Attila, though utterly ruthless, had a more pragmatic attitude to violence. Although his name has become a byword for tyranny, he was not regarded as a tyrant by his fellow Huns. His personal enemies might have suffered an agonizing death by impalement, but for the most part Attila relied not on terror but on personal charisma and successful war leadership to keep the Huns obedient to his rule. A Greek prisoner who had decided to remain with the Huns after being freed compared Attila's rule favourably with that of the Roman emperors with their high taxes and corrupt officials.

Little is known about Attila's movements until the spring of 447 when he again invaded the Eastern Roman Empire, on an even larger scale than in 441. This time Attila brought with him contingents drawn from his Germanic subjects. In January of that year Constantinople had suffered a series of severe earthquakes and a large section of the city walls, including fifty-seven towers, had collapsed. As the people of Constantinople laboured frantically to rebuild their walls, Attila approached, leaving the usual trail of smoking ruins behind him. This time, however, Roman resistance was stiffer. Near Marcianopolis, Attila met the Roman field army and, though he defeated it, he incurred heavy casualties. Learning that the walls of Constantinople had been restored, Attila turned aside and ravaged through the Balkans and into

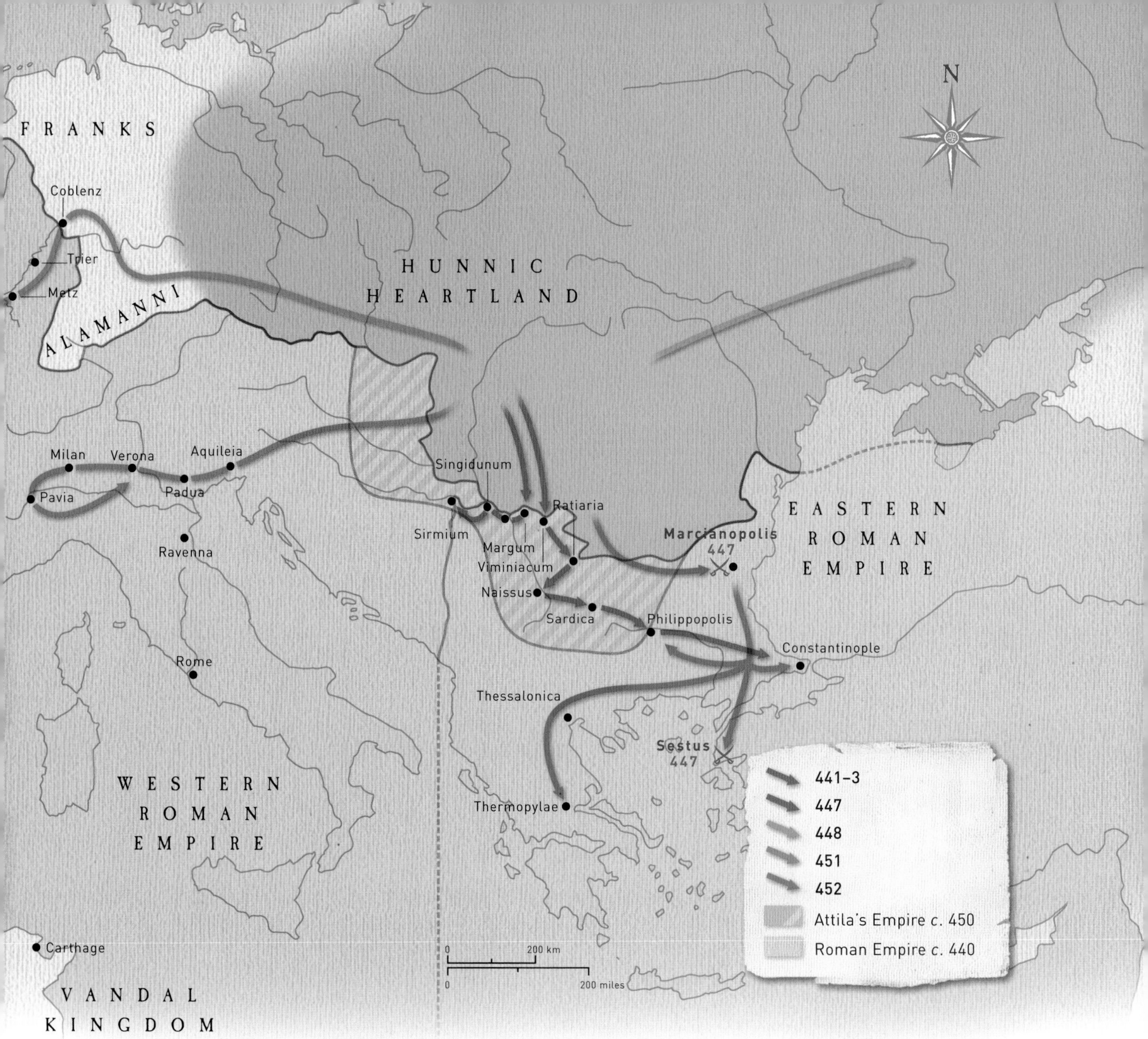
FRANKS
Coblenz
Trier
Metz
ALAMANNI
HUNNIC
HEARTLAND
Milan
Verona
Aquileia
Pavia
Padua
Ravenna
Rome
Singidunum
Sirmium
Margum
Viminiacum
Ratiaria
Naissus
Sardica
Philippopolis
Marcianopolis
447
EASTERN
ROMAN
EMPIRE
Constantinople
Thessalonica
Sestus
447
Thermopylae
WESTERN
ROMAN
EMPIRE
Carthage
VANDAL
KINGDOM
N
0
200 km
0
200 miles
441–3
447
448
451
452
Attila's Empire c. 450
Roman Empire c. 440

THE CAMPAIGNS OF ATTILA THE HUN, 441–452.

Greece. The price of peace for the Romans this time was to cede a strip of territory south of the Danube that was five days' travel wide (about 120 miles). The following year Attila left the Romans alone and campaigned in the east, conquering the Acatziri, a nomadic people who lived on the steppes between the Black Sea and the Caspian Sea. The attack was probably provoked by the emperor Theodosius' attempt to forge an anti-Hun alliance with them.

The Romans now resorted to desperate measures. In 449 Theodosius' government, hatched a plot to assassinate Attila using a diplomatic embassy as cover. The plot was betrayed, however, and the ambassadors, who had not been told that their mission was just a diversion, counted themselves lucky not to be executed on the spot. Attila's show of mercy made it easier for him to exploit Roman embarrassment over this treacherous breach of diplomatic protocol to extract another huge payment

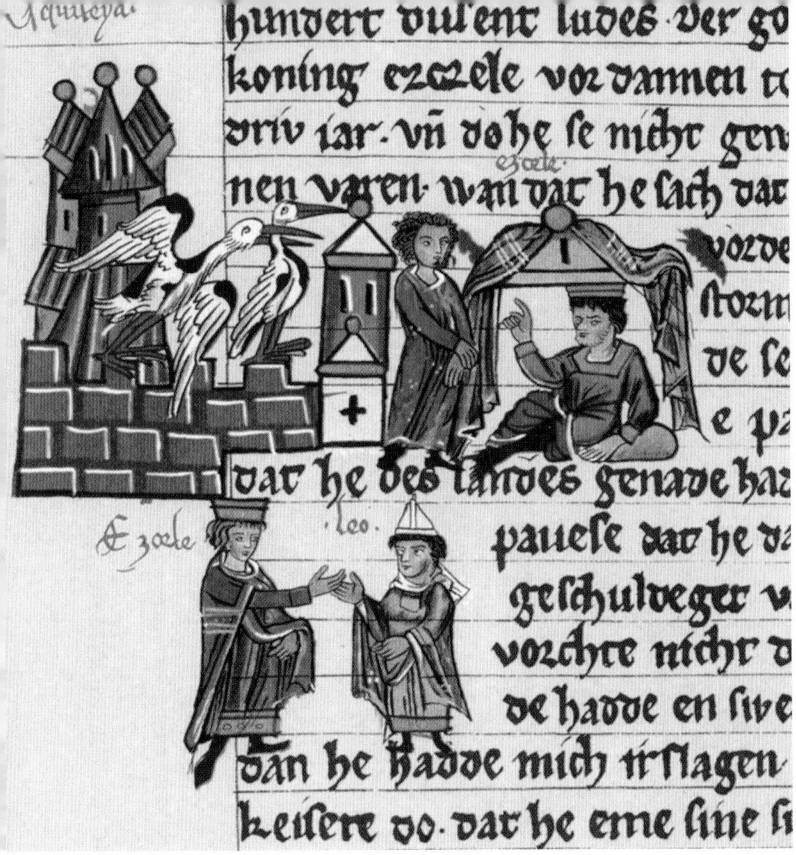
Aquileya
hundert dusent ludes · der go
koning ezzele vor dannen
driv iar · vñ do he se nicht gen
nen varen · wan dat he sach dat
Ezzele
Leo
dat he des landes genade ha
pauese dat he
geschuldeger
vorchte nicht
de hadde en sive
dan he hadde mich irslagen
keisere do · dat he eme sine

A fifteenth-century manuscript illustrating a legend about the siege of Aquileia in 452. When he saw storks flying away from the city, Attila inspired his men to greater efforts by telling them that the birds had foreseen its fall and were escaping while they still could. Shown below is the meeting at which Pope Leo I offered Attila tribute in return for his agreement not to attack Rome.

of tribute. Satisfied that the Eastern Empire was now no threat to him, Attila turned his attention to the Western Roman Empire. Nominally ruled by the weak emperor Valentinian III (r. 425–455), real power in the west lay with the master general Aetius (d. 454). In his younger days, Aetius had been a hostage with the Huns and he had maintained close and friendly relations with them ever since, often employing them as mercenaries. Aetius had even made Attila an honorary master general in the Western army.

Glittering prizes beckon

In early 450 Attila announced his intention to attack the Visigothic kingdom in Aquitaine as the ally of Valentinian. The Visigoths had been a problem for the Romans ever since they had entered the empire in 376 as refugees from the Huns, and the destruction of their kingdom would have served Roman interests. It is likely that Attila intended to make his honorific military rank into a real one, replace Aetius as commander of the western armies and so win effective control of the Western Roman Empire. Attila received further encouragement in the spring when a messenger arrived from Valentinian's sister Honoria with a plea to rescue her from an intolerable marriage. Attila demanded that Valentinian hand her over, together with a dowry of half the Western Empire. He refused. In the summer a succession dispute broke out among the Franks, one party appealing to Aetius for support, the other, a minority party, to Attila, giving him another reason to intervene in the west. Then Theodosius died in a riding accident and Marcian, the new eastern emperor, refused to pay any more tribute to Attila.

Attila continued with his planned campaign in the west – if successful he would easily be able to deal with Marcian. As in 447, he called on the services of his Germanic subjects and he crossed the Rhine near Coblenz with a massive army, and invaded Gaul. However, Attila had bungled the diplomatic preparations for the invasion. By threatening the interests of the Romans, Visigoths and Franks all at the same time, Attila drove them into an alliance. Attila got as far west as Orléans but, failing to take the city, he withdrew to the Catalaunian Plains (Champagne). There, somewhere between Châlons and Troyes, he was met in battle on 20 June 451 by Aetius, at the head of a mixed army of Romans, Visigoths, Franks and other Germans who had settled in Gaul. The two armies fought themselves to a standstill by nightfall, each suffering heavy casualties. During the night Attila briefly considered immolating himself on a pyre of saddles but thought better of it. In the morning Aetius watched as the Huns withdrew in good order. By September Attila was back in Hungary, and sending raiding parties into the Balkans to keep Marcian guessing about his plans.

Though he was still determined on marriage with Honoria, Attila learned from his mistakes; the next year he forced the Romans to face him alone by invading Italy, which the Visigoths and Franks had no interest in defending. Aetius, believing that Attila would be ready to negotiate peace after his defeat, had failed to guard the Alpine passes so the Huns faced no opposition until they reached Aquileia. Here Attila was held up for several weeks by the heroic resistance of the garrison, before his Huns scaled the walls and sacked the city so thoroughly that it never recovered. Attila swept west along the Po valley, sacking city after city, until at Milan he was met by a delegation led by Pope Leo I (r. 440–461) with offers of tribute in return for peace. It came none too soon. Italy was in the grip of famine and Attila would have been forced to retreat soon for lack of supplies. He returned home to discover that, in his absence, Marcian had sent troops to raid Hun territory.

The collapse of Attila's empire

Though the world still quailed at the mention of his name, Attila's position at the end of 452 was surprisingly weak. The Italian expedition had certainly been profitable in terms of plunder and tribute, but casualties had been heavy, and these came on top of the losses suffered in Gaul the previous year. He had not married Honoria and was no nearer controlling the Western Empire. The Huns' horses were tired and had returned home too late to benefit from summer grazing, so no campaign could be launched the following year until they had had a chance to fatten up again in the spring. The Balkans had been ravaged so often that there would be little profit in raiding them again and Attila knew, from previous experience, that Marcian was safe from his vengeance so long as he remained behind the walls of Constantinople. Yet Attila had an imperative need to maintain a constant supply of plunder to maintain his hold on power: it was impossible for him to do nothing.

In spring 453, while he was still contemplating what to do about Marcian's defiance, Attila decided to add a

The massive land walls of Constantinople, built by the emperor Theodosius II (r. 408–450), resisted all assaults until finally breached by Turkish cannon in 1453. Attila himself never dared to challenge them.

> '**The vigour with which Attila wielded the sword of Mars convinced the world that it had been reserved alone for his invincible arm.**'
>
> EDWARD GIBBON, *THE HISTORY OF THE DECLINE AND FALL OF THE ROMAN EMPIRE* (1776–88)

After his death, Attila's name became a byword for savagery and wanton destruction. This romanticized nineteenth-century painting shows the victorious Huns riding across a plain with female captives and decapitated male heads on their spears.

beautiful German girl called Ildico to his collection of wives. It has been speculated that she was a princess, handed over to Attila by a German king as a form of tribute. The wedding celebrations were long and Attila got as gloriously drunk as any self-respecting barbarian should do on such occasions. Retiring for the night with his new bride, Attila passed out on his bed. During the night, he suffered a severe nosebleed while lying unconscious on his back and quietly drowned in his own blood. The death of such a terrifying figure could not go unnoticed in heaven and, it was said, on the same night Marcian dreamed prophetically that the bow of Attila was broken. Deprived of his charismatic leadership, the Hun empire quickly disintegrated. As Attila's sons fought over the kingship, their German subjects rebelled, and at the Battle of Nedao in 455 they overthrew the Hun empire. Bands of surviving Huns scattered back to the steppes, within a century losing their identity as a people.

Attila's legacy

Any objective assessment of Attila's career must conclude that he achieved nothing beyond perhaps hastening the decline of the Western Roman Empire by diverting forces that were needed elsewhere. True, Attila spread terror, destruction and death across much of Europe, and he relieved the Romans of a great deal of treasure, but he never even began to lay the foundations of a lasting state. He lacked the political imagination to make the transition from barbarian war leader to statesman. Despite

Attila

this, Attila's reputation continued to grow after his death. By the eighth century the legend that he had called himself 'the Scourge of God' had gained wide currency and he was firmly ensconced in Germanic and Scandinavian legend, and in dozens of spurious tales of miraculous deliverances from Attila and of gory martyrdoms at his hands. Only among the Hungarians, or Magyars as they call themselves, is Attila regarded as a national hero. Even this is a legend, however; the Magyars, a Finno-Ugrian people originally from Siberia, are actually completely unrelated to the Turkic Huns. The Hungarians, despite appearances, did not get their name from the Huns – the term derives from a Slavic mispronunciation of On-Ogur ('Ten Arrows'), the name of the Magyar confederation that conquered the area in the late ninth century.

A Hunnish skull, showing the deformation caused by head-binding in infancy. Their unnatural appearance only added to the Huns' fearsome reputation.

THE HUNS AT WAR

DESPITE HIS MANY VICTORIES, there is no evidence that Attila was an innovative commander. The secret of Attila's success was mainly down to the Huns' style of fighting. Although by Attila's day the Huns were becoming increasingly sedentary, they continued the traditions of warfare that they had developed when they still lived on the Eurasian steppes. Like all the steppe nomads, they spent much of their lives on horseback, constantly moving with the seasons in search of fresh pasture for their flocks of sheep and herds of cattle and horses, and they made natural light cavalrymen. Blood feuds and fights with other nomad peoples over grazing rights were an everyday fact of steppe life. The favoured weapon of the Indo-Iranian nomads, such as the Sarmatians and Alans, who had dominated the western steppes before the arrival of the Huns, was the lance and both rider and horse wore scale armour like the cataphracti of the Persian and Roman armies.

In contrast, the Huns were horse archers. They rarely wore armour and relied on speed and manoeuvrability for protection. Using their powerful composite recurved bows, the Huns could pour down a deadly and demoralizing hail of arrows on slower-moving armoured cavalry and infantry long before they could get close enough to retaliate. Made by gluing together layers of wood, horn and sinew, the composite bow's compactness made it ideal for use on horseback. The bows used by the Huns had the added refinement of a unique asymmetrical design that almost doubled its power, so that it could pierce armour at a range of up to 100 yards. This was comparable to packing the power of a medieval English longbow into a weapon half its size and weight. The importance of the bow to the Huns was such that it was a symbol of authority, and chieftains would be buried with gold-sheathed bows. When they arrived in Europe the Huns had no experience of siege warfare. By Attila's time they had learned to make siege weapons, probably from the Romans, which they carried with them on campaign in their wagons. They also carried rafts with them for crossing rivers.

The effectiveness of their cavalry was enhanced by their nightmarish appearance. The Huns practised deformation of the skull. Infants' skulls were tightly bound above the eyebrows so that as the skull grew it would be deformed into a long flat shape with a low forehead. The Huns also practised scarification of the face, which left them with little facial hair. Soldiers who had not encountered the Huns before must have found their appearance very unnerving, and stories that they were really the offspring of witches and wild beasts were widely believed.

> 'The life of Theodoric represents the rare and meritorious example of a barbarian who sheathed his sword in the pride of victory and the vigour of his age.'
>
> EDWARD GIBBON, *THE HISTORY OF THE DECLINE AND FALL OF THE ROMAN EMPIRE*

THEODORIC

c. 454–526   JOHN HAYWOOD

KING OF THE OSTROGOTHS FROM 471 TO 526, Theodoric conquered Italy in 489–493 and founded the most sophisticated of the barbarian kingdoms. Throughout his reign he fought to protect and preserve his people and win for them a prosperous and secure homeland. In achieving this he showed great military and diplomatic abilities, as well as inspiring leadership, personal bravery and ruthlessness.

Born in 454, Theodoric was the son of Thiudemir, who, with his brothers Valamir and Videmir, was king of the Ostrogoths. He belonged to the Amal family which claimed to be descended from a long line of illustrious, semi-legendary kings. Later tradition had it that he was born, auspiciously, on the same day that his uncle Valamir won a great victory over the Huns. The Ostrogoths ('Eastern Goths') were descendants of the Greuthungi, a branch of the Goths who had been conquered by the Huns around 374 (the other main branch of the Goths, the Tervingi, had escaped into the Roman Empire, where they became known as the Visigoths or 'Western Goths'). The Ostrogoths kept their own kings under the Huns and played an important role in Attila's campaigns in the 450s. Following the death of Attila in 453, the Hun empire disintegrated and the Ostrogoths became independent. Shortly after this, the Romans allowed them to settle as semi-autonomous *foederati* ('allies') in the province of Pannonia on the middle Danube.

In 461 Theodoric was sent as a hostage to Constantinople where he remained for ten years. As a high-ranking hostage Theodoric was well treated and became a favourite of the emperor Leo I (r. 457–474). His upbringing in what was then the world's largest and most splendid city made a great impression on Theodoric, but if Leo thought that this would make him into a compliant puppet of the empire he was to be disappointed. Throughout the time that Theodoric was in Constantinople, the Ostrogoths were fighting their German neighbours and wandering remnants of the Huns. During these wars Valamir had been killed, leaving Theodoric's father Thiudemir as the senior Ostrogothic king. On his return to his people in 471, Theodoric set out to prove himself a war leader. The Sarmatians had recently captured

Theodoric

the Roman city of Singidunum (Belgrade) and Theodoric, still aged only 18, raised an army on his own initiative and drove them out. Instead of returning the city to the Romans, he kept it for the Ostrogoths. For this Theodoric was acclaimed king, alongside his father and uncle Videmir.

In 473, Thiudemir and Videmir decided that war-ravaged Pannonia was no longer a suitable homeland for their people. To pressure the Romans into relocating them, they decided that Videmir would invade Italy while Thiudemir would attack the Eastern Empire. Videmir's campaign failed: he died in Italy and the survivors went to Gaul and joined the Visigoths. Thiudemir launched his campaign from Singidunum and advanced as far as Nish. From there he sent Theodoric, with a couple of grizzled veterans as advisers, to lead a raid through the Balkans and into Greece. Thiudemir followed up his son's success by laying siege to Thessalonica. Negotiations followed and the Romans allowed the Ostrogoths to settle in Macedonia. Shortly after, probably in 474, Thiudemir died and Theodoric succeeded to sole kingship of the Ostrogoths. The settlement in Macedonia proved to be unsatisfactory, however, and a few years later the Ostrogoths were moved by the Romans to Thrace.

Rival leaders

The next few years of Theodoric's reign were dominated by his rivalry with Theodoric Triarius, the leader of a separate band of Goths that the Romans had settled in the Balkans as *foederati* some years previously. The eastern emperor, Zeno (r. 474–491), was only willing to support one Gothic leader, so the two Theodorics had to compete for imperial recognition. When Triarius rebelled in 478, Zeno allied with Theodoric to mount a joint attack on him. In the event, Zeno failed to supply the troops he had promised and Theodoric found himself facing his rival alone. However, the Goths refused to fight one another and the two leaders were reconciled. Zeno broke up this alliance by offering Triarius a generous settlement, including a generalship, and abandoning Theodoric and the Ostrogoths. Angry at his betrayal, and with his people facing starvation, Theodoric led his men on a campaign of plundering and indiscriminate killing through the Balkans until Triarius rebelled again, forcing Zeno to open negotiations. As the price of his support, Theodoric demanded that he be given Triarius' command and Roman citizenship. Wary of replacing one troublesome barbarian general with another, Zeno refused. Zeno's hand was strengthened when the Roman general Sabinianus ambushed an Ostrogothic baggage train in 479, taking five thousand prisoners and two thousand wagons. Sabinianus then blockaded Theodoric in Epirus until 482,

A gold solidus minted by Theodoric after his conquest of Italy. Theodoric ruled officially as the viceroy of the eastern Roman emperor Anastasius whose name, rather than Theodoric's, appears on the legend.

Theodoric

when Zeno ordered his execution on suspicion of treason. Sabinianus' less able replacements failed to prevent Theodoric escaping.

Theodoric's position was simplified in 481 when Triarius, once again in rebellion, was fatally injured in a riding accident. His son Recitach took over but was murdered by Theodoric when they met for a banquet in 484. Recitach's following of around thirty thousand joined the Ostrogoths, raising their strength to around one hundred thousand men, women and children. In these years Theodoric swung between loyalty to the empire – in 484 he was made consul – and rebellion. This reflects the difficulty of his position. Although the Romans were not strong enough to expel the Ostrogoths, the Ostrogoths were not strong enough to dictate terms to the Romans. Theodoric's rebellions were even becoming counterproductive: the Balkans was now so war-ravaged that the land could hardly support his people.

> 'I would be more splendidly dressed today than for any festival. If the enemy do not recognize me by the violence of my assault, let them recognize me by the brilliancy of my raiment. If fortune gives my throat to the sword ... let them at least say, "How splendid he looks in death."'
>
> THEODORIC BEFORE THE BATTLE OF THE ISONZO (ACCORDING TO HIS COURT POET, ENNODIUS)

Zeno's commission

Zeno provided the solution to Theodoric's problem: in 488 he gave him a commission to invade Italy, overthrow its ruler Odovacer and govern it until 'the emperor should come to claim his supremacy'. Odovacer was a German general who in 476 had overthrown Romulus Augustulus, the last, powerless, Roman emperor of the west, and been proclaimed king by the German (mainly Herul and Rugian) mercenaries he commanded. Zeno accepted Odovacer's face-saving offer to rule Italy as viceroy, which at least maintained the legal position that it remained part of the Roman Empire. From Zeno's point of view, sending Theodoric west was a win-win situation. If Theodoric lost, that would be the end of the Ostrogoths, and if he won, at least they would be a long way from Constantinople. The offer was attractive to Theodoric, too. He was well aware that the Ostrogoths were in a very insecure position in the Eastern Roman Empire and Zeno's commission gave him the opportunity to win legitimate control of a rich kingdom. The question of what would happen if Zeno actually did 'come to claim his supremacy' was left hanging.

Invasion of Italy

The Ostrogoths gathered at Novae (Cezava) and set off for Italy in the autumn of 488, perhaps an unpromising time of year to begin what was not so much a military campaign as a migration of a whole people, but it would have been easier to find (buy or plunder) food supplies so soon after the harvest. The early stages of the route, up the lower reaches of the Sava river valley, lay across territory occupied by the Gepids, old enemies of the Ostrogoths, who refused them passage. The Gepids held a strong position on the opposite bank of the River Ulca, somewhere near Sirmium, and they repulsed all attacks until Theodoric led a charge across the river in person and broke the Gepid line. Part of the plunder from the battle was a Gepid wagon train loaded with grain.

A twelfth-century stone carving from the church of San Zeno, Verona, showing Theodoric (left) jousting with Odovacer, his rival for control of Italy. There is no evidence that the two men actually met face to face in battle.

Once out of Gepid territory Theodoric followed the same route through the Julian Alps that Alaric the Visigoth had taken when he had invaded Italy eighty years before. The Ostrogoths moved slowly, encumbered as they were by thousands of wagons, pack animals, herds of cattle, flocks of sheep, and non-combatants. Of the one hundred thousand or so Ostrogoths, only around one third would have been able-bodied men capable of bearing arms; the rest would have been women, children and old people. It is unlikely that the migrating horde could have made much more than about 4½ miles a day, so it was not until summer 489 that they began to descend to the plains around Aquileia. Odovacer had prepared his defences and was waiting for the Ostrogoths in a strongly fortified camp overlooking a ford crossing the Isonzo river. On 28 August Theodoric forded the river, stormed the camp and put Odovacer to flight. Nothing is known about the conduct of this crucial battle: most of the descriptions of Theodoric's battles come from the work of his court poet Ennodius and, though strong on heroic imagery, they are almost totally lacking in tactical detail.

Odovacer retreated to Verona and built another fortified camp outside the city, on the east bank of the Adige river. By placing their backs to the river, and by

Theodoric

THE SIEGE OF RAVENNA

LAYING SIEGE TO RAVENNA was a daunting prospect. The city was a natural stronghold, being surrounded by malarial marshes that were not only difficult to cross, but would make life uncomfortable and unhealthy for any besieging army. As capital of the Western Roman Empire from 402, and Odovacer's capital from 476, Ravenna had been heavily fortified, and it was also a port, so it could be supplied and reinforced from the sea. Moreover, Theodoric did not have enough troops to seal off Ravenna completely from the outside. His main siege camp was in the Pineta, a strip of sandy pine forest lying between Ravenna and the open sea, a healthier environment in which to camp than the marshes.

In September 490, Theodoric began to send out regular mounted patrols to stop any traffic going to the city by road but, lacking a fleet, Theodoric was unable to stop ships delivering supplies. Odovacer sent out raiding parties to harass the Ostrogoths at every opportunity. To protect his rear, Theodoric sent death squads throughout Italy to eliminate as many of Odovacer's supporters as they could find, but Odovacer's general, Tufa, remained at large with an army in Lombardy.

In mid July 491 Odovacer received reinforcements from the Heruls, who lived beyond the Danube, and tried to win back the initiative with a surprise night attack on Theodoric's camp. After hard fighting, and heavy casualties on both sides, Theodoric again prevailed and again, as he had throughout the war, showed his ability to rally his soldiers in difficult situations. The leadership of his opponent, on the other hand, was consistently

Ships in the harbour of Classis, the port of Ravenna, shown in a sixth-century mosaic from the church of Sant' Apollinare Nuovo, Ravenna. The fact that it had good sea communications was a major reason why Ravenna was chosen as capital of the Western Roman Empire in 402 and, subsequently, as capital by both Odovacer and Theodoric.

breaking the bridge that linked his camp to Verona, Odovacer hoped to force his men to fight more stubbornly than they had at the Isonzo. Once again leading from the front, on 30 September Theodoric stormed the camp. Odovacer and some of his followers managed to break out of the self-made trap and fled south to Ravenna, his capital. Theodoric continued west and in October occupied Milan. There, Odovacer's chief of staff Tufa, together with a large body of German troops, surrendered to Theodoric. In a rare error of judgement, Theodoric took Tufa and his men into his own service, sending them to besiege Odovacer in Ravenna. Once there, Tufa reverted to his old allegiance and the Ostrogoths Theodoric had sent with him were handed over to Odovacer and murdered.

On hearing of Tufa's betrayal, Theodoric immediately moved to Pavia, a more easily defended position than Milan, being protected on two sides by rivers. The Ostrogothic non-combatants would remain there, in crowded and uncomfortable conditions, for the remainder of the war. Both kings spent the winter of 489–490 in lacklustre. Still the siege dragged on. In August 492 Theodoric captured Rimini, which was still held for Odovacer, and with it a fleet of *dromons*, a type of light and fast war galley. He did what perhaps he should have done earlier – began to blockade Ravenna from the sea, cutting off all supplies. By January 493 the population of Ravenna was beginning to starve, and on 27 February, with no hope of relief, Odovacer surrendered. Theodoric entered Ravenna, to the welcoming cheers of its people, just six days later.

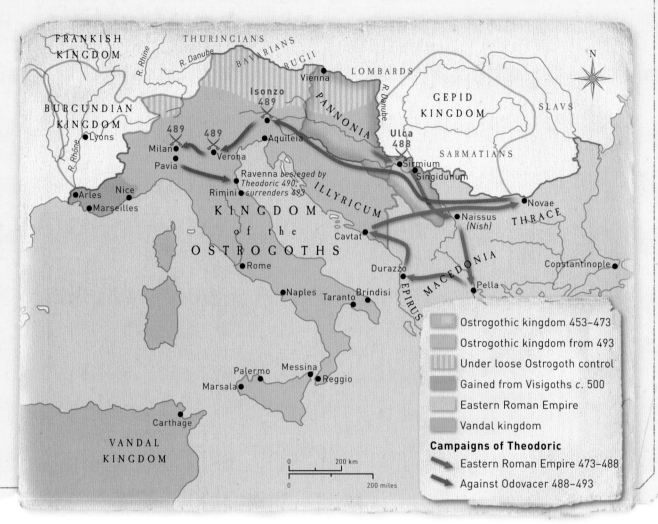

diplomatic activity. Theodoric won support from the Visigoths, while Odovacer persuaded the Burgundians to invade Italy by playing on their fears of encirclement by Goths. While Theodoric was distracted with the Burgundians – he was eventually able to negotiate their withdrawal – Odovacer began to reassert control in northern Italy. By the summer he was in Milan, which he treated roughly for having been too welcoming to the Ostrogoths. With an army of Ostrogoths and Visigoths, Theodoric left Pavia, and on 11 August he inflicted another heavy defeat on Odovacer at the River Adda, 10 miles east of Milan. Odovacer fled back to Ravenna and prepared for a siege.

The siege lasted for two and a half weary years, during which one of Theodoric's allies, a Rugian prince called Fredericus, went over to Tufa and occupied Pavia on his own account. Though his own family was at Pavia, Theodoric held fast to the siege and it seems that no harm was done to the Ostrogothic non-combatants by the Rugians. Finally, on 27 February 493, Odovacer surrendered to Theodoric on seemingly generous terms. Theodoric agreed not only that Odovacer's life should be spared but

THE CAMPAIGNS OF THEODORIC AND THE KINGDOM OF THE OSTROGOTHS in the late fifth and early sixth centuries.

that the two of them would share the kingship of Italy. On 15 March Theodoric invited Odovacer to a feast to celebrate the peace. When he had been separated from his guards, Theodoric drew his sword and with a single blow cut Odovacer in half, from the collarbone to the groin. Surprised by his own strength, Theodoric is said to have commented that he always knew that Odovacer was a spineless wretch.

The outstanding problem of Fredericus and Tufa solved itself in 494 when the two fell out over a division of plunder. Fredericus killed Tufa and then vanished from history. At no time throughout the long war had the Roman population of Italy taken sides; what was it to them which barbarian ruled them?

A system of military apartheid?

Like Odovacer, Theodoric continued to rule Italy as if it were still part of the Roman Empire. Theodoric never described himself as king of Italy (because of its implication of territorial sovereignty), only as king of the Ostrogoths in Italy. He respected the right of the emperor in Constantinople to appoint the consuls of Rome and even his right to make laws. Though he always ruled from Ravenna, Theodoric consulted the Roman Senate, continued the dole of free grain to the Roman poor and sponsored games in the circus. Whatever his failings, Odovacer had ruled Italy competently through the existing Roman institutions, and Theodoric continued this policy, his

The mausoleum of Theodoric at Ravenna.
Begun some years before Theodoric's death in 526, the roof of the mausoleum is carved from a single block of limestone weighing 300 tons. Theodoric's remains were removed after the city was captured by the Byzantines in 540.

government being run entirely by Roman bureaucrats. The military, on the other hand, was the exclusive preserve of the Ostrogoths: under the veneer of civilian government, Theodoric remained a barbarian warlord. Goths were even forbidden to have a Roman education lest it sap their martial vigour. Romans were forbidden to carry any weapon larger than a penknife. The separation of Roman and Ostrogoth extended into all aspects of life, amounting to a system of apartheid that was intended to maintain the dominance of the Ostrogoths and to prevent their assimilation into the far more numerous Roman population. Romans and Ostrogoths could not legally marry and they were judged in different courts. Religion was a major obstacle to assimilation. The Ostrogoths were Arian Christians and were regarded by their Catholic subjects as heretics. To maintain their cohesion as a people, Ostrogothic settlement was concentrated in the Po valley and in smaller military settlements at strategic locations. The Ostrogoths lived on the revenues from estates allocated to them and on annual donatives. To preserve the link between the king and his warriors, the donatives had to be collected in person from Theodoric himself.

After the fall of Ravenna, Theodoric never personally led an army in the field again, but he continued to direct campaigns run by able subordinates. By the year 500 he had extended his frontier as far north as the Danube and as far east as the Rhône, establishing a common frontier with the Visigoths. Theodoric regarded the Visigoths as kin and he intervened to help them preserve their kingdom after their king Alaric II was killed by the Frankish king Clovis (r. 481–511) at the Battle of Vouillé in 507. In 508 Theodoric fought a short war with the Eastern Roman Empire, as a result of which the emperor Anastasius (r. 491–518) recognized his control over Illyricum. When, shortly afterwards, the Visigoths recognized his sovereignty, Theodoric had gone a considerable way towards reuniting the Western Roman Empire under his rule. The edifice of Romanitas survived more intact in Italy than in any other barbarian kingdom and this undoubtedly lent a quasi-imperial majesty to Theodoric's rule. Indeed, Theodoric saw himself, and was widely accepted, as the elder statesman of the barbarian kingdoms.

Under Theodoric, Italy enjoyed thirty years of peace and prosperity but, in his later years, he began increasingly to question the loyalty of his Roman subjects and his rule became more oppressive. This may have been because he feared for the future of his kingdom, having failed to father a son. When he died of dysentery in 526 he was succeeded by his 8-year-old grandson, Athalaric, under the regency of his daughter Amalasuntha. She was never able to assert her authority over the Ostrogoths, who could not accept being ruled by a woman. Her murder in 535 gave the emperor Justinian (r. 527–565) the pretext to initiate the reconquest of Italy by his general Belisarius.

It is difficult to assess Theodoric's achievements. Was his separation of Goth and Roman doomed to failure, as many historians argue? Or did he lay the foundations of a sustainable state on which a more able successor might have built? Theodoric was certainly the most powerful of the barbarian kings of his day and a great military leader. Even the Frankish king Clovis, whose reign saw an unbroken succession of conquests, would back down rather than risk outright war with Theodoric. However, unlike Clovis' achievements, which continued to have a seminal impact on European history, Theodoric's, perhaps through no fault of his own, died with him.

> 'I find it hard to go on seeing these Arians occupy a part of Gaul. With God's help let us invade them. When we have beaten them, we will take over their territory.'

CLOVIS JUSTIFYING HIS WAR AGAINST THE VISIGOTHS IN 507; FROM GREGORY OF TOURS, *HISTORY OF THE FRANKS*

CLOVIS

465–511

JOHN HAYWOOD

THE FIRST GREAT KING OF THE FRANKS, Clovis (r. 481–511) was arguably the most successful of the Germanic conquerors of the fifth century. Energetic and ruthless, Clovis led the Franks on successful military campaigns that transformed them from a minor people into a great power that, more than any other, shaped the future of medieval Europe.

The son of Childeric (r. 460–481), king of the Franks of Tournai in modern Belgium, Clovis was born in 466 and brought up as a traditional Germanic pagan. He belonged to the Merovingian dynasty, named for his grandfather Merovech (d. 456), an obscure chieftain who, legend claimed, was the son of a sea monster.

Clovis was only 16 when he inherited the throne, but very soon displayed outstanding abilities. The situation that Clovis inherited was a complex one. The Franks were not a united people and Clovis was only one of several kings, each with a small kingdom based usually on a former Roman town. Most of the kings seem to have been related to one another either by blood or marriage.

Frankish kings were set apart from their subjects by their long hair, which embodied the mystique of kingship. To cut a king's hair was to depose him. Childeric, Clovis' father, was probably the most powerful of the Frankish kings of his day but he was still little more than a local warlord whose power was based on his personal retinue of household warriors. These men expected to be rewarded for their service with a share of plunder, so a king who was not a good leader in war would not keep his army for long. Clovis would have been well aware that the advantage he inherited from his father would not last unless he proved himself as a war leader too.

Clovis

Salians and Ripuarians

Though older tribal identities still survived, the Franks were gradually coalescing into two main groups, the Ripuarians and the Salians. The Ripuarians inhabited the traditional Frankish homeland on the lower Rhine, from Cologne northwards almost to the sea. The Salians were descended from Franks who had migrated west into Toxandria (roughly northern Flanders) in northeast Gaul in the middle of the fourth century. The Romans, who were distracted with campaigns elsewhere, allowed the Franks to settle as *foederati* ('allies') as a temporary expedient until they got the chance to expel them. This never happened and, as the Franks were mostly loyal to their alliance, the Romans left them alone. This may seem an unspectacular migration compared with those of the Vandals and Goths, but the Franks were able to put down deep roots in Toxandria, which remains part of the Germanic-speaking world today, and it made a secure base from which to expand into Gaul when Roman power entered its final decline in the middle of the fifth century. By the time Clovis became king, Frankish territory extended as far west as the River Somme and south over the Moselle valley.

The Visigoths also exploited Rome's decline and seized most of Gaul southwest of the Loire, and the Burgundians built a kingdom centred on Lyons and the Rhône valley. Britons had crossed the Channel to settle in Armorica (soon to become known as Brittany, after them) and were pushing east under their king, Riothamus. Seafaring

[Opposite] **A copy of the seal ring of Clovis's father,** Childeric I. The original was found in Childeric's richly furnished grave, discovered near the cathedral of Tournai in 1653. It was stolen in 1831, along with most of the other grave goods, and melted down. Among the few objects not stolen were these fragments [below] of a Frankish sword with gold and inlaid garnet ornamentation.

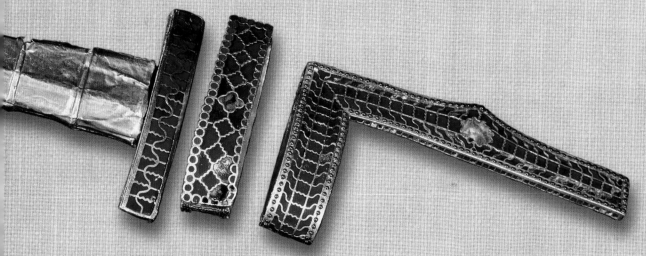

Saxons had founded colonies on the Channel coast of Gaul and around the mouth of the Loire. The last vestiges of Roman authority in Gaul were to be found between the Loire and the Somme. After the deposition in 476 of the last Roman emperor of the west, the Gallo-Roman cities in this area became, in effect, independent under the leadership of their bishops and local magnates who could afford to maintain armed retinues recruited from redundant Roman soldiers.

The defeat of Syagrius

It was against the Gallo-Romans that Clovis enjoyed his first major military success. In 486 he allied with Ragnachar, the king of the Franks of Cambrai, against Syagrius 'king of the Romans' who was based at Soissons. Syagrius was the son of a Roman general, Aegidius, who had fought to maintain Roman authority in Gaul in the dying days of the Western Empire and, left to his own devices after 476, had created some sort of kingdom for himself. Clovis won an annihilating victory over Syagrius' army, after which he was able to conquer the whole area between the Somme and the Loire. Syagrius fled to the Visigoths but their king, Alaric II (r. 484–507), handed him over to Clovis, who imprisoned him and later had him secretly murdered. Clovis was still very much the leader of a war band at this point in his career. (After the defeat of Syagrius, a bishop came to Clovis to ask for the return of a sacred vessel looted by the pagan Franks. Clovis was agreeable but had to ask his warriors if they would give him the vessel above his agreed share of the loot.)

In 491 Clovis conquered a small group of Thuringians who had settled between the Franks and the territories of the Alamanns and the Burgundians. The Alamanns responded to this move by invading Frankish territory in 496. In an important first step towards establishing his authority over all the Franks, Clovis united the armies of all the Salian and Ripuarian kings under his leadership to repel the invaders. Clovis also enjoyed the support of at least one Gallo-Roman magnate, Aurelianus, who brought his own warriors to join the Frankish army. The two armies met at Tolbiac (Zülpich), about 30 miles south of Cologne, and the Alamanns were defeated. Clovis proceeded to take over the bulk of the Alamannic kingdom but was warned against attacking any Alamanns who lived south of the Danube by Theodoric, the Ostrogoth king of Italy, who regarded the river as the border between the Frankish and Ostrogothic spheres of influence.

'Just think of all Clovis achieved, Clovis, the founder of your victorious country, who slaughtered those rulers who opposed him, conquered hostile peoples and captured their territories, thus bequeathing to you absolute and unquestioned dominion over them!'

GREGORY OF TOURS, *HISTORY OF THE FRANKS*

The conversion of Clovis

By the time of his victory over the Alamanns, Clovis had married Chlothild, a Catholic Christian princess of the Burgundian royal house. Chlothild tried unsuccessfully to persuade Clovis to convert to Christianity but he refused, partly because of a lack of conviction, but also because he feared it would alienate many of his warriors, most of whom were still pagans. He finally made his decision to convert after supposedly calling on the Christian God for help at a difficult moment during the battle of Tolbiac and he was subsequently baptized into the Catholic church by Bishop (later Saint) Remigius at Reims. This was a turning point in Clovis' reign but its immediate impact was much as he had predicted: thousands of the warriors he had led against the Alamanns defected to Ragnachar of Cambrai.

Such a serious loss of manpower begs the question, why did Clovis convert? He may indeed have had some profound religious experience but he was such a ruthless and cynical man that this can hardly be the whole story. His conversion may have been a deliberate overture to his Catholic Gallo-Roman subjects, who, since his defeat of Syagrius, now outnumbered his Frankish subjects. Winning their active collaboration would have more than made up for the loss of a few thousand warriors.

Other barbarian peoples, such as the Goths and Vandals, had long since converted to Christianity but they belonged to the Arian sect, which Catholics regarded as heretical because it denied the true divinity of Christ (the Burgundians were divided on the issue; some, such as Clovis' wife Chlothild, were Catholic, others Arian). This created an unbridgeable gulf in the other barbarian kingdoms between the German minority and the 'Roman' majority and prevented them forming any sense of loyalty to their rulers. This proved to be a fatal weakness, and those barbarian rulers that clung to Arianism did not survive long. Even those Arians, like the Visigoths, who eventually adopted Catholicism, remained tainted in their subjects' eyes by their association with heresy. This was not a problem for the Franks because they converted to Catholicism directly from paganism. The Gallo-Roman bishops gladly ignored the unsavoury side of Clovis' character and lent him their support and administrative expertise in return for his protection and patronage. In addition, Clovis gained diplomatic support from the papacy and the eastern Roman emperor Anastasius, who awarded him the rank of consul, so legitimizing his rule in the eyes of his Gallo-Roman subjects. This made possible, over the next century or so, the complete assimilation of the Gallo-Romans to Frankish identity. By the seventh century, Gaul had become known as Francia.

THE CONQUESTS OF CLOVIS, 486–507.

The map is labelled with the following places and features:

BRITONS; ANGLO-SAXONS; FRISIANS; SALIAN FRANKS; RIPUARIAN FRANKS; SAXONS; R. Meuse; R. Rhine; Cologne; Tolbiac 496; Tournai; Cambrai; Reims; Mainz; R. Mosel; Trier; Paris; Soissons 486; BRITTANY; R. Somme; R. Seine; Nantes; Orléans; Dijon 501; Strasbourg; ALAMANNI; N; Tours; R. Loire; R. Danube; Vouillé 507; Saintes; KINGDOM of BURGUNDY; Bordeaux; AUVERGNE; Lyons; KINGDOM of the OSTROGOTHS; R. Rhône; Avignon; BASQUES; Toulouse; Arles; Carcassonne; KINGDOM of the VISIGOTHS; 0 100 km; 0 100 miles

Map key:
- Frankish territory 481
- Clovis conquered by 497
- Clovis conquered by 508

A family affair

Clovis' marriage to Chlothild drew him into the complex politics of the Burgundian royal family. Kingship of the Burgundians was shared between two brothers, Godigisel and Gundobad. In 500 or 501 relations between the two brothers broke down and Godigisel secretly appealed to Clovis for help against Gundobad in return for an annual subsidy and some territorial concessions. As Gundobad had murdered Chlothild's parents, Clovis had a ready-made justification for intervention. When Clovis invaded the Burgundian kingdom, Godigisel appealed to Gundobad, who knew nothing of his brother's plotting, to take the field with him to repel the Franks. When the three armies met near Dijon, Gundobad was taken completely by surprise when his troops were attacked by both his brother and by Clovis. Though his army was crushed, Gundobad escaped and took refuge in the fortified city of Avignon. Clovis pursued and laid siege to the city, whereupon Gundobad negotiated a peace settlement, agreeing to pay Clovis an annual subsidy if he withdrew. Once free of Clovis, Gundobad settled scores with Godigisel, capturing and killing him and his family. A few years later Gundobad refused to pay any more tribute to the Franks,

Clovis

only escaping retribution because Clovis needed his support against the Visigoths.

Clovis' next campaign was against the Bretons, although the exact date is uncertain. He was again victorious and the Bretons became in some way tributary to the Franks because they supplied troops for his armies. Some of these troops were the descendants of Roman soldiers and, when they went to war, still marched under the old legionary standards of their fathers and grandfathers.

War against the Visigoths

Clovis' greatest military campaigns were against the Visigoths who ruled a kingdom comprising Aquitaine and most of Spain from their capital at Toulouse. According to the Gallo-Roman churchman Gregory of Tours, whose *History of the Franks* is the main source of information about his reign, Clovis was motivated by Catholic zeal to overthrow the heretical Arian Visigoths. However, it is clear that Clovis had already captured Visigothic territory as far south of the Loire as Saintes in the early 490s, some years before he converted to Christianity. In 496 the Visigoths recaptured Saintes, perhaps taking advantage of Clovis' war with the Alamanns. In 498 the Franks returned and captured Bordeaux but

Alaric II, king of the Visigoths, kneels in submission before Clovis in this illustration from the fifteenth-century *Chroniques des Rois de France*. The peace between Alaric and Clovis, agreed in 502, lasted only five years.

seem not to have held it for long. In 502 a temporary peace was agreed when Clovis and Alaric II met on neutral territory, an island in the Loire, the river that marked the border between their two kingdoms. It is likely that Alaric agreed to pay tribute to Clovis and also that he tried to do so using debased coin. If this was true, then it is no surprise that the peace treaty did not last.

After putting down a resurgence of Alamannic resistance in 506, Clovis went back to war with Alaric in 507. Clovis was mindful of the propaganda value of his Catholicism and he ordered his men to respect church property when passing through Visigothic territory and to take nothing but water and grass for horses. He is said to have killed one of his own soldiers who robbed an old man. His advance was slowed by bad weather, but his army reached the vicinity of Poitiers and brought the Visigoths to battle at Vouillé, about 10 miles northwest of the city. The outcome was a crushing defeat for the Visigoths. Clovis deployed archers and spear-throwers to the rear of his formation to shower the Visigoths with missiles over the front ranks of his army, who engaged the enemy in hand-to-hand combat. Clovis fought and killed Alaric in single combat but came close to being killed himself when he was attacked by two Visigothic spearmen. He was saved by the strength of his leather cuirass and the speed of his horse. Many Gallo-Romans took part in the battle, commanded by 'men of senatorial rank', though it is not clear whose side they fought on. King Gundobad of the Burgundians had helped divide the Visigothic forces by invading from the east at the same time as Clovis invaded from the north.

In the aftermath of the battle Clovis captured Bordeaux, this time permanently, and spent the winter there. He sent his eldest son Theuderic to mop up Visigothic resistance in Auvergne. The following year Clovis seized the royal treasury at Toulouse and ousted an isolated Visigothic garrison from Angoulême. Obviously intending that his readers should see Clovis as a latterday Joshua, Gregory informs us that God made the walls of Angoulême fall down of their own accord. In the same year, Clovis laid siege to Carcassonne while another Frankish-Burgundian force laid

Late Roman and Visigothic period walls at Carcassonne, unsuccessfully besieged by Clovis in 508.

siege to Arles. This attempt to seize a foothold on the Mediterranean coast was challenged by Theodoric, who sent Ostrogothic troops to support the Visigoths, and Clovis was forced to withdraw. Despite this failure, Clovis had added a prosperous and very Romanized region to his kingdom, nearly doubling its size.

The unification of the Franks

This succession of conquests had established Clovis as by far the most eminent of the Frankish kings and he now felt strong enough to unite the Franks under his sole rule, managing during this period to achieve the codification of the law of the Salian Franks. But it was during these years of his reign that his cynicism is most clearly revealed, as he used bribery, deceit and murder to eliminate his rivals one by one and take over their kingdoms. The last to die was Ragnachar, after which his pagan warriors joined Clovis and submitted to baptism. Gregory of Tours tells the story that in his last years Clovis would tearfully express his regret at having murdered all his relatives so that he was condemned to lonely isolation. But, Gregory says, 'he said this

FRANKISH ARMIES IN THE AGE OF CLOVIS

AS WITH OTHER ASPECTS of Clovis' military activities, there is little evidence to explain the organization of his armies. His army was built around his retinue or *trustis*. The *trustis* included the *pueri* ('lads') or household warriors that Clovis kept with him at all times, and the *leudes* or sworn military followers. The *leudes* were men of high social rank, many of whom brought warrior retinues of their own to the army. The loyalty of the *leudes* was essential; Clovis was able to overthrow his rival Ragnachar by bribing his *leudes* to desert him. After the defeat of Syagrius in 486, Gallo-Roman magnates were admitted to the ranks of the *leudes* and they added their own armed retinues to the Frankish army. Though they did not fight in person, the Gallo-Roman bishops also kept armed retinues to defend their sees in the turbulent conditions of post-Roman Gaul and no doubt these too served in Clovis' armies. Clovis probably also inherited some remnants of Roman military institutions as the sources mention *laeti*, a term used to describe barbarian settlers who were given farms in return for military service. In Roman times the Franks had been pirates and in the sixth century they still maintained a fleet somewhere near the mouth of the Rhine.

Frankish armies were not large: for Clovis' war with the Alamanns the Salian and Ripuarian Franks could raise only around six thousand warriors between them. Though their leaders might fight on horseback, most Franks were foot soldiers. The most distinctive Frankish weapons were a barbed spear called an *ango*, a throwing axe, known after them as the *francisca*, and the *scramasax*, a long single-edged fighting knife also popular with the Anglo-Saxons. For protection most warriors relied on a large round shield and probably a hardened leather cap and cuirass. Swords, iron helmets and body armour were the preserve of high-ranking warriors only. There is little evidence of the battlefield formations used in Clovis' time. The Franks probably fought like other Germans, forming up behind a wall of overlapping shields for both offence and defence. Siege warfare was not something in which the Germans had great expertise but in his later campaigns Clovis had engineers who could build siege engines.

A seventh-century Frankish battle axe, found in the River Marne near Villevenard. The axe was a favourite weapon of the pagan Franks.

not because he grieved for their deaths, but because in his cunning way he hoped to find some relative still in the land of the living whom he could kill'.

Clovis died in 511, aged 45, at his favourite residence at Paris and his kingdom, according to the Frankish custom of partible inheritance, was divided between his four sons. Murderous family politics resulted in the kingdom being reunited under Clovis' last surviving son Chlothar in 558. On his death in 561, the kingdom was divided between his four sons and the whole bloody process began again. Division in no way inhibited the expansion of the Frankish kingdom, however, and by 536 Clovis' sons had conquered the Burgundian kingdom, Bavaria, Thuringia and Provence, at last gaining a foothold on the coast of the Mediterranean Sea.

The reign of Clovis was one of the most significant in early medieval Europe. His military campaigns turned the Franks from a minor, disunited people of the North Sea region into the major power of western Europe, and his political abilities ensured that they would retain this position long after his death. He is often presented as being the first king of France but this is anachronistic.

Clovis with his wife Chlothild and their sons, in an illustration from the fourteenth-century *Les Grandes Chroniques de France*. Murderous feuding thinned the ranks of the Merovingian royal family under Clovis' successors.

France as a political entity was born of the break-up of the Carolingian empire in the late ninth century. Nevertheless, his reign was critical for the formation of France as it was from the assimilation of the Gallo-Romans and the Franks, which began in his reign, that the French national identity would eventually develop. As a war leader, Clovis was brave, leading from the front, but there is simply too little evidence to assess other aspects of his military leadership. But he was undoubtedly one of the great commanders of his age, as the far-reaching results of his campaigns testify.

BELISARIUS
c. 505–565

JOHN JULIUS NORWICH

'By the union of liberality and justice he acquired the love of the soldiers, without alienating the affections of the people. The sick and wounded were relieved with medicine and money, and still more efficaciously by the healing visits and smiles of their commander ... In the licence of a military life, none could boast that they had seen him intoxicated with wine; the most beautiful captives of Gothic or Vandal race were offered to his embraces, but he turned aside from their charms, and the husband of Antonina was never suspected of violating the laws of conjugal fidelity ... The spectator and historian of his exploits has observed that amidst the perils of war he was daring without rashness, prudent without fear, slow or rapid according to the exigencies of the moment; that in deepest distress he was animated by real or apparent hope, but that he was modest and humble in the most prosperous fortune.'

A gold coin with a portrait of Emperor Justinian I (r. 527–565).

It is not often that Edward Gibbon allows himself such an unqualified paean of praise. Admittedly its subject lived in the sixth century, and early medieval sources are always inadequate; even those few that have come down to us are seldom entirely reliable. (We are lucky indeed to have the highly educated Syrian-Greek Procopius of Caesarea, who was an eyewitness to much of what he records and is thus a good deal more trustworthy than most of his fellow chroniclers.) Such evidence as we possess, however, suggests that although the emperor Justinian's most brilliant and celebrated general – like every other military leader of his time – could be capable on occasion of considerable brutality, he may otherwise have been something approaching the paragon described by this normally least charitable of our historians.

The *Nika* riots

Belisarius was, like his master, a Romanized Thracian. His early career was meteoric. His military gifts were unquestioned; his personal courage was proved again and again, and he was a natural leader of men. In 529, while still in his twenties, he had inflicted an overwhelming defeat on a far

superior Persian army at Dara, a few miles northwest of Nisibis. He achieved still greater prominence, however, in Constantinople itself at the time of the most serious political crisis of Justinian's reign, the so-called *Nika* riots. There were several reasons for these disturbances, the most important of which was the division of the populace into two rival factions, the Blues and the Greens. Their names had originally referred to the colours worn by the two principal teams of charioteers in the Games, but the factions themselves had long since left the narrow confines of the arena. By now they existed as two independent semi-political parties, both of which wielded a dangerous amount of power. Once secure on the throne, Justinian had therefore embarked on a policy of firm repression, depriving them of their privileges and curbing their excesses with harsh, sometimes even savage, punishments.

Thus it was that when, on 13 January 532, Justinian took his seat in the Hippodrome, his appearance caused uproar. Now, suddenly and for the first time, the Blues and the Greens were united; and their cries of '*Nika! Nika!*' – 'Win! Win!' – were no longer addressed to their favoured teams. The word had now become a menacing chant, directed against the person of the emperor. The races began, but were soon abandoned. The mob poured out of the circus, hell-bent on destruction, and for five

Justinian and his court, as they appear in a mosaic in the sixth-century Basilica of San Vitale in Ravenna. The man behind the shield on the left is probably Belisarius.

Belisarius

SOUTHERN EUROPE AND THE MEDITERRANEAN in the sixth century.

days smoke lay thick over the city as nearly all its principal public buildings went up in flames. A panic-stricken Justinian was preparing to flee in disguise and was restrained only with difficulty by the empress Theodora, who preferred death to flight. If she had to die, she said, the imperial purple would be the noblest winding-sheet.

Fortunately, Belisarius was present in the palace. He rallied his soldiers – principally Scandinavian mercenaries – and marched on the Hippodrome, bursting in and taking the mob by surprise. Meanwhile the commander of the imperial bodyguard, an elderly and deceptively frail-looking Armenian eunuch named Narses, had stationed his men at the exits with orders to cut down all who tried to escape. What followed was a massacre. The number of dead is said by Procopius to have been thirty thousand. It was a heavy price to have paid, but Belisarius had almost certainly saved the lives of the imperial couple. He may well have saved the Byzantine Empire. His reputation was made.

In the period of relative domestic tranquillity that followed the riots, Justinian was at last able to concentrate on the primary objective of his reign: the recovery of the Roman Empire of the west from the Vandals and the Goths. And Belisarius was, he knew, the one man to whom this task could confidently be entrusted. He sailed first to Carthage, then capital of the North African Vandal kingdom occupying roughly the site of modern Tunis, where a nobleman named Gelimer had recently seized the throne. On the flagship, together with Belisarius himself, were Procopius – serving as his military secretary – and, as usual, his wife Antonina.

Antonina nearly always accompanied Belisarius on his campaigns – perhaps so that he could keep an eye on her. Her background had been not unlike that of the empress, of whom she was a close friend. The relationship was valuable to them both. Theodora knew that she could always control Belisarius – who by now, after Justinian himself, was the most powerful man in the empire – through his wife, while Antonina could rely on the empress to protect her from the consequences of her countless adulteries. Like Theodora, Antonina had also been brought up in the theatre and circus. Both women had a lurid past; but, unlike the empress, Antonina had made no attempt to reform her character after her prestigious marriage. At least twelve years older than her husband – Procopius claims twenty-two – she had already had several children, in and out of wedlock, and in the coming years was to cause her husband much embarrassment and, occasionally, anguish; but his love for her remained, none the less, deep and enduring.

A brief account of Belisarius' conquest of Carthage is given separately (see p. 241). It was typical of him that on the occupation of that city he should have given his men strict orders to respect the local people who, despite a century of occupation, technically remained Roman citizens like themselves. There was no swagger, no insolence or arrogance; everything bought in the shops was properly paid for. On his return to Constantinople Belisarius was awarded a triumph – the first non-imperial recipient to be granted such an honour for five and a half centuries, and the last ever to receive one.

The conquest of Italy

Belisarius was now ready to take command on the second stage of the emperor's master plan: the reconquest of Italy. It was to prove a good deal harder than the first. He sailed for Sicily in the summer of 535 with seven thousand five hundred men, and took the island almost without a struggle; the only show of resistance was made by the Gothic garrison in Panormus (Palermo). Belisarius is reported to have massed his fleet so close inshore that its masts rose above the town walls. He then filled the ships' boats with men and hoisted them up to the yard-arms, whence they could fire their arrows down on the defenders and, we are told, leap directly down on to the battlements. Before he could cross the straits, however, he was called urgently to Africa to deal with a serious mutiny in the imperial army of occupation; not until the late spring of 536 did he land on the Italian mainland.

Belisarius' advance was once again unchallenged until he reached Naples, the citizens of which defended their city stoutly for three weeks. He had

Theodora and members of her court, in a detail from a mosaic in the Basilica of San Vitale in Ravenna.

warned them that if they resisted he would be unable to restrain his semi-savage barbarians from the murder, rapine and pillage that they would consider their just reward, and the Neapolitans now paid a heavy price for their heroism. The Huns, pagan to a man, had no compunction in burning down the churches in which their intended victims had sought asylum.

The next objective was Rome. King Vitiges – an elderly general whom the Gothic leaders had recently appointed to the throne – had announced that he would not be defending the city, and Pope Silverius had accordingly opened the gates to the imperial army; but if the Pope and his flock imagined that by so doing they had avoided the miseries of a siege they were to be disappointed; Belisarius entertained no such delusion. He suspected, with good reason, that Vitiges was merely giving himself an opportunity to consolidate – and he was right. The siege that followed lasted for a year and nine days, during which time the besiegers cut all the aqueducts, dealing Rome a blow from which it would not recover for a millennium. But the walls of Rome held. Not until March 538 did the Goths finally withdraw; as they retreated northwards along the Via Flaminia, Belisarius pursued them and fell on them at the Milvian Bridge – the same spot where Constantine the Great had routed the forces of his rival Maxentius 226 years before – leaving several hundred drowned in the Tiber.

A few days later the general himself headed north; but trouble awaited him. While he was at Ancona, reinforcements arrived from Constantinople under the command of the most powerful member of the imperial court – the eunuch Narses. Narses was no soldier. His life had been spent in the palace, and even his command of the bodyguard had been more of a domestic appointment than a military one. His presence can thus have had but one explanation: Justinian was beginning to have

The siege of Perugia by Totila, king of the Ostrogoths, in 548, as imagined in a fresco by Benedetto Benfigli (1420–96) in the Palazzo del Popolo in Perugia.

THE CONQUEST OF CARTHAGE

ON MIDSUMMER DAY 533 the great expedition set sail from the Golden Horn. It consisted of five thousand cavalry and twice as many infantry – at least half of them barbarian mercenaries, mostly Huns but with a strong contingent of Scandinavians. They travelled in a fleet of five hundred transports, escorted by ninety-two *dromons*. (The *dromon* was the smallest type of Byzantine warship, carrying a crew of only twenty rowers at a single bank of oars.)

After brief stops in Sicily and Malta, the expedition landed at the easternmost point of the Tunisian coast and headed north towards Carthage. The army of the Vandal king was waiting near the tenth milestone, where the road from the south entered a narrow valley. His plan of attack was threefold: his brother Ammatas would attack the vanguard, his nephew Gibamund would sweep down on the centre and he himself would deal with the rear. Unfortunately for Gelimer, his communications let him down. Ammatas moved too soon; Belisarius was ready for him, and in the ensuing battle Ammatas was killed. The soldiers around him lost heart and fled. The flanking attack was no more successful; the Byzantine cavalry was composed of Huns, hideous and implacable. The Vandals took one look and ran for their lives. All now depended on Gelimer. At first he seemed to have the advantage – but then he came upon his brother's body. He refused to move until he had seen the corpse carried from the field. Belisarius seized his chance, bore down upon the Vandal host and scattered it. Carthage lay open.

On Sunday 15 September the victorious general made his formal entry into the city. Gelimer, however, was still at large, regrouping his army and rallying support from the local Punic and Berber tribes; one more battle was necessary before Belisarius' task was done. It was fought in mid December. This time it was Belisarius who took the initiative, charging three times into the thick of the Vandal ranks. Once again Gelimer hesitated; his soldiers, seeing his indecision, began to draw back – and once again the Huns charged, quickly turning the Vandal retreat into a rout. Gelimer fled back into the wilds of Numidia, his army pell-mell after him. The imperial army lost fifty men, the Vandals eight hundred. This time it was the end. Belsarius advanced to the city of Hippo – which opened its gates at once – and took possession of the royal treasure. Then, with a train of Vandal prisoners behind him and his wagons loaded with plunder, he returned to Carthage.

doubts about Belisarius. He was too brilliant, too successful, too rich – and, being still only in his early thirties, too young. He was, in short, the stuff of which emperors were made; more disturbing still, he was the stuff of men who made themselves emperors. The eunuch's instructions confirmed the fact. He was to obey Belisarius in all things, *so far as seemed consistent with the public weal.* In other words, he could overrule him in all major decisions of state policy. His arrival effectively split the army down the middle. Some generals remained loyal to Belisarius, whereas others would obey only Narses. It was as a direct result of this division that the imperial garrison in Milan was starved into surrender, all the male citizens massacred by the Goths and not a house left standing.

The catastrophe had one useful consequence. Justinian immediately summoned Narses back to the capital leaving Belisarius, meanwhile, to move on to Ravenna. The city was already surrounded – on the landward side by his army; on the seaward by the imperial fleet, which had set up a virtually impenetrable blockade. One night a secret emissary arrived in the imperial camp with an extraordinary proposal: Vitiges would resign his throne to Belisarius, on the understanding that the latter should then proclaim himself Emperor of the West. Many an imperial general would have leapt at the chance. The bulk of the army would probably have supported him, and with the Goths at his back he would have been more than capable of dealing with any punitive expedition from Constantinople. But Belisarius was nothing if not loyal; in the words of Procopius, 'he hated the name of usurper with a perfect hatred', and it is unlikely that he gave the Goths' proposal a moment's consideration. Here, however, was an ideal means of

bringing the war to a quick and victorious end. He accepted. The gates were duly opened, and the army marched in.

But there was no proclamation. The Goths soon realized that they had been deceived. Vitiges and his court were led into captivity, but there is no indication that Belisarius suffered any qualms of conscience. The proposal itself had been perfidious, and he had saved untold bloodshed on both sides. His triumph after the capture of Carthage had been magnificent; how much more so might be his reward for returning the whole Italian peninsula, including Ravenna and even Rome itself, to the empire?

The emperor's jealousy

Alas, he was disappointed. Every victory he won now increased the emperor's jealousy. There was certainly no feeling of victory in the air when in June 540 he returned home to learn that the Persian king Chosroes had captured Antioch. His presence would be required, not in the Hippodrome, but on the eastern front. And another shock, too, awaited him. Antonina, who had not accompanied him to Italy, had embarked on a passionate liaison with her godson, actively abetted by the empress herself. This delayed him for some time in Constantinople; but the Persian campaign was anyway to prove indecisive, owing to an outbreak in both camps of bubonic plague. In 542 Chosroes was forced to retire; but Belisarius returned to more trouble. Justinian had succumbed to the epidemic, and Theodora had taken control. Accused of having enriched himself unduly with barbarian treasure, Belisarius found his household disbanded; anything of any value that he possessed had been transferred to the imperial palace. Not until the emperor's recovery the following year was he partially restored to favour.

And just in time: under their young king Totila, the Goths in Italy had retaliated and had already recaptured Naples. Belisarius was despatched back to the peninsula – but with a lesser rank, little authority, less money and only a handful of inexperienced troops. He did his best, but by now it was no longer just the Goths who were hostile; it was virtually the whole population. Justinian reluctantly sent reinforcements, but Belisarius was unable to prevent Totila from capturing Rome. Although fighting continued up and down the peninsula, it was soon clear that a stalemate had been reached. After the glory of his first Italian campaign, the second had brought only frustration and disappointment. But he had saved Italy, at least temporarily, for

The interior of the Hagia Sophia, the church of the Holy Wisdom in Istanbul, originally constructed on the orders of the Byzantine emperor Justinian I between 532 and 537. The Islamic medallions and furniture date from its time as a mosque after the Turkish conquest of Constantinople in 1453.

the empire. He had laid the foundations for reconquest, making it easy for his old rival Narses – possessed of all the resources for which he himself had appealed in vain – to win the victories that should rightfully have been his own. In 549 Belisarius returned disconsolately to Constantinople.

Last years

Justinian gave him a warm welcome. The two had been kept apart by Theodora, who had continually poisoned her husband's mind against Belisarius; but Theodora had died in 548, and with her death his trust had quickly revived. The general's career, however, was drawing to its close. He was to fight two more minor campaigns, regaining Corsica from the Visigoths in Spain and successfully dealing with a Hunnish tribe known as the Kotrigurs, who had suddenly swarmed into imperial territory, advancing eastward through Thrace to within 20 miles of the capital. By this time he was in his middle fifties, but although it was ten years since he had seen serious action in the field, he had lost none of his energy or his tactical imagination. With only a few hundred men at his disposal he organized a brilliant guerrilla campaign, drawing the Kotrigurs into a carefully planned ambush and leaving four hundred dead where they had fallen. It must have been a considerable surprise to him when Justinian awarded himself a triumph, suggesting a great and glorious victory for which Belisarius alone had been responsible. That old jealousy that had always smouldered in his heart had suddenly flared up again, for the first time since Theodora's day.

Belisarius doubtless took note, and retreated once more into the background. Even then, probably no one was more surprised than he when, in the autumn of 562, several distinguished citizens were accused of plotting against the emperor's life, and one of them named him as being among those implicated. Nothing, of course, was ever proved; but he was shorn of all his dignities and privileges, and lived for eight months in a state of disgrace until Justinian, finally persuaded of his innocence, reinstated him. (It was presumably this incident that gave rise to the legend of his being blinded and thrown out into the streets with a begging-bowl. The earliest authority for this story dates from more than five centuries later, however, and can safely be rejected.) After his final return to favour it is pleasant to record that Belisarius lived out his life in tranquillity and comfort, dying in March 565 aged about 60. Antonina, now possibly well into her eighties, survived him.

After fifteen centuries, the name of Belisarius is still remembered as one of the great generals in world history. Was his reputation deserved? It is not easy to judge – we simply do not know enough about him, either as a strategist or as a tactician. The only real evidence we have is the evidence of his success in almost every military expedition that he ever undertook. The exception is, of course, his second Italian campaign; but here the blame can be laid squarely on the emperor himself. Had Justinian conquered his instinctive – but wholly unjustified – mistrust of his greatest general, had he given him not only the authority and the troops he needed but also his fullest trust, there can be little doubt that the second campaign would have been as victorious as the first, and that of Narses would have been unnecessary. On the other hand, the story – which Robert Graves turned into the superb novel, *Count Belisarius* – would have been far less interesting. Military history provides few examples of a career in which human frailty plays so significant a part.

> 'Stick to jihad and you will be in good health and get sufficient means of livelihood.'
>
> THE PROPHET MUHAMMAD

MUHAMMAD

570–632

EFRAIM KARSH

'I WAS ORDERED TO FIGHT ALL MEN until they say "There is no god but Allah".' With these final words, the Prophet Muhammad summed up not only the international vision of the faith he brought to the world but also his own life story and political career.

Born in AD 570 in the merchant town of Mecca in the Hijaz, the northwestern part of the Arabian peninsula, Muhammad ibn Abdullah is believed to have experienced his first divine revelation at the age of 40. Initially the Meccans viewed his claim to prophetic powers with indifference, but this turned to outright hostility as Muhammad launched a frontal assault on their most cherished beliefs and values, deriding their gods, emphasizing the perdition of their ancestors who had died in disbelief, and demanding an unequivocal profession of belief in Allah, as Muhammad called his god, and total submission (the meaning of 'Islam' in Arabic) to His will.

For a while Muhammad managed to hold his ground, but as his position became increasingly untenable he began to look for an alternative home from which to spread his divine message. As early as 615 he sent a group of his followers to Ethiopia to escape persecution and to explore the possibility of cooperation with its Christian king. But Ethiopia was too remote and isolated to serve as a permanent base of operations, so Muhammad began to look closer to home. After a humiliating rebuff by the notables of Ta'if, a hilly town some 60 miles southeast of Mecca, and a string of abortive overtures to neighbouring Bedouin tribes, Muhammad eventually reached an agreement with a group of Muslim converts from the town of Yathrib, some 275 miles north of Mecca, who gave him their oath of allegiance and undertook to fight with him against his enemies. In the early summer of 622, about seventy of his followers quietly left Mecca in small groups for Yathrib. A few months later, on 24 September, Muhammad himself arrived in the town.

From preacher to leader

The *Hijra* – the migration of Muhammad and his followers from Mecca to Medina ('the city'), as Yathrib would hitherto be called, was a watershed in Islamic history, aptly designated after the Prophet's death as the official starting point of the Muslim

Muhammad

era. Almost immediately, Muhammad was transformed from a private preacher into a political and military leader and the head of a rapidly expanding community, while Islam graduated from being a persecuted cult into a major religious and political force in the Arabian peninsula.

Muhammad created this inextricable link between religious authority and political power in the 'Constitution of Medina', set up shortly after the *Hijra*, which organized his local followers (*Ansar*) and those who had migrated with him from Mecca (*Muhajirun*) into 'one community (*umma*) to the exclusion of all [individual] men', designed to act as a unified whole against external enemies and internal

Muhammad leads his nascent Muslim army into battle against a superior Meccan force in the Battle of Badr (624), in a fourteenth-century book painting in the Topkapi Museum, Istanbul. Victory at Badr was pivotal to his consolidation of local power.

The Battle of Mecca (630) in a miniature from a nineteenth-century manuscript. Abu Sufian ibn Harb (left) defends Mecca against a Muslim force led by al-'Abbas, Muhammad's uncle, in the battle in which Muhammad gained control of his city.

dissenters. The document wisely refrained from specifically abolishing existing tribal structures and practices, yet it broke with past tradition by substituting religion for blood as the source of social and political organization, and by making Allah, through the aegis of His chosen apostle, the supreme and exclusive sovereign: 'If any dispute or controversy likely to cause trouble should arise it must be referred to God and to Muhammad, the apostle of God. God accepts what is nearest to piety and goodness in this document.'

Having established himself as the *umma*'s absolute leader, Muhammad spent most of his Medina years fighting external enemies and domestic opponents. During the first eighteen months after the *Hijra* he carried out seven raids on merchant caravans as they were making their way to Mecca. This was an attempt to build up the wealth and prestige of his followers, who had lost their livelihood as a result of their move to Medina, and to weaken Mecca's economic lifeline. It was also the logical thing to do. The caravans from Syria to Mecca passed between Medina and the Red Sea coast and were militarily unprotected, which made them easy prey for potential raiders who could intercept them at a substantial distance from their base and then disappear before the arrival of a rescue party. Yet as the Muslims lacked military experience, having themselves been merchants rather than fighters, they normally returned home empty-handed. It was only in January 624 that Muhammad scored his first real success. A small raiding party of eight to ten Muslims, disguised as pilgrims, ambushed a convoy at Nakhla, southeast of Mecca, killed one of its attendants, captured another two (the fourth attendant managed to escape), and led the caravan to Medina. Yet as the raid occurred during the holy month of Rajab, when bloodshed was forbidden according to pagan convention, it was met with a wave of indignation in Medina. The embarrassed Muhammad claimed that his orders had been misunderstood and waited for a while before distributing the booty. Eventually a new Qur'anic revelation appeared to

Muhammad

246

justify the raid, and two months later the incident was all but forgotten as a Muslim contingent headed by Muhammad himself routed a numerically superior Meccan force near the oasis of Badr, southwest of Medina, carrying home substantial booty and a few dozen prisoners.

Eliminating potential rivals

The Battle of Badr boosted Muhammad's position in Medina and allowed him to move against his local opponents. The first to find themselves in the firing line were Medina's three Jewish tribes (the town had originally been established by Jewish refugees fleeing Roman persecution and their local Arab proselytes), whose refusal to acknowledge the validity of Muhammad's revelations weakened the appeal of the nascent faith, and whose affluence made them a natural target for plunder. Using a trivial incident as a pretext, he expelled the weakest of these tribes, the Qainuqa, from the town and divided its properties among the Muhajirun. (Muhammad had originally meant to kill the Qainuqa men but was dissuaded from doing so by a local sheikh.) In March 625, after a Muslim defeat in the Battle of Mount Uhud, near Medina, had dented Muhammad's prestige in the eyes of the neighbouring Bedouin tribes, it was the turn of the second tribe, the Nadir, to pay the price of the Prophet's setback: after a few weeks' siege they were driven from the city and their lands were taken over by the Muslims. The last and most powerful Jewish tribe – the Quraiza – suffered more profusely following the abortive Meccan siege of Medina in the spring of 627. Charged with collaboration with the enemy, the tribe's six to eight hundred men were brought in small groups to trenches dug the previous day, made to sit on the edge, then beheaded one by one and their bodies thrown in. The women and children were sold into slavery and the money they fetched, together with the proceeds from the tribe's possessions, was divided among the Muslims.

On to the offensive

By now Muhammad had consolidated his power to a considerable extent. The Uhud defeat, where over seventy Muslims were killed (including some of Muhammad's oldest and most trusted followers and his formidable uncle Hamza), was a humbling experience for the Prophet. Yet the Meccans failed to achieve their strategic goal of destroying the *umma* and were increasingly forced to rely on a network of alliances with Bedouin tribes in their fight against the Muslims. Muhammad, however, was not to be easily overcome. He managed to maintain the loyalty of the tribes around Medina, conducted a string of successful raids throughout the peninsula, and even resorted to the assassination of

'The gates of Paradise are under the shadow of the swords.'

THE PROPHET MUHAMMAD

Muhammad

political rivals. These efforts did not prevent the Meccans from forming a grand alliance against Muhammad, yet they kept many potential participants out of this grouping, thus ensuring a more equal balance of forces in the final encounter.

This came at the end of March 627, when a 10,000-strong Meccan–Bedouin force advanced northward and laid siege to Medina, only to be confronted with a number of tactical surprises. To begin with, the Muslims had dug a trench around the city wherever it lay open to cavalry attack, a defence method hitherto unknown in Arabia. This caused considerable operational confusion among the Meccans, whose hopes of victory largely rested on their superior cavalry. This was further compounded by Muhammad's negotiations with the main Bedouin group in the coalition, the Ghatafan, aimed at bribing them out of the war. While the talks came to naught, since the Medinese considered such a deal to be beneath their dignity, the Ghatafans had been sufficiently compromised in the eyes of their Meccan allies to preclude a cohesive military effort. After two weeks of abortive attempts to break the resistance of the far more committed and disciplined Muslims, the coalition disintegrated and its members went their separate ways.

The Hudaibiya agreement

With the failure of the siege of Medina, Mecca ceased to pose a threat to Muhammad, and in the spring of 628 he felt confident enough to attempt to make the 'little pilgrimage' (*umra*) to his native town. As the Meccans vowed to prevent him from doing so, Muhammad stopped in the small nature spot of Hudaibiya, some 10 miles northwest of the town, where the two sides negotiated a ten-year truce. The Muslims were given the right to carry out the pilgrimage the following year and the Meccans agreed to vacate the town for three days in order to allow them to perform their religious duties unhindered. Muhammad agreed to send back anyone who came to him from Mecca without the explicit permission of his guardian, while the Meccans were not obliged to reciprocate this move.

Many Muslims viewed these conditions as an unnecessary and humiliating surrender. They were particularly resentful of Muhammad waiving any reference to himself in the treaty as Allah's Messenger, and were indignant at the loss of booty attending the stoppage of raids on the caravans to Mecca that was implicit in the agreement. To deflect this simmering discontent, Muhammad found a handy scapegoat that had served him well in the past: the Arabian Jews. Having eliminated the Jewish presence in Medina, he now

THE EASTERN MEDITERRANEAN AND THE ARABIAN PENINSULA in the seventh century.

turned to the affluent Jewish community in the oasis of Khaibar, some 90 miles north of the town. After a month of siege the Jews surrendered. They were then stripped of their possessions before being granted free passage with their women and children. Yet when Muhammad was unable to find the necessary manpower for tilling the site, he relented and allowed the Jews to stay on their land in return for an annual tribute of half of their produce. A number of neighbouring Jewish communities surrendered shortly afterwards under the same terms, thus laying the ground for what would become the common arrangement between the *umma* and its non-Muslim subjects (or *Dhimmis*).

In the end, Muhammad proved more far-sighted than his critics. Far from diverting him from the ultimate goal of occupying his native town, the Hudaibiya agreement actually turned out to be a Trojan horse, facilitating the attainment of his objective. Besides putting the *umma* on a par with Mecca, the treaty gave both signatories a free hand in their dealings with the nomadic tribes. On the face of it, this provision was of a reciprocal nature. In fact it worked in Muhammad's favour, as increasing numbers of tribes, including some that had previously been aligned with Mecca, sought to associate themselves with the *umma*.

The Battle of Mecca

When, in 629, Muhammad performed the deferred 'little pilgrimage', it made a great impression. A fresh influx of converts flocked to the Prophet's camp, and Muhammad took immediate advantage of the opportunity. Using the killing of a Muslim by a Meccan in the course of a private dispute as a pretext for reneging on the Hudaibiya agreement, on 1 January 630 he set out from Medina at the head of a formidable force. Ten days later, without offering any serious resistance, Mecca surrendered.

The capture of Mecca was the ultimate prize for Muhammad. Less than eight years after his undignified departure, the ridiculed and despised preacher had returned as the city's undisputed master and Arabia's most powerful leader. In the course of the following year a steady stream of tribal dignitaries from all corners of the peninsula would flock to the warrior-prophet to profess their subservience. For many of them, this was more a pragmatic response to the newly established balance

A schematic view of Mecca, showing the Ka'ba, the black stone temple which stands in the central court of the Great Mosque, considered by Muslims to be the most sacred spot on earth.

of power than a true conversion to Islam. Yet being the astute politician and statesman that he was, Muhammad was prepared initially to content himself with a merely verbal profession of faith and payment of tribute. Paganism, as a social and political phenomenon, was virtually a spent force, so there was no need to bring about an instantaneous transformation of these independent-minded tribes. As long as they gave him their political obeisance and financial tribute, he could afford to wait and allow the socioeconomic dynamics, which now favoured Islam, to run their natural course. Even in Mecca Muhammad refrained from following up his victory with mass conversions, leaving the population very much to its own devices, and incorporating many of the local leaders into his administration. Some of them were given handsome rewards, including his arch-enemy and the town's grand old man Abu Sufian ibn Harb and his two sons, Yazid and Mu'awiya, the future founder of the Umayyad dynasty.

An Islamic painting showing the revelation of Qu'ranic verses to Muhammad during an unnamed battle.

Preparing for Allah's empire

As we have seen, the formation of the *umma* created a sharp dichotomy between Muslims and 'infidels' and presupposed a permanent state of war that would only end with the establishment of a global political order in which all humankind would live under Muslim rule as either believers or subject communities. In order to achieve this goal it is incumbent on all free, male, adult Muslims to carry out an uncompromising struggle 'in the path of Allah', or jihad. As the fourteenth-century historian and philosopher Abdel Rahman ibn Khaldun wrote: 'In the Muslim community, the jihad is a religious duty because of the universalism of the Islamic mission and the obligation [to convert] everybody to Islam either by persuasion or by force.'

Muhammad devised the concept of jihad shortly after his migration to Medina as a means of enticing his local followers to raid Meccan caravans, and he developed and amplified this concept with the expansion of his political ambitions until it became a rallying call for world domination. The Qur'anic revelations during this period abound with verses extolling the virtues of jihad, as do the countless sayings and traditions (*hadith*) attributed to the Prophet. Those who participate in this holy pursuit are to be generously rewarded, both in this life and in the afterworld, where they will reside in shaded and ever-green gardens, indulged by pure and virtuous women. Accordingly, those killed while waging jihad should not be mourned: 'Allah has bought from the believers their soul and their possessions against the gift of Paradise; they fight in the path of Allah; they kill and are killed ... So rejoice in the bargain you have made with Him; that is the mighty triumph.'

But the doctrine's appeal was not just otherworldly. By forbidding fighting and raiding within the *umma*, Muhammad deprived the Arabian tribes of a traditional source of livelihood. For a time, the Prophet could rely on booty from non-Muslims as a substitute for the lost war spoils, which is why he never went out of his way to convert all of the tribes seeking a place in his Pax Islamica. Yet given his belief in the supremacy of Islam and his relentless commitment to its widest possible dissemination, he could hardly deny conversion to those wishing to undertake it. Once the whole of Arabia had become Muslim, a new source of wealth and an alternative outlet would have to be found for the aggressive energies of the Arabian tribes: it was, in the Fertile Crescent and the Levant.

As early as the summer of 626, Muhammad sent a small force to fight some hostile tribes in the area of Dumat al-Jandal, some 500 miles northeast of Medina. The ease and rapidity of the operation seemed to have whetted Muhammad's appetite, and in the following year he sent his freedman and adopted son Zaid to Syria on a trading mission. This failed to produce concrete results, but another mission in the same year resulted in a treaty of alliance with the Dumat prince.

At this stage, Muhammad was apparently not interested in occupying these territories on a permanent basis, or converting their largely Christian populations to Islam. Yet during the last three years of his life he attempted to incorporate the tribes on the road to Syria into his Islamic order and even made overtures to tribes in the direction of Iraq. Muhammad was also reported to have sent emissaries to a number of prominent Arab and non-Arab rulers, including the Byzantine, Iranian, and Ethiopian emperors, with the demand that they embrace Islam. In October 630 he ventured toward the Byzantine frontier at the head of a 30,000-strong army. Advancing as far as the oasis of Tabuq, some 500 miles north of Medina, Muhammad camped there for twenty days, during which time he negotiated a peace treaty with the Christian prince of Aylah (the biblical Eilat), at the northern tip of the Gulf of Aqaba. In return for an oath of allegiance and an annual tribute, the Christians were placed under the protection of the *umma* and granted freedom of worship. At this point Muhammad decided to return to Medina, having apparently realized the impracticability of his Byzantine ambitions. Yet this did not imply the disappearance of his interest in northern expansion. No sooner had he returned from his pilgrimage than he began preparations for a campaign in Transjordan and southern Palestine, which were only brought to an abrupt end by his sudden death on 8 June 632. And while it is unlikely that Muhammad had imagined the full scope of Islam's future expansion, let alone planned it in detail, he left behind a new universal religion and a community of believers organized on its basis – an unprecedented phenomenon in Arabian history that not only accounted for the prophet's military exploits but also made Islam's worldwide expansion inevitable.

> 'Charlemagne never withdrew from a campaign which he had once begun simply because of the difficulties involved, and danger never deterred him.'
>
> EINHARD, *THE LIFE OF CHARLEMAGNE* (c. 829)

CHARLEMAGNE

742–814

JOHN HAYWOOD

NO RULER OF THE EARLY MIDDLE AGES has made a greater impression on posterity than the emperor Charlemagne (r. 768–814). Even within his own lifetime he was called Charles the Great, or in Latin *Carolus Magnus*, from which the Old French name Charlemagne derives. In a lifetime of constant campaigning, Charlemagne united a larger area of western Europe into a single state than any ruler since of the demise of the Western Roman Empire. After his death he attained legendary stature and is claimed as a national hero by both the French and the Germans.

Charlemagne was born in 742, the eldest son of Pippin III, then mayor of the Franks. He was given the usual education of an aristocratic Frank, being taught to ride, hunt and fight. He was also a man of considerable intellect who spoke Latin fluently and had a keen interest in astronomy and theology. Pippin's elevation to kingship in 751, however, dramatically changed Charlemagne's prospects. On Pippin's death in 768, the Frankish kingdom was divided equally between Charlemagne and his younger brother Carloman. The two brothers did not get on well, and when, soon after his accession, Charlemagne faced a serious rebellion in Aquitaine and asked for Carloman's help, this was refused. Charlemagne gathered what forces he could and moved swiftly and decisively to crush the rebellion. When Duke Lupus of Gascony gave sanctuary to the fugitive leader of the Aquitainians, Charlemagne invaded and forced him to submit to Frankish rule. Charlemagne had made his first conquest. Two years later, Carloman died and the Frankish kingdom was reunited under Charlemagne's sole rule: he was now indisputably the most powerful ruler in western Europe.

The conquest of Italy

Charlemagne's first conquest after he became sole king of the Franks was the Lombard kingdom of Italy. Early in 773 envoys arrived from Pope Hadrian I (r. 772–795) asking for Charlemagne's help against King Desiderius of the Lombards, who had seized papal lands. Charlemagne's father had only become king with the support of the papacy, so this was a summons he could not ignore. Hoping to force Desiderius to divide his forces, Charlemagne led one army into Italy over the Mont Cenis Pass, while sending another through the Great St Bernard Pass. Charlemagne's weight of numbers counted for little in the narrow Alpine valleys, however, and both his armies found their way blocked by Lombard defences. After a brief stand-off, Charlemagne's scouts found an alternative route through the mountains; in order to prevent himself being outflanked, Desiderius withdrew his forces to his heavily fortified capital at Pavia, being followed there by Charlemagne, who laid siege to the city.

The Lombards had faced Frankish invasions before and knew from experience that they always withdrew in the autumn to avoid getting cut off in Italy when winter snows closed the Alpine passes. As it was already September when Desiderius retreated to Pavia, he was probably confident that the siege would be short. It was a fatal miscalculation: Charlemagne had no intention of withdrawing. With Desiderius and his army bottled up in Pavia, he was free to spend the winter taking over the rest of the Lombard kingdom. Pavia finally surrendered in June 774. The Lombards submitted to Charlemagne, and Desiderius was deposed and imprisoned in a monastery. Though Charlemagne returned the lands seized by Desiderius to the papacy, he took the title 'Patrician of the Romans' and left Hadrian in no doubt as to who was the ruler of Rome. This was an important moment in Charlemagne's reign, paving the way as it did for his assumption of the imperial title in 800.

A silver-gilt reliquary made in c. 1350 to house the head of Charlemagne, now in the treasury of Aachen cathedral, where the emperor was buried.

The Saxon wars

In the opinion of Charlemagne's friend and biographer Einhard, 'no war ever fought by the Franks was more prolonged, more full of atrocities and more demanding of effort than the conquest of Saxony'. It took dozens of campaigns spread over thirty-three years before Saxon resistance was completely extinguished. In the eighth century, the Saxons were still a decentralized tribal people, divided into four main groups: the Westphalians, the Angrarians, the Eastphalians and the Nordliudi. Despite the efforts of Anglo-Saxon missionaries, who felt duty bound to bring the benefits of Christianity to their continental cousins, the Saxons were still committed pagans, and there was a long history

Charlemagne

ET SYRIAM SOBAL · ET CONVERTIT
IOAB · ET PERCUSSIT EDOM IN VAL
LE SALINARUM · XII MILIA ·

Frankish cavalry, in a ninth-century psalter from the monastery of St Gall in Switzerland. Elite cavalry units known as *scaras*, capable of operating independently in enemy territory, formed an important part of Charlemagne's military machine.

of conflict between them and the Franks. The Saxons frequently raided across the border and the Franks retaliated by invading and imposing tribute, which the Saxons stopped paying at the earliest opportunity. From the beginning of his reign, Charlemagne was convinced that the only way to reach a lasting settlement with the Saxons was to conquer them and to convert them to Christianity by whatever means necessary.

Charlemagne began the conquest of the Saxons in 772 by capturing the most important of their pagan shrines. He plundered the shrine of its treasure and provocatively destroyed its great idol, the Irminsul, to demonstrate the superior power of the Christian god. The need to intervene against the Lombards in Italy prevented him from following up this campaign until 775, and by 777, when the Saxon war leader Widukind fled to Denmark, Charlemagne felt his control of Saxony was secure enough to hold the annual general assembly of the kingdom there (at Paderborn). Charlemagne's declaration of victory was premature. When in 778 the Saxons heard that Charlemagne had suffered a defeat in Spain, they rebelled, massacred the Frankish garrisons, burned churches and ravaged the Rhineland. More Frankish campaigns followed. Pitched battles were rare; the Saxons generally avoided battle with the better equipped Franks, preferring to fight a guerrilla war. Charlemagne's strategy was usually to establish a camp deep in Saxon territory and send out fast-moving cavalry units, called *scaras*, to ravage the surrounding countryside and wear down Saxon resistance.

By 780 the Saxons again seemed to be pacified. Charlemagne divided Saxony up into counties, the normal unit of local government in the Frankish kingdoms, and punitive laws were introduced to suppress paganism. But once again Charlemagne was premature. In 782 a new rebellion broke out under Widukind, who had returned from exile, and the Saxons inflicted a serious defeat on a Frankish army in the Süntel mountains, which had rushed into battle without adequate scouting. As the Frankish royal annalist commented, 'since the approach had gone badly, badly also went the battle'. The Franks were surrounded and few escaped: the dead included twenty-six high-ranking members of the nobility. Charlemagne's revenge was swift and brutal: he ordered the execution of 4,500 Saxon prisoners at Verden. Widukind escaped capture and continued to lead resistance until 785, when he finally submitted and accepted baptism. Saxony enjoyed seven years of peace, but in 792 another widespread revolt broke out while Charlemagne was campaigning in the east. Once again churches and the clergy were attacked, but this was the Saxons' last effort. By 797 Charlemagne had broken Saxon resistance south of the Elbe. Resistance continued north of the Elbe until 805, however, when Charlemagne finally deported and dispersed most of the population.

It may seem surprising that Charlemagne took so long to subdue the tribal Saxons when he was able to conquer the wealthy and centralized Lombard kingdom in less than ten months. However, in the early Middle Ages, political centralization was not always the advantage it seems. In a centralized kingdom, where power and leadership were concentrated in few hands, an invader could simply remove the political elite and then use the institutions of the state to control the rest of the population. This is what happened to the Lombards (and also to the English in 1066). After deposing Desiderius, Charlemagne simply took his place, adopting the title king of the Lombards, while the Lombard kingdom kept its separate identity, laws and institutions. In Saxony, this approach was impossible. The Saxons had many different chiefs, so there was little chance of eliminating the elite in a single campaign, there was no-one with whom to negotiate a lasting peace, nor were there any institutions of government to be taken over. Charlemagne probably did not appreciate this, apparently believing, wrongly, that the submission of one Saxon tribe could be binding on the others.

THE CONQUESTS OF CHARLEMAGNE AND THE EXPANSION OF THE FRANKISH KINGDOM, 768–814.

Disaster at Roncesvalles

As well as conquering the Lombards and Saxons, Charlemagne campaigned against the Avars, Spanish Moors, Bretons, Bavarians and Slavs, Venetians and Byzantines, approximately doubling the size of the Frankish kingdom. Other than towards the end of his long reign, when his health was failing, there were few years in which he did not lead a military campaign in person, and only one when a Frankish army was not campaigning somewhere on the empire's borders. The year in question was 790, when the royal annalist remarked simply that 'this year, the Franks were quiet'.

The death of Count Roland at the Battle of Roncesvalles in the Pyrenees, depicted in a thirteenth-century manuscript. Here Roland is shown blowing his horn, Oliphant, to summon Charlemagne (top), who mourns his death on the battlefield (bottom). The defeat of Charlemagne's rearguard by the Basques at Roncesvalles in 778 was so severe that it was covered up in official records for over twenty years.

Charlemagne was undoubtedly a great military leader but, ironically, his most celebrated campaign was also his greatest failure. In 777 Ibn al-Arabi, the Moorish governor of Zaragoza in northern Spain, rebelled against his overlord, the emir of Córdoba, and offered to hand over his territory to Charlemagne in return for his protection. The following year, Charlemagne invaded Spain in massive strength. He himself led one army across the western Pyrenees from Aquitaine and advanced on Zaragoza to enforce Ibn al-Arabi's offer of submission. A second Frankish army crossed the Pyrenees from Provence and approached Zaragoza from the east. After receiving hostages from Zaragoza, Charlemagne returned to Aquitaine over the pass of Roncesvalles, where his rearguard was ambushed and massacred by the Basques. It was a major disaster, with several important nobles among the dead, including Roland, the count of the Breton March. After the battle the Basques melted away into the mountains, frustrating Charlemagne's attempts to exact reprisals against them. The battle was later immortalized in the Old French epic *The Song of Roland*, though a generous amount of poetic licence has transmuted the Spanish campaign into a prototype crusade. The expedition produced no lasting results to compensate for this defeat – Ibn al-Arabi soon went back on his word and Charlemagne never again led an expedition to Spain. However, through the efforts of the margraves (border lords who were given considerable freedom of military action) and, later, his son Louis the Pious, the frontier was pushed slowly south. The capture of Barcelona in 801, after a two-year siege, firmly established Frankish power south of the Pyrenees.

Military service

All freemen were expected to attend the annual general assembly of the kingdom and all were liable for military service and expected to provide their own equipment. For infantry this usually comprised a spear, bow, shield, mail coat and helmet. In addition to these arms, horsemen were also expected to own two swords. These duties were beyond the means of poorer freemen and various measures were used to ease the burden on them. However, even in Charlemagne's time unscrupulous lords deliberately made repeated demands for military service to impoverish freemen and force them into serfdom. For administrative purposes, Charlemagne's empire was divided into around six hundred counties, each governed by a count, whose responsibility it was to raise the levy in his county, lead the men to the assembly and command them in battle. The core of Charlemagne's armies was made up of his military vassals. These were men who had commended themselves, and become sworn dependants of the king in return for which they received a benefice, usually an estate, so that they could devote themselves to military service. Such agreements were the basis of what has become known as feudalism (from *foedus*: 'agreement').

Imperial coronation

As Charlemagne's realm expanded, his rule became increasingly imperial in character. Much of his legislation and relations with the church were clearly modelled on the practice of the Christian Roman and Byzantine emperors. The culmination of this development came on Christmas Day 800, when Charlemagne was crowned emperor by Pope Leo III at Rome. The exact meaning of the imperial coronation has been debated by generations of historians, but it is likely that Charlemagne believed that he was restoring the Roman Empire, which, to medieval Europeans, represented the ideal of Christian unity.

A sincerely pious Christian, Charlemagne believed that he had a responsibility to defend Christendom against unbelievers and to support the church in creating an orderly and just Christian society. To this end, he was an active legislator and promoter

Supply wagons with Charlemagne's army, from a fourteenth-century Venetian manuscript. Charlemagne paid close attention to logistics and his armies set out on campaign with supplies for three months.

THE AVAR CAMPAIGN

PITCHED BATTLES WERE RELATIVELY RARE EVENTS in early medieval warfare. Charlemagne is known to have led an army in battle in person on only two occasions, both in 783 and, though he won both, nothing is known about the tactics he used. His general strategic approach to campaigning is much clearer. As ruler of the largest kingdom in western Europe, Charlemagne had considerable manpower at his disposal. This enabled him to deploy two or more separate armies on major campaigns, so forcing opponents to divide their forces. Meticulous planning was a characteristic of Charlemagne's campaigns and armies set out with three months' supplies in waterproofed wagons, siege engines and entrenching tools. Where possible, fleets were deployed on inland waterways to transport troops and supplies.

The most meticulously planned of Charlemagne's campaigns were those he fought against the Avars, a pagan nomad people who had settled in Pannonia (roughly modern Hungary) in the sixth century. Charlemagne's first Avar campaign in 791 involved a total of three armies. Two of these armies were gathered at Regensburg on the Danube. One army was ordered to march along the north bank of the river; the other, under Charlemagne's personal command, along the south bank. A fleet accompanied the armies, to carry supplies and to ferry troops across the river if either army needed reinforcements, and to bypass the fortifications that the Avars had built on the riverbanks. At the Avar border the armies halted for three days of fasting and prayer to ensure that the campaign had divine support. A cavalry *scara* was sent to invade the Avar kingdom from Italy. Seeing the massive forces arrayed against them, the Avars simply abandoned their positions and for several weeks the Franks ravaged their territory at will.

Charlemagne's preparations for a follow-up campaign were even more ambitious and imaginative. These included the construction of a portable pontoon bridge and an unsuccessful attempt to link the Rhine and Danube with a canal to speed movement

of troops and supplies to the front. In the event, no further major campaigns were needed. A civil war broke out among the demoralized Avars, and a Frankish army led from Italy by Duke Eric of Friuli met little opposition when it captured the Avar capital, a fortress at an unidentified location known as the Ring, in 795. A vast hoard of treasure, looted by the Avars during centuries of raiding, was carted back to Francia. The conquest of the Avar kingdom was completed in 796 by Charlemagne's son Pippin, who led another army from Italy to destroy the Ring and carry off the Avars' remaining treasure.

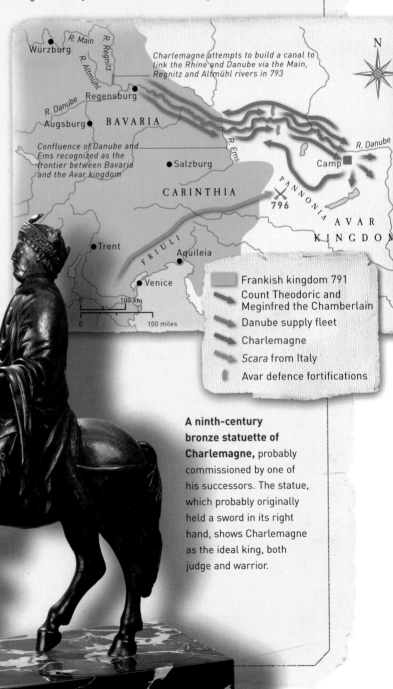

Charlemagne attempts to build a canal to link the Rhine and Danube via the Main, Regnitz and Altmühl rivers in 793

Confluence of Danube and Ems recognized as the frontier between Bavaria and the Avar kingdom

Würzburg · R. Main · R. Regnitz · R. Altmühl · Regensburg · R. Danube · Augsburg · BAVARIA · Salzburg · CARINTHIA · R. Ems · R. Danube · Camp · PANNONIA · 796 · AVAR KINGDOM · Trent · FRIULI · Aquileia · Venice

0 — 100 km
0 — 100 miles

Frankish kingdom 791
Count Theodoric and Meginfred the Chamberlain
Danube supply fleet
Charlemagne
Scara from Italy
Avar defence fortifications

A ninth-century bronze statuette of Charlemagne, probably commissioned by one of his successors. The statue, which probably originally held a sword in its right hand, shows Charlemagne as the ideal king, both judge and warrior.

of monasticism and learning. Today, these are seen as non-military aspects of his reign, but Charlemagne would not have recognized the distinction. Medieval Christians believed that success in all human enterprises ultimately depended on the will of God. Good laws and a well-educated clergy would encourage Charlemagne's subjects to live more Christian lives, and so win God's favour for his kingdom and his armies.

The Viking threat

By the time of Charlemagne's imperial coronation, the Frankish empire was reaching the practical limits of expansion and there were few significant territorial gains after the capture of Barcelona in 801. New threats to the empire emerged in the shape of raids by Muslim pirates in the Mediterranean and by Vikings on the North Sea and Channel coasts. Charlemagne delegated the defence of the Mediterranean coast to subordinate commanders, but he personally oversaw the preparation of defences against the Vikings. Fleets were stationed on all the major navigable rivers, and coastguard garrisons were stationed in forts at harbours and vulnerable river mouths. His decision to concentrate defences in these places shows clearly his mastery of the strategic and tactical situation.

Charlemagne understood that rivers, in particular the Rhine, Scheldt, Seine, Loire and Garonne, were the key to an effective defence against the Vikings. If raiders penetrated these river systems they could roam at will in the empire, as they were to do later in the century. Fleets and fortifications at these points could, with luck, prevent the Vikings from getting into the heartlands in the first place or, if this failed, the raiders' escape to the sea could be blocked and they could be brought to battle. Charlemagne showed similar tactical sense in stationing a fleet at Boulogne to control the bottleneck of the Straits of Dover. There was, however, little that could be done to protect the open coastline from attack. In 810 the Danish king Godfred launched a major raid on the exposed Frisian islands. Charlemagne mobilized the fleet and immediately set off for Frisia with an army, but the Danes had already set off home before all his forces had gathered. This was to be the last time that Charlemagne, now nearing 70 years old, led his troops in person.

Despite this kind of occasional failure, Charlemagne's coastal defences prevented any Viking incursions inland for over twenty years after his death. Similar success was enjoyed by Frankish naval forces in the Mediterranean against the Muslims. However, the effectiveness of Charlemagne's military system depended on the maintenance of strong royal government that ensured that subjects performed their military duties. During the years of expansion, men served willingly enough because of opportunities to plunder enemy territory. They were less enthusiastic about serving on defensive campaigns, however, when they incurred the same costs and ran the same risks but, being on friendly territory, had no opportunity for plunder. This was already a problem in Charlemagne's later years. When, under his less able successors, royal authority collapsed, so too did the defences against the Vikings and Muslim pirates and, as a result, the Frankish lands suffered years of devastating raids.

'It is our function ... externally to defend Christ's holy church by force of arms against the incursions of the pagans and the devastations of the infidels, internally to strengthen it in the knowledge of the Catholic faith.'

LETTER OF CHARLEMAGNE TO POPE LEO III (796)

Charlemagne

'I desired to live worthily as long as I lived, and to leave after my life, to those that should come after me, the memory of me in good works.' ALFRED THE GREAT'S TRANSLATION OF BOETHIUS' *CONSOLATION OF PHILOSOPHY* CH.XVII

ALFRED THE GREAT

JUSTIN POLLARD

c. 849–899

WHEN ALFRED THE GREAT ASCENDED to the throne of Wessex in 871, the old kingdoms of Anglo-Saxon England stood on the brink of collapse. What had driven them to this point was a new threat that had emerged in the late eighth century and which today we call the Vikings. During the ninth century Viking raiding parties on the English coast had rapidly expanded into full-scale invasion armies, and one by one the crowns of Northumbria, East Anglia and Mercia had fallen, leaving only Alfred's Wessex. Even that came briefly under Viking control, but after months hiding on the Isle of Athelney in the Somerset Levels, Alfred managed – in a brilliant counter-attack – not only to defeat his enemy, but also to create an in-depth system of defence that would protect his people from future attacks and lay the foundations of the English nation.

Alfred was an unlikely king. As the youngest of the four sons of King Aethelwulf he is not even mentioned in the chronicles during the reigns of his two eldest brothers, and only when his closest brother Aethelred succeeded to the throne did he emerge into the somewhat dim political spotlight of the ninth century. Aethelred's Wessex was a country fighting for its life. The threat posed by the Vikings was new in both its type and its scale. Even amongst the martial Anglo-Saxon states, warfare had developed particular rules. Armies attacked other armies; soldiers fought other soldiers and fighting was reserved for the summer when food supplies were plentiful and the fyrd (the peasant levy that made up much of the army) was not required on the land. Truces and treaties were backed by religious sanctions, the swearing of Christian oaths usually being enough to ensure compliance in what was then an overwhelmingly Christian society. The Vikings neither understood nor cared for any of these rules of engagement. They operated guerrilla armies, and were happy to attack rich undefended sites such as monasteries and slaughter the occupants who, to them, simply seemed ludicrously unprepared. Caught in a tight corner they would swear Christian or pagan oaths (and even convert to Christianity, sometimes repeatedly) but just as easily break that oath as soon as their situation improved, unbothered by the threats of supernatural retribution.

Yet the Vikings were not simply the demons portrayed in the Anglo-Saxon chronicle. Their form of warfare was not only new but also brilliantly effective in three key areas against the old Christian states of Europe. First, they moved quickly, thanks to ocean- and river-going ships, which could carry invasion forces across the open sea and could both infiltrate and exfiltrate raiding parties deep inland without being noticed. For them the rivers of England were not boundaries between states (as Anglo-Saxons tended to see them), but highways. Second, they fought practically, hitting hard but seeing no dishonour in then rapidly retreating before a response could be mounted. Third, and perhaps most important of all, they had an acute understanding of the power politics behind the fault lines in Anglo-Saxon society, playing rival aristocratic families off against each other and allowing internecine warfare to cripple their targets before simply stepping into the bloody void left behind.

The early campaigns

The history of Alfred's campaigns against the Vikings follows his slow and painful realization of their tactics and tells of how, at his lowest moment, he created a series of brilliant and innovative strategies for countering them. Alfred's first experience of the Vikings was in 865, with the arrival in England of what the chroniclers call 'The Great Heathen Army'. Unusually large for its day, this Viking warband certainly numbered in the thousands (although no accurate figures are available). Led by two of the most feared names in ninth-century Europe – Halfdan and Ivarr the Boneless – the Vikings landed in East Anglia where the king, Edmund, agreed to let them overwinter and probably paid them tribute in return for a promise to leave. The following year, as good as their word, they left East Anglia and marched to the kingdom of Northumbria; here their real intentions became only too apparent. Dividing the rival aristocratic families, the Vikings seized control and installed their own puppet ruler, before striking back south into the once great nation of Mercia.

With a Viking army camped in Nottingham, the Mercian king Burgred decided to take the diplomatic option and paid them off. But this proved to be a major tactical mistake. The following spring the Great Heathen Army did leave Mercia, to put down a revolt in Northumbria, but they then marched straight back to where they had been paid off before – East Anglia. Here they slaughtered King Edmund (later

Saint Edmund), destroyed his army and took over his kingdom. For Wessex and Mercia it was only a matter of time before Halfdan and Ivarr applied the same tactics to them.

The first assault on Wessex

In fact Aethelred's Wessex became the target the very next year. Towards the end of 870 the Great Heathen Army moved to Reading and began a series of probing raids into the Wessex heartlands. Here Alfred finally met them in a series of battles which taught both sides important lessons for the future conflict. Of these, the most notable was Ashdown, where Alfred was said to have entered battle raging like a wild boar whilst his brother Aethelred remained at his prayers. The battle was a shock for the Vikings, who had expected a weaker and less organized defence; instead they found themselves driven from the field. The West Saxons failed to follow up on this, however, perhaps due to the failing health of King Aethelred who died in the spring of 871, possibly from battle wounds. Just a month after Alfred's accession, and reinforced by another army which had arrived at Reading from the continent, the Vikings attacked Alfred at Wilton. Rather optimistically, the chroniclers give Alfred the credit for another victory, but the outcome seems to have been far less certain; his decision following the engagement to pay Halfdan to leave Wessex would suggest that, if it was a victory, it was certainly a Pyrrhic one.

In paying off the Vikings, Alfred must have been aware that he was only postponing the next battle. The following year they would want more money and, crucially, it was clear that they were intent not simply on extortion, but on invasion. Money might buy them off temporarily, but only long enough to give them time to regroup, plan and execute the inevitable attempted conquest of the country.

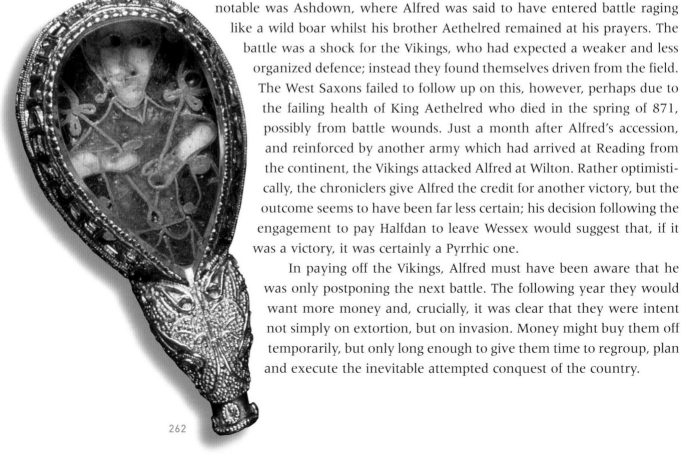

Wessex

English Mercia

Viking territory

Viking Mercia

VIKING ASSAULTS ON THE ANGLO-SAXON KINGDOMS, 866–895.

Yet fortune smiled on Alfred after Wilton. The Vikings did not return for the following five years, which they spent annexing Mercia. Alfred failed to use the time wisely, however, and no records survive from this period to indicate that any attempt was made to reorganize or fortify his kingdom. Perhaps blinded by his success in the Battle of Ashdown, he seems to have still been unaware that the old-fashioned forms of Saxon warfare would ultimately prove inadequate against this enemy.

The Vikings' return

The second invasion of Wessex began in 875, with the Viking army making an impressive dash from Cambridge, right through the Wessex heartland to Wareham on the Dorset coast. Having outrun their supplies, the Vikings now agreed to terms, which this time included giving hostages as well as oaths. Alfred was about to learn another important lesson. Believing he had again protected his kingdom, he stood back and watched as his enemy flouted their oaths, abandoned their hostages and simply moved their base to Exeter. Here though, the Vikings' luck failed them. Their breaking of the terms of the Wareham treaty was predicated on their knowledge that a reinforcing fleet was at that time heading along the south coast. When the army arrived at Exeter, however, they learnt that the fleet had been wrecked off Swanage and that they would not be relieved. Further oaths and hostages followed and this time the Heathen Army did retire back into Mercia.

Alfred's tactic at this stage seems to have been to buy time, in the hope that Halfdan's men would tire of years in the field and eventually settle down to divide up the kingdoms they had already conquered. If this was the case, he was mistaken. The Vikings had no intention of abandoning their dream of seizing the richest prize – Wessex – and even if this army did disband, there were many more Vikings in Scandinavia. So it was, and in 878 a third invasion of Wessex was mounted, led by a new warlord, Guthrum.

The Alfred Jewel: discovered in a cart rut at North Petherton, near Athelney in Somerset in 1693, this late ninth-century jewel is probably one of the *aestels* or bookpointers Alfred mentions in his writings. Around the edge it bears the legend +AELFRED MEC HEHT GEWYRCAN – 'Alfred Had Me Made'.

Alfred the Great

Guthrum's invasion

This time Alfred was caught entirely unawares. It was mid winter, a Christian holiday, and a truce was in place. But on Twelfth Night the Viking army, probably in collusion with elements of Alfred's own court, crept up on Chippenham, where the king was spending the holiday, and attempted to seize him. A last-minute warning saved Alfred's life and he escaped into the mazy marshes of the Somerset Levels, but Wessex was now, to all intents and purposes, a Viking state.

Alfred was deposed but safe and entering into the period of his life most associated with myth and legend. This is the period in which the famous story of Alfred burning the cakes is set, when a despondent king, left to watch some cakes in the oven of a peasant's house, fell to dreaming and let them burn, only to be scolded by the housewife who was unaware of her noble guest's identity. In the light of his military campaigns up to this point, this can clearly be seen as an allegory. Alfred is the man who took his eye off the ball, who wasted the time he had bought and now saw his kingdom fall to ruin. In return he had been scolded by his people. Now he had to take that reproach and recover.

In fact, having failed to capture Alfred or drive him overseas (like Burgred of Mercia) it was Guthrum who found himself in a difficult position. He was now the static ruler trying to organize a large state and Alfred was the guerrilla, moving quickly and silently through difficult terrain that he knew better than his enemy. During that winter and early spring, Alfred seems to have been able to re-establish contact with key members of his court who did not support the new regime, and news that he had survived and was still in Wessex prevented the collapse in resistance that had been witnessed in East Anglia and Mercia. So it was that in early May 878 Alfred emerged from Athelney and rode to the unidentified site of 'Egbert's Stone' (possibly Kingston Deverill in Wiltshire) where the fyrds (or partial fyrds) of Somerset, Wiltshire and Hampshire awaited him. He was ready to retake his kingdom.

Alfred the Great

The recovery

News that a large Saxon army was in the field must have reached Guthrum at Chippenham very quickly, presenting him with a choice – to play the king and meet this army in open battle, as Alfred wanted, or continue to play the Viking, sue for peace or slip away in the night. Significantly, Guthrum chose to play the king, and on the ramparts of the old Iron Age fortress of Bratton Camp, on the escarpment above Eddington in Wiltshire, the two sides met in battle. As with all battles of this date we have no detailed accounts of tactics, troop movements or even the order of events. What the chronicles make clear is that the Viking army was routed, and fled back to Chippenham where they were besieged until, starving and exhausted, they surrendered.

Alfred's terms were lenient by Viking standards. Guthrum gave hostages, Alfred gave none (a first, as the chroniclers proudly state), the Vikings would retreat into their territory to the east of Watling Street and Guthrum himself would be baptized, Alfred becoming his godfather. This treaty was a magnificent piece of realpolitik on the part of Alfred. He could have slaughtered the Viking garrison – indeed they probably expected that – but that would simply have left a vacuum for another younger and more hungry warband to fill. Alfred chose instead to make Guthrum the Saxon-style king he had shown he wanted to be. He would have his land in East Anglia but on Saxon terms, under rules of kinship that both sides could understand, with Alfred as the overlord restraining and protecting his protégé. It was a good deal for Guthrum too. Viking warlords who survived their enemies were often deposed by their own men. Alfred was offering him the position of an anointed king with all the protection offered by that role; in return Guthrum would be a restraining hand on any future Viking army intent on invading England, as he was now a part of that land.

A new England

Freed from the imminent threat of invasion, Alfred finally put the lessons of the war to use by completely reorganizing his country and the means it adopted to deal with this new form of threat. This was perhaps a greater victory than Eddington. First, he reorganized his court and defences, putting his administration and army on a shift basis; in the case of the army,

> **'Alfred's name will live as long as mankind shall respect the past.'**
>
> PART OF THE INSCRIPTION ON THE STATUE OF ALFRED THE GREAT IN HIS BIRTH TOWN OF WANTAGE, BY COUNT GLEICHEN

The weapons of war: the sword and round boss (from the centre of a hide-covered wooden shield) are the weapons of a wealthy warrior, even iron-tipped spears being expensive items in the ninth century. Many of the fyrd entered battle with little more than agricultural implements.

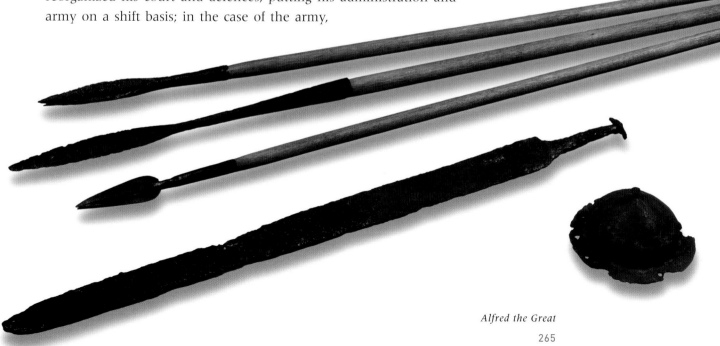

Alfred the Great

The Fuller Brooch: this late ninth-century silver and niello ornament is typical of the work of the Alfredian renaissance brought about by the king's military and social reforms. It depicts the five senses, from top left clockwise – taste, smell, touch, hearing and sight (centre).

this meant that half were on duty at any one time, allowing the other half – who were largely, of course, a peasant levy – to work their fields. He also built a coastal patrol force, the first tentative step towards a royal navy, allowing him to exploit the same rivers and coastal waters which had given the Vikings their great mobility.

But defence has to be funded and it was here that Alfred really changed the whole structure of the kingdom. He created a system of burhs – small towns about 20 miles apart from each other. When invading, Vikings traditionally headed for the capital of a state and decapitated the regime there to seize control, but with all these towns there was no one place to strike, as they formed a distributed defence network. Wessex was neither wealthy nor organized enough to build and permanently man forts, however. Alfred's solution, uniquely, was therefore to invest in his people. He granted land to inhabitants in each burh so that they could set up in business. The same roads that helped armies to march between towns also encouraged trade, so these people profited. The burhs were defended market towns, not forts, and their inhabitants provided the means and the manpower to defend them because the financial success of the towns gave them the wealth and the desire to do so. The success of the scheme is indicated by the fact that these towns founded by Alfred – which include Winchester, Chichester, Hastings, Southampton, Shaftesbury and Oxford – are still the backbone of the south of England's economy today.

Finally, Alfred instituted a programme of education, and most importantly literacy. He understood that ruling this new country with its new network of towns required a new level of communication. Few men in his administration before this time were literate, and orders had to be given by word of mouth. With a literate administration, government orders, military orders, intelligence and information could all be carried and distributed quickly and widely in written form – another crucial advantage over the largely illiterate Viking enemy.

The last battle

Alfred was right to prepare. The Vikings did return in 892 under the leadership of the near legendary warlord Hastein (or Haesten, to use the Anglo-Saxon spelling of his name). This Viking war proved very different from the first one, however, illustrated by the fact that Hastein's army arrived in 330 ships but left in just five. Alfred had learnt the lessons of this new form of war. He had watched the old states of Anglo-Saxon England collapse, and had seen his own crown nearly fall from his grasp. But intelligent, educated Alfred had studied his opponent and learnt. He knew this was an enemy too flexible and too driven to ever simply 'go away', so he used his victory not to crush them but to remould them into something that he could live with. He then proceeded to remodel his entire country and administration to prevent such attacks ever happening again. When he died in 899, Wessex was secure, and his scheme of burhs, his organization of the military and his style of government spread, until his descendants could call themselves not kings of Wessex but kings of England.

ALFRED'S SECOND VIKING WAR

THE VIKINGS THAT RETURNED to Alfred's coast in 892 found a very different country from the one Guthrum had invaded. Wessex no longer yielded easy pickings, and during their initial raids they were confronted at Farnham not by a fyrd exhausted after months chasing an elusive enemy, but by a highly mobile force supported by local burh garrisons. The result was a Viking rout in which they were forced to flee across the Thames to an island then known as 'Thorney'.

Before these raiders could be fully contained, however, news reached Alfred of other attacks at Exeter and on the north Devon coast and, having detached a small force to march to London, he had no choice but to head back west.

This probably co-ordinated attack gave the Viking leader Hastein the chance to regroup at Shoebury, where he was joined by new East Anglian and Northumbrian contingents. Realizing now that attacking the heart of the shires and their well-organized fyrds was simply too costly, he decided to try his luck in the wilder territories of the Welsh marches and, skirting the Wessex burhs, he cut along the Thames and then up the Severn to Buttington.

The fyrd followed in hot pursuit and, thanks to improved communications, found when they arrived that the men of Somerset, Wiltshire and Wales were waiting for them. This cosmopolitan army then besieged the Vikings until they faced starvation, and a desperate attempt to break out led to a comprehensive defeat.

For Hastein there followed another dash back across England to Essex, then north, further from the burhs of Wessex, skirting the lands where Alfred held sway, until they came to the deserted Roman city of Chester. The fyrd pursued them all the way, seizing the crops and animals in the immediate vicinity before leaving the bitter winter to do their work for them.

By the early spring of 894, hunger forced Hastein to leave, but he did not dare set foot in Mercia. Instead, he picked his way back south through Viking-held territory to the island of Mersea, in Essex. With Alfred bearing down on them, the Vikings escaped up the Thames and the Lea to the vicinity of Hertford, where they dug in to overwinter.

Alfred reacted quickly. Surveying the river environs south of the enemy camp, he found a suitable bottleneck where the surrounding landscape constricted, and set about building a fortress there on each side of the river. As soon as his enemy became aware that he was preparing to choke off their escape route, they ran. Eventually they reached Bridgenorth, which is the last place we hear of them. The following summer they left Alfred's lands for good.

Viking figurehead: a Viking dragonhead decoration from the Oseberg ship, a beautifully preserved Viking *karve* (longship) built *c.* 815–820 and buried under an earth mound as part of the burial of two Viking women at Oseberg farm near Tønsberg in Vestfold county, southern Norway.

Alfred the Great

> 'Torch the town. Take the captives and as much spoil as possible to the ships. Let the tillers of the soil of this land feel that we have busied ourselves in their territory.'
>
> HASTEIN AT THE SACK OF LUNA, 860 (ACCORDING TO DUDO OF ST QUENTIN)

HASTEIN
fl. c. 856–895

JOHN HAYWOOD

HASTEIN WAS ONE OF THE MOST SUCCESSFUL, and notorious, Viking leaders. In a career that lasted forty years, Hastein (who is called 'Haesten' in English sources) left a trail of destruction behind him in France, the Low Countries, the Mediterranean and in England, yet probably survived to old age. The early eleventh-century Norman writer Dudo of St Quentin (d. *c.* 1043) described Hastein in lurid terms as a 'cruel and harsh, destructive, troublesome, wild, ferocious, infamous and inconstant, brash, conceited and lawless, death-dealing, rude, ever alert, rebellious traitor and kindler of evil' and, as if this were not enough, a 'double-faced hypocrite and an ungodly, arrogant, deceiving, lewd, unbridled, contentious rascal' to boot. Sources as hostile as this need to be treated with caution, but other writers are agreed that Hastein was exceptionally ruthless and cunning, very much the archetypal Viking freebooter of popular imagination.

Though he was certainly a Dane (as, in fact, were the majority of Vikings), Hastein's origins are obscure. One tradition has it that he was the son of a peasant farmer, but it is more likely that he came from the chieftain class. The driving force of the Viking age was the beginning of state formation and political centralization in Scandinavia. Scandinavian society had a large class of men who, by possession of royal blood, were eligible for kingship. However, the progressive centralization of power meant that opportunities to rule were severely reduced. Competition for power was intense and civil wars were common. For the losers in these struggles, the best option was to become a Viking and go on plundering raids, to win wealth and a military reputation, either to support a renewed bid for power at home or for the chance to carve out a new kingdom abroad. Possessing the charisma of royal blood made it easy to raise an army, and it was not actually necessary to possess a kingdom to be recognized as a king. Scandinavian kings were still essentially rulers of men rather than territory. Such landless kings were known as 'sea kings'. According to the Norman writer William of Jumièges, Hastein began his career as the councillor of one such sea king, Björn Ironside, who is said to have been exiled by his father, the semi-legendary

Viking Ragnar Lodbrok. Hastein is never described as a king, and his lack of royal blood may be why, for all his success, he seems never to have attempted to set up a kingdom of his own, but continued to live by plunder throughout his long career. In this, he was probably unusual. Most 'rank-and-file' Vikings were not full-time professional pirates: raiding was considered to be a short-term option to raise funds to buy a farm or win a share of land conquered abroad.

The early raids

Hastein's earliest exploits were in the Frankish empire in 856–859. With Björn Ironside, he sailed up the River Seine sacking the monasteries of St Quentin, St Médard, St Eloi, the royal abbey of St Denis, and finally St Geneviève in Paris. This was meat and drink to the Vikings: the first securely dated Viking raid was an attack on the famous monastery of Lindisfarne on the coast of northeast England in 793. Early medieval monasteries were wealthy and unguarded because no Christian would dare risk the wrath of the saints by attacking them. This, of course, was of no concern to the pagan Vikings. Because they often doubled as trade and craft centres,

An Anglo-Saxon gravestone amid the ruins of Lindisfarne Abbey, Northumberland, depicts what may be axe-wielding Viking warriors. The sack of Lindisfarne in 793 was the earliest securely dated Viking raid. Hundreds of abbeys in western Europe were raided during the Viking Age.

Hastein

The West Frankish king Charles the Bald

(r. 843–877) receives the gift of a Bible in this illustration from a contemporary manuscript. Charles ordered the fortification of many towns to protect them from Viking attack and built fortified bridges to block the progress of Viking fleets up the Loire and Seine rivers. He generally preferred to buy off Viking raiders rather than risk battle, however.

monasteries were also commonly sited on the coast or navigable rivers and so they were highly vulnerable to Viking hit-and-run raids.

Hastein first came to prominence when, with Björn Ironside, he led a fleet of sixty-two ships on a plundering expedition around the western Mediterranean in 859–862. Algeciras and Pamplona in Spain, Mazimma in Morocco, Narbonne, Nîmes, Valence (nearly 125 miles inland on the River Rhône) and Arles in France, and Pisa, Fiesole and Luna in Italy were among the many places attacked. Dublin's slave market was reported to have been flooded with Moors captured during the expedition.

According to Dudo's colourful but surely legendary account, Hastein mistook the Italian city of Luna for Rome and was determined to capture it. Judging the city's defences to be too strong to storm, he tried to gain entry by a ruse. Viking emissaries approached the townspeople, telling them that they were exiles seeking provisions and shelter for their sick chieftain. On a return visit the emissaries told the townspeople their chieftain had died and asked permission to enter the city to give him a Christian burial. The townspeople agreed and a procession of Vikings followed their chief's coffin to the grave, at which point Hastein, very much alive and fully armed, leapt out of the coffin and slew the city's bishop. In the resulting confusion, the Vikings sacked the city. When he was told that he had not, after all, sacked Rome, such was Hastein's disappointment that he had Luna's entire male population massacred.

This story was repeated by many Norman writers and the same ruse was attributed to later Norman leaders such as Robert Guiscard, Bohemond of Taranto and Roger I of Sicily – evidence that medieval warriors admired cunning as much as bravery and skill at arms. Although the daring nature of this raid established Hastein's reputation as a great commander, in fact the Vikings had faced fierce resistance everywhere. Only twenty of Hastein's ships made it home, and the Vikings never returned to the Mediterranean. After the expedition Björn and Hastein split up. Björn headed back to Denmark, perhaps to launch a bid for the throne, but he never made it and died in Frisia. Hastein went to the Loire where he became a thorn in the flesh of both the Bretons and the Franks.

Hastein

Raiding on the Loire

Soon after his arrival on the Loire, Hastein hired himself out as a mercenary to fight for Duke Salomon of Brittany. In 866 he helped Salomon defeat the Franks at the Battle of Brissarthe (near Le Mans), where he killed two Frankish counts, and he was probably also the leader of raids on Bourges in 867 and Orléans in 868. In 869 he turned on his former ally, Duke Salomon, and forced him to pay 500 cattle for peace during the grape harvest season. In the same year, King Charles the Bald (r. 843–877) ordered the fortification of Tours and Le Mans, so that they could act as refuges from Viking raids, and Hastein had to move quickly in order to extort protection money from the two cities while he still had the chance. When in 872 he seized Angers on the River Marne, a tributary of the Loire, King Charles allied with Duke Salomon and laid siege against him, surrounding the town with earth-works, then diverting the course of the river to leave his ships high and dry. This persuaded Hastein to agree to withdraw from Angers, but he soon re-established himself in a base on an island near the mouth of the Loire and continued raiding. Finally, faced with the prospect of a crushing attack by King Louis III of the West Franks, Hastein agreed to leave the Loire in 882, but he went no further than the Channel coast. Vikings were not military supermen and when forced to battle they lost as often as they won. They committed atrocities to sap their victims' will to resist, but generally avoided battle if they could and were more than happy to be bought off by payments of Danegeld. Hastein's success may be due, in large part, to his skill (and duplicity) as a negotiator of such deals.

Hastein's movements for the next ten years are uncertain. A late, and unreliable, source says that he was with the large Viking army that unsuccessfully besieged Paris in 885–886. However, no contemporary source mentions Hastein as one of that army's leaders and he may, instead, have been in England. By 890 he had moved to Flanders and built a fort at Argoeuves-sur-Sommes near Amiens. In a rather unprincipled attempt to save his abbey from destruction, the abbot of St Vaast, near Arras, reached an agreement which gave Hastein free rein to plunder the surrounding countryside so long as he spared the monastery. Hastein had no intention of keeping his word. After plundering the monastery's lands, he allied with another Viking band to launch a surprise attack on the abbey. However, the Franks were getting used to his treacherous ways, and Hastein was repulsed by the troops that the abbot had ready.

An iron Viking helmet with face protection from a tenth-century chieftain's grave at Gjermundu, Norway. Viking helmets only ever had horns in the imaginations of nineteenth-century romantics.

Returning to England

In 892 an unusually hot and dry summer caused crop failure and famine across northern Francia. Because they had to live off the land, the Vikings were forced to leave. Most made for England, which had seen little Viking activity since Alfred the Great's victory over the Danes at Eddington in 878. A major Danish army had landed in England in 865 and had quickly conquered East Anglia, North-umbria and eastern Mercia. Alfred had saved his own kingdom of Wessex only by the narrowest of margins. However, England in 892 was much better prepared for a Viking attack than it had been in 865. During the years of peace, Alfred had reorganized his army, created a navy, and founded a network of fortified garrisoned towns across his kingdom, which were intended to deny the Vikings their greatest advantage – their freedom of movement.

The main Viking army in northern Francia gathered at Boulogne and sailed to Appledore in southern Kent in 250 ships supplied by the Franks. Presumably they thought the ships a small price to pay to be rid of their unwanted guests. Shortly after, Hastein arrived with a fleet of eighty ships in the Thames estuary and built a fort at Milton Regis opposite the Isle of Sheppey in north Kent. His fort was well sited across the main road from London to Canterbury, and with easy escape to the

The *Helge Ask* is an accurate modern repro-duction of a small Danish longship of the eleventh century. The ship was 56 feet long and could reach 9 knots under sail and 5 knots when propelled by its twenty-four oars. Drawing only 18 inches of water, it was ideal for operations in shallow coastal waters and rivers.

open sea if things went wrong. Alfred responded by placing his army in mid Kent between the two Viking armies. A long stand-off followed. Alfred could not concen-trate his forces against one Viking army without leaving the other free to plunder as it wished, but with a large English army in the field, the Vikings were also reluctant to stray far from their camps. At some point Alfred entered negotiations with Hastein. These resulted in the baptism of Hastein and his family and a payment of Danegeld in return for his promise to withdraw. Christian rulers commonly demanded that Viking leaders accept baptism as a way of sealing a peace treaty, as had Alfred himself when negotiating the Treaty of Wedmore with the Danish king Guthrum in 878. Many conversions secured in this way were certainly insincere – some Vikings are known to have been 'converted' more than once – and, in the event, Hastein did not keep his side of the bargain.

Hastein

The arrival in spring 893 of a third Viking army in Devon broke the stalemate by forcing Alfred to split his forces. It had proved too easy for Alfred to contain the Vikings in Kent, so both armies decided to move across the Thames estuary to East Anglia, where they could count on support from local Danish settlers. Hastein built a new fort at Benfleet in Essex, while the Vikings at Appledore sent their ships to Mersea Island, also in Essex, and then set out to join them by marching overland through English territory, plundering as they went. Weighed down by their booty, the Vikings moved slowly and were intercepted by Alfred's son Edward at Farnham in Surrey and badly mauled. The survivors withdrew to Mersea, but their king had been so badly injured that he could not provide effective leadership. Many of the Vikings defected to Hastein at Benfleet, reflecting the fluid nature of Viking armies.

Encouraged by this reinforcement to his army, Hastein set out on a plundering expedition in the east Midlands. In his absence, the ealdorman Aethelred raised an army from London and stormed Hastein's camp at Benfleet, capturing all his ships, booty and his wife and two sons. Many of the ships were broken up and burned, the rest taken to London and Rochester. Hastein built a new fort at Shoebury, 10 miles east of Benfleet, where he received new reinforcements from the East Anglian Danes. Undeterred by the defeat at Benfleet, Hastein launched a raid into the west Midlands. Harried by English and Welsh forces, he was besieged on an island in the River Severn. Hastein fought his way out, but suffered heavy casualties and retreated back to Shoebury. Reinforced by more East Anglian Danes, Hastein set out for the Midlands again in the autumn. This time he captured Chester, but the English cleared the surrounding countryside of food. With winter coming on, he again retreated, this time to Mersea. Alfred now returned Hastein's family to him as one son was his godson, the other was ealdorman Aethelred's. Alfred's generosity was not reciprocated.

Areas plundered by Hastein with dates

Bjorn and Hastein's expedition 859–862

Borders c. 870

N

0   200 km
0   200 miles

NORWEGIANS

SWEDES

GÖTAR

KINGDOM of the SCOTS

NORTHUMBRIA

STRATHCLYDE

DANES

FRISIA

SLAVS

IRISH KINGDOMS

DANELAW

892–895

Chester

WELSH KINGDOMS

MERCIA

London   Benfleet

WESSEX   Milton Regis

890–892

Boulogne

Arras

EAST FRANKISH KINGDOM

Amiens

856–859

FLANDERS

BRITTANY

NORMANDY

Paris

Nantes   Angers   Le Mans

Orléans

Tours

866–882

Bourges

KINGDOM of ITALY

WEST FRANKISH KINGDOM

Valence

Luna

Nîmes   Arles

Pisa

Fiesole

Narbonne

KINGDOM of GALICIA & ASTURIAS

Pamplona

Rome   LOMBARD DUCHIES

EMIRATE of CÓRDOBA

Balearic Isles

Córdoba

Orihuela

Seville

Algeciras

Asilah   Mazimma

IDRISID EMIRATE

VIKING ARMIES

THE VIKING ARMIES of the ninth century had a loose segmentary organization. The basic military unit was the *lið* (pronounced 'lith'), a king's or chieftain's personal retinue of warriors, the size of which depended on the wealth and status of its leader. The warriors of a *lið* formed a sworn fellowship or *félag*, which was bonded together solely by mutual loyalty. Discipline was maintained mainly by the individual warrior's fear of dishonour if he abandoned his companions in the thick of battle. Warriors expected to be rewarded for their loyalty with a share of plunder, and could transfer their allegiance to another leader if their own was unsuccessful in battle. A Viking army was essentially a group of *liðr* which had come together for a common purpose, and when a campaign was over the army simply broke up into its respective fellowships to settle, return home or join another army somewhere else. Because of their segmentary nature, Viking armies often had joint leadership, but a leader with an established reputation, like Hastein, could sometimes exercise unchallenged command. Because contemporary annalists usually described the size of Viking armies in terms of the number of ships in which they arrived, it is uncertain how large they really were. The ninth-century Viking ship from Gokstad in Norway had a crew of at least thirty-three men. If this was typical, the fleet of eighty ships that Hastein took to England in 892 would have carried a force of over two thousand, six hundred men, a substantial army for the time.

When on campaign, Viking armies built forts to use as raiding bases and to protect their ships, loot, and the women and children who sometimes accompanied them. Though women did not fight, they cooked and tended the wounded. The favoured battle tactic of Vikings was to form a defensive shield wall or *skjaldborg* ('shield-fort') to meet the enemy attack. In attack, a wedge-shaped formation called a *svinfylkja* ('swine-wedge') was often adopted to try to break the enemy shield wall. The Vikings' main military advantage was not superior weapons, tactics or organization – most northern Europeans waged war in a similar way at the time – but mobility, which kept them one step ahead of the defenders. Their fast longships drew only about 18 inches of water and were ideal for hit-and-run raids on coastal settlements or transporting armies along rivers. On land the Vikings campaigned as mounted infantry, covering long distances quickly on commandeered horses but dismounting for battle. Usually, by the time local forces had gathered in sufficient strength, the Vikings were long gone with their loot. Once their opponents found ways to curtail their freedom of movement, even experienced Viking commanders like Hastein could achieve little.

Hastein

In 894 Hastein sailed up the Thames and built a new fort on the River Lea, north of London, but was forced to abandon his ships in 895 when Alfred built a stockade to block the river. Another Danish raid into the west Midlands that summer also failed. Though the Danes had not suffered a decisive defeat, the English had denied them the freedom to plunder. Frustrated, the Danish army broke up, some to settle in the Danelaw – that part of England under Danish law – others to return to Francia.

Hastein's last years

A twelfth-century English source says that Hastein returned to Francia in 895. According to a story recorded by Dudo, Hastein acted as a negotiator on behalf of King Charles the Simple (r. 893–922) with another, more politically astute, Viking leader, Rollo, who became the founder of Normandy. The negotiations collapsed, fighting broke out and the Franks were put to flight. There is some suggestion that Hastein was playing a double game and had used the offer of talks to lure the Franks into a trap. However, Hastein's star was now fading. Before the talks, without revealing his identity, he asked some of Rollo's men, 'Did you ever hear anything of Hastein, who was born in your country and sailed here with a great army?' They answered, 'We've heard of him. A good fortune was foretold of him, and he began well; but a bad outcome in the end is his lot.' Hastein's ultimate fate is unknown. By the mid 890s, he must have been in his sixties, which in those days was a good age. A later tradition claimed that Hastein died in 931, fighting against Raoul, the count of Burgundy, but this is improbable as he would have been getting on for 100 years old by then. The death in battle of so notorious a Viking would surely have been trumpeted by contemporary chroniclers, so it is, perhaps, more realistic to imagine that he finally settled down in Normandy or the Danelaw, his raiding days behind him, and died in relative obscurity of natural causes – not such a bad outcome after all.

(Opposite) **Discovered in a burial mound in Norway** in 1880, the Gokstad ship is the best-preserved Viking ship to have survived. Built of oak *c.* 900–905, it is 76 feet long and had a single square sail and sixteen pairs of oars. There was certainly room in the ship to carry more than the minimum crew of thirty-three. The Gokstad ship is thought to be an example of a type of longship called a *karve*, used as the private travelling vessel of chieftains and kings.

'With words and deeds he has challenged the king of the Franks who, with his followers, has dolefully remained inside the cities. He rages around the walls of the garrisons as does a wolf around the pens of sheep.'

DUDO OF ST QUENTIN

WILLIAM THE CONQUEROR
c. 1027/8-87

JOHN GILLINGHAM

WILLIAM THE CONQUEROR'S REPUTATION as a great commander rests securely on that most familiar of dates – 1066 – and on his victory in one of the most decisive conflicts in military history, the Battle of Hastings. The Norman Conquest meant that England received not just a new royal family, but also a new ruling class, a new culture and a new language. Some of the castles William built, at Colchester and at London (the Tower, for example), were the largest buildings of their kind to be erected in northern Europe since the fall of Rome, and they stand to this day as monuments to a duke who conquered a kingdom that was much larger and richer than his duchy.

The Norman Conquest was one of the most astonishing military achievements in European history. Yet in any serious assessment of William as a commander, the almost mythical fame of this one year should not be allowed to block out the fact that he spent his whole adult life, some forty years, in making or preparing for war.

The risks of battle: Val-ès-Dunes, 1047

When William, as his father's only son, inherited the Duchy of Normandy in 1035, he was at most 8 years old, and ambitious Norman nobles seized the opportunity to build castles and make themselves more independent. On coming of age, William's first important lesson in war came when he began the fight to restore ducal authority. He was fortunate in being able to call upon the aid of his own lord, King Henry I of France, whose rank and long experience of war meant that he was the one in command when king and duke overwhelmed Norman rebels in the Battle of Val-ès-Dunes in 1047. Even though their leader, Guy of Brionne, did not surrender until Brionne fell after a long siege, it is clear that the battle had broken the back of resistance, and William had learned that a pitched battle could be decisive. In the fiercely competitive world of eleventh-century France, small-scale wars were the normal continuation of local politics by other means.

By 1066 William had become a highly experienced commander, with at least twenty campaigning seasons behind him. Yet in not one of these campaigns did he

William the Conqueror

ANGLI

himself take command in a pitched battle. A moment of confusion or panic in battle and the work of months or years might be undone, with catastrophic consequences for the losing side. This does not mean that William was unusually cautious. In that age political morality required that rulers who sent men to war must themselves share in its perils – rather than, as today, lurk many miles behind the danger zone. If the imminent prospect of battle brought to all soldiers the terrible fear of injury or death or shame, how much worse must this have been for the commander himself. It was widely acknowledged that the surest way to win was to kill or capture the opposing leader; the flight of the English when they learned that King Harold was dead is only the most famous example of the outcome of a battle being decided by the fate of the commander. Harold's own victory two weeks earlier, when he defeated the Norwegians at Stamford Bridge, had been sealed by the killing of the Norwegian commanders, Harold Haardrada and Tostig. At Hastings, the duke's chaplain, William of Poitiers, reported that William had three horses killed under him. If so, it may have been merely a matter of luck as to which of the two leaders was killed first.

A commander who sought battle was thus putting himself in great personal jeopardy. Not surprisingly, battles were rare events. Only the over-confident ignored the advice given by the 'soldier's Bible', the *De re militari* composed by Vegetius, one of the most influential of all handbooks on the conduct of war. His advice on giving battle was simple: Don't. Just possibly you might, if you heavily outnumbered the enemy, if their morale was low and they were tired and poorly led, but otherwise, no. 'Battle', he wrote, 'is the last resort. Everything else should be tried first.'

The final scene of the eleventh-century embroidery known as the Bayeux Tapestry: the Normans (including a mounted archer) pursue the defeated English, whose mutilated and despoiled bodies are represented in the lower border. The word 'Angli' is the last word of a text which ties together King Harold's death and the English flight.

William the Conqueror

The capture of Domfront

In the years after 1047, William proved himself a master of 'everything else'. In the struggles for power and territory between the princes of northern France, among them the King of France (who ruled over little more than the region around Paris), castles were both the main bones of contention and the focal points around which campaigns revolved. In 1051 William established his reputation as a brilliant soldier by capturing the fortress-town of Domfront (on the border between Normandy and Maine) from the most formidable warrior of his generation, Count Geoffrey Martel of Anjou. After an initial attempt to take it by surprise, he settled down to the only possible alternative: an attack on Domfront's economic base. He mounted a blockade by building four siege castles. To keep his own garrisons supplied, William of Poitiers reports, 'he rode out on patrol by day and night, both to defend his foragers against attack and to ambush those trying to bring provisions or messages into Domfront'.

Geoffrey Martel responded by bringing up an army, not so close as to risk battle, but close enough to inhibit William's foraging and threaten his supply lines.

At this point Geoffrey had the upper hand. But William's scouts reported that the defences of Alençon, 30 miles away, were in a poor state. William rode through the night and attacked at dawn, calling upon the defenders of a small fort across the river to yield. They refused, and made insulting jokes about his mother's status. He responded by taking the fort by assault and then cutting off the defenders' hands and feet, an act of such ferocity that it persuaded the people of Alençon to surrender rather than risk the same fate. Leaving a garrison there, William rapidly returned to Domfront, which, on hearing the news, also decided to yield. In what turned out to be a closely supervised strategy of attrition, William succeeded not only because he moved with great speed and was prepared to be brutal, but also – frequently riding on patrol for the purpose – because he made sure he was well-informed.

> '**Victory will go to the commander who is prepared to be generous not only with his own property, but also with that of his enemy.**'
>
> DUKE WILLIAM TELLING DOUBTERS WHY HE WILL DEFEAT HAROLD

The 1050s: the defence of Normandy

Alarmed by his success, neighbouring princes sought to cut William down to size. In 1053, 1054 and 1057 the King of France and his allies invaded Normandy. In 1054 Henry launched a two-pronged attack, one army under his own command and another under his brother's. According to William of Poitiers, 'burning and looting, the invaders were intent on reducing the whole land to a miserable desert'. In other words, like all armies of the time, they sent out foraging parties and whatever they could not take with them by way of provisions or plunder, they destroyed. This was the gospel according to Vegetius: 'The main and principal point in war is to secure plenty of provisions for one's self and to destroy the enemy by famine.' Simultaneously foraging and looting while ravaging suited both the commander's overall campaign strategy and the individual soldiering for private profit. A method that worked on so many levels at once was a supremely efficient way of conducting war. How was it to be countered without running the risk of battle? Certainly not by the defender shutting himself up in his castle and allowing the invaders a free hand. William put forces into the field to shadow both armies. By moving close enough to deter them from spreading out to ravage and forage, while at the same time taking care not to risk being forced into a battle, his troops harassed the invaders. William himself shadowed the king's army; the outcome was stalemate. But the commanders of the other French army failed to discipline soldiers who, naturally enough, saw looting as the main point of going to war. As soon as William was informed of this he dispatched an elite force, which rode through the night, and at dawn caught the enemy off guard. The Battle of Mortemer, as it is conventionally called, was essentially an attack on troops who were enjoying ravaging too much to be prepared for battle; its effect, however, was to persuade King Henry, on hearing the news, to call off the invasion.

Three years later, in 1057, William defeated another invasion of Normandy when, at Varaville, King Henry and Count Geoffrey Martel allowed the rear of their army to get separated from the rest. William, shadowing them with a small rapid reaction force, at once seized the chance, cutting to pieces those who had been left behind.

The conquest of Maine

By coincidence, both King Henry and Count Geoffrey Martel died in 1060, and this transformed the situation. Throughout the 1060s, the second phase of his military career, William could take the strategic offensive. His first target was the city of Le Mans and the county of Maine. He adopted precisely the same methods as had Henry and Geoffrey in their attacks on Normandy. The first step was to ravage the whole region, 'sowing terror in the land by frequent and sustained invasion', in the words of William of Poitiers. Deprived of its economic base, Le Mans capitulated in 1063.

The ruined keep of the castle of Domfront. Castle building was on such a scale in eleventh-century Europe that by William's day – and for centuries thereafter – the conduct of war was dominated by the struggle to control fortresses such as this. In 1066 William began a systematic programme of castle building in England.

Crossing the Channel

The death of Edward the Confessor in January 1066 gave William an excuse to challenge Harold's right to the English throne. His ship-building preparations for the invasion of England, on a scale unprecedented in Norman history – and extraordinary enough to warrant illustration in the Bayeux Tapestry – spurred Harold to take defensive action. From May onwards an English army and navy was stationed along the south coast. By August, the large army which William assembled at Dives-sur-Mer was probably seven to eight thousand strong, with one in four being mounted. Throughout that month he sat at Dives, despite the logistical problems caused by immobility. Possibly the winds in the Channel were against him, but it seems more likely that William was unwilling to take the huge gamble of disembarking an army in the presence of hostile forces. But Harold too faced logistical problems, and on 8 September, after keeping his forces together for well over three months, he was forced to disband them. Now at last William had his chance to strike. Despite bad weather, his fleet put to sea on 11 September. But the wind was unquestionably against him now. Some of his ships sank and the rest were forced to seek shelter in the Somme estuary. Harbour-bound for two weeks at St Valéry-sur-Somme, William prayed for a south wind. What he got was something even more fortunate; the arrival in the Humber estuary of the invasion fleet of Harald Haardrada, king of Norway.

Harold raised an emergency army and marched north. By the time he reached Tadcaster on 24 September, Haardrada had already defeated the northern levies at Fulford Gate. But Haardrada had underestimated the speed of Harold's response and, presumably made over-confident by recent victory, had failed to send out reconnaissance patrols. Encamped at Stamford Bridge just outside York, the Norse king and his allies, believing themselves secure, were overwhelmed on 25 September. Just three days later the wind in the Channel changed direction. On the evening of 28 September, while King Harald's men were still celebrating their victory and recovering from their exertions, the Norman fleet set sail. The next morning William, after managing to keep most of his several hundred ships together during the night crossing, made an unopposed landing in Pevensey Bay. This news brought Harold south as fast as he had gone north. By the time he reached London, William had established a fortified bridgehead, exploiting and strengthening the ancient forts at both Pevensey and Hastings.

Not all of the ships in William's invasion fleet can have been newly built for the purpose, but so many were that the designer of the Bayeux Tapestry chose to interrupt his represen-tation of scenes from aristocratic life and – for once – show us labouring men at work.

BRINGING HAROLD TO BATTLE

IN OCTOBER 1066, for all his twenty years' experience of war, William faced a challenge unlike any he had dealt with hitherto. Enormous odds were against his being able to continue governing Normandy and hold his cross-Channel bridgehead during the coming winter months. He would not be able to keep what was, by the standards of the age, an unusually large army together for much longer. Only if he defeated Harold in battle could he make gains in any way commensurate with the scale and cost of his preparations. All this must have been obvious from the start, however. For the first time in his military career he had launched a campaign with the intention of forcing a battle. So great was the potential prize that for once it was a risk worth taking. But it takes two to make a battle. Almost always the commander with most to lose could avoid it. The problem for William was how to lure Harold into a position in which the Englishman had no choice but to stand and fight.

Ever since they disembarked, the Normans had ravaged the region around Hastings. All kings felt under some pressure to protect their subjects, but for Harold there was an extra dimension: this was East Sussex, an area in which many of his family estates lay; the landholders here were his tenants, many of them people he would have known personally. The ravaging of East Sussex was in part intended as a provocation to draw Harold into striking range. But it may also be that, elated by his great victory at Stamford Bridge, Harold aimed at repeating the trick, choosing to take risks in the hope of once again taking invaders by surprise.

But any miscalculation Harold may have made was punished only because William, as he did throughout his career, moved fast and took great care to be well informed before so doing. William of Poitiers noted that although all leaders were accustomed to send out scouts, Duke William often went on reconnaissance himself, as he did again after landing in England.

On the evening of 13 October William's scouts informed him that Harold was approaching. He hurriedly recalled those of his troops who were out foraging; fearing a night attack, he made those in the camp stand to arms till dawn. In this anxious moment, William put his hauberk on the wrong way round. But the feared attack never came, the English having decided to rest for the night. At first light the whole Norman army advanced rapidly, giving Harold no chance of withdrawing in good order. The moment for which William had long been preparing had come. Battle was now unavoidable. Achieving this in what was, for him, an unprecedented strategic situation, was William's masterstroke.

(Above) **'Here', wrote the Bayeux Tapestry designer,** 'a house is set on fire.' Destroying enemy resources was standard military strategy. William would have agreed with Henry V's dictum, 'war without fire is like sausage without mustard', and with an early commentator on international law: 'if sometimes the humble and innocent suffer harm and lose their goods, it cannot be otherwise'.

The great battle: 14 October 1066

The Bayeux Tapestry shows both English and Norman warriors wearing similar armour. The English, however, intent on holding their ground, fight on foot, forming a shield wall to keep the Norman cavalry at bay. It was, wrote William of Poitiers, an unusual fight, with one side all movement and the other seemingly rooted to the spot.

But Harold still had time to draw up his army in a strong defensive position on the ridge at what is now called Battle. All he needed to do was to hold his ground. William had no choice but to gamble on an all-out attack. The surviving sources are not remotely good enough to allow us to reconstruct the events of that autumn day (which has not stopped many historians from trying), but it is possible that William's army possessed a decisive advantage in its missile-delivery systems – either a technological edge in the shape of the crossbow, a weapon with which the English were unfamiliar, or perhaps just an advantage in the numbers of archers present. Courageous warrior though Harold was, he lacked William's many years experience of command. For the last fifty years, except on the Scottish and Welsh borders, the English had had little direct experience of war. The stories of the Norman cavalry's feigned flights, drawing some of the English out of their strong position, suggest

practice on one side and inexperience on the other. Even so, the battle was fought hard and long. It was already getting dark when Harold was killed, in circumstances which remain a mystery. William of Poitiers, the contemporary writer who knew most about what happened, chose to stay silent. When the remaining English turned and fled, they were hunted down. The day ended with a massacre which shocked contemporaries. It sent a signal, no doubt deliberately. To make himself King of England, there was no step from which the duke would shrink.

The conquest of England

Their leadership dead or in disarray, and lacking a plausible candidate for the vacant throne, the English were unable to put up any significant resistance as William's army marched on London, taking a circuitous, but strategically astute, route via Dover, Canterbury, Winchester, and Wallingford. On Christmas Day 1066 William was crowned in Westminster Abbey. Early in 1067 he returned in triumph to Normandy. But the Normans celebrated too soon. There were risings every year from 1067 to 1070: in Kent, in the southwest, the Welsh marches, the fenlands, above all in Northumbria. By 1069 William had realized that the north posed military problems well-nigh insoluble for a king of England who was also Duke of Normandy. Virtually cut off from the rest of England by the Humber marshes and the Pennines, Northumbria lay wide open to Danish and Scottish intervention. William's solution, pushed relentlessly through during the winter of 1069–70, was the 'Harrying of the North', the calculated destruction of a region's winter food supplies and seed corn: massacre by famine. The wreck of the Yorkshire economy was still visible years later in the Domesday Book (1086). In strategic terms William had solved the problem of the north, turning it into a cordon sanitaire, a wasteland of no interest to predatory

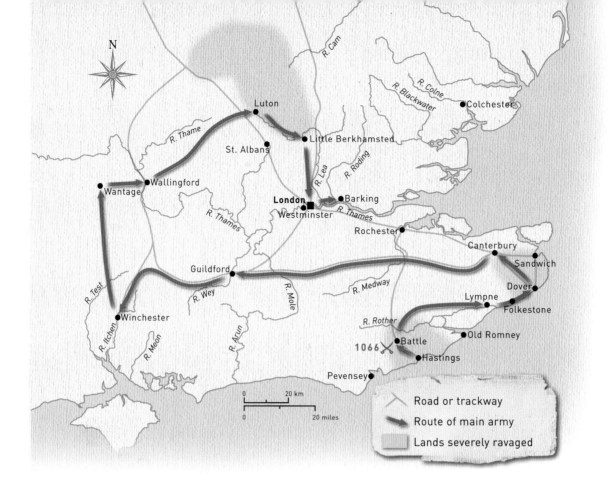

neighbours. In 1070 the kings of both Denmark and Scotland revisited, and both soon went home again.

After 1071, William's hold on England was fairly secure, made more so by his policy of building castles in all towns of any importance. But the citizens of Le Mans had taken advantage of his absence to throw off Norman rule. In 1073 he returned to Maine, bringing English troops with him. In the words of the Anglo-Saxon Chronicle: 'they laid it waste, destroyed the vineyards, burned down the towns and completely devastated the countryside, bringing it all into subjection'. It was back to business as usual. As a new king of France and Count of Anjou flexed their muscles, William's homeland was much more vulnerable to sudden attack than his island kingdom. From then on diplomacy and war on the Norman frontiers took up most of his attention. As he grew older, not everything went his way. In 1087 the garrison of the French fortress of Mantes raided Normandy. While William's troops sacked Mantes in retaliation, he received the injury from which he died.

Known to his contemporaries as William the Bastard, his mastery of all the disciplines of eleventh-century warfare, the routine, the exceptional and the brutal, means that he unquestionably deserved the name by which he has been known for the last eight centuries: William the Conqueror.

'Bohemond was implacable and savage both in his size and glance ... he was so made that courage and passion reared their crests within him and inclined him to war ... his wit was manifold and crafty, in conversation he was well informed ...'

ANNA COMNENA, BYZANTINE PRINCESS AND HISTORIAN

BOHEMOND I

c. 1055–1111

JONATHAN PHILLIPS

BOHEMOND OF TARANTO, Prince of Antioch, was arguably the greatest soldier of the First Crusade (1095–9). When the crusaders captured Jerusalem, people across Latin Christendom perceived it as a miraculous event – 'a renewal of biblical times', as one writer exclaimed. Bohemond's skilled generalship and bravery in battle were fundamental to the survival and the success of the Crusade, and created a huge reputation in his own lifetime and for generations to come.

When he travelled to France in 1106, people crowded around him; William of Malmesbury wrote that knights wished 'to see in action at close quarters that living image of valour, whose glorious fame made him talked of everywhere'. He was a leading figure in the *Chanson d'Antioche*, one of the most popular epics of the twelfth century and a tale embedded at the heart of chivalric culture. He was also a benchmark for future crusaders: as Richard the Lionheart's dejected warriors turned back from Jerusalem in 1192, they recalled Bohemond's valour and remarked how 'God raised [his] deeds to great heights'; heights they seemed unable to attain for themselves.

Bohemond's early years

Bohemond was born in about 1055, the eldest son of Robert Guiscard, foremost amongst the dynamic Norman adventurers who carved out their lands in southern Italy. His baptismal name was Mark, but such was the infant's size that, after hearing a story about an eponymous giant, his father called him Bohemond and the nickname stuck. Bohemond was soon exposed to harsh political reality when Guiscard divorced his Norman wife to marry a southern Italian princess and it was their offspring who were designated to succeed to the duchies of Apulia and Calabria, leaving his eldest son without an inheritance. Nevertheless, Bohemond soon established himself as a warrior of great prowess and by 1081 he rose to be second-in-command to his father.

Guiscard's relentless territorial ambition turned him towards the struggling Byzantine Empire, and in 1081 he invaded Greek lands. Bohemond led much of the campaign and he gathered considerable military experience, steering the Normans to victories in Albania and Bulgaria. These were tough wars, fought in difficult terrain

Bohemond I

against a wily enemy; it required sharp leadership to counter the full range of Byzantine strategies, such as the use of fast chariots and horse-traps. The defeat of formidable opponents such as the famed Varangian Guard, and the completion of a series of sieges, further extended his military repertoire. But by 1085 a combination of sterner Greek resistance and the effects of a plague in the Norman camp saw the expedition collapse; Guiscard himself died on Corfu in July of that year. It was rumoured that he had planned to make Bohemond the ruler of the territory conquered from Byzantium, but at the time of his death no provision had been made for his eldest son.

To establish a domain for himself, Bohemond needed to fight his brother Roger, and this he duly did, acquiring lands in Apulia that included the important cities of Taranto, Brindisi and Bari. Interestingly, in 1089, 1092 and 1093, Bohemond also met Pope Urban II and became a papal vassal. Within two years of the last of these meetings the pontiff had launched the most radical and enduring idea of the medieval age – the Crusade.

The crossing of Asia Minor

Urban's appeal to the knighthood of western Europe to free the holy places from the hands of the Muslims in return for the remission of all their sins was an incredible success. People from all walks of life flocked to take the cross and grasp this chance of salvation. It is unclear from our sources whether Urban contacted Bohemond

Bishop Adhémar of Le Puy carries the Holy Lance at the Battle of Antioch, 28 June 1098, in an illumination from an Old French manuscript of William of Tyre's *History of Outremer, c.* 1250. The Holy Lance, supposedly the spear that pierced Christ's side as he was dying on the cross, was 'discovered' by a monk named Peter Bartholemew during the second siege of Antioch in mid June 1098.

Bohemond I

THE EASTERN MEDITERRANEAN IN THE LATE ELEVENTH CENTURY, showing the route and principal battles of the First Crusade.

directly about his plan. The main eyewitness account for the campaign – a southern Italian cleric who wrote the *Gesta Francorum* (the 'Deeds of the Franks') – describes how his lord, on seeing a group of men heading towards the Holy Sepulchre, was inspired by the Holy Spirit to cut his most expensive coat into crosses and to join the expedition. In a climate of such intense religiosity it is inevitable that Bohemond would have been concerned to make good the many sins that he had committed; it is also undeniable that he, perhaps above all the crusaders, would have been determined to carve out a territory of his own in the Levant.

Bohemond gathered a force of several hundred knights, including his nephew Tancred, another warrior who would gain a considerable reputation on the crusade, and headed towards the Christian forces' main rendezvous, Constantinople (where Bohemond met the emperor's daughter, Anna Comnena, whose *Alexiad*, written some fifty years later, describes both his physical appearance and his presence in vivid detail). Given events in the 1080s this was a delicate diplomatic moment. The Byzantine emperor Alexius was, in part, responsible for the calling of the crusade, having sought Urban's help against the Seljuks of Asia Minor. He had not, however, anticipated that a series of armies, numbering perhaps sixty thousand in total and inflamed with religious zeal, would head towards his lands. The fact that one contingent was led by Bohemond – his bitterest enemy – was a further complication.

Bohemond I

In the event, Bohemond kept firm discipline amongst his men and worked hard to establish good terms with the emperor. Alexius required all the crusade leaders, such as Raymond of St Gilles, Count of Toulouse, and Godfrey of Bouillon, Duke of Lower Lorraine, to swear oaths of fealty to him and to promise to return any lands that were former possessions of the Byzantine Empire. In return they would receive food, guides and military support. Some were reluctant to make such a commitment but, given the practicalities of the situation, there was little alternative.

In the early summer of 1097 the crusaders and the Greeks moved into Asia Minor. The crusaders laid siege to the city of Nicaea, but when the Byzantine army arrived with reinforcements, the defenders surrendered to Alexius. The emperor gave some compensation to the crusaders, but from this time onwards, relations between the two parties soured and the Franks (as they were collectively known) pressed on alone. As they passed near Dorylaeum on 30 June, Bohemond's camp was attacked by a force of Seljuk mounted archers. The Normans fought bravely for over six hours, but it was only the arrival of Godfrey and Raymond's contingents that enabled the crusader forces to form a new battle-line, and in a concerted charge they drove the Turks from the field.

The arduous march across the Anatolian plateau (in the height of summer) saw the loss of many valuable horses; numerous poorer people deserted, unable to endure the hardships of the journey. By the autumn of 1097, however, the crusaders reached the city of Antioch in northern Syria. This immense metropolis was the gateway to the Holy Land, and as recently as 1085 had been in Byzantine hands. Now it was the Turks who guarded its formidable walls and towers, in part skirted by the River Orontes and all overlooked by a citadel perched high above. The city was too big to surround effectively but the crusader armies settled down to try to squeeze it into submission.

A mid nineteenth-century engraving of Antioch, showing the city in the foreground and, above it, on the vertiginous slopes of Mount Silpius, the citadel.

THE SIEGE OF ANTIOCH

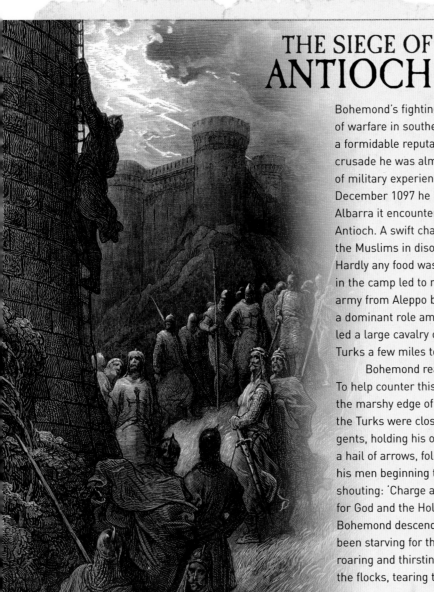

AT FIRST, SUPPLIES OF FRUIT, corn and wine were plentiful, but by the early winter the surrounding land was beginning to be stripped bare. It was at around this time that Bohemond's fighting capabilities most clearly emerged. His years of warfare in southern Italy and Byzantium had already gained him a formidable reputation – compared to the other leaders of the crusade he was almost certainly the man with the broadest range of military experience, which he now brought to the fore. In December 1097 he led a major foraging expedition, but near Albarra it encountered a strong Muslim force heading towards Antioch. A swift charge by the crusader heavy cavalry drove back the Muslims in disorder and brought the attackers some plunder. Hardly any food was found, however, and the continued privations in the camp led to more desertions; news of the approach of an army from Aleppo brought further gloom. Bohemond now assumed a dominant role amongst the senior nobles. Taking the initiative, he led a large cavalry contingent away from the camp to confront the Turks a few miles to the north by the Lake of Antioch.

Bohemond realized that his forces were numerically inferior. To help counter this, he positioned his troops between a river and the marshy edge of the lake. Once his scouts had ascertained that the Turks were close by, he drew the crusaders up into five contingents, holding his own at the back in reserve. The Turks began with a hail of arrows, followed by a cavalry charge. When Bohemond saw his men beginning to buckle, he hurled himself into the fray, shouting: 'Charge at top speed like a brave man, and fight valiantly for God and the Holy Sepulchre!' The *Gesta Francorum* records that Bohemond descended on the Turkish forces 'like a lion that has been starving for three or four days, and so comes out of its cave roaring and thirsting for the blood of cattle and recklessly falls upon the flocks, tearing the sheep apart as they flee in all directions'.

The Battle of Antioch

The crusaders break into Antioch at dawn on 3 June 1098, as imagined by the illustrator Gustave Doré (1832–83). Firuz, the renegade Armenian inside the city, has lowered a ladder and a crusader prepares to ascend, watched by Bohemond himself.

After an eight-month siege (see above), the crusaders took most of Antioch in early June 1098. But in spite of their victory, their position was about to take a turn for the worse; the besiegers were about to become the besieged. The reasons the First Crusade made such headway in Asia Minor and northern Syria were, crucially, the political and religious divisions of the Muslim Near East. The years before the crusade had seen the deaths of many powerful figures and a fragmentation of central authority; the result was a series of minor lordships in competition with one another. Understandably, they had not realized that the crusaders were engaged in a war of religious colonization and the caliph of Baghdad had shown little interest in the situation. It was not until the summer of 1098 that he authorized Kerbuqa of Mosul to lead a serious response.

The arrival of Kerbuqa's huge army soon pushed the Franks back into the city and the Muslims in the citadel also began to attack. Under such pressure even more men fled. Those who remained were so short of food that they were forced to eat their precious horses, while the poor were reduced to boiling the leaves of thistles for

Inspired by the sight of their leader's banner flying deep in the Turkish ranks, the main body of crusaders regained courage and threw their enemy back, killing the Muslims and looting from them as they fled.

Meanwhile, the siege ground on, with the Franks continuing to struggle for supplies and the prospect of further Muslim relief armies a constant threat. In the spring of 1098 Bohemond made contact with Firuz, the Armenian warden of three towers on the city walls. The crusader offered him untold riches if he would let the invaders into the city, and Firuz consented. This was, in fact, an almost identical ploy to that used by his father in 1082 at the siege of Durazzo during the campaign against the Greeks, when the prospect of an advantageous marriage induced one of the defenders to betray the city to Guiscard. At this point we can see Bohemond's political ambitions emerging. He approached the other crusade leaders and persuaded them to agree that if one of them could engineer the downfall of the city he could keep it for himself, although it would be surrendered to Alexius when, as the emperor had promised, he came to help them. On 3 June a group of Bohemond's men approached the towers guarded by Firuz. Soon the crusaders were swarming over the walls and began to descend into the city, slaughtering anyone in their path. Once the gates were opened the crusader army poured in and put the place to the sword. Antioch had not fallen entirely, however; high on the mountain the citadel remained intact.

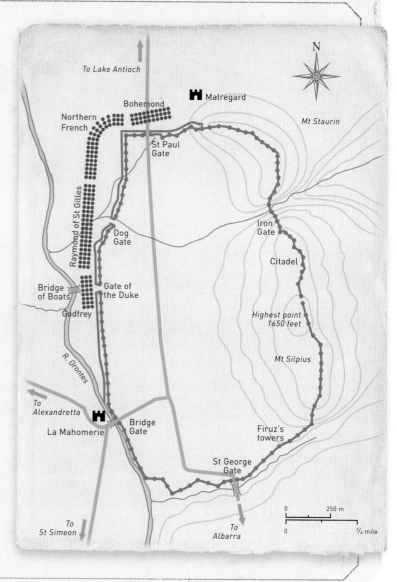

food. The deserters met Emperor Alexius who, as he had agreed, was crossing Asia Minor to support the Christians. The deserters convinced him that it was pointless going to Antioch at all and so he turned back, a decision that would have serious consequences for Bohemond. In mid June the 'discovery' of an object recognized as the Holy Lance inspired the troops and after almost a month pinned between Kerbuqa and the citadel, it was time for the crusaders to act.

Bohemond once more acted as commander for this crucial battle. On 28 June the crusaders marched out of the city and deployed in five contingents; Bohemond again kept his own force at the rear. With few remaining horses, the Franks must have presented a sorry sight, yet in terms of discipline and coordination they were now a well-drilled fighting force; an acute sense of desperation focused their efforts to an even greater extent. Bohemond directed his troops with authority and vision and once they had resisted early Muslim attacks, the crusaders charged and drove their enemy from the field. Seeing this disaster, the defenders of the citadel soon surrendered and handed over the fortress to Bohemond himself.

Bohemond's power established in Antioch

After such a monumental effort the crusaders took months to recover. Within the crusader camp there was huge tension between Raymond of St Gilles and Bohemond, each wanting possession of Antioch for himself; the former tried to insist that it should be held for the emperor Alexius, as had been agreed, while Bohemond began to act as if he had full authority over the city for himself, issuing privileges and confirmations of rights. Further campaigning in northern Syria – in which again Bohemond fought prominently – merely postponed the dispute until, under pressure from the pilgrim masses who were intent upon reaching Jerusalem, Raymond headed south. Although Bohemond would miss the capture of the crusaders' ultimate goal, he could now establish control over his new lands and begin to call himself Prince of Antioch. He rejected requests from Alexius to hand over the city and claimed that because the Greeks had failed to provide the assistance they had promised, he was under no obligation to do so; one imagines a deep satisfaction on Bohemond's part in dismissing the claims of his old enemy. It was not until Christmas 1099 that he felt secure enough to travel south and formally complete his pilgrimage at the Holy Sepulchre.

Over the next few months Bohemond continued to extend his lands in the north, but in early August 1100 he made a rare mistake. For once it seems that he let slip his usual caution and advanced without being properly armed and prepared for battle. The Turks ambushed the Franks and, much to their delight, took Bohemond prisoner; 'the whole of the Persian nation rejoiced and was happy; for the infidels had regarded him as the veritable king of the Franks and all of their people had trembled at his name', as Gregory the Priest, a contemporary local Christian reported. Bohemond remained a prisoner for three years before his ransom of 100,000 gold pieces was paid.

Within a year of his release, the situation in Antioch began to deteriorate rapidly. The Greeks started to make attacks from the sea and through Cilicia; the Muslims of Aleppo pressed from the east and Bohemond's old rival, Raymond of St Gilles, caused trouble to the south. Money was extremely short (partly due to the ransom), and there was a desperate lack of fighting men. In these circumstances, Bohemond decided to return west to raise support.

A thirteenth-century depiction of the siege of Antioch from an Old French manuscript of William of Tyre's *History of Outremer*, c. 1250. Muslim defenders are hurling rocks and firing arrows at the attacking crusaders.

Bohemond's tour of Italy and France

It is in the course of this journey that we can see just how great a reputation the hero of the First Crusade had gained. Assisted by the fact that his cousin travelled ahead to conduct some canny pre-arrival publicity, Bohemond's presence induced great excitement. One reporter noted that people came to look at him 'as if they were going to see Christ himself'! Bohemond met Pope Paschal II and it is clear that he planned to launch a new campaign against the Byzantine Empire before going on to the Holy Land. Paschal gave him a papal legate to help recruitment, although – and this is a matter of ambiguity amongst contemporary chroniclers – it is unlikely that he formally proclaimed a crusade against the Greeks.

Bohemond I

'Bohemond the famous prince of Antioch came to France ... he had won fame and renown among the people of the East and the Saracens themselves praised his noble deeds, which could never have been done without the help of God.'

SUGER, ABBOT OF ST DENIS

Bohemond travelled north to France where he made a high-profile visit to the tomb of the patron saint of prisoners, St Leonard of Noblat, to give thanks for his freedom. He then moved around France presenting relics to religious houses and making what amounted to a victory tour; people flocked to hear him and wanted him to be the godfather of their children; it is said that the name Bohemond, from being virtually unused in France, was suddenly highly popular. His promises of land and money (presumably in Byzantium) lured many to join him, and by September 1107 he was ready to sail from Bari to invade Greek lands in Albania. As in 1081, he besieged Durazzo, but this time he failed; by the summer of 1108, illness, a lack of supplies and the desertion of some of his men compelled him to swear a humiliating treaty with Alexius, in which he agreed to hold Antioch as an imperial vassal and to preserve the interests of the empire at all times.

The mausoleum of Bohemond at Canosa, Puglia, in southern Italy, shows the influence of Islamic styles on the architecture of Norman Sicily. Inscriptions on the mausoleum record Bohemond's triumphs in Greece and Syria.

Bohemond returned to southern Italy where little is known of his final years; he was taken ill and died in March 1111. He was buried in Canosa where his tomb – a striking combination of Byzantine and Islamic styles – remains.

While his career ended in relative ignominy there is no doubt that *Boamundus magnus*, as his son styled him, was regarded as a figure of immense achievement and ability. While it was his exploits on the First Crusade that propelled him to international fame – in the Catholic west, amongst the Christians of the Middle East and in the Muslim world – the wealth of experience that he had accrued through decades of campaigning in southern Italy and Byzantium meant that he was brilliantly prepared to take the leading part in the expedition to the Holy Land. He was brave, enormously ambitious, and at times entirely unscrupulous. He was also a sharp conversationalist and negotiator; perhaps he is best summed up by Romauld of Salerno, a southern Italian writer, who commented that he was 'always seeking to do the impossible'.

Bohemond I

FREDERICK BARBAROSSA
1127–90

JONATHAN PHILLIPS

IN THE SUMMER OF 1190 Frederick Barbarossa battled across Asia Minor en route to the Holy Land. His relentless advance deeply worried Saladin, the conqueror of Jerusalem, because, as the most powerful warrior in the West, Frederick would present the sternest of challenges to his hold on the Holy City. The emperor had a vast range of military and diplomatic experience: a veteran of the Second Crusade (1145–9), Frederick had led six major campaigns into northern Italy; he established his dominance over the German nobility, and, in the course of the Third Crusade (1189–92), swept past both the Greeks and the Seljuk Turks.

(Opposite) **Frederick I Barbarossa,** Holy Roman Emperor, leader of the Third Crusade, and the most feared warrior of his age. This celebrated twelfth-century gilded bronze bust of Frederick, a masterpiece of German gothic art, is housed in the abbey church of St John the Evangelist at Cappenberg in North Rhine-Westphalia.

Just when he was poised to enter northern Syria he died – probably of a heart attack – as he crossed the River Saleph in southern Asia Minor on 10 June. The relief in the Muslim world was immense: 'If the king of the Germans is broken, then after him the unbelievers will be building on a shattered foundation', as one contemporary wrote; even with the armies of Richard the Lionheart still to come, the most potent warlord of the age had perished.

Frederick's early years

Frederick was born in 1127, the son of Frederick, Duke of Swabia, and Judith, the daughter of the Duke of Bavaria. At the age of 20 he took the cross and joined his uncle, King Conrad III of Germany, on the ill-fated Second Crusade. In the autumn of 1147 the Germans attempted to force a direct route through the heart of Asia Minor, but, weakened by a lack of food and water, their footsoldiers were decimated by the Seljuk Turks' cavalry. The Germans spent the winter recovering and then linked up with King Louis VII of France in the Holy Land. In July 1148 the crusaders besieged Damascus, but after only four days, news of the imminent arrival of relief forces from Aleppo compelled them to lift the assault and return home, angry and humiliated at this dismal performance.

Four years later Conrad died and Frederick – his nephew – was elected king of Germany, thus becoming the ruler of the largest territory in Christendom. He was a cheerful, pragmatic and clever young man; tall, strongly built, with blond curly hair and a close-cropped red beard. He was undoubtedly physically tough because, given the demands placed on him, he had to be on the move for most of his reign. He regularly attended mass and was said to be eloquent, moderate (but not frugal) in eating, drinking and entertaining, as well as a noble warrior and a keen huntsman; a contemporary described him as 'the most vigorous prince in the world'.

The kingdom of Germany was formed by a series of powerful lordships, such as the duchies of Bavaria, Saxony, Austria and Bohemia, whose leaders could (and often did) challenge royal authority. But Frederick was not just the ruler of Germany; his imperial inheritance – which had emerged from the remains of the Carolingian empire – included the kingdom of Burgundy in eastern France and much of the Italian peninsula. In addition to his election as king of Germany he was also entitled to be crowned emperor in Rome by the pope. It was relations with the papacy and dealings with the Italian city-states that would absorb most of his energy and would lead him to become enmeshed with the aggressive kings of Sicily and the mighty Byzantine Empire; his desire to extend the boundaries of Christendom into the pagan territories of northeastern Germany was a further ambition. In assessing Frederick's performance as a military leader, therefore, we have to bear in mind the extraordinary demands these challenges placed upon his political skills, and to see that he faced a massive and complex task to realize imperial authority in the form that he desired.

Frederick's first campaign in Italy, 1154–5

In 1154 Frederick marched towards Rome for his imperial coronation. He also wanted to impose his will upon the towns and cities of Lombardy, a region long accustomed to minimal interference from Germany and, in an age of growing communal identity, unwilling to acknowledge Frederick and give the rights and taxes traditionally owed to him. He took Tortona after an eight-week siege in early 1155, then continued south to confront the Romans. Hostilities broke out on the streets of the city, but he was crowned emperor on 18 June 1155 by Pope Hadrian IV (the only Englishman ever to hold the title). An outbreak of plague forced Frederick to leave Rome, although he took Ancona and Spoleto from the Sicilians before heading home. While relations between the papacy and emperor had, to this point, been reasonably cordial, in 1156 Hadrian chose to signal his disquiet at Frederick's power and signed a treaty with King William I of Sicily, a decision that would bring the pope and the emperor into direct confrontation for over two decades.

Frederick's Italian campaigns, 1158–62

Milan was at the centre of resistance to the imperial forces and its citizens constructed an enormous 3-mile-long earthen rampart, surrounded by a water-filled moat, to protect themselves. The first assault on the city, in the late summer of 1158, lasted for only a month and was characterized by exchanges of siege artillery, skirmishes and the ravaging of crops. On 7 September a truce ended the attack, but the decrees that Frederick issued at the Diet of Roncaglia in November 1158 provoked even more anger. He set out a vision of imperial rights which made plain that city consuls were subject to his authority, which required oaths of fealty from the populace, and, in addition, contained renewed financial demands. Unsurprisingly, these decrees soon provoked dissent and Milan rebelled, followed by Crema and Brescia.

Frederick Barbarossa with his sons Henry (left) and Frederick (right), in a late twelfth-century manuscript illumination from the Abbey of Fulda, in Hesse, central Germany.

Frederick increased the size of the imperial force and drew on his allies in Germany, Bohemia and Lombardy itself. The sieges of Crema and Milan required a variety of military techniques to bring them to a close – their success stood amongst Barbarossa's finest military achievements and, for a period at least, gave him the ascendancy in his struggles with the Italians.

The siege of Crema was a particularly arduous, vicious and important episode, because it paved the way for an attack on Milan itself. Crema was formidably well defended with river defences, a large moat, a double circuit of walls and good stocks of food and water. To break through these obstacles Frederick employed some highly specialized engineers, including a man from the kingdom of Jerusalem who claimed to have had a successful career in the Levant (he may have been present at the siege of Ashkelon in 1153). Frederick's Italian allies provided the money, materials and labour to build a huge oak siege-tower that stood six storeys high, at around 100 feet. The lowest level reached the height of the city walls and had a bridge; at its top, archers and crossbowmen could rain arrows and bolts down into the city below. Hides and padding protected a structure that took five hundred men to move along on giant rollers. It needed a massive *testudo*, or armoured roof, to shield the men who laid down the rollers, a covering that also gave protection to the attackers as they attempted to fill the moat in order to bring the device right up to the walls. Frederick needed more local support, and he called on the citizens of Lodi, who provided two thousand cartloads of earth and wood to be cast into the moat to create a causeway.

Frederick Barbarossa

In September 1159 the siege intensified as the tower was inched towards the fortifications, yet the defenders were well prepared and their own artillery inflicted serious damage on the device. They also used machines, described by contemporaries as human-sized mousetraps, to harass the attackers. To try to break their morale, Frederick ordered local captives to be suspended by ropes in front of the tower. A contemporary German writer – ignoring the part his own side had played in this episode – was horrified that the Cremasce continued to fire:

> *This is a thing unheard of even amongst barbarians … And so several children died miserably, struck by the stones, while others though remaining alive, suffered yet more pitifully, hanging there … You might have seen children fastened to the machines beseeching their parents, reproaching them for their inhumanity … [but the parents] consoled themselves for the necessity of their act by taking thought of the miseries they must endure if they were made subject to their enemy.*

THE CAMPAIGNS OF FREDERICK BARBAROSSA IN ITALY, 1154–76.

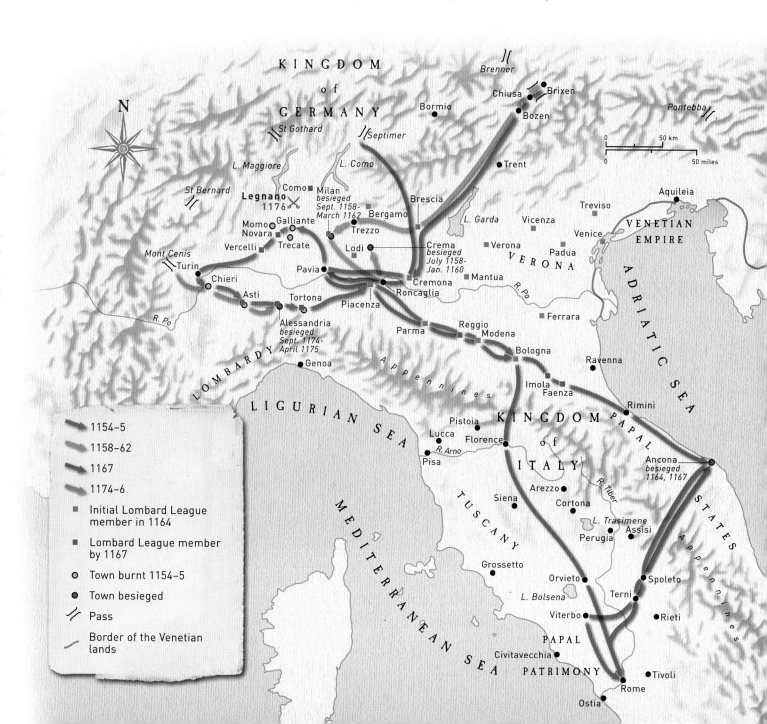

Meanwhile the *testudo* was redeployed to protect a ram, which smashed a jagged hole in the outer wall. The defenders' resourcefulness was admirable; they built an earth and timber barricade and used it as a sally point to assault the *testudo*; they also set up swinging hooks and booms to hurl incendiaries, iron weights and barbs on to it. The battle became even more vicious – the Cremasce scalped one imperial warrior and made another crawl along after his hands and feet had been severed. As is so often the case in a finely balanced struggle, it took a defection to make the crucial difference. In January 1160 the Cremasce's chief engineer, Marchesius, deserted to the emperor, and he recommended the construction of another bridging platform to go alongside the existing tower. The new machine was, of course, well protected and could extend 30 feet forward, enabling archers to deliver a sustained bombardment and a sufficient numbers of knights to cross from both the tower and the new bridge to take the walls.

On 21 January 1160 the onslaught began; initial progress was good, with imperial troops seizing the outer walls; but stern resistance at the inner walls and the destruction of the siege-tower's bridge broke their momentum. None the less, with Frederick's men now inside the walls, the defenders were forced to capitulate; given the harsh treatment of captives earlier in the siege, the fear of even more terrible reprisals was a strong motivating factor. Crema surrendered on 27 January and all its fortifications were destroyed. The colossal expense of the siege (over 2,000 silver marks) and Frederick's determination to enforce it over the winter, demonstrated his ability to hold troops in the field and to keep his allies on side. To the Milanese it was a sign that he would be hard to withstand.

The emperor's first encounters with the Milanese were tentative and not especially distinguished; there was one attempt on his life by a man of exceptional size, described by contemporaries as a lunatic, and who was in the camp as 'entertainment' for the troops. But after coming to Frederick's tent and trying to drag him towards a nearby cliff, the would-be assassin tripped over the tent-ropes and was caught and killed.

The Italians had a formidable army that included a hundred chariots with scythed wheels, as well as archers and heavy cavalry, so Frederick prudently chose to avoid battle for a while. In 1161 he began his assault on Milan in earnest, his tactics emphasizing attrition rather than assault. He initiated a substantial blockade and destroyed crops and trees within a 15-mile radius, taking particular care to deny the Milanese the annual harvest. Roads were closely monitored, and anyone carrying food for the defenders was punished by having his or her right hand amputated; by 1 March 1162 the citizens were so desperate they had no choice but to surrender. Milan's fortifications were demolished, its churches destroyed, its moats filled in; the population was dispersed and the commune abolished. Once again, Frederick had managed to preserve a large army, made up of a confederation of German forces and Italian allies, for a sustained and focused campaign – a tribute to his wealth and his skills as a commander.

Frederick in Italy, 1167–76

In 1167 Frederick crossed the Alps once more. His relationship with the papacy had, by this time, deteriorated to the point whereby he had established an anti-pope to rival Alexander III (1159–81). In July 1167 the emperor entered Rome and enthroned his own candidate, Paschal III, but an outbreak of disease killed many of Frederick's senior advisors and his best knights and compelled him to retreat. More significantly, December 1167 saw the formation of the Lombard League, a confederation of sixteen cities opposed to him. Needless to say, Alexander III supported the League, as did the Byzantine emperor Manuel Comnenus (1143–80), who saw a chance to assert himself as the sole, or certainly the dominant, ruler entitled to imperial status and to be the true successor to the Roman Empire.

Six years later Frederick sent another army into Italy. The most symbolic place to attack would be the new city of Alessandria, constructed in 1168 by the Lombard League, and named after the pope himself. The city posed an unusual challenge; instead of stone walls it relied on a huge earthwork, topped with a palisade and fronted by a wide, deep, water-filled ditch. Autumn rains frustrated the Germans' early assaults because the resultant quagmire meant it was impossible to bring forward siege machinery. This time a Genoese engineer directed imperial operations and, as the weather improved in springtime, he used a huge mobile roof to allow the creation of

a causeway and then sent a ram to break down one of the gates. Somehow the defenders still managed to resist, but the Germans sent in a siege tower which became the focus of the struggle. Sustained determination frustrated the imperial forces and Frederick decided to resort to subterfuge. During a truce over Easter 1175 he ordered his men to complete a series of tunnels, intending his troops to emerge within the city and open one of the gates. The Alessandrians detected the noise made by the miners, however, and quickly collapsed the tunnels; in the resulting confusion a swift foray enabled them to burn the precious siege tower and put the imperial operation in jeopardy. News of an approaching relief force compelled Frederick to leave, and a city derided for having straw roofs and mud walls was able to celebrate its resistance.

The following year saw the Battle of Legnano, on 29 May 1176. By now Frederick was facing destructive levels of dissent within the empire; Henry the Lion, the powerful Duke of Saxony, for example, had declined to fight in Italy. Meanwhile the Lombard League gathered over three thousand five hundred cavalry – a huge number for the time – as well as several large groups of footsoldiers, and challenged him to battle. The League's forces were bigger than Frederick's, but the emperor refused to lose face by avoiding the fight. Initially the imperial troops did well and a fierce struggle developed around the *carroccio*, an ox-drawn wagon on which the League's flags and priests were based. Frederick led the attack, but in their defence of this symbol of communal identity the Italians managed to unhorse him. Some imperial troops believed him dead. Unlike William the Conqueror at the Battle of Hastings, famously remounting and raising his helmet to reassure his men that he was still alive, Frederick was unable to show his troops that he had survived, and he could not, therefore, prevent their wholesale flight. The Treaty of Venice (1177) brought this

Frederick Barbarossa

An illumination from the *Liber ad honorem Augusti* ('The Book to Honour the Emperor'), by Peter of Eboli, c. 1196. The top part of the illumination shows scenes from the Old Testament. Below, Frederick Barbarossa appears with his sons Henry (left) and Philip (right). At the bottom, Frederick orders forests in Hungary to be cut down to allow his crusading army through.

campaign to an end, and six years later the Peace of Constance marked a conclusion to the imperial effort in Italy. In spite of the defeat at Legnano, Frederick's diplomatic skills ensured that by 1183 he was in a hugely powerful position, having preserved the majority of his governmental powers and secured an oath of loyalty from the League, as well as a promise of assistance if he entered its lands. In short, imperial rule in Italy was greatly intensified.

Frederick and the Third Crusade, 1188–90

The final military episode of Frederick's career was also, potentially, the most momentous. In July 1187 Saladin recaptured the Holy City of Jerusalem; western Europe steeled itself to fight back. This was an opportunity for Frederick to take on the highest aspect of the imperial dignity, the protection of the Church – to regain Jerusalem would be the ultimate expression of this and, as such, the pinnacle of his reign.

In March 1188 he held a court at Mainz, a *curia Jesu Christi*, and the emperor, his son and thousands of others took the cross. Oddly, Frederick decided to take the land route to the East, rather than sail, as Richard the Lionheart was to do; it brought a further level of complexity to the enterprise and opened up the possibility of a repeat of the troubles of 1147–8. The emperor had perfectly good relations with the Venetians, so why did he not go by sea? The size of his army may be one explanation; another is that a soothsayer predicted the emperor would die in water and he therefore wished to avoid sailing. Given his final demise, if true, this forecast would indeed be ironic. In his preparations we can see the legacy of Frederick's experiences on the Second Crusade. He made sure that only men with sufficient money were allowed to take part and he worked strenuously to establish firm agreements for markets and prices with the Hungarians, Byzantines and Seljuks. Crusaders who behaved badly were punished by mutilation or death.

The German army set out in the spring of 1189 and made excellent progress until Emperor Isaac II Angelous of Byzantium, an ally of Saladin, began to hinder the troops. Such was the size of Frederick's army, however, that he was able to compel the Byzantine ruler to let him cross into Asia Minor at Gallipoli. At this point the expedition hit trouble; relations with the Seljuks became hostile and, beset by lack of food and water, the crusaders had to mount a fighting march towards the Seljuk capital of Iconium in central Anatolia. In spite of his troops' weakened state, Frederick was determined: 'With the help of our Lord Jesus Christ, whose troops we are, the road will have to be opened with iron', he wrote. In mid May Iconium fell to the Germans, thus avenging one of the Second Crusaders' defeats. The march towards Armenia continued successfully, but when Frederick perished in the River Saleph in June, army morale collapsed and many returned home; others, weakened by their suffering across Asia Minor, died at the siege of Acre in 1190–91.

There remains, however, a further part of Frederick's story. Legends emerged: he remains in an enchanted sleep in Mount Kyffhausen in Thuringia, waiting to reawaken on the Day of Judgement, his red beard having grown so long as to twice encircle the stone table at which he sits. Just like those surrounding King Arthur, these tales reflect a combination of nationalism and regeneration, and while they may originally have been connected with Frederick II (1198–1250) they are now firmly associated with the mighty Barbarossa and his vision of imperial glory, a vision underpinned by a long and varied military career.

A view of the River Saleph (now the Goksu river) in southern Turkey, in its final stretch before it flows into the Mediterranean, with the Taurus Mountains in the background. It was near here that Emperor Frederick I Barbarossa – bound for the Holy Land and intent on the recapture of Jerusalem – drowned on 10 June 1190, to the relief of his Muslim opponents and the despair of his crusading army.

GENGHIS KHAN

c. 1167–1227

JUSTIN MAROZZI

THE MILITARY RECORD OF GENGHIS KHAN places him comfortably at the top table of world conquerors, together with Alexander the Great and Tamerlane. Yet even this accolade scarcely does him justice. Genghis Khan could arguably lay claim to being the most successful commander and empire-builder who ever lived. At the time of his death in 1227, the Mongol empire he had created from nothing stretched from the Pacific to the Caspian, and covered an area four times the size of Alexander's realm. Unlike Tamerlane's empire, it proved remarkably robust and continued to expand after his death, doubling in size under his sons and grandsons.

Possessed of a savage genius both for warfare and for the civil administration of government, Genghis struck terror across Asia. Those who surrendered without opposing him could expect to be spared his trademark outrages. As a rule, though there were exceptions, they were shown mercy. But cities that chose to resist him forfeited their right to exist: they were razed to the ground, their populations subjected to hideous tortures before falling victim to wholesale slaughter. When the indefatigable Moroccan traveller Ibn Battutah journeyed through Central Asia in the 1330s, more than a century after Genghis's ravages, many of the celebrated cities of antiquity he encountered, such as Merv and Balkh, still lay in ruins. For Muslim chroniclers, Genghis occupied the heights of infamy as the Evil or Accursed One.

A heavenly destiny

There is a good deal of obscurity surrounding Genghis's life, particularly his early years, which is not entirely unexpected when studying a hitherto illiterate nomadic race of the late twelfth century, a people that despised the settled life of cities. The precise year of his birth remains controversial, varying from 1155 to 1167.

Acknowledging the difficulties of such a shadowy subject in a landmark study of the Mongols, the nineteenth-century historian Henry Howorth wrote, 'If we wish to enter upon a branch of inquiry which seems utterly wanting in unity, to be as

disintegrated as sand, and defying any orderly or rational treatment, we can hardly choose a better one than the history of the Asiatic nomads.'

In seeking to make sense of Genghis's career of conquest, historians have necessarily relied heavily on *The Secret History of the Mongols*, Mongolia's first written work, compiled by scribes in 1228 to record his momentous deeds. Although it is of questionable reliability, few contemporaries among his shamanistic brethren would have quibbled with its opening sentence, which baldly states: 'Genghis Khan was born with his destiny ordained by Heaven above.' No other possible explanation could account for Genghis's extraordinary mastery of his fellow men; nothing else could justify a wrath and destructive power that appeared almost divine in its vengeful fury.

At the height of his power, Genghis did little to discourage such suggestions of a heavenly mandate to rule. There was, according to John Man, one of his most recent biographers, 'an odd division between the arrogance of one chosen to unite, lead and conquer, who was justified in using every means to achieve Heaven's purpose, and the humility of an ordinary man awed by the inexplicable nature of his assignment'. It was this internal dichotomy, Man suggests, 'that lay at the heart of the paradoxical whirlwind of destructiveness and creativity, of ruthlessness and generosity, that constituted Genghis's character'.

Genghis Khan, Ruler of the Universe, founder of the Mongol empire and one of the world's most famous – and infamous – conquerors, in an eighteenth-century Chinese portrait from the National Palace Museum in the Taiwanese capital of Taipei.

Genghis Khan

From inauspicious beginnings

If heaven had marked him out for special things, it kept such promises well hidden during his earliest years. He was born near the present-day Mongolian capital of Ulan Bator, the eldest son of a minor chieftain, Yesugey, and given the name Temujin after a Tatar captured by his father. *The Secret History* records, no doubt apocryphally, that he was born with a clot of blood in his right hand, a harbinger, according to Mongolian tradition, of future greatness.

Having noble blood conferred considerable advantages, but they proved short-lived. When Temujin was 9, Yesugey departed to find his son and heir a suitable girl to marry. The mission was successful – the girl's name was Borte – but Yesugey was poisoned on his return home, leaving his wife with six young children to bring up alone. Temujin had lost his protector. Abandoned by their relatives, the family was forced to survive by foraging for fruits and roots, fishing and hunting.

With extreme adversity came certain benefits. It was probably during this time that Temujin honed his skills in the saddle, an essential foundation for future leadership and conquest. In a desolate landscape, survival itself – primarily through the hunting of meat – demanded the same set of talents required on the battlefield. Military techniques were thus learnt from the earliest age among the Mongols. As soon as a boy could ride, he was well on his way to becoming a soldier. Temujin would have learnt to master his horse and to manoeuvre it with the greatest finesse, to gauge the distance between himself and his quarry, and to shoot with deadly accuracy. It was the perfect training for a mounted archer, the backbone of Genghis's army, equipped with the lethal composite bow of horn, sinew and wood. As the

'... where there had been a hundred thousand people there remained, without exaggeration, not a hundred souls alive ...'

ATA-MALIK JUVAYNI, *THE HISTORY OF THE WORLD CONQUEROR*

eighteenth-century historian Edward Gibbon remarked, 'the amusements of the chase serve as a prelude to the conquest of an empire'.

The Secret History records Temujin's first kill, at the tender age of 13. His victim, felled in cold blood, was his half-brother Bekter, with whom he had quarrelled over the capture of a lark and minnow. It was the first indication of a ruthlessness that came to characterize his later career. Tales of bravery and derring-do accumulated steadily during his youth. He survived kidnaps and raids, made hair-raising escapes, and on one occasion launched a daring rescue mission to retrieve his family's stolen horses, upon which its survival depended.

Once married, he began to demonstrate there was far more to his abilities than mere military prowess. Evidence of his prodigious political talents came to the fore as he assembled a coterie of allies and protectors. Already joined with his sworn blood brother Jamuka, he added a more powerful; his father's blood brother Toghrul. Together, the two men helped Temujin put a combined army of twelve thousand into the field to retrieve his wife Borte, kidnapped by a rival Mongol clan. Temujin's fame spread and soon he was emerging as much more than his family's protector. Indeed, in time both Jamuka and Toghrul would be sacrificed on the altar of his overweening ambition.

Genghis Khan

Unleashing the Mongols

By around 1200, Temujin had managed to unite about half the traditionally feuding Mongol clans under his leadership. Jamuka and Toghrul, however, stood in the way of sole command. Over the next several years, after a bewildering period of opportunistic, shifting alliances, battles, triumphs and reversals, they were finally eliminated from the field, removing the last obstacles in Temujin's rise to power. *The Secret History* shows a magnanimous Temujin allowing his defeated blood brother Jamuka a noble execution – although another chronicle says he suffered an agonizing death by dismemberment.

In 1206 a kuriltay or national assembly was summoned at the source of the Onon river. Temujin, the man who had 'unified the people of the felt-walled tents', was proclaimed Genghis Khan, Oceanic Khan or Ruler of the Universe. Though the tribes subsumed under his command were many, henceforth they came to be known simply as the Mongols. The Mongol conquests, a period of catastrophic terror and destruction for the peoples of Asia, could begin.

Genghis took immediate steps to underpin his military command, starting with a fundamental reordering of tribal loyalties. His army was organized according to the traditional decimal system of the steppe: platoons of 10, companies of 100, brigades of 1,000 and divisions of 10,000 soldiers. Genghis's radical innovation was to create these units from mixed races and tribes, thereby undermining traditional loyalties and creating a new force united in its allegiance to his person. This was in addition to a brand new creation, an elite imperial guard of 10,000. Staffed by many of the sons of his regimental commanders, it acted as an insurance policy against disloyalty in the wider army and a buttress to his unrivalled personal command. General conscription was introduced for all men between 15 and 70.

Genghis Khan and his terrifying Mongol cavalry at war, in a gouache illustration from the *Jami al-Tawarikh* ('Compendium of Histories') by the Persian historian Rashid al-Din (1247–1318).

THE CAMPAIGN AGAINST SULTAN MOHAMMED OF KHOREZM

In 1219, A MONGOL ARMY of two hundred thousand swarmed into Central Asia. Otrar, in what is now Kazakhstan, was put under siege and captured. Genghis's sons Ogedey and Chaghatay seized its governor and executed him by pouring molten gold into his eyes and ears. It was the first sign of the terrifyingly vicious campaign to come. The suddenly feeble Mohammed fled in terror, closely pursued to an island on the Caspian Sea where he died in mysterious circumstances. The rest of his kingdom was not so fortunate.

Arriving in fabled Bukhara, 'dome of Islam' and richest city of the kingdom, Genghis mounted the pulpit of the Kalon mosque and warned the terrified inhabitants that God had sent him to punish them for their sins. From Bukhara, the Mongols rode southeast across the steppe to Samarkand, driving thousands of captured prisoners before them to create the impression of an irresistible army on the move. The city's defensive forces were no match for the massed Mongols, who by now had been joined by Ogedey and Chaghatay. Samarkand's speedy surrender in 1220 failed to prevent its plunder in another orgy of bloodletting. Thirty thousand artisans were deported to Mongolia and – an infinitesimally small mercy – only the clergy were spared.

North of the Oxus the Mongols fell upon the ancient city of Termez, where legend had it that a woman who begged to be spared the massacre, telling her captors she had swallowed a pearl, had her stomach ripped open and the gem removed. Genghis then ordered his men to disembowel every corpse. Balkh, the celebrated former capital of the Bactrian empire, collapsed before the Mongol

onslaught, followed in 1221 by the city of Merv, where the forces of Genghis's son Tuli were said to have massacred seven hundred thousand. For four days, the captive population was rounded up and driven onto the plain. Each soldier was ordered to execute three to four hundred prisoners and bring the severed ears of the victims to their commanders to prove they had done so.

Another siege was mounted against Gurganj (Urgench), homeland of the shahs. After seven months of resistance, the city was stormed and taken street by street, Mongol troops hurling flaming naphtha into houses. A small number of artisans – and women for the harem – were spared and the rest were put to the sword. The Persian historian Juvayni records that fifty thousand soldiers were commanded to kill twenty-four prisoners each, a death toll of 1.2 million. Even allowing for the notorious unreliability of the chroniclers, the slaughter was immense.

In 1221, Nishapur fell in a frenzy of killing. The heads of men, women, children – even cats and dogs – were piled into dreadful pyramids in the streets. By the end of the year Herat and Bamiyan had fallen amid similar horrors. It was only in the dying months of 1221, when Mohammed's son Jalal al-Din was defeated at the Battle of the Indus, that the campaign was over.

(Below) **A view of the sky-scraping minaret** of the Kalon Mosque in Bukhara, sole monument that escaped the razing wrath of Genghis Khan's invasion in 1219. The nomadic warrior of the steppes, invariably contemptuous of settled civilization, was said to have been so taken by this triumph of verticality that he ordered his men to spare it.

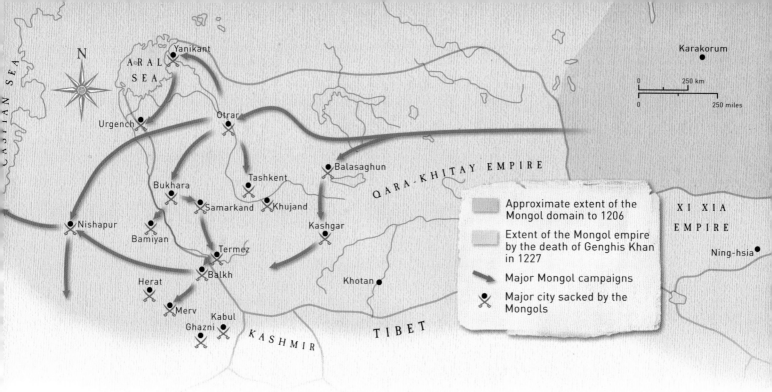

Once created, this vast fighting force, which probably numbered at least one hundred thousand at this stage, needed to be kept occupied in the field. Soldiers did not receive salaries and were only paid with plunder from defeated enemies and ransacked cities. If the army was not kept busy campaigning, the likelihood was that it would quickly fracture into the time-honoured pattern of feuding tribal factions, thereby destroying the foundation of its master's new-found authority.

Genghis looked south across his borders and decided to strike. Across the Gobi desert lay the Tanguts of Xi Xia, his weakest neighbours, and a people whose cultural obscurity to this day can largely be attributed to the genocide meted out by Genghis's ferocious army. It was, of course, a taste of things to come. The Tanguts were an easy stepping-stone towards a richer, more powerful adversary, the Jin empire of northern China.

His army, noted for its exceptional horsemanship and superb archery, swept across Asia like a tsunami, flattening every enemy it encountered. In 1209, the Turkic Uyghurs in what is today Xinjiang offered their submission. Two years later, undeterred by a Jin army numbering several hundred thousand, the Mongols invaded the northern Chinese empire.

Beijing, its capital, was one of the most powerful, heavily defended cities in the world. With 10 miles of walls, nine hundred guard-towers, and a bristling arsenal of heavy weaponry such as catapults that could hurl fire bombs at attackers, it was Genghis's greatest challenge yet. He starved it into surrender. Beijing fell in the late spring of 1215.

For the first time a civilized city felt the full destructive terror of a Mongol onslaught. Within minutes, the looted palaces and public buildings were going up in smoke and the first of many massacres was underway. The campaigns against northern China rumbled on for the next two decades. To Genghis's growing arsenal of military weapons was added the machinery and techniques of siege warfare. Once mastered, they offered him a wider canvas on which to paint the world red.

THE CONQUESTS OF GENGHIS KHAN in Central Asia.

Genghis Khan

The invasion of the west

The Qara-Khitay, nomads who controlled lands from their base in the Altaic steppes of northern China, had fallen under the rule of one of Genghis's earliest enemies, Kuchluk, former king of the Naimans who was now persecuting his Muslim subjects. In 1218, Genghis's general Jebe rode to Kashgar with a corps of twenty thousand men, where he fomented rebellion by reminding the downtrodden Muslims of Genghis's precept of religious toleration and freedom. The Qara-Khitay revolted, Kuchluk was captured and killed and Mongol dominion had seeped further west with barely a sword raised.

The victory brought the frontiers of Genghis's nascent empire rubbing uncomfortably close to those of Sultan Mohammed, the Muslim Khorezmshah who ruled over most of Persia and Mawarannahr, with his capital in Samarkand. It is debatable whether Genghis was looking to fight this formidable Asian ruler at this time, but after a caravan of four hundred and fifty Muslim merchants from his territories were butchered in cold blood in Mohammed's border city of Otrar on suspicion of being spies (which they probably were), and after reparations were refused, invasion was the only course open to him. The Sultan compounded his offence with the

A romanticized hand-coloured engraving of Genghis Khan, published in France in 1780.

unpardonable folly of killing one Mongol ambassador and shaving off the beards of two others. Genghis's blood was up.

This was a man who revelled in war and bloodshed, who believed, as he told his generals, that 'Man's greatest good fortune is to chase and defeat his enemy, seize all his possessions, leave his married women weeping and wailing, ride his gelding, use the bodies of his women as night-shirts and supports, gazing upon and kissing their rosy breasts, sucking their lips which are as sweet as the berries of the breasts.'

The three-year campaign that followed was one of the most blood-soaked in history. It has been likened to the genocidal outrages committed by the Assyrians in ancient history and by the Nazis in more modern times. The Mongol storm broke west in 1219 and quickly enveloped city after city. Sultan Mohammed, who had divided his forces by stationing them in smaller detachments across the region, fled ignominiously, leaving his kingdom in the hands of his rather braver son Jalal al-Din and at the mercy of the Mongol invaders. After his flight, there was a terrible inevitability about the Mongol triumph, their greatest to date. Genghis's empire stood poised on the fringes of Europe.

Writing shortly after this campaign in the Middle East had concluded in 1221, the Arab historian Ibn al Athir was in no doubt of the magnitude of the calamity and the epochal horrors it had inflicted. It was, he wrote, 'a tremendous disaster such as had never happened before ... It may well be that the world from now until its end ... will not experience the like of it again, apart perhaps from Gog and Magog.'

Taking the scenic route home

The conclusion of the campaign against Sultan Mohammed did not spell an end to Mongol conquest in the region. The lust for blood and treasure had not been sated.

While Genghis took a break from the action, the section of his army under the generals Jebe and Subedey continued north around the Caspian Sea, rolling over every enemy in their path. Cities were razed and depopulated, prisoners slain or ordered to march as shields before the army in full battle formation. Riding through Azerbaijan, the invaders sacked the Christian kingdom of Georgia, flattening the capital of Tiflis (Tbilisi) in 1221. Through the Caucasus and the Crimea and along the Volga they advanced, routing Bulgars, Turks and Russian princes as they hugged the northern shores. Twenty nations were defeated in this astonishing, megalomaniacal circuit of the Caspian.

Mourners surround the coffin of Genghis Khan on his death in 1227, in a Persian gouache of the Ilkhanate period. To this day, the exact place of his burial in Mongolia remains unknown, just as the great conqueror intended.

In 1225, after a couple of years hunting in the steppes of Turkestan, brushing up on his philosophy in discussions with a Taoist sage – from whom he sought the elusive elixir of immortality – and discussing religion with the Islamic priests of Bukhara, Genghis set out for home.

Although by now an old man, Genghis's appetite for war remained undimmed. By the end of 1226 he had put the rebellious Tangut capital of Ning-hsia under siege. The city, and its inhabitants, went the way all flesh did when confronting Genghis. Chinese chronicles lament the battlefields piled high with the bones of their countrymen.

He lived to see his eldest son and troublesome heir, Jochi, predecease him in 1227. The succession was bestowed upon Ogedey. Later that year, Genghis Khan, the Ruler of the Universe, died, master of an empire which spanned an entire continent from China to the gates of Europe. Rarely have the sword and sceptre been so brilliantly – and brutally – held by one man.

Genghis Khan

KUBLAI KHAN

1215-94

JUSTIN MAROZZI

MOST EMINENT DESCENDANT of the royal house of Genghis, Kublai Khan was the fifth Great Khan of the Mongols and founder of the Yuan dynasty in China. With the tumultuous conquest of China finally completed in 1279, he became the most powerful man on earth, his authority acknowledged by the junior branches of the Mongol empire throughout Asia, right up to the borders of eastern Europe.

After the barbarous savagery of his grandfather Genghis's conquests, the rule of Kublai ushered in a new era of civilization. Where Genghis had been the archetype of the nomad conqueror of the steppes, Kublai was master of a noble, sedentary society. The famous study of the emperor from the National Palace Museum in Taipei shows a benevolent old sage rather than the demonically fierce warrior that was Genghis. Heavily influenced by his cultivated Chinese court, Kublai, without ever forgetting the martial ferocity of the Mongols that was instilled into his very nature, was a lavish patron of literature, culture and science.

Though his campaigns lacked the irresistible momentum of Genghis's armies during their whirlwind conquests, Kublai's enduring triumph was the astonishingly successful incorporation of China into the Mongol realm. Completed in 1267, his magnificent new capital T'ai-tu ('Great Court'), popularly known as Khan-Balik ('City of the Khan'), was an appropriately splendid monument to the genius of Mongol military might throughout the thirteenth and fourteenth centuries. Fuelled both by the high-spirited tales of Marco Polo and, half a millennium later, by Samuel Taylor Coleridge's opium-inspired poem about Kubla Khan and his 'stately pleasure dome' in Xanadu, it gave rise to the sense of romance and wonder that still greets Kublai's name today.

Troublesome relatives

In a culture that regarded Genghisid blood as the sine qua non of military and political leadership, Kublai, second son of Genghis's son Tuli, was blessed from birth with considerable advantages. Not for him the humble scrabbling about for followers that

Kublai Khan

marked the early years of both Genghis and Tamerlane. While at an age when both of these men had been grubbing about in adversity and complete obscurity, Kublai, together with his younger brother Hulagu, founder of the Ilkhanate dynasty of Persia, were joining their world-famous grandfather on his last campaign in 1226–7. Neither boy was yet a teenager. A Mongol chronicler records how Genghis singled out the young Kublai for future greatness while on his deathbed. With his father away much of the time campaigning with Genghis, Kublai learnt to ride, shoot and hunt under the watchful eye of his mother Sorkaktani, a woman of enormous political mettle.

After Genghis's death in 1227, the succession passed to Ogedey, who established the seat of the Mongol empire in Karakorum and consolidated its hold over northern China before his rule collapsed as he descended into alcoholism. After Ogedey's death in 1246, his son Kuyuk became Great Khan, a brief and unhappy reign which ended just two years later with his premature death from a fatal combination of gout and alcoholism. Sibling rivalry between the various branches of the Genghisid family now burst out into the open and rival courts were established. It was only through the deft manoeuvring of Kublai's mother, by then Tuli's widow, that Kublai's older brother Monke was installed

A late thirteenth-century portrait of Kublai Khan, now housed in the National Palace Museum in the Taiwanese capital of Taipei. The posthumous portrait depicts him at the height of his powers in the 1260s, serene, masterful and alert. In his later years he became a corpulent alcoholic.

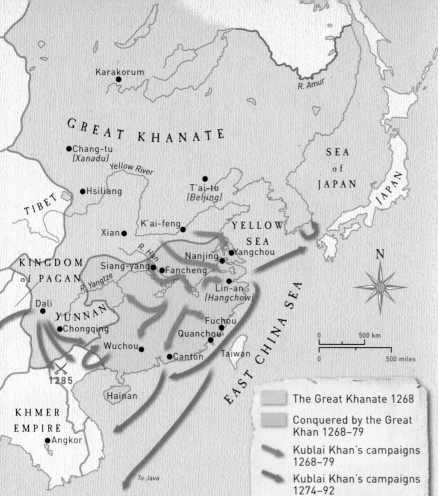

Map labels:
Karakorum
R. Amur
GREAT KHANATE
Chang-tu (Xanadu)
Yellow River
SEA of JAPAN
JAPAN
Hsiliang
T'ai-tu (Beijing)
TIBET
Xian
K'ai-feng
YELLOW SEA
KINGDOM of PAGAN
R. Han
Siang-yang
Nanjing
Yangchou
Fancheng
R. Yangtze
Dali
Lin-an (Hangchow)
YUNNAN
Chongqing
Fuchou
EAST CHINA SEA
Wuchou
Quanchou
N
Canton
Taiwan
1285
Hainan
KHMER EMPIRE
Angkor
To Java

The Great Khanate 1268
Conquered by the Great Khan 1268-79
Kublai Khan's campaigns 1268-79
Kublai Khan's campaigns 1274-92

THE CONQUESTS OF KUBLAI KHAN.

as Great Khan in 1251, though not without more opposition from within the perennially feuding Genghisid clan.

It was not until 1251 that Kublai played any more than a cameo role in the Mongol story. Though his blood was unquestionably noble, he had plenty of relatives who could make the same boast. Genghis had not been backward in spreading the Mongol seed. Kublai was merely part of the extended royal family, no more, no less. Critically, he was not a member of the senior Ogedey branch from which all future Great Khans had to be chosen. Monke's elevation, however – effectively a coup by the house of Tuli against the house of Ogedey – immediately tore up the old script and thrust Kublai into greater prominence.

Early glory in China

If martial success was an overriding characteristic of the Mongol khans, it was invariably twinned with an insatiable hunger for territorial conquest. With his brother Hulagu blazing through the west, Monke looked east to continue the Mongol march deep into China. The unfathomably rich, unconquered southern Sung dynasty, ruler of 50 million subjects, was an affront to a race that believed its heavenly destiny was to rule the world.

Kublai was a natural choice to prosecute this ambitious effort in the east. He owned lands around Xian and already had experience of governing in China. In 1252, Monke gave him command of an army to take the modern-day province of Yunnan. Once conquered, it would serve as the base for the conquest of the south. This was Kublai's first opportunity to prove himself on the only testing ground that really mattered to the Mongols – the battlefield.

Kublai marched south with his army more than a year after receiving his orders, accompanied by Uriyangkhaday, the son of Genghis's greatest general, Subedey, having devoted the intervening time to intensive preparations for his debut campaign. Unlike his father Tuli and Monke, who had both commanded expeditions in their teens and early twenties, Kublai was by now in his mid thirties. He was resolved to make his mark.

In the event, Kublai's first foray into war was a brilliant success. His complacent enemy was undone by a three-pronged offensive and, after a surprise night-time attack across the Upper Yangtze, the Mongols prevailed. After only a handful of executions, the capital of Dali was spared and the king became a Mongol puppet with minimal disruption. Kublai had won his spurs.

Kublai Khan

A bigger prize

In 1257, after several years of governing and extending his Chinese estates with an increasingly cosmopolitan caucus of advisers, Kublai's next commission was to lead one of Monke's four armies sent to conquer the Sung dynasty, thereby uniting the north and south under Mongol rule. The campaign was interrupted in 1259 by the sudden death of Monke, a severe blow to the Mongol body politic. It marked the collapse of unity and the end of further Mongol conquest in Asia Minor and the Middle East. For the first time, the succession from one Great Khan to the next would be decided by the use of arms.

Rather than hurrying north to press his case for supreme command of the empire, when asked to return Kublai refused, choosing instead to continue the campaign, perhaps reasoning that a military triumph would only improve his chances. The army pushed on south of the Yangtze, forcing the Sung into a defensive position. With his younger brother Arik Boke gaining ground in his bid to succeed Monke, Kublai was forced to put the campaign on hold. He called a kuriltay, the traditional national assembly convened to select a new emperor, and on 5 May 1260 in Chang-tu, or Xanadu – henceforth his summer capital – Kublai was duly made Great Khan.

Winning the civil war

A month after Kublai's coronation, Arik Boke was proclaimed Great Khan in a rival ceremony in Karakorum, Genghis's former capital. With the early backing of Berke, khan of the Golden Horde, and Alghu, Chaghatay khan of Central Asia, together with many in Monke's family, Arik had an early edge over his older brother, who could count only on Hulagu, embattled in the west. Quite legitimately, Arik argued that Kublai's kuriltay was invalid, since it had been convened outside the Mongolian

A fantastically imagined illustration of the historic encounter between the irrepressible Venetian adventurer Marco Polo and Kublai Khan. The miniature is taken from a copy of Marco Polo's sensationalist and relentlessly self-aggrandizing *Livre des Merveilles du Monde*.

homeland. The two men, though brothers, were poles apart. Arik represented the traditional Mongol values of the steppe, opposed to the despicable luxuries of settled life and arguing that the centre of the Mongol empire should be in Mongolia. Kublai, on the other hand, was a more pragmatic ruler steeped in the culture of his Chinese subjects, who recognized the need for accommodation between the relatively small Mongol political class and the far more numerous people they ruled.

The rivalry had to be resolved on the battlefield. Arik, hampered by an inability to secure enough grain and weapons for his army, ended up in a distracting fight with his former ally, Alghu. With Chinese support behind him, Kublai consolidated his hold over Mongolia, in 1264 forcing Arik to make a humiliating surrender. Within the space of a year, the deaths of Hulagu, Berke and Alghu had cleared the diplomatic field for him. In 1266, Arik, too, died suddenly. The unproven suspicion remains that Kublai had him poisoned. Whatever the truth, all of the main challenges to his authority had been removed in short order. Though his cousin Kaidu, head of the house of Ogedey, continued to oppose him, and though there were always Mongols who resented Kublai's Chinese ways, his position at the helm of the most powerful empire in the world was never seriously unsettled again.

The coronation of **Kublai Khan** as Great Khan of the Mongols in 1260. The ceremony took place in Chang-tu, or Xanadu, which was to become his magnificent summer capital, and the inspiration for Samuel Taylor Coleridge's opium-assisted poem 'Kubla Khan' (1816).

A Chinese dynasty for China

With these internal matters resolved, Kublai could turn once more to his main preoccupation: China, specifically the incorporation of the elusive southern Sung dynasty into the Mongol realms. Part of his genius lay in the way this was accomplished. Genghis might have looked upon such an undertaking as a purely military exercise. For Kublai it was profoundly political, too.

It was for this reason that, at the outset of his reign, Kublai moved his capital from Karakorum to T'ai-tu, Marco Polo's dazzling city of Cambaluc, today's Beijing. As J. J. Saunders wrote in his classic work, *The History of the Mongol Conquests*, for a man such as Kublai, who had spent almost his entire life in China, 'it seemed natural that he should transfer the centre of empire to a Chinese city within the Great Wall and that he should aspire to reign as Son of Heaven rather than as a Mongol khan'. It was a seismic shift in the history of the empire. The imperial capital was now a settled city built by Chinese architects on Chinese soil. Under Kublai's command it grew to the height of magnificence, surrounded by 15 miles of walls 30 feet high and 30 feet thick. A second set of walls screened the Imperial City, a third hid the royal palace and a fourth created a palace within a palace. It would become the richest city on earth.

Northern China might have fallen into the hands of foreign barbarians, but Kublai did his best to disguise this obvious truth. Hence the new Chinese name for his new dynasty: Yuan, meaning first, principal, fundamental, the ultimate source,

Kublai Khan

A map showing Cambaluc, the imperial capital of Kublai's world-spanning empire. Mongols knew it as Khan-balik, literally the City of the Khan. In time it became the richest city on earth, on the site of modern Beijing.

cannily plucked by Kublai from the *I Ching*, the hallowed book of divination. A master of imperial administration, Kublai sustained his new dynasty with a subtle amalgam of Mongol and Chinese traditions and officials.

Defeating the Sung

Kublai's initial attempts to wrest control of southern China from the Sung were diplomatic. Initially, limited self-rule was offered in return for acknowledgement of his authority. The Sung were unimpressed and detained his envoy for sixteen years. Throughout the 1260s Kublai remained committed to the cause, encouraging defections from the Sung army, giving land, clothing and oxen to those who rallied to his side. It was also during this time that Kublai brought Tibet within his expanding sway, through astute patronage of a Buddhist lama and prince, Phags-pa.

Conquering the Sung was the Mongol empire's most formidable challenge to date. Unlike the steppe homeland, southern China was a land of cities and rivers. Its conquest required a mastery of both siege and naval warfare. The key to success in the south lay on the Han river, a tributary of the mighty Yangtze; it was the prodigiously strong and well-defended city of Siang-yang.

The siege of the city began in 1268 and continued for five years, ending with its complete capitulation to the Mongol forces supplemented with large numbers of Chinese troops, Muslim experts in siege warfare from Persia and a fledgling navy of some five hundred boats. Its fall opened the way to the Sung capital of Lin-an (Hangchow), then the world's richest and most populous city, with a population conservatively estimated at 1.5 million.

From Siang-yang, the Mongol army turned east, commanded by Kublai's most trusted general, Bayan. Towns and cities folded before their advance, prompting the dowager empress Hsieh to sue for peace on favourable terms. But it was too late.

Kublai Khan

Bayan was interested only in unconditional surrender, finally achieved in 1276. Further resistance from Sung loyalists who had been forced further south continued to test Kublai's resolve and patience. It was only when the 9-year-old child emperor Shih died, following the shipwreck of his fleeing supporters in 1278, that Kublai finally extinguished the dream of Sung independence for good.

It has been said that Kublai was emperor of a greater population than had ever acknowledged the supremacy of one man.

The later campaigns

Gloriously successful at home, where his political skills eclipsed his military talents, Kublai proved less impressive overseas. It is difficult to avoid the conclusion that his later adventures overseas, particularly his ill-conceived campaigns against Japan, Java and Vietnam, dulled the gloss on what had, until then, been an exemplary military record. So why did Kublai launch such campaigns? Because he was a Mongol and this is what a Mongol emperor instinctively did. Imperial expansion was not so much a choice as a necessity. It came almost as a hereditary obligation. It is only because they are so rare that we tend to be disproportionately shocked by Mongol defeats. If, for much of the twentieth century, the British Conservative Party was seen as the natural party of government, for much of the thirteenth and fourteenth centuries the Mongols were seen as the natural masters of warfare and empire.

Kublai's first attempt on Japan was launched unsuccessfully from his vassal state of Korea in 1274. A second attack, with an army of forty-five thousand Mongols and one hundred and twenty thousand Sino-Koreans, followed in 1281, but it was wiped out by the defenders of Kyushu and a vicious typhoon. It was Kublai's most catastrophic loss and destroyed the Mongols' long-treasured aura of invincibility in the East. A third punitive campaign was only prevented by the refusal of Chinese shipbuilders to produce the vast numbers of boats Kublai demanded. There were repeated campaigns against the recalcitrant little kingdom of Pagan (Burma) from 1277. But even when the wily king eventually offered tribute in 1287, the blood and treasure it had cost Kublai to mount these expeditions was far more than anything derived from it. Further embarrassing overseas failures followed, first in Vietnam and then, in 1292–3, in Java.

'He was the first of his race to rise above the innate barbarism of the Mongols.'

ENCYCLOPAEDIA BRITANNICA, 1911

With rebellions breaking out in Tibet and Manchuria, in 1287 the 72-year-old Khan of Khans, laid low by gout and rheumatism, took to the battlefield in person to see off his cousins, rebel leaders Nayan and Kaidu. Marco Polo described the encounter as 'the most parlous and fierce and fearful battle that ever has been fought in our day'. It resulted in the capture of Nayan, who was bound and trussed, rolled inside a carpet and beaten to death in the traditional bloodless execution the Mongols favoured for a royal prince. Kaidu remained at large. The disappointments of Kublai's later years were crowned with the crushing deaths of his favourite wife Chabi in 1281 and his crown prince Chen-chin in 1285. Kublai's response was to consume spectacular quantities of food and wine, ballooning into a vastly overweight alcoholic in the process. He died in his eightieth year, diminished through age and gluttony, but with his reputation as one of the Mongols' most brilliant commanders deservedly intact.

Kublai Khan

THE SIEGE OF SIANG-YANG

THE ZENITH OF KUBLAI'S MILITARY CAREER was unquestionably the conquest of southern Sung China, a victory that guaranteed his posterity as one of the Mongols' finest commanders.

The heart of the Mongols' armies had always been their superb cavalry, trained almost from birth and deployed with devastating effect across the battlefields of Asia. To take Sung China, however, required a concerted input from Kublai's infantry and an impromptu navy, allied with a breathtaking level of logistical support and the world's latest siege machinery – all of this for a campaign that would rumble along for a decade. Few, if any, Mongol expeditions had ever attempted anything so ambitious.

The siege of Siang-yang and the adjacent city of Fancheng was the longest confrontation of this sustained campaign, lasting from 1268 to 1273. It was rightly singled out for special notice by the Persian historian Rashid al-Din, Marco Polo and the Chinese chronicles. The two cities on the opposite banks of the Han river were the heavily fortified gates to the Yangtze basin and the south. Siang-yang, said Rashid al-Din, was defended by a 'strong castle, a stout wall and a deep moat'. To take it demanded a complete blockade of the Han.

The cosmopolitan background of the commanders Kublai chose to prosecute this campaign demonstrated his flair for promoting non-Mongols to important positions, which was a key factor in his military triumphs. Two were Chinese generals, including a recent defector. The chief Mongol was Aju, son of Uriyangkhaday, the grandson of Genghis's legendary general Subedey. From Persia came the siege engineers Ismail and Ala al-Din. His ships were built by Koreans and Jurchens.

An order was given to build 500 boats in order to draw a noose around Siang-yang. Next came fortifications south of the city to prevent boats bringing in supplies. There were periodic attempts to break the blockade. In August 1269, the Sung general attacked with 3,000 boats, only to be trounced by Mongol forces. In March 1270, 10,000 Sung soldiers and cavalry, together with 100 boats, tried to break through and again were defeated.

The siege, however, was drifting into stalemate. Kublai sent to his nephew Abakha, the Persian Ilkhan 4,000 miles away, for siege engineers, and in late 1272, a huge counterweight trebuchet started raining down enormous missiles on the two cities. 'These took effect among the buildings, crashing and smashing through everything with huge din and commotion,' Marco Polo wrote. With such formidable artillery support, the Mongol

army was able to storm the fort at Fancheng, which quickly fell in late 1272. Ten thousand soldiers and civilians had their throats slit within sight of Siang-yang.

The city held out until the following spring, but the blockade and artillery barrage proved too fierce. The garrison, Polo wrote, 'took counsel together, but no counsel could be suggested how to escape from these engines. They declared they were all dead men if they yielded not, so they determined to surrender.' Siang-yang's fall led Kublai's army to the Sung capital Hangchow, which quickly folded. Its fall was the crowning glory of Kublai's career, a landmark conquest of the Mongols' toughest ever adversary.

Kublai Khan

ALEXANDER NEVSKY

ISABEL DE MADARIAGA

1220/21–1263

PRINCE ALEXANDER YAROSLAVICH NEVSKY was born in Pereyaslavl' Zalessky, in northeastern Russia. Whilst still a young man, Alexander was appointed by his uncle, Grand Prince Yury Vsevolodovich, to rule in the Republic of Novgorod, and in 1238 and 1242 commanded Russian forces in two seemingly minor engagements, both of which he won, and which later added to his great fame as saint, prince and warrior.

(Opposite) **A detail of an early sixteenth-century fresco** of St Alexander Nevsky in the Cathedral of St Michael the Archangel, in the Moscow Kremlin.

Russia's reigning dynasty in the early thirteenth century descended from the possibly legendary Scandinavian prince Riurik. In the late tenth century, Grand Prince Vladimir had presided over the conversion of Russia to Orthodox Christianity as practised in Constantinople. Russia's principal city was Kiev, on the Dnieper river, from whence the Scandinavian–Slavonic settlements spread out. The number of Russian princes multiplied over the centuries, and there were frequent and violent disputes over the succession to the lands belonging to the various branches of the princely family. In a practice adopted by many other ethnic groups at this time, the throne did not normally descend from father to son but from the ruler to his eldest brother. The succession then went from brother to brother and, when there were no further brothers, to the eldest son of the eldest brother, then to his next son and, if the heirs failed, to the son of the next brother in line. Non-ruling princes were often temporarily allotted lesser principalities of their own, which they might pass to their own brothers or sons.

By the late twelfth century, Kiev had been replaced by the city of Vladimir-in-Suzdal as the stable political centre of the dynastic lands; its ruler was also called 'grand prince' and charged with appointing princes to the other principalities of northeastern Russia. In the early thirteenth century Yury II was grand prince, and his heir was his brother Yaroslav, the father of Alexander Nevsky.

To the northeast of the lands of the Rus' princes lay the city republics of Novgorod ('new town') and Pskov, both within easy reach of the Baltic Sea. Novgorod was a prosperous, self-governing trading community, owning vast lands that extended as far as the Arctic Ocean. Rich in furs, wax, honey and hides, it traded

Alexander Nevsky

extensively down the Volga river to the Caspian Sea and the Far East; down the Dnieper river to the Black Sea and the Eastern Roman Empire; and through the Baltic Sea to the west, by means of its relationship with the German Hanseatic League. Novgorod had a special arrangement with the Grand Principality of Kiev, whereby it appointed a prince from the ruling dynasty, by contract, to organize and lead the defence of the city and to supervise its administration; the town assembly comprised the mayor and the wealthier citizens, and the archbishop also played a prominent political role in the government of the city.

In the early thirteenth century the land of Rus' faced serious enemies: in the north, the Swedes and members of a German crusading order in Livonia; further west, the pagan Grand Principality of Lithuania, not yet dynastically linked with Poland but advancing already against the Russian principality of Polotsk; and in the east, the even more serious threat of the Mongol empire of Genghis Khan.

The Mongol invasions

By the end of the twelfth century, the Mongols were united under the rule of Genghis Khan in his distant city, Karakorum, in what is today Outer Mongolia. A first exploratory raid on southern Russia took place in 1222–3, as part of a carefully planned Mongol attack on Central Asia which culminated in a Russian defeat on the River Kalka, on the Sea of Azov. Although Genghis Khan died in 1227, a further assault on the West was made in 1234, the Mongols this time advancing to Moscow, which they burnt, then storming Vladimir-in-Suzdal and killing the inhabitants, including Grand Prince Yury's wife and two of his sons.

Alexander Nevsky

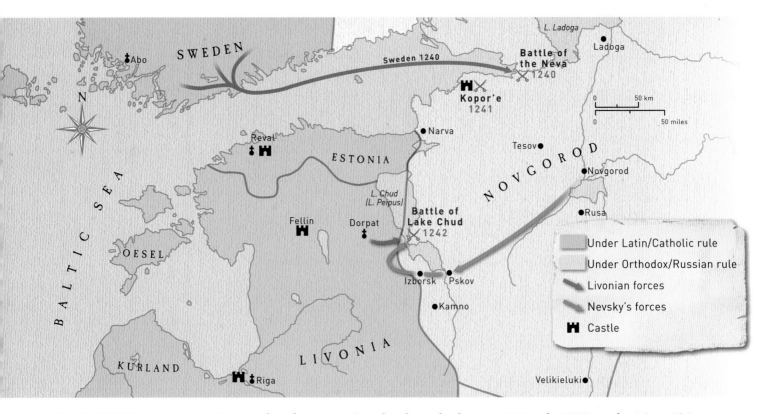

THE CAMPAIGNS
AND BATTLES OF
ALEXANDER NEVSKY
against the Swedes
and the Germans.

A second and more serious battle took place on 4 March 1238 on the River Sit', in the province of Vladimir, in which the Grand Duke Yury himself was killed, together with three of his nephews. With the approaching spring thaw, however, the Mongols turned south, to where they could find the vast pastures necessary for the maintenance of their huge cavalry army. After a year's rest the Mongol army renewed its assault and on 6 December 1240 stormed into Kiev, destroying the city and massacring all who lived there. The Mongol advance into Europe continued under Genghis Khan's grandson Batu, and on 9 April 1241 the Mongols defeated the joint German–Polish forces at the Battle of Liegnitz in Silesia and, continuing into Croatia, reached the coast of Dalmatia. The campaign was called off, however, on the news of the death of the Khan in faraway Karakorum in the spring of 1252.

The first appearance of Alexander Nevsky

As ruler of Vladimir-in-Suzdal, Grand Prince Yury II had occasionally sent his young nephew, Alexander, to rule in Novgorod. On the death of Yury in the battle of Sit', his next brother, Alexander's father Yaroslav, became Grand Duke, and the young Prince Alexander Yaroslavich was again sent to Novgorod. As a result, Alexander's first independent experience of battle was against the Swedes, who had been converted to Christianity by Catholic priests and monks and had been briefly under the tutelage of Cardinal Nicolas Breakspear (later Pope Hadrian IV).

Unfortunately for the Rus', the Christian Church of Rome considered the Orthodox Christians of the Church of Constantinople to be schismatics, as bad as pagans. The Catholic Swedish Vikings, in a crusading spirit, thus felt entitled to attack as heathens the small Russian settlements on the southern shore of the Gulf of Finland. Indeed, it has been suggested that the Swedes were moved at this time, by pressure from the papacy, to embark on a crusade against the schismatic Russians in order to extend the lands under Catholic control, but there seems to be no strong evidence to support this otherwise convenient theory. What is certain is that Sweden was anxious to control the narrow isthmus that dominated communication between Finland and Lake Ladoga, which would enable the Swedes to defend themselves against constant attacks by local tribes.

The evidence of events in the early thirteenth century is firstly based almost entirely on the many versions of local Russian and Livonian chronicles, produced in various redactions and at various times, usually by monks, in the interests of various princes; and, secondly, on the many versions of a 'Life' of Alexander Nevsky – part biography, part hagiography – probably composed some forty years after Alexander's death by someone who had known him personally, possibly under the supervision of Metropolitan Cyril. The most systematic chronicle, the genealogical *Book of Degrees*, dates from the mid sixteenth century, and introduces much material which emphasizes Alexander's role as a saint and a prince, but not as a military commander.

According to the 'Life' of Alexander, as remodelled in 1563, the king (Erik) 'of a land of the Roman faith' to the North (Sweden), hearing that the Rus' were suffering from the ravages of the Mongols, 'thought it a good time to conquer the rest of Rus'', to 'reduce the Slavs to slavery' and to take Grand Prince Alexander 'alive with my own hands'. The Swedish forces, therefore, with the support of Norwegian, Finnish and Karelian contingents, landed near the mouth of the River Neva in July 1240, with the aim of seizing the settlement of Ladoga, advancing on Novgorod the Great, and enslaving the people of Rus'.

Russian military organization

There was at this time no Russian national army, because there was no national centre or state. The armament reflected the time and the enemies faced by the Russians, comprising mounted and armour-clad western knights and the fleet cavalry of the steppe nomads. Russian armed forces consisted of cavalry from the local prince's personal retinue, supported by their own mounted retainers and supplemented by a locally based militia raised in the cities and the villages. The higher-ranking princes and boyars (noblemen) supplied the cavalry. They were armed with shields, helmets and chain-mail tunics; in illustrations, Russian helmets with noseguards are usually spiked and German ones round. The cavalry sometimes also fought on foot, though the militia normally supplied the foot soldiers and baggage train.

Firearms began to be used at the end of the thirteenth century. Weapons consisted of double-edged swords, sabres, long and short spears, axes, bows and arrows. Troops were divided into '*polki*', usually translated as regiments, but at this time more realistically viewed as 'units' of between five hundred and a thousand men, depending on the size of the total force, which could be stationed as three or five or more units and could be flexibly deployed around the enemy centre. There were few castles and fortified townships in this marshy land.

'My children, you should know that the sun of the Suzdalian land has set. There will never be another prince like him in the Suzdalian land.' METROPOLITAN CYRIL, AT ALEXANDER NEVSKY'S FUNERAL

The Battle of the Neva

The 'Life' describes the young Alexander as fearing God, keeping the commandments, keeping himself clean in body and soul, and being a virtuous young man, pleasing to God. His enemies trembled at the sound of his name. In response to the Swedish challenge, Prince Alexander called upon divine help and prayed in the church of Saint Sophia in Novgorod.

There is no information about the numbers engaged on either side in the Battle of the Neva, and indeed some historians think that no such battle actually took place, since it is not even mentioned in Swedish sources. To reconstruct Alexander's strategy, Russian authors have had to rely on the various redactions of the 'Life', and on an entry in the first *Novgorod Chronicle*. They have also drawn upon descriptions of fifteenth-century conflicts.

Divine intervention

The Swedes are said to have landed on the southern shore of the Gulf of Finland, not far from the confluence of the River Izhora with the Neva. Alexander had assembled a mixed force of cavalry and foot soldiers, also mainly mounted, and by forced marches had covered the 90 miles from Novgorod to the shores of the gulf in two days. He confronted the enemy on 16 July 1240. According to historical reconstructions of his tactics, he deployed five '*polki*', disposed in 'echelons', which enabled them to advance in waves and to re-form.

Battle began with a cavalry charge by knights armed with lances, and very fierce fighting. Alexander himself slashed the leader of the Swedish forces across the face with his sword. The battle then split up into encounters between individuals or small groups. One modern historian, drawing on the earliest version of the *Novgorod Chronicle*, has suggested that among the Russian knights there were perhaps twenty killed, and among the soldiers perhaps over one hundred; the total number of men involved in the battle could thus be counted in hundreds rather than thousands.

But Alexander had other allies: one of his scouts spotted the two Russian eleventh-century princely martyrs, the brothers Boris and Gleb, being rowed in a boat towards the land. Boris called out to Gleb to row harder so as to hasten their arrival to assist Alexander. When informed of the presence of the saints, Alexander bade his followers not to mention it, until God had proclaimed his will. Defeated by the intervention of angels, the Swedes rushed to their ships, threw their dead into three of their vessels, which they sank in Lake Nevo, and fled. According to the 'Life', great multitudes of men struck down by God's angels were found dead on the opposite shore of the Izhora, where the prince's troops had not even set foot. His victory earned Prince Alexander the name of 'Nevsky,' given to him much later.

The attack from the Catholic West

The people of Novgorod were not, however, grateful to Alexander for his victory, and the grand prince left, taking his troops and his family with him. There was always tension between Alexander and the republican city, the princes wanting to increase their rights and authority, the Novgorodians wanting to preserve their independence. But hostilities of a different kind soon broke out. The German crusading Teutonic Order (formed by the merger between the Livonian Brothers of the Sword and those members of the Order of the Temple who remained after the collapse of the crusader kingdoms at the end of the twelfth century) had undertaken the task of converting the peoples of the Baltic shore by conquest and colonization – a tale enshrined in the Livonian *Rhymed Chronicle* (1290), and in a *Novgorod Chronicle*. Grand Prince Yaroslav of Vladimir sent his second son Andrey to defend Novgorod, and Alexander and Andrey cooperated in demolishing a fortress built by the advancing Germans in Kopor'e, and in freeing Pskov, which had been seized by the Teutonic Order. Re-establishing his authority in Novgorod by executing a number of 'traitors' and advancing into Estonian land, Alexander prepared for battle against the Teutonic Order on Lake Chud (also known as Lake Peipus), which took place on 5 April 1242. The combined Russian forces numbered at least three 'regiments' according to one authority, and there was also a contingent of archers.

Four miniatures from *The Life of Saint Alexander Nevsky*. (From left to right) Saints Boris and Gleb row to assist Prince Alexander; the heavenly hosts drive the Swedes into the Izhora river; the Battle on the Ice – the Livonians and the Russians draw up for battle; 'And there was a great and cruel slaughter of the Germans on the Chud ...'

Was this a turning point in Russian history?

The idea of the Battle on the Ice has fascinated subsequent students of historical myths in Russia, and it features dramatically in *Alexander Nevsky*, Sergei Eisenstein's film of 1938 – where Alexander is hero, prince, common man, splendid general, and charismatic saviour of Orthodox Russia from German conquest and from the Roman Catholic aggression of the papacy. (The film was withdrawn during the Nazi–Soviet

Alexander Nevsky

THE BATTLE ON THE ICE

ACCORDING TO A RECENT RECONSTRUCTION based on a battle in 1268, the Novgorodian troops, on reaching the shores of Lake Chud on 5 April 1242, retreated, or feigned a retreat, on to the ice on the lake. Their feint drew the German troops, drawn up in their usual 'wedge', or 'hog' form, on to the frozen surface of the lake in pursuit. The Russian archers then attacked the knights on both flanks, but left the hand-to-hand fighting to the Russian cavalry advancing on both sides. Again there is very little evidence of what actually happened, but according to the 'Life' of Alexander, there was now 'a great and cruel slaughter of the Germans on Lake Chud, and a loud noise from the breaking of spears, and the clashing of swords. The frozen surface of the lake seemed to move and the ice could not be seen for the blood that covered it.' Alexander's forces pursued the fleeing Germans on the ice for seven versts (4½ miles).

The battle did not involve large numbers. According to the first *Novgorod Chronicle* four hundred German knights were killed and fifty taken prisoner. There were, however, fewer than four hundred and fifty knights in the Teutonic Order at the time, so the figures must be an exaggeration. The Livonian *Rhymed Chronicle* speaks only of twenty knights killed, and six taken prisoner. There is still considerable disagreement between Russian historians about this battle, some arguing that, like the Battle of the Neva, it never took place at all. Yet the battle and the personality of Alexander Nevsky have become embedded in historical memory.

The actual feasibility of a battle on the ice is questionable. A group of mainly American historians has recently discussed the surviving evidence in some detail, partly because there is no mention of knights being drowned in the early sources. The 'Life' of Alexander speaks of the ice 'beginning to move' (*zadvigat'sya*) in the course of the battle, and the sixteenth-century miniatures clearly show a few knights sinking in water, surrounded by shards of broken ice. But there are mentions of battles on ice at earlier times and in different places which may have influenced the historical memory. Moreover, are historians thinking of horsemen merely crossing frozen rivers on the ice, or are they thinking of actual fighting taking place on frozen rivers and lakes? Some have argued that 'it was safe to act on the thick ice' and that the Mongol contingent of the Russian force preferred campaigning in winter because it was easier for the small Mongol horses, possibly unshod, to gallop on frozen ground and rivers. It has been suggested that the horses were equipped with crampons. The greater weight of iron carried by German knights might have reduced their mobility on ice just beginning to thaw. However, underwater investigations carried out in the 1950s in what seems to have been the right places in Lake Chud revealed no remains of dead German knights in armour in the relatively shallow waters of the lake.

(Left and above) **A SPECULATIVE REPRESENTATION** of the disposition of forces involved in the Battle on the Ice.

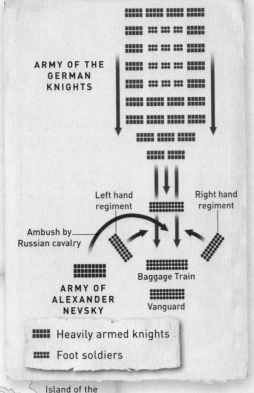

ARMY OF THE GERMAN KNIGHTS

Left hand regiment

Right hand regiment

Ambush by Russian cavalry

Baggage Train

ARMY OF ALEXANDER NEVSKY

Vanguard

▦ Heavily armed knights
▦ Foot soldiers

LAKE CHUD (FROZEN)

Island of Potka

LIVONIA

LIVONIAN FORCES

Island of the Stone Crow

Lake Chud 1242

Samolva

Forest

Mehikoorma

Forest

NEVSKY'S FORCES

NOVGOROD TERRITORY

Forest

Alexander Nevsky

pact of August 1939 but released when Germany invaded Russia in June 1941.) But there is really no agreement on the significance in Russian history of these two minor battles won by Alexander Nevsky.

Alexander succeeded his father in 1252 after Yaroslav, who had been confirmed as Grand Prince of Vladimir by the Mongol overlord, died in 1246 on the return journey from Karakorum. Alexander himself journeyed twice to Saray, the Mongol capital on the Volga, and once all the way to Karakorum, also dying on the return journey. Apparently believing that Russia was too weak to oppose Mongol supremacy, Alexander pursued a policy of appeasement of the Mongols, coupled with a number of victorious engagements against western forces. He cooperated with the Khans in imposing a census on Novgorod, levying the tribute for the Mongols, recruiting Russians for service in the Tatar army and influencing the choice of princely rulers. His 'great deeds' in defence of Russia and the confidence which his charismatic personality inspired (he took the highest monastic order on his death bed in 1263) led many (though not the Novgorodians) to overlook his pro-Mongol policies, and to regard his tomb in the church of Vladimir-in-Suzdal as a shrine. He was proclaimed a saint in Russia in 1547.

'Cet Ulysse parmi les saints'

The final apotheosis of this 'Ulysses among the Saints', in the words of the French scholar Pierre Pascal, came when Peter the Great, after his defeat of Sweden, planted wooden crosses in 1704 near the site of the Battle of the Neva, and made St Alexander Nevsky patron saint of his new city of St Petersburg, as a warrior, not a monk. His widow, Catherine I, founded the Military Order of Knights of St Alexander Nevsky in 1725 in his honour. The intimate association of St Alexander Nevsky, first with his direct descendants, the tsars of Moscow, then with St Petersburg and the Romanovs, raised him to the highest level of Russian heroism and sanctity.

Alexander Nevsky (right) in personal combat with a Teutonic Knight, in a still from Sergei Eisenstein's eponymous film of 1938.

'The sultan stood among his comrades like a sun among the bright stars and like a lion among the cubs it protects. He trained to fight the unbelievers and continued the holy war day and night.' *THE LIFE OF BAIBARS, BY 'ABD AL-ZAHIR*

BAIBARS
c. 1229–77

JONATHAN PHILLIPS

SULTAN BAIBARS CAN JUSTLY CLAIM to be the most formidable warrior of the medieval Islamic world. He rose from being a reject on the slave-markets of Syria to become the foundation stone of the Mamluk dynasty – for over two hundred years one of the world's great powers. His own career encompassed the crusade of Saint Louis (1248–54); the defeat of the previously invincible Mongols at the Battle of 'Ayn Jalut (1260) and a seventeen-year period as the ruler of Egypt and Syria (1260–77).

While Saladin (d. 1193) stands as the emblematic figure of the Muslim–Crusader conflict – as an icon of chivalric virtue in the West and, for present-day Islamists, the man who recaptured Jerusalem from the Christians (1187) – it was Baibars who really broke the Frankish stranglehold on the coast and made their expulsion from the mainland Levant almost inevitable. If it is Saladin who dominates the popular imagination of today it was, until modern times, Baibars' reputation that loomed the larger. Apart from the biographies written during and after his lifetime, it was in the fifteenth century that we find the first references to the oral folk epic, *Sirat Baibars* (*The Story of Baibars*). With the heroism, humanity and piety of its hero burnished to the dazzling levels appropriate to the genre, it remained an immensely popular work for hundreds of years; in the early twentieth century it still had at least thirty specialist reciters on the streets of Cairo alone.

A mounted Mamluk archer, depicted on the 'Baptistère de Saint Louis', an early fourteenth-century inlaid brass basin produced by the master craftsman Mohammed ibn al-Zain. A masterpiece of Islamic art, the basin is now in the Louvre in Paris.

The origins of the Mamluks

The principal feature of Baibars' regime – and that of his successors – was the dominance of the army; the sultan himself was the product of a military upbringing. He was born in around 1229 to a family of Kipchak Turks who had fled from the southern Russian steppes to the Crimea in the face of Mongol invasions. As a youth Baibars was enslaved, but his first purchaser returned him because of a white mark in one of his pupils, while another buyer turned him down because of his supposedly evil eye.

At the age of 14, he was purchased cheaply in the slave markets of Aleppo by a local noble, but before long he ended up in Cairo at the court of as-Salih Ayyub, the ruler of Egypt and a descendant of Saladin himself. There he was sent to join the Bahriyya Mamluks, a body created by Ayyub to be the elite force of his army. The Muslim rulers had long used Mamluks (slave soldiers, literally meaning 'owned') purchased from central Asia or the Crimea, but the youths from this particular group were separated

SELJUK SULTANATE of KONYA

KINGDOM of ARMENIA

Sis

Tarsus

Mamistra

Corycus

Alexandretta

Syrian Gates

PRINCIPALITY of ANTIOCH

Trapesac

Gaston

Antioch

St Simeon

Cursat

Aleppo →

SYRIA

Saone

Latakia

Jabala

Apamea

Margat

Maraclea

Masyaf

Shaizar

Tortosa

Ruad

Hamah

Chastel Blanc

Krak des Chevaliers

Homs 1281

KINGDOM of CYPRUS

Kyrenia

Agridi

Nicosia

Gastria

Famagusta

Limassol

Paphos

MEDITERRANEAN SEA

Tripoli

Botron

Gibelet

Baalbek

Beirut

ANTI LEBANON

Sidon

KINGDOM

Beaufort

Damascus

Tyre

Tibnin

Banyas

of

Scandelion

Toron

Chastel Neuf

L. Huleh

Casal Imbert

JERUSALEM

Jacob's Ford

Acre

Montfort

Safad 1266

Haifa

Nazareth

L. Tiberias

Château Pélerin

GALILEE

Tiberias

'Ayn Jalut 1260

Jisr al-Majami

Caesarea

Belvoir

Jenin

Beth Shean

Arsuf

Nablus

Jaffa

SAMARIA

Lydda

Ramla

Jericho

Ibelin

Jerusalem

Ascalon

Bethlehem

Gaza

Hebron

DEAD SEA

MAMLUK

Darum

Kerak

N

SULTANATE

Muslim conquests 1263–71
Muslim conquests 1285–90
Muslim conquests 1291
Christian lands after 1291
Castle
Battle
Siege

0   50 km
0   50 miles

Baibars

and sent to the island of al-Rawda in the Nile, where they were converted to Islam. They lived a communal life in barracks and trained hard – the need for conversion aside, in these other respects they were comparable to the prime strike force of the Christian armies, the Military Orders. After completing their training the Bahriyya Mamluks were emancipated and formed the sultan's combat household.

One of the earliest occasions when this group came to the fore was at the Battle of Mansourah in February 1250. The previous summer King (later Saint) Louis IX of France had landed in Egypt at the head of the Seventh Crusade, the best-organized of them all; now he advanced down the Nile and threatened Cairo itself. The sultan Ayyub had recently died, and on 8 February the crusaders crossed the river and devastated the Egyptian camp, killing their commander as he took his early morning bath. The Christian cavalry thundered on towards the town of Mansourah – a fatal error; with Baibars at the head of the Bahriyya Mamluks, the Muslims regrouped. Described by a contemporary as 'lions in battle and the champions of cut and thrust' the Mamluks mounted a vicious counter-charge and the Christians scattered. Then, trapped in the dense warren of Mansourah's streets, the Muslims killed the crusaders' horses and slowly picked off the exhausted, thirsty knights. Probably fifteen hundred of the finest crusader warriors perished, including two hundred and eighty Templars. For Baibars and the Bahriyya, it was a famous victory. In a society that so valued fighting prowess this was a vital example of strength and, of course, of divine favour – two factors that would be advanced later to help justify Baibars' seizure of power.

Two images from *Nihayat al-su'l*, a fourteenth-century Mamluk cavalry training manual, attributed to Muhammad ibn 'Isa al-Hanafi al-Aqsara'i. The top image shows a Mamluk mounted archer, with a spear-carrying warrior beneath.

The Mongol invasion and the Battle of 'Ayn Jalut

The Seventh Crusade eventually collapsed, although not before Ayyub's heir, Turanshah, had been murdered by the Bahriyya for failing to reward them for their efforts at Mansourah. Into this dynastic void an unsteady combination of Ayyubid and Mamluk rulers emerged, led in the late 1250s by Baibars' rival, Qutuz. It was this man who had to face the most dangerous threat of all: the Mongols. In 1258 an army of over one hundred thousand nomadic horsemen smashed their way into Baghdad, the greatest city in the Near East, and destroyed the Sunni caliphate. The Mongols were emboldened by their belief in a divine mandate, which entitled them to treat anyone who confronted them as enemies of God and deserving of obliteration. On this basis, in late 1259, they advanced on Syria, Palestine and Egypt; some cities, such as Frankish Antioch, submitted; others, such as Muslim Aleppo, tried to fight but were crushed. In the early summer of 1260, however, a large part of the Mongol army retreated to seek better pasture and Qutuz took this as his cue to resist. With Baghdad and Syria in Mongol hands, the survival of Islam in the Near East rested with the Egyptians. Invoking the jihad, or holy war, against the Mongols, Qutuz cut their envoys in half in a brutal declaration of hostility.

In September 1260 Qutuz, now accompanied by Baibars, marched into Syria to confront the invaders. The two armies, each numbering about twelve thousand men, met at on 25 September at 'Ayn Jalut – the Springs of Goliath; an appropriate place for a supposedly weaker party to take on an allegedly invincible opponent. Unlike a battle between contemporary Christians and Muslims, the two forces were relatively similar, with both sides formed principally of mounted archers, rather than the heavy cavalry intrinsic to Frankish warfare.

A crucial element in the Mamluk victory was the work of Baibars' scouting party, who repeatedly tangled with the Mongol vanguard, only to drop back and lure his opponents to the Mamluks' chosen battle-ground at 'Ayn Jalut, a valley with wooded ridges, water supply and an adjacent plain. The Muslim troops arrayed themselves on the hillside while the Mongols faced the strong early morning sun. The Mamluks marched slowly down the slope, constantly beating their drums and calling upon God's help. At first the Mongols looked the stronger, but the Mamluk left wing had been reinforced with extra cavalry and was able to push back the Mongol right. Then, on the Mongol left, the ruler of Homs, a Muslim ally of the nomads, broke and fled,

Mamluk horsemen carry out training exercises in a hippodrome, in an image from *Nihayat al-su'l* (see caption opposite).

Krak des Chevaliers in western Syria, described by T. E. Lawrence as 'perhaps the best preserved and most wholly admirable castle in the world'. First built by the emir of Aleppo in 1031, it was taken over by the Franks after the First Crusade and then given to the Knights Hospitaller in 1144. After a huge earthquake in 1202 the castle was massively enlarged into the form it retains today. The fortress fell to the Mamluk sultan Baibars in 1271.

leaving the centre to be surrounded. The remaining Mongols fought fiercely and tried to battle up the hill, but Baibars led the pursuit and they were routed. Ibn 'Abd al-Zahir, Baibars' contemporary biographer, described how:

> *He stood before the enemy and bore the first shock of their onslaught. The enemy saw his bravery, the like of which was never heard before ... [He] followed them up the hill ... People heard about his efforts on the mountain and they climbed up to him from every direction, while he was fighting like one who staked his very life. The foot soldiers began to collect the heads of those he had killed.*

The Mongol general was among those slain, and his remaining contingents in Syria were swiftly driven out. For the Mamluks this was a supreme moment – the aura of Mongol invincibility was broken.

Baibars takes power

Qutuz was not able to savour his achievement for long. On the journey back to Egypt he was murdered by Baibars near Gaza on 23 October 1260. Given his own heroism in the battle, Baibars could claim a large part of the responsibility for the Muslims' victory; more importantly, 'Ayn Jalut allowed him to pose as the true defender of Islam, the saviour of the faith; usurper or not, God must have approved of the Mamluks to permit them such a famous triumph.

Baibars moved fast to capitalize on 'Ayn Jalut and had himself elected as sultan; he also initiated a clever propaganda push. Ibn 'Abd al-Zahir wrote: 'When God had granted him victory over the Tartars at 'Ayn Jalut, the sultan ordered the erection of the Mashhad al-Nasr (a victory monument) to make plain the importance of this gift of God and the spilled blood of the enemy.'

When Baibars became sultan, his absolute priority was to organize the defences of Syria and Egypt against a possible Mongol counter-attack; the continued declaration of jihad was an integral part of this. Baibars himself was a devout Muslim and part of his success came through a close identification with holy war. To assist in this he resurrected the Sunni caliphate after its destruction at Baghdad in 1258. The sultan found a 'relative' of the last caliph and in 1262 invested him with the title. The man was kept under a close watch and with such 'guidance' he provided a source of spiritual legitimacy for Baibars, who could then act in the tradition of Saladin and Ayyub as leader of the jihad.

Baibars' organization of the army

Baibars required a military machine of the highest order, and under his command the numbers of cavalry rose considerably, in part boosted by refugees from areas now controlled by the Mongols; these were trained men incorporated into existing forces. It was amongst the Mamluks themselves, however, that the most significant changes took place. From a group of about one thousand, Baibars increased the number to nearer four thousand, a substantial body of highly skilled men who were to form the backbone of his army. These troops were fully professional soldiers who received rigorous training and were imbued with the ideas of jihad. They were exceptionally formidable warriors: heavily armed, bearing a bow and arrow, a sword, an axe, a lance, shield and wearing body armour, while riding horses (also with frontal protection) that combined the mobility of Arab mounts with the sturdiness of the Cyrenaica breed that could adapt to rougher terrain.

Baibars himself ordered the construction of special hippodromes in Cairo, and inspired his men through his wholehearted involvement in drills to practise the skills of equitation, fencing (one thousand hits a day on a target), archery, and the use of the lance (seventy-two separate exercises had to be mastered). The sultan's iron discipline was also famous; he held regular inspections of the troops and anyone who failed pass muster was executed. Political challengers to the sultan were brutally dealt with, and drowning, crucifixion, banishment and blinding were amongst the summary deterrents meted out to those who opposed him.

Baibars paid great attention to logistical matters. Immediately after he became sultan he set up a 'pony express' style system of riders who could carry messages from Cairo to Damascus in three days – a distance of over 400 miles. He also used signal fires and a pigeon post to spread news, and he ensured that land routes were in good condition, improving roads and bridges where practical. He was particularly keen on espionage and would disguise himself to discover an opponent's strengths and weaknesses. At Tripoli in 1268, for example, he dressed as an equerry to meet Prince Bohemond VI in person, although his primary aim was to 'explore the town and find the points it could be stormed' according to Ibn 'Abd al-Zahir.

'You would have seen your [Christian] knights prostrate beneath the horses' hooves ... your women sold four at a time ... the crosses in your churches smashed, the pages of false testaments scattered ... fire running through your palaces, your dead burned in this world before going down to the fires of the next.'

FROM A LETTER WRITTEN BY BAIBARS IN 1268 TO THE PRINCE OF ANTIOCH

Baibars' campaigns against the Franks

Baibars certainly exploited this combination of military expertise, practical support and intelligence gathering; his remarkable energy allowed him to lead campaigns in almost every year of his rule, and he took on Franks (the name given to Christian settlers in the Levant), Turks, Mongols, Arabs and Armenians with equal determination and calculated ferocity. He made a series of truces with the Franks, usually when he needed to confront other opponents, but readily broke them when it suited him.

A summary of his efforts against the Franks gives an impression of his vigour: in 1261, he raided Frankish Palestine; in 1263, he attacked Acre; in 1265, he took Caesarea and Arsuf; in 1266, he captured Safad; in 1267, he raided Acre; and in 1268, he captured Jaffa and Beaufort before marching further north and taking Antioch. In 1269, he threatened Tyre, and in 1270 he raided near Krak des Chevaliers and captured it the following year along with Safita and Akkar. This schedule was in addition to the almost annual need to visit Damascus, to inspect his other Syrian lands, and to campaign in Nubia, the Yemen and Asia Minor. In 1269 he also made the haj to Mecca and Medina.

Baibars' raids against the Franks were so harsh that even Muslim writers characterized them as malicious: harvest crops were ravaged, trees felled and villages and livestock destroyed. From time to time various tricks were employed. On one occasion his men carried banners captured from the Templars and Hospitallers so as not to alarm agricultural workers close to the city of Acre; when the defenceless peasants realized the deceit it was too late to escape and five hundred of them were killed and then scalped, the trophies being strung on to a cord and hung around a tower on the castle of Safad.

THE CAPTURE OF SAFAD

PROBABLY THE MOST IMPORTANT BATTLE of Baibars' career was 'Ayn Jalut but, as we have seen, he was not yet the commander. The Mamluks' greatest victory came a couple of years after his death when they routed the Persian Mongols at the Battle of Homs in 1281, although this is generally agreed to be a consequence of the military expertise generated by Baibars. The sultan himself led his troops in many successful sieges and the investment of Safad in June 1266 gives a sense of the formidable range of weapons – military, psychological, and economic – that he would bring to bear upon an opponent.

The Franks had spent huge sums of money on this Templar fortress in northern Palestine. Ibn 'Abd al-Zahir described it as 'a lump in Syria's throat, an obstacle to breathing in Islam's chest'. As usual, soon after the siege began, Baibars offered the defenders gifts to try to induce them to surrender; much to the sultan's fury, however, these were adopted as ammunition and hurled back by mangonels (stone-throwing siege machines). Baibars brought up his own heavy siege engines from Damascus

to fire naptha and huge stones. After a few days he took the barbican, although in doing so the Muslims suffered heavy losses. Worried by this, Baibars offered the Syrian Christians – but not the Templars – safe conduct; he then renewed the attack. Because the castle seemed about to fall, a Templar official went out to negotiate. But Baibars still nursed a grievance over the insult concerning the gifts, and in revenge for the slight to his honour, he substituted a double of himself in order to offer safe conduct to everyone but then kill the Christians. Baibars told the Templar envoy his plan and gave him a simple set of alternatives – if he wanted to live and be rewarded, he was to go along with this stratagem, otherwise he would be killed most cruelly. The man picked the former option. The defenders duly made their agreement with the false sultan and on 22 July 1266 they surrendered. The following night, as they made their way towards Acre, the Christians were seized and beheaded. In a typically macabre display, the sultan had their bones and heads placed inside a small circular wall so that they could be seen; a gruesome example for those who presumed to defy him.

The sultan's policy with regard to Frankish castles was cited by Ibn al-Furat: 'One part of the Muslim armies uproots Frankish fortresses, and destroys their castles, while another rebuilds what the Mongols destroyed in the east and increases the height of their ramparts [compared with what they were].' The idea behind dismantling those on the coast was to deny any forthcoming crusades a bridgehead. As the writer here noted, however, fortresses inland were often repaired after the damage of a siege and could be used as a base to control the surrounding districts, to intimidate Christian lands, and to defend against possible Mongol incursions.

Baibars and the Mongols

The threat from the Mongols of Persia required Baibars to show flexibility and inventiveness in his warfare. In the early years of his rule, he created a scorched-earth zone in the east of his lands to deny the nomads pasture for their horses. Then, needing more time in which to build up his own forces, he used diplomacy; first, as noted above, by making treaties with the Franks, but also by working with the Mongols of the Golden Horde, a group based in southern Russia who had become Muslims. Invoking a shared faith, Baibars exploited the deep-seated rivalry between the Golden Horde and the Mongols in Persia to take the pressure off his own lands. There were occasions, however, when the Mongols did invade. In 1273 they surrounded the castle of al-Bira on the Euphrates. The sultan skirted around the enemy with camels and wagons on which were carried boats in kit form; he then reassembled the boats and launched a devastating attack that utterly routed the Mongols. He continued to push back the nomads in Asia Minor, and victories here and in Cilicia were among the last of his career.

Baibars died on 20 June 1277. He was taken ill while watching a polo match during which he had drunk some qumiz, a highly alcoholic brew made from fermented mare's milk (not the wine he so frowned upon). Given his atrocious record of murder and deceit, rumours of poisoning abounded, but no one was identified as responsible. He was buried in the Madrasa Zahiriye (formerly the house of Saladin's father) and the domed chamber, decorated with polychrome marble and mosaic work, can still be seen today.

Both ruthless and calculating, Baibars created an empire that ran from Asia Minor, through Syria, Palestine and Egypt down to Nubia and the Yemen. He successfully resisted the most lethal military force of the day and arguably took over that mantle for his own superb armies. His skills broke Frankish Syria beyond repair, and in spite of his harsh rule he governed successfully for seventeen years – a remarkable achievement for the slave-boy from the Crimea.

A polychrome marble mihrab (a niche showing the direction of Mecca) in the Mausoleum of Baibars in Damascus. This is located in a *madrasa* (teaching college) founded by Baibars's son after the sultan's death in 1277. Above the *mihrab*, a band of mosaic work imitates that found in the courtyard of the Great Ummayad Mosque of the same city.

TAMERLANE
1336–1405

JUSTIN MAROZZI

IN THE CLOSING DECADES of the fourteenth century, the world's greatest conqueror surged forth unannounced from Central Asia. Tamerlane blazed through the continent like a firestorm, toppling kings and empires with contemptuous ease, riding to victory after victory at the head of his ferocious army of mounted Tatar archers. One by one the great cities of the East were stormed and sacked: Antioch and Aleppo, Balkh and Baghdad, Damascus and Delhi, Herat, Kabul, Shiraz and Isfahan – all were left in flaming ruins, their populations tortured without mercy, slaughtered and decapitated. On every battlefield Tamerlane's soldiers built soaring towers from the heads of their victims, deadly warnings to anyone who dared oppose them.

With each new triumph, his sparkling imperial capital of Samarkand, Pearl of the East, grew richer and more magnificent with the treasures plundered from across Asia, a booty that included waves of captive scholars and silk-weavers, poets and painters, musicians and miniaturists, armourers, gem-cutters, masons, architects, silversmiths and calligraphers. The sweep of his conquests was staggering. By the time of his death in 1405, after thirty-five years of constant campaigning, Tamerlane remained undefeated on the battlefield and had outshone both Alexander the Great and Genghis Khan in the annals of empire-building and warfare. Little wonder that two centuries later, in his celebrated play *Tamburlaine the Great*, Christopher Marlowe should christen him 'The Scourge of God'.

That all this could be achieved by one man is astonishing. That it is the record of a military leader crippled down his right side is scarcely credible. Excellence in the martial arts was an absolute prerequisite for success and self-advancement in the turbulent world of fourteenth-century Central Asia. As a local proverb had it: 'Only a hand that can grasp a sword can hold a sceptre.'

Tamerlane's beginnings were relatively humble. Unlike Alexander, he was not the son of a mighty king, nor of royal blood. According to tradition, he was born in Shakhrisabz, south of Samarkand, on 9 April 1336 to a minor noble called Taraghay of the Barlas tribe. His name was Temur, meaning 'iron'. An injury in his youth gave

Tamerlane

rise to the Persian version Temur-i-lang, Temur the Lame, which became further corrupted to Tamburlaine and Tamerlane.

Unlike Genghis Khan and his Mongols, he did not have a homogenous people to lead to war. Central Asia was a melting-pot of feuding tribes, riven by divisions and shifting alliances. It took a leader of outstanding charisma and bravery to forge these disparate peoples into one formidable army that was to prove so irresistible in the field. Any assessment of Tamerlane's extraordinary career must take into account these important distinctions.

The sheep-rustler who would rule the world

The fifteenth-century court chronicle of Sharaf ad-din Ali Yazdi, a masterpiece of florid sycophancy, has the young Tamerlane aspiring to world dominion. A much harsher verdict comes from Ahmed ibn Arabshah, Yazdi's Syrian contemporary, who as a young boy saw Tamerlane put his native city of Damascus to the sword in 1401. Arabshah lays much emphasis on the conqueror's early years as a sheep-stealer and petty brigand. It was during one such foraging mission that Tamerlane appears to have received his debilitating injury, probably shot by arrows to his right arm and leg while roaming the deserts of southwest Afghanistan in 1363.

Though the sources are generally quiet about Tamerlane's childhood and youth, there are glimpses of the relentless cunning that throughout his life would see him outwit and outmanoeuvre opponents both on and off the battlefield. If martial prowess was a constant throughout his career, so too was a quick intelligence coupled with meticulous preparation. His army was always superbly organized and equipped. Tactically and strategically he was masterful, with a love of the unexpected. Few commanders in history have been as bold.

A magnificent statue of Tamerlane on horseback dominates the square that bears his name in the heart of the Uzbek capital of Tashkent. In Soviet times he was banned from Uzbek literature and history as a nationalist threat to unity. When Uzbekistan became independent in 1991, he returned to national life with a vengeance.

In 1360, he vaulted out of obscurity and into the official histories with a characteristically audacious move. His homeland of Mawarannahr, the land beyond the river, had been invaded by the Moghul khan. Haji Beg, chief of the Barlas clan that ruled the Qashka Darya valley where Tamerlane lived, decided to flee rather than fight. The youthful Tamerlane told his leader he would stay behind to prevent the invading Moghuls from seizing more land. He did nothing of the sort. Recognizing the superiority of his enemy's army, he immediately offered his services to the Moghul khan as a vassal ruler. The offer was accepted. At the age of 24, Tamerlane had successfully claimed leadership of the entire Barlas tribe.

In another, more outlandish example of his cunning in the years before he rose to power in 1370, he was summoned to pledge his loyalty to a hereditary khan or face him on the battlefield. Since he did not have an army strong enough to deploy, he pretended he was sick and drank a basinful of wild boar's blood before receiving the khan's envoys. During the interview he

Tamerlane's soldiers present their emperor with the severed heads of their enemies after the sacking of Baghdad in 1401. The chronicles report 90,000 heads piled into 120 towers around the ruins of the city.

started vomiting blood copiously, convincing his visitors that he was at death's door. The envoys returned to their master with news of their adversary's imminent demise. Tamerlane, who was encamped nearby, chose this moment to strike. Catching the hapless khan and his courtly entourage entirely unawares, he slew them where they lay.

By 1370, the opportunist sheep-stealer had seen off his one-time ally Amir Husayn, grandson of the last Chaghatay khan. He had himself crowned imperial ruler of Chaghatay in Balkh, the celebrated seat of power that had attracted both Alexander and Genghis Khan before him. His royal titles, nothing if not premature, were harbingers of the great conquests to come: Lord of the Fortunate Conjunction, Emperor of the Age, Conqueror of the World.

The horizons expand

From 1370 until his death in 1405, en route to war with the Ming emperor of China, Tamerlane hardly stood still. Apart from a two-year stint in Samarkand from 1396–8, during which he threw himself into a grandiose building programme with a fury usually reserved for the battlefield, he was always on the move. Samarkand was the hub around which his restless campaigning revolved.

Conquest was only possible for as long as he could keep his armies in the field. Steppe tribesmen traditionally would remain loyal to a leader for as long as he proved victorious in battle. There were no salaries. Temur understood this acutely. His military career was one long campaign, punctuated with only the briefest of interludes; he needed to keep his armies on the move.

Surveying a map of his conquests, the first decade or so of his reign from 1370 looks very much like a dress rehearsal for the main performance. It was during this time that Tamerlane started to consolidate his power in Mawarannahr and the surrounding region, the necessary precursor to projecting his force much further afield. In 1379, he sacked the city of Urgench. Roving west in 1381, he added Herat to his nascent empire with barely a murmur, and by 1382 Tamerlane was lord of the Caspian.

Wars of terror

It was also during this period that he developed a style of warfare that sent collective shudders across Asia and, in many instances, defeated opponents before they had even set foot on the battlefield. His soldiers, motivated by prospects for plunder, were willing agents of this policy of inflicting terror on their enemies and the civilian population alike.

As Sir John Malcolm, the nineteenth-century historian of Persia, wrote, 'Such a leader as Timour must have been idolized by his soldiers … he was careless of the opinion of other classes in the community. His object was fame as a conqueror; and a noble city was laid in ashes, or the inhabitants of a province massacred, on a cold calculation that the dreadful impression would facilitate the purposes of his ambition …'

News of what today we would call war crimes spread fast across the Asian steppes. Kings and princes came to appreciate the wisdom of acknowledging his suzerainty quickly. Those steadfast or rash enough to challenge his might were despatched with appalling brutality.

In 1383, Tamerlane had 2,000 prisoners cemented alive into towers in the city of Isfizar to punish the rebels of Khorasan. In 1387, infuriated by an uprising in the Persian city of Isfahan, which had already surrendered to him, he ordered a general massacre, in which 70,000 were slaughtered. Poised on

'He ran to the ends of the earth, as Satan runs from the son of Adam and crept through countries as poison creeps through bodies.'
AHMED IBN ARABSHAH IN *TAMERLANE THE GREAT AMIR*

the outskirts of Delhi in 1398, he ordered the army to kill in cold blood the 100,000 Indian prisoners he had captured, who had made the mistake of celebrating the Tatars' initial reversals during the early skirmishes with the Indians outside the city walls. Two years later, 3,000 Armenians were buried alive in the Turkish city of Sivas, this being Tamerlane's way of honouring a promise not to shed any blood after it had surrendered. After the fall of Baghdad in 1401, as the Tigris ran red with blood, Tamerlane had another terrible girdle of 120 towers piled around the city, this time the vultures having 90,000 heads to feed on.

Though Tamerlane bequeathed a splendid architectural legacy characterized by monumental blue-tiled mosques and madrassahs with domes of iridescent blue rising high above elaborate portals, it was neither these remarkable buildings, nor the exquisite parks and palaces he designed during his reign for which he was best remembered. The much more ephemeral towers and pyramids of human heads, often

THE BATTLE OF **ANKARA**

AT AROUND 10 O'CLOCK ON THE MORNING of 28 July 1402, Tamerlane surveyed his army on the Chibukabad plain, northeast of Ankara. There were up to two hundred thousand professional soldiers drawn from the farthest reaches of his empire, from Armenia to Afghanistan, and from Samarkand to Siberia. They had never been defeated in battle.

The left wing was commanded by the emperor's son, Prince Shah Rukh, and his grandson, Khalil Sultan. Its advance guard was under another grandson, Sultan Husayn. Tamerlane's third son, Prince Miranshah, led the right wing, his own son, Abu Bakr, at the head of the vanguard. The main body of the army was under the command of Tamerlane's grandson and heir, Prince Mohammed Sultan.

The Ottoman sultan Bayezit I had put a similar number of troops into the field. There were twenty thousand Serbian cavalry in full armour, mounted Sipahis, irregular cavalry and infantry from the provinces of Asia Minor. Bayezit commanded the centre at the head of five thousand Janissaries – the makings of a regular infantry – supported by three of his sons, the princes Musa, Isa and Mustapha. The right wing was led by the sultan's Christian brother-in-law, Lazarovic of Serbia, the left by another of his sons, Prince Suleiman Chelebi.

Even before battle commenced, Tamerlane's brilliant tactical manoeuvrings had comprehensively wrong-footed the Ottomans, knocking their morale and leaving them exhausted and thirsty. Only a week earlier they had occupied the higher ground on which their adversary's army now stood. Feigning flight, the Tatars had outmanoeuvred them, diverted and poisoned their

The Ottoman sultan Bayezit I is brought before Tamerlane after his calamitous defeat at the Battle of Ankara in 1402. This was the only time in Ottoman history that, humiliatingly, the sultan was captured in person. This image comes from a sixteenth-century manuscript of *Zafarnama – Book of Victory*, compiled by the court chronicler and tireless sycophant, Sharaf ad-din Ali Yazdi.

illuminated by beacons at night, the hallmark of his battlefield victories, were his most feared and dreadful signature. They represented a powerful and highly effective disincentive for an independent city to resist or a subject city to rebel.

Taking care of his nemesis

In 1386, shortly after capturing Sultaniya, Tamerlane received disquieting news. His former protégé Tokhtamish, who with Tamerlane's repeated military support in the 1370s had become khan of the Golden Horde, had sacked the city of Tabriz in a direct challenge to his one-time mentor. Tamerlane's response was swift: the three-year campaign against Persia. The army marched west from Samarkand, taking Tabriz, quickly followed by the Georgian capital of Tiflis (Tbilisi). After one of his worst massacres, Isfahan fell in 1387, prompting Shiraz to surrender (wisely) without a fight. While Tamerlane was campaigning in Armenia and Asia Minor, word came that

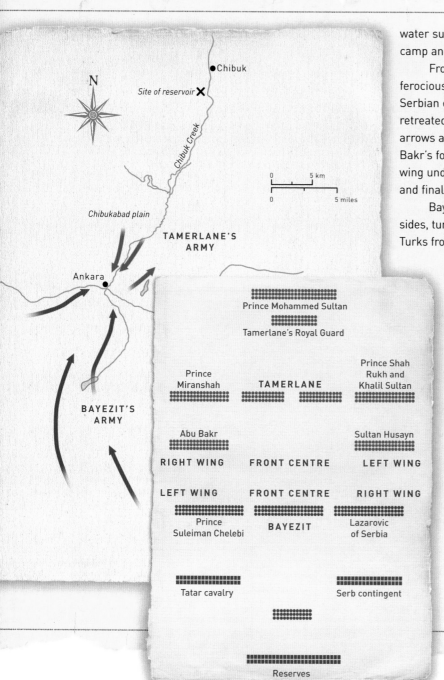

water supply, doubled back, plundered their undefended camp and taken their position.

From the first blows struck the fighting was ferocious. Charging across the plain came the formidable Serbian cavalry. Under pressure, the Tatar left flank retreated, defending itself with volley after volley of arrows and flames of naphtha. On the right wing, Abu Bakr's forces, advancing against Prince Chelebi's left wing under cover of a cloud of arrows, fought like lions and finally broke through their enemy's ranks.

Bayezit's Tatar cavalry chose this moment to switch sides, turning suddenly against Chelebi's Macedonians and Turks from the rear. It was a decisive moment, which broke the Ottoman attack. Tamerlane had engineered the defection of the Tatars in the months before the battle by playing on their sense of tribal loyalty and holding out the prospect of richer plunder. Chelebi judged the battle lost and fled the field with the remainder of his men.

The elite Samarkand division, together with a body of the emperor's guards, charged the Serbian cavalry, who buckled under the attack and followed Chelebi in retreat towards Brusa. Bayezit's infantry were now the only forces left intact. Worse was to follow. The Tatar centre now moved forward to settle the affair with eighty regiments and the dreaded war elephants. The Ottoman infantry was routed.

Bayezit's forces defended their sultan valiantly to the last, but the Tatars' greater numbers eventually told. For the first and only time in Ottoman history, the sultan was captured in person. Tamerlane's greatest victory was complete.

Tamerlane

Tokhtamish, by now emerging as a formidable foe, had been laying waste to Mawarannahr.

In the harsh winter of 1389–90, with snow up to his horses' flanks, Tamerlane ordered his army north to hunt out and destroy his rival. For five months and almost 2,000 miles his men rode across the bleak Siberian steppe in ever worsening conditions. Tokhtamish's army, retreating into the shadows, refused to engage them, luring Tamerlane to certain destruction deep inside enemy territory.

Eventually, on 18 June 1391, the two armies came face to face. In a show of calculated contempt for his adversary, Tamerlane ordered his men to unpack and erect his sumptuous, fur-lined tents and pavilions and calmly lay out his carpets. According to the chronicles, this exercise in psychological warfare had its intended effect, shattering the morale of the Golden Horde. The next day, in the heat of the battle, Tokhtamish fled, leaving Tamerlane once more victorious.

> 'If some partial disorders, some local oppressions, were healed by the sword of Timour, the remedy was far more pernicious than the disease.' EDWARD GIBBON

On 22 April 1395, the two rivals faced each other again for the last time. For three days, both armies manoeuvred for position on opposite banks of the Terek river in modern-day Chechnya, Tokhtamish holding the advantage. At this point, as the confrontation was drifting towards stalemate, Tamerlane played his master card. As night fell, he ordered the women in his camp to dress up as soldiers, while his men made a three-day forced march back to a ford, the only crossing point available. Battle was then joined, with Tamerlane's men having seized the advantage. For the second time Tokhtamish fled during the battle. The Golden Horde was pillaged and put to the sword.

Outdoing his predecessors

Though his enemies within the Muslim world considered him an infidel barbarian, Tamerlane was a cultured man, a keen student of history and religion, and a peerless chess player. When, in 1398, he announced a campaign against India, having just concluded the successful, blood-soaked five-year campaign against Persia and Georgia, he did so consciously, to eclipse the achievements of Alexander and Genghis before him.

His princes and amirs were aghast at the logistical challenges of moving an army of one hundred thousand across the roof of the world. How would they cross the mountains and the rivers that lay between Samarkand and Delhi, they asked? How would they overcome the Indians' terrifying fighting elephants, clad in steel armour with tusk-mounted scimitars and flame-throwers, archers and crossbowmen in protected turrets on their backs? Tamerlane silenced them. Such feeble objections counted for nothing to the man who had never known defeat.

It was a whirlwind mission. Once the treacherous route across the mountains had been negotiated, with the elderly emperor at one point having to be lowered on a litter over a 1,000-foot precipice, the rest of the campaign proceeded as though on auto-pilot. Ruthless as ever in his preparations for war, Tamerlane ordered his men to make caltrops, three-pronged iron stakes, and leave them on the plain around Delhi. Camels were loaded with bundles of dried grass and wood. When battle was joined, the Indian war elephants found themselves being charged by roaring camels on fire. Wheeling around in terror, they retreated pell-mell through their own ranks, hobbled by the deadly caltrops, scattering the Indian troops who fled in blind panic. With a tortured gasp, one of the richest cities in the world slipped into Tamerlane's dominions. The extraordinary wealth accumulated by generations of India's sultans was plundered within the space of several days. Decapitated bodies lay putrefying in the streets. Towers of skulls loomed over a scene of unspeakable carnage. Famine and disease were rife. It took more than a century for Delhi to recover.

A pilgrimage of destruction

Barely pausing for breath after his triumphant homecoming to Samarkand, Tamerlane levied his army for the Seven-Year Campaign. It would be his final push. Age had not softened him. After his burying alive of the Armenian garrison at Sivas in 1400, he continued southwest into the heart of the Egyptian empire, striking first at Aleppo, which collapsed before the onslaught. The Tatars gave no quarter. Men, women and children were cut down where they stood, thousands of heads being piled into mounds as the army marched further south, leaving behind them scenes of appalling slaughter.

In 1402, he faced his most powerful enemy in the corpulent form of Sultan Bayezit the Thunderbolt, Sword Arm of the Faith (see pp. 336–7). He prevailed once again and, having sacked Asia Minor, stood on the shores of the Aegean with Europe at his mercy. Instead, he set his eyes east towards the greatest prize yet: the Celestial Empire of China, the only significant adversary against which he had yet to test himself.

In the winter of 1404, the Tatar army marched from Samarkand with the wizened 68-year-old emperor at its head. Temperatures plummeted, winds gusted and the snows fell. Beards and moustaches froze on men's faces, said the chronicles. In Otrar, in what is today Kazakhstan, Tamerlane fell ill. Court doctors attended to him with hot drinks laced with drugs and spices but still the fever worsened. At 8 o'clock at night on 18 February 1405, he breathed his last. His blood had barely cooled when the internecine conflicts that he had warned against on his deathbed exploded. The empire he had laboured so carefully and cruelly to build started crumbling away. Within a century of his death it had vanished altogether.

The subterranean sarcophagus of Tamerlane in the magnificent Gur-i-Amir Mausoleum in Samarkand. A plaque reads: 'This is the resting place of the illustrious and merciful monarch, the most great Sultan, the most mighty warrior, Lord Temur, Conqueror of the World.'

'I shall do in this place what I was sent to do, to harass and humble its inhabitants, and to make war on all those who have defied the authority of my father.' THE PRINCE TO THE CARDINAL OF PÉRIGORD, 1356, FROM THE *CHRONICLE* OF ROBERT AVESBURY

THE BLACK PRINCE

1330-76

JONATHAN SUMPTION

EDWARD, PRINCE OF WALES AND AQUITAINE, the eldest son of Edward III, has been known as the 'Black Prince' since at least the sixteenth century. To his contemporaries, however, he was simply 'the Prince', a man whose fame in his own time was so great that no other description was called for. If generalship is the art of winning pitched battles, then Edward was unquestionably the greatest general of his day, and one of the greatest of the European Middle Ages. He commanded the Anglo-Gascon army which defeated and captured John II of France at the Battle of Poitiers in September 1356, one of the most complete military victories of the Hundred Years War. Eleven years later, at Nájera in northern Castile, he led another Anglo-Gascon army to overwhelming victory against Henry of Trastámara, the pretender to the throne of Castile. These were remarkable battles. If they were not decisive, it was because generalship is more than battlefield tactics and politics more than force of arms.

The Prince was born into a world in which military methods were evolving rapidly. For several centuries, the chief instrument of war had been the heavy cavalryman, mounted on a powerful charger, protected from head to toe by chain mail, and armed with lance and buckler, axe and sword. Yet however powerful the impact of their charge, heavy cavalry were generally ineffective against disciplined men fighting on foot in prepared positions. Moreover, they were vulnerable to mass archery, which could wreak havoc among the dense mass of unprotected horses, breaking up their formations and inflicting heavy casualties. In 1302, in a remarkable and widely noted demonstration of the superior strength of defensive formations of infantry, the army of the Flemish towns destroyed the chivalry of France at the Battle of Courtrai. The suicidal charge of the English cavalry against the disciplined squares of Scottish pikemen at the Battle of Bannockburn in 1314 was an awesome lesson, better learned by the English, perhaps, than by any other European nation.

Over the next half century, the English devised battle tactics which revolutionized European warfare. The hallmark of the English method was the use of dismounted cavalry fighting on foot, both defensively and offensively. The horses

The Black Prince

were taken to the rear at the outset of any engagement, to be used only for the rout at the end and the pursuit afterwards or, if things went badly, for flight. At the same time, dismounted infantry formations were supported by dense lines of archers, generally at least a third of their strength, rising to two thirds by the end of the fourteenth century. The English, alone among European nations, made the longbow a formidable battlefield weapon. With their longer range and rapid rate of fire, longbows completely outclassed the crossbows which had become the standard item of equipment in other European armies. Traditional infantry was gradually eliminated from English armies, and had almost vanished by 1350. It was the co-ordinated use of dismounted cavalry and longbowmen that enabled Edward III to destroy a Scottish army at Halidon Hill in 1333 and a French one at Crécy in 1346. Crécy taught the French the lesson that they had failed to learn at Courtrai. In the second half of the century, their military method developed along English lines, with smaller, all-mounted armies fighting on foot, and increasingly composed of full-time professionals.

These developments taxed the skills of generations of army commanders to come. The co-ordinated deployment of dismounted men-at-arms and archers called for commanders to exercise a far greater degree of control over formations in the course of the battle than had been necessary before. Manoeuvring large bodies of men-at-arms who had never trained together was one of the perennial problems of medieval battlefields. It required not just outstanding judgement but battlefield staff, a rudimentary chain of command, and some means of communicating with subordinates. These requirements presented a considerable challenge at a time when orders

A gilt bronze effigy on the tomb of Edward, the Black Prince, in Canterbury Cathedral. He died in 1376, just one year before his father, King Edward III, on whose death the throne of England passed to the Prince's infant son, Richard II.

were transmitted to section commanders by trumpet, occasionally by messenger, and thence by shouting. Signals could be complex, and difficult to hear inside a vizored helmet. The Prince rose to the challenge better than any of his contemporaries.

The Battle of Crécy, 1346

The Prince first saw action in 1346, when he took part, under his father's command, in the campaign in northern France which culminated in the Battle of Crécy on 26 August. He was then 16 years old, and in nominal command of one of the three divisions which made up an English army of about fourteen thousand men. They had fought a difficult campaign, landing from the sea in southern Normandy, and making their way first to Paris, then across the Seine west of the city, and finally, hungry and exhausted, across the great plain of Picardy. At Crécy the Prince, guided by experienced military commanders in the king's confidence, commanded the vanguard. We cannot know what impact the experience made on the young man. But some lessons must have been learned, for the battle was perhaps the classic demonstration of the English tactical method at a time when it was new to continental warfare, as well as a terrible warning of the consequences of a commander losing control of his own army.

The first division of French cavalry charged en masse with neither warning nor orders, trampling their own archers underfoot. The rest of the cavalry careered pell-mell after them, and ran into the rear of the first division. The English bowmen, stationed at the wings of the army, inflicted carnage on the Genoese crossbowmen – who provided the archery arm of the French army – before they could even come within range. They broke up the lines of the approaching masses of heavy cavalry, the latter being finally stopped by the lines of dismounted men-at-arms. The French horsemen repeatedly wheeled and charged, but without regard to what was happening elsewhere on the field. As a result, they were overwhelmed by a smaller but more skilful and disciplined enemy.

The Poitiers campaign

After the battle, the Prince played an increasingly prominent part in his father's wars against France. He served in the eleven-month siege of Calais which followed the Battle of Crécy, fought in the battle outside Calais in January 1350 and fought again in the great sea-battle off Winchelsea later that year. But he did not exercise an independent command until 1355, when he served as his father's lieutenant in the English duchy of Aquitaine in southwestern France. The Prince arrived in Bordeaux by sea in September 1355, accompanied by a small English army of eight hundred men-at-arms and fourteen hundred mounted archers. Most of his strength was to be recruited after his arrival from the Gascon nobility. Between October and December 1355, the Prince's variegated army got used to fighting together in the course of a long and spectacular raid into the French province of Languedoc, which took them from the Atlantic coast at Bordeaux to within sight of the Mediterranean at Narbonne.

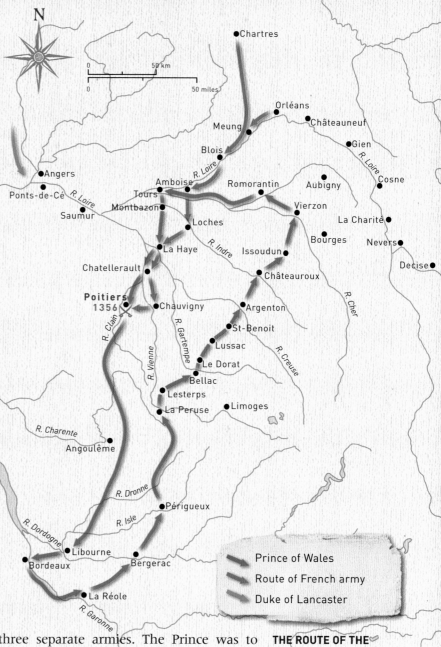

THE ROUTE OF THE BLACK PRINCE'S OFFENSIVE, August–September 1356.

The real purpose of the Prince's presence in Aquitaine, however, was to take part in the great offensive against the heartlands of the French kingdom which had originally been planned for the autumn of 1355, but in the event had to be deferred to the following year. In its final form this plan had been formulated by the fertile strategic minds of King Edward III and his cousin Henry of Grosmont, Duke of Lancaster. It called for the co-ordinated invasion of France by three separate armies. The Prince was to advance north from Bordeaux. A small English army was to land in the Cotentin peninsula under Lancaster's command, and join forces with English garrison troops in Brittany and a substantial contingent of men loyal to Charles of Evreux, the French King of Navarre, then embroiled in a bitter civil war with the French monarchy. A third, much larger army, was to cross to Calais under the command of the king himself and come down from the north. All three English armies would join up in the Loire valley.

The Prince set out with his own army at the beginning of August 1356. Allowing for troops that had to be left behind to guard the marches of Aquitaine, he must have had between six to seven thousand men at his back, at least two thirds of whom were Gascon cavalrymen. There were about one thousand English archers. The army reached the Loire at Tours on 7 September, only to find that the northern claw of Edward's pincer movement had failed. The king had been forced to cancel the army of Picardy. Lancaster had set out from Normandy, but the great barrier of the Loire prevented him from joining forces with the Prince. Every crossing of the river was either broken or heavily defended, and Lancaster was obliged to retreat. The French king, John II, had collected an army of about eight thousand heavy cavalry and three thousand infantry. If the three English armies had been able to join up, he would have been seriously outnumbered. As it was, he was able to confront the Prince's army on its own. The Prince, concerned about numbers, supplies and communications with his base in Gascony, appears at first to have tried to retreat to Bordeaux. But the French king crossed the Loire and came south in pursuit. On 16 September 1356 he caught up with him in the great plain east of Poitiers. There, his army was defeated and largely destroyed in a great battle on the following day (see p. 346).

The outcome of the Battle of Poitiers was largely determined by differences at the level of command. The French king, although he had the larger army, tried to attack a strong defensive position without any local superiority of numbers, and proved incapable of modifying his plans as the battle developed. His divisional commanders had received their orders before the battle, and carried them out with grim persistence and outstanding courage, regardless of what was happening elsewhere. By comparison, the Prince was able to improvise plans in the heat of battle, and redeploy formations, communicating his orders with impressive speed to those who had to act on them. It was an outstanding demonstration of courage, discipline and generalship.

Yet it went a long way to show how evanescent were even the greatest victories if there were no means of following them up. The English in France in the fourteenth century never had the financial or administrative resources to occupy and hold enemy territory for more than short periods. They relied on the moral impact of defeat on their enemies, and on the sheer scale of physical destruction that they were able to inflict, rather as advocates of area bombing did in the Second World War. After the battle, the Prince returned with his army and his prisoners to Bordeaux. Even the capture of the king of France was an advantage that ultimately proved hard to exploit. The battle provoked a prolonged and bloody political crisis in France. Yet it took nearly four years to force the French to ransom their king and agree terms, and even then these terms proved to be short lived.

'Thus died the last hopes of the English. For while he lived, they feared no enemy invasion, no threat of battle. Never, when he was present, did they fail or desert the field. And, as is said of Alexander the Great, he never attacked a nation which he did not conquer, or besieged a city which he did not take.'

THOMAS WALSINGHAM MOURNS THE PASSING OF THE BLACK PRINCE IN HIS *GREAT CHRONICLE*

Prince of Aquitaine

It is perhaps unfair to blame the Prince for the limitations of medieval warfare or the failure of a strategy devised by his father. Yet when his own turn came to govern, he showed much the same inability to grasp the political framework in which all military action occurs. Between 1364 and 1371, the Prince was the independent ruler of the English principality of Aquitaine, a vastly enlarged territory comprising about a quarter of France which emerged from the treaties of 1360. In one sense it was the reward of his victory at Poitiers. Yet it was thrown away by a series of political misjudgements. Characteristically, the greatest of these misjudgements was about what could be achieved by mere force of arms.

In 1366, the Prince agreed with the deposed king of Castile, Pedro I, to invade Castile in order to restore him to his throne. It was essentially a financial transaction, under which the Prince was putting his army at Pedro's service in return for his expenses and a suitable fee. The Prince does not seem to have asked himself whether Pedro could afford to pay him, or how he would enforce the debt if he had to. He did not consider how Pedro could be maintained on his throne once the army which put him there had gone. He did not wonder what impact the venture would have on the future relations between England and the Iberian kingdoms.

The Battle of Nájera

Nájera is a small town of northern Castile, a short distance south of the River Ebro. West of its walls is the site of the Prince's last great battle, which was fought on 3 April 1367. His army was slightly larger than the one he had commanded at Poitiers, about eight to ten thousand men. Its make-up was very similar, consisting of a core of English men-at-arms and archers, with a much larger number of Gascon cavalry. The army ranged against him, however, was a good deal less formidable than the host of John II in 1356. The Pretender of Castile, Henry of Trastámara, had gathered together an army which was rather larger than the Prince's, but weaker in cavalry and both technically and tactically backward. Its main strength lay in the presence in its ranks of about one thousand experienced French veterans commanded by the future Constable of France, Bertrand du Guesclin. Like the Prince, they were there for money.

Henry was wrong-footed from the outset when a large section of the Anglo-Gascon army approached his forces by an unexpected route, from behind a line of hills beyond their left flank. Attacked from two directions at once, the Castilians and their French auxiliaries tried to take the offensive, only to be met by a rain of arrows from the English lines which broke up their formations and enabled them to be defeated in detail. It was all over in minutes. The Castilian light cavalry, which refused to demean itself by fighting on foot, was wiped out. As at Poitiers, the Prince's victory was due mainly to his intelligent exploitation of the lie of the land, his willingness to try an unconventional manoeuvre, and his ability to follow and control the movements of his dispersed forces.

BATTLE OF POITIERS

WHEN DAWN BROKE on 17 September 1356, the English were dug in to a strong defensive position on gently rising ground south of the French army. Their front was protected by a thick hawthorn hedge. Their archers were stationed in their traditional position on the army's wings, their flanks protected on one side by deep trenches, and on the other by a marshy expanse of ground by the banks of the River Miosson. The French had decided on their tactics at a quarrelsome council of war the previous evening. They resolved to abandon the mass cavalry charge which had been the main feature of their battle tactics for more than two centuries, and deploy the greater part of the cavalry on foot. Interestingly, these dispositions were made on the advice of the Scottish knight, William Lord of Douglas, who was fighting with the French army and who reminded his colleagues of the fate of the English at Bannockburn.

The first French attack was a cavalry charge by two small formations, directed against the English wings. It was designed to scatter the archers and open the way for the main force. It came at the worst possible moment for the English. A short time before, the Prince and his advisers had decided to retreat, mainly, it seems, because they had run out of food. The force of the initial French cavalry charge struck the two flanks of the English line just as the retreat was beginning. However, regrouping with great difficulty, the archers succeeded in inflicting terrible casualties on the approaching horsemen and their mounts. All this was hidden from the lines of French men-at-arms by the brow of a hill. Ignorant of the fate of the cavalry, their first line was already advancing on foot towards the English positions under the young Dauphin of France. When they reached the hawthorn hedge, they crammed into the gaps to attack the enemy. After two hours of fierce hand-to-hand fighting, they were forced into retreat. In order to protect the Dauphin, he was hurried from the field with most of his men. The second French line took this as a signal to withdraw and followed after them. It was left to King John II to try to save the day by leading the reserve against the triumphant English. Attacking the whole of the English army with just a third of his own, John was driven back down the hill and overwhelmed in the fields below. At the critical point, one of the Prince's Gascon captains remounted about one hundred and sixty of his men and took them round the rear of the French to attack from behind. Another cavalry force, commanded by Sir James Audley, attacked from the side, completing the rout. Among the many famous French prisoners of the day was John II himself.

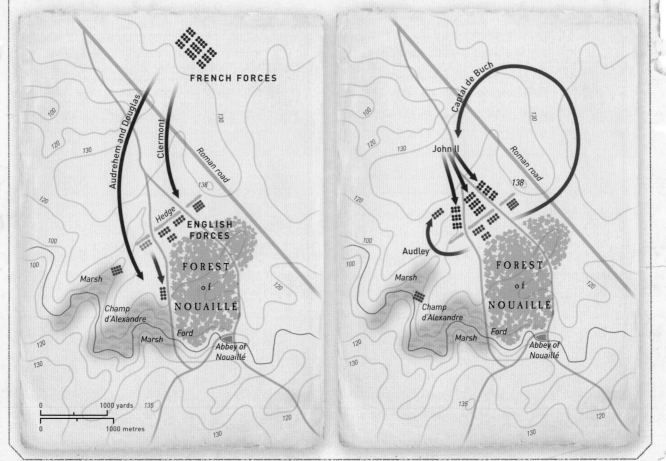

Decline and death

As after Poitiers, however, the Prince was unable to exploit his victory. In spite of an attempt to occupy territory in Castile as security for his claims, he was forced to return, bankrupt and ill, to Aquitaine. Henry of Trastámara himself barely escaped alive from the field of Nájera. Yet three years later, he had defeated and killed his rival, and permanently secured his possession of the Castilian throne. The financial claims of the Prince's Gascon followers, aggravated by his own lack of political finesse, ultimately led to a major rebellion against the Prince in Aquitaine which enabled Charles V of France to recover all the territory that France had lost in 1360. Weakened in body and mind, the Prince's one attempt to command his armies in person was the siege of the rebel city of Limoges in 1370. The siege became notorious for the massacre of the inhabitants that followed the successful assault, but had almost no impact on the inexorable advance of the French into his principality. The Prince returned a broken man to England at the end of 1371. He died at Westminster on 8 June 1376, a year before his father. Such was the prestige enjoyed by the profession of arms in the late Middle Ages, that no one recalled his political incompetence or questioned what his victories had really achieved. It was enough that the Prince had been physically impressive, courageous in the face of danger, and had won every battle that he had fought.

John II, king of France, surrenders to the Black Prince at the Battle of Poitiers, 1356, in a contemporary manuscript illumination. John was later imprisoned in various locations in England. After four years of ransom negotiations, at the Treaty of Brétigny in 1360 the French agreed to hand over no less than a third of the land of France in full sovereignty.

The Black Prince

'It is well seen that victory lies not in the multitude of people, but in the power of God.'

A LETTER TO HIS FATHER, AFTER HENRY HAD DEFEATED A MUCH LARGER
ARMY OF WELSH REBELS AT GROSMONT IN 1405, WHEN HE WAS 17 YEARS OLD

HENRY V

ROBERT HARDY

1387–1422

'"THOU LIEST, THOU LIEST, MY PORTION IS WITH THE LORD JESUS CHRIST!": the dying cry of one of the greatest commanders in the long history of English wars. He had been confronted in his sleep by a demon of doubt and fear that all he had achieved was evil, and damned him to Hell, in which he certainly believed. That cry had brought him upright in his bed; but then he lay back in his confessor's arms and a little later murmured "In manus tuas, Domine, ipsum terminum redimisti", and died "as if he slept".'

(THOMAS RYMER X. 253, *VITA HENRICI QUINTI, MONSTRELET*, ET AL.)

It was midnight, 20 August 1422, that Henry Plantagenet, King of England, heir of France, father of a baby boy who would be crowned King of France and England, died in the Château de Vincennes, outside Paris, a few weeks short of his thirty-fifth birthday; in another six weeks and a day he would have outlived his troubled and defeated rival, Charles VI of France, and become by solemn treaty inheritor of the crown of France.

Henry, Shakespeare's Hal – which let us call him for the moment – was born on 16 September 1387 in Monmouth Castle, the first surviving child of Henry Bolingbroke and grandson of John of Gaunt, Duke of Lancaster. The facts of his early upbringing are few. By the time he was 11, Hal's father had been banished by their cousin, King Richard II, partly because Bolingbroke had ousted some of the king's favourites, partly because of a dangerous quarrel with the Duke of Norfolk whom he accused of treachery, but also because his father was John of Gaunt, the king's uncle, whom Richard loathed and whose brother Gloucester the king had had murdered at Calais the year before. Hal was called to Court, as hostage for his father's good behaviour abroad, where Bolingbroke was now nursing his anger and planning revenge.

Gaunt died in 1399 and his absent son should have become Duke of Lancaster, but the king declared both title and lands forfeit to the Crown. Fortified with this extra money to pay his troops, Richard invaded Ireland, taking young Hal with him and dubbing him knight for a conspicuous piece of bravery during the abortive campaign.

Enraged by Richard's denial of his rights, Bolingbroke landed in England. The news reached the king in Ireland, who called Hal to him, and said, 'Henry, my boy, see

Henry V

what thy father hath done to me ... through these unhappy doings thou wilt perchance lose thine inheritance'. The 'doings' gathered pace and power; Bolingbroke said he had only come to claim his rights, but the speed of chance and events bore him faster and further than that, and in that same year, 1399, Richard was deposed, 'uncrowned' in Westminster Hall, and Bolingbroke became King Henry IV of England.

From the first Bolingbroke insisted his sons should succeed him, in a strong Lancastrian dynasty, so Hal, sent for by his father from Richard's side, though pleading his loyalty to Richard, met Henry at the Tower of London. Later, seated next to his father at the coronation, he was declared Prince of Wales, Duke of Cornwall, Earl of Chester, and soon afterwards, Duke of Aquitaine. In November he inherited the dukedom of Lancaster; he was heir to the throne a mere two months after his twelfth birthday.

But all was troubled, and Hal was in for a hard and insecure life. His father was a usurper; deposed Richard was in prison and shortly murdered at Henry's command; a growing number resented the usurpation. The new monarch was short of money, short of support beyond his rigidly controlled adherents, there was a threat of civil war and the Welsh were already in arms, with a new and splendid leader, Owain Glyndwr, who in September 1400 proclaimed himself Prince of Wales and invaded England. In October the king and Prince Hal led an army into Wales to meet him. As would happen so often in these wars, the Welsh melted away among the mountains. Hal was put in charge of his principality with a council of which another Henry, Henry Percy (called Harry Hotspur), son of the Earl of Northumberland, was the principal member. Hal became his friend, and learned from him much of military matters, though he soon began to have his own ideas of strategy and tactics in the field. He took from Hotspur much of the fierce courage of the older man, but not the reckless, dangerous bravura that cost Hotspur his life.

Hal wrote frequent despatches to his father, in precise forthright style, usually begging, often without result, for troops

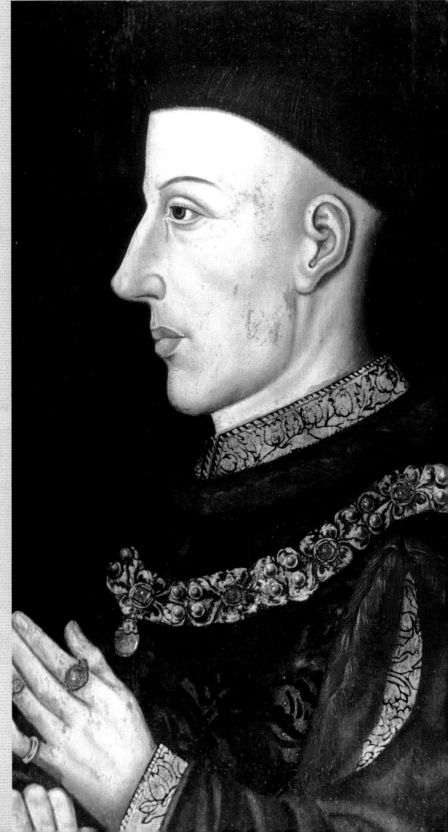

King Henry V, portrayed by a fifteenth- or sixteenth-century artist. Battlefield victories and strategic alliances so strengthened Henry's negotiating hand that, by the Treaty of Troyes (1420), he was made heir to the French throne.

A late fifteenth-century engraving of the Battle of Shrewsbury (1403), from the Beauchamp Pageant. Probably the most accurate representation of late medieval archers, it is well worth close study.

and money to pay them, having pawned all his own 'little jewels'. He witnessed all the horrors of war, the barbaric executions after battle. He did not shrink from it; 'War without fire', he once said, 'is like sausage without mustard.' He could be cruel, certainly to our eyes, but even the French, after his death, said he was 'ever just'.

Those battles were in March 1404. Two years before, Hotspur, returning north to repel a Scottish invasion, had a great victory, won entirely by his longbowmen. But this had led to a profound dispute between the Percies of Northumberland and the king, the several reasons for which led to a massive rebellion which came to a head in 1403.

Hal, as commander in chief of the forces on the Welsh border, was at Shrewsbury. Hotspur marched south, on his way gathering large forces from counties still loyal to Richard's memory. He aimed to capture the prince before aid could reach him, but the king, hearing the news at Nottingham on 12 July, by remarkable forced marches arrived just before the rebels, so that when Hotspur and his uncle Worcester caught sight of the walls of Shrewsbury on 20 July, they saw the royal standard flying beside the prince's above the castle. The rebels' hope had been to join with Glyndwr's forces before any battle, but the Welsh prince was far distant at a siege and never arrived.

Hotspur chose his ground well, a long, south-facing slope 2 miles north of the town, ideal for his archers looking down on the enemy below. Henry's army, approaching from the southeast, had to be content with the low ground. The battle was the first fearsome fight between two armies with equal numbers of skilled longbowmen, and a grim encounter it was, a foretaste of the horrors to come in the War of the Roses.

Early on, Hal, in command of the royal left wing, was wounded in the face by a rebel arrow; his companions tried to persuade him to leave the field, but he would not, and went on to alter the balance of the battle, which was going badly for the king. Moving his wing round Hotspur's right, Hal outflanked him, bringing on the final mêlée in which Hotspur was killed, possibly by an arrow in the face, or more likely struck down in the thick of battle in his last desperate charge at the king.

Shrewsbury Field must have been a grievous one for Hal; he was 14, he had been a leader of those forces that caused the death of his friend and old tutor, Henry Percy, and he was badly wounded. His courage in refusing to leave the field is the more extraordinary when you hear the extent of the wound from the surgeon, John Bradmore, who operated on him days later in Kenilworth Castle; his royal patient 'was struck by an arrow next to his nose on the left side … the which entered at an angle, and … the head of the arrow remained in the furthermost part of the bone of the skull for a depth of six inches.'

The manner of a prince

So what did this calmly determined, strange young man look like? A monk of Westminster with frequent opportunity to observe him tells us that his limbs were well-formed, his bones and sinews firmly knit together, he had a broad forehead, a spherical cranium, brown hair, cut short all round, above the ear (for ease in a hot helmet), with a straight nose, eyes bright, large and hazel, teeth 'even and white' and his chin 'divided'.

Maître Jean Fusoris, an eminent French savant who came with the last French embassy before the war of 1415, saw Henry at Winchester and said that though he had the manner of a prince, he seemed more like a priest, less a soldier than his brother, the Duke of Clarence. This was a misjudgement of real character. Clarence was a sort of Hotspur soldier, later killed in a rash attack, Henry a superb and meticulous planner, strategist and tactician. He treated all men equally, with courteous affability but never wasting words; to any who failed him he was ice and fire.

> 'Night and Day, in storm and calm alike, he went the rounds of the camps ... with sleepless energy.'
>
> TITUS LIVIUS 63, VITA 188

We must leap over the years of Hal's well-substantiated wildness when not engaged in Wales; the years when he rose to power, with his own allies, a power often exercised against his father's rule, which became so dangerous to the king's government that he was dismissed from the Council; the prince's virtual rule of England during his father's illness, the quarrels between father and son; the king's death; these must fly past, until we see that an astonishing transformation came over him on his accession as Henry V in 1413. He now prepared to put the kingdom in order, dealing with those disloyal to his father either by stern action or by restoration of deprived lands and titles on condition of loyalty to himself.

Preparing for war

In 1414 Henry demanded from France the restoration of all lands granted to his great-grandfather, King Edward III at the Treaty of Brétigny in 1360, following the English victories of Crécy in 1346 and Poitiers in 1356, and soon pushed further: he claimed, like Edward, his right to the throne of France. If any Englishman could make such a claim, it was Edward, Earl of March, through Edward III's mother, the daughter of King Philip IV of France. But Henry was a visionary. He was destined, he believed, to unite the warring factions in France, the Burgundians and Armagnacs, unite all Christendom under one pope as a defence against the Infidel, and finally unite the armies of all Europe to recapture Jerusalem. It was even a possibility. France's king was mad a good deal of the time, religious and dynastic divisions were tearing the country apart; there were two, at one time three, popes; now Henry must step in and make an empire under his rule.

There was much diplomatic activity, spying, promising and reneging until a gross insult by the Dauphin, accompanied by a gift of tennis balls, as appropriate to his youth, offered an excuse for Henry to declare himself at war with France.

Henry V

Immense preparations were made under Henry's supervision, backed by a nobility hungry for conquest and honour, and a country with a newfound sense of itself and a feeling of patriotic confidence. Soldiers by thousands, weapons of war in vast quantities, tens of thousands of yew longbows, millions of arrows, ships built or impressed, guns such as never seen before, men and still more men for all the tasks of war; and in July and August 1415, a massive army moved towards Southampton, to await the fleet there.

All was ready, the king was in Southampton, when suddenly the Earl of March, the rather fearful claimant to the throne, revealed to Henry a plot to kill the king and install March in his place. Henry acted fast: the ringleaders were arrested, summarily tried, and executed. That done, fair stood the wind for France. On Sunday 11 August 1415 the ships of the expedition moved into Southampton Water. One ship caught fire, which spread to two others alongside, probably started either by French spies, or remnants of the late plot. The joyous mood fell at this omen. Henry made much of the better augury of a group of swans among the ships. Then trumpets blew, the sails unfurled, and a fleet of ships bearing some 2,500 men at arms and lances, 8,000 archers, horses, grooms, varlets, cooks, esquires, and the king, set sail for the open sea; their secret destination Harfleur, on the coast of Normandy.

Two days later, in the afternoon of 13 August, the armada sailed into the estuary of the Seine and anchored off the Chef de Caux, which the soldiers christened 'Kidcocks'. The next morning, after a reconnaissance, the landing commenced. There was no sign of French resistance, though from the shore to the city of Harfleur defensive ditches and dykes had been built. By Saturday 17 August the unloading was complete and the advance began towards the city, over the marshes and mudflats in broiling weather. The king sent a message through the ranks: 'fellows be of good cheer; breathe you and cool you and come up with your ease, for with the love of God we shall have good tidings.'

Henry kept strict control of his army; there was to be no looting, no mistreatment of the inhabitants; women, priests and churches were to suffer no harm, and army discipline was severe – all on pain of punishment, even death. Though some French talked later of devastation, others admitted that French armies behaved far worse. By Sunday night, 18 August, the city was encircled. Henry was to prove from then until his death in 1422 that he was a Caesar in siege warfare, and after one great battle whose name resounds today, most of his campaigns in France were a series of sieges, planned with meticulous care, with a Caesarian eye for detail and the morale of his men.

The surrender of Harfleur

The city did not surrender until 22 September, when its leaders, with ropes around their necks, were received by Henry, who was clad in cloth of gold, and seated on a throne. Henry entered the city barefoot, went to the church and gave thanks to God who had delivered Harfleur 'to its rightful owner'. The question was, what next? His army was depleted by casualties, disease and desertions, and a fleet with relief forces had been scattered by a storm. Should he march on Paris? Return home to raise more money and troops? His Council advised return to England; the siege had taken too long, the season was late, the weather turning bad. Yet Henry's belief in his own destiny put aside all argument. He would march north to Calais, by treaty an English town, and show his banner through France. Some say it was a retreat, but as Winston Churchill and others have contended, 'his decision shows his design was to tempt the enemy to battle'. Henry said, 'We will go, if it please God, without harm or danger, and if they disturb us on our journey we shall come off with victory, triumph and very great fame.'

On 8 October the army marched north, with eight days' rations. It was a dreadful march in foul weather, denied by the French any crossing of the Somme, having to march inland to find an unguarded ford, kept going by the will and determination of a leader who somehow maintained the spirits and discipline of his men. At last they reached two fords, at Voyennes and Bethencourt, where Henry himself supervised the crossing.

On 20 October he let the army rest and rode ahead, to be met by a French party, whose leaders 'inform thee that before thou comest to Calais they will make thee to fight with them'. Henry replied calmly, 'without his face changing colour', that he would march straight to Calais. They moved on, dogged now by the French, and sixteen days after leaving Harfleur, on 24 October, crossed their last river, the little Ternoise at Blangy, soaked, cold, hungry and exhausted.

Preparing for battle

Henry was called to the advance guard at the top of the slope beyond the river. He saw the French, as his chaplain described it, 'in compact masses, battles and columns, their numbers not comparable to ours … they took up a position facing us, a little more than half a mile to our right … and there was only a little valley, not so very wide between us.' The valley can be seen today, to the right of the Calais road, not a mile above the river. Here Henry

> very calmly and quite heedless of danger, gave encouragement to his army, drawing them up in their battles and wings to go at once into action … then the enemy withdrew to the far side of a certain wood, and our king believing they would either circle it and attack us by surprise, or else move behind woods in the distance and completely encircle us, immediately moved his lines again, always positioning them so that they faced the enemy.

But the light was gone. In the dark, in incessant rain, Henry quartered his army in and around the tiny village of Maisoncelles. Whether, as Shakespeare has it, he went among his men we do not know, but it was his constant practice. He forbade the army to make any noise, and in their silence they could hear the French camp half a mile away.

The Battle of Agincourt

Before dawn on 25 October Henry was up and armed; he heard three masses, then with his captains drew up his army, men-at-arms four deep in a single line, divided in three battalions; his longbowmen, five times more numerous, were grouped between the battalions and thrust forward on the wings of the army, and probably deployed across the front of the host, but able to withdraw among the armed men when the armies clashed. Before their main groups, archers hammered stakes into the ground, their sharpened points chest high to horses.

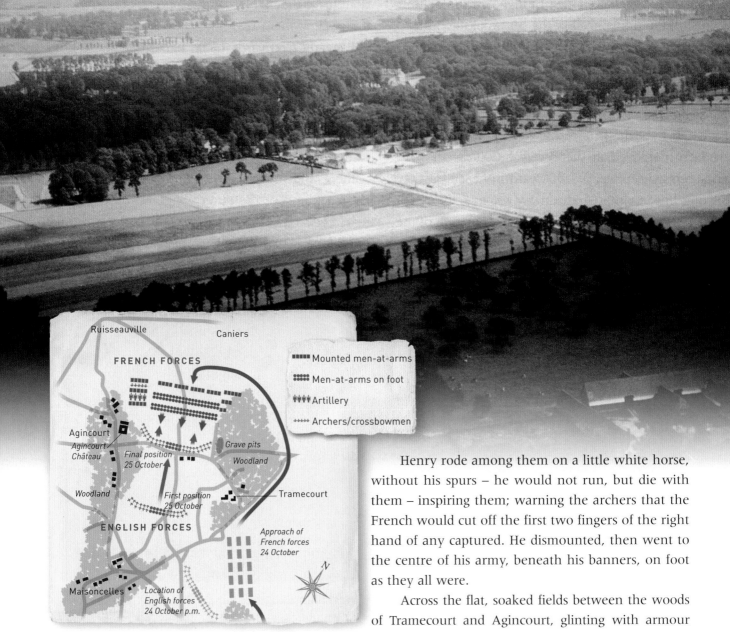

Ruisseauville   Caniers

FRENCH FORCES

▦▦▦ Mounted men-at-arms
▩▩▩ Men-at-arms on foot
⩚⩚⩚ Artillery
┉┉┉ Archers/crossbowmen

Agincourt
Agincourt
Château
Final position
25 October

Grave pits
Woodland

Woodland
First position
25 October
Tramecourt

ENGLISH FORCES

Approach of
French forces
24 October

N

Maisoncelles
Location of
English forces
24 October p.m.

(Top) The author's aerial photograph of the battlefield of Agincourt (1975). Though the woods on either side are much thinned since 1415, the bottleneck into which the French advanced, from the left (NW), can still be clearly seen. The village of Agincourt is just below the picture, the line of trees squares the site of the castle, and the clump of trees at the upper left marks the massive grave pits.

Henry rode among them on a little white horse, without his spurs – he would not run, but die with them – inspiring them; warning the archers that the French would cut off the first two fingers of the right hand of any captured. He dismounted, then went to the centre of his army, beneath his banners, on foot as they all were.

Across the flat, soaked fields between the woods of Tramecourt and Agincourt, glinting with armour and weapons, bright with banners, was the massed French host. Yet nothing happened.

The only movements among the crowds of French were to do with breakfast, and arguments about positions; their archers and crossbowmen and gunners were being pushed to the back. Henry could not stay still; his army would starve. He ordered the archers to pull up their stakes, and the whole force to advance. They trudged through the mud, stopping several times to maintain formation. Within bowshot of the French – 250–300 yards – they halted. Henry watched for any movement from the enemy while so many of his men had their backs to them, as they drove in their stakes again, and then re-formed. The marshal of the army, Sir Thomas Erpingham, hurled his baton into the air; the army gave wild shouts, and five or six thousand archers let fly into the French.

This stinging, murderous cloud of arrows forced the French to attack, first with cavalry on the wings, ploughing through thick mud, aiming to roll up the wing archers; they came slowly, floundering into the stakes, and as they laboured, the archers shot and shot, wounding and killing until the maddened horses that still lived, arrows wagging in their wounds, turned back, and crashed into their crowded vanguard, pushing forward

Henry V

on foot. Disorder made the crowding worse, but they came on, the narrowing woods pressing them inwards, heads down against the rattling arrows, until their vast weight of numbers hit the English and drove them back. But Henry's line held, and held; he was in the thickest of it; the archers, now too close to shoot, threw bows behind them and joined the men-at-arms, with swords and battle hammers, killing without pause, until great heaps of dead and wounded French were piling in the mud, on which the archers climbed, dinging, thrusting, slashing at those below, who, pressing up behind the French front ranks, forced an ever tighter pack, unable to use their weapons freely, endless victims of their hacking enemy.

The French were surrendering in droves and, pushed behind the English line, stood, numbed by defeat. Word suddenly came that the French rear was mounting a fresh attack; the English baggage had been raided, its treasure stolen, unarmed people killed. Henry saw a fearful danger: hundreds of French captives could pick up weapons that strewed the ground and attack his rear. He ordered that the prisoners be killed; many were, until it was clear there would be no more fighting. To us, an infinite cruelty, to contemporaries, in England and in France, merely logical. The battle was over by about two o'clock, and Henry named it after the nearest little castle – Agincourt. It was a long way from Monmouth.

It was a victory of discipline and calm, fearless command, which Henry continued to exercise for seven successful years of campaigning in France, and organization at home. What would have happened if he had lived another twenty years? That fine medieval historian Bruce MacFarlane said of him: 'Take him all round he was, I think, the greatest man who ever ruled England.'

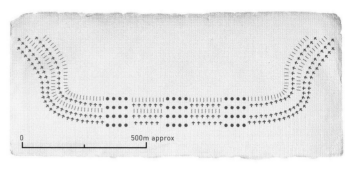

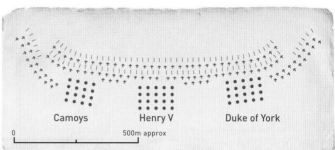

Camoys   Henry V   Duke of York

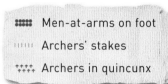

■■■■ Men-at-arms on foot

ııııı Archers' stakes

ʇʇʇʇ Archers in quincunx

TWO POSSIBLE PLANS of the Anglo-Welsh army at Agincourt, with which the author tries to interpret contemporary accounts and practical likelihood.

The Battle of Agincourt, in an illumination from *Les Vigiles de Charles VII*, a chronicle of France's wars with England by the fifteenth-century French poet Martial d'Auvergne.

'I am a commander of war ... sent here by God, the king of Heaven, to drive you all out of France.'

LETTER FROM JOAN TO THE ENGLISH, 22 MARCH 1429

JOAN OF ARC

c. 1412–31

ANNE CURRY

JOAN OF ARC IS UNIQUE. In this collection of great commanders she is the only woman, and one of only two saints. These characteristics suggest that there is something very special – if not odd – about Joan as a military leader. She was not canonized because of her role in saving France from English rule, of course, but her achievements in that context are substantial. After raising the siege of Orléans in early May 1429 and defeating the English at the Battle of Patay on 18 June in the same year, she then led the Dauphin Charles to his coronation at Reims on 17 July and to the reconquest of many towns previously held by the English and their Burgundian allies, until her capture by the latter at Compiègne in May 1430.

That she was not made a saint until 1920, almost four hundred years after her condemnation for heresy and her burning at the stake in Rouen on 30 May 1431, demonstrates that Joan was as controversial in death as in life. After all, few whom the Roman Catholic Church has condemned as heretics have been made saints by that self-same body.

Joan's military career was fleeting, yet we know more about her than her gender and social status might have predicted. She speaks to us directly in response to questions at her trial in 1431 (the *procès de condemnation*), the procedure and outcome of which were nullified at a second trial in 1456 (the *procès de nullification*, later called 'the Rehabilitation') at which no fewer than 115 of those who had known her gave testimony. These witnesses included childhood friends as well as companions-in-arms and the commanders of the French army. At a time when 'women were excluded from the deeds of men', as one late fourteenth-century military treatise put it, she was a phenomenon: not surprisingly, then, her deeds were recorded in chronicles, letters and governmental records. Even so, it remains difficult to 'explain' Joan. Much ink has been spilled in attempts to do so, but we need to strip back the accretions of later centuries to find the real Joan and to understand her place as a military leader.

Joan the woman

We do not know when Joan was born. When asked at her trial, she replied that 'as far as she knew, she was around 19 years old'. At the time that she relieved Orléans in 1429, therefore, she was no more than 17. Although there are examples of those who were military commanders at an early age, these are men of royal or noble status whose birth committed them to leadership. Joan was of humble birth. Admittedly her family were not impoverished: they were middling farmers, and an uncle had entered the priesthood. Joan's father was the *doyen* or sergeant of Domrémy (now in the

la pucelle

An illustration from a late fifteenth-century manuscript, which combines the impression of Joan as a simple shepherdess with that of a warrior. She is dressed in women's clothes but provided with a sword, a halberd and spurs, and extends her hand as if directing events.

département of Vosges), responsible for representing his fellow villagers and for assisting in the collection of the taxes they owed to the Crown. After her military successes Joan remembered not only her family – two brothers who served alongside her were elevated to noble status on 25 December 1429 – but also her community. Two weeks after his coronation on 17 July 1429, Charles VII removed Domrémy's tax liability 'in honour of and at the request of Joan La Pucelle considering the great and profitable service which she has done and does each day'. For each year until the French Revolution, the tax registers record simply '*néant* (nothing) – La Pucelle'.

Joan appears to have been an ordinary village girl in upbringing and interests. Asked during her trial if in her youth she had learned a craft, she said 'yes, to sew linen and to spin', and she 'did not fear any woman in Rouen when it came to sewing and spinning'. Here is a brief glimpse of the bravado and self-confidence that assisted her

Joan at the court of Charles VII in an illumination from *Les Vigiles de Charles VII* (1484) by Martial d'Auvergne. The image is thought to represent her reception at court after her success at Orléans rather than at her initial meeting with the king. Her soldiers wait expectantly at the door as she addresses him.

later military command. As she herself explained, her 'voices' had told her that she should leave home and come to the French king to save the kingdom. A witness in the Rehabilitation said that Joan first approached Robert de Baudricourt, her local lord and captain of Vaucouleurs, in May 1428, but he sent her packing. Two months later, her patriotism, and her determination to serve, were heightened when she and her family were forced by incursions of Burgundian soldiers to flee their village and take temporary refuge in the nearest town, Neufchâteau. When the siege of Orléans, laid by the English in October 1428 as a major push into the Dauphin's territory south of the Loire, dragged on into the New Year, her voices spoke of a more specific intention: she would raise the siege. De Baudricourt was finally persuaded, and provided a sword, horse and escort as she set out for the Dauphin's court in Chinon on 22 February 1429. It was at this point that she adopted male clothing and cut her hair short.

The making of Joan the warrior

Joan had no experience of war, and no experience of leadership. She was, like all women of the day, excluded both in theory and practice from the world of the warrior. How, then, did she become a commander at all? The answer must be found not only in the military and political context but also in contemporary religious sensibilities. The English had suffered a setback at the start of the siege of Orléans with the death of their commander, Thomas, Earl of Salisbury, who was an early victim of gunshot. They had strained their resources to keep an army surrounding the city over the winter, but thanks to Sir John Fastolf's victory at the 'Battle of the Herrings' near Rouvray on 12 February, they managed to bring in much-needed supplies to continue the siege. Faced with this situation, the Dauphin's advisors looked for other solutions.

Joan of Arc

An embassy under Poton de Xaintrailles (one of Joan's later companions) was sent from Orléans to the Duke of Burgundy, trying to persuade him to drop his alliance with the English in return for a power-sharing arrangement with the Dauphin. Nothing came of this, but shortly afterwards a dispute between the duke and his allies prompted him to withdraw his troops. The moment was therefore ripe for a French attempt to raise the siege.

Arriving in Chinon on 4 March 1429, and meeting the Dauphin two days later, Joan had appeared at exactly the right time. This may not be coincidence. Charles was known to be fascinated with signs and predictions. Historians have suggested that Joan was put forward by one of the factions at court, the Angevins, who were related to his wife, Marie of Anjou. We know that before Joan's last interview with de Baudricourt she had visited the Duke of Lorraine, father-in-law of Duke René of Anjou, asking him to persuade his son-in-law to give armed support. When Joan arrived at the Dauphin's court, the other factions were not impressed with her, but Charles was soon in her thrall. All that was needed was proof of her virginity: a brief physical examination carried out by his mother-in-law reassured him. He decreed that Joan should be allowed to go to raise the siege, 'to show a sign of divine approval before Orléans'.

Whilst an army of several thousand was gathered under the Count of Dunois, Joan prepared herself – and was also coached – for her intended role. She had told her voices that 'she was a poor girl who did not know how to ride on horseback or lead in war'. Yet by 22 April, the Lord of Roteslar could write that 'the Pucelle every day rides on horseback, armed with a lance in battle, as all the other armed men guarding the king are accustomed to doing'. The Duke of Alençon, himself a patron of astrologers and one of Joan's main supporters, also reported in 1456 that he had seen her at Chinon riding before him with a lance, and was so impressed by her skills that he gave her a horse. Unless Joan had been practising in Domrémy (which is highly improbable given medieval gender expectations), we can envisage a crash course in basic military training where she proved an eager, if not star, pupil. 'Designer armour' was provided by the king. That Joan was new to wearing it may be suggested by the observation of one of her companions-in-arms in 1456 that she was very bruised on her arrival at Orléans because she had slept fully armed the night before. An 'Excalibur' was found for her, somewhat predictably, perhaps, buried behind the altar at the church of St Catherine de Fierbois on 2 April. But in Joan's own words, she loved her standard forty times more than her sword. It bore 'the image of our saviour sitting in judgement on the clouds of heaven … an angel holding in his hands a fleur-de-lys which the image of Christ was blessing', alongside the names 'Jesus Maria'. The standard was a symbol of Joan's purpose as a spiritual as well as military leader. As she herself said at her trial, she 'carried her standard to avoid killing

The earliest known attempt to portray Joan is this doodle in the margin of the Register of the Parlement of Paris, an institution at that time dominated by the English and their Burgundian allies. It is placed against the entry for 10 May 1429 which noted her success at Orléans.

Joan of Arc

359

THE SIEGE OF ORLÉANS

BY THE TIME JOAN ARRIVED at Orléans in April 1429, the English-laid siege, now in its seventh month, was flagging. The city was too large and well defended to surround completely. Burgundian troops had already been withdrawn. The English army was distributed in a series of specially constructed temporary fortresses. They were particularly weak on the eastern side. At the Rehabilitation, the crossing of Joan and her men to the north bank of the Loire was ascribed to a miracle, in which God responded to her prayers that the wind change direction to help them to sail across the river. In reality, it was more likely the *sortie* of the defenders of Orléans against the English at the outwork of Saint Loup, launched once they heard of the imminent approach of French troops and supplies, that enabled Joan to enter the city on 29 April. According to Dunois' testimony in 1456, she was furious that there had not been immediate engagement with the English. Indeed, there is evidence to suggest that Dunois was initially hostile to her involvement in the proposed action. How could she fulfil her mission if he would not allow her to fight?

In the early days of May, Joan harried the English with religious invective, targeting particularly William Glasdale and his men, who were defending Les Tourelles, the southernmost defence of the bridge over the Loire. She also rallied support within the city

itself as well as reconnoitring the English defences. Meanwhile, Dunois sought reinforcements at Blois. Once achieved, Saint Loup could be captured on 4 May. Two days later, Augustins was captured. This assault was Joan's first experience of action and it was exhausting and costly. But she urged that the next day, on 8 May, an attack should be launched on Les Tourelles. She was wounded by an arrow 'which penetrated her flesh between her neck and her shoulder for a depth of half a foot', as Dunois later recalled. The fight went on almost all day and Dunois advised withdrawal. But Joan asked

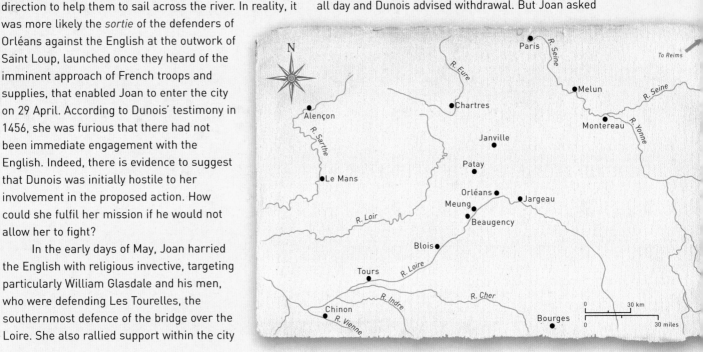

anyone'. In all of her successful engagements, her presence with this standard – its image created to show God's approval for the French cause and for Joan herself – was vital. Time after time, in chronicles and in the testimonies of 1456, we are told that French soldiers were hesitant and anxious until she appeared with her standard and encouraged them to advance, in the name of God as much as of the French king.

Through Joan, the rescue of Orléans (see above), and the war against the English as a whole, was made a religious as much as a military mission. The intention was made clear in a letter dictated by Joan on 22 March urging the English to surrender not simply the city but all their conquests. It was not couched in the standard terms of a commander but in those of an impassioned teenager and fervent believer:

> *God will send greater strength to the Pucelle, both to her and her good men-at-arms than you English could overwhelm in all your assaults. The one who has greater right from God in heaven will be revealed by this exchange of blows.*

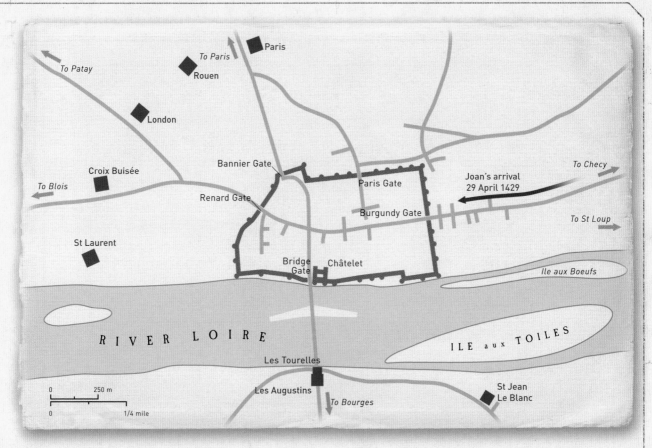

him to wait until she had prayed. Returning, 'she took her standard in her hands and placed it on the side of the ditch, and instantly, once she was there, the English became afraid and trembled, and the soldiers of the king regained their confidence and began to climb up'. According to her own testimony, she was the first to put her ladder against the wall. After hard hand-to-hand fighting, the English were defeated. Those in the remaining defences chose to withdraw from the siege. Orléans had been saved. For the next two days, its streets resounded with cheering for Joan and her troops, and its churches with prayers of thanksgiving.

Although Charles did not give her formal command, his captains were subordinated to her because, as one contemporary observer put it, 'counsel from God supersedes any judgement from a military council'. When the advance guard set off for Orléans she had priests walk ahead singing *'veni creator spiritus'* ('come, holy spirit').

From success to failure

Despite her success at Orléans, Joan could not continue her action against the English without more men. Once reinforcements arrived, she moved against the other English-held strongholds on the Loire since until the whole area was secured and the enemy driven back towards Normandy, it was dangerous for the Dauphin to attempt a move to Reims for coronation. What is clear, however, is that Joan's success at Orléans boosted confidence in her and her mission. Troops rallied to her support, and in their turn the English were afraid to offer resistance. We can only imagine the psychological effect of Joan's presence on the English. She was linked to the worst military disaster they had faced since their king, Henry V, had reopened the war in 1415, thereby putting into their minds the notion that God had deserted their cause for that of the French. Joan was now joined by the Duke of Alençon, who proved the most enduring of her supporters. At the Rehabilitation he told how some of the French captains, despite the success at Orléans, were reluctant to chance an attack on Jargeau because of the strength of the English garrison, and that it had been Joan who had persuaded them that all would go well because 'God was conducting their work'. In fact, it seems to have been French artillery that softened the town enough to allow an assault. Other successes followed at Beaugency and Meung-sur-Loire, and advance was begun towards Reims. The French constable, Arthur de Richemont, then arrived with more troops, making it possible to confront the English at Patay. Joan's role here is uncertain, a reflection, perhaps, that her limited military skills were adequate for encouraging soldiers in a siege but not for pitched battle.

'She is supreme captain of our brave and able men. Neither Hector nor Achilles had such strength.'

CHRISTINE DE PISAN, 'LA DITIÉ DE JEANNE D'ARC', 31 JULY 1429; A POEM WHICH IS ONE OF THE EARLIEST CELEBRATIONS OF JOAN'S SUCCESSES

Joan continued to regard the war as a religious mission. As she wrote to the inhabitants of Troyes on 4 July, 'Joan the Maid commands you on behalf of the King of Heaven our rightful and sovereign lord in whose royal service she serves each day, that you should obey and recognize the gracious king of France'. But opposition to her within the French command was increasing even before the entry into Reims and the coronation of the Dauphin as Charles VII on 17 July.

Joan of Arc

Although at the crowning she stood by his side carrying her banner, the anointing of the king transformed him into God's chosen one as well as the supreme military commander. From that point onwards, Joan was surplus to requirements. Whilst she lobbied for the continuation of the war, Charles preferred a political solution through negotiations with the Duke of Burgundy. He also refused to heed her increasingly desperate urgings to move quickly against the English in Paris. She was determined to take the city, but underestimated how difficult this would be. If Orléans could not be taken by siege, there was little chance Paris could be, and the English had drawn back into it many of their troops from the Loire valley and Normandy as well as bringing a new expeditionary force from England. On 8 September she launched a

premature attack against the St Honoré gate to the west of the city. Struck by a crossbow bolt, she urged her men on, but this time, unlike the action at Les Tourelles, her men were disheartened by her wounding and withdrew. Within a few days the king ordered the attacks to cease, and brought his army back to the Loire, discharging the Duke of Alençon. Joan's enemies had triumphed. The king no longer had confidence in her: she had prophesied that he would enter Paris, but her predictions had proved untrue.

Joan of Arc at the stake, 30 May 1431, in an illumination from *Les Vigiles de Charles VII* (1484) by Martial d'Auvergne. Although Joan recanted her heresy and was sentenced to perpetual imprisonment, a few days later she relapsed and was handed over by the church to the English authorities for burning in the Vieux Marché at Rouen. The site is now marked by a church.

Joan fought on in the upper Loire, but now with what were little more than mercenary companies and without much role in command. Although Saint-Pierre-le-Moutier was taken, the king refused to send more men or supplies to continue the advance, so that her attempt shortly before Christmas 1429 to besiege La Charité-sur-Loire failed. It is unlikely that after this point she was ever in the royal presence again. The remainder of her career saw further failure. She rushed to the defence of Compiègne when she learned that the Burgundians had defaulted on their rapprochement with King Charles and were preparing to lay siege to the town. She arrived in time to enter the town, but on the very next day, 23 May 1430, she led an ill-advised sortie in which she was captured. There is even some suggestion that she was betrayed by the French captain of Compiègne, Guillaume de Flavy, who, according to the chronicler, Perceval de Cagny, 'had the bridge raised and the gate shut' so that she could not return to the town. A few days later, the University of Paris demanded that she be handed over to the Inquisition. Sold to the English in November, she was taken to Rouen just before Christmas 1430. The preliminaries of her trial for heresy began in early January, with Joan being presented to the court on 21 February. Her last battle began, not against soldiers and fortifications, but against theologians. As an uneducated woman, and a woman who had usurped a male role, this was a battle she had no chance of winning. Yet she remained steadfast in her support for her king. Intriguingly, at her trial she denied that she had called herself a 'commander of war' in the letter sent to the English before her arrival at Orléans, but she never denied her belief that she had acted in God's name. Her war was a religious mission. As much as serving the king of France, Joan of Arc, the maid of Orléans, saw herself as serving the king of Heaven.

'The spider weaves the curtains in the palace of the Caesars;
The owl calls the watches in the towers of Afrasiab.'

LINES FROM A PERSIAN POET, MURMURED BY THE SULTAN IN THE IMPERIAL PALACE ON THE DAY OF THE FALL OF CONSTANTINOPLE

SULTAN MEHMET II
1433–81

JOHN JULIUS NORWICH

SULTAN MEHMET II – always known to modern Turks as *Fatih*, the Conqueror – changed the course of history. In May 1453, after a furious siege of fifty-five days, he and his army smashed their way through the great land walls of Constantinople, captured the city and so put an end to the Byzantine Empire. That empire had lasted for 1,123 years, a period of time comfortably longer than that which separates us from the Norman Conquest; and as it was essentially only a continuation of the old Roman Empire, Mehmet could be said to have destroyed that also. It was an astonishing achievement for a young man not yet 22 years old.

The Ottoman sultan Mehmet II ('the Conqueror'), as portrayed by the Venetian artist Gentile Bellini (1429–1507). The portait hangs in the National Gallery in London.

Few people in Europe knew much about the inscrutable young prince who had recently succeeded to the throne of the Ottoman Turks. Born in 1433, Mehmet – the name is the Turkish form of Muhammad – was the third son of Sultan Murad II. He had had an unhappy childhood. His father had made no secret of his preference for his two elder half-brothers Ahmet and Ali, both children of well-born mothers, whereas Mehmet's own mother had been a mere slave-girl in the harem and probably – though we cannot be sure – a Christian to boot. At the age of 2 he had been taken from his birthplace at Adrianople (the modern Edirne, on the present Turkish–Bulgarian frontier) to Amasa, a province in northern Anatolia of which his 14-year-old brother was governor; but Ahmet had died only four years later and Mehmet, now aged 6, had succeeded him.

Then, in 1444, Ali was found strangled in his bed, in circumstances still mysterious. Mehmet, now heir to the throne, was summoned back urgently to the capital, now at Adrianople. Hitherto his education had been largely neglected; suddenly he found himself in the care of the greatest scholars of their day and with them, over the next few years, laid the foundations of the learning and culture for which he was soon to be famous. At the time of his succession he is said to have been fluent not only in his native Turkish but in Arabic, Greek, Latin, Persian and Hebrew.

'But,' wrote Edward Gibbon, 'it cannot be denied that his passions were at once furious and inexorable; that in the palace, as in the field, a torrent of blood was spilt on the slightest provocation; and that the noblest of the captive youth were often

Sultan Mehmet II

dishonoured by his unnatural lust.' Twice, in the last six years of his life, Sultan Murad had abdicated in favour of his son; twice – knowing these faults all too well – his Grand Vizir Halil Pasha had persuaded him to continue. After Murad's second reluctant return to power he gave up all thoughts of retirement and settled down again in Adrianople, banishing his son to Magnesia in Anatolia; and it was there that news was brought to Mehmet that his father had died, on 13 February 1451, of an apoplectic seizure.

The young sultan

It took Mehmet just five days to travel from Magnesia to Adrianople, where he held a formal reception at which he confirmed his father's ministers in their places or, in certain cases, refused to do so. At this time Murad's widow arrived to congratulate him on his accession. He received her warmly and engaged her for some time in conversation; when she returned to the harem it was to find that her infant son had been murdered in his bath. The young sultan, it seemed, was not one to take chances.

Some days later there arrived an embassy bringing congratulations from the Byzantine emperor Constantine XI. To this Mehmet is said to have replied almost too fulsomely, swearing by Allah and the Prophet to live at peace with the emperor and his people. Perhaps it was this that put Constantine on his guard; immediately he began to strengthen the city's defences. He seems to have been one of the first to sense that the sultan was not all that he appeared – that, potentially, he was very dangerous indeed.

All too soon, the emperor's suspicions were confirmed. By autumn, Mehmet had decided to build a great castle on the Bosphorus, at the point where the channel was at its narrowest. Another castle, built by his great grandfather Bayezit I, already stood on the Asiatic side; with the two opposite each other he would have complete control of the strait. There was one small technical objection to the plan: the land on which his castle was to be built was Byzantine. But this he ignored. All that winter he collected his workforce, with a thousand professional stonemasons. In the early spring all the churches and monasteries in the neighbourhood were demolished to provide additional materials, and on Saturday, 11 April 1452, the building operations began.

**EASTERN THRACE AND
THE BOSPHORUS** in the
mid fifteenth century.

The castle of Rumeli Hisar still stands, essentially unchanged since the day it was completed – Thursday, 31 August – just beyond the village of Bebek. It is hard to believe that its construction took, from start to finish, only nineteen and a half weeks. When it was ready the sultan mounted three huge cannon on the tower and decreed that every passing ship, whatever its nationality, must stop for examination. That November a Venetian ship failed to obey. It was blasted out of the water; the crew were all executed, the captain impaled on a stake and publicly exposed as a warning to anyone else who might think of following his example.

The preliminaries

The Ottoman fleet assembled off Gallipoli in March 1453. It seems to have comprised no fewer than six triremes and ten biremes – vessels with respectively three and two rowers per oar – fifteen oared galleys, some seventy-five fast longboats, twenty sailing-barges for transport and a number of light sloops and cutters. A week or two later it made its way slowly across the little inland Sea of Marmara, to drop anchor beneath the walls of Constantinople.

Sultan Mehmet II

367

The army, meanwhile, was gathering in Thrace. Turkish sources suggest it comprised some eighty thousand regular troops and up to twenty thousand irregulars, or *bashi-bazouks*. Included in the former category were about twelve thousand Janissaries. Though legally slaves, these elite troops had been recruited as children from Christian families, forcibly converted to Islam and subjected to rigorous military training. Mehmet was proud of both his army and his navy; but he was proudest of all of his cannon. Cannon, in its primitive form, had been used for a century or more; but it was not until 1452 that a German engineer named Urban sought an audience with the sultan and offered to build him a weapon that would blast the walls of Babylon itself.

This was just what Mehmet had been waiting for. He gave Urban four times his requested salary, and was rewarded only three months later by the fearsome monster at Rumeli Hisar that had accounted for the Venetian ship. He then demanded another, twice the size of the first. This was completed in January 1453. It is said to have been 27 feet long, with a barrel 2½ feet in diameter. The bronze was 8 inches thick. When it was tested, a ball weighing 1,340 pounds hurtled through the air for well over a mile before burying itself 6 feet deep in the ground. Two hundred men were sent out to prepare for its journey to Constantinople, smoothing the road and reinforcing the bridges; and at the beginning of March it set off, drawn by thirty pairs of oxen, with a further two hundred men to hold it steady.

On 5 April the sultan joined his army before the walls of the city. Under a flag of truce, he at once sent the emperor the message that was required under Islamic law, undertaking that he and all his subjects would be spared, with their property, if they made immediate and voluntary surrender. If on the other hand they refused, they would be given no quarter. As expected, he received no reply. Early in the morning of Friday, 6 April his cannon opened fire.

The defenders

To defend Constantinople and his empire (and by now that empire amounted to little more than the city itself), Constantine's forces were pathetically small. Moored in the Golden Horn – that long, narrow, deep-water creek that runs northwest from the city and provides it with a superb natural harbour – were just twenty-six ships, including eight Venetian, five Genoese and one each from Ancona, Catalonia and Provence. Where manpower was concerned, the situation was even worse. To defend 14 miles of land and sea walls against an army of a hundred thousand, the population, dramatically reduced after nine separate visitations of the plague, yielded – including monks and clerics – rather less than seven thousand able-bodied men.

The land walls, on the other hand, first built more than one thousand years before, running from the Marmara shore to the upper reaches of the Golden Horn, formed the most elaborate and impregnable bastion ever constructed in the Middle Ages. Both inner and outer walls boasted ninety-six towers, and outside them lay a deep ditch some 30 feet across, which could be flooded to a depth of about 30 feet in an emergency. But the builders had reckoned without the sultan's cannon. The great walls were now subjected to a bombardment unprecedented in the history of siege warfare. On the very first day, a central section was reduced to rubble. The Turks repeatedly tried to smash their way through, but were always forced to retreat under a hail of missiles until nightfall sent them back to their camp. By morning the wall had been completely rebuilt.

The siege

On 11 April the last cannon was trundled into position, and the bombardment resumed, to continue uninterrupted for the next forty-eight days. Although some of the larger pieces could be fired only once every two or three hours, the damage they did was enormous; and although the defenders worked ceaselessly to repair the damage behind makeshift wooden stockades it was clear that they could not continue indefinitely. None the less, a surprise attack on the night of the 18 April was courageously beaten off; after four hours' heavy fighting the Turks had lost two hundred men, at the cost of not a single Christian life.

At sea, too, the Byzantines scored notable successes. Two attempts by heavy galleys failed miserably to break the heavy chain across the entrance to the Golden Horn (see p. 370); soon afterwards, four ships hired by the Pope and one sent by the King of Aragon appeared in the Marmara. The sultan personally gave strict orders to his admiral: they must be captured or sunk before they reached the city. The admiral did his best, but the superior height of the Christian ships saved the day. The small cannon mounted on the Turkish galleys lacked the necessary elevation; the balls all fell short. Grappling and boarding an enemy vessel that stood substantially higher in the water was virtually impossible, involving as it did a climb up the side under showers of arrows, while the defending crews wielded heavy axes that lopped off heads and hands indiscriminately.

The sultan had watched every moment of the battle from the shore, occasionally in his excitement riding his horse out into the sea until his robes were trailing in the water. He was famous for the violence of his rages; such was his fury as he watched the humiliation of his fleet that those around him began to fear for his sanity. The unfortunate admiral was bastinadoed and deprived of both public offices and private possessions. He was never heard of again.

The final assault was planned for Tuesday, 29 May. At half-past one in the morning, the drums, trumpets and blood-curdling Turkish war-cries signalled that the attack had begun. The sultan knew that he must attack in wave after wave, allowing the exhausted defenders no rest. First he sent in the *bashi-bazouks*, then his trained Anatolian regiments, finally the Janissaries. It was still early morning when the wall was finally breached – there is a theory that a small postern had been insecurely bolted – and the Turkish army poured into the city. The emperor, seeing that the battle was lost, plunged into the fray where the fighting was thickest. He was never seen again.

By noon the streets of Constantinople were running red. Houses were ransacked, churches razed, women and children raped and impaled. Sultan Mehmet had promised his men the traditional three days of looting; but after an orgy on such a scale, there were no protests when he brought it to a close soon after sunset.

The walls of Constantinople, built in the fifth century AD. By the mid fifteenth century the once-mighty Byzantine Empire was little more than a glorified city-state. However imposing its walls, Constantinople was ultimately powerless to withstand the big guns and large forces of Sultan Mehmet II in 1453.

Sultan Mehmet II

369

TAKING THE
GOLDEN HORN

FROM THE BEGINNING OF THE SIEGE, Mehmet knew that somehow he must gain control of the Golden Horn. Having failed to break the chain across the harbour mouth, he had set his engineers to work on a road running from the Bosphorus shore just to the east, behind the suburb of Galata, over the hill (near today's Taksim Square) and down, meeting the Horn beyond the chain. Metal tracks had been laid and iron wheels cast. His carpenters, meanwhile, had been busy fashioning wooden cradles large enough to accommodate the keels of medium-sized vessels. It was a Herculean undertaking; but the sultan had enough men and materials to make it possible. On 21 April 1453 the work was complete; and on the 22nd the Genoese colony in Galata watched dumbfounded as some seventy ships were hauled by innumerable teams of oxen over a 200-foot hill and then lowered down to the water.

The Byzantines had known nothing of the sultan's plan. Seeing the Turkish ships in the Horn, they found it difficult to believe the evidence of their own eyes. Not only was their major harbour no longer secure; they now had 3½ more miles of sea wall to defend. They were still hoping for a relief expedition from the west; but even if it were to arrive, how could it now be received in safety?

Mehmet now compounded the insult by throwing a pontoon bridge across the channel. Previously all messengers between his army beyond the walls and his fleet at the entrance to the Bosphorus had to make a long detour around the top of the Horn; henceforth they would be able to complete the journey in less than an hour. The bridge had other uses too: broad enough for a regiment marching five abreast, it could also accommodate heavy carts and – on special rafts attached at intervals to the sides – cannon which could be used either to cover the army's advance or to bombard the sea walls of the city. Now, if not before, Byzantium's fate was sealed.

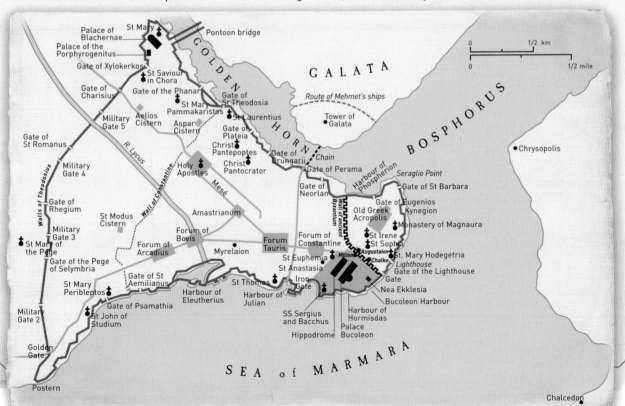

He himself waited till the late afternoon before entering the city. Then he rode slowly down the principal thoroughfare to the great church of St Sophia. Dismounting outside the central doors, he stooped to pick up a handful of earth which, in a gesture of humility, he sprinkled over his turban. He had already decided that the Church of the Holy Wisdom should be converted into the chief mosque of the city; he now entered, and touched his head to the ground in prayer and thanksgiving.

(Opposite) **The siege of Constantinople, 1453,** in a fifteenth-century book illustration. On the left, the Turkish ships are being lowered into the Golden Horn, behind Mehmet's pontoon bridge.

The later years

Four years later the sultan was once again on the march in Europe. By the end of 1462 he had eliminated the last vestiges of an independent Serbia – though the vital bridgehead of Belgrade had been saved by the Hungarian John Hunyadi – seized the principal islands of the northern Aegean, then swept southward to expel the Florentine dukes of Athens and the brothers of the last emperor, who had established themselves in the Peloponnese. Two years later he was master of Bosnia, and in 1480 a separate expedition (of which he was not in personal command) captured the important Venetian colony of Negropont – the modern Euboea.

By this time his health was failing, and when in the same year he attacked the Knights of St John on the island of Rhodes, he once again delegated the command. The Knights had summoned the greatest architects of the day to ensure that the fortress city of Rhodes was as near impregnable as any city could be; but they were hopelessly outnumbered, and after a two-month siege the Turks had actually broken through the walls when, in the face of a massive counter-attack, they suddenly turned and fled. Why they did so remains a mystery.

For Mehmet, triumph was from one moment to the next transformed into disaster. Furious, he immediately began preparing a fresh army, which he resolved to lead in person against Rhodes the following year. Had he done so, the Knights would have stood no chance; their defences could never have been repaired in time. But in the spring of 1481, as he was riding through Anatolia on his way to take up his command, he was stricken by a sudden attack of dysentery. A day or two later he was dead.

It is, in more ways than one, a tribute to Sultan Mehmet II that his portrait by Gentile Bellini (p. 365) should hang in the National Gallery in London; for the painting commemorates not only him but the breadth of his culture. No other Muslim ruler for centuries would summon a European painter to his court and then sit for his portrait; but if contemporary evidence is to be believed, Mehmet was almost certainly the most civilized man in his empire. Of course he was cruel; had he not been, he would never have survived. But he was a great ruler, and a superb commander. He captured Constantinople at the age of 21, and the world was never the same again.

Sultan Mehmet II, by an unknown Turkish artist.

Sultan Mehmet II

> 'And Cortés was as feared and worshipped ... as Alexander the
> Great, or Julius Caesar ... among the Romans, or Hannibal
> among the Carthaginians ...'

BERNAL DÍAZ, *HISTORIA DE LA CONQUISTA DE LA NUEVA ESPAÑA* (COMPLETED c. 1568)

HERNÁN CORTÉS
c. 1484–1547

FELIPE FERNÁNDEZ-ARMESTO

HERNÁN CORTÉS had, as far as we know, no innate or early vocation for war, and never served as a professional soldier. As strategist and tactician, he was at best unremarkable and sometimes inept. Yet, from 1519 to 1521, he led an expedition of a few hundred adventurers – ragged, ill equipped, cut off from all hope of retreat and reinforcement – against the orders of his superiors and the laws of his king, through the perils of previously unexplored environments and unknown enemies, to the conquest of one of the most dynamic and aggressive empires of the day. The outcome was startling because of the disparity of the forces and the disadvantages under which the victorious commander laboured. It was world-transforming, because Cortés's victory established the first substantial overseas land empire in what was to become a long history of European imperialism. The annals of warfare record no story harder to understand or more compelling to investigate.

Cortés was born probably in about 1484 in Medellín in southwest Spain – a nursery of conquistadores. His family belonged, technically, to the nobility, but suffered derogating poverty. Cortés's parents wanted him to be a lawyer: he acquired rudimentary legal training and a smattering, at least, of Latin in his teens. But something held him back – maybe poverty, maybe lack of aptitude. In 1506 he took the obvious route out of a society of restricted social opportunity: he crossed the Atlantic to Hispaniola, the island of adventure that Columbus had discovered and colonized in the previous decade.

It was an option many *pícaros* tried. Most settlers were more or less desperate; they had to be to cross 3,000 miles of barely explored ocean and face a future in a land notorious for savagery and sickness. For Cortés, the fact that a distant relative was governor of the island raised hopes of patronage. He became the town scribe of a new Spanish settlement – a few huts on the south coast – before escaping again, as secretary to a conquistador. When

Hernán Cortés

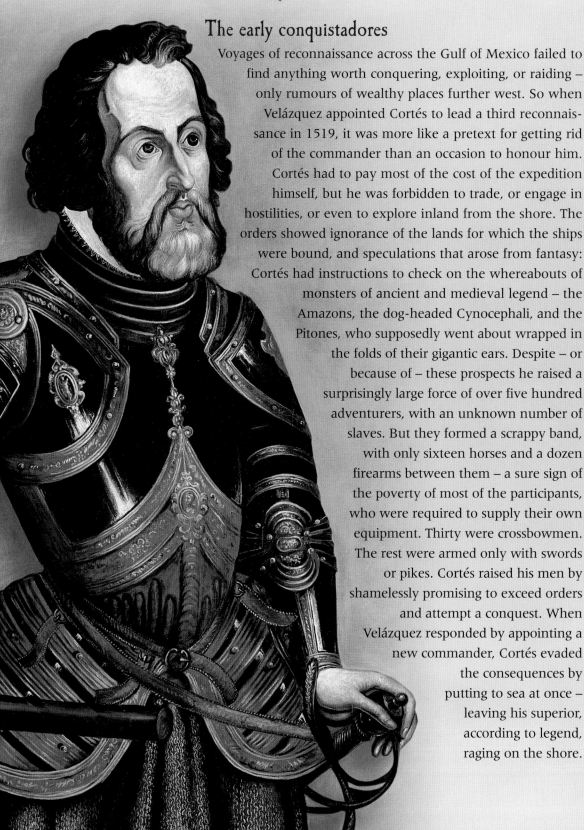

Diego Velázquez set off on the conquest of Cuba in 1509, Cortés accompanied him. There he acquired substantial property, a native mistress, and a Spanish bride, whom he married only after being gaoled for breach of promise. But his ascent was precarious. He fell out with Velázquez, who suspected his loyalty, mistrusted his ambition and doubted his reliability.

The early conquistadores

Voyages of reconnaissance across the Gulf of Mexico failed to find anything worth conquering, exploiting, or raiding – only rumours of wealthy places further west. So when Velázquez appointed Cortés to lead a third reconnaissance in 1519, it was more like a pretext for getting rid of the commander than an occasion to honour him. Cortés had to pay most of the cost of the expedition himself, but he was forbidden to trade, or engage in hostilities, or even to explore inland from the shore. The orders showed ignorance of the lands for which the ships were bound, and speculations that arose from fantasy: Cortés had instructions to check on the whereabouts of monsters of ancient and medieval legend – the Amazons, the dog-headed Cynocephali, and the Pitones, who supposedly went about wrapped in the folds of their gigantic ears. Despite – or because of – these prospects he raised a surprisingly large force of over five hundred adventurers, with an unknown number of slaves. But they formed a scrappy band, with only sixteen horses and a dozen firearms between them – a sure sign of the poverty of most of the participants, who were required to supply their own equipment. Thirty were crossbowmen. The rest were armed only with swords or pikes. Cortés raised his men by shamelessly promising to exceed orders and attempt a conquest. When Velázquez responded by appointing a new commander, Cortés evaded the consequences by putting to sea at once – leaving his superior, according to legend, raging on the shore.

Hernán Cortés, in a copy of a painting by the Master of Saldana in the Museo Nacional de Historia in Mexico City.

Hernán Cortés

373

Turning to conquest

Cortés had little incentive to obey orders. If he returned to Cuba without further risk, he would be poorer than before and would probably face further victimization at Velázquez's hands. If he turned his reconnaissance into a conquest, he might encounter monsters or riches or both, and become the real-life hero of a chivalric romance, of the kind he and most other modestly literate people read. Tales of knightly derring-do, involving fantastic voyages, contests with monsters and conquests of fabulous realms were the late medieval equivalent of station-bookstall pulp fiction today. He landed at what is now Veracruz in August 1519. Abjuring Velázquez's authority, he constituted his men as a civic community and had himself elected mayor. As a device for self-legitimization, it was little more than a fig-leaf. But it was almost a reflex action in the circumstances. Whenever Spaniards met on a wild frontier, they founded a city, just as Englishmen, in similar circumstances, might found a club.

Cortés and his followers on their way to meet the Aztec paramount Motecoçuma in Tenochtitlan, August 1519.

Beaching his ships, Cortés proceeded 'with no fear that once my back was turned, the people left in the town would betray me.' Rumours of Aztec wealth steeled a resolve, which, with the ships grounded, was literally to conquer or die. 'Trusting in God's greatness and in the might of their Highnesses' royal name', 315 Spaniards struck inland to seek Motecoçuma, the Aztec paramount, 'wherever he might be'. Some of the men claimed later that the boat-beaching was the result of a collective decision. But it was important for the conquistadores' self-esteem to represent themselves as acting in knightly companionage, consistently with their self-perception as heroes of chivalric romance. The real decision-making, however, lay with Cortés.

To the Aztec city of Tenochtitlan

The state for which he was bound was one of the most rapidly expanding conquest states in the world. The Aztecs' principal city, Tenochtitlan, was perched like an eagle's eyrie, 7,500 feet above sea level in the central valley of Mexico, in the midst of a lake surrounded by mountains. Like an eyrie, it was strewn with its victims' bones – literally so, because the Aztecs made human sacrifices of thousands, perhaps scores of thousands, of their captive foes, piling their skulls at the foot of the great temple. Tenochtitlan was a robber-city of enormous dimensions – probably of some eighty thousand inhabitants, despite the unconducive altitude and site. The lakebound position made it impossible to grow enough food for such a huge metropolis. The location was too high for the cotton on which the community depended for clothes and quilted armour. It was far from the source of the tropical luxuries – chocolate, rubber, exotic plumage, ocelot pelts, jade, incense – on which the elite way of life depended. Only war and tribute could supply the city with what

Hernán Cortés

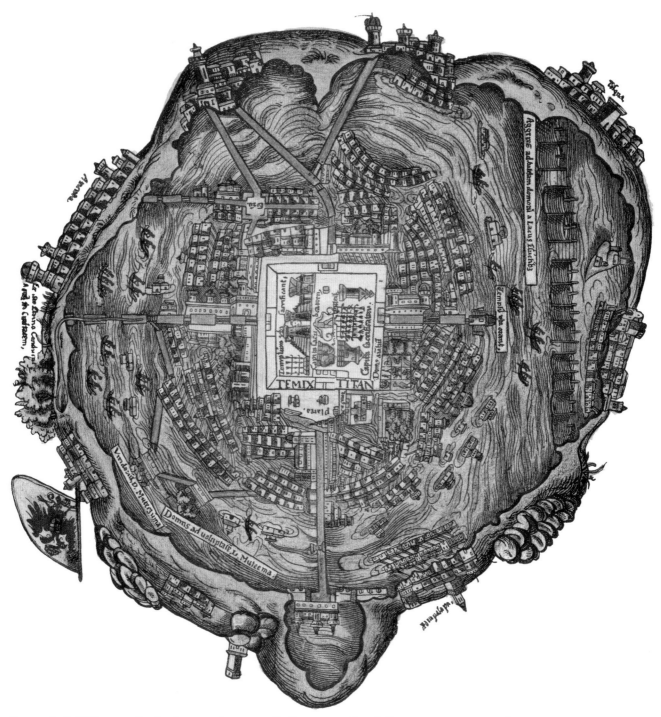

it needed. This was both the weakness and the strength of the Aztec system. The tribute exhibited the reach of Tenochtitlan's power. But it also showed the vulnerability of Aztec hegemony to the dissolution that must ensue if tribute were witheld.

Dependent on war to replenish supplies of tribute and sacrificial blood, the Aztec state was expanding faster, perhaps, than any almost other political community in the world at the time: only the empires of the Inca and the Ottomans were comparable in their dynamism. During the reign of Motecoçuma, the Aztecs conquered forty-four communities, spread over vast distances from the Pánuco river in the North to what is now the Guatemala frontier, raising the number of tributary cities within the system to nearly three hundred and fifty. The empire was, perhaps, over-extended, but it was confident, dynamic and aggressive. The encounter between Aztecs and Spaniards was a clash of rival imperialists.

A map of the Aztec capital city of Tenochtitlan, published with a Latin translation of the letters of Hernán Cortés to Emperor Charles V at Nuremberg in 1524.

Hernán Cortés

A copy of a mid sixteenth-century Tlaxcalan representation of the battle for the causeways leading into Tenochtitlan. Tlaxcalan versions of the Spanish conquest always show Tlaxcalan warriors in the vanguard and Doña Marina, Cortés's native concubine, in a position of command.

teçiquauhtitlã

The land of Tlaxcala

Cortés's route inland was, presumably, one recommended by the native hosts – enemies of the Aztecs – who welcomed him on the coast. It seemed consciously chosen to penetrate the most inaccessible patches of the Aztec world, where Tenochtitlan's most reluctant tributaries and most defiant enemies would be found. The Spaniards climbed from Jalapa by a pass 'so rough and steep that there is none in Spain so difficult', emerging with the conviction that they were now in the Aztec realm. 'God knows,' wrote Cortés, 'how my people suffered from hunger and thirst and ... hailstorms and rainstorms.' They fought their way through the land of Tlaxcala, home of the Aztecs' most implacable enemies. Though the battles seemed fierce enough to the Spaniards, the Tlaxcalan forces were seeking only to test them to see whether they would make worthy recruits for their war against the Aztecs. As a reward for their courage, the Spaniards acquired the alliance of the fiercest pocket of resistance to the Aztecs between Mexico and the coast.

The thread on which their morale hung frayed quickly. They were thousands of miles from home. They were cut off from hope of help and knew that if a force followed them from Cuba it would be to punish rather than assist. They were surrounded by a hostile and awe-inspiring environment and hundreds of thousands of menacing 'savages' whom they could not understand. They had to breathe an unaccustomed, rarefied atmosphere; to endure extremes of heat and cold; to eat a debilitating diet without the red meat and wine that Spaniards considered essential for health and high status. They were at the mercy of native guides and interpreters who might choose to betray them at any moment. At Cholula, Cortés resorted to terror. To pre-empt, he said, an Indian conspiracy, but, more convincingly, to alleviate the Spaniards' stress, or simply *pour encourager les autres*, he massacred, by his own account, more than three thousand people. Most indigenous sources cast a different light on the massacre: the Tlaxcalans, they maintained, induced Cortés to undertake it, making him an agent of their own vengeance against neighbours they detested.

Meeting Motecoçuma

Most Mesoamerican cultures venerated strangers. When he arrived at Tenochtitlan in November, Cortés was honourably received. Traditional explanations of this are incredible. It is nonsense, for instance, to suppose that the Aztecs mistook him for a god or the envoy of a god: there is no contemporary evidence for this legend, which myth-makers extemporized long after the conquest. In his own account of his meeting with Motecoçuma, Cortés put a fanciful speech into the paramount's mouth, resigning sovereignty in favour of the ruler of Spain: this obviously self-interested bit

Hernán Cortés

of propaganda deserves no credence. Even more ridiculous is the early colonial myth that corroded morale undermined Aztec resistance. The so-called portents that are supposed to have influenced them derived not from Aztec tradition but from ancient Roman and Jewish traditions about the fall of Rome and Jerusalem. The simplest explanation for Cortés's reception is the best: decision-makers at the Aztec capital wanted to detach Cortés from his alliance with Tlaxcala. They therefore showered him with the gold he demanded, even after he had taken advantage of their hospitality to make a prisoner of Motecoçuma and – in effect – to hold him to ransom. It was a characteristically bold strategy. How practical it was in the long run is doubtful, as it was vexatious to the Aztecs, unprofitable to the Spaniards' native allies, and unsatisfactory to Cortés's men, who squabbled over the division of the spoils.

In April 1520, when the situation was already tense, a force of nine hundred men arrived in Mexico from Cuba, with a commission from the crown, to arrest Cortés and restore the expedition to obedience to its official superiors. Cortés responded with customary resolution. He mustered a force of three hundred, subverted the newly arrived army with bribes, and launched a surprise attack that resulted in the capture of the leaders and the incorporation of the task force into his own army. His absence from Tenochtitlan, however, had left his garrison there dangerously weak. The commander, egged on perhaps by Tlaxcalan admonishers, attempted a pre-emptive strike against the Aztec leadership; when Cortés returned, the situation was desperate. Motecoçuma died – perhaps in an accident of war, perhaps murdered by Spaniards who realized that he had outlived his usefulness to them. Cortés felt obliged to save as much as he could of his garrison by evacuating the city with heavy losses.

Doña Marina's man

Cortés's native allies seemed to lose confidence in him after this humiliation. Had they turned against him, the Spaniards would have been massacred. But the Spaniards enjoyed the favour of a native leader whose influence proved decisive. A native

HERNÁN CORTÉS'S INVASION OF MEXICO, 1519–20.

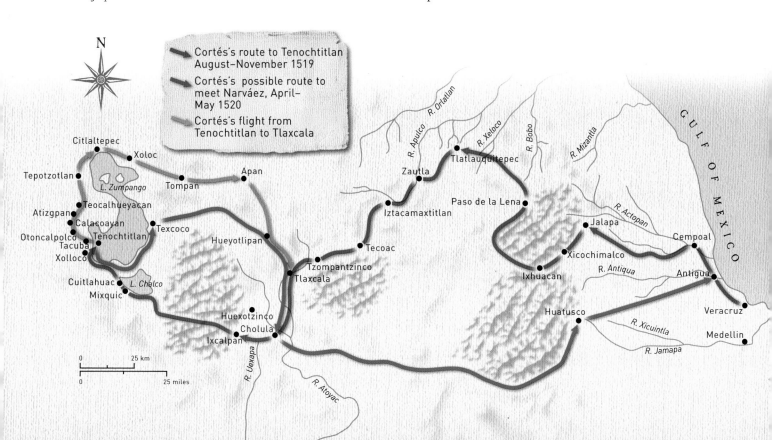

THE SIEGE OF TENOCHTITLAN

THE INTERRUPTION OF TENOCHTITLAN'S TRIBUTARY LIFEBLOOD made the outcome of the siege a foregone conclusion. But it took a long time, owing to ferocious resistance. The defenders launched a fleet of canoes, drove stakes into the lake to trap Spanish vessels, mustered a large garrison and made deadly sorties. Ultimately, they armed women rather than surrender.

Spanish technology had little influence. Horses (even though reinforcements had brought their numbers to forty) are useless in street-fighting in the middle of a lake. Heavy Spanish armour was an embarrassment in the rarefied air of Mexico: Spaniards largely discarded it in favour of the quilted cotton armour of the natives. Guns are of marginal value without access to renewed powder and shot.

In any case, native allies did most of the Spaniards' fighting. Reinforcements had expanded Cortés's Spanish contingent to over a thousand men, with ninety horses; but the native allies, by Cortés's own reckoning, numbered one hundred and fifty thousand. In one respect, however, Spanish ingenuity was important: Cortés had twelve brigantines built, each of 50 feet or more in length, which dominated communications across the lake.

In April 1521, the reduction of outlying lakebound and lakeside outposts began. Cortés only just eluded capture in the battle for the first of them, Xochimilco. For the next two months, progress was slow, for the attackers, under constant harrassment, were unable to rebuild a causeway for an assault across the lake. On 1 June, the defenders, using hundreds of canoes, mounted a concerted attack on the brigantines. They drove the flagship aground, boarded it, and almost succeeded in capturing it. In general, however, the Spanish craft outclassed the canoes, scattering and overturning them with ease. From this point, command of the lake was so complete that the Spaniards could protect the engineers who were at work on the causeways, use the brigs as pontoons, and get close enough to the city to set parts of it on fire.

On 10 June the attackers at last managed to cross the lake and penetrate the city, but the defenders drove them back. After a further attempt a few days later, Cortés resorted to demolishing the city bit by bit in order to deny the rooftops to enemy snipers. The desertion to Cortés's coalition of all the remaining neutrals in the region showed how the battle was unfolding. By the end of June, Tenochtitlan stood virtually alone, with only the neighbouring community of Tlatelolco fighting alongside it. Yet street fighting raged for two more gruelling months, until typhus, dysentery, starvation and, perhaps, smallpox brought resistance to an end. On 13 August, the Spaniards found no defenders in the streets – only frantic, often suicidal refugees, and piles of the dead.

CONQVISTA DE MEXICO POR CORTES. N7

Hernán Cortés

378

woman whom the Spaniards called Doña Marina had joined the expedition in its early days as an interpreter and as Cortés's concubine. She hailed from central Mexico, perhaps from Tlaxcala itself. Long captivity near the Gulf Coast had made her fluent in the only native tongue which any of the Spaniards knew. She rapidly learned Spanish, and used her unique position to mastermind the negotiations that put together a coalition capable of overthrowing Tenochtitlan. Indigenous sources show her, rather than Cortés, in control of the anti-Aztec forces. She appears both in a central diplomatic role, and as a field commander, directing operations – massacres included. Most natives called Cortés by a name which meant, in effect, 'Marina's man'.

Cortés's resolve and his mistress's diplomatic skill proved to be a successful combination. After much hesitation, Tlaxcala held firm on the Spaniards' side. The next most important adherents were the Huexotzinca, whose own records show their contingents marching out to support Cortés, with vast quantities of supplies and *matériel*, for the siege of Tenochtitlan (see p. 378). Cortés spent the next few months putting together an alliance that eventually encompassed all but one of Tenochtitlan's tributary neighbours.

'Even should I fall still further from Your Majesty's favour ... I shall remain content with doing my duty and knowing that all the world knows.'

HERNÁN CORTÉS, LETTER TO EMPEROR CHARLES V, 26 SEPTEMBER 1526

The glory of conquest

For the rest of his time in the New World, Cortés remained a participant in – and a major beneficiary of – internecine indigenous wars, collaborating with some of his allies, turning against others, extending control over the whole of the former Aztec realm, and into what are now Honduras and Guatemala. He ended enriched, ennobled – and embittered, dissatisfied with his rewards and frustrated at finding no more gold-rich empires to conquer.

However deficient he was in military experience, tactical sagacity, strategic mastery, or battlefield prowess, Cortés had shown outstanding qualities of leadership – which are, perhaps, nine-tenths of what it takes to be a great commander. By striking out for the conquest of Mexico on his own initiative, he showed how quick and bold he was in decision-making, as did his breathtaking insubordination and his decisions to beach his boats, capture Motecoçuma, and follow up the fall of Tenochtitlán with a series of ever wider-ranging expeditions of conquest. His men were under his spell. One memoirist, who resented the way Cortés garnered all the glory of the conquest, and much of the profit, admitted that there was never a better leader in the world, and recounted how the men would sing his praises around their campfires.

Cortés inaugurated a new era in world history by acquiring the first of many great European overseas land empires. His efforts extended contact between the different civilizations in world-changing fashion. Formerly, Spanish outposts in the New World had been of marginal importance: only modestly productive, barely significant for the lives of most people in Eurasia. Cortés put them in touch with one of the most populous and productive regions on earth. The great belt of rich sedentary civilizations that stretched across Eurasia could now begin to exchange life-forms and culture with those of the Americas. A line of communications – still imperfect, still precarious – was beginning to bind the world together.

(Opposite) **The capture of Tenochtitlan** by Cortés, as depicted by a sixteenth-century Spanish artist. The attackers finally managed to cross the lake into the city in June 1521, using hundreds of canoes as a pontoon bridge. It was not until 13 August that the siege ended and the city was finally conquered.

Hernán Cortés

'It saddens me to force that brave old man to leave his home.'

SULTAN SÜLEYMAN, OF THE GRAND MASTER OF THE HOSPITALLERS, AFTER THE FALL OF RHODES, 1 JANUARY 1523

SÜLEYMAN THE MAGNIFICENT

1494–1566

JOHN JULIUS NORWICH

DURING THE FIRST HALF of the sixteenth century, four giants bestrode Europe. They were the Habsburg Emperor Charles V, King Henry VIII of England, King Francis I of France and the Ottoman Sultan Süleyman the Magnificent. Of the four, Süleyman was arguably the greatest. He was, like the others but in his own oriental way, a son of the Renaissance: a man of wide culture and a gifted poet, under whom the imperial potteries of Iznik (the ancient Nicaea) were at their most inspired and the imperial architects – above all, the celebrated Sinan – adorned the cities of the empire with mosques and religious foundations, schools and caravanserais, many of which still stand today.

(Opposite) **Süleyman I,** in a painting *c.* 1530, by an unknown Venetian artist from Titian's circle. Europeans called him 'the Magnificent', for the splendour of his court, but to the Ottomans he was 'the Lawgiver', for the many regulations imposed by his government.

Like his Ottoman forebears, however, he was also a conqueror, whose overriding ambition was to achieve in the west victories comparable with those of his father Selim the Grim in the east, simultaneously extending ever further the frontiers of Islam. Thus he was to swell his already vast empire with conquests in Hungary, the Balkans, Central Europe, Persia and the Mediterranean.

The bombarding of Belgrade

Succeeding to the throne in September 1520, the 26-year-old Süleyman was the only member of his family whom his father had left alive: on his own accession Selim had his two brothers and five orphan nephews – the youngest of whom was aged 5 – strangled with a bowstring. (He was also suspected of having poisoned Bayezit II, his own father.) The young sultan, confident of his own position, was thus free to begin his programme of conquest. His first objective was the kingdom of Hungary – which was, since the collapse of the Bulgarian and Serbian empires and the fall of Constantinople, his major enemy in eastern Europe. Reaching Belgrade, that vast fortress at the confluence of the Sava and the Danube, he bombarded it for three weeks, until at last, after a huge explosion had destroyed the largest tower, the garrison surrendered. Most of the captured Hungarians were put to the sword; the Serbs were rounded up and taken back to Istanbul, where they were settled in a nearby forest, still known today as the Forest of Belgrade. This was Süleyman's first great victory, opening up as it did not only Hungary, but also Austria and even Germany and northern Italy to Turkish raiding parties.

The capture of Rhodes

Encouraged by his first success, Süleyman now turned to the Christian enemy that had always been a thorn in Ottoman flesh: the Knights Hospitaller of St John – who from their headquarters on Rhodes, only 10 miles off the Anatolian coast, continued to harass Turkish shipping. They were comparatively few, with neither an army nor a navy that was any match for his own, but – as his great-grandfather Mehmet had discovered to his cost forty years before – they were determined fighters. In those forty years they had worked unceasingly on their defences, building huge angled towers and strengthening the ramparts against the heavy cannon which had smashed those of Constantinople in 1453 and by which they themselves had been so nearly defeated in 1480. They would be hard indeed to dislodge.

On 26 June 1522, their Grand Master Philippe Villiers de l'Isle Adam having ignored the sultan's letter demanding the island's surrender, the first ships of the Ottoman fleet appeared on the northern horizon. They were joined a day or two later by the flagship carrying Süleyman himself and his brother-in-law Mustafa Pasha, who had marched down with the army through Asia Minor. Against this host of perhaps two hundred thousand were only some seven hundred Knights – even after their numbers had been swelled by contingents from their commanderies throughout Europe – together with five hundred Cretan archers, some fifteen hundred other mercenaries and the Christian people of Rhodes. On the other hand their defences were as near as possible impregnable, and they had laid in supplies of food, water and munitions to hold out for months.

By the end of June the heavy bombardment had begun in earnest. The Turkish sappers, too, were busy. Within weeks they had drilled some fifty tunnels running in various directions under the wall, and it was not long before a mine exploded, creating a gap 30 feet across. The Turks poured in, and there followed two hours of bitter hand-to-hand fighting before the Knights somehow prevailed and the surviving attackers retired exhausted to their camp. Gradually, however, the defenders weakened. Süleyman's cannon were even more powerful than those of Mehmet, capable of hurling stone balls a yard in diameter a mile or more. By December the Knights were at breaking point, with well over half their fighting force dead or disabled. Although the sultan offered honourable terms, the Grand Master favoured fighting to the last; it was the native Rhodiots who finally persuaded him that continued resistance would mean a massacre, of Knights and people alike. And so he invited the sultan personally into the city to discuss terms – and Süleyman accepted. As he approached the gates he is said to have dismissed his bodyguard with the words: 'My safety is guaranteed by the word of a Grand Master of the Hospitallers, which is more sure than all the armies of the world.'

The Süleymaniye Mosque, Istanbul, founded by Süleyman and designed by the architect Sinan (1550–57). The water-colour above, dating from *c.* 1588 and now housed in the Bodleian Library, is probably Turkish in origin. The photograph (opposite) of the mosque's interior dome shows the magnificence of the Ottoman craftsmanship.

On the day after Christmas, de l'Isle Adam made his formal submission. The sultan treated him with all the respect he deserved, congratulating him and his Knights on their tenacity and courage. A week later, on the evening of 1 January 1523, the survivors sailed for Crete. For the next seven years they wandered homeless; then, in 1530, Charles V gave them the island of Malta. There, after a still greater siege in 1565, they were to inflict upon Süleyman his last defeat.

The Hungarian campaign

At some time in 1525, the sultan faced a revolt by his crack fighting troops. As the result of a rumour that he had decided against any further military expeditions, the Janissaries, who lived for war and plunder, had ransacked the Jewish quarter of Istanbul. Süleyman acted fast, personally killing the three ringleaders with his bare hands; many senior officers were also put to death.

Süleyman the Magnificent

The rumour was in any case untrue. The sultan was already preparing his next campaign. Europe was once again to be his battlefield; it was there that he could extend the territory of Islam, there that his three great rival sovereigns could be brought low. As always, the key to Europe was the kingdom of Hungary. In the days of the great John Hunyadi and his son Matthias Corvinus, it had served as the continent's principal bulwark against the Ottomans; but now, after two feckless rulers, it was hopelessly divided. The *voivode* (governor) of Transylvania, John Zapolyai, was intriguing for the crown; the Magyar nobles felt little loyalty to the reigning king, Lewis II, and were violently anti-German at a time when they needed all the imperial help they could get.

And so Süleyman, together with his brother-in-law and Grand Vizier Ibrahim Pasha, left Istanbul on 21 April 1526 at the head of one hundred thousand men, together with three hundred cannon. The weather was dreadful; storms had swollen the rivers, washed away the bridges, flooded the roads. But discipline was never relaxed. All provisions were paid for; soldiers trampling on sown fields were executed. At Osijek a 1,000-foot bridge was thrown across the Drava river in five days; as soon as his army was

Süleyman the Magnificent

safely across, Süleyman had it destroyed, making it clear that there was no question of retreat. From there it was only some 40 miles to the plain of Mohacs, where King Lewis was waiting.

The battle was fought in the afternoon and early evening of Friday, 29 August (see p. 386). Its result was a foregone conclusion. Like the last two Byzantine emperors in the previous century, Lewis had appealed to all western Europe for help against the Ottoman threat; like theirs, his appeals had been largely ignored. When the moment came, he refused to wait for the reinforcements promised by Zapolyai, or even for another detachment of Croatians known to be on its way; despite a small contingent provided by King Sigismund I of Poland, his army of some thirty thousand was consequently outnumbered by more than three to one. Finally, there was the factor of discipline. That imposed by Süleyman was, as always, stern and unbending; the Hungarian knights scarcely knew the meaning of the word. They fought with immense courage; but heroism was powerless against Turkish cannon.

SOLIMANVS·IMPERATOR
TVRCHARVM, 1526.

Süleyman the Magnificent on campaign, in a sixteenth-century German woodcut.

The Vienna expedition

Three years later, Süleyman was again at Mohacs, investing Zapolyai as his vassal-king of Hungary. He then continued to Buda, at that time occupied by the troops of Charles V's brother Ferdinand. The city fell in less than a week, and the new king was formally enthroned; but now the sultan made his fatal mistake. Had he continued his advance immediately, he could hardly have failed to take Vienna. Instead, he delayed until the high summer. Throughout his life he was unlucky with the weather; and the summer of 1529 in Central Europe was even worse than that of 1526. Not until 27 September were his one hundred and twenty thousand men and three hundred cannon all in place before the walls.

The siege continued for nearly three weeks. On 7 October the sultan was within sight of victory when the Austrians mistimed a sortie and paid the usual price – that evening saw a heap of five hundred Christian heads outside the Carinthian Gate – yet somehow the defences held. Then the foul weather returned; a week later it snowed uninterruptedly for eighteen hours, and the snow was followed by incessant rain. It was a long way back to Istanbul, and the Janissaries – deprived of their expected plunder – were growing restive. Reluctantly but wisely, Süleyman gave the order to return.

The Persian campaign

Süleyman had long been considering a campaign against Shah Tahmasp, the Safavid ruler of Persia; by 1533 it was clear that this could no longer be postponed. Over the past decade the Shah had grown steadily more powerful, intensifying his persecution of the

Sunnis of Mesopotamia; executing their leaders, destroying their shrines and converting their mosques to Shia use. That autumn the army under Ibrahim Pasha set off across Anatolia, making straight for Tahmasp's capital, Tabriz. It fell without a struggle, the Shah having fled only a few weeks before. Ibrahim then settled down to await his master, who joined him two months later. Together they then headed southward to Baghdad.

It was an appalling journey. Winter was approaching, the weather deteriorating fast. The Zagros mountains took their toll on the animals, and caused the heavy cannon to be abandoned. Now the Turks' principal enemies were cold and hunger, for in that barren terrain food was desperately scarce; one of their officers was actually to die of starvation before the army finally reached the Mesopotamian plain. There Süleyman expected to find Tahmasp's army, which he was determined to bring to battle; but it never appeared.

The sultan entered Baghdad on 4 December 1534. The city was but a shadow of what it had been in the days of the Abbasid caliphate three centuries before; but he immediately initiated an ambitious programme of restoration and reconstruction, returning all the mosques to the Sunni rite. He repaired the defences, instituted a survey of property and distributed fiefs. By his departure in April 1535, Baghdad was well on its way to a new period of prosperity.

Kheir-ed-Din Barbarossa

For the previous thirty-odd years, the Barbary coast of North Africa had been dominated by a number of corsairs, led by Kheir-ed-Din Barbarossa. Son of a Greek-born Janissary, Barbarossa and his brother Aruj had conquered most of what is now Algeria, and after Aruj's death Barbarossa dominated the central and western Mediterranean. By 1533, after the Genoese admiral Andrea Doria had won several sea victories over the Turks, Süleyman summoned Barbarossa to Istanbul and commissioned him to reorganize his entire navy.

Barbarossa did so, with remarkable success. His last years were spent not as a corsair but as admiral of the Ottoman fleet, operating above all against Venice. Hitherto, Venice had pursued her mercantile activities virtually unopposed – thanks, it was said, to the goodwill of Ibrahim Pasha; but in 1536 he was murdered at the

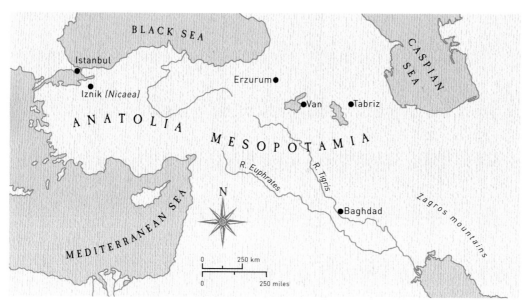

THE EASTERN MEDITERRANEAN AND MESOPOTAMIA

at the time of Süleyman's Persian campaign of 1533–5.

Süleyman the Magnificent

THE BATTLE OF MOHACS

O N 29 AUGUST 1525 IBRAHIM PASHA took up his position
with the Rumelian troops in the front line; the sultan,
with the Anatolian divisions and the cannon, were directly
behind him. Rather than making a direct head-on attack
on the Hungarian cavalry, Süleyman's basic strategy was
to open his own ranks, let the Hungarians through and
then close in on them. This tactic brought the Hungarians
very close to Süleyman himself; had it not been for his
Janissaries, who surrounded him and hamstrung his
assailants' horses, he is unlikely to have survived.

The second phase of the battle belonged to the
cannon. It was this that proved decisive; the Hungarians
had nothing to match the power of the Turkish artillery
and were blown to pieces. They fought furiously, none
more courageously than their commander-in-chief Paul
Tomori, Bishop of Kalocsa; but finally they fled the field,
many of them – including King Lewis – drowning in the
surrounding rivers and marshes.

On the following morning two thousand heads,
including those of seven bishops, were piled in a pyramid
before the sultan's tent. The total number of the dead was
estimated at thirty thousand; Hungary never completely
recovered. An old Hungarian folk song tells of a series of
domestic disasters; after each comes the chorus: *'But no
matter: more was lost on Mohacs field.'*

The Battle of Mohacs,
29 August 1526, in an
image from an Ottoman
manuscript of 1588
devoted to the military
campaigns of Süleyman
the Magnificent.

instigation of Süleyman's wife Roxelana, and his successor felt very differently.
Although the Turkish siege of Corfu failed – largely, once again, owing to the
appalling weather – other Venetian islands and harbours were less fortunate: Skyros,
Aegina, Patmos, Ios, Paros, Astipalaia and the Peloponnesian ports of Nauplia and
Malvasia (Monemvasia) fell one by one. It was the end of Venice's hegemony in the
Mediterranean.

Persia and Prince Mustafa

Since the previous campaign against Tahmasp, there had always been unrest along the
Persian frontier. Safavid agents were still active, spreading Shia propaganda
throughout eastern Anatolia, where Ottoman authority was growing ever more
uncertain. In spring 1548 the sultan took personal command of his army. His first
objective was the lake fortress of Van, which he had taken in 1534 but which the Shah
had since regained. It soon surrendered and Süleyman moved on to Aleppo for the
winter. The following year saw the capture of 31 towns, the demolition of 14 fortresses
and the construction of 28 others. His twenty-month campaign had successfully
consolidated his authority, but he had failed in his main objective: to destroy Tahmasp's
army once and for all. He was to make one more attempt, in 1552; but this was interrupted by a crisis which ended in the execution, on his own orders, of his eldest son.

Mustafa was 37, capable and intelligent: he would have made a worthy successor to his father. Unlike his three surviving brothers, however, he was not the child of Roxelana, and he knew that on Süleyman's death he would be in mortal danger: either he must – in traditional Ottoman fashion – kill his brothers, or they would kill him. Whether or not he was actually planning a coup is unknown; but Süleyman summoned him to his Anatolian headquarters and accused him. Mustafa protested his innocence, and was still doing so when his father raised his hand in a signal to a party of mutes who were waiting in readiness. A minute later the prince was dead. His young son Murad soon followed him to the grave.

Apparently unmoved, Süleyman continued his campaign. Once again, the Persians refused to meet him in the field; he was allowed to advance virtually unhindered, ravaging and plundering as he went, until finally Tahmasp had had enough. An ambassador was despatched to the sultan's headquarters at Erzurum with proposals for an armistice. Süleyman, equally tired of the war, accepted at once. The resulting treaty, signed in May 1555, put an end to the long quarrel. The Shah agreed to stop his propaganda campaigns; the sultan promised unrestricted entry for the Shia into the holy shrines of Islam.

The invasion of Malta

Süleyman had plenty of time to regret the mercy he had shown to the Knights of St John after his capture of Rhodes. They had promised never again to take up arms against him; never had a promise been so repeatedly broken. Furthermore, Malta promised to be a useful stepping-stone between Turkish-held Tripoli and Spanish Sicily, on which he had long had designs. His immense invasion fleet sailed in May 1565 with well over two hundred ships, carrying some forty thousand men, plus horses, cannon and ammunition. But the sultan made one mistake: regretfully deciding that at 71 he was too old to lead it in person, he divided the command between two men who detested each other and quarrelled constantly.

The three-month siege has gone down in history. It nearly succeeded – and, under Süleyman's leadership, almost certainly would have. Malta was saved by the heroism of the Knights – as always, hopelessly outnumbered – and by the dysentery that spread through the Turkish camp. When, on 7 September there arrived the *Gran Soccorso* – the Great Relief – of nine thousand men sent by the Spanish Viceroy of Sicily, the surviving Turks saw that they were beaten and returned to their ships.

The last campaign

Scarcely had the army returned to Istanbul when war broke out again in Hungary. Süleyman had not led an expedition for ten years, but he desperately needed a victory over the Christians to expunge the shame of Malta. He could no longer ride a horse, and the rough roads made travelling by carriage a nightmare; even when the stops, on his orders, were as few and as short as possible, the journey to Belgrade took seven weeks. From there he marched on Szeged; the city fell in early September 1566, but Süleyman never knew it: he had died on the night of the 5th, in his tent.

GONZALO DE CÓRDOBA

1453–1516

NICCOLÒ CAPPONI

GONZALO FERNÁNDEZ DE CÓRDOBA was born on 16 March 1453 in Montilla, near the city of Córdoba, with cold steel running through his bloodline. Ever since the kings of Castile had reclaimed most of Andalusia from the Moors in the thirteenth century, Gonzalo's family had been fighting the Muslims of the kingdom of Granada, and, more often than not, rival Christian lords in the area. Gonzalo's father, Don Pedro Fernández de Córdoba, Count of Aguilar, died when his son was 2 years old, leaving his widow, Doña Elvira de Herrera, to rear his children in the true Fernández de Córdoba tradition. Sharing her former husband's mettle, the Countess of Aguilar – connected by blood to some of the most powerful Castilian families – raised Gonzalo and his elder brother to be warriors and accustomed to danger from their earliest years.

Gonzalo took eagerly to soldiering, and years later would describe his attitude to martial training: 'I would take a sword and for hours fence in a room alone, away from the gaze of others. Swordsmanship came to me naturally as walking or running, and I perceived it as perfectly suited to the natural movement of the body.'

As soon as he could sit on a saddle, Gonzalo participated in raiding expeditions or joined in the relief of some beleaguered ally. The counts of Aguilar carried on a long-standing feud with the Fernández de Córdoba counts of Cabra, and minor *hidalgos* living on the Andalusian border, often related by blood to both factions, frequently changed sides at whim. Usually, but not invariably, the warring parties closed ranks when facing the Grenadine Muslims. Gonzalo mastered the hit-and-run tactics typical of border warfare and learnt how to survive the vagaries of frontier politics. The guerrilla and diplomatic skills he developed during this period would serve him to no small degree in later years.

Once Gonzalo reached the age of 14, his mother sent him to train at the court of Castile, royal service being an acceptable profession for a younger son. He was originally attached to the household of Don Alfonso, the king's brother, but after his master's untimely death Gonzalo become a retainer of Princess Isabella, heir

Gonzalo de Córdoba

presumptive to the Castilian throne and the wife of Ferdinand of Aragon. Returning to Córdoba in 1473, Gonzalo became one of the officials in charge of the municipality's administration, and it was whilst he was in office that civil war broke out in the city between the *conversos* (Jews who had converted to Catholicism or their descendants) and the so-called 'Old Christians'. The origins of the upheaval were both social and religious: the 'Old Christians' not only resented the fact that the *conversos* occupied political offices, but also doubted the validity of their Christian beliefs. On Good Friday 1474, an incident occurred during a procession between 'Old Christians' and *conversos* that rapidly escalated into violent street fighting. Gonzalo, himself of *converso* descent, fought against the 'Old Christians' until he and his brother Alonso were forced to retreat to Córdoba's citadel. Eventually the two had to fight their way out, pursued by the troops of the Count of Cabra. Retreating to his fortress of Santaella (a gift from Alonso), Gonzalo eventually fell into the hands of his enemies and was carried off to Cabra in shackles.

His imprisonment lasted until the end of 1476, when he regained his freedom thanks to the personal intervention of Isabella of Castile, now queen following the death of Henry IV. Gonzalo participated in the last stages of the war of Castilian succession against the supporters of the late king's illegitimate daughter Juana, commanding a company of 'lances' (heavy cavalrymen with their retinue) and earning the praise of the grand master of the Order of Santiago, Alonso de Cárdenas, for his performance at the Battle of Albuera in 1479. He had, by this time, earned a well-deserved reputation for personal bravery and for being a careful, calculating commander.

The ten-year war for Granada brought Gonzalo more laurels, his reputation boosted by a series of skilful and daring exploits, including that of saving Queen Isabella and her retinue from a Moorish sortie. When the last Muslim stronghold in Spain finally capitulated in January 1492, he was one of the officers selected to arrange the surrender, being rewarded for his services with an estate in Loja. In the course of the conflict Gonzalo not only refined his guerrilla tactics, but he also gained knowledge in

A nineteenth-century bust of '*El Gran Capitán*', inspired by a near-contemporary portrait. The expression captures well Gonzalo de Córdoba's steely determination, as much as his reflective mind and wry sense of humour.

Gonzalo de Córdoba

Ferdinand of Aragon and Isabella of Castile enter the captured town of Granada, the last Muslim stronghold in Spain (1492), in a wood carving from the early sixteenth century. Isabella was Gonzalo de Córdoba's greatest mentor, and her unwavering confidence in his abilities proved a huge asset for the Spanish crown.

the use of artillery and field fortifications. Moreover, Ferdinand and Isabella's employment of Swiss mercenaries allowed Gonzalo to see at first hand their revolutionary fighting techniques, which were far removed from those traditionally used – and cherished – by the Spaniards.

Defeat and reform

Gonzalo did not have to wait long to put his newly acquired knowledge into practice. In September 1494, a strong French army under Charles VIII of Valois descended on Italy, with the aim of conquering the kingdom of Naples from the Aragonese of Sicily. An adroit use of diplomacy, military might and terror tactics, coupled with the indifference – when not the open complicity – of the majority of Italy's governments and

Gonzalo de Córdoba

of the Neapolitan ruling elite, enabled Charles to conduct the equivalent of a blitzkrieg campaign, entering Naples at the end of February 1495. The dispossessed Neapolitan king, Ferrante II, appealed to his cousin Ferdinand of Aragon for help in the name of mutual dynastic interests, with the understanding that the latter's son Juan would be the next ruler of southern Italy should Ferrante die without legitimate male offspring.

Ferdinand of Aragon was only too happy to oblige his cousin's request. Charles VIII's high-handed behaviour had managed to alienate practically everyone in his newly conquered territories; moreover the creation by Italy's rulers of an anti-French league had forced the Valois king to retreat home leaving a reduced military presence in the kingdom of Naples – too small to control it efficiently. The man chosen to lead the expeditionary force to succour Ferrante was none other than Gonzalo Fernández de Córdoba, thanks to the influence of Isabella of Castile. The queen could not forget her former retainer's long-standing devotion and his exploits during the siege of Granada, and considered Gonzalo, a relatively junior commander, to be the right man to manage a campaign requiring diplomatic skills as much as brute force. Ferdinand and Isabella realized that without the support of the slippery Neapolitan nobility, any victory in the field would be useless.

Gonzalo sailed for Italy in May 1495 with a small army of about eighteen hundred men, mostly sword-and-buckler infantrymen, plus a small contingent of crossbowmen and harquebusiers and a few hundred light cavalrymen. He linked up with Ferrante in Calabria, discovering to his dismay the king determined to deliver

Spanish harquebusiers depicted in an early sixteenth-century tapestry. Gonzalo de Córdoba's understanding of the changing art of war revolutionized the Spanish way of fighting, successfully combining firepower with shock tactics. These same harquebusiers were largely responsible for Córdoba's stunning victory at Cerignola in 1503.

a knockout blow to the French forces in the region. Ignoring Gonzalo's warnings never to fight on ground chose by the enemy, Ferrante led the joint Spanish–Neapolitan army to Seminara, confident that his 6,000 men would easily defeat the 4,000 fielded by the French commander Robert Stewart d'Aubigny. Gonzalo knew better, for if about half of d'Aubigny's soldiers were Calabrian militiamen of dubious quality, the same could not be said of his 1,000-strong Swiss contingent and the 1,200 French cavalrymen – 300 of which were heavily armoured gendarmes. Initially, Gonzalo's horsemen met with some success, but Ferrante's Neapolitans mistook the Spaniards' hit-and-run for a rout and retreated in panic from the field. The attack by the French gendarmes and Swiss infantry smashed the enemy line to pieces and Gonzalo and Ferrante barely escaped with their lives. Gonzalo retreated with his remaining men into the hills, from where he conducted a vigorous guerrilla-style war, pinning down the enemy and at the same time avoiding pitched battles, carefully

Gonzalo de Córdoba

THE BATTLE OF CERIGNOLA

THE BEGINNING OF 1503 saw Gonzalo Fernández de Córdoba confined to Barletta, in Apulia, by superior French forces under the command of the Duke of Nemours. Undaunted, the Great Captain kept the enemy under constant pressure by means of daring sorties and raids, but none the less his situation looked bleak. The French naval blockade of Barletta's harbour not only threatened to starve the Spanish army, but also obstructed the arrival of desperately needed reinforcements. The situation changed dramatically the following February, when a Spanish maritime victory allowed seven Sicilian ships loaded with grain to disembark. Even more important, at the beginning of April two thousand landsknechts sent by Emperor Maximilian I landed near Manfredonia. Gonzalo, not yet fully trusting the capacity of his own infantry to defeat the French alone, now believed he had the troops who could match the Swiss soldiers in Louis XII's service. The defeat near Rutigliano of a strong French contingent by Pedro Navarro balanced the forces in Gonzalo's favour, giving him sufficient confidence to seek battle.

On the morning of 28 April the Spanish army marched out of Barletta towards the French-held stronghold of Cerignola. The Great Captain had about nine thousand five hundred men under his command, including the landsknechts, about eight hundred Spanish–Neapolitan heavy cavalry under Prospero Colonna and as many light cavalrymen under Fabrizio Colonna. The latter troops proved to be particularly useful, screening the advance of Gonzalo's main force and thus preventing the enemy from

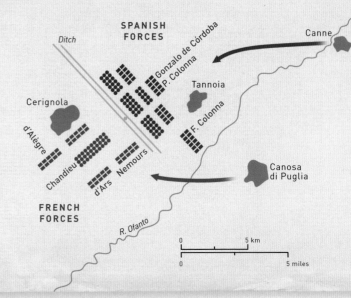

seeing its strength and advance route. Arriving in front of Cerignola, Gonzalo deployed his troops on a vine-covered ridge behind an irrigation ditch, which he immediately proceeded to excavate and strengthen. He placed his pikemen and swordsmen at the centre of the line, with harquebusiers in front and on the sides. Behind stood half his heavy cavalry, the rest being used as a tactical reserve. Fabrizio Colonna's horsemen covered the Spanish left flank, while Gonzalo's sixteen field pieces guarded the right.

Nemours arrived some time later and, seeing Gonzalo's deployment, hastily convened a war council. Many of the most experienced commanders advocated

husbanding his meagre monetary and human resources. Through force and treaty, he slowly brought over to his side the cities and towns of the region. In July 1496 Ferrante retook Naples after a daring amphibious operation, and helped by the willingness of the Neapolitans to be rid of the French for good.

Ferrante's sudden death two months later put Gonzalo in an awkward position, since his successor was the king's illegitimate uncle Federico and not – despite all previous agreements – Ferdinand of Aragon. Gonzalo therefore eagerly accepted Pope Alexander VI's request to help him expel the Valois troops occupying Ostia, at the mouth of the River Tiber, and distinguished himself by being one of the first into the breach, earning both the pontiff's gratitude and a spectacular entry into Rome at the head of his troops, which now included infantrymen carrying 10-foot pikes.

The lessons of Seminara had not been lost on Gonzalo. He realized that for Spanish soldiers to be successful in the field, their traditional fighting methods had to be drastically reformed. This implied not just a change of practice, but also, for the rank and file, absorbing and integrating the changes brought by the military revolution in

Gonzalo de Córdoba

ADRIATIC

Barletta

Andria

N

prudence, but Nemours never-theless decided to fight, having confidence in his Swiss pikemen and French heavy cavalry. He placed his Swiss, Gascon and Italian infantry at the centre, flanked by two wings of respectively heavy and light cavalry. Behind the main line stood the twenty-six French field pieces. Nemours planned to attack first with half his cavalry, immediately following them with the infantry grouped in three squares, and keeping the remaining horsemen for the decisive blow – a total of nearly eleven thousand men. With dusk fast approaching, Nemours gave the order to attack.

As the French men-at-arms approached the ditch they were met with the withering fire of Gonzalo's harque-busiers. Unable to jump the trench, the heavy cavalrymen fell in droves, Nemours among them. Fabrizio Colonna's horsemen repulsed the French light cavalry's attempt to turn the Spanish left flank, as Gonzalo's hand gunners opened gaping holes in the advancing Valois infantry. Falling back, the French infantry collided with the rest of their mounted troops, as the Spanish infantry moved in for the kill. In only half an hour the French had suffered a crushing defeat, leaving four thousand men on the field against about two hundred Spaniards.

Years later Fabrizio Colonna would comment that the ditch had been the real victor at Cerignola. While partially true, it is without doubt that the Great Captain's adroit use of technology had inaugurated a new season in the history of warfare.

Europe. The Spanish sword-and-buckler men were excellent troops, but alone could do little against Swiss-style infantry or heavily armoured horsemen. Gonzalo's reform implied integrating them with pike-wielding footmen and an increased number of harquebusiers instead of crossbowmen, backed by heavy cavalry units. Such changes required time, but to implement his reorganization Gonzalo could rely on a core of professional junior officers, many coming from the ranks of the *Santa Hermandad* (the Spanish royal police force) and veterans of the Moorish wars. While it would be wrong to attribute these military reforms solely to Gonzalo, his drive and determination accelerated a process already under development at the time of the Granada war.

Kingdom come

Gonzalo sailed back to Spain in the summer of 1498, having earned from the Italians the sobriquet of '*il Gran Capitano*' ('*el Gran Capitán*' in Spanish). Isabella and Ferdinand rewarded him with land, titles and honours, before sending him off to quash a Muslim rebellion in Andalusia. In September 1500 he sailed for the island of

Pikemen and artillery feature prominently in this depiction of the entry into Naples, *c.* 1498, of Fabrizio Colonna and the Count of Popolo. Charles VIII of Valois' whirlwind campaign in Italy provoked Spain's intervention in the peninsula, starting a struggle that was destined to last until the signing of the Peace of Cateau-Cambrésis in 1559.

Cephalonia, at the head of an expeditionary force to help the Venetians recapture the island from the Ottomans. No sooner had he completed the task than he was once more ordered back to Italy. Unbeknown to him, Ferdinand of Aragon had signed a secret treaty with King Louis XII of France, aimed at the joint conquest of the kingdom of Naples. Against such formidable foes, Federico of Aragon, after putting up no more than token resistance and agreeing to become one of Louis' pensioners, could do little but surrender. However, the ambiguous wording of the Treaty of Granada caused the French and the Spanish to quarrel immediately over the partition of the newly conquered kingdom.

Confronted by French superior forces, Gonzalo once more resorted to guerrilla-style tactics and the stubborn defence of key strongholds in Calabria and Apulia. But now he could also count on the aid of the powerful *condottieri* of the Colonna family; moreover, the alliance between Ferdinand and Emperor Maximilian I meant the arrival of reinforcements in the form of two thousand landsknecht heavy infantry. His confidence thus boosted, Gonzalo marched out of his headquarters in Barletta on 28 April 1503, and in the evening won a spectacular victory at the Battle of Cerignola (see pp. 392–3). The defeat by his lieutenants of the French forces in Calabria allowed Gonzalo to take Naples the following month.

Louis XII still held the Neapolitan territories north of the Garigliano river, having built a series of formidable field fortifications along its banks and receiving constant reinforcements from the nearby port of Gaeta. Undaunted, and despite his inferior numbers, Gonzalo followed the advice of the Italian *condottiere* Bartolomeo d'Alviano, and on the night of 28 December 1503 crossed the river on a hastily built pontoon bridge and took the French by surprise. In the ensuing running fight Louis' soldiers were utterly defeated; the surrender of Gaeta a few days later meant their complete eviction from southern Italy.

Thanks to Gonzalo, the kingdom of Naples had been permanently conquered and would remain a Spanish possession for the next two hundred years. Moreover, he had completely transformed the structure of Spain's armies, a process finalized in 1503 by his creation of large tactical formations called *coronelías* (roughly, regiments) composed of 3,000 infantrymen, 400 men-at-arms, as many light cavalrymen and 11 field guns. By pairing two such units, Gonzalo created the first divisions – effectively small, self-contained armies much like the old Roman legions.

Added flexibility was obtained by dividing each regiment into companies with a proportion of one harquebusier for every five foot soldiers – half of the remaining troops being pikemen and the rest armed with swords and bucklers. This combination of shot and shock would eventually develop into the famed Spanish *tercios*, the dominators of European battlefields until the mid seventeenth century.

The Great Captain's accounts

Gonzalo de Córdoba received the title of Viceroy of Naples for his exploits, but the death of Isabella of Castile in 1504 deprived him of his strongest patron. By then his fame had aroused the jealousy of Ferdinand of Aragon, who in 1507 replaced him as viceroy and, according to a well-known if uncorroborated story, asked him to show his accounts. A miffed Gonzalo delivered a sarcastic breakdown of his expenses, ending with: 'One hundred million ducats for the patience needed to listen to a King who asks accounts from the person who gave him a kingdom'. In truth he did present detailed accounts of his spending over the years; none the less, Ferdinand recalled the Great Captain to Spain, conferring on him the dukedom of Sessa and promising him the Grand Mastership of the Order of Santiago. It was not long before the king reneged on the latter commitment, granting him instead the town of Loja as a fief. Gonzalo moved there with his wife and daughter, remaining loyal to his unfaithful monarch even during the 1508 rebellion of the Andalusian nobility. Never receiving further military employment, he died peacefully in Loja on 1 December 1516.

> 'He not only vanquished his foes with his great courage and vigorous efforts, but also surpassed them by his intelligence and wisdom.'
>
> HERNAN PERÉZ DEL PULGAR ON GONZALO DE CÓRDOBA

The Great Captain's military heritage would survive him for another century and a half, his military reforms allowing Spain to dominate European battlefields until the Thirty Years War. In addition, a number of the conquistadores who conquered large swathes of America for the Spanish crown had previously served under Gonzalo de Córdoba, thus carrying his legacy to the New World.

AKBAR THE GREAT

1542–1605

FRANCIS ROBINSON

JALAL AL-DIN MUHAMMAD AKBAR was the most successful military leader of the able line of 'Great Mughals' who ruled in India from 1526 to 1540 and from 1555 to 1707. The grandson of Zahir al-Din Muhammad Babur (1483–1526), who founded the Mughal dynasty in India, and the son of Humayun (1508–56), whom he was to succeed as Mughal emperor, Akbar was profoundly aware of his family's traditions of conquest and empire, which reached back through his ancestor Timur (Tamerlane) to Chinghiz (Genghis) Khan.

He was still a teenager when he began what was to be a continuing series of successful military campaigns, which first consolidated the Mughal empire in the quadrilateral formed by the north Indian cities of Agra, Ajmer, Lahore and Allahabad, then expanded it, so that by the end of his reign the empire stretched from Afghanistan's Helmand river in the west to Bengal's Brahmaputra in the east, and from the Deccan's Godavari river in the south to the Himalayan mountains in the north. Akbar's success flowed in part from his qualities as a leader on the field of battle, and his willingness to develop gunpowder technology; but in part, too, from his gifts as an administrator and ruler. His regime played an important role in creating the circumstances whereby the subcontinent came to support one-third of the world's Muslims.

Akbar was 13 when he came to the throne, after his father died in January 1556 as a result of falling down the stone steps of his library. In the previous year Humayun had restored Mughal power to northern India; the immediate problem after his death was to sustain it. At this stage, rule was in the hands of Bayram Khan, a successful commander whom Humayun had appointed to be Akbar's guardian, but the regime was soon threatened by a vastly superior combination of Afghan and Rajput forces; in November 1556, however, assisted by fortune, these were defeated at Panipat, north of Delhi.

Akbar's development into a ruler

As Akbar progressed through adolescence he clashed increasingly with Bayram Khan, eventually aligning himself with a court faction opposed to his guardian, led by Adham Khan, the son of his wet nurse. In 1560, Akbar dismissed Bayram Khan, who

was subsequently assassinated. As Adham Khan and his mother began effectively to wield power, the young Akbar again asserted himself by appointing his own prime minister, whom Adham Khan then killed, violating the privacy of the harem in order to do so. Akbar immediately had him thrown to his death from the harem balcony. A further incident in which Akbar demonstrated his growing authority took place in 1561, when two victorious generals refused to send him the treasure and war elephants won in conquest, as they were required to do. Akbar immediately marched several hundred miles to their camp and forced them to submit. From then on, aged 19, Akbar was firmly in charge.

Akbar spent much of his time in the field. Successful campaigning kept the treasury full and the people reminded of his power. Akbar had no fixed capital city. During his reign his armies set out first from Agra, then Fatehpur Sikri, then Lahore and then again from Agra. The Mughal court travelled in Akbar's highly organized camp, in which the whole administrative apparatus of empire, registers and ledgers and so on, would be carried by elephant, camel and bullock cart. The use of different bases at different times followed the changing strategic emphases in the expansion of Mughal power.

A drawing of Akbar.
Probably made in the last year of the Mughal emperor's life, it seems to reflect the sadness of his old age, when he not only lost his mother and two of his sons, but was also estranged from his remaining son, Selim. After Akbar's death in October 1605, Selim ascended the Mughal throne and ruled as the emperor Jahangir.

Akbar the Great

Akbar's campaigns from Agra, 1564–71

Akbar's first major campaign from Agra began in 1564, when his Uzbek nobles revolted and invited his half-brother, Hakim, who ruled Kabul, to invade India in 1566. Matters worsened when a group of Timurid princes (that is, descended from Tamerlane), also challenged him. Akbar ignored the princes, moved quickly to confront his half-brother at Lahore, who retreated to Kabul, and then turned to drive the Uzbeks from the cities and fortresses they occupied east of Agra. The key to his success was speed and daring. Before the Uzbeks realized what was happening, he

had arrived on the banks of the Ganges opposite their encampment. Although this large river was swollen by monsoon rains, Akbar led a surprise night river-crossing and attacked the rebels at dawn. The Uzbeks were overwhelmed, and the Timurid princes promptly fled, to take refuge with the Sultan of Gujarat.

These rebellions of Uzbeks and Timurids from outside India convinced Akbar of the need to enlist indigenous nobles. Some were recruited from Muslim families but significant numbers came from the Hindu Rajput clans, the heads of whom gave him their daughters as wives. The Rajputs surrendered all control over their territories, and revenues from them were collected by Mughal administrators and adjusted against their salaries. This alliance between the emperors and the Rajputs was one of the great pillars of Mughal rule. Not all, however, gave in without a fight. In 1568 Akbar was forced to besiege the Rana of Mewar in his great fortress of Chitor (see p. 401), and in 1569 Rai Surjan was besieged in his fortress of Ranthambor. These two forts controlled the trade route to the Arabian Sea, and their capture underlined the will and power of Akbar, as well as the futility of resistance. The sieges have been described as 'spectacular public events'.

Akbar's campaigns from Fatehpur Sikri, 1571–85

In 1571 Akbar moved his capital 26 miles west from Agra to Fatehpur ('City of Victory') Sikri, which he was building in order to reflect the cultural inclusiveness and Islamic legitimacy of his regime. He became interested in linking Gujarat, the province on the Arabian Sea to the southwest, with its rich agriculture, textile production and busy seaports, to his territory in the fertile Indo-Gangetic plain. He was also interested in suppressing the Timurid princes who had established themselves in the south of Gujarat. In July 1572 he occupied Ahmadabad, the capital, and by January the following year he had received the submission of the sultan and all the Muslim nobles. The Timurid princes fled south to the Deccan.

Then, three months later, the nobles of Gujarat, disappointed because they had not been incorporated in the imperial service, allied with Afghans and Rajputs to drive out the Mughals. The crisis showed Akbar at his best. He put together a contingent of three to four hundred men who, mounted on swift camels, rode 500 miles to Ahmadabad in

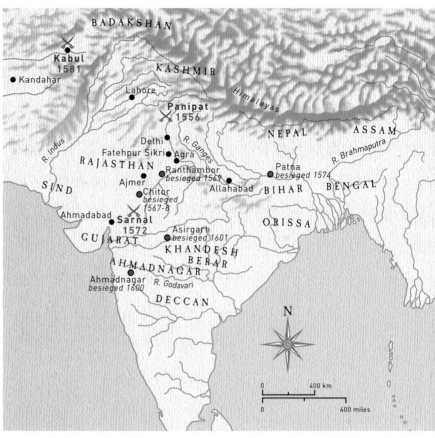

INDIA IN THE SIXTEENTH AND EARLY SEVENTEENTH CENTURIES, showing the principal victories of Akbar the Great.

nine days – a distance that caravans would then have taken two months to travel. On reaching the rebel army of twenty thousand men at Sarnal, he ignored the objections of his officers and immediately attacked, using the advantage of surprise to force the rebels to submit. Although the respective sizes of the two armies are those given in the *Akbar Nama*, the official history of Akbar's reign, other sources suggest the more believable figures of three thousand Mughal troops and fifteen thousand rebel troops. Whatever the precise figures, however, it is clear that Akbar achieved another great feat of arms in which speed and daring were vital. Forty-three days after he left, he was back in Fatehpur Sikri, his reputation for invincibility much enhanced.

In 1574 Akbar turned east to Bihar and Bengal, where Afghan nobles and Hindu rajas still held power. He besieged and captured the Afghan-held fortress of Patna and then forced the Afghan Sultan of Bengal to retreat before him, and eventually to flee to Orissa. Akbar then left the consolidation of the Mughal position to his able revenue minister, Todar Mal, although it was not until the late 1580s that all opposition was extinguished.

Akbar's campaigns from Lahore, 1585–98

In February 1581, Akbar's half-brother, Hakim, invaded northwest India from Kabul and took Lahore. Akbar immediately set off from Fatehpur Sikri with a major force of fifty thousand cavalry, five hundred war elephants and vast numbers of infantry. As soon as his forces approached Lahore, Hakim fled. Akbar pursued him into Afghanistan, defeating his army outside Kabul. In August, Akbar held court in Kabul. A proposal was put forward that Hakim should be executed, but Akbar showed his half-brother mercy, restored him to the throne of Kabul and returned to India.

(Opposite) **Akbar was a man of unusual energy** and courage. In November 1561 at Agra, to the consternation of his ministers, he rode the mighty elephant Hawa'i in a fight with another elephant named Ran Bagha. This image, from the *Akbar Nama* of Abul Fazl, shows Akbar riding Hawa'i as he chases the defeated Ran Bagha across a bridge of boats over the River Jumna.

Akbar the Great

Two images from the *Akbar Nama* of Abul Fazl, illustrating the use of mining and gunpowder in the Mughal siege of Chitor, 1567–8: (left) the explosion of a wrongly laid gunpowder charge in December 1567 causes numerous Mughal deaths; (right) Akbar kills the Rajput commander Jaimal in February 1568, having created a *sabat*, or covered way, to create a breach in the city walls.

This campaign in the northwest was the overture to thirteen years spent campaigning in order to establish Mughal power firmly in the region. The spur was the death of Hakim in 1585 and the conquest by the Shaybanid Uzbek ruler, Abd Allah Khan, of the northeastern Afghan province of Badakshan, thus threatening Kabul. Akbar responded by sending an army to occupy Kabul and by bringing the region under Mughal imperial administration. To consolidate and expand Mughal power further in 1585, he moved his capital to Lahore.

One of Akbar's major concerns in the northwest was to foster the rich caravan trade between this region and Iran, Central Asia and China. In one direction came goods such as textiles and spices from India; in the other, horses, silks and porcelain. The trade was particularly vulnerable to lawless Afghan tribes, in this case, the Yusufzais. In 1586 a royal army which recklessly attacked the Yusufzais was ambushed in the mountain passes, and eight thousand Mughal soldiers were killed, including one of the two commanders, Akbar's friend and court wit, Raja Birbal. Over the next six years Akbar responded by building a military system to control the region and protect the caravan trade. He succeeded in doing what few others have been able to do since that time.

In 1585 Akbar sent an army north to invade Kashmir which, by June 1589, he brought fully under Mughal control. In the following year, he sent another army into the lower Indus valley to conquer Sind. By 1593 its ruler had made a formal

THE SIEGE OF CHITOR

AKBAR'S ALLIANCE with the Rajput princes was a pillar of his rule. Full Rajput acceptance of Mughal sovereignty was only achieved by military victory. Akbar's successful siege of Chitor, which lasted from 20 October 1567 until 23 February 1568, was the key victory. Chitor was the fortified capital of Udai Singh (r. 1540–72), the Rana of Mewar, who as head of the Sisodia clan had the highest status of all the Rajput princes and chiefs. Once he had submitted, the others would duly follow.

Chitor stood on a rock outcrop 3¼ miles in circumference and rising over 600 feet above the Rajasthan plain. As Akbar approached, Udai Singh withdrew, leaving eight thousand troops with supplies to withstand a long siege. After devastating the surrounding country, he then fled to the hills. Forty thousand peasants took refuge in the fortress.

On investing Chitor, Akbar encircled it with batteries and even had a massive mortar cast on the spot to intimidate the defenders. His bombardment, however, was ineffective. In addition, despite all precautions, it was undertaken at the cost of two hundred Mughal lives a day. Despite many being killed around him, Akbar exposed himself to enemy fire without evident fear.

Faith was then placed in mining the walls. On 17 December Akbar asked that two separate gunpowder charges be placed under them, but the engineers chose to connect them. In consequence, when after the first explosion, the flower of young Mughal nobility charged through the breach, two hundred of them were then killed in the second explosion. 'Though the garrison showed exultation', Abul Fazl tells us, 'H.M. the Shahinshah was tranquil, for he knew that there had been a want of plan and gradual progress in regard to the siege ... patience and planning were necessary ...'

Akbar now placed his faith in a *sabat*, a covered way wide enough for ten horsemen to ride abreast and tall enough for a man on an elephant to hold a spear erect. Its side walls were made of rubble and mud to absorb cannon shot, and its wooden roof was held together with ropes of hide. Screens of hide concealed those building the *sabat* in the very dangerous position at the front. The *sabat* took a sinuous course to the foot of the wall, at which point those inside it began to tear the wall down, Akbar himself directing operations from a small pavilion on top of the structure.

In February 1568 the *sabat* reached the wall and a breach was created. Akbar noticed Jaimal, the Rajput commander, in the breach directing operations and killed him with his favourite musket 'Sangram'. Realizing that it was all over, the Rajputs burned their women to death, the act of *jauhar*, and prepared to sell their lives dearly. On 23 February the Mughals charged through the breach with fifty elephants in the van, killing thirty thousand Rajputs. Udai Singh remained at large but ineffective; whereas Akbar, at the shrine of Muin al-Din Chishti at Ajmer, gave thanks for his victory.

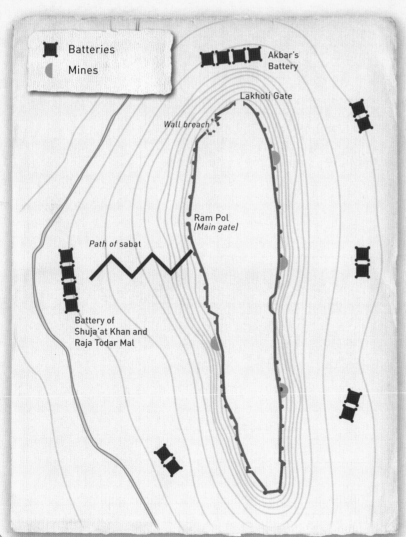

Batteries

Mines

Akbar's Battery

Lakhoti Gate

Wall breach

Ram Pol *(Main gate)*

Path of sabat

Battery of Shuja'at Khan and Raja Todar Mal

submission to Akbar in court at Lahore and his lands had become the Mughal province of Thatta. Finally, in 1595, Akbar was able to round off his control of the northwest by retaking Kandahar, when its disgraced Safavid commander surrendered to him. This important city, which had long been out of Mughal hands, controlled the caravan route which skirted the south of Afghan territory on the way to Iran.

Akbar's campaigns from Agra, 1598–1605

In 1598 Abd Allah Khan died. Akbar clearly thought that this event, together with his own military and administrative achievements, left the northwest secure enough for him to move the capital once more to Agra. One of the reasons he may have chosen his original capital over Fatehpur Sikri was the fact that he was now faced with an increasingly rebellious eldest son, Selim – and Agra was well defended.

Akbar now turned his full attention to the five Muslim sultanates in the Deccan to the south. Indeed, his armies had already been in action there, leading in 1596 to the incorporation of Berar into the empire. Subsequent Mughal armies under his sons, Murad and Daniyal, achieved only moderate success, so in September 1599

> # 'A lofty genius is the key to difficult enterprises ...'
> ABUL FAZL, *AKBAR NAMA*, ON AKBAR AT THE SIEGE OF CHITOR.

Akbar took control of operations in person, with notable results. In August 1600, Mughal forces stormed the fortress of the Sultan of Ahmadnagar; then in January 1601, after his last major military operation, Akbar secured the surrender of the great fortress of Asirgarh and the submission of the Sultan of Khandesh.

Akbar's last years were clouded by the deaths of his sons Murad and Daniyal from alcoholism and by major acts of rebellion from Selim, with whom, however, he was reconciled before his death in Agra on 25 October 1605.

Akbar's gifts as a ruler

Akbar's achievements as a commander owed much to his gifts as a ruler. To some degree his armies helped to pay for themselves through treasure captured from defeated enemies. But they were also maintained by able revenue administration. Akbar and his ministers created a system based on accurate statistics of production, which was measured field by field and crop by crop. The Mughal state levied between one-third and one-fifth of the value of the harvest as tax. Accurate measurement, and the use of averages over a ten-year period, enabled the state to achieve the desirable end of extracting a high proportion of rural productivity while leaving enough to encourage the cultivator to produce more. By the end of his reign the Mughal treasury was producing annual surpluses of between 4–5 million rupees.

Important, too, were Akbar's inclusive religious policies. As a Muslim he made men of all faiths welcome as contributors to his imperial project, his leading Hindu commanders, for instance, including rajas Todar Mal, Birbal and Man Singh.

Especially important in holding the imperial framework together were the nobles who filled the senior administrative and political positions in the system, and whose bureaucratic skills, military prowess and entrepreneurial abilities made it work. They all had rights to receive revenues from land assigned to them, in return for which they maintained contingents of cavalry, according to their rank – war horses, elephants and so on – all of which were at the disposal of the emperor. Managing the nobles was crucial to Akbar's success: they were moved frequently from post to post; court ceremonial required frequent acts of submission; and towards the end of his reign their loyalty was encouraged by membership of his Din-i Ilahi cult, which entitled them to wear his portrait on their turbans. At this time the nobles were responsible for one hundred and forty thousand cavalry and consumed 82 per cent of the imperial budget.

These policies enabled Akbar to fashion and maintain an effective war machine, the major features of which were organization, discipline and gunpowder technology. Observers were astonished by the size and symmetry of the imperial camp. Arranged with streets and bazaars, it was the same wherever it was pitched, with an immense white royal pavilion at the centre. The army on the march operated under rules designed to maximize its security and to minimize its impact on the local people, providing they were acquiescent. Disobedience in the ranks met with instant and exemplary punishment. Although the cavalry and composite bow remained staple weapons, gunpowder technology, in which Akbar took much personal interest, was important to its success. Indeed, so important was it to Akbar that the *Ain-i Akbari* describes it as 'a wonderful lock for securing the August edifice of royalty and a pleasing key to the door of conquest'. The royal household maintained a monopoly over artillery, which was parked in front of the emperor's pavilion in camp. In 1596 the army comprised one hundred and forty-seven thousand cavalrymen and thirty-five thousand musketeers.

Speed and daring were the hallmarks of Akbar's battlefield generalship. This illustration from the *Akbar Nama* of Abul Fazl depicts the Battle of Sarnal in Gujarat in 1572 when, after riding 500 miles in nine days, he defeated a vastly superior rebel force.

At the head of this war machine Akbar won victory after victory and fashioned what was, along with Ming China, the greatest of the early modern Asian empires. In measuring his achievement we must realize, as historian John F. Richards states,

that the Mughal empire met determined enemies who commanded substantially well-equipped, well-motivated armies. Most battles were desperate and bloody; the sieges difficulty and lengthy. On numerous occasions Akbar could have been wounded or killed when leading his troops in battle. Luck and his military skills saved him. The builder of the Mughal empire was undoubtedly a superb military commander in a generally bellicose society.

ODA NOBUNAGA

1534–82

STEPHEN TURNBULL

VILIFIED BY GEORGE SANSOM in his *History of Japan* as a 'cruel and callous brute', Oda Nobunaga is still a controversial figure in Japanese history, a man whose military genius remains his only undisputed quality. Nobunaga embraced western military technology with an enthusiasm that none of his contemporaries could match, applied it with an eye for strategy and tactics that others lacked, and achieved results with an utter ruthlessness that others only feared. Through a series of military victories, achieved by a loyal and well-organized army, Oda Nobunaga began the process that was eventually to lead to the reunification of Japan, a goal that only an untimely and violent death prevented him from achieving for himself.

The violent episode by which Nobunaga met his end – he was ambushed by the army of a treacherous subordinate while resting overnight in a temple – was no more than typical of the age into which he had been born. Since the tragic Onin War of 1467–77, the central authority of the Shogun, Japan's military dictator, had rapidly declined in favour of a number of independent *daimyō* (warlords). Nobunaga's father, Oda Nobuhide, provides a classic example. His family had overthrown the Shogun's provincial deputy, after which they ruled much of their native province of Owari. When Nobunaga succeeded to the family headship in 1551 he inherited a reputation for valour and daring, two qualities that he required in abundance when he united the province under his rule. This process, which involved fighting members of his own family, was an almost exclusively military undertaking, small in scale but indicative of the challenges that he would face from the powerful enemies who surrounded him. Their first major move in 1560 was to mark the emergence of Nobunaga's military career on to a national stage.

The Battle of Okehazama

The most powerful *daimyō* among Nobunaga's near neighbours was Imagawa Yoshimoto (1519–60), who controlled the provinces of Mikawa, Tōtōmi and Suruga. In 1554 and 1558 Nobunaga had suffered attacks from Yoshimoto, whose growing confidence, boosted by judicious alliances, was such that by 1560 he was contemplating a march against Kyōto, Japan's capital. The first unfriendly territory that Yoshimoto would have to cross in his drive against the Shogun's rule was Oda Nobunaga's province of Owari.

Contemporary accounts of the resulting Battle of Okehazama, Oda Nobunaga's first significant military victory, paint a picture of a battle won against overwhelming odds. Ota Gyūichi, the author of *Shinchō-kōki*, Nobunaga's first biography, written in 1610, may be exaggerating somewhat when he states that Imagawa Yoshimoto marched west with an army of forty-five thousand men against his master's two thousand, but the discrepancy was certainly considerable. Yoshimoto's first objective was to capture Nobunaga's frontier forts, which he did with ease, after which he rested his army while he performed the traditional ceremony of viewing the severed heads of the defeated.

The place chosen for Yoshimoto's temporary field headquarters was a small gorge with restricted access near to the hamlet of Okehazama. It was an area Nobunaga knew well, so after rigging up a dummy army of flags a safe distance away he led his men around the hills to within close distance of the unsuspecting Imagawa army. His final movements were concealed by a fortuitous thunderstorm and a fierce downpour, at the end of which Nobunaga's men attacked. Yoshimoto's guards were caught completely by surprise and could not prevent Nobunaga's raid from sweeping right into the inner circle of Yoshimoto's bodyguard. Yoshimoto initially thought that a brawl had broken out among his own men, but no sooner did he discover the truth than his head was sliced from his body.

The death of Yoshimoto set in motion the rapid collapse of Imagawa influence and the consequent rise to power of Oda Nobunaga, whose willingness to take on overwhelming odds and to act swiftly and decisively confirmed his unique military skills. One response to this demonstration of talent was the recruitment of more followers to his flag and the considerable enhancement of his original *kashindan* (retainer band). The way in which Nobunaga organized his army around a nucleus of devoted followers,

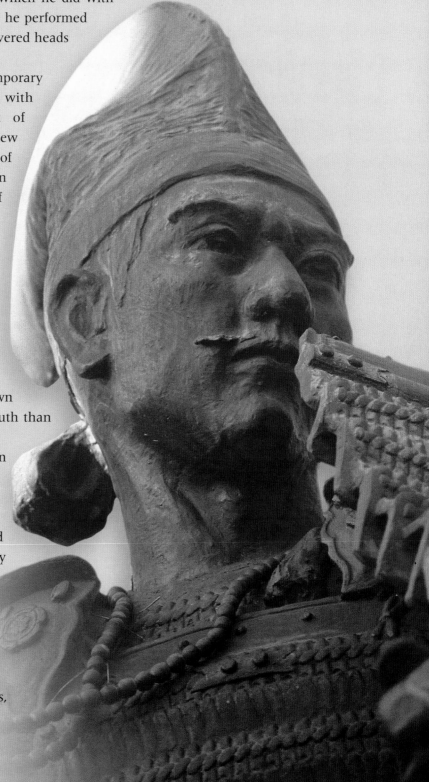

The statue of Oda Nobunaga on the site of his castle of Kiyosu, which Nobunaga captured in 1555, and later used as his operational base.

adding to it by incorporating defeated enemies into its ranks, was one reason for his continued martial success. Contrary to the popular image of the vanquished samurai seeking nothing but death, it was common practice for entire armies to enter a victor's service when a daimyō was eliminated. The distinguished Shibata Katsuie (1530–83), for example, was in joint command of an army that supported Nobunaga's younger brother for leadership of the family. He was defeated in 1556 and went on to become one of Nobunaga's most trusted generals. Similar considerations were made when the province of Mino passed into Nobunaga's control in 1567, although it became the practice to place most of these later newcomers under the command of existing generals in a subordinate role known as *yoriki*.

The *Shinchō-kōki* account of the Battle of Okehazama records the active part played by Nobunaga's *o uma mawari* (horse guards), who formed the core of his army. As his elite mounted force, the horse guards had responsibilities that went beyond guarding Nobunaga's person. In 1568, for instance, they were to lead the attack on Mitsukuriyama castle, and enjoyed a unique social status. (As shown by a bizarre account of a New Year reception Nobunaga held in 1574, when, after dismissing his ordinary retainers, Nobunaga continued with a second party for the horse guards, whose sake drinking was enlivened by a private viewing of the severed heads of the Asai and Asakura *daimyō*, nicely presented with an attractive coating of gold paint.)

Oda Nobunaga accompanied by his standard bearer, from a hanging scroll in Gifu Castle Museum.

The other main divisions of Nobunaga's army consisted of his *ichimon* (kinsmen) and his *koshō*, a word best translated as pages or squires. The latter tended to be young men, often the sons of senior retainers who served in the Oda Nobunaga household. Along with an emerging officer corps they went to make up a trusted leadership under a charismatic commander.

The master of musketry

Perhaps because of the heavy rain, there seems to have been little use made at Okehazama of harquebuses, or *teppō*, the weapons with which Nobunaga is most

Oda Nobunaga

closely associated, although Yoshimoto's troops had used them during their advance. These simple muskets were fired by dropping a lighted match on to the touch hole. First introduced by Portuguese traders in 1543, the *teppō* was soon copied and mass-produced by those *daimyō* who understood its potential. Oda Nobuhide, Nobunaga's father, was one of these, and arranged for his son to receive instruction in firearms techniques from a certain Hashimoto Ippa. He also arranged Nobunaga's marriage in 1549 to the daughter of Saitō Dōsan, and it was on a visit to his father-in-law that Nobunaga was able to demonstrate his early appreciation of the value of firearms, when he paraded in front of Dōsan with five hundred of the weapons.

By the mid 1550s the *teppō* had become widely disseminated throughout Japan. In 1555, for example, Takeda Shingen (1521–73) sent three hundred harquebuses to help in the defence of Asahiyama castle. It was Oda Nobunaga's early appreciation of the best way in which these clumsy weapons could be used, however, that was his outstanding contribution to the development of firearms in Japan. In contrast to the bow, which could deliver more missiles in a shorter space of time, the harquebus required less training but more discipline. To entrust simple *ashigaru* (foot soldiers) with the weapons, to place them en masse at the front of an army – the place traditionally occupied by the bravest and most noble mounted samurai – and then to control them to deliver organized volleys, was a considerable conceptual leap for any general to make. Yet Nobunaga seems to have achieved all three by the year 1554, when he attacked the Imagawa outpost of Muraki on the Chita peninsula.

The *Shinchō-kōki* account tells us that Nobunaga set up his position on the very edge of the castle moat, and ordered three successive volleys against the loopholes in the castle defences. The harquebusiers appear to have been organized in squads that fired in succession, confirming Nobunaga's sophisticated battlefield control, and it has been further argued that the Muraki action represents the first use of rotating volleys in Japanese history, a technique with which Nobunaga is credited during his epic Battle of Nagashino in 1575.

> 'The King of Owari would be about 37 years old, tall, thin, sparsely bearded, extremely war-like and much given to military exercises ...'
>
> LUÍS FRÓIS, *CARTAS QUE LOS PADRES Y HERMANOS DE LA COMPAÑIA DE JESUS QUE ANDAN EN LOS REYNOS DE JAPON ESCRIVIERON*, ALCALÁ, 1575

Nobunaga the Ruthless

Nobunaga's appreciation of the potential of massed harquebuses in the hands of lower class warriors had not escaped the attention of the leaders of the armies who were to prove to be the deadliest enemies of his entire career. Over a period of ten years between 1570 and 1580, Nobunaga was frequently occupied in fighting the Ikkō-ikki, the fanatical warriors drawn largely from the lower echelons of the samurai class and farming communities who were united by their religious affiliation to the True Pure Land sect of Buddhism. Motivated by a belief that heaven was the reward for being killed in battle, and contemptuous of the authority over them that the samurai assumed, they ruled territories comparable to those of the *daimyō*, from self-governing communities with well-stocked arsenals. In 1570 Nobunaga led an attack on Noda and Fukushima, two outposts of the Ishiyama Honganji, the Ikkō-ikki's 'fortress cathedral' built on the site of present-day Osaka castle. The defenders had

VICTORY AT NAGASHINO

THE BATTLE OF NAGASHINO, Nobunaga's operational master-stroke, came about as a result of a move to lift the siege of the castle of the same name. Nagashino, which stood on a promontory where two rivers met, had been holding out against the army of Takeda Katsuyori (1546–82), the heir of the famous Shingen. The great strength of the Takeda lay in their mounted samurai, whose ability to overrun and disorder foot soldiers, even when they were armed with harquebuses, had been demonstrated as recently as the Battle of Mikata ga Hara against Nobunaga's ally Tokugawa Ieyasu in 1572.

On approaching Nagashino, Nobunaga made his plans accordingly. First, instead of simply falling on to the rear of Katsuyori's army, he took up a planned position a few miles away at Shidarahara, where the topography enabled him to restrict enemy cavalry movement. Bounded by mountains to the north and a river to the south, Nobunaga's position was not susceptible to outflanking manoeuvres. Second, Nobunaga erected a loose palisade of lashed timber that provided protection to his army while allowing some gaps through which a counter-attack might be launched. Third, he arranged a welcome for Takeda Katsuyori in the form of massed ranks of harquebusiers.

The popular view of Nobunaga's victory at Nagashino is that it came about entirely as a result of the third of these factors. A. L. Sadler credits Nobunaga with choosing 'three thousand specially selected marksmen' who would 'pour in alternate volleys. It was the machine gun and wire entanglement of those days'. This latter quotation, and Sansom's conclusion that 'the musketeers were divided into three sections, firing in rotation' has become the accepted view of Nagashino, and the notorious final scene depicting the battle in Akira Kurosawa's film *Kagemusha* makes the action look as though the bullets were indeed delivered by machine guns.

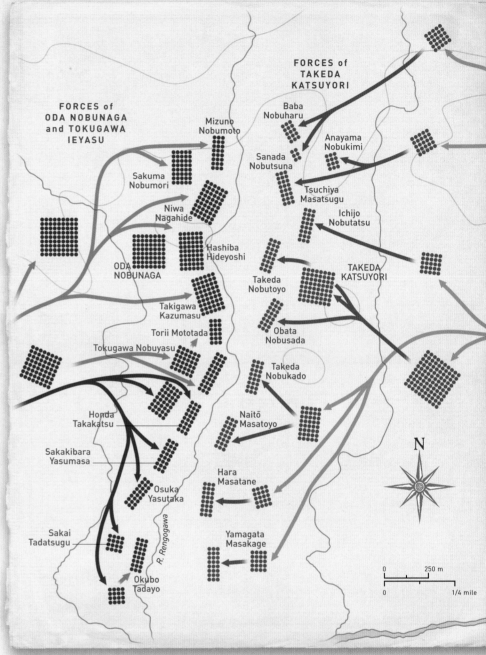

The reality of the situation is somewhat less dramatic, yet it detracts nothing from Nobunaga's generalship on the day. The first point concerns the number of harquebuses deployed. *Mikawa Go Fudoki* (Sadler's source) says three thousand. The more reliable *Shinchō-kōki* has one thousand. Nor need we necessarily conclude from the observation that different squads of harquebusiers fired alternate volleys, that this was an early application of the system of rotating volleys. Such a scheme, associated in particular with the military

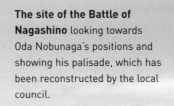

The site of the Battle of Nagashino looking towards Oda Nobunaga's positions and showing his palisade, which has been reconstructed by the local council.

(Below) **Oda Nobunaga's firearms break the Takeda charge,** from a modern reproduction of the famous painted screen of the Battle of Nagashino in Gifu Castle Museum.

innovations of Maurice of Nassau, required the front rank to discharge their pieces then move to the rear to allow the second rank to do the same, a manoeuvre known as the counter-march. Yet even the Dutch were to discover that a minimum of six ranks, and preferably ten, were required to keep up a constant fire.

At Nagashino, Nobunaga did not possess the resources to mimic machine guns. Many of the harquebusiers he arranged behind the palisades were not his own troops but had been supplied by allies and subordinates a few days before the battle took place. There was therefore no time to drill them in the counter-march. Alternate volleys were certainly delivered, but should be understood as a response to the successive waves of attack launched by the Takeda cavalry under the iron discipline of the five *bugyō* (commissioners) whom Nobunaga had placed in command of the squads. *Shinchō-kōki* records each of the five attacks, naming the Takeda generals who advanced to the beat of drums and were met by gunfire. *Mikawa Go Fudoki* breaks the action down further, noting that three hundred harquebusiers in the sector held by the Okubo brothers faced a charge by three thousand men under Yamagata Masakage. Interestingly, this is precisely the situation illustrated on the contemporary painted screen of the Battle of Nagashino owned by the Tokugawa Art Museum in Nagoya. Horses are shown falling dead and throwing their riders, in classic images of a broken cavalry charge. Yet the Battle of Nagashino still had several hours to run,

and from this point onwards the spears and swords of the samurai came into their own. Protected by the long spears of other foot soldiers, whose contribution to the battle was in no way inferior to their harquebus-firing colleagues, Nobunaga's armies took on the Takeda on a battlefield of their own choosing. Takeda Katsuyori was decisively defeated by a skilled general who used a combination of arms to its best advantage.

three thousand harquebuses, to which Nobunaga responded with guns of his own, so that 'the thunder of the guns of both friend and foe made heaven and earth shake by night and by day'.

In 1576 Nobunaga suffered a slight wound when he was hit in the leg by a bullet fired from Ishiyama Honganji, but by then it had already become clear to him that he was not able to defeat this mass movement by the application of firepower alone. With a ruthlessness driven by necessity and made palatable by his utter contempt for the 'rabble' that opposed him, the dark side of Nobunaga's military genius asserted itself against the Ikkō-ikki. Yet it was not the Ikkō-ikki who were the first to experience his wrath. That was to be the fate of the 'soft target' of the Enryakuji, the ancient monastic complex situated on Mount Hiei to the northeast of Kyōto, revered for centuries as the guardian of Japan's capital city and its major centre of monastic learning. In 1570 its monks had unwisely provided sanctuary to certain of Nobunaga's defeated enemies, so on the last day of September 1571 Nobunaga's troops surrounded the mountain and slowly advanced up it, burning and killing every living thing in their path. The horror of the attack was noted by the Jesuit Luís Fróis, who fully appreciated the message that it sent out to Nobunaga's other better-armed Buddhist rivals.

In 1574 the indiscriminate weapon of fire was brought to bear upon the defenders of Nagashima, a major fortress of the Ikkō-ikki located among a maze of muddy islands in a river delta. Nobunaga had failed to take Nagashima in both 1571 and 1573, but in 1574 the application of superior force enabled him gradually to drive the defenders into an area of the delta that was sufficiently small to allow him to erect wooden palisades around the complex and then burn to death at least twenty thousand people.

But his most notorious act of ruthlessness was to be reserved for 1575, the year of his triumph at Nagashino. In a well-organized operation involving the coordination of three armies, Nobunaga moved into Echizen province, which the local Ikkō-ikki army had captured from him the previous year. The province was retaken within a few days, but then the retribution began. The former magnanimity with which Nobunaga had incorporated defeated enemies into his own army was not extended to the twelve thousand five hundred prisoners taken from the lower-class 'rabble' of the Ikkō-ikki. Instead words such as 'eradicate' and 'wipe out' were used. In Echizen, Nobunaga's *koshō* (pages) were given the grisly task of either executing the prisoners or overseeing their removal as slaves. Nobunaga described his triumph in a letter to his *shoshidai* (representative) in Kyōto, Murai Nagato-no-kami: 'Within the town of Fuchū dead bodies lie everywhere with no empty space between them. I would like you to see it. Today, hunting mountain by mountain, valley by valley, I have to complete the task of seeking out and exterminating them.'

The death toll in Echizen may well have reached forty thousand men, women and children, but this undisputed stain on Nobunaga's character has to be seen in the context of the times. By eliminating the Ikkō-ikki from the equation, Nobunaga spared his successors Toyotomi Hideyoshi (1536–98) and Tokugawa Ieyasu (1542–1616) from having to engage in dishonourable warfare. Their opponents were, by and large, of similar stock, for whom magnanimity in victory was regarded as appropriate, and it can be argued that their concern over the threat posed by Christianity in Japan was based on a fear that Japanese Christians might become a second Ikkō-ikki. As it was, Nobunaga had done their dirty work for them.

In conclusion, Oda Nobunaga deserves to rank with the greatest generals of all time. His willingness to embrace new military technology with thoughtful application, his ability to think strategically and respond appropriately, having created and maintained a loyal and cohesive army, sit well beside the ruthless pragmatism with which he discharged his role. If Nobunaga, like his fortunate successors, had needed only to fight fellow samurai then his calculated ruthlessness may well have been seen as an additional martial virtue.

The charge of the Takeda samurai, as depicted by life-sized dummies at Ise Sengoku Mura on the outskirts of Futami in southwestern Japan.

CONQVISTA DE MEXICO POR CORTES. 7

FURTHER READING

THUTMOSE III

E. H. Cline and D. O'Connor (eds), *Thutmose III: A New Biography* (University of Michigan Press, Ann Arbor, 2006).

I. Shaw, *Egyptian Warfare and Weapons* (Shire Publications Limited, Princes Risborough, 1991).

M. Lichtheim, *Ancient Egyptian Literature: A Book of Readings. Volume II: The New Kingdom* (University of California Press, Berkley, Los Angeles, and London, 1976).

RAMESSES II

K. A. Kitchen, *Pharaoh Triumphant: the Life and Times of Ramesses II* (Aris and Phillips Limited, Warminster, 1982).

M. Lichtheim, *Ancient Egyptian Literature: A Book of Readings. Volume II: The New Kingdom* (University of California Press, Berkley, Los Angeles, and London, 1976).

I. Shaw, *Egyptian Warfare and Weapons* (Shire Publications Limited, Princes Risborough, 1991).

J. A. Tyldesley, *Ramesses: Egypt's Greatest Pharaoh* (Viking Penguin, London, 2000).

JOSHUA BIN NUN

The Bible, Book of Joshua.

R. S. Hess, 'Early Israel in Cana'an; A Survey of Recent Evidence and Interpretations', *Palestine Exploration Quarterly*, 125, 1993.

KING DAVID

The Bible, I Samuel 16–31, II Samuel 1–24, I Kings 1–2.

Jonathan Kirsch, *King David: The Real Life of the Man who Ruled Israel* (Ballantine, New York, NY, 2001).

TIGLATH-PILESER III

Mark Healy, *The Ancient Assyrians* (Osprey, London, 1991).

Doyne Dawson, *The First Armies* (Cassell, London, 2001), chapter 5.

SUN-TZU

Sun Tzu, *The Art of War*, translated and with introduction by Samuel B. Griffiths (Oxford University Press, Oxford, 1963).

C. P. Fitzgerald, *China, A Short Cultural History* (Cresset Press, London, 1950).

Marcel Granet, *Chinese Civilisation* (Barnes and Noble, London, 1957).

Mao Zedong, *Selected Works* (Lawrence and Wishart, London, 1955).

CYRUS THE GREAT

Pierre Briant, *From Cyrus to Alexander: A History of the Persian Empire*, translated by Peter T. Daniels (Eisenbraums, Winona Lake, Indiana, 2002).

Tom Holland, *Persian Fire: The First World Empire and the Battle for the West* (Little, Brown, London, 2005).

Josef Wiesehöfer, *Ancient Persia*, translated by Azizeh Azodi (I. B. Tauris, London, 2001).

LEONIDAS

Herodotus, *The Histories*, translated by Aubrey de Sélincourt (revised edition, Penguin Classics, Harmondsworth, 1996).

Paul Cartledge, *Thermopylae: The Battle that Changed the World* (Macmillan, London, 2006).

Tom Holland, *Persian Fire: The First World Empire and the Battle for the West* (Little, Brown, London, 2005).

THEMISTOCLES

Herodotus, *The Histories*, translated by Robin Waterfield (Oxford University Press, Oxford, 1998).

Robert Lenardon, *The Saga of Themistocles* (Thames & Hudson, London, 1978).

Barry Strauss, *The Battle of Salamis* (Simon and Schuster, New York, 2004).

N. G. L. Hammond, 'The Expedition of Xerxes', in John Boardman *et al.* (eds), *The Cambridge Ancient History*, *Volume 4* (second edition, Cambridge University Press, Cambridge 1988).

THUCYDIDES

Nigel Bagnall, *The Peloponnesian War* (Pimlico, London, 2004), which includes a good map of the Sicilian expedition.

Simon Hornblower, *Thucydides* (Duckworth, London, 1987).

Robin Lane Fox, *The Classical World* (Penguin, London, 2005).

Thucydides, *The Peloponnesian War* (New English Library, London, 1966).

ALCIBIADES

Thucydides, *The Peloponnesian War*, translated by Rex Warner, revised by Tim Rood (Penguin, London, 2008).

Xenophon, *A History of My Times*, translated by Rex Warner (Penguin, Harmondsworth, 1979).

David Gribble, *Alcibiades and Athens: A Study in Literary Presentation* (Oxford University Press, Oxford, 1999).

Walter Ellis, *Alcibiades* (Routledge, London, 1989).

XENOPHON

Xenophon, *The Expedition of Cyrus*, translated by Robin Waterfield (Oxford University Press, Oxford, 2005).

J. K. Anderson, *Xenophon* (Duckworth, London, 1974).

Robin Waterfield, *Xenophon's Retreat: Greece, Persia and the End of the Golden Age* (Faber & Faber, London, 2006).

PHILIP II OF MACEDON

M. Andronikos, *Vergina: The Royal Tombs and the Ancient City* (Ekdotike Athenon, Athens, 1984).

G. T. Griffith, 'Philip as a General and the Macedonian Army', in M. B. Hatzopoulos and L. Loukopoulou (eds), *Philip of Macedon* (Heinemann, London, 1981).

N. G. L. Hammond, G. T. Griffith, *A History of Macedonia II* (Clarendon Press, Oxford, 1979).

N. G. L. Hammond, *Philip of Macedon* (Duckworth, London, reprinted 2002).

N. Sekunda, *The Army of Alexander the Great* (Osprey, London, 1984).

ALEXANDER THE GREAT

J. F. C. Fuller, *The Generalship of Alexander the Great* (Eyre & Spottiswoode, London, 1958).

N. G. L. Hammond, *Alexander the Great: Commander and Statesman* (Chatto & Windus, London, 1981).

Robin Lane Fox, *Alexander the Great* (Allen Lane, London, 1973; reprinted Penguin, London, 2004).

N. Sekunda, *The Army of Alexander the Great* (Osprey, London, 1984).

HANNIBAL

Gregory Daly, *Cannae: The Experience of Battle in the Second Punic War* (Routledge, London, 2002).

Adrian Goldsworthy, *The Punic Wars* (Weidenfeld & Nicolson, London, 2000).

J. F. Lazenby, *Hannibal's War* (Aris and Philips, Warminster, 1978).

SCIPIO AFRICANUS

H. Scullard, *Scipio Africanus: Soldier and Politician* (Thames & Hudson, London, 1970).

Adrian Goldsworthy, *The Punic Wars* (Weidenfeld & Nicolson, London, 2000).

Adrian Goldsworthy, *The Fall of Carthage* (Cassell Military Paperbacks, London, 2003).

B. Liddell Hart, *Greater than Napoleon – Scipio Africanus* (William Blackwood & Sons, Edinburgh, 1930).

JUDAH MACCABEUS

I and II Maccabees, English translation, available at *http://st-takla.org/pub_ Deuterocanon/Deuterocanon-Apocrypha_ El-Asfar_El-Kanoneya_El-Tanya__ 8-First-of-Maccabees.html* and *http://st-takla.org/pub_Deuterocanon/ Deuterocanon-Apocrypha_El-Asfar_ El-Kanoneya_El-Tanya__ 9-Second-of-Maccabees.html* respectively.

B. Bar Kochva, *Judas Maccabaeus: The Jewish Struggle against the Seleucids* (Cambridge, Cambridge University Press, 1989).

POMPEY

P. Greenhalgh, *Pompey: The Roman Alexander* (Weidenfeld & Nicolson, London, 1980).

P. Greenhalgh, *Pompey: The Republican Prince* (Weidenfeld & Nicolson, London, 1981).

Adrian Goldsworthy, *In the Name of Rome* (Weidenfeld & Nicolson, London, 2003).

JULIUS CAESAR

Adrian Goldsworthy, *Caesar: The Life of a Colossus* (Weidenfeld & Nicolson, London, 2006).

J. F. C. Fuller, *Julius Caesar: Man, Soldier and Tyrant* (Eyre & Spottiswoode, London, 1965).

T. Rice Holmes, *Caesar's Conquest of Gaul* (Oxford at the Clarendon Press, Oxford, 1911).

ARMINIUS

Adrian Murdoch, *Rome's Greatest Defeat: Massacre in the Teutoburg Forest* (Sutton Publishing, 2006).

Tony Clunn, *The Quest for the Lost Roman Legions: Discovering the Varus Battlefield* (Spellmount, Stroud, 2005).

Dieter Timpe, *Arminius-Studien* (Winter, Heidelberg, 1970; untranslated).

Rainer Wiegels and Winfried Woesler (eds), *Arminius und die Varusschlacht: Geschichte, Mythos, Literatur* (Schöningh, Paderborn, 2003; untranslated).

TRAJAN

J. Bennett, *Trajan: Optimus Princeps* (second edition, Routledge, London, 2001).

S. S. Frere and F. Lepper, *Trajan's Column* (Sutton Publishing, Stroud, 1988).

I. Richmond, *Trajan's Army on Trajan's Column* (The British School at Rome, London, 1982).

ZHUGE LIANG

Luo Guangzhong, *The Romance of the Three Kingdoms*, translated by Moss Roberts in four volumes (Beijing, Foreign Languages Press, 2005).

Rafe de Crespigny, *The Three Kingdoms and the Western Jin in East Asian History* (Australian National University, Canberra, 1991).

ALARIC I

Peter Heather, *The Goths* (Blackwell, Oxford, 1996).

Peter Heather, *The Fall of the Roman Empire* (Macmillan, London, 2005).

AETIUS

There has never been a biography of Aetius in English (although there was one in French a hundred years ago).

J. B. Bury, *The History of the Later Roman Empire. Volume 1* (Macmillan, London, 1923; latest reprint Dover, New York, 2003).

Peter Heather, *The Fall of the Roman Empire* (Macmillan, London, 2005).

ATTILA

John Man, *Attila: The Barbarian King Who Challenged Rome* (Bantam Press, London, 2005).

Edward A. Thompson, *The Huns* (Blackwell, Oxford, 1999).

THEODORIC

Thomas Burns. *A History of the Ostrogoths* (Indiana University Press, Bloomington, 1984).

Peter Heather, *The Goths* (Blackwell, Oxford, 1998).

Thomas Hodgkin, *Italy and her Invaders. Volume 3: The Ostrogothic Invasion* (second edition, Oxford, 1896). Or better, the Folio Society reprint of 2001 entitled *The Barbarian Invasions of the Roman Empire. Volume 3: The Ostrogoths* with an introduction by Peter Heather. Although old, this is detailed Victorian narrative history at its very best.

CLOVIS

Edward James, *The Franks* (Blackwell, Oxford, 1988).

Ian Wood, *The Merovingian Kingdoms* (Longman, London and New York, 1994).

BELISARIUS

John Julius Norwich, *Byzantium*, volume I (Penguin, London, 1990).

Procopius, *The Secret History of the Court of Justinian* (The Echo Library, Teddington, 2006).

Robert Graves, *Count Belisarius* (Penguin, Harmondsworth, 1955).

E. Gibbon, *The Decline and Fall of the Roman Empire*, abridged (Penguin, Harmondsworth, 2000).

Robert Browning, *Justinian and Theodora* (Thames & Hudson, London, 1987).

MUHAMMAD

Michael A. Cook, *Muhammad* (Oxford University Press, Oxford, 1983).

Efraim Karsh, *Islamic Imperialism: A History* (Yale University Press, New Haven and London, 2006).

Hugh Kennedy, *The Great Arab Conquests: How the Spread of Islam Changed the World We Live In* (Weidenfeld & Nicolson, London, 2007).

CHARLEMAGNE

Alessandro Barbero, *Charlemagne: Father of a Continent* (University of California Press, Berkeley, 2004).

P. D. King, *Charlemagne* (Methuen, London, 1986).

P. D. King, *Charlemagne: Translated Sources* (Lambrigg, 1987). This includes translations of the main contemporary sources relating to Charlemagne's campaigns.

ALFRED THE GREAT

Richard Abels, *Alfred the Great: War, Kingship and Culture in Anglo-Saxon England* (Addison, Wesley, Longman, Harmondsworth, 1998).

Justin Pollard, *Alfred the Great: The Man Who Made England* (John Murray, London, 2005).

Simon Keynes and Michael Lapidge (translator), *Alfred the Great: Asser's Life of King Alfred and Other Contemporary Sources* (Penguin, Harmondsworth, 1983).

John Peddie, *Alfred, Warrior King* (Sutton Publishing, Stroud, 2001).

HASTEIN

John Haywood, *The Penguin Historical Atlas of the Vikings* (Penguin, Harmondsworth, 1995).

Gwyn Jones, *A History of the Vikings* (Oxford University Press, Oxford, 1968).

WILLIAM THE CONQUEROR

Matthew Bennett, *Campaigns of the Norman Conquest* (Osprey, Oxford, 2001).

Stephen Morillo (ed.), *The Battle of Hastings: Sources and Interpretations* (Boydell, 1996). This includes John Gillingham's essay 'William the Bastard at War'.

David Bates, *William the Conqueror* (Sutton Publishing, Stroud, 2001).

M. K. Lawson, *The Battle of Hastings 1066* (Tempus Publishing, Stroud, 2002).

Jim Bradbury, *The Battle of Hastings* (Sutton Publishing, Stroud, 1998).

BOHEMOND I

Gesta Francorum et aliorum Hierosolimitanorum ('The Deeds of the Franks and the other Pilgrims to Jerusalem'), edited by R. M. T. Hill, translated by R. A. B. Mynors (Clarendon Press, Oxford, 1962).

J. France, *Victory in the East: A Military History of the First Crusade* (Cambridge University Press, Cambridge, 1994).

R. B. Yewdale, *Bohemond I, Prince of Antioch* (Princeton, 1924).

FREDERICK BARBAROSSA

Otto of Freising, *The Deeds of Frederick Barbarossa*, translated by C. C. Mierow (Columbia, 2004).

P. Munz, *Frederick Barbarossa: A Study in Medieval Politics* (Eyre & Spottiswoode, London, 1969).

R. Rogers, *Latin Siege Warfare in the Twelfth Century* (Oxford University Press, Oxford, 1992).

GENGHIS KHAN

Paul Ratchnevsky: *Genghis Khan: His Life and Legacy* (Blackwell, Oxford, 1991).

John Man: *Genghis Khan: Life, Death and Resurrection* (Bantam Press, London, 2004).

J. J. Saunders: *The History of the Mongol Conquests* (Penn, Philadelphia, 2001).

KUBLAI KHAN

Morris Rossabi, *Khubilai Khan: His Life and Times* (University of California Press, Berkeley, 1990).

John Man, *Kublai Khan: The Mongol King who Remade China* (Bantam, London, 2006).

David Morgan, *The Mongols* (Basil Blackwell, New York, 1987).

ALEXANDER NEVSKY

John Fennell, *The Crisis of Medieval Russia: 1200–1304* (Longman, London and New York, 1983).

Mari Isoaho, *The Image of Aleksandr Nevskiy, Warrior and Saint* (Brill, Leiden and Boston, 2006).

BAIBARS

Ibn 'Abd al-Zahir, edited and translated by F. Sadeque, *Baybars I of Egypt* (Oxford University Press, Dacca, 1956).

R. Amitai-Preiss, *Mongols and Mamluks: The Mamluk–Ilkhanid War, 1260–1281* (Cambridge University Press, Cambridge, 1995).

P. Thorau, *The Lion of Egypt: Sultan Baybars I and the Near East in the Thirteenth Century* (Longman, London, 1992).

TAMERLANE

Justin Marozzi, *Tamerlane: Sword of Islam, Conqueror of the World* (HarperCollins, London, 2004).

Beatrice Forbes Manz, *The Rise and Rule of Tamerlane* (Canto, Cambridge, 1999).

Harold Lamb, *Tamerlane the Earth Shaker* (Thornton Butterworth, London, 1929).

THE BLACK PRINCE

Richard Barber, *Edward Prince of Wales and Aquitaine: A Biography of the Black Prince* (Boydell Press, Woodbridge, 1978).

Jonathan Sumption, *The Hundred Years War*: i, *Trial by Battle* (Faber and Faber, London, 1990); ii, *Trial by Fire* (Faber and Faber, London, 1999).

HENRY V

J. H. Wylie and W. T. Waugh, *The Reign of Henry V* (Cambridge University Press, 1914–29) three volumes.

Christopher Allmand, *Henry V* (Methuen, London, 1992).

Robert Hardy, *Longbow: A Social and Military History* (Patrick Stephens/Haynes Publishing, Sparkford, 1976–2008).

Anne Curry, *Battle of Agincourt: Sources and Interpretations* (Woodbridge, 2000).

Juliet Barker, *Agincourt* (Little, Brown, London, 2005)

Matthew Strickland and Robert Hardy, *The Great Warbow: From Hastings to the Mary Rose* (The History Press, Stroud, 2005).

JOAN OF ARC

Kelly DeVries, *Joan of Arc: A Military Leader* (Sutton Publishing, Stroud, 1999).

Joan of Arc: La Pucelle, edited by Craig Taylor (Manchester University Press, Manchester, 2007).

Marina Warner, *Joan of Arc: The Image of Female Heroism* (Weidenfield & Nicholson, London, 1981).

SULTAN MEHMET II

Steven Runciman, *The Fall of Constantinople* (Cambridge University Press, Cambridge, 1969).

Patrick Balfour Kinross, *The Ottoman Centuries: The Rise and Fall of the Turkish Empire* (William Morrow, London, 1979).

John Julius Norwich, *History of Byzantium, Volume 3: The Decline and Fall* (Penguin, Harmondsworth, 1996).

HERNÁN CORTÉS

The Codex Mendoza, edited by Frances Berdan and Patricia Anawalt, four volumes (University of California Press, 1992)

Hernán Cortés: Letters from Mexico, translated and edited by Anthony Pagden (Yale University Press, New Haven and London, 1986).

Matthew Restall, *Seven Myths of the Spanish Conquest* (Oxford University Press, New York, 2003)

Bernardino de Sahagún, *Florentine Codex*, edited by A. J. Anderson and C. E. Dibble, thirteen volumes (University of Utah Press, 1975)

Hugh Thomas, *Conquest: Cortés, Montezuma, and the Fall of Old Mexico* (Pimlico, London, 2004).

SÜLEYMAN THE MAGNIFICENT

A. Clot, *Suleyman the Magnificent* (translated from the French) (Saqi Books, London, 1992).

Patrick Balfour Kinross, *The Ottoman Centuries: The Rise and Fall of the Turkish Empire* (William Morrow, London, 1979).

John Julius Norwich, *The Middle Sea: A History of the Mediterranean* (Chatto, London, 2006).

GONZALO DE CÓRDOBA

G. de Gaury, *The Grand Captain: Gonzalo de Córdoba* (Longmans, Green and Co., London, 1955).

A. L. Martín Gómez, *El Gran Capitán: Las Campañas del Duque de Terranova y Santángelo* (Almena, Madrid, 2000).

J. J. Primo Jurado (ed.), *El Gran Capitán, de Córdoba a Italia al Servicio del Rey* (Córdoba: Publicaciones Obra Social y Cultural Caja Sur, 2003).

M. J. Quintana, *Memoirs of Gonzalo Hernandez de Cordova, Styled the Great Captain*, translated by J. Russell (E. Churton, London, 1851).

P. Pieri, *Il Rinascimento e la crisi militare Italiana* (Einaudi, Torino, 1970).

M. Purcell, *The Great Captain* (Alvin Redman, London, 1963).

AKBAR THE GREAT

Abul Fazl, *The Akbar Nama*, translated by H. Beveridge, three volumes, reprint (Ess Ess Publications, Delhi, 1993).

John F. Richards, *The Mughal Empire: New Cambridge History of India* (Cambridge University Press, Cambridge, 1993).

ODA NOBUNAGA

Jeroen P. Lamers, *Japonius Tyrannus: The Japanese Warlord Oda Nobunaga Reconsidered* (Hotei, Leiden, 2000): the only biography of Oda Nobunaga in the English language.

Two articles in John Whitney Hall, Nagahara Keiji and Kozo Hamamura (eds) *Japan Before Tokugawa: Political Consolidation in Economic Growth, 1500 to 1650* (Princeton, 1981) give insight into Nobunaga's political role.

Further Reading

INDEX

Figures in italics refer to illustrations

PICTURE CREDITS

Quercus Publishing has made every effort to trace copyright holders of the pictures used in this book.
Anyone having claims to ownership not identified below is invited to contact Quercus Publishing.

Rex Features **34**

British Library, London **47, 246, 326, 327, 350**

Werner Forman Archive **59, 85, 87, 197, 267, 315, 397**

TopFoto **60, 66, 104, 349**

Getty Images **65, 216, 218, 394**

Tom Holland **73**

Fotis Kerasaridis **77**

Ancient Art & Architecture Collection **83, 86, 91, 154**

Corbis **75, 134, 252, 261, 269, 272, 274, 291, 299, 333, 335, 339**

History Today archive **109**

The Rosen Collection **114**

Ralph Sawyer **194**

John Haywood **217, 233**

Stephanie Pollard **264**

BPK **106, 212**

SCALA **110, 210, 223, 236, 237, 239, 242, 265, 297, 345, 393**

Hellenic Republic Ministry of Culture Archaeological Receipts Fund **128**

Mary Evans Picture Library **137, 287**

RMN – Droits réservés **148**

The Bodleian Library, Oxford **205**

Alamy / Neil Turner **247**, AA World Travel Library **279**

National Library of Russia **320–321**

Dr Stephen Loud **328**

Robert Hardy **354**

Niccolò Capponi **389**

Stephen Turnbull **405, 406, 409, 411**

Dedicated to Johnnie Heffer and Matthew Sadler

First published in Great Britain in 2008 by
Quercus
21 Bloomsbury Square
London
WC1A 2NS

Compilation copyright © Quercus 2008

A CIP catalogue record for this book is available from the
British Library.

Cloth case edition: ISBN 978 1 84724 259 4

Printed case edition: ISBN 978 1 84724 515 1

Printed and bound in China

10 9 8 7 6 5 4 3 2 1

PUBLISHING DIRECTOR Richard Milbank
PROJECT EDITOR Penny Gardiner
DESIGNER Austin Taylor
PICTURE RESEARCH Elaine Willis
CARTOGRAPHY The Maltings Partnership

ELEANOR THE QUEEN

by

DOUBLEDAY & COMPANY, INC.,

Norah Lofts

THE STORY OF THE MOST FAMOUS WOMAN
OF THE MIDDLE AGES

Eleanor the Queen

GARDEN CITY, NEW YORK

With the exception of actual historical personages
identified as such,
the characters
are entirely the product of the author's imagination
and have no relation
to any person or event in real life.

ELEANOR THE QUEEN

Part One

CHAPTER ONE

Just before the moon rose to full glory over the city of Bordeaux in
that June of 1137, a young man who had been moving swiftly and
secretively through the deserted streets came to the end of his journey at the foot of a tall round tower. There he stood for a moment
in the shadow and then, emerging cautiously, moved away a little,
took in his right hand one of three small stones which he carried
in his left palm, and aimed it at the narrow, unglazed arrow-slit
near the tower's top. His aim was accurate and the stone disappeared into the opening. He stepped back into the shadow and
waited while a man might have counted, with deliberation, to fifty.
He was fingering a second stone when a door close beside him
opened silently and a voice whispered,

"Richard?"

In his excitement he momentarily forgot to be cautious and said,
"Eleanor . . ." in a loud, normal voice. The girl who had been
waiting for him said,

"Sh! Danger everywhere!" She drew him into the complete black
darkness of the tower and guided his hand to the wall. "Keep to
this side," she whispered. "There are eighty-four steps; be careful."
She closed the door, which swung silently on its well-oiled hinges,
but she did not replace its heavy iron bar.

The eighty-four steps were worn hollow and smooth and dangerous, for they were part of the original castle and in the far-distant times of the Roman occupation of Aquitaine had formed the main approach to the lookout turret at the top of the tower; for the past two hundred and fifty years they had been used only by those on secret errands, by lovers and assassins, by grave men on worthy but unadvertised business, by hurried men carrying secret messages from popes and kings and sultans to successive Dukes of Aquitaine. The staircase ended at a doorway, always locked and concealed by a hanging tapestry within arm's reach of the bed in the Duke's own sleeping chamber. Tonight this door stood open and, as young Richard de Vaux rounded the last curve of the spiral staircase, he could see the glimmer of light ahead. Moving more swiftly, he gained the room and stood aside as Eleanor, who had been hard on his heels, entered and half closed the door behind her.

"It might be necessary for you to leave quickly," she said, "so I will leave it ajar. If anyone should come to *that* door," she nodded towards the door on the other side of the room, a heavy, bolted door, "waste no time. Run. For once you know the secret, your life will be in real danger!"

"What secret?" he asked. "Oh, Eleanor, what is all this? Why did you send for me so secretly? And it's been so long . . ." He took her hand and brushed it with his lips as he realised that, after so long a separation, they had hardly greeted one another, that her first words to him had been a warning of danger. "What has happened?" he asked again.

"So many things," she said heavily. "Terrible things, Richard. Perhaps it was wrong of me to send for you . . . but I couldn't bear for you to hear it all from the lips of a casual gossip. And I've been virtually a prisoner ever since . . . ever since . . ." Her voice broke and Richard reached out a comforting arm which she ignored. "Sit down, dear heart, and I'll try to tell you everything. You would do well to drink some wine . . . pour for me, too. Richard, the first thing is . . . my father is dead. He died six weeks or more ago, in Compostella."

Richard set back the flagon he had lifted.

"My sweet!" he said and, taking both her hands, began to blurt out some muddled words of sympathy. Words never came easily to him, and now shock and bewilderment made him less than usually vocal. Eleanor listened for a moment and then drew away.

"Yes, you were fond of him, too; and he of you, Richard. And I've hardly had time to realise or grieve for him properly . . ." She steadied herself. "I didn't send for you to tell you that only, there is so much more to say, and perhaps not much time." She looked at the barred door, and as Richard began to speak she went on hurriedly, "Let me tell you first about how the news came and then you'll understand why I am frightened for you. You know that, when my father left to go to Spain on this pilgrimage, he put Sir Godfroi of Blaye in charge here. Sir Godfroi behaved, as usual, very kindly to me and we enjoyed one another's company; we had actually been out hawking together one morning six weeks ago when a man on a half-dead horse arrived at the gate just as we were entering. He gasped out that he had news from Spain, and Sir Godfroi immediately dismounted and dragged him into the guardhouse and turned the guards out. I stayed outside and I was worried; I knew that my father had set out a very sick man and I was afraid that he was worse. Presently Sir Godfroi came out and took my arm and said there was news which he would tell me later. Something made me suspicious and I asked to speak to the man. Sir Godfroi said that was impossible, the man was dead. That I didn't believe. I'd seen the fellow on his feet only five minutes before, so I pulled myself free and pushed into the guardhouse. There the man was, very blue and swollen in the face, and dead. No, don't interrupt me . . . Sir Godfroi had choked him, I am sure of that, but he gave out that the man had died of plague and, within the day, he had men posted on every road that leads to Spain, with orders to turn back, or if necessary kill, anyone who attempted to enter Aquitaine. He said it was to prevent the plague being brought in again. Very reasonable and very clever."

"To hide the fact that our Duke is dead? Our dear liege lord dead in a distant land and we, who should be saying masses for his soul, kept in ignorance, what is clever about that?"

"Wait," she said. "That is what I have to tell you. Drink some wine, Richard." She lifted her own cup and drank. "That same day Sir Godfroi took me aside and told me what I already knew—that I am now my father's heir, Duchess of Aquitaine, Countess of Poitou. He said also what I did not know, but which I see might well be true, that the moment the news was out there would be at least six ambitious, ruthless nobles ready to take and marry me —by force if needs be."

The young man's face hardened and his eyes narrowed as, without speaking, he nodded his head in understanding and agreement. Heiresses, the world over, were regarded as fair game, prizes to be won by trickery or by violence. Even when the women themselves were old, or ugly, or of known ill temper, men would squabble and fight to marry them and rule their lands . . . even small estates. And Eleanor . . .

As though answering his thought she went on, in deliberately steady voice, "This heritage of mine is very tempting, Richard; so wide: even I hardly realised, until Sir Godfroi showed me the map of its bounds, how wide it is. From east to west it runs from Auvergne to the sea, north and south it stretches from the Loire to the Pyrenees, and its cornfields and vineyards and orchards are the richest in the world, as is well known. A prize indeed for any man. . . ." Her voice changed, became brisker. "I pointed out to Sir Godfroi that in the marriage ceremony the bride is asked for her consent and if any man used force to me I should scream and protest up to the very altar; but he laughed and said that I was not the first to think of that device. With such a prize to gain, any man, he said, could find a priest who, for a bribe, would go on with the ceremony even with the bride screaming.

"He gave me instances where such a thing had happened. Once

the news was out, it would be merely a question of who could get here first with a strong force; and, once that one had married me, there would be no lack of others, wildly jealous, to set about him and start bloody civil war in Aquitaine. You know as well as I, Richard, how turbulent our nobles are, how ready to seize on an excuse for war. In the end he convinced me and I agreed to his plan—which was to stay in my own apartments, pleading a slight indisposition, to conceal my grief, and to keep the news secret until he had decided what was best to do and had made a plan which would settle my future peaceably, in seemly fashion and with dignity."

She checked the headlong rush of her story and looked half shyly at the young man's face, and then away. He did not speak, but she knew that they were both remembering the same thing. Richard's father had been killed in one of the Duke's minor wars, and the boy had come, years ago, into the castle, to be trained in the arts of knighthood. He had been first her chosen playfellow and then her tutor in all the unfeminine pursuits which appealed to her and which her indulgent father allowed. The affection between them had ripened, had been on the point of change, when, a year ago, Richard had returned to his own estate at Paullac. There had been then a half-understanding that when she was sixteen, when Richard had won his spurs, when her father had returned, in restored health, from his pilgrimage to Compostella, a formal betrothal between the pair was not unlikely. The Duke, as well as Sir Godfroi, had realised that, whoever married her, would become extremely powerful, and he had decided it might be better to take as his son-in-law a simple, well-bred knight of small estate than a great lord who might become *too* great and whose luck would lead to jealousy among the others. Nor had he, as a kind father, been blind to Eleanor's liking for the boy.

Now all was altered . . . the half-promise, the unspoken understanding, was all part of a past which suddenly seemed very far away; her father was dead in distant Spain; she was alone, doomed to pick a careful path through a quagmire of shifting policies, threatening schemes, dark intrigues.

And time was short; she must say what had to be said, and Richard must go.

"I made a grave mistake, Richard," she said, beginning to speak more rapidly. "I told Sir Godfroi that, although no fuss had been made because of my father's illness, you and I were betrothed, with my father's consent, before he left for Spain. It was *nearly* true! And I said 'If I marry Richard de Vaux, I shall be safe from other suitors, however ambitious; and there will be no cause for jealousy between the great nobles, since he is not of their number.' I urged him to send for you and to let us be married immediately."

Still Richard said nothing. The secret message, the furtive way he had been admitted by the secret stair, was proof enough that this plan had found no favour in Sir Godfroi's eyes.

"All that I did by that speech, Richard, was to put you in danger —such danger that it is wrong of me to have you here tonight. But I wanted so much to see you again, and to tell you myself. And I have been careful. I asked Sir Godfroi's permission to make a little vigil and say my prayers in this, my father's own room. That door is locked and no one but I knows about the secret stair. We are safe enough, I think, for a little time. But we must be quick."

He reached out and took one of her hands in his. Her long slim fingers, icily cold, closed over his warm ones with a force and strength which reminded him of how often in the past he had been astonished by the vigour and vitality concealed in her apparently delicate frame, and how those hands, which looked fit only for handling a needle or a lily, had proved themselves so apt and skilful at archery and horsemanship.

"Go on," he said, "tell me what has been decided."

"It all sounds so complicated, and so far removed from us, standing here hand in hand, with so many things to remember. Capet and Plantagenet, France and England, what have they to do with us? But Sir Godfroi made it clear to me; alas, very clear. Stephen is King of England now, but many men think that the Empress

Matilda should, of right, be Queen, and it seems likely that when Stephen dies, Matilda's son, Henry, is to have the throne. Henry will then be King of England as well as Duke of Normandy, Duke of Anjou, and Count of Brittany; he'll be far more rich and powerful than the King of France . . . unless the King of France can add to his domains. The rivalry between the two houses is very strong and the King of France would stop at nothing, Sir Godfroi says, that would strengthen his position. Aquitaine would do that and, unless it goes to the French by means of a peaceful marriage, France will attempt to take it by force. I would hate to be the cause of a war, Richard." She released his hand and turned away, making a great show of snuffing one of the guttering candles and though, when she turned back to him, she kept at a distance, he could see that tears had brimmed her eyes and were only kept from falling by a supreme effort of will.

"I can't marry *you*—Sir Godfroi would have no hesitation in killing you to prevent it; and, if he failed in that, the Capets, hungry for Aquitaine, would never rest until they had persuaded the Pope to grant an annulment . . . and they would have grounds; my father never publicly acknowledged our betrothal and the King of France could claim his rights as overlord. I have thought and thought about it all and I can see that Sir Godfroi's plan is the only way out of the muddle which can be followed with peace and dignity. So it is done. He sent a secret message to the King of France, and Prince Louis set out, as though on a hunting trip, and has moved quietly southward. Yesterday he reached Larmont. As soon as he arrives here, we shall be married and, before any Aquitainian noble or Plantagenet duke knows that I am for sale, I shall be sold to a bidder whose claim cannot lightly be disputed."

She spoke the last words bitterly, but Richard hardly noticed. He was thinking how rapidly, how thoroughly, she had mastered all the facts, the rules of the political game. It seemed only yesterday that they had played together and he, by virtue of two years or so seniority and his superior sex, had been her mentor, devoted but patronising. And now . . .

But it was not only for his good looks, his gaiety, and his skill with weapons and horses that she had chosen him long ago from the rabble of youngsters in her father's castle. Faced now with all this talk of kings and princes and power politics, he hooked his thumbs into his belt and said diffidently but with spirit and firmness:

"There is an alternative. A strange alternative to being Queen of France, my sweeting . . . you could come away with me, now. My horse could carry us both back to Paullac, where I could get fresh ones and what money I could lay hands on; then we could ride to La Rochelle and take ship. The world would be open to us. King Stephen in England could find use for a good swordsman, so could the Emperor of Germany, or the Emperor of Byzantium. We'd find a place and I would see to it that you did not want. It'd be a life without luxuries; but if you come with me and leave them to hammer out who shall have Aquitaine, we'd be together and I'd . . . I'd hack you out a place with my sword and serve you with my whole heart as long as I lived."

Colour came to her face; her eyes sparkled as she cried:

"How like we are. It was my first thought! I remembered my Uncle Raymond in Antioch; he'd welcome a good swordsman, and he'd stand by any action that was bold and free. Oh, I would do it with such a glad heart. The whole world . . . wide open. I thought of that . . . but it is impossible." She swung away from him as she spoke the last word and began to pace up and down the long room. "And don't think, never, never think, that my decision has been influenced by the prospect of being Queen of France. I am Duchess of Aquitaine and that is enough for me; and if I could leave Aquitaine safe and sound behind me I would dispense with all titles. But how should I leave it? We would go secretly and, until we were safe in some far-distant place, no one would know what had happened to me; think of the accusations that one would bring against the other; think of the Prince of France arriving and finding the bride promised him gone. That would mean war, the towns burning, the villages robbed, the vineyards ravaged. Compare that with what is in my power to do. This union of Aquitaine and France will mean such peace as this land has not known for six hundred years . . . no one would dare to challenge so strong an alliance. And if I have a son, he will be, by right that none could question, king of the widest realm in Christendom. I have no choice."

He stared at her gravely, offering neither protest nor persuasion. He knew that he would love her and remember her all his life, but he knew also that, even if events had not taken this turn, any number of other obstacles might have prevented their marriage. The troubadours might sing songs of love and how it conquered everything, but marriages were still made for other reasons—convenience, policy, greed. Having made his offer, he accepted her rejection of it just as he would have accepted it if the Duke had returned from Spain with some other plan for his daughter's future. The dream had been too wonderful to be realised. . . .

It was Eleanor who, with an abrupt change of mood, cried:

"God's fingers! What a state to be born to! The lowest little stinking goosegirl has freer rein for her fancy. We could have been so happy, Richard. Now I must say good-by to you, and to all our play and our plans. They were childish, I see now, but sweet nonetheless. And wherever I go and whatever happens to me, I shall remember you. Always."

She stretched out both hands to him and he took them; and thus, drawing her toward him, he saw all the colour drain out of her face, her eyes fly wide open with dismay. He whirled round and saw what she had seen over his shoulder—the massive, ominous figure of Sir Godfroi, filling the doorway that led to the secret stair. His right hand was on his sword hilt, his left fingered the dagger at his belt.

Before either Eleanor or Richard could speak, he stepped into the room and said in a mocking, jovial voice,

"So this, my lady, is how you keep vigil! It cuts me to think that my handling of your affairs should lead you to believe me so easily fooled."

"It is not what you think," said Eleanor, moving swiftly between them.

"And how do you know what I think?" Sir Godfroi asked, still amiably. His eyes, brown and opaque, but glistening like wet pebbles, travelled over Richard's face and figure in a long calculating stare. "I think that so handsome a young knight may well cherish high . . . aspirations."

"If to act as my falconer and kennel-hind is an honour—yes, he does," Eleanor said. "That is why I sent for him, Sir Godfroi; my birds and my hounds know him and he will tend them while I go on my , . . journey and handle them so that they are workable when I return."

"A very sensible arrangement," Sir Godfroi agreed. "And rightly contrived in secret, since such a commission from you, my lady, is a favour and likely to raise jealousy amongst the many other knights." His voice changed. "Spare us the mummery, madam. I am not yet blind or senile. I know why he is here and what you have been telling him. I grant you, it was not easy hearing for him." He looked directly at Richard. "If I greeted you churlishly, young sir, it was because I do not care to be deceived; and because I have much on my mind, as you—knowing what you do—will understand. I must ask you to swear on your honour that no word of what you have heard tonight will be repeated."

"I swear, on my honour."

"Then take your leave and go, as you came, secretly," said Sir Godfroi, not unkindly; then, as they stretched out their hands to one another again, he ostentatiously turned his back upon them and stared about the bedchamber, which was for its period unusually comfortably and luxuriously furnished. Several of Eleanor's ancestors had visited the East, either on crusades or for their private purposes, and they had brought back smooth silky rugs for their floors, cushions for their benches, curiously carved chests, and even rare looking glasses. Sir Godfroi found plenty to look at while Eleanor said briefly,

"There is no more to say, Richard, save that I wish with all my heart that things had been otherwise; and I shall always remember you."

"Remember most of all that, if at any time I can be of service to you, my heart and my sword are yours to command." He lifted her hands to his lips.

"This green-sickliness strikes us all in youth, and we all survive to laugh at ourselves," said Sir Godfroi; and the hearty words, for all their tactlessness, seemed to indicate a desire to comfort. "I will see you down and bar the door behind you," he went on.

"I will light you down," Eleanor said and stepped to the table by the bed where a five-branched silver candlestick stood. As she did so, Richard passed through the door and set his foot on the stairs; Sir Godfroi followed and Eleanor, moving forward bearing the light, was in time to see him whip out his sword and, with the calm deliberation of a man spearing a gobbet of meat from a dish, run the blade through Richard's body. There was a choking cry from the stairway, a shrill wild scream from the door. The spitted body sagged, hung for a second from the sword, and then fell forward into the darkness. Sir Godfroi turned back and, with the bloody blade dripping from his right hand, took the candlestick as it dropped from Eleanor's nerveless fingers. He stood it safely aside, then closed the door and let the tapestry fall into place over it.

"The outer door I barred when I entered," he said. "And I hope, my lady, that all your intrigues will be handled as discreetly." Then, as she swayed forward, he caught and laid her on the great bed.

Three weeks later, when the whole vast plot had been brought to a successful conclusion, when Eleanor, Duchess of Aquitaine, had been safely married to the Prince of France and all the unruly nobles of her domain had knelt to the young Prince, laid their hands in his, and promised to be his liege men, old Sir Godfroi, well pleased with himself, well pleased with the rich manor which had been given him by King Louis as his reward for the handling of a very tricky and dangerous business, sat himself down and engaged in the—for him—unfamiliar and difficult business of letter writing. The letter, when at last completed to his satisfaction, he confided to a monk by the name of Odo who had accompanied the Prince from Paris, and whom his shrewd old eye had picked out as being a man both cunning and discreet.

"This," he said, "is for the King's hand alone. On no account must the Prince or the Lady Eleanor know of its existence."

Odo, fully as cunning and discreet as Sir Godfroi had judged him, placed the letter in his pouch, and guarded it well. To deliver it to the King of France was beyond his power, however, for while the cavalcade with the Prince of France, and his new Princess, the nobles of his train, and a few Aquitainian knights who were following their lady to Paris, was still travelling the hot, dusty summer roads of Touraine, Louis the Sixth of France, for long a sick man, died and was buried.

The letter troubled Odo and, as soon as they arrived in Paris, he went straight to his Abbé, Bernard of Clairvaux—since the King's death, the most powerful man in France. Odo explained the situation, saying, "The old knight was very explicit in his instructions, my father. 'Not to the Prince,' he said. But now that the Prince is King . . ."

"An interesting problem," said the Abbé. "Give me the letter!"

Without hesitation he broke the seal and read the words so badly, painfully, and yet so clearly penned. The letter began by referring to the plot, now happily brought to fruition; then it went on:

The Lady Eleanor, behind a courteous manner, conceals a deep and devious disposition that will bear watching. I tell you this for your guidance, the more so as my lord the Prince, her husband, has been taken with her charms beyond what might have been expected in a match so hasty and so contrived. I have of late had excellent proof of her cunning and wilfulness and of her desire to manage all things in her own way.

"You did well," said Abbé Bernard. "The letter is purely personal, mainly in praise of the Prince, and the words addressed to his father, the King, now in the tomb, would only hurt his tender feelings. Put it in the fire, Odo."

But Sir Godfroi had judged Odo well. Something went into the fire, something crackled and flamed; something else went into hiding in Odo's sleeve. There were now two men in Paris who had been warned that, behind a courteous manner, their new Queen concealed a cunning disposition and a desire to manage. And since that description applied exactly to themselves and they wanted no competition, they watched her as closely and as coldly and as distrustfully as even Sir Godfroi could have wished.

CHAPTER TWO

By midwinter of Eleanor's first year in Paris, most of the nobles and knights and ladies who had followed her thither had, on one excuse or another, gone home. Whatever reasons they gave for leaving, she knew, because she passionately shared, the feelings which led to their departure. Paris, both as a town and as the centre of a court, had been a most dismal disappointment to her, to her friends, to anyone who had known the gaiety, the warmth, the stir and movement and colour of her father's castles in Bordeaux, in Tours, and in Poitiers.

The city, which in later ages was to become a byword for frivolity and to be known as "Gay Paris," was at that time a collection of ancient grey buildings and dark narrow streets huddled together on an island in the Seine. The castle to which Louis the Seventh conducted his young Queen had been built as a fortress in the troubled times of the Merovingian kings and, since nothing had been done to alter or improve it, it was crumbling in decay. The northern sun—so pale, so fleeting to eyes accustomed to the long hot summers in the South—could never reach the small apartments set deep in the thick walls behind the narrow slit windows; and all that winter when the Queen, sick for home, hungry for some distraction, pressed close to the windows and stared out, all that met her gaze was the grey water of the Seine running below the grey buildings under the grey sky. And when at last spring came, slowly and late, there was nowhere to walk except in the crowded, narrow, and dirty streets, or in the palace garden, none too spacious and planted with discouraged fig trees and cypresses, least cheerful of trees. There was no room in the narrow city for open gardens or orchards—they, like the woods which Eleanor loved, were on the riverbank across the water and only to be reached by crossing the bridge which linked the island with the mainland.

But it was not in a physical way only that Paris was dull. The city, even the dingy palace, would have been bearable if the life that went on in them had been lively and cheerful; if the young Queen had been able to introduce some of the customs of her homeland. At the Duke's court, anyone with a good song to sing, a good story to tell, or a good trick to display had always been welcome, so entertainment was never lacking; moreover the young men and women about the court, not to be outdone, vied with the professional musicians and poets and thus became skilful in amusing themselves and one another. At the King's court, only two kinds of people were welcome—grave churchmen and serious soldiers. Only once a year—during the Twelve Days of Christmas—was anything like gaiety encouraged, and even then Eleanor knew that Louis heaved a sigh of relief when the carols were finished, the evergreen wreaths taken down, and the Lord of Misrule, who had governed the revels, put aside his wand for another year.

It was not a court to attract gay, lively people, so it was that, one by one, the Aquitainians who had accompanied their Duchess to Paris seized upon, or invented, excuses to go home. Eleanor bore them no grudge, though their going left the dull palace a little more dull. She thought herself fortunate that one particular favourite remained, a young woman of her own age, gently born, intelligent, and not without wit. Her name was Amaria and her father had been gravely injured in that same war in which Richard de Vaux's father had lost his life. Useless for fighting, too demented to govern his estate properly, and given to terrible rages, the knight had lived on, growing poorer each year and using his children very ill. In the end, the Duke, hearing of his plight, had granted him a small pension and taken on the responsibility of the knight's family: setting one son up as a wine merchant in Bordeaux and another in the silk trade; marrying off, with adequate dowries, the two daughters of marriageable age; and taking the youngest, Amaria, into his household. Her nerves had been ruined by her father's rages and the bustling gay court terrified her until one day Eleanor noticed her and decided to befriend her. The lonely child responded wholeheartedly to the first kindness she had ever known. She repaid it with devotion, exerting herself to become not only a skilful waitingwoman but a companion upon whom Eleanor came to rely more and more. Amaria was invaluable in the lonely days, the dull days which followed the Christmas of 1137, when the court settled down to its usual routine, which, for Eleanor and her ladies, meant rising, eating, going to church, reading a few books over and over again, and tapestry work or embroidery, a little gossip, a little music with lute or harp, or sleep.

Eleanor waited. She told herself that Louis was newly come to kingship; there was much to do, many people to consult on serious business; and he had not yet moved out of the shadow of the cloister in which he was raised. Later things would be different. And the spring *would* come.

Spring came that year to Paris with a shout, with a blustering warm wind, with a race of white clouds across a blue sky, on a day in April. Eleanor and Amaria, up before the other ladies, walked in the palace garden before going to church. The solemn fig trees, the funereal cypresses, hardly recognised the change of season, but across the river, which surely ran less grely this morning, the orchards and woodlands on the far bank held up their shining buds to the sun and seemed to float in a pinkish-purple haze, freckled here and there with clear pure green where some branch, ahead of the others, had shaken free a few fresh leaves.

Suddenly Amaria said, "Oh, listen! The cuckoo!" It came again, the gay yet wistful call that is the very voice of spring.

Amaria's mind slipped back to the time when she had first known happiness. Incautiously she said, "Oh my lady, do you remember how on such a morning we would ride out . . ."

"All too well," Eleanor said shortly, thinking of the gay cavalcade setting off to greet the sun, the dew-jewelled grass, the laughter, the jokes, and the songs . . . and the way Richard could imitate the cuckoo's cry so that the lonely elusive bird would answer him. Amaria thought, Ah, she is homesick and small wonder!

"Come," Eleanor said briskly, "we shall be late for mass."

They breakfasted with the other ladies as usual, and afterwards Amaria said resignedly, "At least we might carry our work into the garden."

"Not I," cried the Lady Ursula, the elderly chief lady in waiting. "It is well known these spring days are treacherous, blowing hot and cold like a fickle lover. Do you sit in the garden if you wish to court the rheum; I stay here."

One or two others echoed her. But Amaria and another, Sybille, looked at the Queen, their young eyes shining and pleading.

"Not I," she said—thinking that they looked like puppies begging to be let free—"I have a better thought. Wait for me and leave the work where it is."

She set out briskly for the King's apartment. Ordinarily she never saw him until the midday dinner hour, for Louis still kept his monastery hours; he rose at first light, attended the first mass, ate his frugal breakfast, and was at work before the Queen was awake. Already, early as it was, the corridors and anterooms on his side of the palace were humming with activity, messengers coming and going, men with appointments waiting patiently, rubbing the sleep from their eyes, and clerks, with three hours' work behind them, beginning to yawn as they scribbled. They all looked at her curiously as she made her way to the plainly furnished, north-facing chamber which lay behind the high, vaulted room where Louis gave his public audiences. The guard on the door, with respect, and some confusion, answered her question, "Is His Grace within?" with,

"Within, my lady, but engaged."

"Nevertheless, I wish to speak with him."

He threw open the door and announced her.

A diffidence, which she had not foreseen, came over her as she stepped into the room, where the very air seemed grey and heavy with concentration. She had been here only once before—soon after her arrival in Paris. It was evening then and Louis was showing her, not without pride, all over the palace.

"This is where I shall work and do all my business," he had said. "My father—God rest him—was for a long time a sick man. He conducted his business from his bedchamber and even an emissary from the Emperor was apt to be jostled by a physician or a leech bearing a plaster. As a consequence, everything grew very slack and informal. But I shall have it otherwise. Only those with business shall penetrate this room." He had given her a warning glance as he spoke, and she had heeded the warning—until now.

In Aquitaine it had all been very different. Her father had taken his executive duties very lightly before he had become ill and, belatedly aware of his many sins, planned a penitential pilgrimage to Compostella. He had been capable of deciding weighty matters in the instant it took him to mount his horse, would stand with one foot on the ground and one in the stirrup and say, "I've made up my mind . . ." And from her earliest childhood she had been accustomed to run to him when she would; even in the manor court he would greet her when she appeared, lift her onto his knee, and say, "Now sweetheart, sit still, listen and watch. This is as good as a play . . ."

This room of Louis' held three tables; two small ones near the door where the most trusted scribes sat working, a longer one at the far end, occupied at the moment by Louis and Odo. Near the end of the table was a tall rack laden with rolled maps. A row of shelves under the window held parchments, supplies of ink, and sand and seals and candles. On account of its situation, the room was always chill, so a fire burned on the hearth, and a very young page sat on a stool with no other occupation in the world than to put—as silently as possible—a fresh log on the fire when it was needed.

A deep, almost religious hush held the whole place in thrall. The noise her heels made on the stone floor as she moved towards the far table sounded like sacrilege.

She looked at Louis, and, as suddenly as it had come, her feeling of diffidence, of being an intruder, left her. As she entered, Odo reached out, took a map from the rack, and unrolled it before the King; in the instant before he looked up to recognise and greet his Queen, the King of France had borne a remarkable resemblance to some rather bullied little schoolboy who had been set a task just beyond his powers. He was only eighteen, slightly built and fair; the life he had led since his coronation had done nothing to lift the cloister pallor from his face. A pang of affection and pity went through Eleanor's heart as she looked at him. It's time he *was* disturbed, and who should do it but I? she thought, and advanced to the table boldly.

Louis rose and kissed her, his gravity broken by a smile which was both sweet and diffident. Odo, unsmiling, rose too, kissed her hand, and said,

"I trust you are in good health, Your Grace."

"She is, thanks be to God," Louis said. "She shines in this dull chamber like a ray of sunshine on a dull morning."

Odo shot him a sharp, suspicious glance and spread the map which had begun to reroll itself as soon as they took their hands from it.

"But it isn't a dull morning, my lord," Eleanor said. "It is a lovely morning, and spring is in the air. It is because of that that I have dared to disturb you. I have a favour to ask."

The King's expression became ambiguous. His lips smiled, his whole face softened. He was very fond of his beautiful wife; at times, indeed, he was as nearly completely in love with her as a man of his cold, monkish nature could be with any woman. He was prepared to do her any favour which did not bring him into conflict with the old men who ruled him and whose good opinion he valued next to that of God. It was this thought which brought a wary, watchful glint into his eyes, even as his lips smiled.

"I thought," Eleanor said, "it being such a lovely morning, we might ride abroad. We could go to the woods and let our falcons free. We would carry our dinner—food tastes so much better in the sunshine. Please Louis . . . in all these months we have not taken a ride together."

He looked relieved.

"Indeed," he said, "I think that might be arranged."

Then, lest she should think that, being so easily arranged, it was a thing which he might himself have suggested, he added, "It is true we have not ridden together. There has been much to do."

"And much remains," said Odo. "Your Grace promised a decision upon this Meridon problem today."

Louis turned almost peevishly and said, "Yes, I did! A place you cannot even find on a map. Perhaps while I am taking the air you would set half a dozen clerks to search for it, Sir Chaplain."

"I know Meridon," said Eleanor. "It is one of my manors, it lies midway between Poitiers and Lusigan." She moved round the table and bent over the map. "Here it is." She placed a pointed finger tip on a name.

"And why?" asked Odo sourly, "should Meridon be writ St. Marine?"

"Because your map is old and out-of-date. My grandfather, the old Duke, had a mighty falling out with the Church, you may remember, and some of his most loyal vassals, to show which side they were on, made the gesture of renaming their manors with worldly names. Gervase One-Eye—he'd lost an eye on crusade with my grandfather—was one of the most loyal, and he changed the name of his manor from St. Marine to Meridon."

"There's a Gervase of Meridon mentioned in *this* dispute," Louis said eagerly.

"You should have asked me," said Eleanor with equal eagerness. "I know them all. This Gervase would be old One-Eye's grandson. . . . The dispute, what is that about? Has William the Hammer renewed his claim?"

"That is so," Louis said uncomfortably. To cover his discomfiture he turned to Odo and said, "Change the name on the map with your quill, Odo—though there should be a newer map somewhere. It should be found."

Odo muttered something about not having his quill to hand, and slipped away from the table. Neither Louis nor Eleanor noticed that he did not come back, for Eleanor, delighted to be of use at last and pleased even to be talking about her own dear Aquitaine, had launched out upon the tale of Meridon: how the rival claims had arisen, how this neighbouring lord supported one claimant because of marriage ties, and that neighbouring lord favoured the other because of an ancient feud with his rival. She talked vigorously, pointing to the map as she talked and making quite a romantic tale of it, especially when she told how One-Eye's son had come back from the wars in Castile with a Moorish wife and was disinherited by his angry father, then excommunicated for refusing to have her baptised against her will.

"And which of the claimants would *you* favour?" Louis asked, so carried away by her story that he forgot his caution, and his instructions.

"They're both good knights and they both have good claims, good *faulty* claims of about equal right," said Eleanor judiciously. "But William the Hammer is old—he must have been over thirty when he formerly made his claim, and unless I am mistaken, he has no son to do knight's duty and inherit. I should give verdict in favour of Gervase. Though that, my lord, may be a little difficult for *you* to do as that family is very unpopular with . . ."

She broke off as the door opened and the Abbé Bernard of Clairvaux entered. Odo had rushed to find him to report that the Queen was in the King's private room, talking as though she were one of the Council.

He greeted the young King and Queen courteously, but his eyes rested coldly upon Eleanor's animated face and his expression hardened as Louis said, "In one moment, my lord Abbé, I shall be all attention," and then to Eleanor, "Unpopular with whom?"

"With the Church," Eleanor said, a little ill at ease. "And now, shall I order the horses and the food while you talk to my lord Abbé, and be ready to ride in half an hour? You will not be wasting your time, Louis; this talk has called so many things to my mind which I can tell you as we ride—things you could not learn by study of that outmoded map!"

Bernard watched her as she walked to the door. He derived no pleasure from the sight of the slim, upright figure, the proud carriage of the head, the lithe, vigorous step; to him they, like her fairness of face and ready wit, were merely possible dangers. She threatened something which he must have in order to perfect his life's work—the complete control of the young King. Bernard, unlike many great churchmen of his day, cherished no personal ambition; he was a saint; he intended that Louis should be a saintly king and France a saintly country. There was no place in his plan for a gay, worldly, beautiful young Queen who exercised influence on her husband. Moreover, both Eleanor's father and grandfather had often been at odds with the Church, and a faint flavour of their defiance clung about Eleanor, though she was herself devout enough.

Seating himself at the table, he now said, "You have been discussing matters of grave importance with the Queen?" His tone was gentle, conversational, even perhaps a little amused.

Dragging up the other chair, Louis said boyishly,

"Indeed yes! Perhaps we should have done so before. At least in this matter of Meridon—which concerns her own domain—she is wonderfully well informed. It seems that the Duke, her father, was accustomed to discussing things with her and encouraged her to take interest in affairs. Which is not strange . . ." Louis went on thoughtfully, "his son being dead. It was wise of him to rear her to the position she was to occupy."

"And that was?" Bernard asked.

"To be Duchess of Aquitaine," said Louis, throwing the Abbé a puzzled look.

"Exactly. But now, you see, she is Queen of France, a very different thing. It is now for *us* to be wise. And I assure you, my son, it would be very unwise to allow her to meddle in affairs of state now. Had it been possible for her to stay and rule in Aquitaine alone, I should have been the last man on earth to question either her policy or her activities—so long as they conformed to God's laws of course. But she did not stay there; she married you and, by that act, made you Duke of Aquitaine. You will remember Christ's words, 'No man can serve two masters' . . . how much less can any country? God called you to rule in France, and in His wisdom added Aquitaine to your domains. You bear the responsibility and you must have the authority, for the two can never, in this world, be divided."

"But to make use of her special knowledge, as in this case . . ."

"Let us consider this case," said Bernard, cutting short the attempt at argument, but noting it against Eleanor as he did so, for Louis seldom argued. "Did she say which claimant should have Meridon?"

"Yes . . . but only when I asked her directly; that is surely permissible."

Bernard could see clearly that, in one half hour, the Queen had made great headway; here was the King sticking up for her against him already.

"And what did she answer?"

Louis told him what Eleanor had said, and why.

"That is precisely what I mean," Bernard said and proceeded to explain at great length, very gently, very firmly, why William the Hammer must be allowed his claim.

Eleanor, hurrying to order the horses and a hamper of food and to invite Amaria and Sybille and two lively young knights to join the outing, was conscious of a great lightening of spirit. She would get to know Louis after all, despite all the barriers which formality and court etiquette and the dull old men around him reared between them. They would learn to work—and to play—together.

She knew that she was not ill-fitted to help Louis; she had always taken an interest in affairs and, under her father's tuition, had learned a good deal about politics and about men. She remembered how he had once leaned towards her when two men were arguing their case in court, both apparently honest but with contradictory stories. "Which is the liar, my pretty?" he asked, and, when she said that she was not sure, he replied, "I am. See how the one with the black beard tucks his thumbs into his fists. He feels the need of something to hold on to. You must mark these things. It is what a man doesn't know he is doing that gives him away."

Once or twice since her arrival in Paris she had made an attempt to talk to Louis about state affairs but he had always put her off, saying, "I couldn't explain; it would take too long," saying, "This is a purely French affair," saying "Don't bother your pretty head about such dull matters." As though anything in the world could be so dull as tapestry work! Still, this morning marked a milestone; she had known what she was talking about, and Louis had really listened.

The horses, gaily caparisoned, were ready in the courtyard, tossing their heads against the hold of the grooms. The falconers with their hooded charges leaned against the sun-warmed wall. Eleanor and her little party waited . . . and waited. A full hour had passed when the little page who tended the fire in the King's room came hurrying out with a note.

"My sweet," it said, "to my infinite regret I cannot ride today. The Abbé brought business which will detain me till supper. The sun should have reached the garden by now; take your ease there."

The poor little boy's schoolmaster would not allow even one day's truancy, Eleanor thought with scorn and pity.

"His Grace cannot ride today," she said, "but we will go nonetheless. Pierre, I observe with pleasure that you have brought your lute. When we have tried the falcons and eaten our food, we will lie under the trees and I will teach you some of the songs of Aquitaine. They are merrier than yours."

At supper Louis asked how she had spent the day.

"Right merrily," she answered. Then observing his pallor and the droop of his shoulders, she said, "The Abbé works you too hard. He forgets that you are young. And we were going to talk as we rode. I have remembered something you should know . . ."

"That is all settled," Louis said hastily, the wary look leaping to his eyes again.

"Oh, and what did you decide?"

"My dear, I have been talking of such things all day. Spare me at supper."

Next day she heard, by chance, that the manor of Meridon had been given to William the Hammer. To Louis she said nothing, but a few evenings later when the Abbé had dined in the palace and the whole court was gathered, waiting for an entertainment of singing by the boys of the Choir School of Notre Dame, she drew him aside and said, "My lord Abbé, was it on your advice that William the Hammer's claim to Meridon was allowed?"

He said genially, "Advice, Your Grace, was not needed. The priority to his claim was evident."

"With due respect, my lord, not so! I heard both cases argued in my father's court. The claims, both flawed, were equal—that was the trouble. It was a mistake to give it to the old, heirless man."

"We mentioned advice," he said, still gently, "may I offer one word of it to you. You would be wise to refrain from meddling."

The hot blood that had come to her from ancestors known for their ungovernable rages flared in her face.

"Meddle, my lord! A word one uses to children who put their fingers in the pin box or the wool bag. How could I *meddle* with something that concerns my own domains, something upon which I am better informed than any man in France."

"Perhaps the word was ill-chosen. I am no courtier, no poet, madam." His eyes remained cold but his self-deprecating smile was disarming. "I should have said that you would be wise not to *concern* yourself with such matters."

"But they concern *me!* Here we have a good manor given to an old man who has no son to do his knight's service or to follow him. And when he dies all will be to do again. You—and I can understand it—approve the choice. But it is not statesmanlike. I know the family of Gervase is in bad odour with the Church; Infidel blood runs in their veins. But for all that, Heaven has shown its approval in giving them four lusty sons."

The Abbé drew in his breath with a little sound.

"I was somewhat at a loss, Your Grace," he said smoothly, "as to how to mention another matter I have in mind; but you have shown me the way. Since you regard the gift of lusty sons as a mark of Heaven's approval, why not endeavour to attain it for yourself? The provision of an heir would be the most valuable contribution that you could make towards the well-being of this great country."

The thrust went home; the colour faded from her face. But she rallied and said with a laugh,

"*Touché*, my lord. You should have been a swordsman; you have a shrewd eye for your adversary's weak spot. I must look to it."

Still smiling, still cold of eye, Bernard said,

"It is now my turn to challenge your use of a word, dear my lady. I am no adversary of yours. I shall pray that your wish be granted."

Bearing his triumph meekly, he turned and left her, his coarse woollen robe whispering on the rush-matted floor.

The child for which she and Louis, indeed the whole of France, was longing and praying was not born until the year 1145, eight years after their marriage, and then, to everyone's disappointment, was a girl, who was named Marie. From this disappointment, Eleanor's valiant spirit was the first to recover. To Louis, who was wondering in what way he had offended Heaven that the gift of a son should be denied him, Eleanor said,

"This is a strong, healthy baby, and pretty, as a girl should be. There will be others. And I shall surely have sons. Once, long ago, a soothsayer came to my father's castle and we all had our fortunes told. He told me that I should be the mother of sons and that one of them would be a king of such renown that his fame would live forever. . . ."

Louis said, with the sourness which was growing on him,

"Maybe Heaven sent us a daughter to show that it has scant respect for soothsayers!"

The little speech gave voice to the mood which was often upon him these days. He was puzzled and resentful—not only by his lack of an heir but by the way in which things in general had been going. He always did his best; he always did exactly what Abbé Bernard advised, but one thing after another had gone wrong. In the eight years of his reign there had been no settled peace; in fact, few of his minor wars had been brought to a successful conclusion. Two of his chief nobles, Count Geoffrey of Anjou and his son, Henry, Duke of Normandy, had been forever on the verge of rebellion; and that was all the more threatening because this same Henry would one day be King of England and Count of Anjou. To the east the Emperor of the Germans, Conrad of Hohenstaufen, acted in an even more threatening manner and seemed to show a particular hatred for Abbé Bernard. And now his first-born was a mere girl. It must be a fault in himself, Louis thought humbly; and he became more attentive to his church duties, more frugal in what he ate, more monkish in his attire; and with every step he took away from the world and his pleasures, he moved a little farther away from his wife, who could never share his unworldliness. In Eleanor life still burned brightly, urgently. Even the eight dull years in Paris, when one outlet for energy after another had been closed to her—so often by the Abbé's hand—she had preserved her interest in people, in affairs, in food and clothes and what chance amusements came her way. Politics were barred to her—she must not meddle; the entertainments she planned were disapproved—"Such worldly amusements set a bad example"; archery and fencing and riding, skills she had learned long ago from young Richard de Vaux, were bad for women who hoped to bear children; even the books she read and the tapestry she worked were subject to criticism. "Is the old pagan story of Europa and the Bull worthy of reproduction or suitable for display when worked? Do not the lives of the saints offer more delicate and dignified subjects for your needle?"

One thing, and one alone, Eleanor said later, saved her sanity during this long dull period. At that time the schools of Paris were the best in the world, and some of the lecturers—notably Master Peter Abélard—had no objection to the presence of women at their classes. Moreover, during the short time in summer when the weather was really warm in this grey city, the cypress-filled garden behind the palace was thrown open to the students, and there in the shade of the trees, with the water of the river running coolly by, the Queen, accompanied by Amaria who shared her interest, would sit and listen by the hour to the lectures and debates. The young men who made the bulk of the classes interested her; she knew several of them by name. There was one, English, Tom Becket by name, whom she marked especially. Women, although permitted to listen, were not allowed to speak in the debates which followed the lectures, and often Eleanor would fume with impatience when some debatable statement was made and whisper to Amaria, "Oh, if only I might answer that"; and often enough, Tom Becket in his plain gown of English wool, and with his handsome face alight with enthusiasm, would get up and clinch the argument with a few well-chosen, often witty words.

"Unless I am mistaken, we shall hear of that young man again," Eleanor said once as she and Amaria walked back to the dark palace. And as she thought of the future . . . of the years to come . . . years which might bring a clever young man to fame and fortune . . . she could not avoid the thought—And what will they bring to me? The years ahead were like a cold dim tunnel, growing narrower as it went on. Sometimes it seemed to her that life, real life with feeling and warmth and excitement in it, had ended with the plunge of Sir Godfroi's sword at the head of that dark stairway. But one mustn't think that way; it led to self-pity. No, one must think, I am only twenty-two, I'm alive and life is full of possibilities. Anything might happen . . . anything . . .

Anything might happen. And one day, far away, on the very edge of the then-known world, something did. . . . So far away that the very news of the happening took months to reach the ears of Louis and Eleanor, and so remote that it seemed to have little to do with the extreme piety of the one, the maddening boredom of the other. Nevertheless, for the King and Queen in the crumbling dark palace set on the grey Seine, life had taken one of its sudden, inexplicable, fascinating turns.

CHAPTER THREE

The crusade in which Eleanor's grandfather had taken part had ended in the year 1099 with the defeat of the Saracens and the crowning of a Christian knight, Baldwin of Boulogne, as King of Jerusalem. Other knights had settled down on the hard-won lands and established a Christian feudal state in the far Eastern country where the Founder of Christianity had lived His life, been crucified and buried, and which was therefore known to all Christendom as the Holy Land. Eleanor's own uncle, her only living male relative, had for his share the rich ancient city of Antioch and the country immediately surrounding it. His neighbour was Count Joscelin of Edessa, whose land lay between Antioch and the unconquered pagan lands to the north. Two generations of peace had followed the ending of the First Crusade, and peace seemed so little threatened that at Christmas in the year 1144 Count Joscelin and all his knights and nobles rode off to enjoy their Christmas festivities in the pleasant country beside the river Euphrates. While he was gone, the Saracens struck; they flooded into Edessa, killing and capturing its Christian citizens, destroying its altars and churches, and showing by their numbers and ferocity that they had recovered from their defeat of forty-five years before and were now on the move once more. Antioch, the rich busy ports on the Eastern edge of the Mediterranean, even Jerusalem itself, were now fearing invasion. Letters of appeal began to pour in from the Holy Land; formal letters from bishops to the Pope, private letters from the nobles of the East to their kinsmen in the West. Raymond of Antioch wrote to his niece, the Queen of France, begging her to influence her husband to come to the aid of Antioch before it was too late. He credited her with power she had never possessed, and eight years of frustration had taught her the folly of even indicating her choice in such matters, since, if the Abbé could move contrary to her wish, he would do so. So she merely passed on the letter to Louis and said nothing. It was the Abbé himself who first suggested to Louis that he should organise and lead the Second Crusade; and Louis, always casting about for some way of gaining Heaven's favour, accepted the idea as warmly and enthusiastically as was possible to his nature; he began mustering his men while the Abbé, now aged and in frail health, travelled about the country, preaching the crusade far and wide.

And now, in a single stride, Eleanor came into her own.

One of the first knights to answer the call for volunteers to drive the Infidels out of Edessa and so save Jerusalem and the Tomb of Christ from the new danger, was Geoffrey de Rancon, the boldest and most faithful knight in all Aquitaine. Coming straight from his great estates at Taillebourg, he seemed not to be aware of the humble position to which Eleanor had been reduced and, in a very short time, he was talking to her exactly as he would have talked to the Duke, her father. One evening in the summer of the year after the fall of Edessa, they sat together under the cypress trees in the garden and talk turned upon the coming crusade.

"It sticks in my mind," Eleanor said at last, "that the Aquitainian knights, on the whole, are hanging back. You have joined, Geoffrey . . . and the Lord of Lusignan and a handful of others . . . but where are the lords of Limoges, of Angoulême, of Thouars? Has the crusading blood that ran so high in my grandfather's knights grown cold and thin in their descendants?"

Lord de Rancon pulled at his beard and thought a little before he answered.

"Not cold, or thin, my lady. Merely cautious. A crusade is not just a war; there is so much besides the fighting. Months of travel for one thing and a . . . a great deal of what I can only call politics."

"And why does that hold them back? The conditions are the same for all."

"No." He eyed her carefully. "The crusading army sets out as a body, united; but naturally disputes arise and have to be settled, and at such times the knights of each nation look to their leader to see that they obtain justice. They need a spokesman, a leader who carries weight at the council chamber. Take for example, madam, me and Thibault of Champagne . . . if we should happen to fall out concerning a camping place, or the turn to water our horses at a well, who would speak up for me?" He brought out the last slowly and with significance.

Eleanor suddenly found herself short of breath. If he meant what she thought, here was her chance! But she had learned not to move too hastily.

"You are the King's liege man," she said, "equally with Thibault, surely you could depend . . ."

"I am an Aquitainian," said De Rancon, "and the King is my liege lord, but he is a Frenchman and so is Thibault. Naturally the decision would go to Thibault." He stirred on the bench. "I am willing to accept such conditions, but there are others who will not. It is this, not lack of courage or care for the Holy Places, which makes your Aquitainians and Poitevins hold back!"

Had he placed a slight but recognisable emphasis on the word "your"? She took the risk.

"Suppose," she said breathlessly, "that *I* came on crusade. Suppose I promised to lead my knights and represent them in the council?"

"You are our Duchess," said De Rancon simply. "They would follow you as they would have followed your father."

"Then, by the rood, I will go. In battle, my lord, you shall lead us, the forces of Aquitaine . . . but in all else where my rank and my tongue and my wits can be of service, there I shall be. Even Bernard of Clairvaux can hardly accuse me of meddling if I, and only I, can bring so many men to the cause which he holds so dear."

"And why?" asked De Rancon innnocently, "should the Abbé in any circumstances accuse you of meddling? You are our Duchess, we are your people. By marrying the King of France you did not forfeit your rights; as your consort, we accepted him as our liege lord—mystified as we were by the choice and the haste . . . but that is an old story. God forbid that I should bring ill luck to the King, poor man, by mentioning his death . . . he looks sick enough . . . but suppose he died. You would still be our Duchess. This King of France is of importance to us only because he is the husband of our liege lady. That should be remembered. There are those, you know—" he eyed her, watching the effect of his words— "I am not among them for I know that you are young and, when one is young and in love, one has no time, no thought to spare— but there are those who feel that, in doing your duty to your husband and your adopted state, you have been neglectful of your duty to your heritage. But that," he hastened on, "will all be mended now."

"It was never true," she said slowly. "The truth is that Louis has always been clay in Bernard's hand. Small blame to him, for he was given into that hand—and a powerful hand it is, my lord— when he was but six years old. I was like a pebble in the clay, so Bernard picked me out and threw me aside." She smiled and her eyes shone. "Now the Abbé is going against the Saracens like David against Goliath, and he is looking for pebbles to use in his

ELEANOR THE QUEEN 38

sling. My lord, will you go out and tell every baron and knight and squire and archer in Aquitaine that I am going on this crusade, and that I call upon them to follow me. And that at the end of Lent next year, when the forces muster at Vézelay, I shall expect *my* followers to outnumber all the rest. You see . . ." the thin, clearly marked brows which arched above the white-lidded eyes knotted themselves where the arrogant little nose met the wide forehead, "I lay myself open to be shamed, Geoffrey. The countless little insults of the last eight years have galled my pride raw. The Abbé will be angry, eager to push me aside again . . . I must not seem a small, negligible pebble. I must have a full force behind me. Tell them that."

"I will," he said. "I will."

And the autumn passed and winter came. This year nobody paid much attention to the Twelve Days of Christmas; there was so much more to think about.

Soon after Christmas the Abbé Bernard, who had been passionately preaching the crusade among the German princes, returned to Paris, and there, one day, he held a grave conversation with the monk Odo—the one man in all the world to whom he could frankly open his heart.

"It is rumoured," he said, "that the Queen has announced her intention of joining this crusade. Had you heard that?"

"I had heard the rumour and also its contradiction," Odo said. "In Aquitaine it is believed; in Paris it is denied. During your absence, my lord Abbé, I stayed close to the King as you advised me and, when the rumour reached his ears, I asked him bluntly whether it were true or not. He said, 'It is only her fancy. When the moment comes, she will realise that the road is too long and too hard for women. But meanwhile,' he said, showing an uncommon shrewdness, 'the belief that she is going is having an effect upon the chivalrous, romantic knights of Aquitaine and Poitou.' There I left the matter, not having had instructions from you, since you had left France before she moved to this decision."

"And there, as always, you were wise. The knights of Aquitaine

must come in, they must take the Crusaders' oath. At the same
time, the Queen must not go with the King to Palestine. The
Prince of Antioch is her uncle; the King is easily led. In no time at
all, the Prince of Antioch would be in charge of the forces from
the West—and he is a very worldly man. When the Saracens were
defeated, he would claim the honour of their defeat and that would
shame . . . what we stand for, Odo." Bernard paused, his pale
wasted face and hollow eyes took on the inspired, fanatical look
which they assumed when he was preaching. "*This* crusade must
be the triumph of Christendom, not the triumph of Raymond of
Antioch, who is so slack-twisted that he allows a Mohammedan
mosque to stand in his city beside a Christian church and allows,
moreover, his knights from the West to take Saracen women in
marriage. Think of that, Odo!" The old man's voice trembled with
genuine horror and disgust. Odo, less easily shocked, said, "Horrible!" and then, after a second's hesitation, added,

"But suppose the Queen insists."

"We must not make it too difficult for the King," Bernard said.
"He is young and she is beautiful—and plausible. But I think it
can be managed so that he has no say in the matter. I shall announce, Odo, that *no* women go on this crusade. I shall say, and
it is true, that in the past many armies have come to grief because
the men took with them their wives and their daughters and their
sweethearts, who held up the marches, caused quarrels, fell sick,
and overburdened the waggons with their luggage. On this crusade,
no women are to go—and that includes the Queen of France."

"What about washerwomen?" Odo asked practically. "There has
never been an army that set out with the idea that the fighting
knights should wash their own linen."

"This one must because . . ." something that was almost a smile
lived for a moment in the hollow eyes, "if I permitted washerwomen, the Queen would most likely say she could wash—and that
might well be true. I think she could do anything she gave her
mind to, and that would be admirable if she gave her mind to
womanly things. As it is . . ."

And so, late in Lent in the year 1146, when all the Frankish forces of the crusade mustered at Vézelay to receive the Abbé's blessing and to take from his hand the white crosses which had been blessed by His Holiness the Pope, the knights of Aquitaine clustered together in a very uncertain and divided state of mind. For months Geoffrey de Rancon had been going among them, swearing that the Queen, their Duchess, was to lead them on crusade; and then, in the last weeks, Bernard of Clairvaux had said that no women of any sort or rank were to set out with the army. Some Aquitainians, caught up in the fever of enthusiasm which was now running high through all the West, said that, having made ready and already having left their homes, they would go on crusade whether Eleanor went or not—but they were in the minority. A greater number, distrustful of the King of France, for all that he was nominally their overlord, announced with some flowery curses that, if the Queen stayed in Paris, they would turn about and ride home. Geoffrey de Rancon, weary of the questions and accusations which met him as one after another of the lords whom he had persuaded to join the crusade came riding in, went at last to the Queen's tent and asked to speak with her.

It seemed to him that there were more women than usual in attendance, and they all seemed to be excited. Some large wicker hampers were being unpacked and he thought wearily, "Clothes, more clothes! A few women travelling from Paris to Vézelay need more baggage than an army on a year's campaign." Some echo of his thought must have reached the women, who slammed down the hamper lids as he stared, and stood looking amused, sly, and secretive.

Eleanor turned her back on them and led De Rancon into a quiet corner, where he asked her bluntly whether or not she intended to ride at the head of her Aquitainians next day. Anxiety made his voice harsh, and Eleanor, listening, knew that he had no idea of her own uncertainty . . . of the hours which she had spent pleading with the King, or of the number of times when she had tried to talk with Bernard, who, since giving out the order about no women accompanying the army, had always made some excuse to avoid her.

"I gave you my promise," she said. "I have not changed my mind. With that you must rest content until tomorrow."

"But the Abbé orders . . ."

"I know." She hesitated and frowned. Then the same shy, amused, secretive look with which the women had slammed down the hamper lids dawned upon her face. "My lord, as you know, there are more ways of unhorsing an adversary than by riding at him point-blank. Sometimes a sideways thrust . . ."

A sideways thrust! She dealt it next day.

Standing upon a simple platform built halfway up a sloping hill-side near Vézelay, Abbé Bernard of Clairvaux looked down upon the thousands of men gathered there, largely as a result of his eloquence, his burning enthusiasm, his tireless energy. The past months of travel, of persuasion, of argument, of prayer, and of fasting had worn him—never very robust—to such a state of frailty that those near enough to see him clearly thought that they saw death in his face and doubted whether he still had the strength necessary to address so great a gathering. He stood there in his plain white robe and lifted his skeleton-thin arms in the air and waited until the core of silence about the platform had spread out-ward to the very fringes of the crowd. Then, in a firm, strong carry-ing voice he spoke of the holy war upon which his listeners must, from this moment, consider themselves engaged, of the loyalty and brotherhood which must unite this great army, of the truce to all quarrels which must fall upon the lands and families they were leaving behind, of the blessing and the forgiveness of past sins which were the reward of taking the cross.

The Abbé spoke with even more than his usual fervour, and no one in the great crowd, where strong men were breaking into tears as the emotional tension grew, could have guessed that one part of his mind had detached itself and was busy and troubled by a prob-lem of its own. He had spent the night keeping vigil by the altar of the great new church in Vézelay, and he would have said that he had not slept at all . . . and yet, and yet, it could only have been a dream. But a dream so strange, so vivid, and so haunting that even at this great moment, when his object was achieved and all the best fighting men of France and Brittany and Anjou and Aquitaine and Burgundy and Champagne were hanging upon his words, he could still not shake himself free of it.

It had seemed to him that he was on his knees in the dim church, lighted only by the altar candles, when a man had entered and knelt beside him; a big fellow, roughly clothed, reeking of fish, onions, and human sweat. It seemed strange that such a man should enter a church in the middle of the night, but it was God's house, open to all. The Abbé continued with his prayers until the man touched him, then he turned, and for all the dimness of the light saw with peculiar clearness that the stranger was offering him something. The big brown hands, scarred and calloused with toil but scoured clean, held what looked like a woman's head veil wrapped around something, and this little bundle he was holding out, inviting the Abbé to accept. Much puzzled, Bernard took the bundle and, as he unfolded the bit of flimsy linen, he was conscious of a sweet scent mingling with the other odours. When all the folds were open, he saw that the scent had its origin in a superb red rose with a diamond drop of dew in its heart . . . and then he saw, huddled near the dewdrop, a hairy black spider, one of the things for which he had an unreasoning, hysterical dislike. At the sight, he dropped the veil, the rose, and the spider to the floor. Then the man spoke. "I'm Peter," he said. "I was just the same when the sheet came down. Only it was Gentiles in my case." Speechless with astonishment, Bernard stared; and the man said with peculiar urgency, "Peter. Simon called Peter. You remember." And then, just as suddenly as he had appeared, he was gone. The veil with its one lovely, one revolting occupant had vanished too; and—I must have been dreaming, Bernard said to himself. He tried to return to his prayers, but his mind was too much disturbed. No determination of his could wrench it away from the thought of Peter, St. Peter, and word by word there came back to him the story of the saint's vision as recounted in Holy Writ—how the sheet filled with unclean things came down three times from Heaven and the Voice said, "What God hast cleansed that call thou not common." And that was always explained as meaning that Peter was to carry the Gospel to the Gentiles, whom, until that moment, he had despised. Gentiles; spiders; roses . . . what could it all mean? Did it mean anything?

Now, out on the hillside in the bright spring sunshine, the Abbé finished his speaking and stood ready to accept the vows of the great lords and to give them the white crosses.

The King of France was the first to come forward and pledge in a shaking, tear-filled voice the services of himself and all those who owed him allegiance, to the freeing of the Holy Places from the Infidel. Bernard could see, ranked behind the King, the lords of France and its domains, all their bright banners lined up beneath the lilies of France. Solemnly Bernard blessed Louis and gave into his outstretched hands the little symbolic white cross. ("I'm Peter . . . only it was Gentiles in my case." What did it mean?)

"God's soldier, servant of the Cross, I pray for you," the Abbé said, dismissing the King, and, as Louis moved away, the old man closed his eyes and murmured his first prayer for the first sworn Crusader of this crusade. And into that prayer broke a clear girlish voice saying,

"I, Eleanor, by the Grace of God Queen of France and Duchess of Aquitaine . . ."

Bernard opened his eyes and with something of the horror with which, in his dream, he had regarded the spider, stared down at the bent head of the woman who knelt at his feet, pledging the services of herself and all those who owed her allegiance to the freeing of the Holy Places from the Infidel.

And immediately it was all clear. The rose stood for the good thing, the thing he wanted—strength for this war; the spider stood for what he hated, female interference; he remembered that in dropping the spider he had lost the rose too. And Peter had rebuked him—just as God had rebuked Peter—for turning away from what was offered just because it was offered in an unacceptable form.

Raising his eyes, Bernard saw behind the slim woman's figure the massed forces of Aquitaine and Poitou—good fighting men all. So many bright banners . . .

With the slow, weighted movements of a sleepwalker, the Abbé placed the little white cross in the slim eager hands. (The Vision, Oh Lord God, I pray that I have interpreted it aright. This is not of my choice . . .)

Aloud he said, "God's soldier, servant of the Cross, I pray for you."

When he next opened his eyes, he was staring down on the cropped hair and bull neck of Thibault of Champagne; the Queen of France, publicly recognised as the leader of the Aquitainian forces, had slipped away, clutching her small but so-symbolic cross.

The momentous day, like those of little importance, ran its course and the dusk came down. The Abbé, too exhausted to walk alone, had been helped to his lodging and there, after refreshing himself with a bowl of mutton broth, which—smelling of onions—reminded him of his dream, or vision, he had a serious talk with Odo.

"From the moment the King leaves France until he is back again, you will remain as near to him as though a chain of ten links fastened your wrist to his. You understand? You will be his guardian, his watchdog, under my orders. When he sleeps in a palace, you share his chamber; when he sleeps in a tent, you lie at its entrance; he attends no council, he receives no message, he gives no order without you." Bernard paused and a look of puzzled bewilderment drifted across his face while Odo, watching, wondered for the twentieth time, Why? Why, having banned all women, had Bernard weakened so suddenly and granted the cross to the most dangerous of them? As though reading his companion's mind, the Abbé went on, "The Queen will tax all your skill and care, Odo. Once they land in Antioch she will have her uncle, the Duke, behind her; they will go hand in glove, and the giddy, worldly influence of the Aquitainians will grow dangerously strong. She must be excluded from the King, and you must seize every possible excuse to prevent her influence from being felt. I cannot tell you how to contrive this, but opportunities will occur. Take any, however small . . ."

CHAPTER FOUR

Watchful as Odo was for any opportunity to come between the King and Queen, none worth mentioning occurred for several months after the great army set out on its journey. From Metz, where they crossed the Rhine, to Constantinople was three months' journey, pleasant on the whole for it was summer and the roads were open, and the latter part of the journey was made by drifting swiftly and easily down the river Danube. At Constantinople the Emperor of Byzantium, Manuel Comnenus, received the great host kindly and seemed to take pleasure in showing the King and Queen of France the splendours and wealth of his city and in lavishing upon them hospitality of such luxury as they had not dreamed of. Nevertheless, the time spent in this half-oriental capital was made uneasy by two facts which Manuel's kindness could not disguise; one was that he himself had just signed a treaty of peace with the Turks, who were first cousins of the Saracens, against whom all Christendom had just declared war (and that seemed odd, since Manuel called himself a Christian); and the other was that the Emperor of the Germans, whom the French host had expected to find waiting at Constantinople, had gone on ahead some weeks earlier.

When, in the early autumn, they set out from Constantinople

they knew that they were facing the most dangerous and difficult part of their journey. The mountains of Asia Minor lay between them and the Holy Land, and in those mountains thousands of earlier Crusaders had died of Turkish arrows, of hunger, and of cold, without ever setting eyes upon the Saracens. So now, as the days shortened and the weather grew colder, they moved cautiously, each band of knights taking it in turn to ride ahead fully armed in order to make sure that the road was not ambushed by Turks, blocked by a fall of rock or a snowdrift, or otherwise rendered impassable.

There came a day when the Aquitainians, led by Geoffrey de Rancon, were to act as pathfinders. Eleanor rode with them; and with her rode the few women who had wished—and had the right —to accompany her. They were the women who had slammed down the hamper lids at Vézelay, the women who were legally included in Eleanor's pledge, "all those who owe me allegiance"; for Sybille of Flanders, Faydide of Toulouse, Torqueri of Buillon, and some half dozen others were all, like Eleanor herself, great heiresses or widows who had kept their property in their own hands. Having once made an exception in the Queen's case and accepted her service and the service of her particular vassals—even female ones— Bernard could not deny the rights of other independent ladies, nor, to do him justice, did he try to. It was better, he thought, for the Queen to have women about her, to have someone with whom to play her unfeminine game of soldiers; that way she was less likely to spend time with the King. So now about a dozen ladies, called with half-mocking affection "the Amazons" after the legendary female warriors of that name, rode alongside the Aquitainian knights, and they seemed to bear the hardships and privations of the journey with similar courage and good cheer. Eleanor herself had designed their simple and practical uniform, a modification of doublet and hose, and they had many secret plans about ways in which they were going to be very useful once the fighting began— they intended to be so useful that no one would ever again say that women were a nuisance or a drawback to an army. They were good plans and doomed to failure; eight hundred years were to pass before another band of bold women brought similar plans to action in the Crimea.

On this day the path, steep and narrow, fit only for goats or sure-footed mountain mules, led high over the Phrygian mountains, in the centre of which was an open tableland where the knights in the van of the army had orders to make camp. When, late in the day, they reached the plateau, they found it raked by a howling wind, laden with snow, which blew in from the northeast. In places the snow lay thickly, freezing as it fell; in others the wind had raked the hard rock bare and, as they sought for a place where it would be possible to pitch a few tents, the wind screamed about them, cutting through wool and leather and flesh to chill the very bone.

Geoffrey de Rancon, with his head wrapped in a peasant woman's shawl, led the exploring party to the edge of the tableland, then rode back to the Queen and the others who had halted while he chose a camping place.

"If we spend a night here," he said brusquely, "we spend it under the sky. No one could rear a tent in this gale, nor is there an inch of soil in which a peg could be driven—but a little farther on the path drops over the edge and the valley there is sheltered from the wind. There is soil there and, in places, grass."

"The plateau was marked as the place to camp," Eleanor said dubiously. "Perhaps . . . in the open, with campfires, it would be bearable."

"And what should we burn on the fires?" asked De Rancon impatiently. "Madam, there are times when even orders must be treated with reason. No one who had compared the two sites could possibly hesitate to choose."

"Very well. We move into the valley."

They moved to the edge of the tableland where the trail led through a narrow gap between piled-up rocks that looked as though a giant child had been playing with a box of giant bricks and flung them down in anger. From the edge they could see far below the valley, free of snow, with a little stream tumbling through it, and patches of green here and there. It looked and, when they reached it, felt like a different country, a country hundreds of miles removed from the wind-scarred ridge above; for the valley had the whole mountain mass of Asia Minor between it and the wind from the north, and lay open to the sun and the warm breezes from the south. Here and there along the banks of the streams the wild anemones, red and pink and purple, were already in flower.

The tents went up, the fires were lighted, and the supper pots hung over them. The horses were turned out to taste the unusual joy of fresh pasture; in the women's tent the Queen and her ladies felt joy in being able to throw off some of their muffling clothes, to take down and comb out their long hair, and put oil on their wind-flayed faces.

Darkness fell and it was suppertime. Still there was no sight or sound of the main army which, until now, had never been more than an hour's march behind the van. Very soon the joy and relief of having found shelter and a hint of spring in the little valley gave way to anxiety. The most likely thing to have happened was that on the tableland the snow had thickened, hampering the wheels of the baggage waggons . . . perhaps even blotting out the view. Moreover, the gap in the piled-up rocks was narrow, not too obvious at the best of times.

"And the King is delicate," Eleanor said suddenly, breaking into Lady Sybille's chatter. "A night in the open, with no fire, in that place . . . Heaven knows what it might do to him." She went for the third or fourth time to the doorway of the tent and listened. Somewhere somebody plucked at a lute, the sweet old song "Lament For a Rose"; the horses stepped with muted sound in the grass and tore at it softly; there was no sound of their weary fellows creaking and straining and slithering down the steep path from the tableland. The bright little campfires burned like fireflies against the immensity of the night, and over the black bulk of the mountains a great white moon was rising, but no moving shadow, snakelike, every scale a marching man, came down the winding path which linked the valley to the tableland.

Anxiety clawed at Eleanor. Louis was so frail . . . what had De Rancon said of him? . . . "Poor man . . . he looks sick enough"; and that was long ago, before all the responsibility and exertion of the crusade had been laid on his shoulders. Delayed, for whatever cause, on that cold hell of a tableland, he would sleep on the bare rock and without even a warm supper in him. He'd shiver and cough and his rheumacticky joints—legacy of a boyhood spent in the damp dark cloister of Notre Dame—would stiffen, and he would be in a creaking, aching misery for days.

Something must be done, she thought, and, turning back into the tent, she began to knot her hair and dress again in the clothes so thankfully discarded two hours before.

The women, drowsy and lulled by the comparative comfort after the gruelling ride, inquired where she was going. It was clear that anxiety and alarm had not touched them yet.

"Only to De Rancon's tent," she said. But, outside her own, she sent a page running to catch and resaddle her horse.

Her arrival at De Rancon's tent caused some confusion, for he and his men had eaten first and then turned their attention to their long-neglected toilet; beards were being trimmed and sore feet were soaking in buckets of hot water.

De Rancon, hastily pulling on a loose robe, came to the doorway where she waited, still looking out into the night and listening. She cut short his apologies,

"Perhaps it is for me to apologise for disturbing you, but, my lord, I am very anxious."

"On what score? Because the main army has not arrived? I take that to mean that they decided to stay and shiver in the appointed place. That can be the only explanation. We know the way was clear and free of foes. And I left men posted by the gap to tell them where we had gone and to point the way. You may rest easy, dear my lady; all is well."

"If all were well, they would be here. The men you left posted would speak of the sheltered green valley within reach. Who but a mad man would stay in that hellish place if he *could* do otherwise? Why, for the sake of the horses' pasture alone, they would ride on."

"You must forgive me for what I am about to say, Your Grace, but is it not true that given a choice between comfort and discomfort the King would choose the latter? I can call to mind two instances when he has deliberately done so. The rest of us may be on crusade for the sake of the Holy Places, but his Grace is on crusade for the good of his soul. To spend the night in what you so rightly call a hellish place when he might have slept in comfort would seem to him a virtue."

Fantastic as it sounded, it was, she knew, just within the bounds of possibility; she remembered that never once had she heard Louis speak of the joys of victory over the Infidels, but he spoke often of the privilege it would be to walk barefoot into the Church of the Holy Sepulchre.

She put that thought away.

"I must *know*," she said. "My horse is ready. I shall ride back."

"I will ride with you, wasted as I think the errand to be. Nevertheless, we too may gain virtue through discomfort." He laughed as he turned away, calling to his squires for his clothes.

The horse Eleanor rode was gifted with the homing instinct of a carrier pigeon. He knew that for the last half year every step he had taken had carried him that much farther from the green meadow by the Seine where he belonged, and he knew that now, at last, he headed for home. Given his head, he would have gone straight through the mountains of Phrygia and Cappadocia, trotted past Constantinople, swum rivers, leapt ditches, found his green meadow, and lain down to die, content. To him the precipitous uphill path was nothing, and all the way Eleanor was forced to curb him in order to keep any kind of company with De Rancon, whose mount, knowing no such compulsion, moved wearily, grudging having been dragged from the first fresh pasture he had known for weeks.

"No need for such speed," De Rancon said on one of the occasions when her curbing and his prodding had brought them within speaking distance. "Madam, what is it that you fear?"

"I know not. Perhaps the Turks."

He laughed. "We saw none. Do you think they let us—a small force—pass from pity—these non-existent Turks—and waited to throw their slight forces against the main army?"

"Perhaps the snow. It *was* snowing. If it thickened, the gap between the rocks might have been blotted out."

"Look at the moon," he said. She looked, and there was the moon, almost full, radiant in the cloudless sky.

"There is something," she said, and let the homesick horse have his head; and he, with the green meadow by the Seine drawing him like a magnet, made easy work of the last stage of the uphill journey. She was alone as she passed through the gap in the rocks and rode into the teeth of the wind which still scoured the plateau.

There was no snow falling; the frozen drifts lay sparkling white under the moon, and the bare rocks were shining black. She gazed upon this vast black-and-white chequered world, lit by the unconcerned, distant moon and swept by a devilish wind. So far as she could see, nothing stirred; no army was camping here. Either it had been delayed much earlier in the day and never reached the tableland, or else the vanguard had seen at once that the place was uninhabitable even for a night and the whole army had camped on the slopes on the other side.

Yet even as she reasoned with herself she felt terror mounting; this was a sinister place where nothing lived, no tree, no bush, no friendly blade of grass. She was alone with the rocks and the snow and the demon wind. And suddenly the wind took voice and howled out the memory of the forty thousand Crusaders who not so very long ago, in her grandfather's time, had perished somewhere in these mountains, maybe at this very spot.

A cold which had nothing to do with the bitter wind fingered her spine, ran through the hair of her scalp, as she thought—This is a haunted place! The horse felt it too; he shivered and moved suddenly sideways, then backed, and tried to turn.

It was with the sweetest relief that she heard the approach of De Rancon, urging his horse up the last incline. He said with breathless reproach as he drew level with her:

"My lady, you should have waited; I did my best to keep up with you. Well?"

"There is nothing here," she said.

"There should be," he said in a different voice. "The men I left . . . where are they?" He stared at the chequered black-and-white of the snow and the rocks, of the moonstruck places and the shadows, and, cupping his hand about his mouth, sent a great "Hullooah" ringing into the wind, which took and shredded it into silence.

"Gaspard! Guillaume! . . ." He called the names one by one and the wind tossed them away mockingly.

"There is nobody here," Eleanor said again; and this time the words were ominous.

Then, as they stared uncertainly, one of the shadows changed shape; one of the flat dark patches on the black-and-white board rose up, humped itself into solidity, and began to move slowly towards them. Eleanor's skin crawled with unwonted, superstitious terror, for this moving thing was like nothing she had ever seen before; low on the ground, humped like a tortoise, and with one long horn erect.

"God between us and all evil," she murmured quickly. And the next second she was brave again; for the crawling thing was a man after all, a dreadfully wounded man with a long arrow completely through his head, the point protruding below his jaw on one side, the shaft bristling from his temple on the other.

De Rancon, with a wordless cry, thrust his horse's bridle into her hand, slipped from the saddle, and began to run towards the crawling man. His horse sighed as his weight lifted, and dropped its head so that the bridle rein moved in her fingers. Her own horse was still quivering and moving restively, ready to run wildly when he had decided which was the least distasteful direction to choose. But De Rancon's horse, she knew, was so tired that he would stand forever; so she knotted the two reins securely and got down and ran towards De Rancon, who had by this time reached the man and was kneeling, holding him in his arms. Unable to speak, the man lifted one hand and laid it for a moment on his lord's; then he moved it and pointed, this way, that way; he made a choking bubbling sound deep in his throat; his uninjured eye screamed out its dumb message of pain.

"Gaspard, can you hear me? Move your hand if you can?"

The hand moved.

"Move it again to answer me 'yes', good man. You were set upon? Many Turks? Much slaughter of our men? The main army killed? Retreated then? Along the road we came? The King? Safe? Dead? You do not know. I'll trouble you no more."

De Rancon drew away his arms and eased the man to the ground again. He and the Queen stood for a moment looking down upon the dreadful mangled mass of broken teeth and bones, smashed tongue, and cheek-flesh of what had been a handsome cheerful face. Shocked past tears and sickened, Eleanor said, "He is doomed, Geoffrey, and in torment. . ."

De Rancon nodded, knelt by the man again, and said,

"My good Gaspard, you have done your duty faithfully and well, and die in defence of Holy Cross. Heaven has opened its gates for you." Without fumbling, he drew his dagger and administered the *coup de grâce*, cutting the man's throat as he would have done a deer's. "Christ in His mercy and God in His glory receive you," he said, and stood up.

"Now, my lady, will you ride back and rouse the camp? I must go on."

"Alone, you can do nothing. The Turks may be lurking still." She looked out across the place of shadows where anything might lie concealed.

"I pray to God," De Rancon said vehemently, "that one at least is lurking and will kill me. Only death now can save me from ever-lasting disgrace."

She knew what he meant. At his command, the advance had, for very good reasons, disobeyed orders and passed on to a more favourable camping ground. That decision had coincided with a Turkish ambush and "great slaughter" of the Crusaders and, although the one might not be directly the result of the other, in the eyes of the world it would seem so. To the end of time men would say that the advance guard had moved on and left the main army to be cut to pieces. And it would be made worse by the fact that it was the Aquitainian force which had moved on. Eleanor wished, for a moment, that she too might ride on with De Rancon and by death escape the reproaches, the shame, the unending calumny. But someone must rouse that sleeping camp. . . .

"I am equally to blame, remember that," she said as they walked back to where the horses were standing.

"Generous, but untrue. But for me you would have camped here."

"And, if I had held to my point, so would you. We share the guilt . . . or the appearance of guilt. Take my horse, my lord; your own is only fit to stumble downhill. I can manage with him."

"And you, dear my lady," said De Rancon, his face ghastly in the moonlight, "take this . . ." He held out the dagger, his only weapon, for he had ridden unarmed, merely pandering, he thought, to a woman's whim. "I think the road back is safe . . . if not, if they have circled behind us, even if I rode with you there would be nothing for me to do but kill you . . ."

"And that I can do for myself," she said, and took the dagger.

She bore him no resentment for leaving her to go back alone; his knight's honour demanded that he should pay for his mistake by riding on into the direction of greatest danger; in his place she would have done exactly the same. She realised that there was a point of desperation where courtesy to ladies, consideration of sex, did not matter any more. And they had reached it. She had no right to be here, or, being here of her own choice, no right to demand preferential treatment. Mounting the tired horse, which sighed again as she settled into the saddle, she spoke to De Rancon as though she were one of his squires.

"If you reach them, my lord, know that we shall be with you at the earliest possible moment. God go with you."

Her horse had had time to feel, through the menace of the smell of blood and death on the tableland, the call of his own green meadow again, and, as soon as De Rancon mounted, he set off most willingly. At the gap, when Eleanor turned for a last look, there was only a shadow, moving swiftly through a world of shadows. She never expected to see De Rancon again.

But the Turks, having made their lightning attack, killed between two and three thousand of the Christians, and captured a number of valuable horses, had dashed away by the mountain tracks which only they knew. The Crusaders, attacked just as they emerged wearily onto the tableland and were engrossed with the difficult business of hauling the baggage trains over the edge, had been taken by surprise and thrown into confusion. For they had been advancing carelessly, with full trust in their advance guard, the Aquitainians, who should have been camped on the tableland, awaiting them.

After the first few moments when they were slaughtered like sheep, they rallied and began to fight back; and then the Turks had withdrawn. Dusk was falling, there were hundreds of wounded to be attended, and a hasty camp had been made just below the edge of the plateau. In the heat of the fight, no one had had time to think about the Aquitainians, except to notice despairingly that they were not where they should have been, but in the aftercalm the question became urgent. The Queen, De Rancon, the whole advance force . . . where were they? Had they also been ambushed with such success that not one man was left to ride back and bring warning?

It seemed possible; it seemed indeed the only explanation. The King, who had aquitted himself very valiantly in the sudden attack and sustained several bruises and cuts, though no serious wound, fell into a frenzy of despair in which remorse had no small part. He was sure that Eleanor was dead, his lovely, gay, gallant Eleanor whom he had held at arms' length all these years in order to please Bernard and Odo.

To Odo he said, weeping, "I blame myself, and shall do so till I die. I was angry with her and jealous . . . yes, jealous, Odo, because the men who had held back when I called for Crusaders rallied to her. So I let her ride with them. Go with *your* Aquitainians, I thought to myself, *they* follow *you*, you lead them, and take your turn with the rest. I should have kept her safe by my side. I was never just to her, Odo, and, in the end, my jealousy sent her to her death."

"But we have no proof of her death, Sire. The first men to step upon the open ground at the top of the pass saw no sign of anything amiss, no sign of struggle. And, amongst the dead and wounded, there was not a single Aquitainian picked up."

"Is it likely that the Turks would attack them at the spot where later they intended to lie in wait for us, where even one body would have given us warning? No, the advance guard was allowed to cross the plateau . . . and then . . ." He rose and pushed away the wet cloths which the physician had applied to his cuts and bruises. "I must go and find out for myself what happened."

"My lord, you are in no fit state . . ." Odo began.

"I have listened to you and your like too long," said Louis in a voice he had never used before to any man in holy orders. "Fetch Thibault to me; he is a man, and will understand how I feel."

Thibault, when he came, said, "Our dear lady's fate has fretted me since the first of those damned Turkish arrows struck. I have had a force standing by this last hour, waiting for the moon to rise. We are just off. At least we can avenge . . ."

"I will come with you," Louis said.

Thibault showed no surprise and, when Odo renewed his protests, turned and said offhandedly, "Tush man, what harm can it do? He has no wound. And anxiety for the Queen would hurt him more than the ride could." Thibault was Louis' man in life and limb, utterly loyal, but he had never before felt the sympathy and unity with his lord which he felt then.

They rode out over what a few hours before had been the scene of the attack, the first battlefield of *this* crusade. In the moonlight, with the help of a few torches, men were searching among the dead and wounded, carrying in the ones for whom there was hope, and despatching with swift mercy those for whom there was none —men who might otherwise linger in pain and thirst after the army had gone on next day. They passed through the ring of Turkish dead and wounded who had fallen after the Crusaders had rallied and begun to fight back; and here, for a moment, Thibault dismounted and walked about, turning over body after body with his mailed foot until he had found what he sought—a Turk with a disabling leg wound, but otherwise uninjured.

"Simon," he said to one of his men, "mount this vermin on your saddle and take him back to camp. Guard him carefully and let the leeches do what they can for his wound. Keep him alive at all costs. We may need him tomorrow."

"Why?" asked Louis as Thibault mounted and rode on.

"Sire—in case we find the Queen neither alive nor dead. Then we shall need to know in what direction the Turks went and where their headquarters are, and that fellow, with the help of a little torture, will tell us. It would do De Rancon and some of his gay knights no harm to cool their heels in a Turkish prison until their ransom was arranged—but I fear for the Queen. Even the Infidels, who prefer women fat, would see that she is a lady of extraordinary beauty."

"Don't speak of it, Thibault. My thoughts are already more than I can bear."

In this mood they rode on, staring ahead into the black and white of the snowdrifts and the rocks, the moonshine and the shadows; presently a shadow moved and took shape and became De Rancon; he was making good speed on his horse, who thought he was going home to a green meadow, which, in fact, he was never to see again.

De Rancon, seeing the chain mail glint in the light, shouted as soon as he was within earshot,

"The King? What news of the King?"

Louis would have answered, but his voice choked with emotion. Thibault shouted back,

"Safe and sound. The Queen?"

"Safe and sound."

Then there was a moment when Louis and Thibault and De Rancon spurring forward met, and, in the overwhelming relief of the most urgent anxieties on both sides, were all talking and laughing and almost crying at once. At that moment the Frenchmen believed that the Aquitainian advance force had been attacked and scattered (why else were they not encamped in the ordered place?) but had survived, at least in sufficient numbers to save the Queen. The belief continued while De Rancon kissed Louis' hand, and Louis patted his shoulder, and Thibault clasped De Rancon's hand and said jubilantly to the King, "God send all your fears should be equally groundless, my lord." But when Thibault asked the natural fellow-soldier question, "Were your losses heavy?" and De Rancon said, "We had no losses. We were not attacked," then the chill fell.

"Not attacked? Why then were you not camped in the place arranged?" Louis asked in a tone of astonishment.

"Aye, by Christ's five wounds, why weren't you there? You could have saved the day for us!" Thibault gasped.

"More than two thousand good men dead, a thousand precious horses gone," Louis said.

Knowing the utter futility, the apparent senselessness of his excuse, De Rancon began his explanation.

It was to be given again and again; it was never to be accepted. Forty, fifty years afterwards, wherever Frenchmen and Aquitainians met, the quarrel would break out anew. Goaded by the question, "Who played that dirty trick in Phrygia?" the Aquitainians invented an insulting explanation of the whole affair.

"Old Turk, he laid there behind the rocks and, when *we* marched through, not many of us, just advance guard but in good order, mark you, he laid low. He dussent tackle us. But when you poor fellows come along, all in a muddle . . ."

The taunt was the bitterer because one of the complaints brought by the main army was that, trusting to the advance guard, they had been marching without much caution.

The King, quite naturally, jumped in one moment from agonising anxiety about Eleanor to fury against her. Like a mother whose child has just escaped death through running out under a horse's hoofs, and who proceeds to shake and slap it, he hurt her in the only way open to him, scalding words and then silence. De Rancon he sent home in disgrace, and when Eleanor pleaded for him, "It was as much my fault. I agreed to seek a better place to camp," Louis said, "That is all the more reason for sending him home. A man who heeds women's whims is no good on crusade."

Odo seized the opportunity which might never come again. He remembered his orders; he also remembered Louis' behaviour when he believed the Queen to be dead or in danger. That had been a very revealing moment. To Louis, at the first chance he said,

"Sire, you must not blame the Queen too harshly. She is but a woman; she does not understand the sanctity of military orders. Nor must De Rancon be too hardly judged. He is a man, and the Queen can wheedle very sweetly; he wished her to camp in comfort and in pleasant surroundings and so forgot his duty, as better men have done for less reason."

He paused to let that sink in and then added thoughtfully:

"But the real culprit in this case is neither man nor woman; it is the Aquitainian *temperament*. Pleasure first, that is their motto, and they should have it embroidered on their banners so that men might be warned. For them all things must be pleasant. In this case the valley looked more pleasant than the plateau. So they bought their pleasure and their comfort at the price of . . . I forget the exact number of men and horses, Sire."

Louis knew; knew to the last man, the last horse; and Odo, without mentioning the numbers, had graved them on the King's mind even more deeply: two thousand, six hundred and eighty-one men, including many good knights, one thousand and twenty-six horses . . . all lost to the crusade because the Aquitainians valued comfort above all else. And Eleanor was Aquitainian . . . not to be blamed, but *not to be trusted,* a wheedling woman who lured men from their duty.

Odo had made his point with great skill. He had also made certain the failure of the crusade—but that he did not know.

CHAPTER FIVE

The private apartment of the Duke of Antioch had been temporarily transformed into a silk merchant's booth. Heaped on the benches and tables and spilling over onto the tiled floor were samples of all the rarest and loveliest fabrics of the East. The four grave turbaned men who had carried the bundles to the palace and opened them reverently for the Duke's inspection now tucked their hands into their billowing sleeves and stood back to wait while he made his choice. The Duke, accompanied by his favourite friend, Gervase, moved busily and happily about, touching the gleaming velvets, the lustrous damasked silk from Damascus, the gossamer gauzes which only the weavers of Gaza knew how to produce, the snowy crisp muslin that had come by camel back from India, and the heavy brocaded stuff which had made an even longer journey from the secret, hidden country called Cathay. The Duke loved colour, loved anything rich and strange, and now, pausing by the bale from which the gauze spilled out, he said,

"It's as though we had netted a rainbow. That purple . . . did you ever see such a colour?"

"That," Gervase said, "is the genuine Tyrian purple; the royal colour, the one the Gospels speak of, 'purple and fine linen'; it is rare for the simple reason that, taken all in all, two men have to die to produce an ounce of the stuff."

"Why? What is it then? Pounded dead men's liver?" asked Raymond, slightly shocked, but as always concealing his genuine feelings by mockery.

"No," Gervase said idly. "It's obtained from some sea snail, down on the coast, near Tyre. Slaves dredge the creatures up, and it's a dangerous business; even the whip won't make the poor wretches face the tide, so they're staked out and only taken in when they've filled . . ."

"How revolting," Raymond said. "You may put this back into the bundle, my good man. We will have no Tyrian purple today!" Then he laughed and said, "Now tell me something equally nasty about this delicious turquoise blue!"

"That I can't do; it's a purely vegetable dye, some brew from a herb that only grows in Samarkand."

"Thank God for that. It's the colour I want for Eleanor. It's almost the colour of her eyes, not green, not blue, both, with a tinge of grey."

"That is a colour even rarer than the purple and will cost you more."

"That is as it should be. She is the Queen, not to mention being my niece. Now, the Lady Sybille is a dark beauty; I think this ruby red for her, don't you? And there's a redhead. I shall have amethyst for her, it's the colour redheads should, but seldom do, wear. Oh and there's one little mouse called Amaria, such a drab timid-looking little creature, you'd never believe she could have survived the journey; still, here she is and . . . what colour does most for a mouse, Gervase?"

"Rose pink," said the young man firmly. "Besides, nine men out of ten men prefer rose pink to any other colour, often without knowing it, so they look at it and make a compliment, then the mouse blushes and is transformed, and is no more a mouse. See?"

When the gauze and the silk and the velvet in matching or harmonious shades had all been chosen, the merchants were paid and dismissed and the sempstresses called in, a group of old Saracen women, all widows, their eyes red-rimmed and nearsighted and their fingers prick-hardened from years at the needle.

They listened to their orders—they were to go to the women's quarters of the palace and spy through the lattices, which had been set up two hundred years ago by the sultan to whom the palace had belonged, in order that he might keep an eye upon the amusements and quarrels of the forty women he called his wives. The old women were to take note of the measurements of the ladies from the West who now occupied the harem quarters; then they were to take the materials into an inner courtyard and cut and sew for all they were worth so that each lady might have a new dress, in Eastern style, to wear for the supper party that evening.

"Now for the jewellers," said the Duke as the old women hobbled away. "This is going to cost me a fortune, Gervase . . . but it will be worth it. I have political reasons for wanting to please Eleanor and get her on my side, of course; but apart from such low motives . . . she does need a little consideration and cheer. They have had a miserable journey. Amongst other disasters, they were stranded at Satalia and had to eat their own horses, which is just a little extreme even for crusaders. And also . . . well, between ourselves, Gervase, and not wishing to decry my royal nephew-in-law . . ." he hesitated, and his companion said, obligingly,

"Once a monk always a monk; and monks should not get themselves married. Is that it?"

"Partly. At least they shouldn't marry women like my niece Eleanor and then make no effort to appreciate their good fortune. All this smouldering resentment about making camp in the wrong place. So tiresome, and so utterly stupid. Every army that has ever crossed those mountains has been set upon; every army that ever crosses them will be set upon. If the Turks hadn't struck the first French to climb on to the tableland, they'd have hung about and attacked the rear. Why blame her? Blame her he does, though in typical fashion his blame takes the form of saying that he *doesn't* blame her. Personally, I'm only too thankful that it was the French and not the Aquitainians who took the brunt of the attack; the Aquitainians—if I can handle Eleanor rightly, and I think I can —are going to be far more useful to me."

"Why?"

"You'll know as soon as we begin to discuss our plans of action. To explain it all now and then again later on would bore me extremely. Let us now turn our attention to these trinkets. Rubies, of course, for the Lady Sybille and amethysts for the red-haired Faydide . . . rose tourmalines for the transformed mouse . . ." He busied himself over the box of jewels as though each selection were a matter of prime importance.

"And for the Queen herself?" Gervase asked at last.

"Ah! None of this bazaar stuff for Eleanor. I am about to make a *gesture*, my dear Gervase. I am going to give her a family heirloom which my crusading grandfather looted from the Emir of Hama and took home to my grandmother, God rest her soul in peace. I was, as you know, very much a younger son, but the old woman always preferred me, and just before I left home to try my luck in the East, she sent for me and said that she had always thought it very harsh that elder sons should inherit everything and younger ones be left to make their own way. 'I have only one thing of my own,' she said, 'for my property was joined to your grandfather's and naturally passed to your father who will hand it on to his son. But this is for you alone. Keep it secret until you are out of Aquitaine!' Whereupon she gave me this, wrapped in a bit of linen." The Duke drew from the breast of his robe a single diamond the size and much the shape of a half-grown jargonelle pear. The narrower end had been pierced and fitted with a ring by which the stone hung on a slim gold chain. Raymond swung it so that the light caught it, and every colour of the spectrum shook and shimmered before Gervase's dazzled eyes.

"It's worth a fortune," he said.

"Only when given," Raymond said, cupping it in his hand. "Or so the story goes. It is supposed to have a long history of bad luck behind it, but my grandmother said it only brought evil to those who took it by force, as indeed most of its owners have done. Certainly it never did me any harm. And I shall give it to Eleanor if only as a token of respect for a woman who could travel herself and persuade a dozen other females to travel without bringing along every bit of gear they owned. I *do* think that for women to set out in those fantastically sensible riding clothes with just two changes of linen and no jewels is quite incredible and rather touching . . . that is partly why I'm being so very lavish with them."

"Lavish indeed," Gervase agreed. "But it sticks in my mind that when they are dressed they'll look like a troupe of Arab dancing girls."

"And what could be more attractive than a troupe of Arab dancing girls *without* that smell of oiled hair and attar of roses which, I must confess, I always find very repellent."

"Oh, I agree. The only thing is, Raymond . . . not that I've seen much of His Majesty of France . . . but I suspect that he will be a little . . . shall we say critical?"

The Duke of Antioch's formal feast of welcome to his guests and allies was set out in what was known as the Hall of Waters. It was a vast apartment, floored and pillared with marble, roofed in, but open to the air on all four sides. A channel of water three yards in width ran the whole length of it in the centre of the floor, and there were five fountains splashing and tinkling in the channel. Marble troughs of flowers and shrubs lined the water's edge, and hanging baskets of flowers alternated with gilded cages in which birds, bright as flowers, chattered and sang in the spaces between the pillars. The Saracens, from whom Antioch and Edessa and Jerusalem and a dozen other towns had been taken in the First Crusade, had devoted great attention to the problem of water in this thirsty land. They had brought to perfection an irrigation system such as the country was not to be blessed with again in eight centuries, and had spared time to install fountains in the city squares, in public and private gardens, and in the houses of the well to do.

Along the marble floor, on either side of the cool water—piped direct from the lake—ran a long, low table; and the two were joined at the far end by one that ran across. On the inner side of the tables no benches were set, so that each guest had a clear view of the water and of those seated at the other tables. Along the outer side, low couches, in the Eastern fashion, were piled with soft brightly coloured cushions.

At the appointed time Duke Raymond ushered in his guests and indicated to the King of France that he should take the place of honour in the centre of the table which ran crossways. The chaplain, Odo, immediately slipped into position at the King's elbow, and Raymond said quietly, "The ladies are invited, and there are enough of them to allow us to sit one and one on this table at least."

Odo stared owlishly and made no move, affecting not to understand the southern, Aquitainian brand of the French language which Raymond spoke. There was an awkward little pause.

Then Louis said, "With your permission . . . I like to have my chaplain by my side. His memory is better than mine and I rely upon it."

"As you wish, Sire. Then the Queen shall sit upon your left, here between us."

Louis appeared little interested in where Eleanor sat; his gaze had travelled towards the lower end of the hall and rested, with an expression of bewilderment tinged with dismay, upon a group of four or five men who had just entered. Their faces were no darker than those of Western men long-exposed to the sun; their garb was no more oriental than that of their host, yet there was that in the shape of their features, in the very way in which they moved, which proclaimed them to be of Eastern origin.

"My lord Duke," Louis asked, "have we Saracen allies so trustworthy that you admit them to your table?"

"None that I know of . . . oh! I see. They are the heads of the leading Pullani families in Antioch."

"Pullani?"

"Mongrels," said Raymond, tactfully lowering his voice and speaking close to Louis' ear. "Sons of Christian knights who married Saracen women, you know."

"A thing which should never have been allowed," Louis said firmly.

"Difficult to prevent with so many young men from the West settling here. And I must say the Pullani are most ardently Christian and Frankish . . . in fact they tend to overdo it. They take their knightly duties very seriously indeed. And if we didn't recognise them and be, if anything, extra civil to them, they'd turn just as seriously Saracen—from resentment. I always take great pains with *my* Pullani."

"So I observe," Louis said in a dry voice.

At that moment the ladies entered the Hall of Waters, and gaiety came with them. In their new dresses they were bright as a cluster of butterflies, and, since the dresses were completely strange to them, gifts entirely unexpected and matched with trinkets both charming and valuable, every lady was excited and therefore more beautiful and animated than usual. A gasp followed by a murmur of admiration greeted their entry.

The Queen, radiant in her fluttering blue-green gown and with the great diamond blazing at her throat, advanced and bent her knee to the husband she had not seen since the landing in Antioch four days previously. He greeted her courteously, "My lady, I hope I see you well," and extended his hand in the formal gesture of aiding her to rise and take her place at his side, but as he did so an expression of hurt surprise moved across his face, and as soon as she was seated he said,

"You, too, have fallen victim to the prevalent disease of Antioch!"

"Disease, my lord? But I am in excellent health."

"I mean this love of Eastern ways!" He looked sternly at her dress and then quickly away.

"But Louis . . . we had no others . . . as you know, what little baggage we brought was lost. And my uncle *sent* us these, surprising us all most delightfully. Would you have preferred us to attend wearing our riding clothes?"

"I do not think that Christian women from the West should take joy in appearing in public in the guise of Eastern houris. But that, as I said, is just a symptom of a grave disease. You have rested for four days; I have inspected Antioch. . . ." The memory of what he had seen darkened his eyes; his voice, always high-pitched, rose to shrillness as he said half hysterically, "I have seen Antioch! And if Edessa were half the sink of iniquity that Antioch is, no wonder it fell so easily to the Infidel! The wonder is that Antioch itself has not been taken long ago!"

On Eleanor's other side Raymond, who had heard every word the King spoke, stirred; he put his hand on Eleanor's arm and gave it a little reassuring, conspiratorial pinch as he said,

"Sire, delay will not improve this unworthy food," and nodded to the Nubian slave who, kneeling, offered a silver dish for the King's attention. But even when the food, delicious in itself and doubly so to people who had half starved in the later stages of their journey, was safely on his plate, Louis managed to ignore it and to scold on about the things which had shocked him in Antioch. The senseless luxury—such a waste of money which should be devoted to providing arms and stores for the crusade; the Godless pursuit of pleasure—in which the Duke himself set a disgraceful example; the astonishing laxness of the Christians—was it believable that, though Antioch had been all these years a Christian province, there were still Moslem mosques standing open in the city? One of them Louis had seen next door, directly next door to a Christian church! And next door to that a heathen temple devoted to the pagan goddess Diana.

"The mosques, of course, are understandable," Eleanor said in an attempt to soothe him. "Serious Mohammedans refuse to stay in a town where there is no mosque. My father had the same trouble in Bordeaux. He had to let the Moorish traders from Spain have their mosque, otherwise he would have lost the trade they brought."

"Typically Aquitainian," Odo murmured. "Pleasure first; trade second."

Louis turned to him, and Eleanor, taking advantage of her release, turned to Raymond. The two pairs of bright, green-blue, rather narrow eyes met in a long look of understanding.

"It is ten years since I saw you last," Raymond said smoothly, "and in such a space tastes change. Do you still love hunting?" Eleanor nodded. "Then, now that you have rested, I will show you some sport. We will hunt gazelles on the Baghras hills and let loose our falcons by the lakeside. I will take you inland by river and show you the mighty ruins of a city as old as time, a place beside which Antioch would look like an anthill. There's a temple there, Eleanor, with fifty-four columns each thirty feet high, and all encrusted with turquoise and lapis lazuli, and no one dares to touch them, even to rob, because of the ghosts that guard the ruins. Oh, there are so many things to show you! If we had time I would take you to the Lebanon, and we would stand on a peak from which, faraway across the ravine, the shining silver roof of the palace of the Old Man of the Mountains can be glimpsed. . . ."

"Ah," said Eleanor, "but time will be lacking. Spring is the time for war in Palestine, I understand. So soon as the stragglers of our host come in from Satalia, we shall be on our way."

The lively look upon Raymond's face gave place to one of great intensity of purpose.

"That is what I must talk to you about," he said. "But not now. A feast of welcome, however inadequate it may be, is no time for serious discussion. Besides, here are the dancers and the acrobats."

As the entertainers trouped into the lower end of the hall, the King of France, accompanied by his chaplain, rose, and with a courteous excuse to his host he retired.

"He looks very tired," Raymond said kindly. "He should have rested, as I advised, instead of driving himself to see Antioch with its shocking sights." His eyes twinkled, but Eleanor did not respond. She said stiffly,

"The King has never spared himself. And no doubt your city *is* shocking to one of his saintly character."

Unmoved by the snub, Raymond said smoothly, "The saddest thing about saintliness, to my mind, is that it is such a handicap to enjoying oneself."

And that, Eleanor thought, is true, Heaven knows. Aloud she said,

"Tell me more about this Old Man of the Mountains."

So Raymond exerted himself to entertain and amuse her; and the dancers wove their intricate patterns, and the acrobats displayed their tricks. The feast went on until the early hours of the morning, mounting in gaiety. At its end Eleanor said, "I *have* enjoyed it. I haven't enjoyed anything so much for—many years."

"And tomorrow we will ride together. I have an Arab mare for you, pure white and swift as the wind."

"And as we ride we can discuss our serious business."

"Oh yes, that too if we must," Raymond said lightly.

CHAPTER SIX

Next day the Duke of Antioch, with delicate skill and immense care, made *his* contribution to the failure of the crusade.

The day was beautiful with the rich transient loveliness of spring in Palestine. Raymond and Eleanor rode through groves of flowering trees which shed scent on the air, and over fields of flowers similar to those of which Christ had said that Solomon in all his glory was not so splendidly arrayed. Finally they stopped their horses on the bank of a little stream which had dwindled since the winter rains ended and now ran narrowly between borders of clean sand; here they alighted and, while the horses drank at the water, stretched themselves in the warm sunshine. Raymond began with his finger to trace some marks in the sand, prodding deeply in certain places and connecting them with lines. Then he said in a voice more serious than his usual one,

"Now, Eleanor, look at this for a moment. Here is Edessa—now in Saracen hands; here is Antioch; here far to the south is Jerusalem. Where I have made holes are Christian strongholds, and these others where I have made mounds are the Saracens'. Can you read a map?"

"Tolerably well."

"Then look at this one carefully and tell me this. Where does the Saracen threat appear to be most dangerous—to Antioch or to Jerusalem?"

The question seemed so easily answered that she feared a trick and hesitated before giving the obvious answer; but at last she said,

"Surely to Antioch."

"Now tell me this. If you wished to deal the Saracens a blow where would you strike—always assuming that this is the comparative position of the two forces?"

Again she hesitated because the question was so simple.

"I should strike at Edessa with the strongest force I could muster *without* leaving Antioch open. I should maintain a squadron of swift horsemen there to cut off any Saracens from the south who attempted to come to the aid of Edessa, or any who tried to get out from Edessa, when I attacked it, to join those in the south."

For a moment Raymond stared at the map in the sand without speaking and Eleanor's face reddened. She had made a fool of herself! What was the right answer then?

Raymond put his arm about her shoulders and quickly kissed her once on each cheek.

"You are my darling, honey-sweet niece," he said, "and worthy to be the daughter of your father! Of course that is the thing, the *only* thing to do."

With self-confidence restored, Eleanor could afford to say with an appearance of modesty,

"I should have to be very blind not to see that."

Raymond scowled. "Your husband is just so blind, sweetheart! Unless we can restrain him, he intends to march straight to Jerusalem."

"But in Heaven's name why?"

"A number of reasons. One—because I suggest attacking Edessa. Two—because recapturing Edessa will make Antioch safe and he doesn't approve of Antioch. Three—because he thinks, he honestly thinks, that Jerusalem is a holy place, *literally* without a sinner or a Pullani or a moneylender or a drunkard in its whole population. He was very much shocked, Eleanor, when I told him that Jerusalem was just like Antioch, Tyre, and Sidon, only bigger and perhaps a little naughtier."

"Is Jerusalem in actual danger?"

"At the moment, no. And if Edessa can be retaken and the Christian kingdom strengthened here in the north, it need never be. But nothing, no amount of argument, can make the King see that."

"Then I must try to make him see it . . . not by argument, Uncle Raymond, he long ago determined never to listen to me on serious matters. The Abbé Bernard and Odo the Chaplain have convinced him that nothing I say is either sensible or trustworthy; I *know* that. I think they make a text of it, 'Be kind to the Queen but never trust her.' But where argument from me fails with Louis, action sometimes answers; it was by taking action, not by talking, that I managed to join the crusade. And I shall take action now."

"What action?"

"I shall lead my Aquitainian and Poitevin knights with yours to Edessa, not with Louis to Jerusalem. They will see the sense of your plan . . . and frankly I do not think Louis would risk moving to Jerusalem without the support of my men."

"I think the mere threat of such action on your part would bring him to reason," Raymond said, well satisfied with the turn affairs had taken. "But you must bear in mind that this will come between you and your husband."

"There are already so many things, so many people, between us," she said bitterly. "Left to ourselves, we might have managed very well—or at least no worse than most people. Louis is kind and well-meaning and was once inclined to fondness for me; upon my part I was fond of him; I married him and I keep my bargains. But none of that matters . . . what matters is this crusade; the success of an action which has already cost so dearly in men and money must *not* be endangered simply because Louis does not like you, your city, or your plan." She stood up, brushing the sand from her clothes and her hands. "We'll go back to the palace now and I will tell Louis, without argument, what I have decided."

The interview which she sought and obtained immediately followed the usual course. Louis was courteous and immovably stubborn, Eleanor reasonable and urgent; Louis became reproachful, accusing her of having gone over to the Duke's side because she shared his frivolous attitude; Eleanor retorted that, so far as she knew, Raymond and Louis were on the same side still. Louis took refuge in the old contemptuous soothing statement that these were matters beyond the understanding of women, things best left to men; and at that Eleanor lost her temper and slapped her hand on the map which was unrolled on the table between them.

"I *do* understand. It is you who are deliberately blind to the truth. When your toe is poisoned and rots, do you cut off your ear? What ails Jerusalem at this moment? Nothing. The Saracens hold Edessa and every day that passes strengthens their hold. Unless they are driven out, by next year they will have Antioch. Can't you see that we must begin at the beginning?"

"I can see," said Louis, angered at last, "that you have learnt parrotwise what the Duke wished you to learn."

"I could see it from one glance at a map before he spoke a word," she said furiously. "And I tell you this, Louis, if you insist on leaving Edessa to its fate and go to Jerusalem, I shall not go with you."

"Madam, you will come to Jerusalem if I have to carry you by force. You are my wife!"

"Use force to me, Louis Capet, and I shall not be your wife long. I shall divorce you!"

The shocking, irrevocable word rang out, and there was a painful drawn-out silence into which Louis said in a small acid voice,

"And how would you set about that?"

"By drawing the Pope's attention to a small detail which everyone agreed to overlook in silence—that we are cousins in the fourth degree and therefore within the forbidden relationship. Not long ago you yourself forbade two marriages between people no more nearly related than we are. It suited you to remember it then, just as it suited you to forget it when you wanted to marry me . . . me *and* my domains!"

Odo, who up to this point had been enjoying the scene which justified so many things he had said about the Queen, now felt things had gone far enough.

"The Queen is not herself," he said, "it is the sudden heat—and she has been riding in the sun. I will call her women."

When Eleanor, still seething with rage, had gone to her own apartments, Odo said,

"Take none of that to heart, Sire, the babbling of a disappointed child, no more. The Duke probably promised her some pleasure to be tasted or some sight to be seen in Edessa, therefore to Edessa she must go." His eyes narrowed craftily. "Nevertheless the suggestion that she is sick from the sun was an inspiration from Heaven; for if it is necessary to take her by force that will serve as an excuse for taking her in a closed litter."

"I pray God that it may not come to that," said Louis, who was already regretting the threat.

Within a week he knew that he was doomed to disappointment again; Raymond refused to give up his carefully laid plan for attacking Edessa, and Eleanor stuck obstinately to her intention to lead her forces with his. The quarrel, beginning at high level with the crusade leaders, spread rapidly downwards until the soldiers of Antioch and the soldiers of France were quarrelling openly in the streets, and any passing Aquitainian would join in on this side or the other, according to his taste. Finally Raymond realised that it was hopeless to attempt to persuade Louis any more, and then, mad with temper, he hurled insults as freely as he had showered hospitality.

"If you are going to Jerusalem," he shouted, "for God's sake go! You came here with your hungry hordes as my ally to help to defend this city from the Infidel; as such, I housed and fed you, but I cannot afford to entertain every idle fellow who plans a pleasant pilgrimage to Jerusalem!"

"We leave tonight," Louis retorted. As Raymond swung on his heel and left the apartment, the King sent a page running to request the Queen to come to the council chamber. He would try once more to persuade her. But Eleanor, convinced of the rightness of her decision, was stubborn, too.

That evening, just as the Moslem call to prayer was sounding from the minaret of the mosque which Louis regarded with such horror, the hastily assembled hosts of the crusade began to stream out through the southern gate of the city and take the long road through Tripoli to Jerusalem. In the midst of the army, well guarded by stern French knights, an angry, helpless woman rode in a swaying, covered litter. At a safe distance from it, the standard-bearers bore high the banners of Aquitaine, and the knights and men of Aquitaine and Poitou followed, bewildered but faithful. They had promised to follow their Duchess and there she was in the litter and here they were behind her, all ignorant of what had caused the sudden change of plan.

It was a triumph for Louis, but one which was to cost him dear. He had used force . . . and Eleanor was a woman who kept her bargains, and her threats.

After the heat, the rough jolting of the litter, the torment of flies and dust and thirst of the journey, Jerusalem was a welcome haven. Its water supply alone provided Eleanor, who had a romantic sense of time, with something to marvel at. The Romans, who long ago, before the birth of Christ, had marched in and taken the city, had built great aqueducts capable of supplying their houses, their great public baths, and their fountains. Christ, looking down upon the great Romanised city, had foretold the time when not one stone of it should stand upon another; and in the seventh decade of the new Christian age the prophecy had been fulfilled. Jerusalem had been sacked and its inhabitants had gone back to drinking the waters of the natural wells, with their ancient names, "the Well of David," "Solomon's Spring." Then, after many years, had come the invasion of the Saracens, who brought with them the practical genius which was to give the world its mathematical symbols, and the Mohammedan emphasis on cleanliness—of a ritual kind—which made men far from water "wash" their hands and feet in the desert sand before they said their prayers. The Saracens had immediately seen the value and purpose of the old ruined aqueducts of the Romans and had put them back into working order. The Christians, conquering Jerusalem in their turn, had inherited the water-ways; and the city, when Eleanor arrived, was a place of singing fountains.

She always remembered in later days that one of the significant conversations of her life took place there—in a bathhouse, where three fountains tinkled and sent their rainbow-hued sprays into the wide flat pool. She was bathing with Melisande, who was the widow of Foulkes, the Christian King of Jerusalem, and the mother of the boy King, Baldwin. Melisande's father had been a Crusader, her mother a Saracen woman; she was, in fact, one of the half-breeds whose very existence Louis so much deplored; but nobody thought of that, probably not even the King of France, for she was a woman of great dignity and character. And of great insight . . . for in the excitement and joy of actually arriving in Jerusalem, the Holy City, all differences had been forgotten, and Louis, weeping with joy, had handed Eleanor out of the litter as though it had been arranged for her comfort, not for her imprisonment. All the crowds who had met them at the Jaffa gate and accompanied them into the city had been shouting their welcome, and Eleanor had been caught up in the vast excitement of being, at last, on this holy ground. There had followed days crowded with sight-seeing: the Holy Sepulchre, the ruins of Solomon's temple, the palace where Pontius Pilate had given his judgement and washed his hands, the hill of Golgotha where the Cross had stood.

Quarrels, even grave differences of opinion, had seemed so small here where sacred history lay in the very stones. There was—Eleanor was sure—no reason why Melisande should suddenly say in the middle of the bathing hour,

"Things are not well with you, Ail-inor? This Louis, he is a very good man, eh? But you are not happy with him. Do I judge right?"

Eleanor said carefully, "Just at the moment we are in ill accord. I was on the side of those who thought that it would have been wiser to attack Edessa."

Melisande laughed, swallowed water, choked, gasped, "Is that all?" and laughed again. "You mean to tell me that you quarrel with your husband about where should go the armies? Oh, these women of the West, how funny you are. Armies are for men, my Ail-inor; for women, women's things."

That sounded well for the woman who had acted—and very skillfully—since her husband's death as regent for her young son, and Eleanor rather grumpily said so.

"Ah, but that is different. Here we have a saying, 'With the birth of her son a woman comes of age.' And there is truth in it, as in many old sayings. Only wait, dear heart. You will find that, when you rock with your foot the cradle of Louis' son, what you say with your mouth will be more listened to. And then you will not talk about armies! It is strange, but so it is. Just the same, what you do not say will stay in the head . . . and in the heart, so that if, as God forbid, you become as I am, you will be wise."

That, Eleanor thought, was a typically oriental speech; in the East a woman had no value save as a mother of sons. But was the Western world any better . . . really? She contented herself by saying stubbornly,

"All the same, I was right about Edessa. Many *men* thought so too. And bundling me into a litter and bringing me here against my will so that my Aquitainian forces followed still doesn't make Louis *right!* He wanted to come to Jerusalem—but he could have made his pilgrimage afterwards. In all these wasted weeks, travelling towards a city still held by the Christians and in no danger, he has given the Saracens warning and time to man their defences."

"It is not for us to decide," Melisande said comfortably. "All such things go as God wills."

And there speaks the East again, Eleanor thought . . . by right Melisande should have said *"Insh'allah"*—"If Allah wills"—a phrase containing the resignation, fatalism, that was the essence of the doctrine of Allah. But God, the God of the Christian world, had given men reason and wits, and He expected them to use them. There lay the difference. And, in Eleanor's opinion, Louis had not used his wits or his reason and so his crusade would come to no good.

So it proved. In the end it was decided to attack Damascus, the busy market town where the roads that linked the great Saracen centres of Egypt and Baghdad met. The Christian forces, with their mounted knights, their horses, their scaling ladders, their mangonels for stone-throwing, and their battering-rams, set out in brave array. But the Damascenes had been warned. Inside the city walls every old well—some disused for years—had been opened and cleaned. Water had been stored in anything that would hold water —from the goatskin which held two pints to the standing tank which held fifty thousand gallons.

They came then, sadly, out of their city and gathered from the gardens, orchards, and fields which lay about its walls everything which was in any way edible by man or beast. That done, they wrecked their aqueducts, destroyed their patiently made irrigation system, down to the tiniest channels which carried moisture through the fields they had reclaimed from the desert, and polluted, or filled with rubbish, all the wells. After that they closed the city gates, rationed their water strictly, and prepared to wait.

The Christian army with its banners arrived to find itself camping in the desert with many miles of scorched earth between them and drinkable water—save that within the walls of Damascus.

Their plight lent their first attack the ferocity of despair; they must conquer the city immediately, or retreat before death in a horrible form overtook them. At one point the King of France, throwing himself with vigour into the one battle of his life which had the full support of his conscience, had almost breached one wall when a cry went up—where started, and by whom carried, nobody ever knew—that a breach had been made on the other side of the city, and that the support of the French troops was needed there to make the entry an overwhelming success. But there was no breach on the other side, and by the time Louis had returned to the place of his original attack the Damascenes had mended the wall and reinforced it.

Soon men and horses were suffering, then dying of thirst. There was nothing left to do but to retreat hastily to the valley of the Jordan.

There the inevitable quarrels between the barons of Jerusalem, the lords of France, the nobles of the Holy Roman Empire, the knights of Aquitaine, broke out with renewed rancour. The false message was debated again and again, the guilt of it laid now at this door, now at that. The Emperor of the Germans said he had taken the Cross and pledged himself to attack the Saracens, and had done so, and now counted himself free to go home.

Louis was heartbroken by his failure. He lingered in Jerusalem, hoping against hope that some opportunity for renewing the war would occur. None did; the quarrels went on; other Saracen cities, much encouraged by the success of Damascus, made ready to use the same means of defence at the first sign of attack. And with the coming of the hot dry summer of the East, the crusading season was over for another year, and this crusade, like those before it and others yet to come, was shipwrecked on the rocks of muddle, rivalry, and unfavourable conditions.

Louis stayed to spend Easter in the Holy City, and had the unforgettable experience of hearing the Easter cry, "Christ is risen," ring through the lovely church which had been built over the very spot where, it was said, the Resurrection had taken place. Then he was ready to go home.

Eleanor went with him. This was no time to talk of divorce; it would have taken a nature infinitely more brutal than hers to entertain the idea of deserting a man so broken with disappointment. She would try again to make a success of this marriage. She remembered Melisande's words, "With the birth of her son a woman comes of age." Perhaps her next child would be a boy. All might yet be well.

It was winter again in Paris; such a winter as even that grey northern city saw but rarely; such a winter that it was to be remembered for more than a century as a measure of severity, with old men saying, "Ah, but this is nothing to the winter of 1149"; and with children saying, "Tell about the time when the river froze." The very water mills stood idle, their wheels set fast in the icy crust that bound the rivers; the gravediggers were also idle, for the ground was too hard to take the dead.

Into this frozen desolate world Eleanor's second child, the Princess Alix, was born. This time Eleanor spoke no brave words about next time, about the sons which a soothsayer had promised. She had seen Louis take the news of the baby's sex sourly, stand for a moment rubbing his thin chilblained hands together, then turn away without speaking. She had failed again.

As she lay in her chamber, with the taste of failure bitter in her mouth, the King, who had been joined by the Abbé, walked slowly back along the cold draughty passage which led to his own apartment. They came to a brazier in which charcoal smouldered, feebly attempting to dispel the icy chill. Louis paused and held his hands over the small warmth.

"Another girl," he said, breaking the silence, "when all France has been hoping and praying for an heir."

"If the ways of God were intelligible to man, He would not be God," said Bernard gravely, answering the spirit rather than the word of Louis' remark. "Mystery is part of the panoply of His majesty, and it is for us humbly to accept His decrees."

His words were utterly sincere; he was voicing the creed upon which he had based a lifetime of toil, self-denial, and unswerving faith.

"But there are signs," Louis said suddenly. "Out of the mystery, He vouchsafes to give us signs."

"Which we interpret amiss," Bernard said, thinking of his dream about St. Peter. Where had that led? To the failure of the crusade, if half the reports were true.

More in an attempt to distract the King's mind from his recent blow than from any wish to convince him, he said, "I once thought I had received a sign from Heaven . . ." and went on to tell about his dream and how, as a result, he had given Eleanor the Crusader's cross. Louis listened, holding his hands nearer and nearer to the brazier. Then, when Bernard had finished his story, he straightened up and said,

"But you see . . . if she had never come to Palestine with me, we should never have quarrelled; she would not have spoken in anger the words I cannot forget—'I shall divorce you.' 'How would you set about that?' I asked, and she said, 'By drawing the Pope's attention to the fact that we are cousins in fourth degree therefore within the forbidden relationship.' My lord Abbé . . . do you not see how this all falls into place? *You* have a sign from Heaven; she comes to Palestine and says those words to me; in the birth of another girl, *I* have a sign from Heaven to take advantage of what she said. We *are* within the forbidden relationship; we should never have married. God in His anger denies us a son. I see it all very clearly now."

Louis raised his eyes and looked with a strange blind stare into the Abbé's face; then, tucking his hands into his sleeves for warmth—his fingers must be supple on the pen—he turned and hurried towards his apartment. Bernard, now very feeble and short of breath, hurried after him.

"My son," he said, panting, "this is not a matter to decide without grave consideration. What of Aquitaine, that rich dower?"

"Of what use," Louis demanded, "is Aquitaine to a man without an heir? Must I leave France to another man's son? God forbid! I have been blinded—first by the great heritage, then by the pretty face, the charming ways. But now my eyes are opened and I see my way . . . my duty, clearly. I go now to write to the Holy Father without delay."

Delay—in various high places—kept Louis waiting for something more than three years before his request for a divorce was granted; but it came at last, in the early days of the year 1152. The final decision was made by a meeting of bishops in Paris and, as soon as it was announced, Louis despatched a message to Eleanor, then shut himself into his own part of the palace, hoping that she would leave without asking a last audience of him. The frail branch of his love for her had never fully flowered, had never really had a chance to flower; she had disappointed him often, angered him frequently and, ever since the moment when he decided to ask for a divorce, he had steeled his heart against her. Occasionally he even felt, comfortably, that he hated her; but now he found himself shrinking from the thought of saying good-by to her. Also his conscience, always active, was uneasy about the children.

Eleanor had asked him to allow her to take the two little girls with her. She had argued that Marie, seven years old, and Alix, still a toddler, were too young to be left motherless; she had argued that the sunnier climate of Aquitaine would be beneficial to their health; she had promised that she would never allow them to forget that they were princesses of France, and, as soon as they were old enough to be betrothed, she would hand them over and take no share in the arrangements for their future. Because they were girls, a constant reminder of his sonlessness, and because they were both pretty in a way which foreshadowed their likeness to their mother, Louis took little pleasure in the children and was, for a while, almost inclined to grant her request. He half hinted to his advisers that he intended to allow the girls to go with their mother to Aquitaine. Immediately there was a storm of protest. The little princesses were the Children of France; they would, in a few years, be very useful pawns in the game of politics, and it would not be easy to marry them off if they came back from Aquitaine headstrong, unfeminine, hoydenish, like—well, was it necessary to say whom? As a tree is trained so shall it stand, did not the proverb say? The girls must stay in Paris and be trained for wifehood, to be meek and pious and biddable; after all, their mother had no right to them, and their father must not ignore his responsibilities.

So the day came—a bright windy spring day—when Eleanor concluded her last-but-one duty in France, the handing over and checking with the chief lady in waiting of the jewelry which belonged to the French crown. As the last casket lid closed, Eleanor said, "So ends one period of my life. Fifteen years."

"I wonder who will wear them next," said the lady in waiting curiously; for though it was taken for granted that the King would marry again without loss of time, since it was desirable that France should have an heir, even the wildest gossip had failed to name, or even hint at, Eleanor's successor.

"Whoever she may be, I hope she will be happier in France than I have been," Eleanor said, and she turned to the completion of her toilet, decking herself bravely in the jewels which were her own, brought from Aquitaine, and with the great diamond from Antioch. Two trinkets, a necklace of amber set in plaques of gold and a little bracelet—which she herself had worn as a child—a wide silver band set with seed pearls and turquoise, she held in her hand as she went to say good-by to her children.

Alix was too young to understand, but Marie, with one of those sudden, disconcerting flashes of comprehension which small children occasionally show, said,

"But you will come back. You went away before and came back."

"This time I may not come back, Marie; but you shall come one day and stay with me. In a very beautiful place where the sun shines and everything is gay."

Spoken with intent to comfort, the promise was genuine. In a short time, Eleanor thought, Louis would marry again and have a second family; then, with the old wounds healed, the old grudges forgotten, he would be prepared to let Marie and Alix visit, at least, in Aquitaine.

There was no need to say at parting, "Be good." Both little girls had inherited, in full measure, their father's tender conscience and unventuresome nature, and, in the orderly, dull routine of their days, there would be little chance for any kind of ill-doing. So it remained for her to lift them in her arms and kiss the soft childish faces—and she must control herself, allow no sign of her own grief at parting to be seen. So soft, so young, so very dear. She gave them the little ornaments, then slipped away and stood in the dim chill corridor until she was in control of herself again.

The children's lady governess, who had been waiting in the next apartment while Eleanor took her leave of them, entered as soon as she heard the outer door close. She found Marie wearing the amber necklace and struggling to fasten the bracelet about Alix's plump dimpled wrist. She swooped down on both trinkets, saying, "You are far too young to wear such things," and succeeded in taking the bracelet. But Marie backed away, clasping both hands over the necklace.

"It's mine," she said. "My mother gave it to me."

"Never mind. Give it to me. I will lay it aside safely and you shall wear it when you are older," said the lady governess.

Still Marie did not move; so the lady governess went near and attempted to unclasp the necklace; and the good, meek little eldest Child of France ducked her smooth little head and set her sharp little teeth in the lady governess's hand and bit it hard.

The King, when this was reported to him, was less shocked than the lady governess had hoped and expected him to be.

"Leave them their gewgaws," he said, "they have lost their mother."

For he, too, was remembering Eleanor, remembering—as though she were dead—her virtues and forgetting all the rest.

"It will do them no harm to remember her," he said rather sadly. "She was a woman of high courage. In that, at least, I hope they will take after her."

The lady governess went away, holding her throbbing thumb.

Part Two

CHAPTER ONE

It was spring again in Aquitaine. In the orchards outside the city of Poitiers the plum and peach and pear blossoms had lost their first brightness and the petals were falling, but the tide of gay wild flowers had run over the orchard grass and over the roadside verges and all the air was full of the sweetness of newly cut hay. The fragrance reached even the high room where Eleanor sat before her looking glass while Amaria brushed her long hair.

Fifteen years since she had seen the spring in her own land! She would be perfectly happy if only the children were here with her. She missed them more than she had expected; for in Paris, owing to all the regulations which governed their upbringing, she had actually spent little time with them. Still they were there and she was always devising little games for them or thinking of amusing things to tell them, so that her visits, though brief, should be gay and have meaning.

She sighed, then said, "Today, Amaria, we'll take a holiday. For ten whole days I have worked at affairs of state, asking and answering dull questions, and going through those dismal accounts. Today I shall leave it all; we'll ride out and watch the haymaking, and take some food and eat it under a tree, then sleep a little and ride back in the cool of the evening. I must admit, Amaria, I find it very delightful to say, 'I will do this, or that,' and not have to ask permission beforehand, or listen to reproaches afterwards."

She could see, in the looking glass, the glumness of Amaria's face.

"What ails you?" she asked, as Amaria stayed silent. "If your head aches, you need not come."

"If you ride, I shall ride. But I think you would do well to stay within the city walls at least, though even there, God knows, you may not be safe. It looks to me as though we may never be safe again."

"Oh come! You make much out of nothing. Two little scuffles on our way down from Paris! Just silly boys' pranks. And we were well protected."

"I lack your stout heart. I can see that when men protect women from other men, some of the blows they aim at one another may fall on the women they are protecting."

"No blow came near enough to us to disarrange our headgear. What has happened, Amaria? You were not so timid when we rode on crusade," Eleanor protested.

"I was always timid. At least, on crusade, we knew our enemies —their clothes and their faces betrayed them. Those boys, as you call them, who lay in wait for you the other day at the ford looked like Christians and we were nearly taken unaware. There are two young noblemen who have tried to take you—run off and marry you —already . . . and greedy, ambitious young noblemen are common as dandelions. Yet there you are, talking of lying down in the sun to sleep! I do beg you, my lady, if we ride out today, to order a strong escort."

"If it comforts you, I will do so. But remember, we are now in my own domain."

"And do the Aquitainian nobles lack ambition or greed?"

"Ah, but I am no longer an innocent young girl, Amaria. Once the thought of being run off with and married against my will did frighten me. The man who tried it now would find that he had caught more than he bargained for. That I do assure you."

"Boldness," said Amaria with a sourness unusual to her, "is mainly

the capacity for underrating danger. With a gag in your mouth
and your hands tied behind you—which is how the Lady Beatrix
was led to the altar not ten years ago—you'd be as helpless as the
next woman." She dropped the tress of hair she was holding and
passed the brush up and down the palm of her hand. "What I'm
going to say may be distasteful, but there's nothing for it but for
you to marry again—and as soon as possible."

"And whom do you propose I should marry? You seem to have
planned it all, Amaria. Boldness in planning, allow me to say, is
mainly the capacity to underrate difficulties."

Amaria, for the first time that morning, smiled.

"I know the man, my lady. And so, I think, must you."

"Well, name him!" She looked into the mirror and her clear
green eyes met Amaria's grey ones in the shadowy depths.

"Henry Plantagenet, Duke of Normandy," Amaria said, and saw
the white lids blink, saw the faintest possible colour creep up from
Eleanor's throat to lose itself in the pale clear rose of her cheeks.
Then, no more than half a second too late, she laughed.

"Amaria, unless that young man has added another birthday to
his tally, he is eighteen years old!"

"What of it? The last fifteen years have gone lightly over you,
my lady. We were saying the other day that you look no older now
than when you left Aquitaine; and the young Duke is a man, whatever his years. More a man, if you ask me, than his father. Surely
you must have marked, when they both came to the French court,
how he always took the lead, how sometimes in their talk his father would look to him before giving an answer, instead of the
other way about. You must have noticed."

"The thing I marked most about him was a strange resemblance
to someone I knew many years ago . . . someone of whom I was
very fond . . ." She brooded for a moment, remembering that first
innocent love. Then she roused herself and said, "Go on with the
brushing, Amaria, or we shall miss the best of the day."

"You'd do well to think over what I have said," Amaria persisted.

"Married to him, you'd be safe. And he admired *you*, I could see that."

"Even so, marriage between us is well-nigh impossible. If the thought entered his head—which I doubt it ever would—he would dismiss it; the King of France would object strongly; after all, these Plantagenets hold Brittany and Anjou from the French crown, great and powerful though they may be."

"Ah well, I didn't mean tomorrow or the next day. By all accounts, the young Duke will be King of England one day, or know the reason why, and then he'll be independent of the King of France. Bear him in mind, my lady; and, in the meantime, take no risks of being married by force." She glanced towards the window. "There'll be no riding abroad today, anyway; a storm is blowing up."

"Don't sound so *pleased*," said Eleanor.

The room grew darker as Amaria looped and coiled the long hair and fixed it with the silver and ivory pins. When it was done, Eleanor went and stood by the window. The black-purple cloud had covered the sun's face, but from its lower edge one ray of concentrated light escaped to fall upon the castle courtyard, the bridge that linked it to the town, and the huddled roofs of the nearest houses. It all looked unreal, a scene from a nightmare.

As she stared, a little knot of horsemen clattered up to the far side of the bridge. One man detached himself to ride on alone and halt for a moment on the bridge, raking the castle with an arrogant appraising stare.

Her breath stopped as she recognised the solid, barrel-chested, long-legged figure, the cocksure set of the head, the red hair showing under the cap with its jaunty sprig of broom—the *planta genesta*, from which his family took its name. She had just said that he would hardly dare to come, and here he was, looking just as he had looked when he came, arrogantly and belatedly, to pay his allegiance to Louis, his overlord—so young, so handsome, so high-hearted. Her eyes had followed him then, and she had thought, Naturally he attracts me, he is the son I should have had. Then, hearing his voice saying brief, downright things, she was reminded of Richard de Vaux and imagined that *there* lay the secret of his attraction for her.

Now, looking down from her high window, she knew that neither of these reasons was the true one.

Suddenly breathless, she turned from the window and said, "Amaria, quick! My best gown. He has come!"

"The Plantagenet? Well, well. They say, 'Talk of the Devil,' do they not?" She hurried towards the great press where the few gowns which Eleanor had brought with her from Paris lay folded, and sprinkled with lavender and rosemary. As she lifted the lid, the lightning struck into the room like a sword and, immediately after, the thunder sounded as though a thousand battering-rams were assaulting the gates of Heaven. White-lipped, Amaria gasped, "He comes with the storm. Oh, what an omen, my lady! What an omen!"

Eleanor swooped across the room, took up a gown, and began to shake it from its folds.

"Don't stand there like an image, Amaria, run out and tell them —De Rancon and the rest—to receive him formally, *formally*; to take him to wait in the anteroom, and offer refreshment. Send Sybille to me, and then run on and tell all my women—their finest clothes—and quickly, quickly."

Henry Plantagenet, Duke of Normandy, acknowledged heir to Anjou, and, in the eyes of many, rightful heir to England, prided himself upon being "a plain, blunt man." Reared in the saddle, the hunting field, and the stern school of war, he had no time and less liking for what he called "nonsense and mummery." In his own court he was as accessible as a farmer or shopkeeper; a man stated his business, was granted an audience, told to say what was to be said as briefly as possible, and dismissed. Today he himself was the one who came asking an audience, and, when he had dismounted and said in his loud firm voice that he wished to speak privately to the Duchess of Aquitaine, he expected to be led straight into her presence and left alone to say his say.

But in the small anteroom, kept waiting, surrounded by the few nobles and knights whom Eleanor had gathered around her in the ten days since her home-coming, he began to feel uncomfortable. These Aquitainians, gay and careless as they could be at times, had a talent for formality and ceremony. He remembered that in the old Duke's time this court had been the cradle of the most elegant form of chivalry. There had actually been a kind of school, called the Court of Love, at which young knights were taught how to behave towards ladies; how to please them by turning pretty speeches, by making music, by singing songs. It was all elaborate, set to pattern, a kind of play acting, in fact, hitherto Henry had dismissed it all as the greatest nonsense and a wicked waste of time. Now he wondered . . . and as he stood, impatiently slapping his leg with his gloves, he gained less pleasure than usual from his thought—"I'm only a plain, blunt man."

When at last he was confronted by Eleanor, wearing all her finery, surrounded by the gaily decked ladies who had been hastily mustered to form as impressive a court as possible, he was annoyed to find himself nervous; and, to the first remarks addressed to him, he gave answers so short and awkward that even in his own ears they sounded unmannerly.

Soon he rallied; he was a plain, blunt man; he had no time to waste; he had something to say which he did not intend to say before this gathering of smiling posturing popinjays, so presently he said,

"Your Highness, I have that to say which is for your ear alone. Can we—or they—withdraw?"

The words rapped out so harshly that Eleanor knew a moment's doubt; perhaps, after all, he had come on some political errand; perhaps he was meditating making war on his overlord, the King of France, and saw in her, the divorced Queen of France, a likely ally. Well, if he wished to be businesslike, she would match his manner. She stood up, abandoning the advantage of the high-backed chair in which she had seated herself for effect, and said, "Come with me, my lord."

When they were alone, he refused the seat she offered him. "I always stand, save when I ride or sleep," he said. Standing stiffly before her, he went on, "It must be clear to you why I am here. A year ago when you were Queen of France and there seemed little likelihood that the divorce would ever be granted, I wished with all my heart you were a free woman. Now you are, and I . . . Madam, I am a plain, blunt man, no hand at pretty speeches, and a sorry figure I'd cut at these courts of love you think so highly of in Aquitaine . . . so I can only offer you my hand and have done with it."

He stared at her with his light, bright, over-prominent eyes, and she could see that he expected her to reply to this proposal in a manner equally brisk. Some of the assurance went out of him when she smiled and said nothing.

He waited; then, with considerably less jauntiness, he went on. "At the moment I can offer you nothing that you haven't yourself, already. Aquitaine is wider than Normandy, wider than Normandy and Anjou; and, if what I have seen during a hard ride is a fair sample, it is richer and more productive. But with God's help—and yours, my lady, if you care to give it—I shall have England, too, before long. And the crown of England will become you better than the crown of France ever did. What's comical in that? Why are you laughing?" The ringing merry laughter, so seldom heard of late, broke irrepressibly from her.

"Not—I assure you—at *you*, my lord Duke. No, I am laughing at all the minstrels and poets with their tales of love. I am told that I am not ill-favoured, and I have travelled farther than most women. I have now received three proposals and not a word of love in any one of them. My lord of France said to me, 'Madam, a marriage has been arranged between us; I trust you do not find me distasteful.' That was forgivable in him, for he was reared to be a monk and monks are not trained to make proposals. Then there was an emir in Antioch who addressed me through my uncle, who knew his language; *he* said literally, 'If you will leave your husband, I will dispose of my eldest wife and you shall rule the others.' There was excuse for him, he was a Saracen. But for you, my lord, I find it hard to find excuse, just as I find it hard to decide whether you really want my hand in marriage—or my help in your bid for the English throne."

She spoke laughingly, teasingly, but no spark of answering amusement lighted Henry's face. He drew away angrily. "By God's head, madam, I thought better of you! A year ago, in the court of France, there was a moment in the talk—you had been sitting there looking as pretty and innocent as a flower—and then you spoke and cut through all the flummery and the nonsense like a sickle through wheat, going straight to the heart of the matter. And I was astonished. A woman in ten thousand, I thought to myself, and to Louis I could scarcely speak civilly on account of the envy that was in me. The moment you are free and it is decent for me to speak, haven't I followed you here? . . . so close that I rode in your dust almost . . . though I know that the moment Louis hears of it he'll call me a faithless vassal and most likely will attack my province."

Henry swung about and began walking to and fro, as was his habit in moments of agitation. In a calmer voice he went on, "I said, 'with God's help, and yours,' but never think I *need* help from you or anyone. It is true that with Aquitaine behind me I should be more formidable, but if all Europe sank into the depths of the sea, leaving me afloat in my nightshirt, I still would have England—or die in the attempt. It is my right; and, if the usurper who drove my mother out and is driving the country to beggary by his mismanagement will not acknowledge my claim, I'll force it from him. When I said, 'with your help,' I meant that when the crown of England was set on your head you could feel it was yours by right—not yours because some creeping politician had arranged it, or because you're fair of face. By the rood, I was fool enough to think that point of view would find favour with you!"

His weather-beaten face had darkened, the light eyes were even more prominent; they stared at her defiantly. After a moment's silence Eleanor said in a surprisingly humble voice,

"Truth to tell, it does. And I have no doubt that with, or without, backing from me you will have your England. I remember your visit to Paris . . . I remember thinking . . ." (For all his dislike of soft speeches, Henry listened eagerly) ". . . thinking that I pitied Stephen of England having you for an enemy."

For the first time Henry smiled. "In Normandy, my lady, we have the saying, 'Good enemy, good lover.' All I ask of you is the chance to prove that I can be one as well as the other."

"Now that," Eleanor said, "is quite a pretty speech."

"It was not so intended," Henry said; but, as though encouraged, he added, "I will tell you another thing. *I* am no monk. A sweet smile, a pretty face, even a stray curl, can bring me down as a falcon brings down a hawk, but since the day when I saw you in Paris I have given no thought to any woman. There's a yellow-headed Hohenstaufen girl—and if *you* think your lands and men will help forward my ambition, think what such a bond with the Holy Roman Empire could do for me. I was on the verge of making an offer for her hand, but, once I'd seen you, she looked as tasteless as a plate of cold porridge—without salt." He seemed to become aware of the fact that he was indulging in the despised pastime of bandying words, "Well, all's been said now. Will you take me or not?"

"It is no decision to make in a moment." Eleanor was grave now. "After all, this will affect all my life—and all yours. And, to be honest with you, the advantage is by no means all on your side. As someone who has my good at heart pointed out only this morning, I must either marry again or go about with an armed bodyguard all my days; a woman alone, a woman of property, seems to be regarded by most men as a plum for picking; and so she shall be while priests can be found to perform the marriage ceremony whether the woman concerned be willing or not."

"Ah!" said Henry; quite unwittingly she had invited him to mount his hobbyhorse. "There you put your finger on it. The Church is wise; no matter what problem arises, the Church has the right, wise answer. The Church foresaw, centuries ago, some poor woman being carried off and married against her will; so it decreed that the priest should ask in a loud audible voice, 'Wilt thou take this man?' and that the woman should say—and be heard by the whole congregation—'I do.' Or, provided she had cause, 'No, I do not.' Holy Mother Church was on guard against the greedy and the unscrupulous. But the *priests* . . . ah, there is the weakness. Sheltered and pampered, they think themselves above the law; they break it with impunity; they defy God, and man . . ." He broke off and swallowed. "Dear lady, this is not the moment . . . but you will find when you know me better that two bees buzz in my bonnet. One is my right to be King of England; the other is that priests should stand level with other men in the sight of the law. Until they do, the whole thing is a mockery. Why, not long since, a woman of some substance, a widow to boot, and sixty years old, was dragged to the altar, gagged and bound, and married to a man who coveted her property. Now that could never happen in Normandy."

"Why not?"

"My priests know my mind. There are loopholes that I have not yet closed—places where canon law and secular law do not fit side by side, but where I rule at least, they are mindful to obey the canon law because it is their bulwark against the other."

Eleanor's heart warmed to him.

He blundered on. "I'm a good churchman, but I'm a soldier, too, and I hold that a priest who breaks the law of the Church, or the law of the land in which he lives, is as guilty as a soldier who deserts to the other side or goes to sleep on guard. Some rogue the other day—he'd come from Venice with some stuff to sell—was telling me about a country where cows were holy. Can you imagine that? They can do no wrong; if they break into your garden and eat all your lettuces, or into your field and trample down your growing corn, you have no redress. It's a poor heathen country, of course, but it seems to me if we're going to let priests disregard all law, they'll end as holy cows. I'm talking too much, wasting time which you need for thinking things over and making up your mind."

But Eleanor already knew what her answer was to be.

Marriage to Henry changed life completely. It was as though for fifteen years she had been stranded in a quiet sluggish backwater and then had been pushed suddenly out into the main stream of a great river, flowing rapidly, and crowded with traffic.

Henry himself was always on the move; up and down his old territories of Normandy and Anjou, and his new ones of Aquitaine and Poitou, he went, ordering and rearranging, looking into the smallest detail; always remembering that any day—tomorrow even—the call might come from England, and he must be able to leave everything settled and running smoothly behind him. He liked in those days to take Eleanor with him, always provided she was ready to mount and ride at a moment's notice, and was willing to travel with little baggage and few attendants. In the year between her marriage and the birth of the first of her Plantagenet children, she rode many hundreds of miles, saw Henry handle dozens of tangled problems, learned something of his methods and ideals, and came to have a sincere respect for his energy and remarkable thoroughness.

The new baby was a boy. They named him William, after Henry's great-grandfather, the great Duke of Normandy who had conquered England, and after Eleanor's own father. Looking down on the red, crumpled face of his first-born, Henry said,

"He will be William the Third of England," and Eleanor remembered the fortuneteller who had promised that her son should be a king of great renown. That prophecy, as well as Henry's about the child's title, seemed likely to be fulfilled for while the child was still in his cradle Stephen of England died, and through the December blizzards of the year 1154 the little family of Plantagenets crossed the Channel to take possession of its inheritance.

Stephen had, as Henry so often complained, "let everything go to rack and ruin," and one of the things which his neglect had allowed to fall into decay was the lovely old Palace of Westminster, so Henry established the family in the smaller Palace of Bermondsey, which had the advantage of being near the Tower, past which London river ran, busy and colourful, the main artery of the city. Ships from every known port, even faraway Palestine, could be seen from the palace windows.

Not that Eleanor had much time for gazing through windows. There was the coronation; there was the coming and going of the great barons and bishops of England to do homage to their new king. There was the discovery that the Norman French—the court language of England—though it resembled the French of Paris, had undergone a change from its sea-crossing and its eighty-eight-year-old exile in this island. If she was to be the Queen to Henry that she wished to be, she must study and practise this new French—perhaps even English, too—for, under the flood of Norman manners, speech, and power which the Conquest had let loose over England, something tough and indestructible had remained and was now pushing upward again.

Then there was her nursery. She had no intention of being cut off from this child, and any others she might bear, as she had been cut off from her small daughters, who from the moment of their birth had lived by rules laid down for "the Children of France."

There was the court, too, to consider. Word of the high standard of manners and the interest in literature and minstrelsy of the court of Aquitaine had reached even this distant island; everyone looked to her to take the lead in such matters. Oh, she was busy, busy, delightfully busy, from morning to late at night. A second boy, a real English prince, born on English soil, and named Henry after his father, was born during the first year in England, and, in the next year, a daughter, named Matilda for Henry's mother. But

there was also the grief of young William's death—he would never
be William the Third and a king of great renown . . . perhaps the
baby Henry would fulfill the prophecy.

In addition to all her other duties, she had a considerable number of responsibilities laid on her by the King. Henry seemed to
have no stupid notions about what was and what was not a woman's
sphere; as a consequence she, who had been pushed aside and accused of meddling while Queen of France, was, in England, not
only allowed but expected to act as Henry's deputy when he was
out of London, which was most of the time.

They had been in England but a few months when, at dusk one
evening, Eleanor was finishing a long day of official work. Of the
three papers handed to her by the clerk, she signed two, glanced
at the other and laid it upon a pile already high.

"That must await the King's return," she said, "I have no power
to deal with it." She stood up, straightening her back and stretching
her arms.

The clerk, with his eye on the pile of documents, said rather
shyly,

"When last we heard, His Grace was in York and no one knew
whether he was coming or going."

That, Eleanor reflected with a smile, exactly summed up Henry's
state since the coronation. He had set himself to clear up what he
called Stephen's "legacy of muck and muddle." To do that he must
visit every part of his realm, riding incredible distances each day,
then working far into the night to deal with the trouble which he
found on every journey. Stephen, never too sure of his throne, had
toadied shamelessly to the great barons of England, who as a consequence had come to regard themselves as above all law, and had
cruelly oppressed lesser men. Hundreds of them had built new unlicenced castles, which were little more than robber dens; and one
of Henry's first orders was that all such unlicenced castles should
be demolished. To see this order enforced would have been a life's
work for an ordinary man; but Henry, rushing round his kingdom
with something of the frenzy of a good housewife cleaning up a

filthy, neglected kitchen, found time to attend to thousands of other details, too. A woodcutter, a miller, a shoemaker—any man however humble—had only to run alongside his horse and cry, "Justice, I beseech you, justice, my lord King," and Henry would halt and listen to his tale, knowing that behind some trivial abuse might lie some serious breach of law. What he called "the common law"— that sturdy mingling of the old English tribal law and the Romanised code of justice introduced by the Normans—seemed ideal to Henry. He meant to enforce it in every village and hamlet in the kingdom, upon the greatest baron as well as the meanest poacher.

Thinking these things, and wondering whither Henry had travelled from York, Eleanor left the official part of the palace and began to walk towards the nursery.

Halfway along the passage, whose unglazed windows gave upon the courtyard and admitted a moist chill evening air which made her shiver, she saw someone—a man who staggered as he walked and put out a hand to reach for the wall, either for guidance or support.

Somebody drunk, she thought. By this time she had learned that in England wine was drunk less frequently than a brew made from barley and hops, called ale, which was extremely intoxicating. For that reason, and also because she wished to encourage the import of wine from Aquitaine and thus benefit her own people, Eleanor deplored the ale drinking. Now she bore down upon the lurching figure, sharp words of rebuke forming on her tongue. As the candlelight strengthened and she came closer, she saw with great astonishment that the man reeling against the wall was the King of England.

"All's well," he cried, recognising her in the same instant. "My legs have turned traitor." She looked down and saw that he had discarded his boots and that his ankles, clad in coarse woollen stockings, were double their normal size.

"Ralph and Foulkes wished to carry me in, but I feared that would alarm you, my sweet; so I distracted their attention and stole in alone. It's nothing; six hours in a bed will set them right. If I may lean on your shoulder . . ."

But before he could do so his attendants came running, and he allowed them to aid his stumbling steps. In his own room he sank gratefully into a chair and consented to prop the swollen legs on a stool.

"Too long in the saddle, that's all that ails me," he said cheerfully. "They say an army's as strong as its weakest horse, don't they? My legs are my weak horse. I must give them more care, or pension them off, eh?"

In a voice made sharp by anxiety she said,

"Henry, where is the sense of building a great empire and killing yourself in the process?"

"I can leave it to my son—and you can run it for him until he comes of age. You'd enjoy that, I think. But never fear. I shall live to see the time when I can sit in this chair in London and give an order and know that it will be obeyed to the Welsh marches and the Scottish border . . . but that can't be done all in a day. I have the tally now of the illegal castles in England, eleven hundred of them, think of that; and all being used to terrify—not to defend—the people of the countryside. If Stephen's reign had lasted another five years, there wouldn't have been an honest man, nor an industrious one, left in England—for who will be honest and work hard when the fruits of his labour can be wrenched away from him by torture? You may find this hard to believe—I would myself if I hadn't seen it with my own eyes—in the dungeon of a new castle near Chester we found . . ."

"Don't think of it now," she said, for into the grey fatigue of his face, the dangerously dark colour had flooded as he remembered the scandalous state of affairs he had uncovered a few days earlier. "You must eat now, and then rest. You should stay in bed tomorrow. I will have the clerks bring the papers to your chamber and you can dispose of them; then the next day, or the day after, you could have half a day's hunting at Windsor. . . ."

"Tomorrow I must go to Winchester—that is why I pressed on to London today. You must be patient, my sweet; you shall have your hunting, but presently, presently."

"It was not of myself I was thinking. . . ."

"Sooner than you think, perhaps," he went on, ignoring the interruption. "Now *this* you will be pleased to hear. I've found the very man to help me; a young ambitious fellow who will take from my hands much of the work that I find so tedious. He's very clever, made a great reputation for himself in Paris and in Rome."

"I should have thought . . . an Englishman," Eleanor said thoughtfully. "Is there no clever ambitious young man in England?"

"This one *is* English, born in London, within a stone's throw of where we sit. He was trained abroad, started to be a churchman, took his deacon's orders, and then made a study of law. His name is Thomas Becket."

"Oh," Eleanor said. A memory sprang: summer in Paris, the group of scholars gathered under the dusty shade of the sad cypresses in the garden beside the Seine; the argument which she longed to take up and might not, being a woman, and the strong confident voice of the young scholar saying the things which she would have said. "I know him, a little. Amaria will tell you that we forecast a great future for him even then. How strange, and how interesting. What will his office be?"

"In England, they call it Chancellor. He will take care of the legal side, and all the scribbling. He'll entertain important visitors —and make a good impression, or I'm no judge. I'm only a plain, blunt fellow; I make a poor show with ambassadors and cardinals and such. I can get on with my hammering of the barons and leave all the rest to my beautiful Queen and my lordly Chancellor, eh?"

The words "lordly Chancellor" went on sounding in Eleanor's mind. Presently she said,

"I'm glad, Henry, that someone has been found to carry part of the load. I've done my best, but even now there is a pile so high"— she measured with her hand—"awaiting your attention. But——" she hesitated. "Henry, I know you laugh at my woman's guesswork, as you call it, right though I often am . . . I have remembered another thing which I thought all those years ago about Tom Becket."

"And what was that?"

"That he had something—I don't know what it was, a look, a tone of voice perhaps—*something* which resembled Abbé Bernard."

"Now you're not to take against him on that account," Henry said hastily; he had heard a good deal about the Abbé's treatment of Eleanor, and knew, too, how impulsively Eleanor took likings and dislikings to people. "Bernard was a fanatic—they're talking, now he's dead, of having him canonized, did you hear that? I'm all in favour of it. He did as much as any man to ruin your marriage with Louis, and I can never be grateful enough for that." He put his heavy arm around her shoulders and gave her a hard, husbandly hug. "But there's nothing of the saint about Tom Becket, never fear that. He's more worldly than I am, keeps a better table, and is far better dressed. Oh, about that, I'll tell you an amusing story. Tom was in York and to save time rode a bit of the way with me towards Chester, while we settled the details of his new office. Just outside York we met a beggar, crippled, filthy, and half-naked. Neither of us had any coined money—Foulkes carries my purse and Becket, aiming only to ride for a mile or so and turn back, had left his at home. So I said, 'Give him your cloak, Tom. You have more than one and there's something in the Scriptures about the man with two cloaks giving one to the poor.' But Tom said, 'This is brand-new—I only put it on in your honour. As for the Scriptures, that is sophistry; everyone knows that the Devil can quote Holy Writ when it serves his purpose.' 'Are you calling me a devil, Tom Becket?' I asked. 'Here I am, hoofs and claws and all!' and I snatched the cloak off his back and tossed it to the shivering wretch. If you could have seen Becket's face!" Henry rolled in his chair with laughter at the memory, and ignored, or put down to women's defective sense of humour, the fact that Eleanor had failed to see the joke.

"Velvet," he said reminiscently, "scarlet velvet it was, and lined with good sable. However, a joke's a joke and I've ordered him a new one, even better."

"But surely . . . if you told him to give his cloak to the beggar,

he should have done so, without protest. Well . . . at least it seems
so to me."

"But how tame! Then there'd have been no fun. If only you'd
seen me, making a face and a noise like the Devil and clawing off
his cloak! And I told you just to show you how wrong you are
about his being like Bernard. *He* would have had a cloak that even
the beggar would have despised and he'd have insisted on the King
parting with *his*. Am I not right?"

"Absolutely. That is exactly what would have happened," Eleanor
agreed. All the same, there was something a little wrong with that
story. A hint, a shadow of things to come. Two men romping like
schoolboys . . . Still, it had brought a little lightness, the blessing
of laughter, into Henry's busy day. He'd ridden on to be scandalised
at Chester . . . poor Henry!

"Come along now," she said, "let's put those poor legs to bed.
I'll help you myself. It looks to me as though nothing less than
the Devil's claws will ever tug off those stockings!"

But her hint of warning, her remark about Becket's lack of obedience, dropped into Henry's mind, went to sleep, was forgotten, lay
dormant as a seed of corn in a winter field.

CHAPTER THREE

The busy, happy years slid along. The appointment of Becket as
Chancellor relieved Eleanor of all the work she had shouldered to
help Henry, and she divided her days between the social round of
the court—now a very adequate imitation of her father's in Aquitaine—and her growing family. In the year 1157 another son,
named Richard, was born. He was the lustiest and the most beauti-

ful of all her babies, and had a remarkable crop of dark red hair. Happily married now, divided by many years and much experience from that old lost love of her extreme youth, she named him for sentiment's sake. Henry's great-grandfather and her own father had been remembered at poor dead William's christening; sturdy young Henry carried his father's name, so her fancy had free rein. This one shall be Richard, she thought; and he shall be *my* heir. For Henry— Normandy, Anjou, and England; for Richard—Aquitaine and Poitou.

There were other children: Geoffrey, destined to be Count of Brittany, was born in 1158; a girl who at Henry's insistence was called Eleanor was born in 1161; then came Joanna; and finally there was John, over whose cradle Henry said with wry humour, "Poor child, there is no title, no land, for him. Poor little John Lackland." The nickname stuck.

Richard was her favourite. However, she treated them all with strict impartiality, awarding praise for good behaviour, punishment for bad—and these were no meek little Capets; they were, as she called them, "young eaglets." But, when they were all in a room together, it was upon Richard that her eye rested most often, not because he was the most handsome—in looks, Henry and Geoffrey far surpassed him—but because something about him satisfied her; he was most like her. By some curious freak of heredity, both Henry and Geoffrey were frivolous; they had their father's fondness of practical jokes, their mother's love of gay and beautiful things. Seriousness seemed to have been left out of their natures. As for the girls, Eleanor often thought they took after her own mother, a model of what a woman should be—lively without being headstrong, gay as well as gentle. But Richard, though he was the wildest of all, was the one who could be reasoned with. He was many-sided, loved music and poetry, could, from his earliest days, make songs and compose tunes to them; was apparently a born horseman and swordsman; excelled, as he grew older, in every manly pursuit. Eleanor loved him but thinking, I must not favour him too much, often slippered him thoroughly.

They were great, vigorous, hopeful days in England. All the world stood back looking with awe at this great Angevin empire which Henry Plantagenet had hammered into unity. "Henry the Lawgiver" they called him now, and they boasted that a man could travel with a pocketful of gold from end to end of the kingdom and not be molested. The unlicenced castles had all come down, their stones used for building sound burghers' houses in the flourishing towns; the sulky barons, no longer able to live by robbery and extortion, were turning their energies to agriculture; and great flocks of sheep gave their fleeces every springtime to build up the wool trade.

Henry turned his thoughts to providing for his youngest son, John "Lackland." For John he would have Ireland . . . that backward, yet potentially productive, little green island should be caught in the Angevin net and become part of this great new empire. Even the Pope—the only Englishman to sit upon the papal throne —approved the scheme.

It was on the way back from one of his campaigns in Ireland that Henry made mock of a superstition and went on to meet a fate, years later, which men of credulous imagination might say was the result of that mockery.

Henry, with a handful of attendants and soldiers—the main body had been left to keep order in the newly conquered provinces in Ireland—was moving towards the border where Wales met England. This was the country of the Marcher barons, trustworthy old soldiers who had been given leave to build castles and possess the land around in return for keeping constant watch and ward against the Welsh, who had never been conquered. Henry had once given the conquest of Wales his serious consideration, but Wales was mountainous, ideal land for the kind of guerilla warfare which mounted knights were least fitted to wage, so he had turned to Ireland instead.

It was late afternoon; the little troop rode in silence save for the sound of the horses' hoofs and the jingle and creak of harness. They had much hard riding behind them and a stormy crossing from Ireland, and behind that, some savage fighting. They were all tired to the bone.

They came to a small, rapidly tumbling stream across which a causeway of hewn stone had been laid; here the water was only ankle-deep. Upstream, where the water came down with force from the hills, there was a mill, its big wheel turning in the water, which next fell into a smooth dammed-up pool, then the stream ran on over the causeway and down, in a series of small waterfalls, to where a great rock loomed out of the water, its base worn out by friction so that it looked like a giant mushroom.

As his horse stepped onto the farther bank, Henry turned to an attendant and said, "Now we are on the English side. There should be a castle or a manor house near by. Go, Ralph, and ask at the mill."

Henry and the others dismounted and allowed their tired horses to drink and rest until Ralph returned, bringing with him the miller, powdered all over with flour, nervous, and stammering.

"He speaks only Welsh, Sire."

"Anyone here understand Welsh?" Henry demanded.

Nobody did and Henry impatiently fell back upon making signs and speaking more loudly, in the world-wide belief that anyone can understand any language provided it is spoken loudly and clearly enough. "House," he demanded, sketching a roof; "Food," he shouted, pointing to his mouth with great vigour; "Sleep," he bellowed, closing his eyes and pillowing his head on his hands.

While the miller racked his brains and stared, anxious only to say or do something which would prevent twelve hungry men and twelve hungry horses from billetting themselves upon him for the night, there was a disturbance, and an old woman, bent almost double and huddled in a shawl, pushed her way through the horses.

"Do I hear the English tongue?" she asked in a high tremulous voice.

"You do, old mother. Well met; maybe you can help us."

"Ah, I knew it again," she cackled. "I lived in England when my man was alive, a drear long time ago that is. But I knew it, though never did I hear such cursed crabbed English as is on your tongue. What is it you want to know, my handsome gentleman?"

The soldier nearest her gave her a poke and muttered,

"Mind your manners, old mother. You are speaking to His Grace, the King!"

"The King is it? The new one who goes round, I'm told, dealing out law and justice? Oh, well met, indeed, Your Highness. I've been needing some justice this long while; and to think it's come to *me!* And, now I'm reminded of it, I did dream last night that a star fell and came and lay on my bed in the shape of a sword. A good sign, a good sign. Now, what *are* the words? I crave justice, my lord King. This villain here . . ." she pointed a gnarled finger at the miller, "he won't let my ducks on his pond. By ancient rights, he must. I've got my copyhold and I had it read out to me by the priest, freehold tenure it says, and the right to swim a score of ducks on the millpond. But he swore he'd wring their necks, and two he did; beautiful ducks they were, too, on the point of laying."

Henry, half impatient, half amused, said,

"With all this water . . . why must your ducks swim on his pond?"

"The copyhold says so. Besides, see for yourself, it's the one still spot in the river."

The miller, seeing eyes looking and fingers pointing up and down stream, guessed at the drift of the talk and burst into stammering speech.

"What is *he* saying?" Henry asked the old woman.

"I'm pleading my own case," she shrilled. "I can't plead his as well."

Henry tired of her. "And I can't give a decision until I have heard both sides of the case. You must carry your case to the nearest court of pleas and, if your copyhold is good, the court will give you justice. That is what it is there for."

He swung himself wearily back into the saddle. The old woman grasped his stirrup, crying, "But they said you gave justice by the ladleful all along the road. Why can't you give me justice now?"

Even then, there was something about her impudence and single-mindedness which prevented Henry kicking off her clasp, but Ralph, leaning down from his saddle, took hold of her skinny old arm and pulled her away with a force which made her totter.

She was suddenly transported with rage.

"So that's your famous justice! I spit on it," she screamed, and spat heartily. Then she raised her arms so that the shawl slipped down and the evening breeze carried locks of her thin grey hair backwards. "Lech-laver will avenge me," she cried. She swung her arms towards the great rock, "Lech-laver, Lech-laver, avenge me on this unjust King!"

"Raving mad," Henry said. "And with all that, we are no nearer a night's lodging. Press we on . . . why man, what ails you? And you? And . . ." he looked in the fading light from one pale stricken face to another. "God's head! Who is this Lech-laver whose very name can strike such terror?"

"Sire," said Ralph in a voice unlike his own, "it is an old . . . evil prophecy. And we are now on Merlin's ground and we are coming back from . . . oh, my Lord, placate her, placate him. . . ."

"I'll placate you," Henry said roughly, "unless you tell me in straightforward fashion whatever it is that can make eleven strong men, fully armed, look like a lot of silly wenches on Allhallow E'en. Who in the Devil's name is Merlin, and who gave him any English ground?"

"He was a wizard, Sire, and he lived in the West country hundreds of years ago . . . but he is still remembered because his prophecies came true . . . some are still to come true. And one was . . . He said, my lord, that a King of England, coming back from conquering Ireland . . . would fall foul of Lech-laver and meet his death."

"And who is Lech-laver?"

The old woman took up the tale malevolently. "There he stands, where he has stood for three thousand years and more, always watchful, always wakeful. There he stands."

"You mean that rock?" Henry asked incredulously.

"You may laugh. The old people were wiser. They knew his powers. Why do you think these stones were laid in the water? To help fools like you across? They were laid there so that, in the old times when men were wiser, they could stand there and lay their offering in the mid of the stream where they'd be carried down to Lech-laver's foot."

She looked up with bright malicious eyes.

"I never, in all my days, heard such a fandangle of nonsense," Henry said. But looking round, he saw that his men did not regard it as nonsense. They were frightened—these bold strong men who had cheerfully faced the wild Irish chieftains. And Henry knew men, knew how the unknown and mysterious can be more frightful than a visible danger; knew how easily panic and rumour can spread; knew that in order to be lucky one must have the reputation for being so. Once let this ridiculous tale get abroad and men would begin to look upon him as a man under a curse, a man sentenced to death. The effect would be incalculable.

"Oh," he said defiantly. "So Lech-laver threatens me, does he? Well, I never yet refused a challenge!" As he spoke, he swung his horse's head around and rode downstream until he was level with the rock. There he dismounted, and from the bank saw that Lech-laver did not stand alone. The big rock was part of a ridge lying athwart the stream; a number of small rocks stood in the foaming water like steppingstones. He stepped from the bank onto the nearest rock in one long stride. Immediately he knew he had acted rashly; at some seasons of the year these rocks must be well below water level and the flow had polished them to the slipperiness of glass. Now, wet with spray, they offered no foothold, and there was nothing upon which to rest his hand to steady himself. Also the wind seemed to have increased in power during the last few minutes; blowing downstream, it was now intent to push him from his precarious perch.

Just for one heart-shaking moment he thought, Perhaps it is true; perhaps by making this extravagant, showy gesture I am doing exactly what the wizard foresaw, and shall die as he foretold. All my plans . . . and the boys so young . . .

But, as always, danger stiffened his pride and courage, and he went on, stepping from rock to rock as though they were patterns in a carpet. He stood under the shadow of Lech-laver, which topped him by six or seven feet and was too smooth to be climbed, so, balancing carefully, he dealt it a buffet with each hand, much as he would have boxed the ears of a careless page.

Then he turned, and in turning slipped, so that for another dreadful moment he stood balanced like a crane on one leg. Then he gathered himself and leapt, failed to regain balance, and knew that his only hope was in speed. He threw himself forward to the next rock, and the next. From the bank it looked nimble, a dancer's progress, and, as the last leap brought him back to solid ground, the watching men voiced their relief and admiration in a ringing cheer which echoed among the rocks. Settling into his saddle, Henry acknowledged it with a lift of the hand. Ralph turned on the old woman, "So much for Lech-laver! And now, before I give myself the pleasure of tearing out your lying, treacherous tongue, use it to tell the nearest decent house where His Grace may lie tonight."

"There's only one place fitting for such a bold beautiful man to rest himself in these parts," whined the old woman. "And that is the house of Sir Walter de Clifford. Aye, a fine house, with a goose-feather bed; proper for such pretty gentlemen."

She gave them directions, edging away from Ralph as she talked, and Henry, conscious of the sweat turning cold on his brow and under his shirt in the chill air, began to ride forward as soon as the last word had left her mouth. As they rode away, they could hear her wild laughter echoing from rock to rock. In their elated mood they shared her mirth.

But it was in the house to which she directed them, on the day when he had defied Lech-laver and Merlin, that Henry Plantagenet first met the young girl Rosamonde Clifford—Fair Rosamonde who was to become a legend. The effects of that meeting were to be far-reaching. The old woman among her displaced ducks, Lech-laver in his cloud of spray, Merlin in the shades . . . they might well laugh!

CHAPTER FOUR

For a long time Eleanor, busy with her children, believed that the change in Henry—a change to which she could not be blind—was due to his quarrel with Thomas Becket. A woman of more simple mind would have been more suspicious, looked nearer home for a more personal reason. But Eleanor was trained and experienced in statesmanship and although, since Henry had found Becket to help him, she had gradually retired from active part in the world of affairs and given her time and attention to her family, she was still woman of the world enough to understand the causes and the graveness of the long-drawn-out quarrel between Henry and Becket. And it gave her little joy to think that Henry had done the very thing she had warned him against . . . and that what she had said *might* happen *had* happened.

Henry and Becket had worked together in a rare and perfect friendliness for six whole years and seemed to see eye to eye on all matters of importance. Not only had they worked together, they had shared their sports, their leisure, and their amusements. When, at the end of six years, the Archbishop of Canterbury died, it seemed to Henry an excellent, even an obvious, idea to appoint Becket in his place. Thomas had hesitated at first, and Henry, thinking his friend suffered from modesty, said heartily,

"To a man of your ability, Tom, it'll mean nothing. You have your deacon's orders already, you can be ordained any day. And, as Archbishop of Canterbury, you will have power over the Church, just as, as Chancellor, you have power over the law courts. What could be better for the peace in the land?"

"And there's the rub! My two offices might one day come into conflict with one another. What then?"

"That could never happen; you're a man of sense, I'd trust you to act sensibly in *any* circumstances."

"But a priest takes certain vows. A priest must put his God and God's church first."

"But of course," Henry agreed. "All Christian men put God first."

"Then they differ as to which God," Thomas said gravely. He persisted that, if he became Archbishop, he must resign his post as Chancellor, but Henry would not listen to that; slapping his friend affectionately on the back, he protested that there was no other man in England whom he could trust with either post; dear Tom, so clever, so faithful, must hold both.

Soon after the appointment was made, Henry went to the Continent and, during his absence, Becket resigned the chancellorship, handing the Great Seal of office to Prince Henry, who accepted it in his father's place.

That news was an unwelcome shock to Henry upon his return, but his first sight of his new Archbishop was a shock even more severe. Gone was the gay, witty, worldly Chancellor who had been finely dressed, fond of luxury and pleasure, and whose table had been recognised as the most extravagant in Europe, feeding hundreds of people on the richest and rarest dishes every day. In his place was a pale, spare churchman, worn with prayer and fasting, wearing a hair shirt under his Archbishop's robes.

"Tom was never one to do things by halves," Henry said to comfort himself. "And there was always a play-acting part to his nature; once the novelty of posing as the perfect cleric wears off, he'll be himself again."

But within a matter of months the famous quarrel, the noise of which reached the utmost parts of Christendom and left echoes to ring down the centuries, had broken out. It was simple in essence. Were clerics who committed an offence to be judged by the ordinary law courts or only by the church courts where the punishments were mild? Hitherto, the latter had been the case; but Henry had spent years drawing up and enforcing the sound, good laws which had gained him the name of "Henry the Lawgiver," and he believed with all his heart that everyone in the land, from the highest baron to the lowest serf, should obey them. Becket was equally stubborn in his belief that churchmen were outside the law of the land in which they happened to live; they were governed by church laws, and answerable only to the church courts.

It was some time before Henry could bring himself to mention the quarrel to Eleanor; he remembered that she had warned him and he feared that she might say "I told you so." But as it continued, he began to feel the need for sympathy and support and one day, having shouted himself hoarse to Becket without moving him an inch, he came storming into Eleanor's apartment and unburdened his mind to her as he had been accustomed to do in the early days of their marriage.

"What it amounts to," he bellowed, "is that it takes two murders to hang a priest. A fellow takes the lowest priest's orders and then breaks somebody's skull in a quarrel; he's hauled into court for murder and immediately squeaks, 'I claim benefit of clergy!' So then he's handed to the church court, where some old woman of an abbot or bishop bleats out, 'You *have* been a bad boy! We can't have you as a cleric any longer. Sentenced to be unfrocked!' Out he comes, free as air, to do another murder if he wills. That isn't fair or just; that makes mock of the law, which should be, which *shall* be, supreme!"

"Put like that, it sounds ridiculous," Eleanor agreed. "But it doesn't happen very often. Few clerics commit *hanging* offences."

"But that isn't all. There you come up against the question 'Who is a cleric?' They're claiming now that anyone who can read or write can claim benefit of clergy. Is that a disgrace? It's worse than that even; we've reached the point where any base fellow, before committing his crime, learns off by heart what they call the 'neck sentence,' just a bit of the Scriptures learned parrot fashion; this he chants out in court, and that, if you please, makes him a cleric —untouchable by English law. What Tom Becket won't see, in his arrogance, is that that kind of thing does the Church no good in the long run. It's only a short step from 'All criminals are clerics,' to 'All clerics are criminals' and, at the moment, it pays all criminals to claim to be clerics. I don't demand that the church courts give up their rights; most of them do good, sound jobs dealing with minor cases. All I demand is that, when a cleric is charged with an offence, he appears before the church court and, if he is proved guilty *there,* handed over to the ordinary law court to be dealt with. Isn't that sane, and reasonable, and just?"

"To me, yes . . . and to you. To all sane, reasonable, and just men, Henry. The trouble is that few men are all three—and Becket is not one of them. He has a mania for power. When he was Chancellor his power was the law, therefore the law could be supreme; now he is a churchman, his power is the Church and, therefore, that must be supreme."

"Not while I live," Henry said. "Unless Tom will meet me halfway I shall fight him until one of us is dead!" He glowered for a moment, visualising the length and sourness of the struggle which lay ahead. Then he said in a milder voice,

"The trouble is that I'm still *fond* of the fool. I look back and remember the good times we had together and how we used to laugh. That time when a beggar stopped us when we were riding—— God's wounds! There's something especially bitter about a friend turned enemy, Eleanor."

She murmured something soothing and exerted her mind to find some cheerful, diverting topic of conversation. But she thought, It is strange he should mention that incident about the cloak at this point, and *still* not see the significance. *I* heard the warning ring clearly then, all those years ago. Should I have spoken more openly? Should I have asked him to think again before adding the archbishopric to the chancellorship . . . and would it have made any difference if I had?

Still she had learned, little by little, the folly of opposing Henry directly—even over the matter of her three girl children. Holding views far in advance of her time, she disliked the system of using young princesses as pawns in a game; left to herself, she would have allowed them to grow to the ripe age of fourteen, and then have some choice as to whom they would marry—not full choice, of course, that was impossible, but *some* choice. But Henry had thought that all out as carefully, thoroughly, and sensibly as he thought out everything else.

"I was not betrothed until I was fifteen," Eleanor had said once in protest.

"You were married at fifteen," Henry said bluntly. "And if these little wenches are to be married at the same age, they must be betrothed *now*, otherwise they'll lose all their fine chances and end up in a convent cloister."

"I did not."

"My sweet, you were a great heiress in your own right. All these pretty little creatures have to offer is the fact that they are my daughters, and whoever marries them will—by that fact—have me for an ally. I shall dower them well, and choose wisely. No father can do more."

So for Matilda, he chose the Duke of Saxony, known as Henry the Lion; for Eleanor, the King of Castile; and for little Joanna, the King of Sicily. He kept his promise about the dowries, too, when the time came, and each English princess went to her husband well provided for.

But that was all far in the hidden future.

Meanwhile in England the quarrel with Becket dragged on. In France the King, who had married a Spanish princess soon after his divorce, became the father of yet a third daughter, the Princess Marguerite who, at the age of three, was betrothed to young Henry Plantagenet and came to join the royal nursery in London. For a while there seemed a likelihood that young Henry Plantagenet might some day rule both England and France, and his son, if he were blessed with one, be king of both countries by right of birth; but the Spanish Queen died, and Louis, married for the third time, realised his long-cherished hope at last, and became the father of a prince. Everywhere, it seemed, hopes were being realised, deep-laid schemes were coming to fruition, children were growing up. Henry, looking at his handsome, unruly boys, had moments when he no longer felt young. Sometimes indeed, looking back, particularly when he remembered the happy days when he and Becket had worked and played together, he felt old—with so much to remember. At such moments he was anxious lest the empire, so carefully and painfully built up and welded together, should fall apart at his death.

In one such moment he determined to revive an ancient custom, common in the days when things were less settled, now falling into disuse, the custom of having the heir to the throne crowned during his father's lifetime.

Becket, the man who should have performed the ceremony, and who would have taken joy in the act since young Henry had been his pupil, and a dearly loved one, was not in England at the time. Despairing of ever making a settlement with Henry himself, he had gone to Rome to lay his case before the Pope and ask for his support. But Henry, determined to carry out this plan as bluntly and briskly as he carried out all others, persuaded Roger, the Archbishop of York, to perform the ceremony, in Becket's absence.

When he told Eleanor and proceeded to suggest dates and the form which the celebration should take, she said suddenly,

"And what about Richard? He is barely two years younger than Henry and—it must be faced—far older in everything that matters."

"Maybe, maybe," said Henry, springing to the defence of his favourite son, "slow growth is no ill omen. A good oak tree takes a hundred years to mature, a wayside weed springs up overnight. Not that I'm calling Richard a weed," he added hastily, then went on:

"But why mention Richard *now?*"

"I think it would be the right moment to install him in his estates—make him Duke of Aquitaine and Count of Poitou."

"That is for you to say."

"I think it would be right, and apt . . . and kind. A boy's pride, you know . . ."

"Very well. We'll go the whole way, and make Geoffrey Count of Brittany at the same time. As for poor John . . . well, he's young yet; and there'll be Ireland for him by the time he can hold it; and we'll find the richest heiress in Christendom for him. And that provides for them all. Was there ever such a fortunate family?" He took her hand, they stood side by side together for a moment, a husband and wife, father and mother, thinking with pride and confident joy of the children they shared.

So all the young eaglets were given their titles, and if any was discontent, it was Henry whose portion was richest of all. "I'm still only the *Young* King," he complained, "nobody calls Richard the *Young* Duke of Aquitaine. I shall probably be the *Young* King until I fall over my own grey beard and die!"

Henry decided that his Christmas court in the year 1170 should be held at Bures, in Normandy. There, in the middle of all the gay festivities, word was brought him that Becket had returned to England, had walked barefoot into Canterbury through crowds weeping with joy, and had threatened to excommunicate all who had taken part in the coronation of the Young King.

The threat at first amused Henry.

"But if he excommunicates all who took part in it, he must excommunicate *me.*"

Roger of York, who had brought the news, said gravely,

"That, Your Grace, is what he threatens to do."

The dark colour rushed so furiously into Henry's face that many in the assembly feared he would be taken with a fit. He spluttered out a few incoherent words and then, with a great effort, mastered himself. When he spoke next, it was with some degree of calm.

"No, no; he would never do that! My lord of Canterbury doubtless feels himself insulted, since none could deny that it was his right to do the crowning; but he is not the man to avenge himself in so petty a fashion, so spiteful a fashion. Why, if he excommunicated me, the whole country would lie under a ban; not a child could be christened, not a corpse buried, not a couple married. Think of the misery that would inflict upon thousands of innocent people, on the very people who, you say, welcomed him back so warmly."

"I assure Your Grace that that is his intention. His visit to Rome has greatly strengthened his determination. His mind is set. Your Grace must give in over the matter of the criminous clerics or suffer excommunication, and all England with you."

It dawned upon Henry that Roger of York, whom he had regarded as being wholly on his side, was wavering. There was a strong hint in this speech that Roger would be willing to see him give in. That and the threat itself combined to spur him, not to red roaring fury, but to an infinitely more dangerous cold white rage.

"The fellow is insolent," he said. "A nobody, a small merchant's son, raised by my hand to high estate, and now he dares to threaten me. And small wonder! Here I sit, surrounded by idle fellows who wear my badge and eat my food, and none of them with spirit enough to rid me of this turbulent priest. He knows how ill I am served or he would not dare so to affront me."

An uncomfortable silence greeted this accusation, and in it two young men looked at one another with slow significance. Young Reginald Fitz-Urse and William de Tracy were both ambitious, eager to attract Henry's attention and gain his favour. Was this their chance?

Henry became aware of the silence. With an abrupt change of mood he said loudly,

"Are we to have our Christmas spoilt? On with the revels!"

The seasonal merrymaking went on, haltingly at first, then with gathering vigour. Nobody noticed that Fitz-Urse and De Tracy had withdrawn themselves, that presently two other young men joined them, and that they had stood in a corner muttering quietly together for a moment, then had left the hall.

On the third evening after Christmas, a frightened monk who had been lighting the candles in the great cathedral for evensong, ran, still carrying his taper, through the door that led to the cloisters and bolted it behind him. Then he sped to the room where Becket was robing himself for the service.

"Four mailed men," he gasped, "in the cathedral. I saw them plainly for a moment, then they vanished into the shadows. They mean you harm, my lord Bishop."

"Mailed men," Becket said calmly, "are permitted to attend evensong."

"Armed men, my lord Bishop. I saw their swords in the candle-light."

"Even so. Young knights, mailed and armed, spend nights of vigil in churches often enough."

"But they went into hiding," the monk insisted.

"Perhaps they feared to alarm you," Becket said with gentle humour.

"They did alarm me. No true men would behave as they did. And now they are lurking in the shadows where a hundred men could skulk until morning. I beg you, my lord, remain here where you are safe and do not venture into the church this night."

"I shall attend evensong as usual," Becket said. "What could harm me at God's altar?"

Was his calm assumed? Was he aware of danger, and determined to die, if die he must, in the cool, orderly performance of his office? Did he place his faith in the power of the Church, which in those days offered sanctuary even to known criminals? No one will ever know.

Accompanied by the group of terrified monks and clerics—for the news had spread rapidly—he went into the cathedral, where the candles made a little island of brightness in a vast sea of darkness, and, when he passed into the choir, he refused to allow the gates to be fastened behind him.

"The altar must not be made into a fortress," he said—perhaps, in his eyes, it was a sanctuary even an assassin dared not violate.

So the four young knights bore down upon him and killed him there in the holy place; and Becket died in the bitter belief that the King, his friend-turned-enemy, had given the order for his death, for the badges of which Henry had spoken so sourly showed clearly in the candlelight as the swords struck.

CHAPTER FIVE

Early in the year 1177, Eleanor came back to England after what should have been a very happy visit to Europe. She had seen her favourite son, Richard, installed as Duke of Aquitaine and Count of Poitou, and had left him busily trying his hand at government. She had thought often that here was a young man of whom her father and her grandfather, and all those other handsome, bold, chivalrous ancestors of hers, would have been proud: for Richard, though acknowledged as the best fighting man of his day, was not just a mass of muscle and courage behind a battle-ax or lance; he was a poet, too, and a musician; in him, of all her brood, the Aquitainian strain ran truest, and the lords and knights of Aquitaine had accepted him with a warm enthusiasm that they had never shown to either of the husbands of their Duchess. Richard was safe with Aquitaine, and Aquitaine was safe with Richard, Eleanor thought.

Moving northward, she had stayed for a while in Le Mans, where her eldest son, Henry—not quite so dear as Richard but still very dear—was trying *his* hand at independent rule. There was a difference between the young men, and Eleanor's eye, fond and maternal as it was, was sharp enough to see it. Henry, the older in years, was younger in spirit; he enjoyed playing at being King; he had gathered about him a group of gay young men and the chief note of his imitation court was frivolity—he wouldn't know how many armed men, how many archers, how many horses, Normandy and Anjou could produce in a moment of need; Richard knew the strength of his domains down to the last blacksmith. It had, in the last months, sometimes shot through Eleanor's mind that Richard should have been the elder, the heir, but she had put that thought aside with a feeling of shame; it was just favouritism; women always preferred the child in whom they could see themselves—themselves as they would have liked to be. Henry was sound at heart, he'd quieten down, some people grew up more rapidly than others, that was all.

But she intended, as soon as she reached England, to have a talk with Henry upon the subject of Young Henry and Richard. His attitude towards them was curious, very fond yet strict and distrustful. He had allowed them, at early ages, to take their high titles, had had Henry crowned; he expected them to behave in public like grown men, conscious of their high estate; yet, in private, he treated them like schoolboys and, when they were out of his sight and reach, had them spied upon and reported about by men he had chosen as their watchdogs and guardians.

All the way back to London, after her visit had ended, Eleanor planned the things she was going to say to her husband: that being so sharply watched and controlled made Henry, who was a boy still, irresponsible and sly, while it made Richard, the man, rebellious and sour; they should both be given rein for a trial period at least and, if Henry remained so thoughtless, he must be checked, but in man-to-man fashion, not as man to child. Nothing but good could come of giving Richard more freedom, she was sure of that! "And there I am again," Eleanor chided herself with a smile.

Henry was not in London when she arrived. He had gone to

Woodstock, but of course no one could guarantee that he was still there. The King, in the seven years since Becket's death, had been, if anything, more restless than ever, moving about as though defying the increasing weight which came with the years, or as though —pious men whispered—to escape the haunting of his conscience. He might now be on his way to Cumberland, or already travelling back to London.

Eleanor decided to go to Woodstock. Afterwards she would remember wryly how that spur-of-the-moment decision was taken. Of late years Henry had somehow moved away from her, but there had remained the strong vital link of the children. He no longer talked over with her the affairs of state or the things that worried him—perhaps he had grown out of that habit during the years when he had had Becket for friend and advisor and, since Becket's death, which had affected him so deeply and so strangely, he had always remembered, perhaps without knowing it, that she had warned him against making Becket the Archbishop. So she had stepped into the background and been content to be the mother of Henry's children . . . and now, as that mother, she went to find Henry at Woodstock, confident that however busy he might be, he would welcome news of their health and doings and, at least, listen when she said what she meant to say about letting them off the apron strings.

The weather was bright and sunny when she began her journey, and in every field the peasants and their ox teams were busy with the spring ploughing. In some sheltered woods the primroses bloomed, palely sweet. Then, as was the way with this unpredictable English climate, there came a change, and she arrived at her journey's end after hours of jogging through a thin drizzle of sleet dropped grudgingly from the claws of a vicious wind. Wretchedly cold, with her wet clothes plastered to her skin, she alighted in the courtyard to be told that the King had left for Shrewsbury on the previous evening. The steward who greeted her with this news looked a little scared, and she said soothingly,

"It is of no matter. A fire to dry me and a meal to stay me is all

I need. You can manage that? If the weather mends, I shall not trouble you long."

The solar, a small withdrawing room—the parlour of that day —lay on the far side of the great hall, and, thinking that in this small space the fire she had ordered would soon be ready, she went straight towards it. On the great hearth, which occupied almost the whole of one wall, a lively fire was already burning. Shrugging off her wet cloak, Eleanor took a stool by the hearth and stretched her hands to the blaze, glad not to be obliged to wait while a servant fumbled with a tinderbox and the first unwilling flames broke through the twigs.

After a moment, rubbing her hands, she looked about her. Near by stood a little table. It bore a shallow dish filled with primroses, carefully arranged in their own green leaves; it bore also a sewing box with its lid—inlaid with silver and mother-of-pearl—propped open. Within were small ivory reels with coloured silks neatly wound on them, three fine needles poked into a pad of damp-defying woollen stuff, a pair of scissors with gold handles, and the glove upon which the owner of all these pretty things had been working. It was of soft leather, its seams very evenly sewn, and on the back was an ornate letter H surrounded by a wreath of broom; the stiff green leaves were completed, the little yellow flowers half done.

As Eleanor stared at this evidence of some woman's presence and activity in Woodstock, the door opened, and that woman entered and stood still, halted by surprise. They stared at one another. Eleanor saw a young, almost childish figure wearing a dress of amber-coloured velvet. Her face was pretty in a vague delicate way, with small smudged features and very soft colouring which was being slowly engulfed by a hot painful wave of crimson. It mounted from the edge of the yellow bodice to the place where the childish hair lay on the rounded brow, then receded, leaving an ashen pallor.

"Who are you?" Eleanor asked.

"I . . . I work here, sometimes. I sew . . ." As though the words had released her, she swooped forward, bundled the glove into the box, and pressed down the lid. As she did so, the rings which decorated her little clawlike fingers caught the firelight and the jewels flashed; Eleanor's stare travelled from them to the gold-studded, buckled belt which clasped the slender waist and on to the necklace about the childish white neck. No sewing maid this.

There came to the Queen suddenly the memory of a day when she had been sitting by a window at Westminster and listening to a boy who played a lute in the courtyard below. Presently he began to sing,

"Rose of the world that flowers in the West . . ." The words were new to Eleanor and the tune wistfully sweet; she had leaned on the sill of the window to hear better and was just in time to see Amaria emerge from a door and deal the lute player a hard buffet on each side of his head and cry, "Don't ever let me hear you tinkle that tune again!" Asked the reason for her sudden wrath, Amaria had scowled and said that some of the words were indecent, and how was a young boy to know right from wrong if his elders didn't point out the difference. It had been rather odd, Eleanor thought at the time, but she had not given it any thought and would have believed the tiny incident forgotten.

Then there was the day when Henry and Young Henry and one or two of their cronies were discussing a design for a new badge for archers and someone had suggested that a wide open rose, with a ring of red petals and a ring of white and a strongly marked gold centre, would be a pleasing device, a kind of beautified target. Neither Henry nor his son had spoken for a second, and then the boy had said, "No roses, I think," and one of the men had agreed, "No, too effeminate for archers!" and someone had clipped a laugh off short. Again trivial, again almost forgotten.

But she remembered now and asked quietly,

"Is Rose your name?"

"Rosamonde," the girl whispered.

Of course, Rosamonde . . . *Rosa mundi* . . . Rose of the World.

"And you have taken my place here . . . and elsewhere. For how long?"

The girl stiffened. Across the little bowl of primroses they stared

at one another again, and the silence grew, stretched itself, an agonizing, nerve-snapping space of silence. Then at last, with a sudden
change of manner, proudly calm, the younger woman said,

"I have never taken your place, madam; who could? I have only
supplied, as best I could, what the King needed from me."

Eleanor looked at the little sewing box, still clasped against the
girl's breast.

"You listen . . ." she said. "You sit there and stitch away making
gloves for him, and he talks, and you listen without saying a word."

"Without understanding even," the girl said rather sadly. "But I
can always tell from his voice whether he wants me to say 'yes' or
'no' when he *does* ask me a question."

"And you always say what he wishes!" She laughed harshly and
then hastened to say, "Child, I am not laughing at *you* . . . only
at the way in which it pleased God to make men and women. You
see . . . I tried so hard to understand everything and to give the
answer which, to my understanding, seemed the right one. So I
failed. Also, I hate to sew, and men seem to find a peculiar satisfaction in watching a woman ply a needle. Tell me . . . do you love
the King very much?"

"To be with him . . . at such times as could be managed,"
Rosamonde said, "I have gone against my father . . . and the nuns
at Godstow who brought me up. And there is no man whom I
can call husband. . . . Also the secrecy, and the loss of good reputation. Yes, I think I should say that I love him. Sometimes, you
know, he is very sad about something that happened such a long
time ago, seven whole years . . . all that sorry business about his
quarrel with Thomas Becket. He'll even shed tears. I always say,
'But you took your beating, and after the beating all boys are forgiven.' That makes him smile."

"Ah, that beating," said Eleanor harshly, "when he knelt by the
tomb and every monk in Canterbury laid on his measure of stripes,
and then he walked barefoot through the streets. To me that
seemed ridiculous. He was right in his quarrel with Becket . . .
and he won. Why smear a triumph with remorse? Admittedly, he

did not wish his opponent to be *murdered,* but he wished to have his own way, and nothing short of murder could defeat Becket . . ." she broke off, aware of the absolute absurdity of this situation . . . the wronged wife and the woman who had wronged her calmly comparing their treatment of the man they had shared. In any song or story they would have busily engaged in tearing out one another's hair! She was, indeed, somewhat surprised by her own lack of malice towards this little creature—but then the simplicity and childishness were very disarming.

"I think I should say . . ." Rosamonde began, and broke off, coughed two or three times in a smothered way, putting one hand to her mouth and then, abandoning herself to the racking bout, she set down the box, stumbled to a high-backed settle and, leaning upon it, coughed and coughed convulsively. Eleanor, looking about the room, saw at its farther end an open, three-tiered cupboard in which stood a pewter flagon, two or three silver-rimmed horn cups, a dish of figs, and a few apples on a plate. She went over to it, lifted the flagon and shook it. There was some liquid in it; she poured it hastily and carried the cup over to the settle where Rosamonde leaned. The girl drank, closed her eyes for a moment and waited, and then, opening them, looked at Eleanor and smiled.

"Thank you. This sounds worse than it is. I caught a cold at Christmas and the cough stays with me."

"A good posset with a linseed and honey and horehound is what you need," Eleanor said. But privately she wondered; as she had held the cup to the girl, she had touched her hand and recognised the dry burning heat of fever. And that kind of prettiness, that ethereal fairness, often marked those with lung fever.

"At Godstow there is a nun, very skilled in herbs and simples," Rosamonde said breathlessly. "I shall carry my cough to her and she will cure me." She smiled again, a smile of such unearthly sweetness that Eleanor thought, Yes, when she was in good health and gay of spirit, she must have been very lovely.

"I'd go without delay," she said brusquely. But her eyes looked at the little sewing box whose hastily forced-down lid had half risen again, revealing the embroidered glove. That will never be finished, she thought, and there was sadness in the thought.

"I'll go tomorrow if the weather mends. It is kind . . ." She broke off again, racked by the cough, gulped at the wine, waited, began again.

"For a long time, Your Grace . . ."

"Don't try to talk," Eleanor said, "it only provokes your cough." But the girl went on trying, saying, "I never tried to take . . ." saying, "Always my conscience . . ." saying, "but faithful to you in his fashion . . ." saying, "so kind and understanding."

She began to cry, sobs mingling with the cough to make her words almost unintelligible.

"This must stop," Eleanor said at last, much distressed. "I must go now; but you should not be alone. Shall I call your woman?"

"There is none . . . better so . . . alone, for secrecy's sake. . . ."

"Most fortunately, I also am without women," said Eleanor. Amaria, stricken with the heavy cold which came to her each spring in England, had been unable to ride with her, and she had come accompanied only by squires and pages. "There will be no gabble about this meeting. Sit now close to the fire and, as soon as may be, get to Godstow. If it comforts you—remember I bear you no grudge."

CHAPTER SIX

"You killed her," Henry said. "I shall never forgive you. Never, as long as I live."

They were his first words when, a month later, he came bursting into the room where she sat, the sweat and dust of his journey still upon him. Then before she could speak, while she stared at him in amazement, half fearing that he had gone mad, he flung himself onto the settle, put his head in his hands, and sobbed the terrible, difficult sobs of a strong man.

"She never hurt you. That was always her thought. That none should know lest you be hurt. And in return for that—you murdered her!"

Eleanor went and put one hand on his heaving shoulder, saying gently,

"You have come from Woodstock? She is dead? I feared it. Death was in her look a month ago."

He shrugged away from her hand and jumped up; tears hung on his bristly lashes, but fury had dried his eyes suddenly.

"Don't touch me!" he said. "Murderess!"

"You think I railed at her, upset her, made her more sick? You are wrong, Henry, so wrong. Strange as it may sound to you, no angry word passed between us. I could see that she was ill. . . . I spoke kindly . . . gave her wine. . . ."

"I know all about the wine," Henry said in a different, cold, heavily accusing voice. "She went that same day to the nuns at Godstow; she told them she had made her peace with you, that you had spoken kindly and given her wine. What was in it? What was in it? What poison did you use so deadly that she died next day?"

"Henry, what are you saying? What has been said to you? Do you realise the vileness of that accusation?"

"I know what I'm saying; and let me tell you this. If I had evidence enough to put before a jury, I'd make that accusation in open court."

"You must be mad," she said, backing away from him. Beneath her surprise and bewilderment, anger began to stir. "Do that," she said. "Accuse me in open court, and give me a chance to defend myself. The wine I poured for her was in the room when I arrived. Am I suspected of carrying poison with me wherever I go? When I went to Woodstock I did not know of the girl's existence. Besides, the nuns at Godstow could tell death from lung rot, and death from poison, as any jury would know. Take me to court, Henry."

"To what end? You have your defence ready. You could outwit Judas Iscariot, if needs be. I know you, your nimble mind, your slippery tongue. The court would acquit you . . . but I never shall, and I shall never forgive you."

"You believe in your heart that I poisoned that girl—because I was jealous?"

"I know you did," Henry said simply. "And she so harmless. My humble, unself-seeking friend, the only friend I had since I raised Tom Becket to be my enemy."

"I have tried," Eleanor said with equal simplicity. "My wonder now is this. If she could cheer and console you as I could not, if you valued her so highly and me so little that you can accuse me of murder without blenching—why did you not divorce me and marry her?"

Henry raised his head and stared at her. There was little subtlety in him; he had blurted out his accusation, but in his next words there was no secret desire to strike a blow at Eleanor's pride; he spoke without forethought, yet no amount of thinking could have provided him with a more hurtful answer.

"That would have lost me Aquitaine and Poitou," he said.

"Oh," said Eleanor. There was no more to be said.

Henry was to live for many more years, but all hope of holding Aquitaine, of governing it peacefully and profitably, was lost to him from that moment.

In a matter of days she was on her way to Poitiers, to Richard. . . .

". . . so then you cut your cable and set your sails for home," Richard said. "And right you were, and right welcome you are!" He set his big brown hands on her shoulders and kissed her heartily once on each cheek. "Nobody cares to be accused of a murder he hasn't committed and, of all people, the King himself should know that, having suffered from a similar false accusation! Maybe . . ." his bright blue eyes twinkled, "he hoped you'd take the false charge as hardly as *he* did Becket's, and go and kneel by the tomb at Godstow, and let the nuns beat *you*."

Possibly, Eleanor thought, the joking speech was not in the best of taste, but it was kindly meant. And Richard's welcome had left nothing to be desired; he had been genuinely glad to see her again, and he had shown it. She said, as though speaking not to her own son but to someone of equal age and experience,

"And so I came to Poitiers. Partly because you were here, Richard, and also because, when he said that unforgivable thing about not wishing to lose my domains, I suddenly saw, very clearly, and of course far too late, what my inheritance had cost me in simple happiness. So I thought that, having suffered so much for its sake, the least I could demand of it was that I should enjoy my latter years there, in the sunshine. . . ."

She was sitting in the window embrasure of the solar of the castle at Poitiers, and the sun was streaming in. She held her hands to the light and noted, without much interest, that they were so thin as to be almost transparent. The events of the last few weeks and the emotions they had roused had left their mark.

"What do you mean by your inheritance costing your happiness?" Richard asked.

"Exactly that. When I was fifteen, because of my rank and lands, I saw the young man whom I loved—oh, so innocently, hardly more than a boy and girl friendship, but doomed just the same— thrust through with a sword before my eyes. *Because* I was an heiress, I married Louis of France so that there might be peace between lord and liege, between France and Aquitaine. And there *was* peace of a sort, uneasy and grudging and temporary. It lasted until, out in the Holy Land *because* I was the rallying point of the Aquitainian forces, Louis must have me with him on his foolish journey and carried me off like a wild animal in a cage."

"I never heard about *that*," Richard said, deeply interested. "I studied his campaign, of course, and everything he did seemed to me mad . . . no! worse than that, madness at least sounds *vigorous,* which his actions never were; let's say flabby and misguided."

"Misguided past understanding, and flabby in everything except the guard kept on me. But that I survived, and in time freed myself," Eleanor said. "So then . . ." she almost laughed, "back to Poitiers I came, much as I have come this time; and, twice on the road, the few men who escorted me had to fight off attacks from ambitious young men who wanted to drag me away and marry me *because* of my heritage. And then your father arrived. You'll find this hard to believe, Richard, but he was better-looking than you are . . . young, full of himself, a knight of renown, and with a most deceptive simplicity. He said that with my help he could conquer England and build an empire, and I remember—oh, how often I have remembered it—I asked him whether it was me or my Aquitainian stores and fighting men he wanted. And he turned that dangerous corner very cleverly . . . he gave a most tempting reason for his choice of words . . . we were to be partners in a high enterprise. So we were," her voice grew bitter. "I gave him advice, which he scorned, and reared his children . . . he wanted somebody who said 'yes' and 'no' and embroidered his gloves! And so, you see, Richard, between them all, they have justified me in saying that my lands have cost me my happiness."

"And that they shall restore to you," Richard said eagerly. "We'll rule together, you and I, and keep a proper court, which you shall govern since I have no time for such things. We'll ride and hunt together, and visit the remotest corners of the realm, and taste all their vintages. And we'll hold the best tournaments in Christendom, and you shall give the prizes to the victors. Be of good cheer, mother; the merry times are about to begin."

"Your father will take it hard that I have come to you," Eleanor said. "Probably at this moment he is thundering out a charge of treachery against us all . . . for your brother Henry received me kindly too, and would have entertained me, but I was anxious to be . . . I felt safer . . . on my own soil."

Richard was silent for a moment; then he said in a deliberately casual voice,

"If father rails against us, he speaks more truly than he knows —yet! Henry and I have decided to rebel against him. We are tired of being treated like children, and simple-minded ones at that, fobbed off with empty titles, and set up as puppets with some governor of his choice always at our heels to tell us when to blow our noses! After all, our lands in Europe are held from the King of France; Henry has already seen him and explained our position and what we intend to do; we shall make our allegiance to *him,* and he has promised to allow us to rule as we wish without interference. . . ."

"But that will mean war, Richard . . . the worst kind of war of all, war between father and sons."

"Only if he chooses to start it." The expression which Eleanor privately called "Richard's red-fox look" slid across the handsome young face. "We only ask to be allowed to exercise the privileges of our age; we only offer our allegiance to the King of France, our legal overlord. If our father wishes to punish such reasonable actions on the part of his sons—well then, of course, there will be war."

Rather sadly Eleanor said, "Both you and Henry *know* that the King of France has always been the enemy of the King of England. Your formal allegiance to Louis was made years ago when you were first given your titles; and it was made with your father's consent. For either of you to visit the French King or the French court now is a challenge to your father . . . and you know it."

"Now isn't that just like a woman," Richard exclaimed. "Not ten minutes ago you were almost weeping over your grievance against him; now you are almost weeping because we mean to avenge your wrongs!" His voice became sour. "Perhaps you would like to go back to England, to the man who thinks you a murderer, and warn him, tell him how naughty the boys intend to be."

The sarcasm brought the hot blood flaring to her cheek and a sharp crushing retort to her tongue, but she checked herself. She must not quarrel with Richard. And she had learned her lesson about men; no man could bear to be crossed, or contradicted, or even reasoned with. She had learned that too late in life for happy marriage, but she had learned it. She seemed to hear again a gentle husky voice saying, "But I can always tell from his voice whether he wants me to say 'yes' or 'no' when he does ask me a question." There, in a few words, apparently lay the secret of being a successful woman! Well, she would try to practise it. She said with admirable lightness,

"Did I ever tell him how naughty you intended to be, and often were? Am I likely to begin now? Am I ever likely to see him or England again? It is just that I am always grieved when war breaks out for stupid, trivial reasons; nothing is gained and everybody suffers in these seesaw wars. Now if you were proposing to fight the Saracens . . ."

"Ah . . ." The change which came over the young face now was startling; it lightened, it glowed, a passionate dream taking form in flesh. "How did you know, mother? I never breathed a word to any living soul. But that is my purpose, my object, my one aim. That, to tell you the truth, is why I've linked my hand in Henry's over this rebellion against father. You see, so long as we're on leading reins, I can never go on crusade. In Poitou and Aquitaine, I'm Your Highness This and Your Grace That, and I train my horsemen and count my archers, and I collect the taxes . . . and then along come father's officials and say, 'Ha, a good year! His Majesty will be pleased!' And into father's coffers the good money goes . . . and away to father's campaign go my trained knights and my archers . . . and away go my hopes of crusade in the Holy Land. Now . . . if Henry and I can gain our independence and shut out his officials, in three years' time I shall be on my way to Jerusalem; and Henry swears that he will guard my lands while I am away and contribute to my expenses. Do you see? Henry is rebelling for the sake of rebelling, because he wants to choose his own friends, live his own life. I'm joining him because . . . ever since I was twelve years old, I have wanted, more than that, *intended*, to be a Crusader." He broke off and drew a deep breath. "I'm reckoned to be a good man in a tournament. I swear to you, mother, I have never levelled a lance without thinking to myself that it pointed to a Saracen breast! You've wondered, I've seen you wondering, why I wear clothes that are threadbare, and mended gloves, scuffed hose. Because I am saving, saving for my great campaign. I live, I breathe—just to go on my crusade."

She remembered suddenly the soothsayer who had said that she would be a mother of sons, and that her son would be a king of such renown that his name would pass into legend. Richard, King of Jerusalem. That was what had been meant. The lively enthusiasm, the glow of the spirit to which, for so long, she had been a stranger, began to smoulder and then to flame. And it was right and fitting, she thought, that this should be her favourite son, the one most like her, the one named for that first innocent, unsullied love.

"Dear Richard," she said, "your aim shall be my aim, and your crusade my crusade from this time on."

"You shall ride with me," he said. "Together we'll redeem that failure; you went on crusade with the wrong man. You shall come with me when I go. We'll ride into Jerusalem together, and feast where Solomon's great temple stood. All in good time, mother."

"Ah," she said, "if only we could. To go on crusade with one leader whom all men trusted . . . and obeyed because they knew him for a good soldier. That would be glorious. But . . . as you say, Richard, all in good time. I think there will be storms to be weathered first." She brooded for a moment and then said more cheerfully, "Of course your father may not attack you even if you make your gesture of rebellion. Despite everything, he is fond of you and Young Henry; he may even yield a little because I am here. Almost his last words to me, cruel as they sounded, were at least an acknowledgement that Aquitaine and Poitou belong to me. He may now decide to wash his hands of it all, to withdraw your advisors, and leave us to go to the Devil in our own fashion."

"That would suit me well. Or, if he decides to make war on me, that suits me too. What I cannot bear, and have no intention of bearing for another hour, is this pretence, this having the title, but not the power, to rule—or, if it comes to that, doing the work and not getting the wages."

It was unfortunate that the Young King's and Richard's final rebellion, their demand to be treated as men and not as children, should have coincided so exactly with their mother's arrival on the Continent. Henry chose to forget that the young men had been fretting, pulling against the rein, for years before that. He loved both his sons—Young Henry especially—and had always been puzzled by their demands. Now, in his simple blunt fashion, he put all the blame on Eleanor. His boys were good boys; he loved them and they loved him; everything had been well until *she,* with her grievance and her notions and her anger, had gone abroad and provoked them to rebellion. He meant, in a kindly paternal way, to teach them both a sharp lesson. A battle or two, which he would win, of course; then he would give them back everything in one magnificent gesture, making it a condition that neither of them saw their mother or harboured her in their courts.

From the same window from which, more than twenty years earlier, she had watched a redheaded young man on a red horse come riding in, Eleanor watched the town of Poitiers burning. The air was thick and heavy, and sour with the scent of smouldering thatch and scorching clay; it was late autumn and the rains had been heavy, and, as each little street was fired, the dampness of roofs and walls had enabled them to offer a momentary, piteous resistance to the flames. Nevertheless, hour by hour, the fires were gaining. War had come to Poitou, and its horror exceeded what she had imagined, clear-sighted and vivid as her imagination had been.

The town's centre, backed by the area overlooked by the castle in which she stood, was still held, she could see, by Richard and the forces which remained to him. Richard had been very unlucky. As soon as the rebellion had broken out—as it had done soon after her arrival, with Richard and Young Henry sending their demands to their father, and Old Henry responding with a laugh and the laying down of even stricter rules—Richard, thinking his brother's lands more easy to attack and less well prepared, had sent to the north all the forces he could spare; more than he could safely spare. He had finally gone himself, but Young Henry's frivolous, fair-weather friends had been halfhearted in the battlefield, and the two brothers had differed over their plans of action. The result was one of those sudden, all-consuming bursts of Plantagenet temper, after which Richard, with some of his men, had come riding hell-for-leather south again in order to put Poitiers in a state of defence.

King Henry, not bothering to complete the defeat of his eldest son, followed hard on the heels of the younger. He thought—rightly—that Richard was the more dangerous of the two; besides, Eleanor was in Poitiers . . . and if he could once get his hands on her . . . !

Now the war was nearing its end; Young Henry was quelled, or almost; and Richard surely could not hold out much longer. Many of his men had stayed in the north; many others had changed sides as soon as the King appeared to be winning; nobles and knights changed sides in those days as easily as they changed partners in a dance. Also—and nobody knew this better than the King—there were those at this minute, standing side by side with Richard in the burning town, who were fully prepared to turn traitor when the time came.

One of these was named Sir Gilbert of Blaye. He was son to that old, crafty knight who had arranged Eleanor's marriage to the King of France and killed her first love with a thrust of his sword. Of that secret story Gilbert knew nothing, for the old man had kept his own counsel to the end; what Gilbert did know, and bore an aching grudge about, was that after her divorce from the French King, in the short period between her marriages while she was completely her own mistress, the Duchess had treated his father very badly indeed! The wide rich manor that King Louis had given him some years back had been taken away; and then, swooping down like a falcon on a pigeon, Eleanor had made a great fuss about several small things which the old man, secure in the favour of the King, had done, or failed to do, for many years. There was a bridge, for example, which it was his duty to repair; he had let it decay so that travellers had been forced to use a ford, farther upriver, where he had charged a fee for every person, animal, or cart. The Duchess had called this "evasion of duty" and "cheating the public," and had fined Sir Godfroi so heavily, so ridiculously severely, that he had died a poor man; died, moreover, of fury which brought on a stroke. For years, Sir Gilbert had hoped for a chance to revenge himself upon his Duchess . . . and the moment was rapidly approaching.

He came into the room where Eleanor, from her window, was watching the progress of the battle. He bent his knee and rose again with just the right degree of courtesy tempered by haste.

"Your Grace," he said, "I come from the Duke, who has need of your services. The enemy is pressing hard, and he is short of men. But at Parthenay—a mere hour's ride away—he has forces stationed with strict orders not to budge. If he sends a page, a jester, or a minstrel—and he can spare no better—the likelihood is that those at Parthenay will suspect a trick and refuse to ride out. So he asks if you dare make the journey. The town is not quite encircled yet, the attack has concentrated to the north; we should stand a chance if we rode out by the south gate, *now!*"

He relied upon the haste and urgency to prevent too close an inquiry into his message, and his carefully concocted tale struck exactly the right note. To Eleanor, who had been standing idle, watching with sorrow and apprehension the inroads of the fire, action—any action—was intensely welcome.

"Of course," she said. "Go back, sir, and tell him that I am on my way and that, within two hours or less, I shall be back, and the reinforcements with me. Go . . ."

"But I am to accompany you, madam."

"I need no company. And the Duke cannot spare an able-bodied man."

"Alas, I am that no longer," said Gilbert, and he reached out the hand which had been behind his back as he spoke. A very blood-stained clout wrapped it round.

"By the same token," he said, "I cannot be trusted with the errand, since swift riding is the direst necessity. But I can, and will, madam, bear up long enough to show you the shortest way out of the town . . . some streets are impassable by reason of the fires . . . but I know my way and, once you are out . . . well, then I can bleed to death, if needs be, and no matter!"

"You are a good man," said Eleanor shortly and, without a thought, suspicion, or hesitation, she led the way down to the court-yard, where two horses waited. The good man (his name she did not know, but she would find out and, if he lived, would reward him; if he died, his family) threw himself into the saddle and gathered the reins in his left hand.

"Follow me," he said.

Down here the smoke was thicker, and the scent of burning so stifling that they coughed as they sped towards the south gate, and their eyes streamed. The south gate was closed and its towers manned, but the noise and fury of battle had not reached it yet; the circle had not yet closed. To the guards Eleanor cried, "I am your Duchess; I go to bring help"; and the men who heard opened the gates willingly, shouting "God speed you" as she and Sir Gilbert trotted through. And, since she knew that Parthenay lay slightly to the northwest of Poitiers, she followed her guide without question, without suspicion, as he led off in that direction.

The road was empty; ordinarily, she remembered, it was a busy road, lively with peasants bringing goods to market in Poitiers; with pack horses and donkeys, with dripping creels of fish coming up from the coast; with pedlars; with goosegirls herding their stately looking charges; milkmaids following the cows with their tinkling bells. Where had they all gone? This was war, she thought, this emptiness, this death in life.

When Sir Godfroi had wished to marry her to the King of France this was what she had imagined would happen to her beloved Aquitaine if she refused to do so and fled. Now . . . after all these years . . . was it happening because she had not been firm enough with Richard? Alas, here she was riding through the deserted countryside, with a burning town behind her.

Away with such thoughts; they served no purpose; they merely weakened, and she needed all her strength at this moment. She glanced at her companion. So far he had ridden a little ahead of her; now he was dropping back and, riding level with him, she could see his face. It wore a peculiar, set expression in which only the eyes were lively; a glancing, sideways look, anxious, almost furtive. She felt pity for him, remembering the blood on the bandage, and his words about seeing her onto the road, then dying if he must. She called to him above the rattle of hoofs:

"Sir! Turn back now. I know the way. I shall make better speed. Just tell me your name and fall back." She gathered herself in the saddle, making herself small, compact, light, leaning low with the instinctive motion, the will-to-help, of the good rider. At the same time, her eye, scanning the road ahead, took note of the bend, the three little haystacks at the curve blocking the view.

"A little further," her companion said; and he looked ahead, then left and right again.

They rode on, rounding the bend. As they passed the stacks, the clear open field lay on their left. Towards the edge of the field there was movement, the glint of light on armour, a tossing plume, lances pointed to the sky. She heard the breath, indrawn or outlet with emotion, hiss in the throat of the man beside her, and it flashed through her mind, on a wave of gratitude, that this was why he had ridden so far with her; he had suspected something untoward at this place. And he had been right, good faithful man.

"Delay, or distract them as best you may," she said and drove her heel into her horse, prepared to make a dash for it. But the hand with the bloodied bandage shot out suddenly and grasped the bridle of her horse, which, thus urged on and checked in the same moment, reared and pivotted round.

"Let me loose . . . I can outride them," she cried; but the man held on, and her horse made another half-turn, twisting the bridle about the clutching hand and driving her foot and stirrup between his stirrup and the body of his horse so that for a second they sat there, tangled, wrestling. And for another, just fatal second, she still thought him a wounded, utterly faithful good man, surprised, overcautious, and taken with panic. Just too late she acted, clenching her fist and bringing it down with all her force, not on the braced hand, but on the point of his elbow. The grasping fingers opened then, and at the same time she jerked her foot free. Her horse swung round. But Henry's men had closed in then, and Sir

Gilbert, flexing and unflexing his elbow, was greeting them with a significant grin.

Two of the long-nosed Normans (to the end of his days it was the men of his own duchy whom Henry trusted most completely and used for any particularly tricky business) seized Eleanor's bridle, one on each side, while a third, approaching from behind, dropped over her head a rope with a running noose in its end. As it fell to her elbows, he pulled, and the noose tightened, pinning her arms to her sides. The fourth man wheeled his horse close to Sir Gilbert's and said courteously,

"Sir, you have done well! You shall have your reward—in Heaven!" and, ripping out his sword, he thrust it home, straight through the body with an action so similar in its suddenness, its treachery, and its skill, to that with which Sir Godfroi had killed Richard de Vaux, that Eleanor, forgetting her present extremity, gave vent to a little cry of horror.

"He was a traitor," said the Norman smoothly, withdrawing his sword. "And we hold that he who will betray one master will betray another. Gaspard, throw him from the saddle and bring the horse along." Turning back to Eleanor, he said, "Madam, we shall ride hard but not far. On our way!"

Part Three

CHAPTER ONE

The larger of the two rooms was fourteen ordinary paces long and twelve wide; the inner, smaller one, into which she was locked at night, measured ten paces each way. So had her wide domains shrunk. Sometimes, if Nicolas of Saxham, her gaoler, was in one of his rare kindly moods, and the weather matched, she was taken down to walk in the little garden which some unknown, more fortunate woman had made in a corner between the brewhouse and the bakery. It was an unthriving, too-shaded little garden, a maze of narrow paths edged by low-growing hedges, the spaces between the paths offering, in due season, a few gillyflowers and primroses, a musk rose or two, a fleck of blue lavender flower on an overgrown bush; but to walk in it and breathe the free air, to see the sky and to hear a bird sing now was something to anticipate eagerly, to remember with joy. She had never counted how many paces it took to walk over every one of the little intersecting paths . . . best not to know; let it be just a walk out-of-doors. So tamed now, and cramped and confined was this most adventurous of women.

She was not alone; the faithful Amaria, left in that other room in Poitiers, had followed, step by step, back from Poitou to England, and at last had risked the King's anger by accosting him and begging permission to join her mistress at Winchester. Amaria had chosen her moment well; Henry had just learned that the King of the Scots, who had taken advantage of his absence on the Continent to make a raid on England, had been taken prisoner and brought, with his legs tied under his horse's belly, to Richmond. Henry was in a good mood and inclined to grant a favour to his other prisoner—his wife. So Eleanor had Amaria.

She had a lute.

She had four books.

She had a tapestry frame and what wool she asked for.

She had a bed, hard and narrow certainly, but she had slept, and slept well, on many worse.

She had three meals a day; a breakfast of bread and thin sour ale, a dinner of some meat or fish, a supper of bread and bacon, or bread and cheese, and more ale. Thousands of people, she often told herself wryly, would be glad to have so much and so regularly. But that self-rebuke invariably brought in its train the thought that to have less, and less regularly, would be more bearable. Food, except to animals and people on the verge of starvation, should do more than merely fill the stomach; it should attract, and sometimes surprise, the eye; it should sometimes wait until one was hungry; it should, above all, be what one had chosen. The sad thing was that, after a long time of bread, ale, meat, fish, bacon, and cheese, always enough, always punctual in appearing, one thought of, dreamed about, and longed for food in a quite shameful way . . . how crisp a fresh apple in September would be between the teeth; how sweetly honey would smell; how smoothly grapes would lie on the tongue.

"But madam, you are well fed," Nicolas of Saxham would say in those early days when she had not learned the uselessness of a request or a complaint. "Three times a day, with unfailing regularity, food of the best quality is set on your table. The household accounts prove that."

"Madam, I only carry out the orders of my master, the lord De Glanville, who receives his from the King . . ."

"Madam, nothing in my orders would justify me . . ."

When the mummers came and everyone else in the castle gathered in the outer bailey to witness, by torchlight, the performance . . . and the torturing sound of laughter, of hands clapped, feet stamped in pleasure, reached the room in which she sat, and she asked permission to go—not to the bailey, she knew that was too much to ask—but to a small window overlooking the scene,

"Madam, I have no orders to that effect . . ."

The days dragged on. Until one had nothing to which to look forward, one did not realise how great a part of life consists of merely looking forward, in thinking, Next Thursday I shall do this or that . . . in April this or that will happen. To look ahead and know that next Thursday will be as like this Thursday as this Monday was like last Monday, that next April will be the blank-faced dragging month that this one is, can be a specially subtle kind of torture.

And she was without hope. Henry believed that she had encouraged her sons to rebel against him; he had captured her by a trick and locked her in prison; and since he was younger than she was, she dared not even look to his death to release her.

She had been in Winchester for three treadmill years when something of interest, of excitement, did happen.

It was a Tuesday in early February, the day dark with snow. The winter had been severe, snow and frost following one another until the roads were impassable; and to make matters worse, of their three precious needles, Amaria had broken one and she herself had lost one down a crack in the stone-flagged floor. So now they could no longer sit companionably together at their work; one must sit idle, and things had come to such a pass that Eleanor, who in Paris, long years ago, had hated needlework, must now say to Amaria, "It is my turn now . . ." and take up the stitching with a sense of relief. Something to do; something to decide . . . which stitch? which colour? which pattern?

She had asked for another needle, making the request to Nicolas some time before Christmas, and he had said in his usual way that needles were not specifically mentioned in his orders, but he would ask De Glanville when he paid his routine visit of inspection. Permission to purchase needles was duly given, but just before the snow and frost set in.

"Between us and the town, madam, the drifts lie eight feet deep. Your needles must await the thaw."

Then on this Tuesday morning, while she and Amaria were playing one of their interminable games of chess—interminable because in reality it was a game of Eleanor against Eleanor, since Amaria was so poor a player that she could be beaten in fifteen minutes, Nicolas of Saxham, jingling his keys, appeared in the doorway of the room and said,

"A crazy pedlar, hot for a penny's profit, has pushed his way through the drifts, God knows how, he's no bigger than my thumb. And he has needles. What kind, and how many, do you ladies require?"

In the old days how blithely she would have said that anything with a point at one end and an eye at the other would do! Now even the choosing of a needle offered a small but welcome break in the dull routine of the day; so she and Amaria began to describe what they would like if the pedlar carried it, and what they could make do with if he didn't, and sometimes they argued, for Amaria, who was very nearsighted, preferred extremely fine needles since she worked with her nose almost brushing the stitches, while Eleanor preferred a stout needle, easily threaded and capable of making bold, stabbing stitches. Nicolas stood there understanding nothing, except that the two bothersome creatures were being as tiresome as possible. Moreover, the room, small as it was for walking about in, was lofty and the smoking fire, beside which the women sat, warmed it very little; he wished to get back to the great seven-foot logs blazing in the big hall; so presently he said, with no notion of the importance of his words, "Oh, stop this clacking! I'll send the fellow in and you can see for yourselves what he carries!"

Alberic the pedlar was shown in by a page who made very plain that he despised the errand and was eager to get back to his game of knucklebones. Retiring, he slammed the door with such vigour that a great billow of smoke sailed out of the chimney and momentarily obscured the room. When it cleared, Eleanor looked at the man who had braved the snowdrifts in order to make a penny profit. He was very squat, mainly because he seemed to have no neck; his head, rather overlarge, appeared to rest on his broad shoulders; his face was reddened and roughened by wind and weather; and he had bright hazel eyes, very lively and candid between their bristly lashes.

"I give you good day, Your Grace," he said, bowing so low that the pack on his shoulders, neatly bundled into a piece of sailcloth, swung forward over his head. Straightening himself, he slipped his arms out of the leather straps and, carrying the pack to the table, opened it and laid its contents out for their inspection. There was nothing of much value, and very little to gladden the eye; it was not one of those packs which, opened, spill out colour like a miniature bazaar. There were a few needles and pins, some small blocks of salt, three or four knives, and a few buckles.

"It's a poor selection," Alberic said cheerfully. "But of course if you, Your Grace, and you, madam, require anything that isn't here, you could give me an order and I could come back . . ."

There was an undertone of meaning in his voice which caused Eleanor to look from his goods to his face. The bright eyes met hers with something of the wish-to-communicate-without-words which she had seen in the eyes of good intelligent dogs. And that look persisted even as he spoke.

"I get about. I'm often in London. And sometimes I go to Dover. I have a friend who has a ship. He could bring me anything from Calais . . . or even Bordeaux . . . if it was ordered. So ask for anything you wish."

"Why do you mention Bordeaux?" Eleanor asked.

"Just to let you know how much I get about, Your Grace," Alberic said, and his bright gaze flicked towards Amaria.

"Amaria and I differ about which thickness of needle is preferable," Eleanor said, "but otherwise we are entirely at one. And the thing we need, the thing we crave most, from London or elsewhere, is *news.*"

In a lifetime of frank speaking, she never said a more sincere thing; the lack of news, the knowledge that outside the walls of her prison things were happening, wars being started, treaties being signed, while she sat here as much cut off as though she were blind and deaf and dumb, had in the last three years been one of the things hardest to bear. Both Richard and Young Henry wrote to her occasionally—she suspected that they wrote more letters than she received—but neither of them told her anything of much interest; perhaps because, knowing her helplessness, they deliberately withheld any news that might anger, or sadden, or excite her; perhaps because they were neither of them skilled in conveying meaning with a pen. They always wrote fondly, always saying that they were nagging at their father to set her free, always urging her to have patience and hope because one day she *must* be free, and Richard had actually said that he would never be friends with his father so long as she was a captive; but of their own doings, the things she longed to hear, they said very little.

"Well now," said Alberic, "news is one thing we pedlars get for nothing, and pass on without charge. What would you wish to hear, madam? You'd best ask questions—I mustn't stay too long."

"Give me news of my sons," Eleanor said.

The pedlar looked at her with compassion; it was true then, what gossip said—that she was locked away, more secluded from the world than a nun in her cell, treated as though she were already dead. In the prime of life, too, thought the pedlar who had a shrewd eye for women, most of his trade being done with them. A lovely, proud-looking lady; just to look at her made you understand the nice songs that were sung about her; and, once you'd seen her, you'd not believe the others.

"Well now," he said again, and swiftly and surely, out of the mass of gossip and hearsay and sheer nonsense which he gathered on his travels, he picked out the bits which concerned her sons. Prince Henry had made peace with his father and come to England for a visit, but they hadn't stayed friendly long; in London people expected fighting between them to break out any day; Prince Richard was still in Aquitaine, knocking his barons about, so they said; last time he and his father came to blows, some of the barons hadn't been as reliable as he wanted, so he was getting them tamed and openly talking about "next time."

It occurred to Alberic, as he gabbled along, that none of this news made very cheerful hearing for the woman who was the mother of the young men and wife of the old one. But then it was a peculiar situation; husbands locking their wives away and sons fighting against their fathers weren't heard of every day! She'd asked for news of her sons and he was giving it, as straightly and honestly as he could. Finally he gave her news of her youngest son, John—most women he met were specially attached to their last-born. The news of John couldn't fail to please her, unless she'd also fallen out with him; he'd been made Governor of Ireland, and there was talk of his having some land on the Continent too.

Eleanor listened without interrupting; she realised that this ped-lar could bring her news of what was being said in the alehouses and market squares, but he could never penetrate below the surface; she took his chatter as he had received it, at face value. But when he had gone, with an order for several trivial items not in his pack at that moment, and had promised that he would bring them back and with them any further news he could gather, Eleanor brooded over the mention of John and spoke aloud to Amaria the thoughts which were troubling her.

"What land on the Continent could Henry give to John without taking it from the others? Unless he conquered France—and, surely, even he would never dream that wild dream. Young Henry has Normandy and Anjou—at least he bears the titles; Richard has my lands, Aquitaine and Poitou; Geoffrey has Brittany. What is there left for John?"

Of her four boys she liked him least; indeed, unnatural as it sounded, she liked him hardly at all. Time and again when he was a child, she had found him to be both sly and cruel, and the treatment which, meted out to the others, had at least checked their faults, had had small effect upon his. She'd slippered him just as she had the others, rapped out the same frank rebukes when he displeased her, but he never minded; he slithered away, moaning when he was punished, and then did the very same thing again. A changeling child, even in his appearance, dark, short, fat—in a family of reddish-blond, lean giants. Against that, one must remember that he had what the others lacked entirely, a prodigious, deliberate charm, and a very subtle intelligence which even rage could not throw out of working order. Any one of the other boys, like Henry himself, was capable of throwing away, in a fit of temper, advantages which had cost years of labour to achieve; Eleanor was a master of the art of "cutting off her nose to spite her face"; but John was different. As a child, he had pursued his secret ways, indifferent to punishment or rebuke; as a man, he pursued his own ends, indifferent to jibes or persuasion. Now, if he had set his heart on more land than his position as fourth son entitled him to, he would plot and plan, and smile his secret smile, and swallow insults, all to that end.

At least, she reflected, Alberic's chatter had given her something outside herself to think about. She was grateful; and, as the months went by, their seasons almost unmarked save by the changes to be seen during the rare visits to the little garden, she had, again and again, reason for gratitude to the pedlar. By some means he had got himself into favour with Nicolas of Saxham and, so far as Eleanor knew, he was never refused admission to her room. Her purchases from his pack were very modest, for she was allowed the smallest amount of spending money, and his profits could hardly have paid him for the time and trouble of the errands he performed. Sometimes she said to him, as she said very often to Amaria, "If ever I regain my freedom, I will make up to you a thousandfold."

Once or twice he carried letters out for her; once or twice he smuggled letters in; but she was cautious. As dull month followed dull month and the years mounted up, her hatred of Henry grew, swelled into a poisonous growth; but the only revenge left to her

—to make further trouble between him and his sons—she shrank from. The memory of the burning town of Poitiers and the deserted countryside around it haunted her. So to Young Henry and Richard, she wrote mild letters which, had they fallen into Henry's hands, could not possibly have led to further ill feeling. Once, for his birthday, she sent Richard a pair of gloves which she had made from strong supple goatskin, embroidering the backs and the gauntlets with a pattern of pearls from a gladly sacrificed necklace.

It was Alberic who brought her, in the sixth year of her captivity, the news that Louis of France was dead. He had been her husband, they had ridden on crusade together . . . but somehow now, to her, sitting by the smoky fire in her narrow prison, the very memory of him seemed remote, hardly concerned with her at all.

"One thing is quite certain," she said to Amaria, "his soul is safe. He was a saint at heart. Even when he dragged me away to Jerusalem and lost all hope of making the crusade a success, he did it from the best motives. Angry as I was, I never doubted his integrity for one moment."

Amaria, sharply conscious that for two women, growing old, locked up together, to begin looking back on the past might be a dangerously depressing business, said briskly,

"Well, they say that Hell is paved with good intentions!"

"And that may be true. I also had good intentions in my time! The thing to remember, Amaria, is that those who make those good intentions are not necessarily the ones who walk that pavement."

"You've not lost your nimble tongue," Amaria said.

"How could I, with you to practise it upon?" asked Eleanor, smiling affectionately upon the faithful woman. Then her mind returned to the news.

"Things will be different now. Louis was King of France and he hated the King of England, but he was a father too, and he never wholeheartedly approved of boys rebelling against their father—what father would? Now that the King of France is young too, and probably as headstrong as all young men seem to be these days, anything might happen."

"Well, one thing that might happen, and that would gladden *my* heart at least," said Amaria, getting up and dealing the sulky fire a blow which sent a cloud of smoke into the room and a shower of sparks up the chimney, "would be if they all got together and made a rebellion and won a real victory. Then you, my lady, might get out of this dungeon before your limbs set fast from the damp."

"It would gladden me more if it could be done peaceably," said Eleanor, "but that is too much to hope for. And somehow . . . no, no matter, just an idle thought." She had been on the verge of saying that she felt that Young Henry would never be the one to score a victory over his father and set her free . . . Richard might. But that was no thing for a mother to say.

And there came the time when she was glad that she had never decried Young Henry, even to the faithful Amaria; for the next news from the outer world, brought this time not by Alberic but by special messenger from the King, was that Young Henry was dead. The rebellion which Eleanor had foreseen, with three young men against the elder, had scarcely begun before Henry, the Young King, was stricken down by fever, and died—so it was said —in an agony of repentance. In his last hours he had sent for his father in order to make peace with him; but Henry suspected a trap and did not go. The gay, frivolous, pleasure-loving young man had made a strange gesture of penitence at the end, bidding his servants spread a bed of cinders and lay him upon it.

The sorry news bore heavily upon Eleanor's already drooping spirits. Her secret preference for Richard—the son most nearly resembling herself—had never blinded her to the charm of his brother; she had loved Henry too. Now, with nothing to distract her thoughts, cut off from the children who remained to her and in whom she might have found comfort, she was in danger of falling into brooding melancholy.

Amaria, ever watchful, was distressed to see how often she would sit, the needle halted in her hands, her eyes staring at nothing and then slowly clouding with tears. "Dear Mother of God," she would pray, "make something happen to take her mind from her loss." And she regarded it as a direct answer to prayer when something quite startling did happen—a visit from Prince John.

He arrived, from Amaria's point of view, in the very nick of time. She had been nagging at Nicolas of Saxham all through the past weeks to grant Eleanor such trivial favours as a change of diet, a little of the wine she loved in place of the ale she loathed, some seasoned logs instead of smouldering green ones for the fire. Often she met with rebuffs; but this morning, windy indeed but with a promise of sunshine, her request for a little outing had been granted, and she had run back to the apartment in high glee to tell her mistress that she might walk in the garden today. Eleanor said, "You begged for it, didn't you, out of your good heart?" Then she walked to the window and looked out.

"All the same, Amaria, I think I shall stay within. It looks very windy. . . ."

"But you love the wind! Over and over again you've said you love the wind, especially when it blows from the east, from Aquitaine. Why, once, I remember, you said it blew so strong and fast that you could smell the vintage . . ."

"Today it would buffet me," Eleanor said; and, turning back from the window, she shuddered and wrapped her arms about herself.

Small, apparently trivial as the incident was, it was significant; it marked a step in the wrong direction. Once let apathy set in and we're finished, Amaria thought . . . once let go and you die. Ten years we've borne up hopefully, turning every tiny thing into a treat, holding on doggedly; and we've kept our health and our sanity. Ten years . . . like rocks repelling the waves of the sea . . . now, if we start to crumble . . .

She said, with great craftiness, "Well, I'm glad. I always hated the wind. I'll mend the fire and pull up the screen and we'll have a nice cosy game of chess. And this morning I shall beat you. You'll see!"

And even that speech had its bitterness; for lately Eleanor had loosened her grip on the chess game, too.

They had just set out the pieces when a commotion was heard outside, and there was the gaoler bowing and scraping and pages pushing and grinning, and in the midst of them . . . John.

He was wise enough not to say anything except the one word "Mother." No explanation of his presence; no reason for his sudden arrival. There he was, alive and smiling, handsome—all her children were handsome—and beautifully dressed. And, just for a moment, he represented them all, all her brood, the three lovely girls, scattered and married, Henry dead, Richard in Aquitaine, Geoffrey in Brittany.

He made a great bustle; he knew, he said, that his sudden coming might disorganise the domestic arrangements, so he had brought his own provender; he sent everybody scuttling to prepare the feast. And he talked, mainly about Ireland. Afterwards, thinking it over calmly, Eleanor realised that he talked about Ireland as though he had been there through the whole time that she had spent locked up in Winchester. But, while he was there, describing with immense humour the customs and manners of the Irish chieftains, such a thought would have seemed churlish, no less. He brought with him a breath of the outer, busy world; relating news of Joanna in Sicily, of Eleanor in Castile—married to the richest king in the world and spending money gloriously in great buildings, tournaments, and pageantry—of Geoffrey and his children, of Richard and his conquests of the turbulent nobles of Aquitaine. Within an hour he had warmed and changed the whole mental climate. She was no longer the woman who had lost one son to death . . . she was the mother of a flourishing family; she was no longer a prisoner without hope; she was a woman whose youngest son, hitherto somewhat discounted, had come to her rescue. For over the venison, the oranges and the figs, and the familiar, longed-for red wine of Bordeaux which John had brought with him, his talk had changed abruptly from the joking gossip, the giving of news.

"Hitherto," he said, "my father has treated me kindly—that I must say to give him his due—but as though I were a child. Now things have changed. Since my return from Ireland and Henry's death, he is more inclined to listen, to take advice . . ."

"Then he has changed as well as the times!"

"But it is so. Dear mother, the quarrel between you two is hardly a matter for you to discuss with me, your son; but I am certain that, properly handled, it could be mended now." He propped his elbows on the table and his chin on his linked fingers and eyed her narrowly. A dozen thoughts ran side by side through her mind. Was it, after all, to be John with his cunning, not Richard with his bluntness, who was to open the prison door? Did the mending of the quarrel mean going back to London and taking her place among people who, in order to please Henry, had for ten years believed her to be a murderess, people who had gone about the streets singing songs about her and Fair Rosamonde, songs in which, oddly enough, the little workbox and the embroidery silks had taken an important, but completely legendary place? And did Henry's new inclination to be advised mean . . . She pushed all the thoughts away and said with something of her old manner,

"John, understand this. Your father wronged me; he accused me falsely; he captured me by trickery; he has kept me a prisoner here for ten years. Sooner than ask him for mercy, or to have mercy asked on my behalf, I would die in this prison. I know what is said and sung about me in the London streets . . . and those words are aimed to please him; that shows what he thinks of me. His wife, Queen of England, I will never be again. If you ask anything for me, ask him to set me free to go back to my own lands."

"To Poitou where the sun shines, to Aquitaine where the grapes ripen, where Richard rules?" John's jewelled fingers tightened on the strip of orange peel with which he had been toying, and it broke with a little squelching sound. "Richard is now—don't forget it— heir to England." Something gritty and harsh had come to the smooth, pleasant voice. "That is what I mean when I say all things have changed . . . and, in my scheming, I have never lost sight of the fact that *you* were a Duchess in your own right before ever you were a Queen. Can you trust me to make a move for you in this game, mother?"

Countless little memories of his trickery, even in very early childhood, swarmed into her mind like wasps, each with its sting. "Slippery John" the other boys had called him.

"What move; and in what game, John?" she asked with something like her old sharpness.

"Ah," he said with a smile, "who can say? I make my plans as I go along; what the move will be I cannot tell you yet; but the game—well, Getting a Queen out of Pawn would be as good a title as any, don't you think?"

Suddenly Amaria, who was present, but carefully effacing herself and seeming to give all her attention to the palatable food, looked up and interrupted.

"Oh, madam, let him *try*. Think what it would mean to be out of this place, free to come and go as we wished, with no bolts and bars and gaolers always saying 'no' to everything. We're neither of us getting any younger, and to think of the years wasting away while we linger here . . ." She burst into tears.

"If you will swear to use only peaceable means," Eleanor said.

"But of course, mother. I am the one who has never used any other kind. Therein lies my power now." He spoke the last words softly, gloatingly.

"Very well then; but remember it is justice, not mercy, I ask; justice, and freedom to go back to my own land."

"That you shall have, I promise," John said.

CHAPTER TWO

John went away and for a little while the flicker of hope, carefully
fanned by Amaria, lived in her heart; but the year ran downhill
towards winter again, the dull cold winter that she dreaded, and
nothing happened; hope, for lack of sustenance, dwindled and died.
Alberic, faithfully plodding the miry roads in November, brought
gossip, but no real news; even John's marriage to Avis of Gloucester
—at which he had hinted during his visit—had apparently not
taken place yet.

Christmas came and went, another landmark, a season without
cheer.

Then, one morning, there came the clatter and commotion of
men arriving in the courtyard. Amaria, huddled in her shawl, went
into the draughty stone passage which linked their apartments with
the main part of the castle and, braving the cold, stood for some
time exchanging the usual half-simple-chatter, half-humourous-in-
sult brand of talk with the guard who was on duty there. He did
not know who had arrived, or why, but he allowed Amaria to stay
with him until a page ran by within hail, and, in answer to a
shouted question, replied that Lord de Glanville had come.

"Oh, we just needed that," said the guard surlily. "Fuss and
bother, fuss and bother, poking his long nose into everything and
finding fault all round. And his chaps gobbling up our fodder. Six
months or more since he showed his face here—living fat in London
and drawing custodian's pay, then popping in here to say we're
idle and overfed."

He realised that he was talking to himself; Amaria, having got what she had come for, had slipped away.

"It's the head gaoler himself," she said, running into the room where Eleanor sat by the smoky fire. "And you in that old dress, madam. That's one thing I do blame myself for not asking the Prince when he was here; he could at least have persuaded the King to send you some of your clothes. All those lovely gowns mouldering away in Windsor and Westminster . . . I could cry to think of them."

"I'm indifferent to the effect of my appearance on De Glanville," Eleanor said. "I only hope he won't do what he did last time he came in winter—set the whole place reeking with his venison roast while we ate our usual eels. And then had the audacity to point out to me that he was out of pocket for our keep because the price of flour had risen!"

"Perhaps it's just as well you look so shabby," said Amaria, pursuing her subject. "Will you ask *him,* my lady, to ask for some of your clothes?"

"I'm asking him no more favours," Eleanor answered. "In fact, this time I shan't even speak to him. Last time, if you remember, I asked him for news—they were fighting then—and he replied that he had no orders to tell me anything. This time I shall stand up, for politeness' sake, when he enters and keep silent until he has gone."

"You'll get no new dress that way."

"Nor any other way."

The now familiar fear pricked at Amaria's heart; despair was loosening her mistress' hold on life; another year and she would be dead, or melancholy-mad. "Holy Mother of God . . ." Amaria began for the thousandth time.

Footsteps and voices in the passage interrupted the prayer.

De Glanville entered the room, Nicolas of Saxham remained by the door. Eleanor very slowly and deliberately rose to her feet and, keeping her vow of silence, made no answer when De Glanville said he hoped he found her well. She did not even look in his direction, and so, by half a minute, she missed the first hint of change. Amaria knew immediately—for both the gaolers had uncovered and bent a knee, and such unusual courtesy could only mean one thing.

"Madam," De Glanville said, "I have been ordered by His Grace to request your presence at Windsor. There are, he says, matters of grave importance to be discussed, and, while regretting any inconvenience which urgency may cause you, he wishes that you should set out today." So much De Glanville said all in a piece, almost tonelessly, a mere passing on of instructions. In a different voice, almost fawning, he went on, "I have done my best to make the journey as easy as possible, my lady. I have a covered litter waiting, and a comfortable lodging for the night is this moment being prepared."

"This covered litter," Eleanor said, speaking for the first time, "did the King order it, or did you think of it?"

"My own thought entirely; thought for your comfort, madam, the weather being so cold."

"Then I shall ride on horseback."

"Oh, my lady," said Amaria, protestingly, "and you so stiff from the damp in this place; and the weather so bitter!"

"I shall ride. You may have the litter, Amaria. I have reason to dislike them." She swung round to Nicolas of Saxham. "You, sir, do you think your wife could lend me a cloak today? Sometime back when I wished to borrow one for a walk in the garden she was unable to oblige me. If she is still so ill-provided, perhaps one of the soldiers could spare me his."

Through the minds of both men shot the same thought—that Henry the King was not entirely enviable. Ten and a half years of strict imprisonment had not tamed the Queen much.

"Go get a cloak," De Glanville said.

"And be sure to say who gave *that* order," Eleanor called; "otherwise your wife will be afraid to show me a kindness. As for you, my lord," she turned to De Glanville with a look of scorn, "your care for my comfort comes too late in the day."

They arrived at Windsor just as the brief winter daylight was fading on the next afternoon. A messenger had been sent on ahead, and both Henry and John were waiting to greet her. Henry had the sense, the good taste, to act very formally, only saying,

"Welcome to Windsor, madam. I trust you are not too tired by your journey. We have many things to discuss, and I hope that we shall reach a settlement which will mend all misunderstanding."

"In that hope I have come," she said with equal formality. Nevertheless, her mood softened as she stared at the man whom she had loved, who had once loved her, whose children she had borne and still loved. He had aged immensely since she last saw him; always thick-set, he was now very stout, but not fleshily; he looked as though the increased weight were due to a thick wooden casing laid over him; even his face looked like a wooden mask, crudely painted, and the harsh lines which ill temper, coarse good humour, and grief and anxiety had drawn upon it might well have been scored there by a chisel. Some of the marks of grief had undoubtedly been caused by the death of Young Henry, the son whom they had both loved. They had shared a grief and, despite everything, that was a link. She made up her mind that, in the discussion later on, she would not allow rancour to sour her demands or sharpen her tongue. She would demand justice and uphold her pride, but spite and the desire for revenge should not influence her behaviour.

Even as she was thinking these things, John came and embraced her with every show of affection; then, drawing away a little, but retaining his clasp on her hand, he smiled his secret, conspiratorial smile and pressed her fingers as though to say, "You see—I managed it!"

Aloud he said, "Richard has arrived and is now washing off the mud; he was mired to the eyes. You also bear the marks of travel. Come, let me take you to your apartments; all the women await you there."

Her meeting with the four young creatures whom she had called her "dear girls" was very different—all flutter and warmth and sentiment. There was the French Princess, Alys, who since childhood had been betrothed to Richard and reared in England; there was Marguerite, Henry's widow, melting into tears at this meeting with her mother-in-law, of whom she was deeply fond; and there was Constance of Brittany, Geoffrey's wife, whom Henry had brought to England at the same time he made Eleanor captive and whom he seemed unwilling to let go again, though he treated her kindly; and Emma of Anjou. They clustered about her, weeping and laughing at the same time and saying how much they had missed her and how delighted they were to see her again. She received their words and their kisses open-heartedly, without grudge; they were not to blame for the ten years' separation; they were all young, all female, helpless in the King's hands, ruled by his lightest whim. She knew that. Henry had probably ordered them to forget her; and, just as probably, he had now ordered them to receive her warmly. All the same, they were pretty and touching and dear, and it was a joy to look at them, to see how the years had developed them, the lightly moving, kind years of youth!

They and the serving-women had opened Eleanor's chests and closets, shaken out, brushed, and aired her clothes. Which dress would she wear for supper tonight when she made her first public appearance in the hall? She chose one of moss-green velvet, the sleeves, bodice, and sweeping hem thickly embroidered with gold thread. It hung loosely upon her body, grown thin on prison fare, and some of them set to work at once to take in the seams.

"I must not look pitiable," Eleanor said. And Emma of Anjou, Henry's much-younger sister, threw her a flashing glance.

"How wise you are! Henry has but one attitude toward the weak —stamp them down. But from you, for the moment at least, he has withdrawn his heel. Look, here are your jewels. Will you choose from them too?"

The young widow Marguerite insisted upon brushing her hair for her, and the others pressed round, exclaiming upon its length and beauty and the wonderful way in which it had kept its colour; and then, as they scattered again, Eleanor and Marguerite spoke of Young Henry, softly and with tears.

Servants hurried in with hot water, soft towels, wood for the fire, and mulled wine, steaming and spicy, to ward off the effects of the cold ride. Eleanor the Queen was back in her castle of Windsor. She even had her mirror again; and what she saw there made her say to Alys who stood by,

"Somewhere amongst my things that were left is a casket which, many years ago, I brought back from the East: it is made of wood, sandalwood, and inlaid with silver and mother-of-pearl. See if you can find it for me."

Alys found it and brought it, brushing off the dust of years with her long hanging sleeve.

Eleanor set it in her lap and opened it. Inside, neatly fitted together, were a number of little flasks and jars and boxes. A sweet, yet musky odour came from them.

"This," Eleanor said, "was given me by a Saracen emir. Not, he said, because I needed it then, but because the years were every woman's enemy, and one day even I might need an ally against them. A pretty speech, don't you think? What interested me at the time was the knowledge that such things have been used in the East since time immemorial, and probably just such a box was used by Cleopatra . . . or Helen of Troy." She began to lift the little lids, remove the stoppers. There were the colours which drained away with one's youth, the rose-pink for the cheeks, the poppy-red for the lips, the lustrous blue shadow for eyelid, the black for brow and lash—all waiting patiently to offer their small challenge to the years and the watching eyes of the waiting world. She used them skilfully, and, when she had done, Alys said almost jealously,

"You outshine us all!"

"Silly child," said Eleanor. "And you with the dew of youth still on you. And with Richard coming. I'll warrant you that at sight of him you'll glow with a brighter rose than these poor pigments could lay on."

Alys' eyes flickered.

"Richard, madam? Does no news reach you at Winchester? His

Grace the King withdrew his favour from that betrothal long ago. He now has in mind to marry me to John!"

"But you and Richard were betrothed fifteen years ago, almost as soon as you were out of your cradle."

"That is so; but every time marriage has been mentioned His Grace has some new excuse to prevent it. And lately I learned why . . . he wishes to marry me to John."

The instinct for politics which, since it had no exercise at Winchester, had slept for ten years, stirred, wakened in Eleanor's mind.

"Richard has Aquitaine and Poitou," she said as though speaking to herself, "and it is good for Aquitaine and France to be bonded by a marriage tie. For that reason I married the King of France." She realised that the girl to whom she was speaking was that King of France's daughter—by his second marriage; but, by the same token, the girl *was* a Princess and understood from the first why and how such marriages were made. She went on in a firm voice, "At least, while I was married to your father, Aquitaine and France had peace of a kind. The marriage failed—and I admit now that the fault was as much mine as his; our natures were ill-attuned. With you and Richard that would not be so, I think. You were playmates as children . . . I used to watch, and think that just for once a cradle match might be a love match. Was I wrong? Have you no fondness for Richard?"

A shutter dropped over the vivid little face.

"Madam, this is all to no purpose. You, of all people, should know the utter hopeless folly of opposing the King. You sit out your days at Winchester. But there are many other strongholds waiting to gulp down those who thwart him. I have not your courage, madam. I shall marry John, or the dwarf jester, sooner than be shut away from the light of Heaven as you have been. I have been watchful, and you have shown me how *not* to behave to the King of England."

"For women this is a hard world," Eleanor said. "But do not despair too soon. Here I am, and at some time or another I will beat out this matter of you and Richard. That betrothal was made in good faith and with the King's consent. And, even in Winchester, I heard that John was promised to Avis of Gloucester."

"And what are promises? Made to be broken at the convenience of the one who has power." The girl's voice was bitter.

"Do you doubt the one I just made you?"

"I only know, madam, that in your place I would be smooth and pleasant. I would agree to anything that would keep me *in* favour and *out* of prison."

"But there are so many kinds of prison! Sometimes, it seems to me, that every woman is born in prison and lives her life there. For poor women the walls are poverty, grinding hard work, and the man's will; for rich ones, schemes and expedients, and the man's will. . . . But this is no way for us to be talking. Rest assured that when the King and I meet and discuss matters I shall not forget you and Richard."

"Madam, against a stone wall one beats one's head in vain," Alys said; and before Eleanor could find anything else to say the trumpets sounded to announce that the food was ready and the King on his way to the table. When Eleanor and the ladies reached the hall, he, Richard, and John were standing together behind the table on the dais; they were engaged in conversation which, even from a distance, Eleanor could see was uneasy. John was smiling and looking about him and, as his eye fell on Eleanor, he plucked Richard's sleeve. Richard looked round and his manner changed from truculent wariness to pleasure; his scowl lifted as he ran forward and embraced her boisterously, crying that it was good to see her, and looking so well, too. In a slightly lower voice he added, as he took her hand and led her towards her seat, "I told you to bear up bravely and all would come right in the end. It takes a battle-ax to drive an idea into the old devil's head, but he's got it there at last. He knows he'd have nothing but trouble from me so long as he kept you caged. Well, he's had his bellyful of trouble, so he's ready to let me take you home to Aquitaine, in return for my promise to be a good boy in future."

It was typical, Eleanor thought, that John should believe that

he had won her release by subtlety, and that Richard should be
certain that he had rescued her by force; and both might be right.
It was also typical, she thought, looking from one handsome son
to the other, that John should be clad in silk and glittering with
jewels, while Richard, save for the size of him and his arrogant
look, might have been any common archer cleaned and reclad after
a battle. There was nothing of any value about him except the
gloves which she had made for him; they were thrust into the plain
leather belt which girded his plain woollen tunic. And even they
showed signs of wear; the goatskin was scuffed and stained, and
some of the pearls had dropped away, leaving the threads bare and
untidy. That he had, at least, a very fine belt, she knew; Henry
had given him one long ago, when he took formal possession of his
titles, Duke of Aquitaine, Count of Poitou. It had been made of
gold chain mail, flexible as leather, and all round it at intervals, and
all over the buckle, were set rubies and sapphires of great worth.
Now, sitting beside Richard at table and helping herself to the first
dish which the servants were handing, she said,

"You must let me have those gloves, Richard; some of the pearls
are loose. And where is your beautiful belt? Your father will be
displeased to see you wearing that thing—it looks like a piece of
harness."

Richard laughed, "Dear mother, you haven't changed! Always
trying to make me compete with John. Isn't he fine enough for two?
As for the belt, I sold it."

"Richard, you didn't! Your beautiful belt! He will be angry."

"He'd be angrier still if he knew that the price I screwed out for
it put armour on the backs of six good men and first-rate horses
under a dozen more. I was hard up, mother; and what use have I
for a fancy belt?"

"But it was a gift . . ." she began. Richard looked at her and
his brilliant blue eyes narrowed.

"When I give anybody a gift—which is, I admit, very seldom—
when I put it into their hand, I take mine off it. The thing is theirs
to use, or pass on, or chuck into the nearest pond if they've a mind

to. There is the trouble with father. He's a great *giver*; high-sound-ing titles, wide acres, cities and towns and castles. He'll give you half a kingdom before breakfast, but, by dinnertime, he'll ask what you've done with it, and shriek like a scalded pig if the answer doesn't please him. . . . But I've said all this before. He beat me once . . . he took you and thrust you into that Winchester dun-geon, but it was only because I'd sent all my best men to help Henry. This time . . ." his face darkened, "I think he knows that he has met his match—hence this family gathering. The price of my peace with His Grace is your freedom; I've made that very plain."

"I wonder then why we are met here." She thought of John and his significant smile.

"Oh, so that he can give us his blessing, make it all neat and sentimental . . . which means that nobody will bear him any grudge."

The supper proceeded. It was plain that Henry had set himself out to please her. Ordinarily, though a man of hearty appetite, he grudged time given to eating, and some courtiers, especially elderly ones with few teeth, complained that the King never allowed them time to eat their fill. As often as not, he would refuse to sit down to table at all, but would walk about, snatching at the food and eating it as he dictated orders or discussed some plan.

Tonight, however, everything was formal: delicate dish followed delicate dish; the wine cups were filled as soon as they were emptied; and from the lower end of the hall, the minstrels played the old sweet songs of Aquitaine. Gradually a half-dreaming sense of well-being came over her; the two days' riding had tired, even though they had refreshed her, and her reunion with Richard, his cer-tainty that she would return to Poitiers with him, had revived her hope. All might yet be well.

At last Henry rose and led the way through the curtained arch-way at the rear of the dais; the seven members of his immediate family followed him into the retiring chamber beyond. A bright fire burned on the hearth, and near by, on stools and table, lay musical instruments, and the needlework with which the ladies employed their evening leisure. Alys, with a glance at Richard, took up her lute, and Eleanor, moving towards a seat by the fire, thought, "They both love music and that would be a bond there."

"I have ordered a fire in the Solomon Chamber," Henry said. "There we can talk undisturbed."

His sombre glance rested upon Richard, and then on John. "You two stay within earshot; we may need you later." He stood hesitant for a second, as though in doubt whether to offer Eleanor his arm, thought better of it, and moved on stiffly to the door at the farther end of the room.

The Solomon Chamber was a gloomy apartment which took its name from a huge tapestry covering one of the longer walls. In colours only slightly faded by the hundred years of its age, it depicted Solomon giving judgement between two women who both claimed the same baby. Solomon had the features and wore the garb of a Norman knight—very probably of that Duke of Normandy who had conquered England—and the two poor Jewish women were dressed as nuns, very neat and demure. Eleanor, who knew what Eastern potentates and poor Jewish women looked like, had been amused by the tapestry when she first saw it, and she looked at it again, after all these years, with a slight, reminiscent smile.

Henry's orders had been obeyed and there was a fire, but it was the first to brighten that hearth for a long while. The room was chilly and its three uncovered walls sweated damp in the candle-light. In the old days, when the court was at Windsor, Eleanor had often used the room; it was a handy place to retire to from the noise and merriment of the outer room, and here she had received many confidences, listened to many secrets, and given a good deal of advice.

Tonight the King of England appeared as ill at ease as any one of the young people who had sought her out in this room in the past. He said abruptly,

"Sit down . . . no, have the big chair, I'll stand." He kicked a log into place, watched the flames leap up, then moved away a little, hooking his thumbs into his belt with a familiar gesture. "First of all, I want you to understand that I'm prepared to let bygones be bygones. We're not here to pick over old bones. It's the future, not the past, that we have to think of. Are you agreed?"

"If you mean am I prepared to bring an open mind to whatever it is you wish to discuss with me—yes. What is it?"

"When it is settled, you understand that you are free to go wherever you will." He paused as though expecting her to say something, then went on. "All this has arisen from Young Henry's death last year at Château Martel—since then, nothing can be the same . . . but we must get used to that and do . . . do the best we can with what's left."

To her great dismay, Eleanor saw that this mention of his dead son had brought tears to his hard blue eyes. One might almost have thought that it was Henry's death which had brought them together; but Henry had been dead for months. Also, with Henry, one must remember, sentiment was never a decisive factor. It was there, running alongside his main purpose; it seldom took the lead. She waited.

Henry made a fresh start.

"Richard has been behaving abominably," he said. "Hobnobbing with young Philip of France; insulting the people I send out to help him rule; trying to cheat the revenues, and wasting money right and left . . ."

"Wasting? That sounds most unlike Richard."

"He's my heir now, bear that in mind," said Henry, ignoring the interruption. "He's the heir . . . and I learned by lesson with poor Harry. Heirs should stay at home and serve their apprenticeship. So what I propose is this; I shall bring Richard home and have him where I can see him day and night; he's going to sit in Chancellory and learn what drudgery ruling is; and sit in the Council and learn how to govern. No more galloping off to these tournaments, inviting any young hothead to break his skull in for him; no more going about arm-in-arm with Philip of France. I'll tame Master Richard if it's the last thing I do!"

"A little late in the day perhaps," Eleanor said. "He is twenty-seven."

"Time he learned sense. And this is where I need your help. . . ." He broke off again and after a second's hesitation said again, "My heir's place is here, by me."

"I agree that he should spend some time in England," she said. England was of great importance, she could see that, had always seen it; an independent kingdom engirdled by the sea, a land of boundless possibilities, not half realised yet, that was beginning, under Henry's strong rule, to emerge as a united country, the Norman blood and the Saxon mingling their peculiar virtues.

It occurred to her that Henry was about to ask her to go to Aquitaine and act as deputy for Richard, while he came to England to serve his apprenticeship in the craft of ruling.

"It would have to be tactfully done," she said. "I think," she checked herself—she must be tactful too! "Wouldn't it be best to do exactly what you did with Henry—have Richard crowned now? That would bring him to England and fix his interest here."

"Oh no, no," Henry brushed that suggestion aside, "that wouldn't do at all! I made a mistake with poor Henry which I don't propose to repeat. I plan no more honours for Richard, who has misused those he has already. That is where I want your help. There's only one way to get the upper hand of Richard, and you are the only one who can do it."

Still unsuspicious, she said, "I . . . well, Richard and I have always been friends, but I should hesitate to claim much influence over him *now*. After all, he has had many years in which to learn to do without me."

"Aquitaine and Poitou belong to you. You chose to cede them to Richard in your lifetime, but they are still yours. You gave them. You can take them back. Stripped of *them*, he'll soon come to heel and be glad to turn his attention to England. And John can have Aquitaine—it's time he had something."

Surprise and dismay held her silent for a moment; then she said slowly,

"You are asking me to take my Duchy from Richard and give it to John?"

Henry nodded, his eyes intent upon her face.

"I should never dream of doing anything so unjust, so mad," she said.

"Now, now, let us not be hasty," said Henry, the effort not to be hasty forcing the dark colour into his wooden-looking face. "You are surprised, you've had no time to think. I have, and I can see all the advantages of the plan. Just sit quietly and think it over, then tell me why you think it unjust and mad."

"I can tell you that without taking time to think," Eleanor said with some spirit. "The first injustice would be to Richard, whom I acknowledged as my heir when he was still a child, whom I took and showed to my people, and who was accepted by them. His ways are not your ways; his methods are not your methods; but in Aquitaine, his rightful place, he has not ruled badly. He has been hampered by the very limited power you have allowed him—driven almost mad at times by the interference of your officials—all the same, he has done a great deal there to establish order and to curb the power of the great barons. The common people love him; the second injustice would be to them. Even these tournaments which you so much deplore endear him to the people—they are very proud that their Duke should be the best and most famous knight in Christendom. They accepted Richard as my heir, and in their eyes —as in mine—he will be Duke until he dies. Apart from everything else, Henry, you establish a very dangerous precedent when you treat a legal claim to land as though it were something to be passed from hand to hand according to whim."

"There is John to consider," Henry said stubbornly. "All this chatter about justice! Is it fair that Richard should have so much and John nothing?"

Eleanor noticed that there was no talk this evening about Ireland —and she knew why.

She said, "Henry, you held many lands before you became King of England; so far as I remember, nobody suggested that when you came to the throne some of your old properties should be taken away and given to *your* younger brother. And there is this to consider, too; to send John to Aquitaine would be a death sentence. Look at the way he behaved in Ireland! Even locked away in Winchester, I heard how he pulled the beards of the old chieftains when they came to do him homage; how he said their stinking breath so tainted his hand, when they kissed it, that they must kiss his foot instead; and how when they tried to do so, he lifted his foot and tipped them over, to the vast amusement of the crowd of raffish young men in his court! There is a talent for ruling, as there is for other things, and it is a talent that John has not. My Aquitainians would not bear with him for a week! Have you forgotten what they did to your man Salisbury when he insulted them? Heaven is my witness, they cut him into such small pieces you could have made a pie. Take away Richard whom they love and give them John, and I tremble to think what would happen."

She awaited his rage; but he stayed patient. Had she been in a mood to notice, she would have seen how ominous that patience was—the patience of the hunter, sure of the kill, moving softly, in no hurry.

"Much of what you say is reasonable. I am aware of John's faults —as I am of Richard's. We must not be hasty." He looked about the room. "I ordered . . . ah, yes, it was remembered. You will drink? It is the best red wine of Bordeaux." He poured the wine into two silver flagons and, raising his own, said, "To the happy solution of this knotty problem. Now, the thing that sticks in my mind like a barb is this, so long as Richard has Aquitaine I shall never have my way with him. . . ."

"Because, from the beginning," said Eleanor, "your attitude towards him has been at fault. Oh, I know you are fond of him and would be more fond if he would allow himself to be led by the nose. But he is a man, ripe for responsibility. He's not a fool. He can sense that you regard his rights, even his titles, so lightly that you can propose removing them and giving them elsewhere. I could make Richard see reason, even to the extent of persuading him to come to England for a long time and serve, as you say, his appren-ticeship to kingship. But not if John had Aquitaine. . . ."

"I do not propose to give John much power in Aquitaine. He is young, he lacks experience, but *that* the council I should appoint could supply. And you, if you wished, could go with him."

"I would not dare," she said simply. "If I played false to Richard and Aquitaine, I should never be able to look him, or my people, in the face again."

Henry's hard-held patience gave way,

"If you persist in this stubbornness, you will never have occasion to. Thwart me now and you go straight back to Winchester!"

So that was the condition.

She stared at the tapestry; its picture and pattern became so much a part of the agonised indecision of the moment that years later she was to say, "Take it down, cut it to pieces, burn it! I cannot bear the sight of it." She knew that, if she went back to Winchester, it would probably be for life; could she condemn herself? The loneliness, the boredom, the endless grey empty days. She con-trasted it with the other life, she and John in Poitou, in Aquitaine in the sunshine. Could she control John, teach him to rule? No; the answer came blunt and inescapable; on such a gross breach of faith, no good thing could be built; the woman who, clear-sighted and deliberate, could commit such a breach merely in order to be comfortable would have forfeited all right to respect.

She said in the cool way which had always had power to madden Henry,

"Why drag in the unimportant? What does it matter where *I* am? It is the whereabouts of Richard and John that we were dis-cussing."

The angry blood surged into Henry's face, reddening his very eyes.

"Give me a straight answer," he demanded. "Will you or won't you?"

"Disinherit Richard? I will not. I cannot. Nor can you, nor any man alive. I am not being stubborn, Henry. I agree with you that

Richard should spend more time in England; I am willing to help you to persuade him to do so, but I cannot take away his legal right. You, with your respect for law, must know that, if he ruled badly, were bedridden, or raving mad, he would still be Duke of Aquitaine."

"You could have done it. But I will still have my way. I can't make John Duke of Aquitaine without your help, that is true; but I can put a stop to Richard's goings on. I'll clap him in the Tower to cool his heels. I've evidence enough of his plottings with the King of France to behead him for treason! That surprises you!"

"Very little. For one thing Richard is bound to be drawn to those who treat him like a man, not as a schoolboy; and your treatment of me has hardly been such as would endear you to any *loyal* son of mine."

"If it has come to a conflict of loyalties, I must bring a little persuasion to bear upon him. He's out there now, tinkling a tune, unarmed and unsuspicious. Unless you change your mind, he shall be in the Tower by midnight, and there he shall stay until I have his full allegiance. And John shall go as deputy to Aquitaine. You underrate him—he can be charming when he chooses; your Aquitainians might like him better than you suspect. At least he won't be always sitting in the King of France's pocket; he is *my* loyal son. I give you one more chance to change your mind; my proposal, or you in Winchester and Richard in the Tower?"

She said smoothly, "The one thing that you *will* ignore, Henry, is that Richard is of age. I can choose for myself, but I would not venture to choose for him. He might well prefer the Chancellory to the Tower—most men would. Why not call him in and ask?"

Henry stared at her; and, slowly, the full significance of that speech dawned on him. How clever she was! Call Richard in and say—"Either you promise to come home and do my bidding, or your mother goes back to Winchester." *She* knew which Richard would choose; and she would have given in while seeming to hold out . . . oh, very clever.

He went to the door and opened it; the sound of music and voices flooded into the room. He called from the doorway; there was a silence; then Richard came, entering the room with the smile dying away in his eyes. It was replaced by that look of wariness with which he always regarded his father.

"It would be best if you explained the situation," Eleanor said. She left her chair and stood by the end of a table where four tall wax candles burned in a branching stand.

"Well, Richard," Henry began, his voice a little too jovial, a little blustering, because, brought face-to-face with his heir, what he was about to propose seemed a trifle farfetched.

"Your mother and I have been . . ." He got no further, for Eleanor gave a scream and began to flap—for a woman of such good sense, in a singularly helpless manner—at her long veil, which had swept across the candles and was, in a second, all ablaze.

Richard ran to her and began to beat the flames with his hands; Henry would have come to help had not Eleanor cried, "Oh my hair, my hair. Fetch water, quickly."

Henry went blundering to the door. In a cool, incisive whisper Eleanor said, "Take a horse and ride to Dover. Stop for nothing. He plans to arrest you."

In the outer room Henry was shouting for water, and somebody said, "Ale will do"; then the King and John and all the young women were thronging into the room. Someone emptied a horn cup of ale over Eleanor's head so that she did not see Richard's going.

She said—not quite untruthfully—"I feel faint," and allowed herself to be led to the settle. Alys mopped the ale and smuts from her face while Marguerite picked the charred fragments of veil from her hair. John brought a stool for her feet, and Henry, tut-tutting at the interruption, awkwardly offered her a cup of wine, which somehow spilled into her lap so that there was more confusion, mopping of the gown, refilling of the cup. And all the time she waited, counting her heartbeats.

There were the inevitable inquiries as to how the mishap had occurred, and, laughing shakily, she said, "I was clumsy. I am not used to such a gauzy veil, nor to seeing four candles in a cluster.

In future I must be more careful!" And because that speech brought Winchester into all their minds, there was a moment of discomfort, then several people began to talk at once.

All in all, it was quite a long time, quite a long, useful time, before Henry looked round sharply and said, "Where's Richard? Where did he go?"

CHAPTER THREE

She was back in Winchester again; and now the conditions of her former imprisonment appeared, as she looked back, to have been luxurious in the extreme. Even in these short winter days, she was allowed but one candle and must go to bed when it was spent; on the coldest day there was nothing but green wood and smouldering turfs for her fire; the food was scantier and more roughly served. There was a change, too, in the manner of Nicolas of Saxham, and—on his rare visits—of Lord de Glanville. They had always been harsh gaolers, now they were insolent, too.

It was clear that Henry had set himself either to break down her spirit and force her to his will, or to punish her every day, in countless small ways, for her defiance.

When she came to her prison room again, she found that her lute, her chessboard and men, and her needlework had all been removed. In their place on the table by the window, where the dust slowly gathered, was something new. An inkhorn, a newly sharpened quill, and a large parchment. The last was a whole sheepskin, and, looking at it with an imaginative eye, one could still see the animal's shape; the head and the legs had been lopped off. The parchment was already covered with writing, very fair writing, three columns

of it, in three languages: Latin up by the neck; the French of
Aquitaine, with its distinctive spelling, in the middle; humble English, only just recognised as an official language, most suitably placed
on the rump, by the tail. All three began in the same way:

"I, Eleanor, by the Grace of God Duchess of Aquitaine and
Countess of Poitou, being of sound mind and acting of my own free
will, do hereby . . ." and in three languages, with many twists and
turns of legal phrases, they all said the same thing—that she withdrew from her son Richard all the powers and titles with which
she had endowed him, and bestowed these same powers upon her
son John. At the foot of each column there was a space for her
signature and her seal. In a little box beside the inkhorn there was
the necessary wax and the small gold seal with which to mark it.

"You are, from this moment, your own gaoler; the key is in your
hand!" Henry had said.

It was when she looked at this document that she was glad that
Henry had seen fit to send her back to Winchester without Amaria.
At the moment it had seemed the most cruel blow of all; but it
was merciful. For Amaria would most certainly have pleaded with
her to sign, to turn the key. But Amaria was gone, and in her place
was an ugly, shambling old woman, chosen by Nicolas of Saxham.
Her name was Kate; in her youth she had been one of the camp-
following washerwomen; she had been in a siege and almost starved
to death; all but one of her teeth had fallen out, and the one remaining hung like a fang over her withered lower lip. The archers
for whom she had washed and with whom she had suffered starvation had been in the service of a queen—Kate had forgotten which
one, but Eleanor, when she heard the story, guessed that it was
Matilda, Henry's mother—and, on account of her sufferings during
the siege, Kate had little use for queens. From the point of view
of Henry and Nicolas of Saxham, she was the ideal companion for
this stubborn Queen, and during the first three months of Eleanor's
new imprisonment, she added to her discomfort in every possible
way.

Deprived of all occupation, all companionship, Eleanor faced an indefinite sentence of what, to all intents and purposes, was solitary confinement, the fate which usually leads to madness. To be alone with one's self, to have only one's thoughts for company, was, for some reason, a thing which only great saints and madmen could bear. What was there? What entertainment could be wrung out of one's own mind—apart from just memories of one's past?—memories so often painful, leading nowhere but to this prison room?

One could remember other things—songs and poems, for example. Better still, one could with some skill and much determination make new songs, new poems.

Now there, she thought, is an occupation. Every morning I will choose one of the songs I have heard in the past; what words I remember I will recite to myself aloud; what words I forget I will search for, wrestle for all day, until I catch them; then I will set myself a new theme and fit it to the measure of that day's song; and sometimes I will make it difficult for myself; I will make each line begin with the same letter or with a letter which is part of a word; I will make patterns with words; I will set myself hard tasks, such as making a whole song without the use of the word "and"; the variety is endless. . . .

Because Kate had deliberately made herself less companionable than a dog, never volunteering a remark and often not answering when spoken to, it was easy for Eleanor to ignore her presence; and because it was necessary, in order to judge the value of one's song to *hear* it, she fell into the habit of chanting her song-poems aloud. Since her life had narrowed down to this one dull empty room, the songs she remembered with most ease and pleasure, the ones she made most successfully, were always songs of great doings, of courage in battle, of adventure by land and sea, of far, strange places, and of people cut to no ordinary pattern.

It was weeks before she noticed that whenever, at the end of the day, she started her recital of the day's work, testing its quality, and grinding its pattern into her mind so that she might have that much more of excitement to remember tomorrow, Kate invariably ceased whatever she was doing—ceased even her endless chewing (for Kate, unlike Amaria, was trusted by the gaolers, had free access to the kitchen, and always had something to mumble upon with her toothless jaws) and would squat down in a corner and listen as a dog might.

One evening in April, when Eleanor had been back at Winchester for three months, she went to the window; outside, the twilight was blue and lingering, and in the garden, where now she was never permitted to walk, the daffodils were blowing golden. She began to try over to herself the verses she had made that day. They were part of a long poem which had occupied her for more than a week; it concerned the story of Helen and the Siege of Troy. Because it was April, winter's end, the supply of salt meat was low in the casks and the portion served to the Queen that day had been even smaller than usual and almost uneatable. More than mere imagination had gone into her description of the hunger of the besieged in Troy, and now she sang with great feeling of how, lying down to sleep with empty bellies, the hungry dreamed of food.

Ending her recital, and on the whole very well pleased with it, she looked down at her hands folded in her lap and wished for the hundredth time that they had left her her lute.

Kate's rough voice emerging from the shadowy corner startled her almost as much as a dog's would have done, had a dog suddenly spoken.

"Thass a masterous true song. Thass just how 'tis when you're famishing. Was you ever hungry, mistress?"

"I'm hungry now," Eleanor said.

A crafty look came into the old crone's eyes.

"If so be I was to fetch you a bite—a good bite, leg off a chicken maybe—would you finish the tale for me? Night arter night I set there and wonder how it'll all end, and night arter night you dole him out like a miser."

"The song isn't finished yet; I'm making a piece each day. But in return for anything you could find me to eat, I could finish the story for you."

Kate hobbled away and was soon back with almost half a cold

fowl, a slice of pease pudding, and a tiny delicious piece of marzipan. Kate's silence, once breached, must not be allowed to close down again, Eleanor thought, so, taking the food, she said,

"Thank you. Now, while I eat, tell me how you know that that was a true song."

"I been in a siege," Kate said simply. "Not in a grut town with towers; a miserable little place it wuz . . . but we held out three months all but a day, we did." In the plain but vivid language of the completely unlettered, she told the Queen her tale. "And me teeth thought, no doubt, I had no use for them no more, not having had a good champ lately, so they dropped away, and when the siege ended and such of us as warded death off was given real food to eat once more, me empty gums was so sore I couldn't take a good bite. I cried then. And I been chumbling something ever since to make up. Now what about that bargain we struck? You've et the food; tell me what happened to them pore chaps locked up in Troy city."

"Well . . ." Eleanor began, "their siege lasted longer than yours; but they held out, and presently the Greeks outside the walls grew tired and impatient. Then one day somebody had a very good idea; he thought of building a great wooden horse and . . ."

Kate interrupted angrily. "You ain't keeping your bargain. You're fobbing me off. I don't like the tale that way. I like it to roll out so that I go like this with my fingers." She tapped out the rhythm of the song.

"Well, for that you must wait until tomorrow. I haven't set the words in order yet."

"Then I'll wait. And to pay for the food I snatched for you, you can say again, proper fashion, the other one, about Roland and the horn and the one who should have come to help him and didn't. I liked that one. ' "Blow and I'll come," he said; "though Heaven fall, blow and I'll come though it be to the earth's end; on the edge of the earth where the demons gibber and clutch; blow and I'll come," he said.' I liked that one."

"I made that song two months ago," Eleanor said. "I fear I do not remember it."

"I do . . . I remember all the words; not the tune, I never could carry a tune. You start, beating it out proper fashion and, when you halt, I'll start you off again."

Deliberately, in the course of the song, Eleanor halted four or five times, fumbling for the word. Always Kate was ready with it. Astonished and excited, Eleanor realised that here, in this old woman, in this primitive, untutored mind, lay a great gift, hitherto unused, the gift for retaining, whole and pure, anything which attracted its fancy. What a discovery!

It had irked her, as the days and weeks went by, that the new song tended to push the older ones aside in her own mind. Songs she had learned in youth seemed to be engraved on her memory forever, but those she had learned more lately tended to slip away. And often she had thought that when, and if, she were ever a free woman again, with minstrels at her service, it would be pleasant to teach them some of the songs she had made; but if she forgot, they would be lost, since she had no parchment, no paper, upon which to write them down. If Kate's mind could act as a store . . . I will write on Kate's memory, Eleanor told herself delightedly.

Cautiously during the following days—for the old woman did not turn into a friend overnight—Eleanor probed Kate's talent. It had, like others, its limits; she never remembered a love song, for instance, nor a lullaby, nor any description of flowers, woods, or weather.

"I give no heed to such," was her answer to any question concerning them. What she heeded were the epic poems, the exciting stories of courage, treachery, bloodshed, and death. And she was inclined to have lapses of memory where anything concerning women was included.

"Me fingers stop twitching when it come to fair ladies," she explained later on when some kind of friendship had been established; "and when me fingers stop, the words slip by like water down a drain." Still, within its limits, her gift was unique, and

Eleanor made the most of it, never allowing the old woman to guess that she was being used. Nowadays the finished songs were resung and the new ones tried over as a favour.

"Indeed I shall not sing to you tonight. You were very rude to me this morning in front of the guard!" or "Kate, I have asked you again and again not to spit while I eat my broth. If you do it again, you'll never know what happened that night in Castle Beauregard!"

Very gradually, and upon Kate's part, grudgingly, they entered upon a new relationship. That was proved by something which happened late in the following autumn.

Kate seldom spent much of the day in Eleanor's room; she fetched water for the Queen's washing (where, if at all, she washed herself Eleanor never knew), kindled the fire, and shuffled away again, to return, in her own good time, with their breakfast. Then she disappeared until dinnertime, after which she slept for a while; went back to her gossip and the better fire, and the chance to pick up something to chew upon in the main hall; and returned in time for the evening's entertainment, bringing the one candle with her.

But one morning she came hobbling in a full hour before dinner-time, and, shifting whatever it was she was chewing into the pouch of her cheek, said,

"There's a pedlar fellow below, call hisself Alberic. He come once afore, a while back. He say back in the old time he useter sell you things. Now he ain't to be let in, so Old Nick say; but if you want to see him—well, Old Nick is out hunting, and I daresay it could be managed."

"I would dearly love to see Alberic . . . but not if it is going to cause trouble. What about the guard on the door in the passage?"

"He wouldn't cross me; he dussent! Besides, I do a tidy bit for all the soldiers, one way and another; washing and mending and such. Well, shall I bring him up?"

"You must warn him first that I have no money—no money at all."

"I told him that in the fust place, but he said that don't matter."

Alberic bustled in, looking just as he had when she saw him

last, a year ago. He threw his pack on the floor and went down on his knees, saying, in a voice tremulous with emotion,

"My lady! I feared I should never be allowed to see you again. Oh, what a sorry state of things!"

"It is good to see you," Eleanor said, almost as much moved as the little pedlar. "Have you news for me?"

Alberic scrambled to his feet and turned to Kate.

"Here, old mother, take this and help yourself to what you fancy. There's raisins and dried plums there; and a bit of a sugar cone. Have what you like." He deposited the pack in the passage just outside the open door. Kate squatted down beside it and began to loosen the straps.

"Now," said Eleanor, "what news?"

He gave it to her quickly; Duke Richard had been rebelling again and attacking his father's strongholds in Anjou, and the King of France had been helping; so King Henry had gone all the way to Gisors, to the great elm tree which was the traditional place for the Kings of France and England to meet and bargain and try to settle their differences. But this meeting had been a failure because the Duke and the King of France had walked away laughing together; the King had been very angry, and the fighting had gone on.

Hardly pausing for breath, Alberic carried his tale to the end. Well, now all the talk in the taverns was about the new crusade. The old heathen had been rampaging about in the Holy Land again, killing folks and burning places, so the Bishop of Jerusalem had sent to ask the King of England to lead a crusade; first he said he wouldn't, but now he was swinging round to the idea because that would be one way to stop all this quarrelling and fighting nearer home. It looked as though he reckoned that the Holy Father in Rome might step in and make all the Dukes and Kings promise to live in peace together while the crusade was on. And, most likely, there *was* something in all this talk because taxes had gone up something shameful. That was all the news he could think of, worth telling. No, no marriages or anything like that. Prince John hadn't married the Lady of Gloucester yet, and it was common talk that one of the things the King of France had against the King of England was that he kept putting off the wedding between Princess Alys of France and Duke Richard. And now, before he went, was there anything madam would like from his pack? He knew about the money but that didn't bother him; them that lived longest would see most, and them that laughed last laughed longest!

"If His Grace goes on crusade, madam, anything might happen. There's a lot of people in England coming round to the idea that you've been ill done by. Bad as the old days under King Stephen it is, to lock anybody up, no trial, no jury, no nothing."

He did not, Eleanor noticed, add "no crime"; on the wings of a popular and very tuneful song, the untrue but romantic story of Queen Eleanor and Fair Rosamonde had been carried the length and breadth of England, and most people believed Eleanor to be a poisoner at least. But they were "coming round," as the English always did come round, to the side of the one who appeared to be treated unjustly, however guilty that one might be.

"Have you anything upon which I could write, Alberic, in your pack?"

"Alas, no, my lady. But I could get it. I'll get it in the town and bring it up tomorrow and smuggle it in. Yon old woman would carry it to you if she's properly asked; and she's not so bad. Back in the summer when I called, I thought she was dim-witted, she was so daft when I tried to wheedle her, but she was all right today and real excited at the thought of breaking the rules."

"Do that, then, my good friend, and I shall be everlastingly grateful to you; and if ever I have a chance to repay . . ."

"Never mind that. It's a pleasure to be of service," said Alberic, and he skipped nimbly away.

He had been right about Kate; next day, when she brought in the dinner, she had a neat parcel under her shawl.

"That pedlar fellow arst me to hand you this and to say that, if you want a letter taken anywhere, he'll hang about for a time down below. Oh, and he still hev his friend what go to Bordeaux, whatever that may mean."

"And would you, Kate, take him a letter, if I wrote one? Secretly, I mean."

"Wouldn't hurt me to, I reckon."

Eleanor sat down straightaway and wrote to Richard, smiling a little as she unstoppered the inkhorn. If Henry could see to what purpose she was putting his ink! She was less careful now than formerly about writing anything which might increase the enmity between father and son. Since her visit to Windsor, she had hardened against Henry, and to hear that he might be going on crusade, to see the East and all its glories, to win himself honour, while she rotted here, hardened her still more. So now she wrote to the son in whom lay her main hope of freedom, "The moment he goes, Richard, come and set me free."

CHAPTER FOUR

With Henry's departure and Richard's coming to look forward to, she settled herself to wait again, to preserve her health by all means possible, and to hold on to her sanity. In these aims old Kate was now an ally, though still gruff of speech and inclined, now and then, to make a gesture of independence. Her raids on the kitchen often brought some tasty, welcome scrap to eke out the meagre diet; her friendliness with the servants often resulted in a log of burnable wood or an extra candle; and at Christmas, when she received, with the other menials, her "dole" of grey homespun cloth, she insisted upon the Queen accepting it and making it into a loose, long-sleeved garment to wear over her gown. Best of all, her insistent demand for stories drove Eleanor to persist in her hobby, even at times when her own interest had flagged.

One day they invented a new game. It arose out of one of Kate's rare references to her own past. In her days as a camp-following washerwoman, she had lived among archers, and had a good opinion of them and of their craft.

"Stand to reason they're the best men," she said. "Do they turn to drinking or loose living, they don't keep their sharp eyes or steady hands for long. And in a battle they ain't got nothing to trust to except their eyes and their arms and the arrows they sharpened up for theirselves—and thass the way men should be. Man in mail on horseback, what is he? Just a little old moving castle and, according to whether he hev money for good mail and a clever steed, he's good or bad. I like archers. . . ." A dreamy, remembering look came into her old eyes. "There was one once taught me to shoot. You can believe this or not, according to your fancy, mistress, but I could split a peeled wand with the best in my day."

"I believe you," Eleanor said. "I practised archery when I was young. I never split a wand, but I once brought down a hawk which was raiding our pigeon cote."

"Did you so?" Kate's voice was tinged with respect. "If you was free to come and go like me, one day we'd hev a match and see how much of our cunning we'd kept down the years. But you can't go in the yard, and this room ain't big enough for taking aim in—leastways not with arrows."

Some days later she came hobbling in carrying a biggish bundle done up in a piece of cloth; her expression was triumphant.

"I been thinking something out," she announced, laying the bundle on the table. "Now we'll see if she'll work or no."

She took out, first, a square board measuring about eighteen inches each way, and bearing upon one side a neat circular target; the centre was red and the surrounding rings alternated black and white.

"See? And here's a nail, and I borrowed a hammer. I reckoned if we nailed her up on that wall there, she'd get what light there is.

And then . . . look at these, I reckon they're a masterpiece. Martin made them for me." She held out a number of miniature arrows; they were four inches long, tipped with iron, but not barbed, and fledged with clipped goose quills. "I thought we could hev a throwing match; that'd test our eyes and our hands at least. What do you think, mistress?"

"I think that is a wonderful idea, Kate. Let's hang it up and try at once."

"I ain't going to nail the board to the wall; I got Martin to put a loop on her back, so she go up and take down easy, and she mustn't ever be up when Old Nick or nobody else make the rounds. For one thing, he'd take it away, and for another, they'd reckon we was up to no good." She balanced one of the little arrows in her hand. "And it's a fact; this here'd kill a man if you sent it full force into his eye, or got the right spot in his neck where the life-blood is." She seemed to derive a sinister pleasure from this thought.

The new game proved to be the source of endless amusement; beginning as a simple test of skill to see which of them could score a hit on, or most nearly on, the red centre of the target, it developed new rules and intricacies as the days went by. A system of points was introduced; a direct centre hit counted twenty; the inmost white circle, fifteen; the inmost black, ten; the outer white, five; the outer black, one. The reckonings were held to this simple form because Kate's arithmetic was limited to what she could count on her fingers and toes. But varieties were easy to find; sometimes, for a whole game, some portion of the target was out of bounds and a hit there took away all the points already gained. There was one rule which Eleanor alone must observe—Kate must not be beaten too thoroughly or too often; she had a childish dislike for defeat and made no attempt to hide her annoyance. Since Eleanor was younger and slightly, but definitely, more skilled, the business of losing often enough, and not obviously, lent an extra zest to the game.

Within the prison walls circumstances had eased a little, but outside the prospect had darkened. Alberic, in the autumn, had spoken to her of the new crusade, and, in the spring of the following year, the Archbishop of Jerusalem himself had come to visit Henry in England to add his persuasions. And Henry had promised that if a truce, the Truce of God as they called it, could be arranged among the quarrelling rulers of Europe—his own sons included—then he would raise and lead an army to fight for the Holy Land.

Now less dependent upon Alberic, since Kate would occasionally report any scrap of news she picked up (but here again, Kate's memory was choosy and she only noticed what interested her), Eleanor heard about the Archbishop's visit and Henry's renewed promise, and hope of a speedy release rose again in her heart. Alberic, when he visited Winchester in the summer of 1185, carried away another letter for Richard. "Promise anything," Eleanor wrote, "so that he goes; and then come for me." There had been no answer to her former letter, though Alberic swore that it had reached Richard; but this one was received and answered with such speed that the faithful little pedlar, in order to deliver it, was back in Winchester a full five weeks before his half-yearly visit was due.

"How can I promise to maintain a truce with him while he holds you in prison?" Richard wrote. "To free you, I must then break the truce and have all Christendom at my throat. Far better to hold my course and beat him in the open field. That I shall do, with God's help. It will take a year. Have patience and be of good cheer for one year more."

One year. What was that to her who had already sat out so many?

Bit by bit, often so late that it had lost all significance when it reached her, the news came in.

Frightening news—Philip of France and Henry of England and Richard of Aquitaine had met and settled their differences; the Truce of God was in being, and Henry could go on crusade. What did that mean? That Richard had changed his mind, after all, and meant to abandon her to this living death?

Heartening news—Philip of France had been the one to break the truce; he had attacked Henry's Norman provinces because

Richard had attacked one of his strongholds. That could mean only one thing; craftily, doggedly, Richard was moving towards that battle in the open field upon which he staked his hope of independence . . . and she, her hopes of freedom.

The new war lasted not one year, but four. And sorrow struck again during that time; Geoffrey died of fever. Only Richard left now . . . and John. And the days going by, leaden-footed as one lived through their long hours, but on wings as one looked backwards and forwards. Sit straight in the chair to keep one's frame from sagging; bargain with Kate for that extra mouthful that mattered; brush one's hair, wash, make the most fastidious toilet possible; amuse oneself with desperate deliberation; cling to health, cling to sanity . . . but all to what end? At any moment, even now as she thought, Richard might be lying dead on the battlefield; and Henry, though he would weep over the body and speak of David and Absalom, would never, never in a thousand years, realise why his son had been his enemy; Henry would never set her free. Not even for dead Richard's sake. She would die here, shut away.

The years passed. New Year's came of the year 1189. On her birthday she would be sixty-seven; she had been in prison for fifteen years.

CHAPTER FIVE

"There's plague in the place now," Kate said one lovely morning in early June. "Martin, what made the arrows for me, and that fat chap, what I made the new jerkin for only last week, they're

both dead. And seven more are sick. Martin they reckoned et something bad, and the other had a cut on his finger that didn't do . . .
but now they know." She gave her report without any sign of feeling. "That don't concern me; I lived through a plague when I was a
bit of a girl; me father and mother, and all me sisters and brothers,
six of them, died—so did the parish priest, so there was nobody to
bury them, I remember that. But I pulled round. And, once you've
had it, you're safe for life; thass one comfort."

She was very callous at heart, Eleanor thought; but even as she
thought thus, the old woman dived into her pocket and brought
out something that looked like a very small hedgehog.

"I made you this pomander ball," she said, holding it out. "The
orange was old and a bit wizened to start with, so I dried it off by the
fire in one night, thinking you'd best hev it right soon. I had a bit
of a job getting the cloves from the cook, I might tell you—they cost
fourpence apiece, or so he say."

Eleanor took the orange, which was dried almost as hard as stone
and studded all over with cloves. Her words of thanks were lost in
a cackle of laughter from Kate.

"Thass a curious thing," the old woman said, "I've just bin thinking . . . when a girl's young, it's good for her to be pretty, 'cause
then men can't refuse her anything; but when she's old, it's best
to be real ugly, 'cause then they *dassent* refuse her on account of
they reckon she's a witch and'll put the evil eye on them. Taken
all in all, I reckon my ugly looks hev done me more good than my
pretty ones did. Anyway, I give him a rare ugly look and he give
me the cloves, so you should be all right."

"It was very kind of you, Kate, and very thoughtful. If I live,
and if I ever get free again, I shall remember this and other things
you have done for me, and I . . ."

But Kate's supply of civility was exhausted; some rudeness was
necessary to restore the balance.

"You won't remember me," she said scornfully. "I know women.
If that door was flung open for you this minute, you'd tramp over
my body to get through it. Moreover, the pomander ball wasn't

meant for kindness, 'twas to save me the bother of tending you on your deathbed." That speech restored her self-respect, and in a very few minutes she was able to say in her normal voice, "Well, how about a game with the arrows?"

Two days passed. There was another death—the cook who had grudged the cloves suddenly sickened. "Turned away from the gooseberry pie he was making, the first this year, spun round like a top, and fell by the wall and died," said Kate. There were no other deaths for a while; and there was no panic. A case or two of plague was almost customary in summertime; most people who had reached their twenties had lived through several plagues and developed some degree of immunity. The really bad times always came after periods when there had been no plague for some years, or when it suddenly changed its nature and its method of attack.

Ten days after Kate had given her the pomander ball, Eleanor woke in the night, suddenly so overheated that the bed felt as though it were on fire. She moved to throw off some of the covers and found that all her joints were stiff and painful; she ached from head to heel. Without the covers she was rapidly chilled, and from burning heat passed to such icy cold that her teeth chattered and her shudders shook the bed on which she lay. She went to pull the covers back, reaching out an arm that ached as though it were on the rack and raising her head. A heavy ball of iron seemed intent upon beating its way through the bones of her skull.

I have plague: I shall die, she thought. And the sweat broke out all over her skin. I need not have worried about the passing of time . . . trying to save myself for the future . . . there is no future. I, Eleanor, by the Grace of God Duchess of Aquitaine and Countess of Poitou . . . but I won't sign; nothing will make me sign; though the crafty wretch knew what a temptation that would be when he said, "The key is in your hand" . . . I won't sign it . . . am about to die. I'm going to die, here in prison, of the plague. I'll die, and they'll shovel me underground and no one will know why I was in prison . . . or care! Even Richard doesn't know what it was Henry tried to make me agree to at Windsor; there wasn't time to tell him then, and I could never bring myself to write it. I didn't want Richard to bear the weight of knowing I was locked away because I would not withdraw his inheritance and let John have it.

John must not have Aquitaine. The way he behaved in Ireland . . . And suppose Richard is killed in this fighting . . . no heir, no heir . . . and that is Henry's fault; he's kept Richard and Alys apart, spinning his webs, making his schemes for John . . . Richard, no heir . . . Then Aquitaine must go to Arthur, Geoffrey's son. I must make a will . . . of course, that's it, I must make a will, a will, a will . . . Thy will be done. There, see how the mind slides from one thing to another when one is sick. I must be calm, wait for morning, and make a will . . .

She lay, willing herself to be calm, while the waves of heat and cold and nausea followed one another.

Mercifully daylight came early in June; the narrow window grew grey, grew pinkish gold, grew blue. Faraway somewhere the cuckoo was calling, calling, an aching, lonely cry; and presently Kate stirred from her slumbers.

"The pomander ball, Kate . . . it didn't work. I am stricken. I feel so ill, Kate, so ill. And there is so much to do before I can die. Kate, you must help me; help me to the table so that I can write."

Brushing the sleep out of her gummy eyes with one hand, the old woman reached out the other and prodded with her fingers beneath the Queen's chin and arms.

"You ain't swelled yet. Mainly they do, big as pullets' eggs. But you're sick, mistress; aye, you're sick." Withdrawing her hand, she stepped back a pace or two. As she did so, stark terror shot through Eleanor. Kate had only to walk away and stay away for an hour or two, as no one would question her right to do, and when she returned it might be to find a dead woman on the bed.

"Don't leave me, Kate. Stay by me now, help me to the table so that I can write; at least do that, Kate. I'll reward you. I must make my will, and the first thing I write shall be that you shall have . . ." (she was about to add "a pension," but, as things were, who could be sure that it would ever be paid?; if Richard lost this war he couldn't, and Henry wouldn't) ". . . my great diamond, Kate. That is entirely mine; it was a gift to me, nothing to do with anyone else, no one can withstand your claim to that . . . if once I get it down in writing. So help me, quickly."

She half raised herself in the bed, and the ball of iron in her skull tried again to break its way through. She fell back weakly.

"Don't fret yourself," Kate said. "Lay easy a minute."

She hobbled into the outer room and, after a little time, came back carrying the flat board on which the painted target was now almost pecked away by the points of the little arrows. Propping it against Eleanor's bed, she went to her own and dragged off the pillow and one cover. Then, with surprising gentleness, she put her hands under the Queen's arms and raised her, inch by inch, wedging the extra pillow behind her and wrapping the cover about her shoulders. She laid the board over Eleanor's knees and shuffled off to fetch the inkhorn, the pen, and the remaining pieces of vellum which Alberic had provided.

The will was very short, two sentences: the first bequeathing "the great diamond given me by my Uncle Raymond of Antioch to Kate, faithful servant and companion to me in prison"; the second stating briefly and clearly that in the event of Richard dying heirless, "all the domains inherited by me from my father, Duke of Aquitaine, Count of Poitou, and now vested in the said Richard Plantagenet are to be passed in their entirety to my grandson Arthur of Brittany, son of Geoffrey Plantagenet."

Not a word wasted; but it took long to write. Sometimes one quill point travelled across one piece of vellum resting on one flat board; then, suddenly, there would be three of each, a dozen, an infinite number of them, shaking and blurring together as though a heat haze hung between them and her eyes; and then again the whole scene would be blotted out, and the darkness would come down, and she would think . . . this is death, the darkness of death . . .

It was done at last, and in a faint breathless voice she said,

"It should have a witness. The priest, Kate, that would be best . . . fetch Sir Wilfred."

"You'll need him anyway," Kate said in her downright, callous way. But, as she hobbled away again, she mumbled, "Dear me, dear me, to think it should all end like this. *And who will sing for me now?*"

Now, before the darkness came down for the last time, there was the letter to Richard.

Her mind was growing incoherent.

"Hold it dear, as it has cost me dear; any moment these five years I could have signed it away from you to John, and gone free."

". . . to Arthur. But better still, oh I do beg you, Richard, marry and rear a boy of your own. John gave proof in Ireland . . ."

It rambled on, but that too was done at last, and still Kate had not returned. Lingering to snatch a breakfast piece in the hall most probably . . .

But presently she came in, moving as swiftly as her stiff old legs would allow, and accompanied, not by the castle priest, Sir Wilfred, but by the crazy fellow, Rolf, the Keeper of the Bees.

"The priest ain't here," she explained. "The town's worse stricken than we are here, and he's down there, busy burying the dead. So I thought of *him*," she indicated the beeman. "He can write like a scribe. And there's nobody else. Old Nick's writing man is out with the steward, rent-gathering."

Eleanor steadied her gaze on the huge, hairy, dirty old man, who, before her eyes, wavered and divided and multiplied and became a dozen, a regiment of huge, hairy, dirty old men.

They all said in a surprisingly gentle voice,

"I'm a clerk, madam, and have, in fact, never been unfrocked. My unfortunate case was still *sub judice* at the time of the tragedy at Canterbury and, before it was resumed, I had discovered how much preferable bees are to parishioners, and so . . ." He broke off as Kate gave him a sharp poke and hissed, "Stop blathering, blockhead."

"I am sorry, madam; I wished only to assure you that I am quite competent to act as your witness; I only regret the sad circumstances which make it necessary."

The exertion of writing her name seemed as great as that demanded for the whole of the will and the letter, but she signed, and then lay back with her eyes closed as the beeman, shimmering in a haze of his many likenesses, came near and wrote his name below hers on the will.

"And may Christ, in His infinite mercy, take your soul into safekeeping," he said.

"Amen," said Eleanor.

She lay for a moment, husbanding her strength. When she opened her eyes, the beekeeper had gone and Kate was standing near the bed.

"Now listen, Kate. You must carry these papers for me . . . not all the way, but to Alberic."

"But how can I do that and . . ."

"Wait . . . please, Kate . . . give me time."

It took time enough, for sometimes the thought would slip away before she had strength to word it; but Kate was listening attentively and, even at such a moment, it was comforting to be able to rely on that memory; no word of this long drawn-out gasping speech would be forgotten.

Alberic, regular as the seasons, was on his way to pay his summer visit to Winchester; he might be as little as two weeks' walk, or as much as five, away. All along the road he was well known. Kate was to set out for Guildford—leaving Winchester secretly, and at each village she must ask if the little pedlar had yet paid his summer visit. If she reached a village where he had been, without meeting him on the way, then she would know that he had turned off the main road, and she must ask which way he went . . . he would be in the district somewhere. And when she had found him, she must give him the letter for the Duke of Aquitaine, and the will . . . the will for . . .

Lying there, racked with pain, she had driven her dizzy brain to the solving of the problem—who was the safest person to entrust with the will. The answer was decisive: the King of France. He would be impartial, and he was the liege lord of the lands concerned.

"This, for the King of France. I will write on it; you, I know, would not forget, but Alberic might. Tell him with all speed, great speed, Kate, for I might die today. You steal out now. I trust you, Kate . . . be swift, be secret, above all things be secret . . . and bless you; may Heaven reward you for what you have done for me."

The faint, thready voice ceased.

"But how can I go and just leave you, mistress, to die like a dog without even so much as a sip of water in your need."

"Kate, you carry the fate of thousands . . . leave the one. I . . . shan't die like . . . a dog . . . I shall die . . . like a Duchess . . . whose will mustn't be . . . sacrificed to sips of water. Go, I tell you. Go."

The effort to impose the order, to speak with authority, was too much; everything, Kate's face, the bits of vellum, the humps her own feet made under the bedclothes, came together and began to spin in a crazy wheel which grew darker and darker . . .

Kate stayed by the bed until late in the afternoon, when the door of the outer room was thrown open. She had just time to snatch up the will and the letter and thrust them into her bodice. But it was only the priest; he had heard that the Queen was sick and her servant searching for him, and had come at once.

"But too late," he said, gazing at the insensible figure on the bed. "Poor lady, she is past all earthly aid. May God have mercy on her; she sinned greatly, but she suffered greatly too; and with patience."

"And now to die unshriven," said Kate. "Sir Priest, come in tomorrow; she might be sensible again then."

"No, no," he said, sadly, "I have seen too many these last days; they die in two ways, falling like an ox under the poleaxe, or drifting away in sleep, like this. The one in twenty that lies and cries and moans and can take bite and sup, that one lives. But I will come, certainly I will come."

"In the morning. Early," Kate said, and something urgent about her voice made the priest look at her curiously.

"My poor soul," he said kindly, "are you frightened to be alone with the dead? You need not, should not, be. The body, after the soul has departed, is nothing more than the empty shell after the bird has hatched."

"But you will come," Kate persisted.

"I will come."

Well, that was done; if the poor mistress lived till morning, the priest would know and carry the news.

When he was gone Kate routed out the shoes which she wore on her rare excursions out-of-doors; they were uncomfortable after the old woollen slippers she shook off, and she grimaced as she pushed her feet into them and thought of the miles of walking she must do. She then set a jug of water and a bowl of pease porridge on a stool by the bed; they would never be needed, she felt sure of that, but it eased her mind to know that she had neglected no precaution.

Before leaving she stood by the bed for a moment. Eleanor's face had changed already; a death mask in dirty wax, the closed eyes sunk into blackish purple hollows, a dark band of shadow round the mouth. And she was hardly breathing; Kate could count all her fingers and toes twice over between one of those painful rattling gasps and the next.

"Well," she said to the deaf ear, "I'm off to carry out your orders, and thass better than staying here moaning when there ain't another thing I can do for you, ain't it?"

The guard at the end of the passage greeted her cheerfully.

"Ain't seen much of you today, old mother. The sleeve's half out of my jerkin, will you oblige me by ramming in a stitch or two?"

"Not tonight," Kate said. "I gotta go in the town; some of me fambly down there is very sick and there's children to be tended. I might hev to stop all night. I might not be back very early in the morning. If I ain't, do me a good turn, will you, and look in at my mistress when you unlock."

"I go off at cockcrow."

"Then pass the word on. Will it be Eddie? He'd do that for me. She's poorly, too, but me fambly come first, and I don't want no hue and cry out arter me if I chance to be a bit late."

"I'll tell Eddie. And you'll mend me up when you get back?"

She nodded absently; his mention of her return brought up a new problem. What were her plans after she had found Alberic and handed over the documents? There was that great diamond to think of too; how could a poor old woman make sure of getting her rights? Better ask Alberic; he was smart, he'd think of something.

She hobbled along to the kitchen and helped herself to food. A young lamb, the first of the season, was turning on the spit, waiting for Nicolas of Saxham's return—he had been out hawking this fine day.

"You can cut me a little nobbly bit off the end of one leg," Kate said, wheedling but prepared to threaten if needs be; "the cut'd seal over and the bit'd never be missed." Heaven knew when she'd get her next square meal. She might carry in her bodice the lawful right to a great diamond, but she'd be a beggar on the road.

Outside the long summer twilight lingered, full of the scent of ripe hay and the soft voices of doves. Some echo of the old spirit of adventure, the wandering haphazard life she had loved, woke in Kate's heart. Her shoes, as they warmed to her feet, ceased their pinching. She hobbled out of the town, on the road towards Guildford at good speed.

When he left the Queen's prison room the priest crossed the castle yard, climbed the seventy steps to his own little chamber, and dropped down onto his bed. Within two minutes he was deep in the sleep of exhaustion, and should have stayed asleep till morning after all the exertions of the last few days. But he had taken with him, across the yard and up the steps and into his very bed, a responsibility which, though he refused to face it, was not to be escaped even in sleep. After four hours, during which he slept like a dog, it nudged him; he woke abruptly, sat up, and faced it, muttering to himself, "Yes, I know."

He knew that in his mind he had never been quite at ease about the Queen. He was an unworldly man; he took no interest in politics or in anything outside the scope of his duties. Fifteen years ago, when Eleanor had first been brought to Winchester, Lord de Glanville had indicated to him exactly how far his duty to the imprisoned Queen extended—he must hear her confession, grant her absolution, impose the necessary penances, and administer the sacraments; that was all. Only once had he stepped over the boundary, and that was long ago, in the winter of 1181, when, visiting her apartments, he had found her and Amaria sitting draped in their bedclothes because the fuel provided for their fire had been too damp to burn. That winter was very severe and the day exceptionally cold, and the two women with their bluish white faces and their fingers like tallow candles had seemed to him so pitiable that, later in the day he had mentioned their plight to Sir Nicolas.

"The room faces north and the fire was barely alight," he said diffidently.

Sir Nicolas favoured him with a hard stare.

"And did my Lord de Glanville entrust you with the Queen's material welfare as well as her spiritual, Sir Priest?"

"No, no, of course not . . . it was just that . . ."

"That you fell victim to those famous bright eyes. Shame on you! No . . . when my lord looked for a custodian for his prisoner —since he could not be expected to stay here and act as gaoler forever—he chose me, knowing that I could withstand that charm, which, they said, could net any man's heart. And how right they were! Even you, you see, even you. And you must be careful, Sir Priest . . . begin with wondering if she is warm enough and, next thing you know, she'll be asking you to carry letters . . . or open the door for her one of these dark nights. And you know what that would be, don't you? Treason. We've heard enough about criminous clerks . . . we can guess what would happen to treasonous ones!"

"Sir, you entirely misunderstand me, it was just . . ."

"Be thankful I do; I have in mind that I understand you too well. With what other fire have you ever concerned yourself? How warm was the guardroom this morning?"

That was enough for Wilfred; he never interfered again.

But death, dying was different. Even old peasant women . . . families gathered . . . there was some kind of ceremony. And there was the Queen of England dying on that tumbled squalid bed, with just that one frightened old woman.

In the dust the priest rose, sighing a little, grudging his broken rest; but he took from the closet and put on his best cassock, washed his hands and face with more care than usual.

Sir Nicolas was just finishing supper; a shallow bowl filled with a high-piled mound of strawberries stood before him, and he was taking each one delicately by its green stalk, dipping it into another bowl which contained a mess of cream and thin honey whipped into froth, and then popping it, dripping, into his mouth. The priest, passing by his own lowly place at the table, proceeded up the hall and stood by his master's elbow.

"If you've come to explain where you've been these last days, don't bother," Sir Nicolas said genially. "You look very peaked, man. All this dismal business. Sit you down; drink some wine. You there . . . a cup of wine for Sir Wilfred . . ."

"Sir . . . I visited the Queen this afternoon and I think you should know . . ." Wilfred began.

"Now this is high June . . . not that fire again!"

Seven years, eight years ago . . . you see, and still remembered, that one false step!

"Sir, she was dying . . . of plague. Four hours ago; she may well be dead now."

Sir Nicolas selected, baptised, and popped into his mouth another strawberry. When he had swallowed it he said,

"So? Very sudden . . . but then plague does strike sharply. When I made my regular visit two days ago . . . But no matter! I think this will be good news for His Grace."

That might well be true, the priest thought; but it was callous and mannerless to say it openly. Disgust gave him courage to say in a manner firmer than usual,

"Men are often stricken with remorse when the object of their dislike is dead. And Her Grace is dying, or lies dead, in circumstances that would be pitiable were she a peasant."

It was the boldest thing he had ever said, and the most effective. Sir Nicolas pushed his chair from the table and stood up.

"We'll look into this. Come with me."

The sense of duty done did not quite compensate the priest for the postponement of his much-needed supper, or prevent him casting a wistful glance at the hacked-up carcass of the lamb as he passed it.

The Queen lay just as Kate had left her; only the noisy breaths, drawn at incredibly long intervals, showed that she still lived. Staring about the bare, squalid, utterly comfortless room, Nicolas of Saxham saw it as though for the first time and, for the first time, was struck by the thought that possibly he had interpreted the order "strict confinement without luxuries" a little too literally. As though defending himself from a criticism which no one yet had made, he seized upon the one point upon which he was safe.

"She should not be alone! Where is her attendant? Curse the old hag. Run off in fright, I suppose."

He stormed into the passage and shouted to the guard, who, loyal to Kate, said that she had just gone out to air herself after a long day in the sickroom. He made it sound as though she would be back at any minute.

"Go and fetch Martha; tell her to bring a broom, and some candles, and some fresh linen, and a clean blanket."

He went back and stood in the doorway between the outer and inner rooms, and thought about what the priest had said about the remorse which came upon men when those they had hated died. He remembered the stories that had gone round about how the King had behaved after the death of Becket—that was murder, of course, and he had ordered it, which made a little difference. Still, he had repented that order; it might well be that after Eleanor's death he would repent the order about "no luxuries."

It was when the candles came that he noticed the target board, the inkhorn, and the quill which Kate, in her casual slovenly fashion, had just lifted from Eleanor's knees onto the floor by the foot of the bed. He stared at them for a long minute, and then went forward and lifted the limp hand which lay outside the covers; as he suspected, it bore inkstains. There were inkstains on the board, too, places where the wet quill had overrun the vellum. He was no fool, and even a fool could see what that meant; recently, in the early hours of her illness, the Queen had written something. Snatching a candle, he hurried into the outer room to the table where the big parchment lay; had *she* at the last moment repented and signed the thing? No. The dust on the parchment was merely another testimony of how ill kept her rooms had been; and in the dust were the marks where the inkhorn had stood and the quill had lain until this morning.

"Stop what you're doing," he said to Martha, who was beginning to tidy the bedroom. "Hunt for letters—anything written on."

He went himself to search the outer room. There was nothing there, and little concealment—the table, two hard wooden stools. The floor was of stone, very scantily spread with rushes which had not been changed for years. The walls were of stone too, without a niche in them.

"There's nothing here but what you see," Martha said when he looked into the bedroom again.

"You've looked in and under the bed?"

"Yes," she said, but she looked at Kate's pallet as she spoke.

"Look in this one."

"It's ill to disturb the dying," the woman said, and drew back.

"Search, I tell you." But the woman just stood and stared; she was terrified of him; all the servants feared him; but superstitious terror swamped all others; it was left for him to go forward, shuddering but determined, and make sure that what the Queen had written in her last conscious moments had not been hidden under the pillows or among the covers.

Sweat broke out on the man's face as he came to full understanding of what this meant. Special orders from the King to De Glanville, and passed on to him, mentioned that there were to be no visitors except by permission, and no written communications. Now, at the last moment, some written communication had been made; and it would be important; people stricken with plague didn't sit up in bed and write trivial things.

The old woman, Kate; that was it.

He flung himself into the passage again.

"Where did that old woman say she was going?"

"Out t-t-to catch a b-b-breath of air, sir."

"You've told me that lie, once. Where? Must I hang you up by the thumbs to get the truth out of you?"

Jerkins, mended or otherwise, were no use to a man hung by the thumbs. Stammering and sweating with fear, the man blurted out the truth, all he knew.

Well, the story about the family might be dismissed for the deception it was; she had gone to deliver whatever it was that the Queen had written. Where would she take it? To somewhere in the town? That seemed to argue a previous arrangement, and this writing, whatever it was, had evidently been done in the stress of the moment—still, Winchester must be searched. The alternatives? Either London or a seaport, and, if a seaport, obviously one of the Channel ports. And thanks to the priest's fit of conscience, very little time had been lost; unless the old crone really was a witch, as some people believed, and had taken to her broomstick, she had not gone far in this time; she'd be on the road to Guildford, if London were her goal; or to Midhurst, if she were making for the Channel ports.

Nicolas of Saxham, custodian of Winchester, had men and horses to command. Most of the men knew Kate by sight; and, as a subject for a search, she was an easy mark—an old woman, rather bent, lame in both feet, with one long tooth hanging over her lower lip; anyone who had seen her would remember her.

Twelve men were sent out on a house-to-house search of the town; three, mounted, left for the Guildford road, and three for the road to Midhurst. The hue and cry was out after her, in full force.

Her shoes, easing to the heat and moisture of her feet, ceased to hurt; she covered four miles in the first hour, and only slightly less in the second. Then the trouble began; there was a limit to the amount of expansion in her shoes, but her feet went on swelling. She was unused to walking; for years she had hobbled about within the castle precincts and, since she had been appointed to the Queen's service, she had hardly been even so far as the town. Soon every step was torture, and at last she removed her shoes and walked, almost a mile, barefoot. It was a relief at first, and she stepped out bravely, but her feet, hating the shoes, in the end hated their unprotected contact with the road even more.

Her last few agonised steps had brought her within sight of a village, quite a number of houses clustered about a little church—there'd be a shoemaker there, she thought. It might seem to be a waste of time—and the mistress had said, "Be swift"—but it would be wise to rest now near the village, and then in the morning seek out the village shoemaker.

Anyway she had little choice—she could walk no farther; and here was a field dotted all over with little new haycocks. She could see them quite clearly for, no sooner had the last rays of the sun faded, than the moon and the stars had come out to light the sky. She flattened a haycock and lay down, and slept so deeply that even the sound of three mounted men clattering past did not disturb her.

In the morning she rose, ate the last sliver of the slice of mutton the spit boy had given her, drank from the ditch, and, hobbling into the village, managed, by dint of her own peculiar brand of cajolery and threat, to exchange her shoes for a pair which the cobbler chanced to have left on his hands through the death of the man who had ordered them. Unfortunately, they were a little too large. Later in the day, however, she passed a place where sheep were grazing; tufts of their wool clung to the bushes against which they had rubbed, and when she had used some of it to pad out the shoes, she walked with more comfort than she had known for a long while. She went along steadily, inquiring at all likely places for Alberic, and usually contriving to beg a bite of food at the same time.

Meanwhile the mounted men had reached Guildford, and had halted.

"We didn't pass her, and she couldn't have got so far ahead—not without help from the Devil," one of them said. They agreed that the best thing to do would be to turn back after they had breakfasted, which they did well, and at leisure. There was no hurry now, since, if old Kate had taken this road—which they doubted—she was coming towards them. They fed and rested their horses and rode back at an easy pace.

By the narrowest margin of chance, they avoided missing her

again. The sun was high in the sky over the little village of Cumford, and Kate had seized the opportunity of inquiring at the alehouse, and had suggested, with a smooth tongue but just that glint of eye and flash of fang, that a mug of cool ale would be acceptable. She was enjoying it in the shadowy little room when the three men, having sighted the inn sign, reined in.

Until that moment the thought of pursuit had troubled her very little. Her simple mind was content with the precaution she had taken; she believed that the Queen would be dead before nightfall and, if in the morning anyone did chance to ask, "Where's old Kate?," the guard had the answer. Nobody knew that the things she carried existed—except the beeman, who would have forgotten before he got back to his hives—so the idea that someone might be searching, might be hot on her trail, never occurred to her.

The three men, having hitched their horses to the post, came stamping in, saw and recognised her, and were for a moment struck dumb by this enormous bit of luck. To the one she was on speaking terms with, she nodded and said, "Good day," and went on calmly drinking her ale.

For lack of anything else to say, he asked,

"What are you doing here, old Kate?"

"Minding me own business. What are you?"

The spell which surprise had laid upon them lifted then; they laughed.

"Looking for you and them writings you're carrying."

Something—not quite fear, more like anxiety—did stir in her then; but she said gruffly,

"You bin drinking, Willie? I got no writings."

"We'll soon see about *that*," he said, advancing towards her.

She got up with the gesture of a cat arching its back in the face of three dogs.

"You keep your hands off me, if you don't it'll be the worse for you." The fang was well bared, the eyes threatened. "Don't you meddle with old Kate!"

"God between us and harm," mumbled Willie, crossing himself

hastily; but the words and the gesture brought no confidence, rather the opposite; the three men stood close together, and the words "witch" and "evil eyes" were handed about.

The innkeeper watched, fingering in his mind the motto of his trade, "Let's have no trouble."

Somebody had brought him, that morning, two pecks of peas in a bag. He turned away elaborately and busied himself with emptying the peas into a basket.

Kate stood, relying upon her reputation for protection.

The men stood, balancing their fear of their master against their fear of the forces of evil.

Casually the innkeeper reached down a mug, advanced to the pyramid of barrels which stood behind Kate. When he was near enough, he whipped out the sack and brought it down over her head.

"That'll take care of the eye," he said. He believed this; it had never been directed at him, so he was in no danger, and, hidden by the sack, it could not be turned effectively on any of the others. Quite at ease, he took off his belt and fastened the sack about Kate's waist. The soldiers, who were quite prepared to believe that one glance of that eye, shot malignantly, could ruin their health, bring them bad luck, work them every imaginable ill, were also equally prepared to believe that a layer of sacking could defeat it. They thanked the innkeeper heartily, drank a good deal of his ale, and paid him in silver. Then Willie lifted the old woman as though she were a parcel—she weighed very light, for, as everybody knew, a witch was light enough to float on water if she were tested that way—and, setting her on the saddle before him, he rode with his companions very happily back to Winchester.

On the third day of the Queen's illness—and she, incredible as it seemed, was still alive—the first rumour reached Winchester; the health of His Grace, King Henry, was causing anxiety. Details were vague; it was said that, in a recent battle, he had received a wound in the leg which had turned green and rotten; a dramatic addition, which some chose to believe, was that the wound had actually been dealt by Richard, his son. It was also said that there was no new wound; an old one, which had long been a source of nagging pain to him, had opened and inflamed anew. In any case, the King was a sick man, could hardly mount his horse, was eating very little, and was miserably low in spirit.

Nicolas of Saxham was bearing this in mind as he studied the two pieces of vellum which he, with his own hands, had been obliged to snatch from old Kate's bodice. Nobody else dared to do it, she had threatened such terrible things; and her curses on her master, when he at last took the risk, were terrible to hear. However, as he suspected, she, like so many other old crones, had exaggerated her powers. So far from being cursed, smitten with sickness, madness, and ruin, he was doing very well. He was now protected on both sides. If Henry recovered his health and lived, Nicolas could present him with the will and the letter, which he could say he had "discovered," and that would give proof of his faithfulness and his watchfulness for the King's interest. If, on the other hand, Henry should die, then the letter and the will would go off in great haste to their proper destinations—and that would make it look as though Nicolas of Saxham had really been on the poor Queen's side, and not too strict a gaoler. Even if the Queen lived, which seemed very doubtful, and went on bearing resentment towards him, she could not deny that in sending off the documents safely he had been doing her a service.

And he was not going to punish Kate for smuggling out the pieces of vellum and giving him such a scare; in fact, he was not going to punish Kate at all. He could safely leave that to others.

Meanwhile the Queen was still alive and, if she should recover, he had plans for making her imprisonment, temporarily, at least, more comfortable; if the King lived, and ever knew that he had relaxed his orders, he could always say that the lapse was due to the lady having been so very ill. Covered on all sides!

Happily, he went off to pay his daily visit to the place where Eleanor lay.

Both rooms had been cleaned; the Queen lay in good linen, and Martha was in attendance.

"Any change?" Sir Nicolas asked.

"About midday she came to herself, leastways her eyes opened, and she drank some water. She's breathing easier, too."

"Good, very good." He went away, his mind busy with his plans . . . rooms on the sunny side of the courtyard as soon as she could be moved; clean rushes on the floor; cushions on her chair; good food on the table, and a little wine each day.

One evening Martha reported that the Queen had become fully conscious and had asked for Kate.

"She's sleeping now, but proper sleep, back in her senses. She seemed very worried about Kate."

"If she asks again, tell her the truth. Kate went into the town to help her sick family, and has not yet returned."

"But, sir . . ."

"You heard what I said. Which would you tell the Queen? What Kate herself said, or some fantastic story that someone made up in an idle moment for other idle people to pass on?"

Coming back to life was very strange, painful at times, and humiliating in its weakness. Eleanor would lie and wonder if she would ever walk again, ever regain the power to think clearly for more than a minute at a time. The new room was pleasant, the new food delightful—but she had little appetite; Martha and the two other women who took turns to sit with her were kind in a shy, dumb way, but she missed Kate, and worried about her for as long as her wavering mind could dwell upon one subject.

However, she was recovering and, now and then, showed flashes of her old spirit. On the day when she was first able to be lifted from bed and set in the chair by the window, Nicolas of Saxham, when he paid his visit, expressed himself happy to see her out of bed at last, and hoped she was comfortable.

"So comfortable," she retorted, "that I fear for the health of His Grace."

"His Grace, so far as we know, is well; and the last two battles ended in his favour," said Sir Nicolas with a bland, innocent look.

"Then you, sir, must be out of your mind! Nothing else could explain your concern for my well-being. Change of heart is impossible to you—you have no heart."

He said patiently, "Madam, you have been at death's door; I have snatched at that as an excuse to deal more gently with you than my orders direct. I do not think that is evidence of heartlessness."

It was evidence of *something*, Eleanor thought, staring at him coldly. He tried again.

"Soon, when you have regained a little strength, you must sit in the garden again; the sun is a good medicine."

"That would be very acceptable," Eleanor said. But she still would not smile.

How he hated her, had always hated her from the moment she was put in his charge, because of her pride, her unbreakable spirit, and the contempt with which she had always treated him.

But now he must be careful; he lied about the King's health; the latest news from the Continent said that Henry's leg was swollen as big as a bolster from hip to heel; that he had to be lifted into his saddle and suffered agonising pain while there. The moment Henry died Richard would be King, and his first act would be to let his mother, that old tigress, out of her cage; and the first person she would turn and rend would be Nicolas of Saxham—unless he was careful now.

Also, just at the moment, he was happily preparing a very sweet revenge—the kind which comes to a man only once in a lifetime. Chance had put it in his power to be kind and indulgent to his prisoner, so that when she was freed she would bear him no grudge, and, at the same time, to make her suffer a far worse thing than mere physical hardship. The Queen would suffer; he himself would enjoy watching her suffer; and he would be utterly blameless. He rubbed his hands in anticipation of the moment.

It came at last; on the thirteenth day of July 1189.

There had been almost three weeks of unbroken summer weather and Eleanor had spent long hours in the garden, where, in the lavender bushes, the bees had been busy all day. The fresh air, the sunshine, and the better food had all contributed to restore her health and, though frail still, she was almost well. Of her nearness to death one mark remained, but that so delicate and decorative that it lay like a caress. One lock of her dark red hair had whitened, just where it grew in a peak from her brow. In later years the court ladies were to go to great pains to bleach one lock in slavish imitation.

Quite early on this lovely July morning she was in the garden, nipping off a few dead flowers from the little border of pinks, and sniffing with great pleasure the scent of those still in full bloom. Nicolas of Saxham strolled into the garden and made some amiable remark about the beauty of the morning and about her restored health. Then he asked if there was anything she wished for.

"I should like to have my lute restored to me."

"Is that all?"

"You know," she said, looking at some point behind his shoulder, "convalescence plays curious tricks with one's senses. My hearing has been affected. For sixteen years whenever I have asked you for anything you have said, 'That is impossible.' Now I'll swear my ears heard you say, 'Is that *all?*' Curious, is it not?"

It cost him an effort, but he managed it, and laughed.

"It pleases Your Grace to jest. I did say, 'Is that all?'; it was in my mind that, the day being so inviting, you might be wishful to ride abroad."

Now he had her attention.

"Have you had orders to remove me from Winchester? If so, you have no need to bait your trap. Even a room in the Tower would be a welcome change!"

Henry knew about the letters, she thought. Kate had been caught. Henry had seized the excuse of treachery . . . The hooded headsman, the bloody block, her own neck bared to the blade, swung dizzily for a moment before her eyes.

"I am prepared to ride wherever you have orders to take me," she said; stooping, she plucked one of the scented pinks and held it to her nose . . . next summer, when these bloom again, I shall be rotting in a traitor's grave. . . .

"You utterly mistake me. In making this suggestion I am dis-obeying my orders with the intent to give you pleasure. . . . I thought a brief outing in a comfortable litter . . . a little change of scene . . ."

"I never ride in a litter. I rode in one all the way from Antioch to Jerusalem and I swore, never again."

"A well-mannered palfrey then."

She looked down at her hands and said derisively,

"A well-mannered palfrey. Yes, that would be the mount for me nowadays." But better, oh better, than nothing. Long years without the sight of a horse, and she loved horses so. Long years without a glimpse of the countryside.

"It will await you in the courtyard at two o'clock. I myself will attend you."

She was still a little dubious of his intention; but when they did not take the London direction, but swung south onto the Ports-mouth road, then turned off onto a track so little-used that grass grew in long green ridges along it, she decided that, unbelievable as it seemed, this was just an outing after all. And it was beautiful. Honeysuckle and a few late wild roses wreathed the hedges, and the corn was, as Sir Nicolas had said, green-gold in the great open fields, and the poppies were everywhere, mingling with the lacy growth of the meadowsweet and the whiter sturdiness of the cow parsley. At one point the road widened out, became a village green, with geese and tethered goats feeding on it, and to Eleanor's unaccustomed eye they were as lovely and strange as the heraldic beasts on a tapestry. Her inborn, indomitable capacity for enjoyment reasserted itself; she was enjoying her ride.

Presently the road joined another, more used, and ran downhill into the shade of some green woods. They passed a man driving a donkey laden with panniers of early yellow plums, a woman with a basket of gingerbread squares on her arm, several little groups of people walking purposefully.

"Is it a holiday? Some saint's day?" Eleanor asked.

"None that I know of. But it might be . . . yes . . . possibly something to do with St. Phocas. The Abbey of St. Phocas does lie this way, now I come to think of it."

As he spoke, the mass of the green wood ended in a froth of bracken and gave way to cultivated ground through which the road ran straight, flanked on one side by a village green, with its little low huts about it, and its geese and its goats, and on the other side by the sombre grey walls and tower of the abbey.

"St. Phocas . . . he is strange to me," Eleanor said.

"And to most of England. A saint from the East, I am told; and the patron saint of gardeners. And it is a curious fact that the vines at this abbey always give a good vintage, even in years when those in other places are ruined by bad weather."

"Ummm," she took her bearings. "They face southwards," she said; "they have the shelter of the abbey itself and of the woods to the north and the east."

"You believe in the practical explanation of all phenomena, madam?"

"If it can be seen—as in this case—with the naked eye. Now if the vineyards were exposed to the northeast wind, which is the bane of this country, then I should give St. Phocas his due."

"As I think these less reasonable folk are doing now. It is plainly some kind of celebration," he said, drawing rein and staring about him with interest. "Something must be afoot. Would Your Grace care to wait and watch for a while?"

They turned onto the green and took a position near one of the little sod houses, so low that its roof was level with Eleanor's shoulder as she sat on the palfrey.

"We shall not be jostled here, and can see what is to be seen," said Sir Nicolas. Something in his voice made Eleanor turn and look at him curiously; he was not the man, she would have thought, to take much interest in the doings of a handful of yokels, or in a village celebration, however unusual; yet his eyes were alight with curiosity, his lips parted eagerly.

More and more people were arriving; but there was no fear of being jostled; the country folk knew their manners. Though some glanced at the two mounted people, none came near, save the man with the plums, who presently approached with his donkey and said humbly.

"Would your honours care to sample my plums? Very sweet they be, and the first ripe this year, thanks to St. Phocas."

"Do they tempt you, madam?" Sir Nicolas asked, and when she nodded he fumbled in the purse at his waist.

"Twenty a penny," the man said, and counted them out into a cool green dock leaf; then, tugging at his donkey's head, he pushed into the thick of the crowd, shouting, "If they're good enough for her ladyship, they're good enough for you. Ripe plums, first of the year, forty a penny!"

"There's a rogue," said Eleanor laughing. "We should have asked him what was happening. If it is bull or bear baiting, I have no desire to watch."

"I see no animal. Do you?"

She raised herself a little and looked towards the centre of the crowd. "No. Just a heap of something . . ."

"We shall soon know. Look . . ." The great gate of the abbey had swung open, and a considerable procession had begun to emerge. At its head walked a monk bearing a wooden cross; and behind him three others carried candles, though the flames were barely visible in the bright afternoon light; and one, somewhere, had a bell which rang at regular intervals—one could count to ten between the strokes of it. In the centre of the procession something was being carried along, and at its very end walked two men with black masks over their faces; they were clad in tight black hose and jerkins, and looked a little like the imps who took part in the Christmas revels. The likeness was increased by the fact that they each carried a blazing knot of pine wood.

The monks advanced, slowly, to a certain position, then stood still and began a soft, mournful chanting. The two masked men went forward, stood one on each side of the heap, and the two who were carrying the bundle went forward with them, placed their burden carefully on the pile, and seemed to be fixing it in place.

"*Not* an effigy of St. Phocas, would you suppose? No, they're making a fire and they wouldn't burn their patron. . . ."

The men with the pine knots bent down and laid them at the edge of the pile, one on each side; the men who had placed the bundle stepped briskly back, one of them as he did so twitching away the dark blanket in which the bundle had been wrapped. At the same moment the low chanting of the monks was drowned in a malicious rhythmical cry from the crowd, "*Death* to the *witch! Death* to the *witch!*" The flames leaped up with a crackle and the thing in the centre of them moved; it was no effigy; it lived; it was an ugly old woman. . . .

"Kate!" screamed Eleanor, and the word cut through the other sounds like a blade. She brought her heel sharply into the horse's side, and the palfrey leaped forward, startled, only to be checked by Sir Nicolas grasping at the rein.

"Have a care, madam. It would be dangerous to interfere with the execution of the sentence of the Abbot's court. And the crowd could be dangerous, too."

"Let go my rein," said Eleanor between her teeth.

"I dare not," he said.

He wore, like any other gentleman riding abroad on a peaceful errand on a fine afternoon, his short sword with its decorated hilt; it hung by his left thigh, convenient to Eleanor's right hand. It left the scabbard with a little slithering sound, wavered a little—heavier in her weak hand than she had expected—then came up, its edge laid to the veins of his wrist as he held the rein.

"Let go," she said; and knowing the sharpness of its well-ground edge, he did so. Under the urge of her hand and heel, the well-mannered palfrey leaped forward towards the fire, and there, not quite near enough, stopped, stiff-legged until Eleanor hit him with the flat of the blade.

The chanting had ceased, but nobody moved as Eleanor, leaning low in the smoke and the sparks, hacked away the cords which bound Kate to a stake in the middle of the faggots; then, with the mightiest effort she had ever made in her life, she lifted Kate bodily upwards and threw her over the pommel of the saddle. The horse, very willingly, leaped away from the fire.

Then the spell of surprise which had bound the crowd was broken. The witch must not be allowed to escape. They all knew about her—the Witch of Winchester, Cursed Kate. The custodian of Winchester Castle had handed her over to the Abbot and, in the court she had dared to say to the Abbot himself, "If you meddle with me, you will be sorry." The man from the alehouse had stood up and said how she had asked him for ale, how he dared not refuse, how she had dared the soldiers to arrest her, and how Satan himself had looked out of her eyes before the sack was dropped over her head. So much evidence was given in court, but what of all the rest? There wasn't a man or woman for miles around who hadn't at some time suffered some affliction, some stroke of ill luck, for which there was no accounting except by the presence of a witch in their midst. When the Abbot had been reluctant to condemn her outright, he'd allowed himself to be persuaded into giving her the swimming test. In the abbey carp pool, that test had been applied; they tied her skirts about her knees and she'd floated like a blown-up bladder. No, she mustn't get away, now.

They closed in, eyes shining, teeth shining like fangs. Like a pack of wolves, thought Eleanor, and she longed for the trained war horse of her crusading days, the horse who would have reared in their faces, crashed down with his iron-shod hoofs, seized and shaken them with his teeth.

She did the best with what she had, backing the palfrey towards the fire again so that she could not be set upon from the rear, and laying about her with the sword. Even so, there would have been no doubt of the outcome had not Sir Nicolas, rallying his wits, remembered that it would be very difficult to explain how the Queen, supposedly in strict confinement, had been torn to pieces on a village green five miles out of Winchester. Riding up to the group of monks who stood as though stupefied, he snatched the wooden cross and, holding it like a club, dashed into the fray, cracking skulls to left and right. Like wolves, the crowd drew back and stood snarling.

They clattered along at a good pace, speeded by curses and a few stones, one of which hit Eleanor on the cheek, another the palfrey on the rump, usefully quickening its speed.

Kate, whose calm throughout had been almost inhuman, now began to sob. "Oh mistress, don't let them get old Kate. Save me, mistress."

"You are saved. None shall touch you now. Are you hurt?"

"No. I was wet to begin with. They ducked me this morning. They . . . oh save me, mistress."

"Leave clutching me, Kate. Hold on to the horse. You make it hard to ride."

"Let me take the sword, madam," Sir Nicolas said. She ignored him, and they rode in silence again until he said half sulkily, "For what are you blaming me? The sentence was set by the Abbot's court; but for my suggestion that we should ride, it would have been carried out. In what way have I offended?"

"You planned it. You took me there to see this old woman, who served me well for five years, die horribly. Did you think I should stand weeping, with folded hands, while she burned? You are a gross fool, sir, as well as a humbugging knave. When I think of the fate you planned for her—for no greater crime than carrying two letters out for me . . ."

"One," he said smoothly, "was addressed to the King of France. To carry it was treason. Do you think His Grace would have dealt more leniently with her?"

"He would have dealt justly, not in this tricky fashion. Mother of God, I have little reason to speak kindly of him, but he would scorn to punish a simple old woman for carrying she knew not what —she cannot read—and then invite the real culprit to watch her death by torture. When His Grace hears—as he shall by *some* means —his scorn of you will match mine."

In such a short time she was to be glad that she had paid Henry that small tribute.

They rode on until the town of Winchester came into view. Then Eleanor said,

"Kate stays with me. The Abbot of St. Phocas may lay claim to her—it is his duty to do so. You will send him to me. You will send me also the two letters. Anything further to be said in this affair can be between me and His Grace, when he returns."

Sir Nicolas' patience, sorely tried that afternoon, gave way.

"By the rood, madam! Are you now giving me orders? I think you are distraught. The old woman was properly convicted of witchcraft—a capital crime in any Christian country—and I shall hand her back to the proper authorities in the morning. The letters are another matter. I shall forward them to His Grace."

"Who will wonder, I think, why you have been so long about it. They are dated. And to make it yet more awkward for you, sooner than see Kate taken and tortured, I shall kill her with this sword; and when she is dead, there will be no one able to contradict what I shall say—that *you* promised to deliver them for me. Well, sir, does she remain with me?"

It was a weak defence, she knew, but all she could think of at the moment. It served to confuse Sir Nicolas, at no time a rapid thinker. She had lived in prison, without hope, long enough to have learned to live from moment to moment. In two days' time he would have thought up some new trick, and she would have to fight him again. Well, that would give her something to think about, would keep her mind busy for a while.

She dismounted in the courtyard of the castle and walked up to her prison room, holding the sword in her right hand and supporting Kate with her left arm. She could not have walked more proudly if she had known that, through the dust-moted sunshine of the late afternoon, the hoofs were beating towards her, bringing the news that would set her free.

Part Four

CHAPTER ONE

Two days later she was on her way back to Westminster. She was Regent of England.

Richard had wasted no time. His first action when the news of Henry's death reached him had been to send William the Marshal speeding to England with orders to go straight to Winchester and rescue the Queen from prison. He, Richard, must stay in Normandy, to bury the dead King and receive the homage of all the vassals of Normandy and Anjou—men who, up to yesterday, had been fighting against him; and the Queen was to act for him, to have complete power in England until he was free to come to London.

William the Marshal was the most honest and the most famous knight in England. He had laid his hands between Henry's and taken the oath of allegiance, and he had kept it faithfully. It was he who in the recent battle had had Richard for a moment in his power—but he had seen, in that moment, not the rebellious prince, but the King's son; he had deflected his blow and killed Richard's horse.

Henry's death ended the war, and Richard and William the Marshal met next by the side of the bed where the great King, Henry the Lawgiver, lay dead.

"Last time we met, Marshal," Richard said, "you tried to kill me." He made the comment without malice . . . just a statement of how things had changed. William, utterly straightforward, without trace of cunning or trickery, said,

"I killed your horse, Sire. I could as easily have killed you, had I wished."

It was all said in that one simple sentence; and Richard, no mean judge of men, knew all that it meant. William the Marshal was the King's man; one inherited him as one inherited the crown.

"I bear you no grudge," he said. And he sent him to England with his orders.

William the Marshal carried them out with such speed that he tried to leap on the Channel-crossing boat before it had been tied to the landing stage, and he was very lame from the injury to his leg when he arrived at Winchester late in the evening of the day of Kate's rescue. His coming, like the wave of a magic wand, changed everything.

As the Queen rode, this time well escorted, along the summer roads, people flocked to see her. In every town and village, at every crossroads, they had gathered to look upon this woman about whom, for so many years, there had been such rumours and counter-rumours, such speculation, and such argument. And when they had done staring, they cheered her and waved their hands, and called, "Heaven save Your Grace," or knelt for a moment and, crossing themselves, murmured, "God save the Queen."

Some of the enthusiasm was the easy-come, easy-go emotion of a crowd moving with the time; but much of it was genuine. Eleanor's feeling that the instinct for justice in the English would eventually turn in her favour had been right enough; in many places, from the City of London to lonely farmhouses, there were people who had thought her ill-used, imprisoned unjustly, and who had always referred to her as "the poor Queen." It was to these that she came most as a surprise; expecting to see a poor, broken-down, old woman (she was sixty-seven, an immense age for those times), ruined in health and looks by her long ordeal, dazzled, and perhaps somewhat overcome by her sudden change of fortune, they saw instead an upright, vital figure of truly royal dignity. She was very thin and very pale, but this fleshlessness and pallor gave her fine-boned face something of the quality of marble, a classic beauty of form with its arrogant nose and smooth brow and hollowed, long-lidded eyes. Even in her prison gown and stuff veil, she was impressive—imagine, they whispered to one another, how fine she would look in proper robes, glittering with jewels.

A trivial happening, just on the London side of Guildford, sealed her popularity, especially with the poor, and spread it among thousands who would never see her face.

Through towns and villages, or past groups by the roadside they rode slowly, but, between times, they made a rattling pace because Eleanor was anxious to get to London and begin the work of receiving—in Richard's name—the homage of the great nobles; and prepare for the coronation, which she was determined should outshine any previous ceremony. So, with Guildford behind them, and an almost deserted road ahead, they were making good speed when they met a trio of men. The one in the centre had his hands tied together with a rope, and the man on each side held one end of it; all three were covered with the whitish grey dust of the road, and the sweat had channelled through it on their faces.

A prisoner of some sort, Eleanor realised with a quick stab of sympathy. To be going dungeon-wards on such a fine hot day!

She reined in beside the three men, who had stepped humbly into the verge of the road to allow this impressive company to pass.

"Where are you taking him?" she asked.

The older of the two rope-holders said—and she noticed that he spoke without pleasure in his task—,

"To Guildford gaol, my lady."

"For what fault?"

The man cleared his throat and assumed a pompous, official voice.

"In that on Saturday last, he entered the King's forest, accompanied by his hound and armed with a bow and arrow, in pursuit of a hind. He stands convicted of an offence against the forest laws of His Grace."

"The beast had trampled and ravished my oat patch twice over," the prisoner said in a flat, matter-of-fact voice.

"And his sentence?"

Before the older man, the village constable, could speak, the prisoner said in that same voice,

"On me, six months in gaol; on my wife and four children, death, for they will surely starve."

The two other men nodded solemnly. With their oat patch ruined and no man to do day labour to make good the loss—yes, they would starve, for in six months it would be winter, when even the most charitable neighbours would have little to give away.

"Turn him loose," Eleanor said. They stared, bewildered, not moving. Even the man seemed either not to realise or to doubt his good fortune. The constable, recovering a little, mumbled something about the manor court.

"By the Queen's order," said William the Marshal.

They loosed the rope willingly enough, and the man fell on his knees, sobbing and calling down the blessing of Heaven upon the merciful Queen.

"That shall be my first act," Eleanor said as they rode on again. "As you will understand, I have a fellow feeling for all those who lie in gaol. Thieves and murderers and those who give short measure, it might be wrong to turn loose on the community—but all those whose only fault is trespass against the game laws, they are to be freed forthwith."

There were thousands of them, for Henry's forest laws had been strict and brutal; and every one of the released men went home to his family, his village or hamlet, a Queen's man for life and death. Richard's man, too—and that was all to the good, for Richard, who had spent his life abroad, who had rebelled against his father and caused so much strife, had no ready-made popularity awaiting him in England; that must be built up, layer by layer, largely by Richard's mother.

CHAPTER TWO

Late on the evening of September third, 1189, Richard, King of England, who had, that very morning, been crowned at Westminster Abbey, strode through the halls and corridors of his palace of Westminster to the Queen's apartments; the noise of music and merrymaking followed him a little way and then grew dim, as his long rapid strides carried him farther from the public halls and courts, where the celebrations were still going on, into the quietude of the more private part of the palace.

Eleanor was alone save for Amaria—now reinstated as her personal maid—and old Kate. She was reclining on a high-backed sofa, her outstretched legs covered by a shawl. The sight of her in this unusual position gave her son a slight shock; he checked in the doorway and then came forward quickly.

"Mother, are you feeling ill?"

"No, merely a little weary . . . as I have a right to be."

He dragged up a stool and sat down by her side, saying in a curious, muted voice,

"Somehow I never thought of you growing weary. And that was very remiss of me."

She said calmly, "If a reckoning had been kept, Richard, of the miles I have ridden, of the audiences I have granted, of the petitions I have dealt with, in these last weeks, I think it would show that I have—as I said—the right to be a little weary."

"You have worked marvels," he said quickly.

"And I have seen you crowned," she said in a voice warm with feeling. "This morning . . . it was such a fulfilment, Richard, such a hoped-for moment, and all so beautiful. In the Abbey, the quietude and the feeling of holiness, and then, outside, those crowds roaring with fervour . . ." She smiled. "I think that is why I allowed myself to feel weary; I feel that my task is done."

"Far from it! At least . . ." He jumped up from the stool and took a few paces up and down, looking at her. "I came this evening to lay another burden on you, mother. A heavy burden. That is why, at the sight of your weariness, I was taken aback. Then I realised how ridiculous was this thing I had planned."

"Because I was resting when you came? You silly boy! Isn't vigour something to hoard and cherish; what would you think of a knight who always rode at the charge and never rested his lance? Here, sit down and tell me what you want of me. You *must* sit down, it gives me a crick in the neck to look up so far." She swung her feet to the ground, gathered the shawl into a bundle, and thrust it behind her back, sitting up very straight. "There, is that better? Sit down by me, Richard, and tell me all that is in your mind."

He sat down on the end of the couch and said a little wryly, "I wanted you to go to Navarre."

It was her turn to be surprised. Navarre, a little independent kingdom in the northeastern corner of Spain, ruled over by a King called Sancho the Wise, an eccentric fellow, who allowed his daughters more freedom than was good for them, and whose tournaments, every spring, were famous.

"I would go to Navarre with pleasure, especially in winter," she said lightly. "And on what errand?"

"Sancho has a daughter, Berengaria. She is very beautiful. I was there, in Pamplona, for the spring tournament two years ago. She looked upon me with some favour, and her father and I have exchanged letters."

Sheer joy rendered her speechless for a moment. If one thing had been lacking for perfect contentment, it was the thought of

Richard's unmarried state, the thought that he might die without an heir. Now he had chosen his bride; all would be well.

Before she could speak he went on,

"The thing is this, mother. I have no time to go a-wooing. The moment I have gathered money and men and gear enough, I am off to Palestine. . . ."

"Oh! Richard!"

"But you knew that! Surely you knew that my dearest dream, my only desire, was to lead a new crusade."

"Yes . . . yes, of course, I *knew* that one day you would go. But so soon? I think you should . . ." she checked herself; that was where she had gone wrong with Louis and Henry; men did not like good advice. "Don't you think it would be wise," she asked, "to spend a little time in England? To show yourself to your people, get to know them, let them get to know and trust you?"

"It might be *wise*," he said, bringing out the word with scorn, "but it is not possible. Mother, since I was fourteen, all I have ever wanted is to get to the East and fight the Infidel. I've never drawn sword, lifted axe, or couched lance without thinking that thus, and thus, would I smite the Saracens. If I linger now, waiting until the seat of my throne is warm, somebody else, Philip of France, or the Duke of Austria, will lead the forces of Christendom into Jerusalem . . . and that I could not bear!"

He spoke with such violence that she knew further argument to be useless; it would merely lead to ill feeling between them. She said soothingly,

"Well then—you leave for Palestine as soon as possible. What of your bride?"

"That was what I was saying; that is why I demand such exertion of you, mother. I can hardly send to Sancho and say that I wish to marry his daughter—but where and when I cannot yet say —and will he send the poor maiden along like a bundle of washing, to be picked up at my convenience somewhere between here and the Holy Land. It would not be seemly; and he would doubt the seriousness of such a proposal. But if you would go to Navarre, and lend your support to my bid for her hand, and then bring her along by gentle, easy stages"—he broke off and did some silent reckoning—"to Sicily. Yes, that would suit me well. I shall stay in Sicily for some weeks, mustering my fleet. Bring her to Sicily, we can be married there."

"Very well." The news, the demand he was making, and the prospect of a long journey to an unfamiliar land had acted as a tonic; she no longer felt tired.

"There's another thing, mother, that you can do for me. You have been on crusade, you know the conditions and can speak with authority—at all costs, prevent her bringing a horde of women with her, or much baggage. Now, how soon can you leave?"

"In an hour," she said. "I must change my clothes and pack a change of linen. Oh . . . and, Richard, I have now a favour to ask you, but that need not delay me. It can all be done in an hour."

He laughed, "You are a woman in a thousand; I always said so. But there is no need for such haste. On such an errand you must ride with a proper escort, and that will take even *me* twenty-four hours to arrange. Say the day after tomorrow? And now, in the meantime, what is this favour?"

"You have hanged Nicolas of Saxham and ruined De Glanville by fines. Concerning them, my enemies, I am satisfied. I have arranged pensions for Kate and Amaria, and so long as they wish they remain under my roof . . . but there is one who was a good friend to me, who served me most faithfully and most imaginatively and asked no reward. I should like to give him something glittering, magnificent. I thought . . . if you have not yet disposed of the Saxham manor, Richard . . ."

"It's his. Nothing could be too fine a reward for one who served you in those dark days," Richard said munificently. "Who is he?"

With a glint of mischief brightening her eyes, Eleanor said,

"Alberic the pedlar, to whom I was indebted, for years, for all the news of you. He not only brought me news but many other things as well, and if I had no money he . . ."

"No need to say more; Saxham is his. And a thought strikes me.

To a pedlar, the manor revenues will seem boundless wealth. Let me think . . . Saxham . . . I looked up the dues when I dealt with that rogue . . . yes, four fully furnished men-at-arms was the Saxham fee. Now a pedlar, suddenly so rich wouldn't jib at ten, do you think? Six extra fully furnished men-at-arms," Richard said delightedly.

"You should have been a pedlar yourself, Richard. Shall we call Alberic in and tell him? He is in the hall. I should like you to see his face when he hears the news."

"Make haste then. I have this escort of yours and a dozen other things to see to," Richard said, but she could see that he was prepared to share her pleasure.

Alberic was found, and he came in looking very unfamiliar. He was without his pack, and had donned his best clothes for the coronation.

"Alberic," Eleanor said, "you have brought me so many things in the past; tonight I have something for you."

"Your Grace, there's no need. What I did I did just to be venturesome. Fust time I visited you, I did it because everybody said *nobody* could get in to see you, so I reckoned I'd have a try. And then, when I'd seen you, I felt sorry for . . ." No, that wasn't the thing to say. "It's a tame life, a pedlar's, Your Grace, and the letters and suchlike . . . they was a bit of excitement. And I made my profit too. I used to go round and say to the women, Here you are, I'd say, this is the very same needle . . . or thread or whatever it was . . . that is good enough for the Queen of England, should be good enough for *you*, I'd say."

"Well, by the same token the Manor of Saxham, which was too good for Sir Nicolas, may just be good enough for you, Alberic."

"The Manor of Saxham?"

"Between six and seven hundred acres, good plough land; a mill . . . two or three smithies . . . I forget the rest. And in return you have to provide me with ten good strong fellows, fully armed," Richard said.

"Well . . . I'm . . . but of course, it'd be a pleasure, Your Grace . . . but I'm struck dumb, and that's the truth of it."

Over the little man's head, Richard caught his mother's eye and laughed.

"Let's make a good job of it, shall we?" he asked. "Down on your knees, man." He drew his sword and touched the broad shoulder which years of pack-carrying had bowed. "Rise, Sir Alberic of Saxham," he said.

It had all been done on the spur of the moment, half in fun. Eleanor's first impulse was one of genuine gratitude; she wanted to reward the little pedlar, and the thought of Saxham had occurred to her as being not only seemly, since Alberic had been kind and Sir Nicolas harsh, but also fantastic, such a magnificent reward. Richard had carried it on to the point of prankishness. . . . But something happened which lifted it to a different plane altogether. Alberic, still on his knees, reached out and took Richard's hand and put his lips to it. Then he stood up and said gravely, and with a dignity which no one could have dreamed lay in that squat, humble man,

"My lord King, you have done me great honour. I swear to be your faithful servant till the day I die. And the ten men I send shall be of the very best, and so shall every buckle and strap about them."

There was a moment's silence. Then Richard said with matching gravity, "I am sure of that, Sir Alberic. I hope that you will have many years to enjoy the reward of your faithful service to my mother."

To lighten the moment Eleanor said, "Now you will have to choose yourself a coat of arms, Sir Alberic."

"I did that when I was down there on my knees," Alberic said. "With your permission, I'll have my old pedlar's pack with ten lances poking out of it; that'll be a link like between the old and the new."

When he had gone Eleanor said, "There is your Englishman, Richard, taking all in his stride. What other breed would have knelt there thinking about the buckles and straps, and then stood up to say that poetical, fanciful thing about the link between old and new?"

Richard said, "It makes me regret that I can't hang every manor owner and appoint a new one!"

CHAPTER THREE

Eleanor left England on one of those prematurely autumnal days when the cold wind fingers and snatches off the first yellow leaves, and the fine rain, falling from a leaden sky, puts a halt to the harvesting. Riding down to Dover, she could not but remember similar days in the autumns of the last fifteen years when the same wind had howled about the walls of her prison with threats of winter days to come. Now she was on her way to the sun; there would be the lingering late-summer days, dripping with sweetness, as she rode through her own provinces; the vintage there should be in full swing, with bare-footed girls, brown in the sunshine, stamping the grapes, laughing and singing as the juice squeezed out between their toes.

The wind would catch up with her again as she reached the roads that climbed, winding and twisting and slow, up through the Pyrenees; on the lower slopes the beechwoods, blazing in autumn glory, would provide some shelter, then she would reach the barren heights which knew no between-seasons, only pitiless scorching sun or merciless biting cold. And then she would ride down into the sheltered valleys on the southern side, where the sun would greet her again.

After that there would be Sicily, where her daughter Joanna,

Queen of Sicily and lately widowed, would be waiting to greet her. And there she would see Richard married. Then they would go on together to the East; and this time the crusade would be a success—how could it be otherwise with Richard at its head?—and they would ride together into Jerusalem.

With the future stretching out so goldenly before her, she thought of the many times during her imprisonment when life seemed to have been over, when it would have been so easy to lie down and die of despair . . . one should *never* despair, that was the truth of it.

So, very happily, she rode down the straight white roads which the Romans had made long ago when they occupied France, and at nightfall she rested at the handiest place, a great castle, a modest manor, a convent, or a wayside inn. Knights and nobles—men she had known in the past, or their sons—would ride out to meet her, and accompany her cavalcade on the next stage of the journey. Often they wore the white cross on their shoulders and, at their leave-taking, would say, "Madam, we shall meet next in the Holy Land." It was all, down to the smallest cup of rough wine, the little ripe apple she ate as she rode, the bunch of wayside flowers offered by a staring, awestruck child, a wonderful and revivifying experience.

But there were times—not many enough to be significant—when she would wake in the night. Towards morning, very suddenly, as though someone had shaken her from sleep, she would wake and think. It was always the same thought, always the same manner of waking. Somebody, something, shook her awake and said, "England. What of England?"

And she had her answer. On the day before she set out on her journey, she had had a talk with Richard, and, encouraged by the knowledge that she was doing him a favour, she had dared to be frank. She had then asked the question, "What of England?" and he had reassured her. England would be all right; when he left for the East he was leaving England in good hands. William Long-champ, a man of humble origin, but greatly gifted, was to be Chan-

cellor with power to act for Richard in all worldly matters; the
Archbishop of York—an honourable and trustworthy man—was in
charge of all spiritual affairs, since the Archbishop of Canterbury
was accompanying the Crusaders; and Prince John, heavily bribed
with many rich manors composed of the best land in England, had
sworn to keep faith with his brother Richard, and to watch out for
his interests while he was away.

These arrangements were all perfectly sensible and, upon hearing them, Eleanor gave her approval. Why then should she wake
in the night and worry, and toss and turn, and feel a responsibility
towards England?

But these were just night thoughts, chased away by the first
morning light, and by day she had no time for brooding. So she
came very happily to Pamplona, where the King of Navarre gave
her a royal welcome. His young, breath-takingly beautiful daughter,
who for two long years had cherished what seemed a hopeless passion for the great red-headed Duke, cried, "I would go with you to
the ends of the earth," when Eleanor explained, a little diffidently,
the journeys by land and by water which would be necessary. Despite her great beauty—she was reckoned the loveliest princess in
Christendom—Berengaria was very modest, almost humble at times.
Eleanor once remarked upon this, favourably, to Sancho, saying
that such mild manners were seldom found in young females of
such outstanding comeliness. Berengaria's father laughed and
stroked his beard.

"Perhaps I should warn you, madam, not to underestimate her.
At the moment things go well. When her will is opposed . . ." he
spread his hands and cast up his eyes dramatically. "I call her an
iron mule, she is so stubborn. For the last two years—ever since
she looked down from the ladies' gallery on the tourney ground
and sighted your son, madam—ah, what have we not endured?
Tantrums by day and tears by night! Isaac Comnenus, Emperor of
Cyprus, wishes to marry her and sends ambassadors—one his own
brother; they make their proposals, they offer her a rope of pearls
that are worth a king's ransom, and what does she do? She throws

back their gifts, calls the Emperor's brother a fat pink pig, and says that she will starve herself to death rather than marry anyone but the Duke of Aquitaine. And at that time it was understood by everyone that he was betrothed to Alys of France." Sancho halted there, challenging Eleanor to explain that broken troth.

"You know," she said, "these childhood betrothals, based upon policy, are tricky things. There were delays, the reasons for which I cannot clearly explain to you for, as you know, I have been far from court for many years. I only know that Richard, grown to manhood, has a mind of his own; he has turned away from Alys, and to your daughter."

She had, all unwittingly, hit upon the right answer, and set Sancho off on one of his favourite hobbyhorses.

"I have *always*," he said firmly, "been against these cradle matches. Poor children used as political pawns, infamous, indecent, disgusting. They are supposed to make for peace between countries, but do they? Look about you, madam, and tell me one instance when war has been avoided because this princess had married this prince. I cannot think of one. What happens is that the men make the wars they wish to make, and the poor women must bear the burden of divided loyalties, as well as the other burdens that are their lot. Mark you," he laughed again, "many times in these last two years I have regretted my softness, and wished I had married off my iron mule before she was old enough to have a mind of her own. How very weary I have become of the refrain, 'I will marry Richard Plantagenet or no one.' Still, you see she was right, and all has worked out well."

"To my great satisfaction and delight," Eleanor said. It was a good thing, a very good thing, she reflected privately, that Berengaria was so much in love with Richard, who was no ladies' man, who would be impatient and neglectful and probably downright inconsiderate at times.

In the late summer and early autumn of the year 1190 the port of Messina was busier than it had ever been in the whole of Sicily's history. Richard of England had chosen it as a mustering place for the fleets which were to carry the great army of Crusaders to the Holy Land.

Every day fresh ships arrived from every port in Europe to join those lying at anchor in the harbour. Inland, whole cities of tents had been set up, their banners and pennants fluttering and shining in the bright air. In every field and pasture all over the island, war horses and pack horses, baggage mules and humble donkeys were grazing. They must feed full now, for their next pasture would be in Palestine, and that was far away.

Richard's arrival in Sicily had been tumultuous. Good old King William, Joanna Plantagenet's husband, had died a year before, and his nephew Tancred, the new King, had refused to allow Joanna to take her dowry and return to England. Now, after a brief struggle, the dowry was in Richard's hands, and Joanna had gone to join her mother and the Princess Berengaria of Navarre, who had lately arrived and been housed in a vast ruined castle some way from the harbour and the camp. Tancred found it wise to conceal his hatred of the King of England and to take his revenge in the form of profits. Before the Crusaders sailed away he would have regained the dowry—and more.

The Sicilians were very happy. There was a thriving market for everything. Every cask of wine, every sack of corn, every bit of vegetable produce could fetch ten times its usual price. Every ship, however old and leaky, could be sold or hired out; every animal, however old and feeble, was worth its weight in gold; and now the King of England was buying up the trees. Someone had warned him that timber was scarce in the Holy Land; the town of Acre, where he intended to land and make his first attack, was said to lie in the centre of a barren belt more than a mile wide in which there was not a bush, not a blade of grass, far less a tree. So Richard was taking from Sicily all that he needed in the way of battering-rams, and the huge wooden slings, called mangonels, which threw stones with great force through the air, and scaling ladders, and the skeleton towers from whose three platforms men attacking a city could fight those defending the walls. All over Sicily the axes were ringing against the tree trunks and the saws were whining as they severed the timber into the required lengths.

The busiest man in the island was the leader of the crusade; Richard believed in keeping his eye on everything, and every detail concerning this campaign had fascination for him. He rose at first light, and moved about with something of the suddenness of lightning all day long. On the very day when Eleanor, with Berengaria and the three ladies who had come with her from Pamplona, arrived in the harbour, he had just come from a camp where men, for no obvious reason, were falling sick and often dying. It was a strange complaint; they burned with fever and shivered and shook at the same time, could not take food, ached in all their bones, seemed to make sudden recoveries, then relapsed, went into delirium. This particular camp lay low, on the ground verging an undrained swamp, and he had that morning decided to have all the tents moved to higher ground. He spoke of the bad air at that level, and one of the physicians—almost as puzzled as he was himself—had admitted that there was a complaint known as "malaria." From this occupation Richard went to welcome his mother and his betrothed, which he did heartily, but standing a little way off and refusing to embrace them.

"I have been handling some sick fellows," he shouted in explanation, "and maybe breathing their bad air. I'll keep my distance for the moment." After promising to visit them as soon as he had changed his clothes and washed, he had seen them off to their castle. That was a week ago, and never once had he found time to keep the promise. Messages and invitations and excuses went to and fro between the camp and castle each day, and Eleanor, who found it harder and harder each time to make Berengaria accept the excuses, had at last sent him an invitation to sup with them, worded with an urgency that even he could not ignore.

He remembered it—having forgotten it all day—just at the right moment, and turned reluctantly away from the harbour, where some of the newly cut wood was being loaded onto a large galley. As he hurried across the beach towards his own pavilion in the town of tents, he saw a little knot of Sicilian fishermen struggling to drag ashore something which had washed to the water's edge. Always curious, he swerved from his path and went near them, and saw that their prize was a large cask branded with his own mark. He remembered that earlier in the day a frail, leaky old boat, transferring casks of beef from one ship to another, had run into a ship's side and broken up so suddenly that there had been no time to unload the cargo. Now the almost imperceptible tide of the Mediterranean Sea had turned, and one cask had washed in. Might there be others? Shading his eyes with his hand and squinting in the level rays of the setting sun, he looked out over the water which lay rippling out, an endless expanse of silk, shot with rose pink and hyacinth blue. Yes, here and there a gently bobbing black dot showed itself.

Berengaria, Eleanor, everything was forgotten. He ran like a mad man to the nearest place where he could be sure of finding a few idle soldiers—a water-front tavern, where six or seven Kentish archers were drinking Sicilian wine and comparing it unfavourably with English ale; and in a few moments he and they were on the beach again.

"It's grab as grab can," he bellowed. "We don't get them, those fellows will, and they'll be selling them back to us in the morning!"

He was too impatient to await the washing in of the casks, but waded out until he was shoulder-high in the water. Some of the men followed him, and others came running to join in the fun, ducking one another in the intervals of waiting for a cask to come into arm's length, shouting, and laughing. An hour went by in a flash; the collection of casks, well guarded on the beach, grew. Suddenly a man said with a good-natured curse, "Blast it! This'll be rare fine eating! Damned old beef be salt enough without soaking itself in the sea."

"You'll eat and be glad, when you're hungry. I could eat a hunk now! Past suppertime, I reckon," said another.

Suppertime!

He knew that if he departed, even if he left them strict orders, they would salvage one, perhaps two, more. Then someone would say, "Don't reckon I see any more, d'you, Tom?" and Tom, conveniently blind, would look at the sky and say, "No, I don't see no more." And off they'd go to supper. That was the way men were, bless them. You could never make them look forward far enough, never make them understand that one day, in some tight corner, *one* cask of beef might just mean the difference between success and failure. No, he couldn't leave them to finish the job, and even if he went now he was late—would be later still by the time he had made himself presentable. . . .

"Does any one of you know where the Queen, my mother, lodges?" One man said he did. "Then you run into camp as fast as your legs will carry you and ask Walter to let you have a good mule. Gallop hard and tell them not to wait for me—the ladies, I mean. Explain what I'm about."

Up in the castle the ladies had prepared a great feast. They had schooled the minstrels in the songs which Eleanor and Joanna had remembered as being Richard's favourites. A full hour before he was expected everything was ready, and they had retired to help one another into their best gowns and to arrange one another's hair. The Princess Berengaria was almost beside herself with excitement; she had been in love with Richard for so long, and seem-

PART FOUR 237

ingly so hopelessly; and the miracle had happened; he had called her and she had come. And she had had but one glimpse of him . . . a whole week ago.

They had been waiting some time, and were worrying about the spoiling of the dishes, when Richard's messenger arrived.

Eleanor tried to make light of the resultant dismay.

"That is the kind of thing which does happen on campaign, my dears! It takes a soldier to turn queens and princesses into mere *waiting*-women!" No smile greeted this pitiable little quip. She tried again. "We should think ourselves lucky that he remembered to send us a message. There was once a knight of Auliac, in Poitou, who was walking one morning in his orchard with his lady and came upon an apple tree nearly uprooted by the wind. He pushed it gently upright again and said to the lady, 'Hold it steady. I'll fetch a stake and a spade.' When he reached his courtyard he found three mounted men who told him of some quarrel that had broken out between their lord—who was his also—and another, and how they were riding into the fray. He said, 'If you wait while I put on my harness, I'll ride with you.' And he did, and was gone three years!"

"And she stood holding the apple tree in place all the time," said Joanna mischievously.

"Well, to be truthful, no! Halfway through the second year the tree turned to her and said, 'Thank you very much, but I'm nicely rooted now. Don't bother any more.'"

It was no good. Berengaria would not smile; though she did, Eleanor noted with approval, restrain her tears until the ladies had withdrawn after the meal—a wasted meal, since no one had appetite to enjoy it. Then the Princess wept; beating her hands against the cushions and crying that tomorrow, since he would not come to her, she would go to him.

"Oh, better not," Eleanor said. "Camps are no place for ladies . . . I speak of what I know. And it may be that the sickness of which Richard spoke a week ago is raging there still. And it is too far to walk, and you couldn't ride a mule in that pretty gown. After all this time, at your first proper meeting, you wish to look your best. He'll probably come tomorrow."

He shall come tomorrow, she said to herself.

No one wished to make music or play any game, so the ladies retired early. Eleanor kissed Berengaria and told her not to cry any more or she would ruin her eyes for tomorrow. To Joanna, who came along to her room, gloatingly taking advantage of every moment of their restored companionship, she said,

"Poor child, if she is going to take everything as hardly as she has done this disappointment, her life will be a misery. I am beginning to think that girls who are married off—as you were—before they know anything about love are perhaps luckiest in the end. And luckiest of all are those women who can accept what is an indisputable fact—that many men, often the best men, are so made that with them their work comes first. It was very *naughty* of Richard to behave like this, but I can see how important those beef casks seemed at the moment. Will you find Gascon and tell him to have a mule—and a lantern—ready in five minutes? I'm going down to talk to Richard."

"To the camp which is no place for ladies?"

"*Young* ladies I should have said."

The castle in which they were lodged stood high. As they went downhill, Gascon carrying the lantern in one hand and holding on to her stirrup with the other, Eleanor could see, faraway, the smoky rose of the campfires at which the men had cooked their suppers. She lost sight of it again as they went through the narrow dark streets of the town, and then, on the far side, they were so near to the camp that they could smell it. She sniffed the unmistakable, unforgettable scent of a great company of men with their horses and their harness, their leather and canvas, their cooking and their fires. She had lived in and moved with it, all the way from Paris to Jerusalem, and her blood ran a little more swiftly in response to its excitement, its earthy reality.

Once inside the camp, where lanterns hung on poles marked every intersection between the serried lines of tents, she could see that, for all its temporary quality, it was a good, orderly camp. There was no rubbish, no filth. One of the contributions to its distinctive odour was the smell of the slowly burning fires which were consuming all the dirt in the camp. Her heart moved towards Richard; he was above all a good soldier, and he never pretended to be anything else. . . . Unless the most unforeseen ill fortune overtook him, he must surely succeed where so many others had failed, and take Jerusalem. And in the face of that great task, that noble ambition, how small seemed the matter of the missed supper.

She passed the large silken pavilion over which drooped the standard of France—once her own; that was a strange thought— and it was strange to think that Louis' son, the son he had longed for and she had failed to produce, was now here, linked with her son, her magnificent Richard. Life was unpredictable, she thought, and the farther you went, the stranger and the more interesting it became. She moved on until she came to a large plain canvas tent with the leopards of England hanging limp from its centre pole. There a tall, bearded man-at-arms dropped a lance with a practised motion across her path and asked her business. Gascon, remembering his duty, ran forward and cried in a loud voice, "Make way there for Her Grace, the Queen Mother of England."

"Make no fuss," Eleanor said. "The King may be busy. I can go in unannounced and, if needs be, wait a little."

It was a long tent with three quarters of its length devoted to trestle tables, from which servants were clearing the remains of the supper. At its far end there was a rough platform of planks forming a kind of dais, upon which stood a plain wooden table, two stools, and a screen which hid, Eleanor knew, Richard's bed and the stand bearing his basin and ewer. From a pole which supported that end of the tent a lamp hung, and its light fell on the table where Richard sat, his head bent over a queer wooden contraption which the man who stood by his shoulder was explaining. A little apart a sturdy, bearded archer stood stiffly at attention holding something wrapped in canvas in his hands.

As she moved nearer she could see that the little wooden toy on the table was the model of a weapon of war; it propelled little balls of clay, like the marbles with which boys played every springtime in the streets. Richard moved its lever, and when the little marble popped out he cried, "It works, Escel, it works!" Presently one of the pellets fell at her feet. She picked it up and tossed it on to the table. Then Richard turned and saw her.

"Mother!" he cried in astonishment. "What brings you here? Is anything wrong?"

"No," she said. "I wanted to talk to you, but I can wait. Go on playing with your marbles."

He came to the edge of the dais and reached out his hand to help her up. "Just my luck, Escel," he said, grinning. "My mother invites me to supper, I say I am too busy, and she comes to find me playing marbles! But it does work. Look, mother . . . a new contrivance for stone-throwing. Show her, Escel. . . . There, isn't that clever? Won't that take the Saracens by surprise? All right, Escel . . . Now you," he turned to the archer. "Let's have a look at that beef."

As the archer came forward Eleanor could see the sweat break out on his brow.

"Your Grace, 'tisn't fit to bring into your tent, leave alone put under Your Grace's nose."

"You were supposed to put it in your mouth, weren't you? Show me."

"My lord, I never meant no harm. I meant it more as a joke like . . ."

"Show me."

The archer laid the bundle on the table and pushed back the canvas, revealing a piece of meat, quite black, save where the white maggots crawled.

Richard gave it half a second's serious attention and then drew back.

"Cover it," he said, "I've known a dead horse smell better! Now . . . you were served this at midday?"

"Yes, my lord."

"Who served it?"

"To us, the sergeant. Rolf the Dispenser opened the cask."

"Fresh opened today?"

"Yes, my lord. But they've been the same this last week or more."

"Then you were right to complain. If that cask was opened to-day, I can trace it back, and, by God's head, when I find the fellow who shipped that . . . But you said a joke. I'd dearly like to know what sort of joke that disgusting offal could give rise to."

"Your Grace, it wasn't much of a joke. I only said . . . well, I said they was giving us this to eat so as to get us ready to eat the old Infidel like . . ."

"I call that a splendid joke," Richard said, and he laughed; but Eleanor, watching, knew that he was not amused. "Now, you go and find Rolf, and tell him I want that cask's brand mark . . . not my mark, the other, the merchant's. Somebody is going to smart for this. Probably we'll all eat rotten meat before we feast in Jeru-salem, but we'll eat it on the battlefield and all together. Good night to you."

The archer jumped down from the dais and went striding away, a man much relieved in his mind. Richard called after him.

"Hi there, you eater of Infidels. What *did* you eat today?"

"I ain't et nothing yet, Your Grace. Rolf served this out at mid-day, and I said what I said and was in trouble straightway."

Richard went to the edge of the platform and called to a servant, "Feed this good fellow; give him the best we have. And bring us some wine—let that, too, be the best." He turned to Eleanor and said, "Have you come to scold me, mother? I trusted *you*, at least, to understand about the beef. Then, before I had changed from my wet clothes, Escel arrived to show me his new toy—a good weapon it will be, too. And so with one thing and another . . . Look, this arrived from England an hour ago, and I haven't yet had time to read it."

"I know," Eleanor said. "Full of excuses, as usual; and every excuse full of reason! I understood, and Berengaria understood, but

she was deeply disappointed. You must visit us soon. After all she
has come a long way. Read your letter now. I crave news of England."

He lifted what looked like a substantial letter and broke its seals
one after another. There was silence as he read.

"Well," he said at last, in a voice that was half amused, half
savage with anger, "here is news indeed. Whose flag do you suppose flies over my keep at Windsor at this very moment?"

"Not . . . John's?" she asked with a sudden feeling of sickness.
After so many years of son fighting against father, pray God that
strife between brothers was not about to begin.

"No. Chancellor Longchamp's! And he's . . . here, read for yourself."

He tossed the letter to Eleanor, who tilted the closely written
page to catch the light and then, with a sinking heart, read news
which confirmed all her worst fears at those moments in the night
when she had waked and thought, "What of England?"

The letter was written by the faithful Archbishop of York. It was
plain that he had written against his will and had delayed the writing as long as he dared. He told how the Chancellor had dismissed
almost all the officials whom Richard had appointed and put his
own friends and relatives in their places; he told how the Chancellor had set up his own private army and never moved abroad
without an armed escort of fifteen hundred men; how he had tam-
pered with the coinage, so that poor people were finding it difficult
to live; how he had signed orders with his own private seal instead
of the Great Seal of England. And all this—oh, how ominous!—he
had done with the public approval of Prince John. The pair were
always together, "laughing and joking like brothers born."

While Eleanor read, Richard had taken up the little model and
had loaded and discharged it with fingers whose jerky action betrayed his excitement; now, as she lowered the page and looked at
him with stricken eyes, he swung round to her and said,

"Well . . . it's a pretty situation, isn't it?"

She said gently, because she knew how grievously he would feel the disappointment and the delay, "There's nothing for it, I'm afraid, but that you should go back to England."

He started as though he had been stung.

"Go back! Now! God's head! My ships are loading, my army ready to move; I have my hand on the thing for which I have longed and worked and scrimped and saved all these years. I wouldn't turn back now, not if England was ablaze from end to end and I could put it out by blowing on it!"

She sat still and in silence did battle with herself. She had come out of Winchester determined to enjoy what life remained to her; she was willing, eager, to help Richard in every possible way, but only in ways that were pleasant. She had, she told herself, learned her lesson—men disliked being advised by women; they resented it even more if the advice proved sound and good. To try to sway their decisions was worse than useless. An inner voice urged her— Stay silent now; stay friends with him. Let him go on his crusade, go with him. Let him make his own decisions. . . .

Yet when she spoke, it was to say in a firm voice,

"England matters, too, Richard."

"Of *course* it matters!" he rapped out impatiently. "It provides me with the sinews of war—money and the best fighting men in the world."

At that cynical statement all caution deserted her.

"Ah, that is where you make your mistake, to look on England as a milch cow or a breeding place for soldiers. England is more than that. I say this, who am not an Englishwoman. But I can see the time coming when he who rules England rules the world. My lands in Europe, rich as they are, your father's Duchies, wide as they reach, are not to be compared, because they will always be dependent on the goodwill of their neighbours, always tangled with the shifting policies of Europe. England stands apart. She could be made impregnable. Don't let England slip from your grasp, Richard. Go back, spend a year if necessary in setting it in order. Jerusalem has waited so long, a year more will do it no damage; but, given a year of this," she tapped the letter, "John and Long-

champ between them will have snatched away the brightest jewel
of your crown."

He had listened, but his face was hard, and between their narrowed lids his eyes were cold, unfriendly. She tried again.

"John was always, from the first, envious of you. He would like
to be King; he craves the glitter, not the responsibility. Longchamp,
reared in the gutter, itches for power. They will work well together;
John will wear the crown; Longchamp wield the sceptre. And who
is to halt their scheme? Who has the power? For that matter, who
but you would *dare* go back and tackle Chancellor Longchamp with
his private standing army and his escort of fifteen hundred men?"

That, she thought, was a good question; it threw out a challenge.
But Richard's ears had heard the call of the East and were deaf to
all else.

"You argue well; you always did! But if what you say were a
thousand times more true than it is I would not budge. I know what
this is—the last desperate trick of the Devil! Everything that could
conspire to stop me has happened—from the obstinacy of Philip of
France to the sickness of a mule; nothing too small, nothing too
ridiculous . . . and I've overcome every obstacle. So now this must
happen! I shall still go on. Maybe the Devil will know he's met his
match and leave me be."

"But you can't . . . just ignore the letter, Richard. It is a desperate plea for help."

"I shall answer the letter. I shall tell Geoffrey of York that, if
Longchamp keeps such high state, it's very plain to me that money
is being spent there which should be on its way to me. I need
money now, this minute. It should have come with this letter. Everything in this damned island is twenty, thirty times its rightful
price. Before God, mother, I'd sell London if I could find a buyer."

"Shh . . ." she said, looking around and seeing with relief that
no one was within earshot. "Don't talk so wildly. Talk like that
travels and gains on the road. Remember the London citizens, the
guilds . . . and what they mean to you, in money if in nothing
else!" She laid her hand on her bodice and felt the slight bulge of

the Antioch diamond that lay on her breast. She said craftily, "I could help you to some ready money, *now*, if you would promise me just one thing in return. Don't just send a letter to England. If you won't go yourself, send a *man*. Geoffrey of York is willing and loyal—proud, too. He would never have written this letter if he had not been at his wits' end. Send him some real support, Richard, and I will give you this."

She pulled at the chain, and the great stone jerked out, spilling its blue and yellow and green and scarlet and purple rays in the light of the smoky lamp.

Richard stared at it; and she remembered how often in the days long past she had bribed him to good behaviour; how sometimes he had taken the bribe and then gone his own way, and how hard she had slippered him.

"Morally, I suppose, this belongs to old Kate; once when I was hard-pressed I willed it to her. But she is provided for now—and if you take Jerusalem, we shall not lack jewels. Take it, Richard— and give me your promise."

To her surprise he made no move. He stood staring at the jewel, not even greedily.

"I hate to take your bauble," he said. "All those long years . . . you never had anything fine or pretty."

"All the better; I learned to live without finery. And this came out of the East; it is fitting that it should go back there, in the form of weapons of war, to help to set the holy places free."

"In that spirit then, and very gratefully, I will take it." He did so and cupped his hand about it, staring at it thoughtfully. Mules and mangonels, sacks of flour and scaling ladders flashed from its rays. He slipped the chain over his head and tucked the stone inside his tunic.

"I know whom I'll send," he said. "Coutance of Rouen."

"Oh Richard!" she said, in instant dismay, "such an old man!"

He laughed, "Well, you're an old woman! And none the worse for that!"

"But he's a churchman . . . and a foreigner. He'll carry no weight at all! At least send a soldier, an Englishman."

"I have none to spare," Richard said curtly. "Every man worth his salt is here with me, and I need every one. We're going forward to hunt bigger game than that little rat playing King o' the Castle. And it is becoming plain to me that *my* army will bear the brunt of *this* campaign. Philip of France will be little help; he goes into a sulk at the first hint of plain speaking."

"He wasn't reared, as you were, in a family of plain-speaking people. Late born into a family of girls, adored by his father . . . probably nobody ever spoke plainly to him in his life. You must handle him softly. . . ." And there I go, she thought, handing out advice again.

"I'll go and see Coutance now," said Richard, jumping from the dais and reaching his hand to help her down.

"And will nothing I say move you?"

"Nothing that anyone could say. I know what I'm about. A good stiff letter to Geoffrey of York, and the overriding power I shall give Coutance of Rouen, and all will be well. Now I'll set you on your way. Why, where's your escort?"

"Gascon and I came alone."

"You are the most reckless woman. You might have been set upon and robbed. It's a wonder you weren't."

"I had nothing a thief would covet."

"You had this!" He touched his own breast. "And there's the mule. They'd take it from under you and sell it back to me tomorrow. Wait a minute. . . ." He chose six archers to escort her home, helped her into the saddle, kissed her kindly, and promised to make time on the morrow to pay a visit to the castle. Then he strode off to find Coutance, and she could hear him singing to himself. The shock of the letter had quite worn off; he had made his stupid, futile arrangements and was satisfied that all would be well.

However, as the mule trotted between the rows of tents into the open, then between the darkened houses of the sleeping town, and began to climb towards the castle, she was aware of a deep and growing depression. She had failed again.

One part of her errand, it was true, had been successfully accomplished; she had set out to persuade Richard to do his duty and visit the Princess, and he had promised. The small, the personal, the woman's part had been well done. Could she not rest content with that? Long years ago the Abbé had warned her against "meddling"; if only she had taken heed, how different her life would have been. Even the disaster of her visit to Woodstock would never have happened if she had not been hurrying to Henry to put before him her views about his treatment of the boys.

And she was old . . . sixty-eight, a great age for a woman. Richard had said, "Well, you're an old woman," with no sense of insulting her. It was true; she was old; surely she could retire now and sit back and learn at last how to play the passive, woman's part. Richard was King of England. Why should she feel a nagging responsibility for a country that was not even her own?

She cast it aside. She thought—I'm going back to the castle, and tomorrow we'll begin to plan the wedding, where and when, and what shall be worn . . . and then I shall begin to hope for grandchildren . . . and I will be a tactful, pleasant, placid old woman with a piece of needlework in my hands and agreeable, complaisant words on my tongue. . . .

They were so far from the camp that when the trumpet sounded its call was sweetened and muted by distance.

One of the archers said, "Your Grace . . . if you would halt for a moment. That is the signal and we *are* within earshot, and the rule is . . ."

He broke off as the trumpet sounded again, and he and the five with him shuffled into an orderly line by the edge of the path. Then, as one man, they raised their right arms and cried, "Help; help for the Holy Sepulchre."

Three times they cried it, and a little thrill ran down Eleanor's spine; she felt her throat thicken. Two minutes earlier there had been eight people on the path together, now there were two groups, the dedicated Crusaders in mystical union, and outside an old woman and a page.

The archer said cheerfully, "Thank you, Your Grace. At your service again."

Over the lump in her throat she asked, "Do you do that every night?"

"Every night, last thing before 'Lights out.'"

He and a hundred thousand like him would go forward and fight and probably die for a cause. He and a hundred thousand like him had responded to that call, "Help; help for the Holy Sepulchre." And she, though she had responded to the thrill of the call and had heard in it the very voice of chivalry, she could now do nothing save drag along in the wake of the army, useless, less valuable than any bit of baggage.

And there came to her—as clear and convincing as the great light and the voice that came to the Apostle Paul on the road to Damascus—the inspiration of what her response to that call could, no, *must*, be.

The cheerful archer laid his hand on the bridle rein, and she said, "No. I must turn about and go back. I have forgotten something."

"One of us could run back and fetch it, Your Grace. You're nearly home now."

He was being kind to an old, weary woman. And he was wrong, ah! how wrong he was. Strength and confidence and power were flowing in towards her from the four corners of the earth. She had a contribution to make, and it was one which she alone *could* make.

"No," she said. "Thank you kindly. I must go back."

The mule, so nearly back in his stable, grunted and sighed as he was turned. She reached out her hand and touched his rough neck encouragingly. Like me, she thought, called on for another effort when he thought the day's work was nearly done.

But who else—save only Richard, who had set his face eastward towards Jerusalem—could go back and set England in order and keep it so? Who else had the power to call John to heel like a whipped puppy? Who else had the right to look up at the Windsor flagpole and ask, "What is that rag doing there?" Who else could make that escort of fifteen hundred men look like the toy soldiers they were?

The rosy glow had faded from above the camp, the fires were out now, and, save for the sound of their own movement through the night, all was quiet as she sat on the jogging mule and planned what she would say to Richard.

She would say—"Send me. I was Regent before, and the people know and trust me. I will hold England for you while you go on to take Jerusalem. I will uphold your authority and rule justly. The gap between your Normans and Saxons, I, being neither, will bridge. I will knit these people together into the great nation I know they are capable of being. I will have them ready to welcome you back with joy. That shall be my contribution to *this* crusade. I can do it because all my life, including even my worst failures, has been schooling me for this task. I shall do it well."

PLANTAGENET

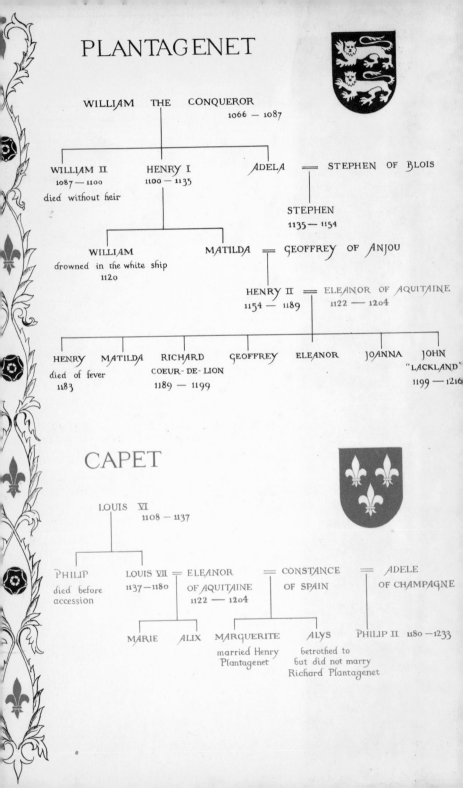

WILLIAM THE CONQUEROR
1066 — 1087

WILLIAM II
1087 — 1100
died without heir

HENRY I
1100 — 1135

ADELA = STEPHEN OF BLOIS

STEPHEN
1135 — 1154

WILLIAM
drowned in the white ship
1120

MATILDA = GEOFFREY OF ANJOU

HENRY II = ELEANOR OF AQUITAINE
1154 — 1189   1122 — 1204

HENRY   MATILDA   RICHARD   GEOFFREY   ELEANOR   JOANNA   JOHN
died of fever   COEUR-DE-LION   "LACKLAND"
1183   1189 — 1199   1199 — 1216

CAPET

LOUIS VI
1108 — 1137

PHILIP
died before
accession

LOUIS VII = ELEANOR
1137—1180   OF AQUITAINE
1122 — 1204

= CONSTANCE
OF SPAIN

= ADELE
OF CHAMPAGNE

MARIE   ALIX   MARGUERITE   ALYS   PHILIP II 1180 —1233
married Henry   betrothed to
Plantagenet   but did not marry
Richard Plantagenet